Advanced Sciences and Technologies for Security Applications

Indexed by SCOPUS

The series Advanced Sciences and Technologies for Security Applications comprises interdisciplinary research covering the theory, foundations and domain-specific topics pertaining to security. Publications within the series are peer-reviewed monographs and edited works in the areas of:

- biological and chemical threat recognition and detection (e.g., biosensors, aerosols, forensics)
- crisis and disaster management
- terrorism
- cyber security and secure information systems (e.g., encryption, optical and photonic systems)
- traditional and non-traditional security
- energy, food and resource security
- economic security and securitization (including associated infrastructures)
- transnational crime
- human security and health security
- social, political and psychological aspects of security
- recognition and identification (e.g., optical imaging, biometrics, authentication and verification)
- smart surveillance systems
- applications of theoretical frameworks and methodologies (e.g., grounded theory, complexity, network sciences, modelling and simulation)

Together, the high-quality contributions to this series provide a cross-disciplinary overview of forefront research endeavours aiming to make the world a safer place.

The editors encourage prospective authors to correspond with them in advance of submitting a manuscript. Submission of manuscripts should be made to the Editor-in-Chief or one of the Editors.

Richard J. Chasdi

Corporate Security Surveillance

An Assessment of Host Country Vulnerability to Terrorism

Springer

Richard J. Chasdi
Department of Political Science
The George Washington University
Washington, DC, USA

ISSN 1613-5113 ISSN 2363-9466 (electronic)
Advanced Sciences and Technologies for Security Applications
ISBN 978-3-031-39549-9 ISBN 978-3-031-39550-5 (eBook)
https://doi.org/10.1007/978-3-031-39550-5

This Springer imprint is published by the registered company Springer Nature Switzerland AG
The registered company address is: Gewerbestrasse 11, 6330 Cham, Switzerland

Paper in this product is recyclable.

This book is dedicated to Sharon M. Applebaum, Rachel Chasdi, Richard A. Fey, Neal A. Tolchin, and Ralph (Yerachmiel) Hollenberg.

Foreword

Although global trade has gone on for thousands of years and companies doing business beyond their borders have existed for centuries, the emergence of multinational corporations with widespread networks of local subsidiaries, offshore manufacturing and outsourcing, global brands selling in markets throughout the world, and modern air travel which facilitated international business travel and tourism all emerged more recently—mainly in the late 1960s and 1970s. This same period saw the rise of international terrorism, so-called because terrorists attacked foreign targets, or international commerce by hijacking or sabotaging airliners, or, in fewer cases, went abroad to carry out their attacks. The coincidence of these two developments led to increasing attacks on businesses doing operating abroad.

Terrorists Target Business

Terrorists found many reasons to attack foreign corporations. Terrorist tactics are always about attracting attention and attacks on foreign targets and were a means of gaining international notice. Diplomats and embassies were frequent targets in the early 1970s, but governments quickly increased their security, and diplomats were more heavily guarded by local authorities, who under international law, were primarily responsible for their protection. In comparison, the business community offered more—and more vulnerable—targets, which also carried less public sympathy.

For those groups motivated by a myriad of anti-capitalist ideologies, businesses could be portrayed as foreign exploiters, stealing the country's natural resources, cashing in on cheap local labor, or simply taking market share from local companies. Attacking foreign companies was also a means of waging economic warfare on the state. Terrorist campaigns discouraged foreign investment as well as foreign tourism, an important source of revenue and jobs, especially in many developing countries. For example, on September 16, 1974, 40 bombs went off in a single day targeting foreign firms in Argentina.

Terrorists saw airlines as stand-in targets for particular nations, not surprising since many were owned at the time by their respective governments. British Airways was not privatized until 1987. Pan Am and TWA, while private, were the only US international airlines for many years and were easily seen as surrogate targets.

Urban guerrillas initially kidnapped foreign diplomats in exchange for jailed comrades. They later kidnapped business executives to force companies to distribute food to the poor or rehire workers who had been laid off. Initially, the guerrilla groups avoided ransom kidnappings, which might make them appear as ordinary criminals and thereby tarnish their political credentials (although they routinely robbed banks, which they described as "proletarian expropriations.") However, they soon overcame this inhibition, opening up a more lucrative means of financing their struggles. In Argentina alone, between 1971 and 1979, urban guerrilla groups carried out 114 ransom kidnappings, most of them targeting the executives of foreign corporations. Ransom demands rapidly escalated from the tens of thousands to the tens of millions of dollars for a single hostage.

A list of foreign terrorist targets attacked by Argentina's urban guerrilla groups in the 1970s tells the story. Targeted companies reflected the biggest international firms of the era. Among others, they include Amoco, Bank of America, Bank of Boston, Bendix, Braniff International, British and American Tobacco Company, Chase Manhattan Bank, Dunlop Tires, Chrysler, Coca-Cola, Eli Lilly, Exxon, Eveready, Fiat, Firestone Tire, First National City Bank of New York, Ford, General Electric, General Motors, Goodyear, IBM, ITT, John Deere, Kodak, Lufthansa, Mercedes Benz, Otis Elevator, Pan American Airways, Peugeot, Parke-Davis, Pepsi Cola, Pfizer, Philips, Remington Rand, Renault, Sheraton, Squibb, Swift Meat, Swissair, Unilever, Union Carbide, and Xerox.

A review of the experiences of the top 100 American corporations ranked by overseas earnings that I assembled many years ago showed that size matters. Of the top 25 corporations, 80% had been the targets of terrorist attacks; 60% of the next 25 had suffered terrorist attacks as had 48% of the third 25, with fewer still for the last 25. The 20% of the top 25 that had escaped terrorist attacks included companies with large overseas sales, but little overseas presence at the time, along with investment banks and others whose business operations were hardly visible.

On the other hand, terrorists routinely attacked corporate names that represented America, like McDonalds restaurants even though these were local franchises, or Marriott Hotels, which were managed by Marriott, but locally owned. Symbolism outweighed imposing economic damage on foreign owners.

Not all terrorist groups targeted foreign businesses. Italy's Red Brigades denounced the "monopolistic multinationals," but carried out few attacks on foreigners. They focused their campaign on Italian corporations and government officials, reflecting their struggle to win the allegiance of Italian workers. The Irish Republican Army focused the bulk of its terrorist campaign on British authorities—police, military, and political officials—which reflected its self-image as an army fighting a legitimate war. But the IRA carried out a bombing campaign against businesses in Belfast, bombed London's tourist sites, and in the 1990s carried out massive bombings in London's financial district.

Bombings were the principal terrorist tactic, followed by armed assaults, sabotage, robberies, kidnappings, and murders. Urban and rural guerrillas also collected "revolutionary taxes"—demands for protection money to protect their employees and facilities against attack. These latter tactics were not uncommon, and payments were made although, since they were negotiated quietly, less information is available.

The Terrorist Threat Evolves

The terrorist threat has evolved over the past half-century. Overall, terrorism increased in volume and escalated in violence. According to the Global Terrorism Database (GTD) maintained by the National Consortium for the Study of Terrorism and Responses to Terrorism (START) at the University of Maryland, which has become the largest terrorism database outside of government, incidents of global terrorism increased from an average annual total of 1192 recorded between 1971 and 1980 to an annual average of more than 10,000 incidents between 2011 and 2020—a ninefold increase [1]. The nature of terrorism also changed.

By the end of the 1970s, most of the urban guerrilla groups in Argentina, Uruguay, and Brazil were destroyed by military governments using brutal repressive tactics. Suspects were "disappeared," often tortured and murdered. Primarily rural guerrilla groups continued to fight in Colombia, Peru, and Central America, and purely criminal kidnapping gangs were active, especially in Brazil and Mexico.

At the same time, with the exception of the Provisional Wing of the Irish Republican Army and Spain's violent Basque separatist group ETA, by the end of the 1980s most of the terrorist groups in Europe had also been suppressed primarily through legitimate law enforcement means. The USA, Canada, and Japan also largely eliminated the tiny extremist groups that had carried out bombing campaigns in the 1970s. The IRA continued its terrorist campaign until a political settlement was achieved in 1998, although splinter groups continued to carry out occasional bombings. ETA did not end its 50 year campaign of violence until 2018.

This period, however, saw the rise of religiously inspired terrorism beginning after the 1979 revolution in Iran and the Soviet invasion of Afghanistan that same year. Shia Muslim extremists carried out bombings and kidnappings in Lebanon during the 1980s, most notably the bombings of the US embassy and US Marine barracks, but also the kidnapping of foreign citizens. Sunni Muslim extremists, inspired by jihadist ideologies, ultimately coalesced around al Qaeda, which launched a terrorist campaign against the USA, culminating with the terrorist attacks on September 11, 2001. As a consequence of internal tensions, al Qaeda later split into two rival organizations, the original al Qaeda and Islamic State, both of which assisted or inspired terrorist operations worldwide.

The threat posed by jihadist extremists differed qualitatively from that posed by the primarily anarchist and Marxist-oriented groups of the 1960s and 1970s. Jihadists were not making statements against capitalism. Instead, they sought to carry out high-casualty events, often employing large-scale vehicle bombings or suicide attacks.

That meant targeting public places where people gathered—tourist sites, hotels, train stations, restaurants, places of worship, concert halls, nightclubs, promenades, beaches, and open-air markets. They also bombed airliners and derailed passenger trains. The targets of these large-scale attacks were Western nonbelievers and those Muslims they considered heretics—in fact, al Qaeda and Islamic State spilled more Muslim blood than that of their declared Christian or Jewish foes. Given their determination to kill in quantity, their attacks were necessarily more indiscriminate. There were no innocent bystanders.

The religiously-inspired extremists carried out attacks on embassies and on occasion launched large-scale assaults on refineries and oil terminals. And they still carried out kidnappings to raise funds. Hotels in Muslim countries where jihadists were active were targeted because they were gathering places for foreign visitors and local elites. Many of the other venues where jihadists carried out attacks were privately owned. Although jihadists were less interested in attacking businesses per se, the 9/11 attacks, in addition to killing almost 3000 people, caused massive damage and resulted in direct and indirect financial losses to the business community reaching into the tens of billions of dollars.

Although fewer business executives were kidnapped, the private sector was still on the front line. From 1970 to 2020, terrorist attacks on business targets as a category increased two and half times in actual number, but they declined as a percentage of the total volume of terrorism.

According to the GTD, between 1971 and 2020, terrorist attacks on business targets comprised 10.6% of the total number of incidents. "Business" as a target category does not capture the full extent of business involvement. Attacks on economic targets, including "airports and aircraft," "telecommunications," "transportation," and "utilities," which were more often than not privately owned, would add another 7.7% to the business column to a total of 18.3% [1].

Confining the inquiry to those listed in the GTD as "business" targets, we see a long-term decline as a percentage. In the decade from 1971–1980, businesses were targeted in 24% of the attacks. This dropped to 14% in the 1980s, 16% in the 1990s, 10% in the 2000s, and 7% in the 2010s. In 2020, the business targets dropped to just 4% [1]. Again, however, the actual volume of attacks on business targets increased, reaching a peak of over a thousand incidents in 2015 when, according to the GTD, the total volume of terrorism also reached its highest volume thus far.

Business Responds

In the early years of terrorism, companies doing business abroad were largely on their own. Local governments, especially in developing countries, had limited resources and were preoccupied with other security concerns. Kidnappings were especially difficult for businesses to deal with. The objectives of the company in ensuring the safe release of a kidnapped employee might conflict with the local government's priority of preventing its guerrilla adversaries from receiving ransom payments, which some governments outlawed.

The US government officially opposed ransom payments, although it did not interfere with private parties making payments. Assistance from local embassies was uneven. Some provided useful information and discreet assistance. Others avoided involvement. Much depended on the attitude of the local embassy security officer and the ability of the company's local security director to cultivate a relationship with local embassy officials.

This uneven relationship was a continuing source of complaint by American firms, which reached the Secretary of State George Shultz in the early 1980s. In response, the US Department of State in 1985 created the Overseas Security Advisory Council (OSAC), a public–private partnership to keep the department's Diplomatic Security Service representatives connected with private sector security professionals from US organizations operating abroad for ongoing threat awareness and crisis support. By 2023, the OSAC enterprise included 5400 organizations and 18,000 individual members [2].

In response to the growing problem of kidnappings in Argentina and elsewhere during the 1970s, Lloyds of London began selling insurance coverage for kidnapping and ransom situations. Other insurance companies soon also began offering K&R covers. By the late 1980s, most large and many medium-size companies doing business abroad, as well as numerous wealthy families, had such insurance policies.

In addition to reimbursing the insured for the ransom paid (with suitable deductibles to incentivize reasonable precautions), the insurance companies offered consultant services to improve security and advise in ransom negotiations. This assistance was critical. Companies were not merely interested in offsetting their financial losses and would have paid the ransom even if not insured, but they were interested in obtaining experienced help in navigating what were invariably complicated crises. For corporate executives faced with ransom demands, it was usually their first time while K&R consultants could bring a wealth of prior personal experience drawn from numerous cases.

Large-scale losses from continuing bombing campaigns and especially from massive terrorist bombings like those in London in the 1990s pushed the British government into serving as the insurer of last resort. The same issue arose in the United States after the 9/11 attacks, leading to the 2002 Terrorism Risk Insurance Program (TRIA). TRIA created a system of shared public and private compensation for specified acts of terrorism. Although considered a temporary response, TRIA was successively renewed and is currently extended through December 31, 2027.

Security Strategy Options

Capitalism is tough. Terrorism came to be viewed as just another risk, along with war, revolution, crime, and natural disasters. Faced with a terrorist threat abroad, corporations theoretically had a number of options.

Divestment. One was divestment. A business could withdraw from the affected country altogether, relocating its operations to a safer environment. Where the subsidiary managed large-scale agriculture enterprises, exploited oil and gas or mineral resources, or had made large-scale investments in infrastructure or manufacturing facilities, this would involve major and possibly permanent losses. Outside of war (including civil war zones) zones, it rarely happened. Manufacturing facilities can be moved. Oil or mineral reserves cannot be. This will continue to be a problem as companies search for strategic minerals, which are often located in politically unstable parts of the world.

Reduce Exposure. A second option was to reduce exposure. Exposed ex-pat employees could be brought home. Some companies practiced "commando management," relocating managers and vital technicians to nearby but safer locations from which they could go in and out of the country for short periods of time. For example, during the wave of kidnappings in Argentina during the 1970s, international company headquarters in Buenos Aires were relocated across the Rio de la Plata to Uruguay. Corporate executives would make only brief trips to Buenos Aires for essential meetings.

Lower Profile. Companies could adopt a lower profile and operate more discreetly, abandoning the practice of naming buildings after their company, removing logos from facilities, and keeping company executives off of the social pages of the newspapers.

Improving Labor Relations. In many cases, leftwing terrorists sought to instigate or capitalize on labor disputes to gain popularity and attract recruits. This was especially true of the urban guerrilla groups active in Argentina whose mentors included veterans of anarchist struggles in Spain, Italy, and France during the early years of the twentieth century. Terrorist attacks in Argentina rose in parallel with often violent labor protests. By reducing labor strife, businesses operating in the country sought to reduce their exposure to terrorism.

Corporate Philanthropy. Businesses could try to reduce potential hostility and improve their image through corporate philanthropy and public relations campaigns that emphasize their importance and contributions to the local community. This had varying degrees of success.

Improving Local Law Enforcement Capacity. In developing countries where local police or national gendarmeries had limited resources and training, private companies may be permitted to contribute equipment—vehicles or communications systems, for example—or assist them in improving their training. The objective was not to turn local law enforcement authorities into company security but to improve their overall capabilities.

Increase Security. This is the most obvious response. Businesses can harden the target by increasing their own physical security and adopting good security procedures. Those exposed to kidnappings can be provided with bodyguards and travel in armored cars driven by specially trained drivers—a common practice in places like Italy during the Red Brigades campaign or Colombia during the peak kidnapping years. Corporate security expenditures correlate most directly with the level of the threat and the value of the investment.

Protection Money. In some cases, guerrilla or terrorist groups imposed "revolutionary taxes" on companies doing business in areas where they operated or demanded that businesses pay for the protection of their employees and facilities. Organized crime and criminal gangs also routinely engage in this kind of extortion. While businesses routinely paid ransoms to guerrilla groups, often with the understanding (which was unenforceable) that the payment would provide immunity against further attacks, paying protection money was a more difficult decision, although many local and some foreign businesses decided they had no choice but to comply.

Hedges Against Losses. The constant threat of terrorism required firms to prepare for shutdown or withdrawal if the security situation deteriorated. Profits were quickly repatriated to reduce loss, contracts, and license fees were designed in advance to permit rapid retreat, and arrangements were made in advance to transfer equipment to local operators in return for equity. Solutions were often creative. To avoid potential loss from destruction or damage, one construction company in Central America sold its equipment to the local government for the duration of the contract, thereby transferring much of its risk.

Insurance. Insuring against losses was the final option. Special covers provided insurance for kidnap and ransom, terrorism, sabotage, extortion, and other extraordinary losses. As more companies offered insurance, premiums declined, and most businesses operating internationally now have such coverage.

Companies operating in higher-risk areas formulated increasingly sophisticated risk management strategies that included combinations of these options. Selection depended on the characteristics of the enterprise, the level of the threat, and the company's tolerance for risk.

Large oil companies and other businesses extracting natural resources were accustomed to operating in the rougher neighborhoods of the world. They seldom pulled out, but instead increased their security and insured against losses, but they also engaged in social projects to improve local conditions. Many companies engaged in corporate philanthropy for reasons of social responsibility—its effectiveness as a means of reducing the threat was questionable. Medium-sized companies had less resources and experience.

Terrorism Databases Permit Quantitative Analysis

The rise of terrorism in its contemporary form prompted increasing government attention and the systematic collection of data for analysis. The RAND Corporation initiated its research program on terrorism in 1972. One of its initial products was a chronology of international terrorist incidents, which became the first formal database of terrorist incidents. The US government started its own terrorism databases during the 1970s, notably the CIA's ITERATE (International Terrorism: Attributes of Terrorist Events[1] and the State Department's Bureau of Intelligence and Research database on attacks against US targets.[2]

Security firms and private consultancies also created terrorism databases beginning with Risks International's in 1978. Ackerman and Palumbo, Control Risks, Pinkertons, Kroll Associates, and others all developed specialized databases, focusing on attacks on business targets. Some were intended to assist companies in the assessment of risk and were available to commercial subscribers. Others—for example, those detailing ransom negotiations and payments—were intended to inform the firm's own team of specialized consultants and, for obvious reasons, were closely held.

Increasing Attention and Increasingly Sophisticated Analysis

In response to the growing number of airline hijackings, bombings of corporate headquarters, and ransom kidnappings of corporate executives, companies and governments paid increased attention to the terrorist threat to business operations. One of the first reports to address the issue was a RAND research project sponsored by the Department of Commerce. In 1981, Susanna Purnell and Eleanor Wainstein published their report, *The Problems of U.S. Businesses Operating Abroad in Terrorist Environments* [3]. Their research was based on RAND's chronology of terrorist incidents and interviews with corporate executives. It analyzed terrorist tactics, how these affected business operations, and corporate responses. Given the time frame, the findings of the research were influenced by the recent experiences of American corporations in Argentina and El Salvador.

The authors addressed not just the visible dangers of terrorist bombings and kidnappings, but the more insidious effects of high-risk environments on business

[1] Edward F. Mickolus, with various co-authors, has published a series of books containing chronologies of terrorist incidents from 1960 to 2022. The chronology is also available online at the International Terrorism Data Center, Vinyard Software, https://vinyardsoftware.com/.

[2] See Dennis A. Pluchinsky, *Anti-American Terrorism: From Eisenhower to Trump: A Chronicle of the Threat and Response*. London: World Scientific Publishing, Ltd., 2020. The first two volumes cover the period from the Eisenhower through the George H.W. Bush Administration. Volumes 3 and 4 are forthcoming.

operations. These included increased security costs, dangers arising from labor relations, difficulty in getting technicians in to install or repair machinery, constant needs to hedge against potential losses and interruptions, and the psychological toll on management.

In the years since this early survey, the analysis of terrorist attacks on business targets has resulted in an extensive and increasingly sophisticated literature, which brings us to this latest volume by Richard Chasdi. It provides a quantitative and qualitative analysis of terrorism against US corporations in five countries: India, Mexico, Brazil, South Africa, and Thailand. Chasdi selected these countries not because they are considered the most dangerous countries in the world, but because they host the most US companies. Chasdi, however, applies a broad definition of the terrorist threats they face. The objective is to better understand terrorist targeting preferences, company vulnerabilities, and strategic responses, which is exactly what we have addressed, albeit briefly and with breathtaking simplification, in this foreword.

This foreword is not the place to summarize the book which follows. The reader need only turn the page to enter Chasdi's thought domain. I have known the author for years and I am an admirer of his uniquely imaginative approaches and always rigorous analysis. His work is invariably intellectually challenging and thought-provoking. Read on.

Santa Monica, USA
2023

Brian Michael Jenkins

References

1. University of Maryland, National Consortium for the Study of Terrorism and Responses to Terrorism, *Global Terrorism Database*. https://www.start.umd.edu/gtd/
2. U.S. Department of State, Overseas Security Advisory Council, https://www.state.gov/overseas-security-advisory-council/
3. Susanna W. and Wainstein, Eleanor S. (1981). The problems of U.S. businesses operating abroad in terrorist environments. The RAND Corporation

Acknowledgements

There are several people that deserve mention for their kind support. I would like to thank my colleague and friend Brian M. Jenkins for his kind attention and insightful suggestions. At The George Washington University, I would like to thank the Chair of the Department of Political Science, Professor Eric D. Lawrence, Professor Cynthia McClintock, and Professor James H. Lebovic. I would like to thank my first-rate editor at Springer, Annelies Kersbergen, for her extraordinary commitment to the project and kind support, and to my top flight clerical staff—my administrative assistant Christine Kreiser, and my graphics designer Nancy Gage for making it possible to produce this book. I would like to thank my George Washington University undergraduate students Mahima Jain, Henry Mann, and Billie Singer for their efforts. Special thanks to my wife, Sharon, my brother David M. Chasdi, Miriam G. Applebaum and Jeffrey A. Nelson, Neal Tolchin, Robin and Jack Matthewman, Mark Bellino, and Fr. Javier Garcia Ocampo for their kind attention and support, particularly during the summer of 2023. I am grateful to Emily, Michael, and Tallullah who help in all ways.

Contents

Chapter 1
Introduction

1.1 Introduction

On December 25, 2021, the recreational vehicle (RV) Anthony Quinn Warner drove to the historical section of Nashville and parked on Second Avenue detonated in front of an AT&T transmission facility. The bomb inside that RV exploded with enough force to decimate a city block. It destroyed buildings, roads, other infrastructure, and automobiles with such intensity that observers at the scene described this "honkytonk" section of Nashville as a "war zone." [2, 28].

Even though Warner's motivations still remain unclear to Federal Bureau of Investigation (FBI) and Alcohol, Tobacco, and Firearms (ATF) investigators, his focus on an AT&T site led to Internet, land-line, call center, and cell phone activity disruption in Tennessee, Alabama, and Kentucky. It also led to the temporary shutdown of Nashville International Airport [28]. Whether on purpose or by default, Warner's Nashville bombing was a significant attack against American United States commercial interests and commercial interests abroad. For business security analysts, the bombing underscored critical infrastructure vulnerability.

The ATT transmission facility bombing underscored an imperative for more effective infrastructure redundancy to keep businesses in operation in times of crisis. Even if Warner's action was simply criminal terrorism rather than political terrorism, his terrorist act, whatever its nature, was significant. It illuminated terrorism's threat to international and domestic business interests linked in a globalized world [13, 1, 3, 183 n1, 184, n10]. Those links between terrorism and commercial targets remain a largely unexplored research area, worthy of further investigation.

This book analyzes terrorism as practiced against business targets in five "host countries" in the developing world with the highest number of active U.S. based multinational corporations. This analysis of "three fifths of the BRICS + 2" provides a quantitative and qualitative analysis of business-related terrorism, either political terrorism, or criminal terrorism or both, in each country. The central notion is to provide American and other business leaders with a comprehensive study of terrorism

R. J. Chasdi, *Corporate Security Surveillance*, Advanced Sciences and Technologies for Security Applications, https://doi.org/10.1007/978-3-031-39550-5_1

events in the near past, that in turn will provide a roadmap of terrorist group behavioral patterns for the international business community.

The business leaders who should profit from this book range primarily from multinational corporation (MNC) leaders, to small and medium-size enterprise (SME) leaders. This book will help business analysts anticipate fledgling terrorist threats by looking at past terrorist targeting trends against commercial interests in those countries. The reason why is that solid data about terrorist targeting trends can help business leaders prepare non-kinetic "soft-line" counterterrorism strategies and tactics in anticipation of future terrorist attacks.

1.2 Host Countries Examined

A breakdown by region where the top five U.S. based multinational corporation (MNC) subsidiaries are found in the developing world included Asia, Latin America, and Africa. The five nation-states examined are India, Mexico, Brazil, South Africa, and Thailand. India ranked first with 643 U.S. based "parent" organizations (2693 "foreign subsidiaries"); Mexico had 604 U.S. based "parent" organizations (4395 "foreign subsidiaries"); and Brazil had 561 U.S. based "parent" organizations (2214 "foreign subsidiaries). In turn, South Africa ranked fourth with 302 U.S. based "parent" organizations (804 "foreign subsidiaries"). Thailand rounded out the five countries under consideration with 283 U.S. based "parent" organizations (899 "foreign subsidiaries") [58].

For definitional purposes, U.S. "parent" organizations are described in *UniWorld* data as publicly owned American "parent companies" of firms in particular countries. In comparison, "foreign subsidiaries," are defined by Hill as "foreign operations," reflective of extended firm operations in "host" countries [29, 348].

The approach of this study was to rank those five countries according to the number of U.S. based multinational corporation "parent" organizations in each country, as of March 2019. The primary reason U.S. based MNC "parent" organizations was chosen as the unit of measurement was because many MNC corporate leaders have strategies to relocate subsidiaries to new country and regional locations in pursuit of profit as international business environment conditions evolve.

For example, "host" country leaders might devalue the local currency to improve sales of their own domestic products. Alternatively, such leaders might impose new business requirements, such as joint ventures between international firms and domestic companies, that put the core competencies of those international enterprises at risk for theft by domestic partners [16, 352–362; 29, 130,137, 378–379; 46, 490] In addition, other factors that produce risk for international firm investment include political factors in host countries, such as ethnic conflict, terrorism, and war.

The numerous reasons behind business leader decisions to make these strategic shifts in geographical locale are well documented in the literature. For example, Flores and Aguilera compare MNC locations in 1980 and in 2000, and spell out some significant factors that influenced MNC leader decisions about where to set up shop.

For the authors, factors included, market size, anticipated wage rates in a "host" country, the prospect of increased transaction costs, and business leader desires to be in close proximity to "host" country markets to skirt around tariffs. In addition, the authors point to cultural affinities and legal system similarities between home and host countries that help influence multinational corporation investment decisions [21, 1193–1194].

Flores and Aguilera found that in most cases, the plant relocation process was piecemeal. It was made incrementally over the twenty-year period examined. For the authors, "first, we discover a strong MNC *de-location* in certain regions, such as Africa, the Caribbean and Central America. This means that U.S. MNCs had subsidiaries in these regions in 1980 and withdrew them by 2000." [21, 1190, 1203; 29].

It follows that change in foreign subsidiary numbers inherent to this relocation strategy makes focus on "foreign subsidiaries" as the unit of analysis a less reliable indicator of American multinational corporation presence and long-run interest in established "host" countries favored by American firms. In other words, focus on "foreign subsidiary" numbers would amount to more of a snapshot in time for an appraisal of the top five developing world host countries with U.S. based MNC operations; only valid for a few years.[1]

1.3 An Operational System of Terrorism

A second key idea in this book is the notion of a terrorism system. For example, a terrorism system can be defined in broad or narrower terms such as an "earth-moon loop system," a region, a country, a city, or a neighborhood [14]. The boundaries of a terrorism system reflect the scope of analysis determined by researchers. A terrorism system is characterized by three component elements. Stakeholders are those nation-state and non-state actors that populate the system and interact with each other directly, and indirectly [51, 5–6, 10, 17–18, 20–21, 63–64, 74].

In turn, explanatory factors are the sources and origins of terrorism threat formation. Lastly, "stressors," are political events and processes, either internal or external to an operational system (or both) that can shock the terrorism system. Such shocks affect interactions between stakeholders, and stakeholders and explanatory factors and can produce second and third order effects [22; 51, 5–6, 10, 17–18, 20–21, 63–64, 74].

[1] The decision to rank countries based on numbers of U.S. based MNC "parent organizations" is also useful because in three out of the five country cases examined (i.e., India, Brazil, and Thailand), the 2019 *Uniworld* rankings of subsidiaries (and their numbers) closely corresponded to the rankings for "parent organizations".

In some cases, the shock from a massive "political stressor" can alter a terrorism system or a broader regional or world operational system in the long haul. For example, many analysts point out the War in Ukraine (2022) led to a structural shift in the economic and political relationships of nation-states and business location strategies when an unprecedented set of economic sanctions were levied against Russian institutions.

Those unprecedented economic sanctions included, but were not limited to, complete removal of Russia from the SWIFT international banking system, efforts to freeze Russian assets in the U.S. and European Union, and sanctions against Russia's Central Bank and "Sovereign Wealth Fund," and efforts to freeze Russian assets abroad owned by Putin, many of his advisors, and many Russian oligarchs. In quick succession, President Joseph R. Biden also issued an American Executive Order to ban Russian oil and natural gas imports into the United States [18, 42, 56].

In addition to primary effects, the anticipated and actual shock to the international political system those economic sanctions caused also produced secondary effects that helped to reconfigure economic relationships between Russia and other countries such as India. In the early days of the war, Prime Minister Narendra Modi, at the helm of the second largest nation-state energy consumer behind China, made a deal with President Putin to purchase Russian oil. Modi's decision was based largely on India's economic needs and its time honored political relationship with Russia and the Soviet Union [60].

Indeed, those coordinated economic sanctions led to third order effects—Russian threats of force against Western business executives in Moscow which in my judgement, amounted to state terrorism. There were reports about intimidation and threats made to Western business executives staying in Moscow within the first three weeks of the war [38]. This example worked to underscore the clear links between political events and terrorist threat formation, and the risk to business executives. More discussion about terrorism systems and the complex systems analysis used to gauge threat formation is found in Chap. 3.

1.4 Terrorism—New Challenges in Research

The study of terrorism in the contemporary world presents certain new challenges for researchers. In large part, those research challenges galvanized because of the continuously evolving nature of globalization. It appears that the end of the Cold War and continued globalization, are factors behind the sources of some of those challenges. For example, some of the traditional theoretical distinctions in terrorism research used to sort out terrorist groups have become much less clear with the passage of time. For example, it is sometimes more difficult to make distinctions between international terrorism, transnational terrorism, where terrorist groups are largely self-sufficient in financial and political terms, and domestic terrorism.

The case of Faisal Shahzad, the so-called "Times Square bomber" who attempted to detonate an SUV full of explosives on May 1, 2010 illustrates the problem. A naturalized American citizen from Pakistan, Shahzad travelled to Waziristan, Pakistan to train with Tehrik-e-Taliban and then back to the United States to commit his attack [43, 120–121, 105, 44]. The Faisal Shazad case clearly showcased the problem with traditional conceptualizations because it is not clear if Shazad's actions qualified as international terrorism, domestic terrorism, or transnational terrorism.

The reason why is Shahzad was a naturalized American citizen, but trained with a foreign terrorist group in Pakistan, and then returned to attack an American target—Times Square. This case also highlights another issue. It begs the question of whether or not this act was carried out by a terrorist group (the Taliban) or a lone operative or both. At a theoretical level, one significant example of conceptual overlap is the distinction between terrorist organizations and criminal syndicalist groups that use terrorism as means to achieve monetary gain. This is a specific focus of this book and in Chap. 4, efforts are made to explore this issue in some depth [20; 37, 129–145; 53; 54].

What complicates the picture even more is that terrorist groups have what Lasswell calls "life-cycles," where terrorist groups can transform into criminal gangs over time. It is also conceivable that criminal gangs could evolve into terrorist organizations. Still, that is probably less likely because of fundamental differences in the nature of both types of organizations [34; 35, 253–263].

This type of evolution should be viewed as on a spectrum where mixtures of criminal and terrorist activities practiced by both organizations happen [20, 37, 54]. The case of the Abu Sayyaf Group (ASG) in the Philippines and Mokhtar Bel Mokhtar's "Battalion of Blood" are as good examples as any of the (de)evolution from terrorist organization to criminal syndicalist enterprise.

What is significant is many terrorist events conducted by criminal syndicalists are characterized by a mix of narrower political themes oftentimes more functional or instrumental in nature [20]. Those criminal actions are dominated by criminal motivations and objectives and usually revolve around economic profit. Still, those criminal syndicalists use terrorism. For example, such terrorist events include organized criminal group efforts to intimidate politicians, judges, and police officials, in efforts to water down anti-drug legislation, reduce police crackdowns or intimidate judges so they impose lighter sentences on criminals.

As the previous example about the War in Ukraine demonstrates, the use of terrorism is not only relegated to terrorist groups and criminal gangs. It has a time honored and long standing place in the historical and contemporary practices of nation-states. One example to be discussed is the 1997 Acteal massacre in the Mexican state of Chiapas.

In this instance, a government militia group known as Mascara Roja ("Red Mask"), slaughtered forty-five indigenous people in a refugee encampment on the bank of a highway in Chiapas's Chenalho municipality. Mascara Roja was one of many government sanctioned militias supported by the Ernesto Zedillo government that recruited from poor Mexico agricultural workers to fight against the Zapatista movement [1, 677–694; 41, 18–25].

From a theoretical perspective, terrorism spans over and into different realms of conflict. Terrorism is used within the context of "total war," where ordinary citizens in a country become legitimate targets and where in many cases, there is full mobilization of a country's research institutions and other resources to contribute to the war effort [43, 120–121, 105]. For example, the bombing of Dresden and Tokyo, the London Blitz, and decision by President Harry S. Truman to drop atomic bombs on Hiroshima and Nagasaki amounted to terrorist events within the context of "Total War" because "the laws of war" were violated. Indeed, "total war" qualifies as state terrorism if non-combatants are purposefully, systematically, or indiscriminately targeted.

1.5 Related Conflict Conditions

The conceptual overlap between terrorism and other related conflicted conditions can be visualized with a Venn diagram. In this diagram, the conflict conditions of oppression, repression, criminal syndicalism, and political protest each have a portion of its domain which overlaps with activities from other conflict condition domains [57, 8]. What that means is a portion of each domain qualifies as (state) terrorism. It follows from this depiction that state-run militaries and paramilitary groups, criminal syndicalist enterprises, lone actors, and political protestors each might have a portion of its activities which overlap with the portion of terrorism practiced by other types of perpetrators.

For example, the January 6, 2021 insurrection, allegedly led by President Donald J. Trump, is a subset of a larger portion of American Republican right-wing protest against the election of President Biden. At the same time, that "protest" against the smooth transition in executive power probably qualifies as terrorism because a substantial number of terrorist acts happened as it unfolded. Threats generally supported by the crowds were made to hang Vice President Mike Pence and kill House Speaker Nancy Pelosi. The symbols of terrorism, including a large noose and platform erected outside the Capitol building were made plain to see.

Moreover, sometimes even within one particular act or acts of protest at a specific moment in time, some protestors might enter into that shared domain of terrorism and become terrorists with use or the threat of illegal force. That would stand in sharp contrast, for example to the threat or use of force for unavoidable self-defense purposes. Frequently, those threats are issued against the police, counter-protestors, or other citizens deemed to be either non-supporters or insufficiently supportive of the political cause at hand.

In other words, while not all of the actions taken by a particular type of stakeholder such as a criminal gang or mob of protestors qualifies as terrorism, some actions that do meet the jurisprudential criteria spelled out in Chap. 2 clearly do qualify as terrorism. For instance, mob violence (i.e., riots) characterized by more explicit or implicit political aims, coupled with the threat, use, or promotion of force as backdrop or context to those political protests, might qualify as terrorism [9, 75, 85; 57, 8] (see Fig. 1.1).

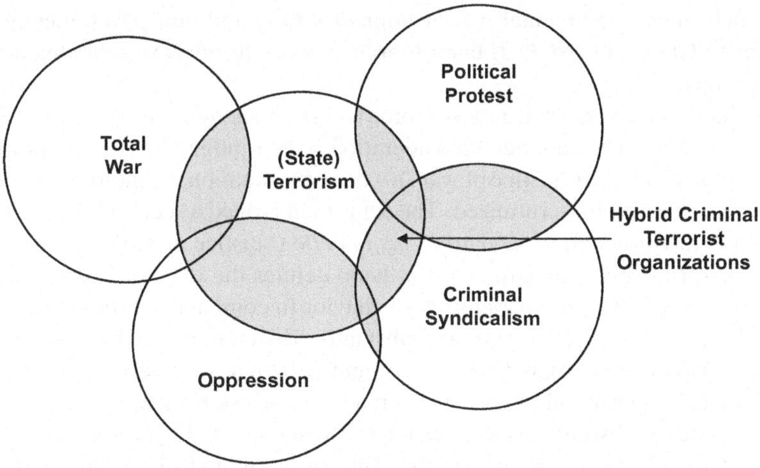

Fig. 1.1 Venn diagram of related conflict conditions

All of the foregoing suggests it is prudent to be very selective about the acts included in a database on terrorism and the definition of terrorism used for data coding purposes. A definition that puts special focus on the political themes found in forceful actions in general, with the capacity to take into account even what ostensibly appear to be (terrorist) criminal actions, is a useful tool for terrorism analysis because of the conceptual overlap conditions previously described.

1.6 Terrorism Definition

The rich body of international law makes it possible to articulate jurisprudential boundaries between the justifiable threat or use of force and illegal threats or use of force. This approach to thinking about where justifiable insurgency ends and where terrorism begins is preferable to more subjective appraisals of terrorism. Those subjective terrorism appraisals oftentimes fall back on who the perpetrator is, or other perpetrator characteristics, such as ideology or geographical locale where the attack happened.

In previous work, I crafted such a definition that is presented in Chap. 2. This terrorism definition is based primarily on "the laws of war" found within international law. The two jurisprudential standards used to define the parameters of actions that might qualify as terrorism include the jurisprudential standards of *jus ad bellum* ("justice of war") and *jus in bello* ("justice in war").

In that definition, terrorism is conceptualized as the threat, use, or promotion of force to change the political attitudes or political dispositions of state or non-state leaders. This definition also accounts for forceful actions taken by state and non-state leaders designed to change government policy, or the policies of non-state actors such intergovernmental organizations (IGO's) and non-governmental organizations (NGO's and INGO's) that oftentimes work to improve relations between ethnic groups.[2]

At a functional level, when an act of force is carried out by a state or non-state actor, it is judged twice. The act under consideration is first judged by the jurisprudential standard of *jus ad bello* ("justice of war"), where the situational conditions associated with the use of force are scrutinized. The act is then judged a second time taking into account the jurisprudential standard of *jus in bello* ("justice in war").

The jurisprudential standard of *jus in bello* defines the rules of law that serve as guideposts for military and paramilitary behavior in combat situations [4, 291–306; 5, 329–351; 6, 129–154]. In this way, substantive distinctions can be made between acts that qualify as justifiable insurgency and acts that are likely to be terrorism, based on whether criminal intent ("mens rea") can be established.

The capacity to distinguish between terrorism and justifiable insurgency is crucial because justifiable insurgency is sanctioned under international law, and that provides benefits. For example, the status of justifiable insurgency affords prisoner of war protections to insurgents that are not available to terrorists. In addition, acquiring justifiable insurgency status also creates the potential to elicit political, economic, and military support from third parties.

Nowadays, those distinctions have become even more complex but at the same time, still vital to consider. One reason why is because the conceptual boundaries between stakeholders, such as criminal syndicalists, terrorist groups, political protestors, and so-called "lone-wolves" have become increasing opaque.

For example, imagine a criminal syndicalist group member, who worked in conjunction with a group in opposition to a government that commits egregious human rights violations. That claim of membership in a justifiable insurgency might have potential to make overall prosecution more complicated politically, if the funds raised were used in support of a conflict that qualified as justifiable insurgency.

Nowadays, the distinction between justifiable insurgency and terrorism has also become more crucial and vital because of the range of terrorism types, now increasingly characterized by conceptual overlap in a globalized world. As previously mentioned, those terrorism types include international terrorism, transnational terrorism, and domestic terrorism. Those designation types, once more easily conceptualized, can have substantive implications for prosecutorial decisions and processes.

For example, what follows a determination of whether or not an act qualifies as terrorism, is the question of making a final decision from among competing claims about primary venue for prosecution. This quickly becomes a complex political issue because legal systems in potential venues of prosecution differ with respect to certain basic jurisprudential practices such as the imposition of the death penalty. Such inconsistencies across legal systems not only have potential to pose bilateral

[2] The neoliberal institutionalist approach puts emphasis on non-state actor efforts, with focus on inter-governmental organizations in particular, to promote cooperation between states.

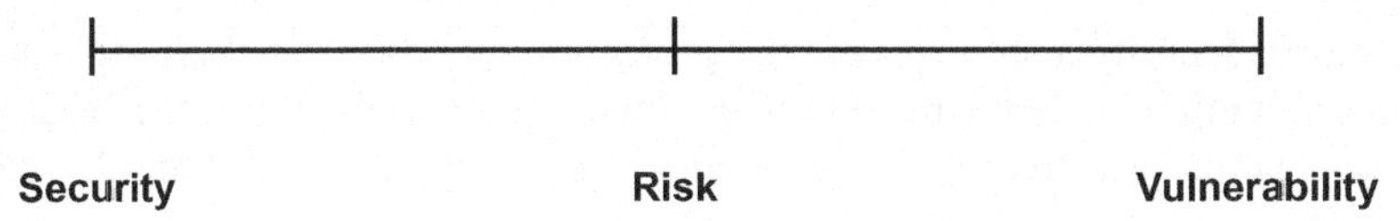

Fig. 1.2 Continuum of security and related concepts

extradition problems in some cases, but increase the prospect of legal manipulations by both prosecution and legal defense teams.

1.7 The Concept of Security

An analysis of the terrorism threat to multinational corporations (MNC) and small, and medium-size enterprises (SME) requires discussion about the concepts of security, vulnerability, and risk and the theoretical links between them. The framework for discussion about what security, vulnerability, and risk are about includes: concept definition; relational and stand-alone comfort level approaches to security; the broader theoretical and functional aspects of each concept. These three concepts are depicted by a continuum where security is placed at the left axis of this spectrum, risk is placed at the middle part, and vulnerability is placed at the right axis of the continuum (see Fig. 1.2).

In the case of security, Buzan reports there is no one widely shared, generally recognizable definition of security [7, 97, 99, 150, 162]. For the purposes of this book, the concept of security can be conceived of in two distinct but interrelated ways. The first standpoint considers security as a psychological condition of comfort obtained, where a small group such as business leaders or an individual, achieves an acceptable level of freedom from worry about specific events, processes, or a threating environment. Under such conditions, the relatively low probabilities for victimization found are acceptable.

The second standpoint views security as a relational concept where the achievement of concrete security benchmarks, defined in economic and political terms for businesses and in political, economic, and military terms for states, lends itself to relational comparisons made with corresponding capacities of competitors. This notion of security draws heavily on the central idea that political scientists such as Morton Deutsch articulate, which is that "power is a relational concept" where neither states, businesses, nor individuals are powerful alone or in the abstract [19; 43, 84–85; 49].

From the perspective that security is a psychological condition of comfort, Morgan states, "security is a condition, like health or status which defies easy definition and analysis" [7, 97, 110].[3] The idea of security as a condition of comfort obtained, extends beyond the individual and small groups, to include the nation-state where in addition to protections to prevent foreign and domestic attacks, Wolfers informs us

[3] Morgan, Patrick. [40] "Safeguarding Security Studies" *Arms Control*, 13(3):466–479)

that national security also involves "the protection of values" such as the values of wealth accumulation, democratization, the inviolability of the human rights regime, and the benefits of a free market economy [7, 114, 225–227; 8, 68; 43, 165; 61, 29–45].

What is significant is that emphasis on psychological comfort also extends to business firms. In the case of business firms, sufficient economic assets, sound organizational structures, political influence, and favorable industry structures (i.e., monopoly, duopoly) work to provide an acceptable psychological comfort level of security. That parallels the psychological comfort level acquired by state leaders with the acquisition of state security assets such as substantial defense budgets and sophisticated weapons and adequate state and societal resilience levels [10, 476–503].

Wolfers' notion of security as "the protection of values" is also critical for the business world. For example, corporate social responsibility (CSR) measures taken by firms in the business world serve to promote and protect certain enshrined corporate values, and to create new norms and values such as the value associated with products that ensure environmental protection. Firms with strong focus on those values include General Electric and Proctor and Gamble [16, 36]. In addition, a firm's efforts to augment worker resilience to be able to cope with environmental "stressors" such as COVID-19 and the War in Ukraine would in my judgement, also qualify as a Wolfers-style norm to protect and enhance business security.

Clearly, this notion of a comfort level obtained is true for security, and for its polar opposite, a "false sense" of security. As Booth suggests, security involves rational discernable beliefs about threat that lead to accurate comfort level appraisals—a process that he calls "objective security." In comparison, its opposite, namely a "false sense" of security, or what Booth calls "subjective security," reflects a condition where risk comfort levels and assuredness about "relative invulnerability" to use Powell's term, are incompatible with actual risk factors in environments readily discernable to other people [7, 105–106, 110]. For Booth, "those who feel safe when they are not (because they do not perceive the threats and risks around them) have a false sense of security, those who feel threatened because they perceive threats and risk that are not present, live with a false sense of insecurity." [7, 110, 105, 149–150; 32, 173–174; 48, 27].

Having said that, security still remains a multi-faceted concept with several dimensions. Even within the context of the "comfort level" psychological perspective, the notion of security as an acceptable level of freedom, free from worry about threat is limited. It is overly reactive and thus only an incomplete part of what security means and is all about. Booth draws on Hobbes' work to suggest a more proactive dimension to security where security is more than basic survival. For Booth, security is a condition that allows human creativity to thrive in effective and sustained ways.

For Booth, "security implies *survival plus*, and for a species with a highly developed consciousness, this means creating space for human self-invention beyond merely existing. Thomas Hobbes understood the instrumental value of security, and thus its role in life beyond simply surviving." [7, 39, 110].

Clearly, that is especially relevant for business firms. The business firm is a structure that produces and capitalizes on "human creativity" through its organizational capacities. In turn, improvements in organizational effectiveness and firm efficiency requires innovation [33, 27]. Such innovation requires political space and distance from direct government involvement. In essence, what the foregoing amounts to is Booth's "survival plus," or namely the capacity to thrive [7, 38–39, 110; 33, 25–27; 59, 105–129].

At the same time, tangible improvements in the human condition, associated with Booth's more proactive security conceptualization of "self-invention," still revolve around a psychological condition or state of mind [32, 173–174].[4] It is, I think, not just about a series of personal, societal, or industrial benchmarks to achieve in relation to others. In other words, it is not necessarily a condition where stakeholders constantly compare their security condition in a relational sense at particular moments of time. At some point in the process of resource and power accumulation, and Booth's "self-invention," a threshold of security comfort is reached where relational comparisons of specific aspects of security become less significant.

This notion of comfort level can also be found in the world of business. In the case of particular industries, this can amount to a monopoly or duopoly condition where barriers to entry for a particular industry, such as production of high-capacity commercial jetliners, are extremely high and where established firms such as Boeing Co. have "first mover advantage." [16, 273; 29, 81, 171–172, 178, 310; 30, 179–180; 36, 290–291]. At some threshold, individual, group, business firms, and nation-state security transforms from being a more relational concept where benchmarks of achievement are frequently compared, to one that is more comfort based and less relational.

In contrast to the psychological comfort approach to security just described, there is the relational concept approach to security. Implicit to this standpoint is an appraisal of security by means of regular and sustained comparisons to competitors or adversaries. A potential problem with the relational concept of security is that approach seems to imply a zero-sum approach to security in ways that discount "win–win" approaches or "win–win" events and processes [3, 517; 43]. That narrower focus about what constitutes a "win" situation from a "zero-sum" standpoint has particular drawbacks in a highly interconnected world.

In the business world "win–win" approaches exemplified by outsourcing for component parts assembly for example, highlight collaborative ventures between firms. Such collaborative ventures are increasingly common because of specialization processes and technological expertise that help to reduce the economic costs of production. For example, aircraft companies such as Boeing outsource to European companies to develop and assemble specific parts of Boeing commercial aircraft. It would seem Booth's notion of "survival plus" lends itself better to a work environment with more collaborate standpoints where there is a cross fertilization of ideas to achieve the creativity required [29, 173, 7, 13; 50, 84].

Furthermore, what constitutes the ability to thrive or flourish at acceptable levels beyond simple survival—what Booth calls "survival plus"—can be a more subjective

[4] This concept draws on Jervis' notion of "subjective security demands," where leaders have various security sensitivities.

interpretation of security, rather than the achievement of quantitative or qualitative benchmarks. For states and ethnic or religious groups for example, what constitutes security might reflect internalized cultural or societal benchmarks that reflect culturally driven notions of success and attainment, rather than reliance on a process of comparison and competition.

For example, Scandinavian countries embrace a notion of security that takes into account quality of life components as internal benchmarks of security. To be sure, this focus on Scandinavian countries might be one way to think about Buzan and Waever's notion of resilient "regional security complexes (RSC's)," albeit from a slightly different angle, where, "...RSC's...are defined (at the more "superficial" or contingent level) by the actual patterns of security practices." In effect, that results in a more expansive notion of security [8, 41, 47, 28, 44, 67, 76, 70, 8, 7].[5]

The notion of security as one that either revolves around achievement of security benchmarks or comfort levels is considered somewhat differently in Patterson and Gleeson Blue's work, which puts a twist on the traditional emphasis on security as a relational concept between actors. In this embrace of the relational approach to security, Patterson and Gleason Blue suggest that greater or lesser amounts of security is a function of greater or lesser degrees of risk.

For Patterson and Gleeson Blue, security is related to a decline in risk in an inverse relationship. In other words, a decrease in risk leads to an increase in security, and vice vera [13, 2, 183 n3, n4; 39, 14–17, 6 n7, 4; 45, 19–20, 35, 41]. The authors also describe risk in spatial terms as a measure of an actor's distance from harm. In this case, the authors demonstrate that an actor (i.e., an individual, group, nation-state, or business) is not secure in isolation from others, but is secure in direct relation to the distance that actor is from harm. For Patterson and Gleeson Blue, removal of risk factors works to enhance security [7, 39, 110; 13, 2, 183 n4; 17, 201–205, 45, 19–20, 35, 41; 49].[6]

1.8 The Concepts of Vulnerability and Risk

Security and vulnerability are conditions where each can be appraised in more abstract psychological terms or in relational terms. Business leaders might feel vulnerable in the abstract without making specific comparisons to other firms if they are aware their business has insufficient assets and revenue flows to stay in business. Alternately, if those leaders compare a firm's assets and revenue flows to other firms in the same industry, vulnerability becomes a relational concept.

It is the notion of risk that serves as the glue that binds security and vulnerability together. The connection between security and vulnerability is an inverse relationship where an increase in security leads to a decrease in vulnerability, and vice versa.

[5] This example suggests the role of culture as one of the determinants to security conceptualization.

[6] Risk, as conceptualized, parallels notions of power as conceptualized by Robert A. Dahl, Anatol Rapoport, and Morton Deutsch.

There are two widely understood ways to conceptualize risk. For Monahan, one approach to risk is "risk abatement," where risk is viewed from an actuarial sciences perspective. From that risk perspective, the mathematical probabilities of victimization in specific environments are calculated [8; 12; 39, 14–17, 6 n7, 4]. Monahan's second approach to risk is "risk reduction."

For Monahan, "risk reduction" involves the removal, constraint, or severe decrease of explanatory factors and their effects in operational environments. From this second Monahan perspective, factors work alone or coalesce with others to cause risk [8; 12; 39, 14–17, 6 n7, 4]. Monahan suggests those different meanings of the term "risk" contribute to policy formulation problems in areas that include business security policy planning, because different analysts might work with different conceptual meanings of risk.

This book's approach to risk conforms to Monahan's second risk approach, described as "risk reduction." Indeed, Monahan's second approach is fundamentally the same approach used by Patterson and Gleeson-Blue. To reiterate, risk reduction from that standpoint involves the removal of explanatory factors or the or constraint of their effects that work alone or coalesce to cause risk in specific operational environments [39, 45, 55].

It follows that firm security depends on the set of risk factors in a specific operational environment, how those risk factors are managed, and how their effects are reduced. In turn, the effectiveness of those protective management processes either work to increase or decrease the intensity of highly emotional feelings of vulnerability. That linkage between risk factor management and feelings of vulnerability appear to hold whether or not the concept of vulnerability is appraised by means of a psychological comfort perspective or from a relational point of view.

The sources of political, economic, social, or cultural risk factors to business are fundamentally internal to a particular terrorism system. At the same time, exogenous factors known as "stressors" can be external to a system and are found at the structural level of the international political system. Those "stressors" can work in conjunction with internal or endogenous risk factors to produce threat.

For example, the war in Ukraine is an exogenous risk factor that has produced economic shocks to commercial interests in countries outside of Russia and Ukraine. The war increased business leader feelings of vulnerability; it affected risk factors associated with business security. For example, reduced availability of supplies led to supply price increases, which contributed to inflation. In turn, inflation and higher interest rates made it harder for business leaders to borrow money to cover costs. Whether or not comparison to the condition of other firms was made, the underlying problem was vulnerability and the desire of business leaders for the conflict over Ukraine to end as quickly as possible.

There are other examples of significant exogenous "stressors" with sources external to a particular operational system of terrorism defined by region or country. Those included global economic shocks such as the Asian economic crisis (1997–1998) and the Great Recession (2007–2009). Indeed, the Asian economic crisis was an explanatory factor that contributed to the rise of Islamic extremism in Indonesia and Malaysia. The rise of Islamic extremism in Indonesia had profound and lasting effects on business on the island of Bali and across the world in 2002 and 2005 [52].

1.9 The Security Issue Agenda

An important question to consider for both the business world and government is how issues make the cut to appear onto the corporate or government security agenda in the first place. What constitutes a set of security issues, or the "securitization" of issues, is a political process found in both the private and public sectors. It follows that issue "securitization" also shapes vulnerability.

While many worthy issues become securitized, there are many other worthy issues that do not. At least in part, this might be due to a psychological mindset in individuals that will not accept fully what risk is all about. As previously mentioned in discussion about the concept of security, this is reflective of Booth's notion of a "false sense" of security [7, 110, 149–150].

In the case of the business world, many critical security matters do not make the agenda or rank low on such agendas because they do not fall within narrower corporate driven norms and values about security that revolve around notions of profit. "Securitized issues" include cybersecurity, workplace violence prevention, economic security by means of product line diversification, multiple organizational structures to account for diverse product lines, and host country macroeconomic policy.

One reason why a narrower range of securitized issues is the norm involves business costs that can be affected by host country government policy. For example, legal requirements exist in many host countries for international firms to keep a certain amount of monetary assets in local currency denominations. Accordingly, government currency devaluations, designed to make domestic goods more attractive than the imported commodities, can work to dwindle international firm assets.

However, one critical issue that for the most part not been securitized in the business world is the threat of terrorism. The reasons why are hard to explain but some point to a two-fold explanation. For some, that reluctance stems from a reduction in profit associated with thinking about anti-terrorism as a fixed or variable cost intrinsic to business operations.

That is compounded by what some see as part of the human condition where efforts to downplay risk predominates until a watershed and catastrophic event happens. Be that as it may, proactive, non-kinetic counterterrorism efforts by international enterprises as a vital part doing business have been makeshift and incomplete at best.

That seems to be a glaring omission because many countries rely heavily on tourism and related sectors to supply essential government revenue. Accordingly, small and medium sized enterprises (SME) become vulnerable and valuable targets for terrorist group leaders who seek to damage the national economies of governments. Such economically calibrated terrorist campaigns have unfolded in various countries throughout the world. Those include Egypt with Islamic extremist terrorist assaults in Luxor, Indonesia with the Bali I (2002) and Bali II (2005) bombings, and in India, Mali, and in the United Kingdom in Northern Ireland [52, 1012–1058].

The interplay of several different factors probably contributes to this condition. For Buzan and Waever, the "issue securitization" process varies on a case by case basis. It is based on a country or a specific region's social and political institutional processes the authors call "vectors," and those specific streams of factor influence are extremely powerful. Such "vectors" include the economy, environmental policy, legal systems, and the human rights regime of a nation-state or region [8, 3, 44, 18, 8, 48, 52, 71–72, 86].

It follows that different political or social sector effects with influence over the securitization process will have different and sometimes unforeseen impacts or outcomes. This seems especially the case when different individuals and groups are involved at local, state, provincial, or department levels of government. It is reasonable to suggest that similar dynamics also play out in multinational corporations (MNC's), other international enterprises, and small and medium sized (SME) domestic firms, particularly as business officials in host countries must interact with government.

Those businesses have to navigate through political and social sectors at various governmental levels to prioritize items in the "issue securitization" process [8, 3, 44, 18, 8, 48, 52, 71–72, 86]. This multiplicity of influences across and within levels of government makes a uniform and standardized ranking of securitized issues extremely difficult for international businesses to make, especially for those firms with business operations in several countries. This notion of "securitization" and the range of non-kinetic counterterrorism policy alternatives available to multinational corporations and other international enterprises, themselves based on that "securitization" process, derive from environmental "contextual factors." Both dovetail well with Brian Jenkins' typology of international enterprise counterterrorism choice presented in the Foreword to this book.

Thus, terrorists with economic disruption goals in mind to target Western countries or capitalism as an ideological system, or to confront targeted governments because of political or economic grievances, have a potent weapon. They know that carefully reasoned terrorist assaults with strategic interests in mind can cause ripple effects in nation-state or regional economies, or as in the case of 9/11, the world economy [15, 47]. For a more detailed discussion, the reader is referred to my book, *Corporate Security Crossroads: Responding to Terrorism, Cyberthreats and Other Hazards in the Global Business Environment* [13].

1.10 Definitions of Business Security

All of the foregoing about the connections between security, risk, and vulnerability, highlights the need for a more precise and meticulous definition of what business security in the broader sense really means. One definition of "business security" that is a good fit with Monahan's work about "risk abatement" and "risk removal" is provided by Spich and Grosse.

For Spich and Grosse, "business security can be defined as a defensive strategy, and a state of organizational readiness to assure and protect (but not guarantee) the functional integrity of the organization's operational systems against purposeful, willful and intentional attempts by agents (inside or outside) to disrupt, damage, dismantle or destroy them." [13, 2, 184 n7; 55, 468]. Both the subjective nature of security and its various dimensions, (such as whether it is proactive or reactive, or reliance is placed on psychological comfort level or relational concept perspectives), make the process of business "securitization" nuanced and complex, with anticipated and unanticipated effects on "a state of organizational readiness." [13, 2, 184 n7; 55, 468].

Spich and Grosse's emphasis on defensive measures in their definition of business security is useful because businesses are prohibited from proactive or reactive kinetic efforts to reduce or eliminate threats in both the physical and virtual worlds. In addition, Spich and Grosse's idea of the importance of business organizational design and its functionality is critical in the context of business security. In no small part, this is because of the characteristics of "intensive globalization."

With respect to business security, those organizational design and functionality issues involve decentralization, supply chain and product manufacturing vulnerabilities, and interdependencies. Those potential vulnerabilities are found up in the "primary activities" value chain in R&D for example, and down the value chain in marketing service response. The importance of those design and functionality issues seems to be compounded and especially important for companies with multiple product lines. Those interdependencies and vulnerabilities are also found in value chain midstream activities such as production [13; 16; 29, 338–339; 30, 342–344].

1.11 The Threat to Multinational Corporations and Small and Middle Size Enterprises (SME's)

Globalization is a time-honored phenomenon that traces an arc back thousands of years, probably to the ancient Greeks and Phoenicians. What is new is our highly connected and conflated world is characterized by widely available computer technology and increased globalization. With the end of the Cold War and the computer revolution, the threat and scope of terrorism has changed as the world has become more politically and economically interdependent. For example, some suggest the frequency of terrorist assaults with conflict sources far removed geographically from terrorist assault venues have increased over the past few decades.

What is significant here is that globalization's continued growth coupled with new technology due to the computer revolution has ushered the world into an era of "intensive globalization." From an economic interdependence point of view, "intensive globalization" is characterized by a set of thicker, but more intricate connections between financial markets and markets for durable goods within the international system.

Moreover, this "intensive globalization" condition has helped to elicit new explanatory factors tied to terrorist threat formation with the potential to affect commercial interests in ways that are unprecedented. It has amplified existing explanatory factor effects at the systems level linked to terrorism such as COVID-19 and climate change. Intensive globalization is also linked to unprecedented refugee flows from the Middle East, Africa, and Latin America.

Because of political and economic interdependencies across states, "intensive globalization" has also enhanced the effects of time-honored explanatory factors linked to terrorism that are found within countries. Those include economic blight, uneven economic development, relative deprivation, and increasing gaps between the "haves" and "have not's" throughout the world [13; 11, 119–131; 20, 4, 15, 188 n47, 76, 95, 102, 109, 114, 149; 25; 26; 27; 24, 203; 23, 82–95; 50, 81–82, 78–79, 87–88, 90, 95–96].

Multinational corporations and other international enterprises confront challenges that stem from this increasingly complex world. As previously mentioned, the structural organizational frameworks designed to account for this new era of intensive globalization are quite fragile, with webs of interconnections prone to disruption and damage. A cursory overview of "matrix," "network," and "transnational" organizational structures provide insight into business organizational complexities that translate into vulnerability. The scope of those structures underscores the degree of vulnerability and risk at stake in today's international economy.

In a "matrix strategy," business leaders sort out firm administrative responsibilities into specialized administrative divisions. Those administrative divisions include monitor and oversight functions for "mid-stream" and "downstream" value chain activities such as marketing, production, distribution, and customer finance options. In the larger world of action, many if not most corporations operate with "hybrid" versions of those organizational structures.

Further, responsibilities in a "matrix strategy" can be funneled even more into administrative units that oversee the locale where firms operate, such as North America, Europe, and the Middle East [36, 321–323]. In this framework, more than one business strategy can be used to take into account the needs associated with product line and geographical diversity. This stands in contrast to "network structures," where multiple strategies are intrinsic to their structure and process [36, 321–323; 16, 326–328].

In comparison, a "transnational network" framework is much more decentralized than a "matrix structure" or "network structure." [16, 326–328; 36, 320–324]. In this case, multiple units in charge of all phases of production and overall marketing strategies are integrated tightly into specific countries or regions. In this decentralized structure, entire units of operation can operate more independently with strategies that focus on local conditions such as local markets, and catering to the tastes and preferences which affect local production and sales.

As a result of their relative autonomy within a "transnational network," foreign subsidiaries are better able to develop and share new knowledge and best practices with corporate leadership within the firm's world-wide network. At the same time, it is clear that terrorist attacks against entire units of operation that characterize a network strategy have the potential to compound the scope and depth of damage to the infrastructure of a firm.

1.12 The "Just-In-Time" Inventory System

Another example of how intensive globalization has created vulnerabilities and risk involves the increasing use of the "just-in-time" inventory strategy. This system revolves around the idea that manufacturers should keep inventory levels in warehouses just sufficiently high to meet more immediate consumer demand [29, 430; 30, 439–440].

The "just-in-time" inventory system is neither a new nor an original strategy to any one industry. Still, its importance has grown apace as a result of new technology development where in specific industries like the computer software and hardware industries, products become outdated within a few years, if not within a few months.

The "just-in-time" inventory system is also compatible with consumer and supplier needs across several industries such as technology, pharmacology, food, and water supply. For example, new biologics medicines such Taltz, Enbrel, Humera, and Cimzia used to treat arthritis are manufactured from living organisms and at present, no generic substitutes are available. Biologics are fragile, vulnerable to high temperature, have a limited shelf-life and are very expensive.

In the case of food supply, the increasing volume of exports and imports that involve the fruit, vegetable, and fish industries has grown with the wider range of goods available due to globalization. That market interdependence condition makes "just-in-time" inventory an indispensable strategy. In addition, "just-in-time inventory" is critical for commercial food production, storage, and distribution activities. That is the case because fresh food is a perishable commodity. Likewise, at geographical locales where clean water is not readily available, the "just-in-time" inventory system is also suitable for bottled water production.

Therefore, the "just-in-time" system has substantial production and distribution vulnerabilities. It is particularly sensitive to supply disruptions by terrorist assaults and criminal activity because product flow can be impeded and illicit activities can cause substantial business losses through a reduction in sales and increased cost transactions, such as transportation costs. In addition, product flow is crucial because climate change exacerbates critical food and water shortages brought on by flood, drought, ethnic conflict or the disease that oftentimes follows such disasters [50, 90, 79].

1.13 Framework of the Book

The framework for this book is comprised of eight chapters. In five of those chapters, the empirical findings about terrorist behavior patterns for the five countries under consideration are presented. In Chap. 2, a three-dimensional typology of terrorist and "hybrid" criminal-terrorist group-types is crafted from which several theoretical propositions subject to empirical analysis are derived.

An underlying aim of this book is to provide business leaders with critical insights into terrorist group formation processes, and terrorist group targeting preferences. Those processes include terrorist group splintering and terrorist group spinoff formation. This book draws on previous work that describes terrorist systems as a bounded operational environment or a complex system. Such complex systems are populated by stakeholders, explanatory factors, and "stressors" that create conditions where terrorism threat is nestled with the potential to grow [13].

In each chapter, a Terrorist Assault Business Vulnerability Index (TABVI) score is assigned to the country under consideration. This score reflects an appraisal of the overall threat of terrorism to a particular country. In addition, the component parts to this TABVI measure lend themselves to a threat assessment appraisal for particular industries under threat in each country. That makes it possible for C-class business executives to make cross comparative assessments of threats to specific industries across countries.

The TABVI score and how it is derived is explained in detail in Chap. 2. In Chap. 2, an operational definition of terrorism that is used as a guidepost to code events is presented. It is based on jurisprudential principles that makes it possible for analysts to distinguish between terrorism, justifiable insurgency, and other related conflict conditions. There is also description about data sources, coding methodologies, and the crosstabulation analysis tests used.

In Chap. 2, a three-dimensional typology of terrorist group-type and "hybrid" criminal terrorist groups is presented. A description of that typology includes how terrorist groups and criminal organizations that use terrorism are sorted out into terrorist group types and hybrid criminal organizations based on political ideology or goals (end goals) and recruitment patterns.[7] Several hypotheses that capture terrorist group attack patterns against commercial interests are tested for validity.

In terms of country examination, Chap. 3 through Chap. 6 are the chapters that present TABVI scores and empirical results for the five case studies in this book. Those case studies include India (Chap. 3), Mexico (Chap. 4), Brazil (Chap. 5), South Africa (Chap. 6), and Thailand (Chap. 7). In each case, the origins and background of major terrorist groups are presented with discussion about terrorist group formation and splintering processes.

---

[7] There was insufficient information in the GTD data and supplemental data available to make accurate determinations about whether or not terrorist group chieftains qualified as charismatic leaders.

In a section of Chap. 7, a comparative analysis is also provided that includes results from a cross country comparison of TABVI scores and empirical results about terrorist group targeting patterns. There is discussion about the implications of those results for multinational corporations, other international enterprises, and in some cases, for small and medium sized enterprise (SME's) business leaders.

Chapter 8 is devoted to discussion about the qualitative and quantitative results of this study, and the rudiments of soft-line, non-kinetic interventions policy, a type of counterterrorism approach that business leaders charged with security responsibilities might consider. Certain findings from previous work about "soft-line" interventions policy, where firms work in conjunction with "host" and "home" governments are discussed. In cases where countries are found in the same region, the interpretation of results will include some preliminary regional observations and comparisons about terrorist group and criminal syndicalist attack patterns.

Chapter 8 concludes with reflections on lessons learned about sources of business related terrorism, more effective counter-terrorism programs for business leaders, gaps in knowledge illuminated, and future directions of research. Possible factors to examine in future work include regime type, imperialism, economic blight, geography, topography, cultural factors such as management-labor relations, work ethic, and (work force) education levels. The foregoing lays the groundwork for future research projects. For example, those projects might consider if certain transnational political, economic, cultural, geographic, or topographical factors are involved in business related terrorism threat formation.

1.14 Conclusions

This book chapter has described the relationships between security, vulnerability, and risk. It posits these interrelated concepts along a continuum where theoretical connections between security, vulnerability, and risk, and the processes which tie them together both for individuals and for groups are depicted. In essence, risk serves as the glue that binds together vulnerability and security in both theoretical and functional terms.

In many cases, those vulnerabilities are choke points for supply chains in the physical and virtual worlds. To be sure, physical supply chains remain vulnerable to terrorist attacks because large swathes of largely unprotected territory and vast littoral areas where supply chain infrastructure is found remains largely unprotected. Those include oil pipelines, trains, and oil tankers laden with resources critical to Western and Japanese industry. Likewise, virtual supply lines are highly vulnerable due to malware and other cyber intrusions.

In addition, these are production processes, supply chain conditions, and vulnerabilities that knowledgeable terrorist group chieftains and criminal syndicalist groups understand well. Those risks and vulnerabilities, many of them new, can be manipulated by terrorists or criminal syndicalists who can use terrorism against multinational corporation assets in home countries and foreign subsidiaries in host countries.

Terrorist organization chieftains and criminal syndicalist group bosses know that inputs for particular value chain "up-stream" and "downstream" activities are sourced and introduced into the value chain system from different countries around the world. Moreover, value chain complexity and vulnerability increase when value chain inputs, such as research and design breakthroughs dovetail nicely with each other and are applied across product lines [16, 185–187; 30, 342–344].

Last, but certainly not least, threat to multinational corporations and other international enterprises also include threats to individual and small groups of business executives en-route. The physical modalities required for connected businesses to function well have exposed business executives to potential criminal and terrorist actions. Even after virtual business communications were refined in response to the COVID-19 pandemic, in person business negotiations remain crucial because of the importance of close interpersonal connections at top tiers of business leadership, perhaps especially so in many Asian and the Middle Eastern countries.

What is also significant here is the link between the need for high level executives to travel and the structural changes made in business organizational frameworks to increase effectiveness and efficiencies. That need for executive travel is also amplified by current trends in organizational structure that emphasize the importance of multinational corporation "subsidiary autonomy." The central notion is that such autonomy helps avoid many of the functional problems associated with cultural differences between home and host countries that impinge on smooth plant operations.

That "subsidiary autonomy" approach, which is perhaps most heavily emphasized in the "transnational network" organizational design, requires corporate officials to travel and conduct on-site monitor and oversight functions to ensure smooth plant operations. Next in Chap. 2, the discussion puts special focus on data acquisition and sources, coding, methodologies, and the statistical techniques used to produce empirical results. There is also description about the TABVI analysis and some of the specific ways research challenges linked to terrorism in the contemporary world have been treated.

References

1. Al S (2015) Local armed uprisings and the transnational image of claim making: the Kurds of Turkey and the Zapatistas of Mexico in comparative perspective. Globalizations 12(5):677–694. https://www.tandfonline.com/doi/abs/10.1080/14747731.2014.991541
2. Allison N, Tamburin A (2020) Retracing the key moments after the Christmas bombing in Nashville. Nashville Tennessean. https://www.tennessean.com/in-depth/news/local/2021/01/10/timeline-christmas-morning-bombing-nashville/6578915002/
3. Barash DP, Webel CP (2002) Peace and conflict studies. Sage Publications
4. Beres LR (1988) Terrorism and international law. Florida International Law Journal 3(3):291–306
5. Beres LR (1988) Genocide, law and power politics. Whitter Law Review 10(2):329–351
6. Beres LR (1990) Confronting nuclear terrorism. The Hastings International and Comparative Law Review 14(1):129–154
7. Booth K (2007) Theory of world security. Cambridge University Press

8. Buzan B, Waever O (2003) Regions and powers: the structure of international security. Cambridge University Press
9. Chasdi RJ (2010) Counterterror offensives for the ghost war world: the rudiments of counterterrorism policy. Lexington Books
10. Chasdi RJ (2014) A continuum of nation-state resiliency to watershed terrorist events. Armed Forces Soc 40(3):476–503
11. Chasdi RJ (2020) Research note—the new frontier of enhanced terrorism with the United States in mind. The International Journal of Intelligence, Security, and Public Affairs 22(2):119–131. https://doi.org/10.1080/23800992.2020.1780075
12. Chasdi RJ (2013) Risks of terrorism, homicide, and illness: a methodological consideration. Perspectives on Terrorism 7(6):126–136. https://www.universiteitleiden.nl/binaries/content/assets/customsites/perspectives-on-terrorism/2013/issue-6/risks-of-terrorism-homicide-and-illness-a-methodological-consideration.pdf
13. Chasdi RJ (2018) Corporate security crossroads responding to terrorism, cyberthreats, and other hazards in the global business environment. ABC-CLIO Praeger, 1–3,183, n1; 183 n4, 184, n10, 184 n7
14. Chasdi RJ (2022) Rudiments of a space security policy framework. The centre for international governance innovation (CIGI), CIGI Papers No. 265, 1–15. https://www.cigionline.org/
15. Collier P, Hoeffler A (2000) Greed and grievance in civil war, policy research working paper no. 2355, World Bank. https://papers.ssrn.com/sol3/papers.cfm?abstract_id=630727
16. Cullen JB, Parboteeah KP (2014) Multinational management: a strategic approach, 6th edn. South-Western Cengage Learning
17. Dahl RA (1957) The concept of power. Behavioral Sciences 2(3):201–205
18. DeBonis M (2022) House votes to strip Russia of trade status, but Congress treads carefully. Washington Post
19. Deutsch M (1973) The resolution of conflict: constructive and destructive processes. Yale University Press
20. Fernandez LM (2009) Organized crime and terrorism: from the cells towards political communication, a case study. Terrorism and Political Violence
21. Flores RG, Aguilera RV (2007) Globalization and location choice: analysis of US multinational firms in 1980 and 2000. Journal of International Business Studies 38(7):1187–1210. https://link.springer.com/article/10.1057/palgrave.jibs.8400307
22. Fuerth L, Faber EMH (2012) Anticipatory governance practical upgrades: equipping the executive branch to cope with increasing speed and complexity of major challenges. National Defense University, Center for Technology & National Security Policy
23. Gurr TR, Harff B (1994) Ethnic conflict in world politics. Westview Press
24. Gurr TR (2003) Terrorism in democracies: when it occurs, why it fails. In: Kegley CW (ed) The new global terrorism: characteristics, causes, controls. Prentice Hall, pp 202–215
25. Gurr TR (1988) Some characteristics of political terrorism in the 1960's. In: Stohl M (ed) Politics of terrorism third edition, revised and expanded. Marcel Dekker
26. Gurr TR (1989) The history of protest, rebellion and reform in America: an overview. In Gurr TR (ed) Protest, rebellion, reform. Vol. 2 of violence in America. Sage Publications
27. Gurr TR (1989) Political terrorism: Historical antecedents and contemporary trends. In Gurr TR (ed) Protest, rebellion, reform. Vol. 2 of violence in America. Sage Publications
28. Hawkins D, Kranish M, Sebastian S, Kornfield M (2020) 63-year-old Anthony Q. Warner is a person of interest in Christmas blast in Nashville, authorities say. Washington Post. https://www.washingtonpost.com/national-security/2020/12/26/after-nashville-blast-tennessee-governor-asks-trump-emergency-disaster-declaration/
29. Hill CWL (2014) Global business today—eighth edition. McGraw Hill Irwin
30. Hill CWL, Hult GTM (2016) Global business today–ninth edition. McGraw Hill Education
31. Hofstede G (1993) Cultural constraints in management theory. Acad Manag Exec 7(1):81–90. https://doi.org/10.5465/AME.1993.9409142061
32. Jervis R (1978) Cooperation under the security dilemma. World Politics 30(2):173–174
33. Kegley C (2007) World politics: trends and transformations, 11th edn. Thomson Wadsworth

34. Lasswell HD (1935) World politics and personal insecurity. McGraw Hill, Whittlesey House
35. Lasswell HD (1978) Terrorism and the political process. Terrorism: An International Journal 1(3/4):253–263
36. Luthans F, Doh JP (2012) International management: culture, strategy, and behavior, 8th edn. McGraw Hill Irwin
37. Makarenko T (2004) The crime-terror continuum: tracing the interplay between transnational organized crime and terrorism. Global Crime 6(1):129–145
38. Miller G, Menn J (2022) Putin's prewar threats to U.S. tech giants fruitful. Washington Post
39. Monahan J (2011) The individual risk assessment of terrorism. Psychol Public Policy Law. https://doi.org/10.1037/a0025792,14-17,6n7,4
40. Morgan P (1992) "Safeguarding Security Studies", Arms Control. 13(3):466–479
41. Nadal A (1998) Terrorism in Chiapas. Bulletin of the Atomic Scientists 52(4):18–25. https://www.tandfonline.com/doi/abs/10.1080/00963402.1998.11456823?journalCode=rbul20
42. Nakashima E, Suliman A, Kuo L (2022) In call, Biden warns China's Xi not to assist Russia. Washington Post
43. Nye JS (1993) Understanding international conflicts: an introduction to theory and history. Harper Collins College Publishers
44. Office of Public Affairs (2010) Faisal Shahzad indicted for attempted car bombing in Times Square. U.S. Department of Justice. https://www.justice.gov/opa/pr/faisal-shahzad-indicted-attempted-car-bombing-times-square
45. Patterson T, Blue SG (2005) Mapping security: the corporate security sourcebook for today's global economy. Addison Wesley
46. Pearson FS, Rochester JM (1998) International relations: the global condition in the twenty-first century, 4th edn. McGraw Hill
47. Pitigala N (2021) The impact of trade and economic contagion on developing and emerging markets. In: Gunaratna R, Aslam MMM (eds) COVID-19: a global security threat. Amsterdam University Press
48. Powell R (1990) Nuclear deterrence theory: the search for credibility. Cambridge University Press
49. Rapoport A (1995) The origins of violence: approaches to the study of conflict. Transaction Books
50. Rogers P (2010) Losing control global security in the twenty-first century, 3rd edn. Pluto Press
51. Ronis SR (2007) Timelines into the future: strategic visioning methods for government, business and other organizations. Hamilton Books
52. Chasdi RJ (2021) Prevention of major economic disruption following acts of terrorism—the case of the Bali bombings of 2002 and (2005). In: Schmid A (ed) Handbook of terrorism prevention and preparedness. ICCT, The Hague, pp 985–1026
53. Shelley LI (2014) Identifying, counting and categorizing transnational criminal organizations. In: Sheptycki J (ed) Transnational organized crime, volume II: definitional and methodological issues, constructionist and critical perspectives. Sage Publications, pp 93–109
54. Shelley LI, Picarelli JT, Irby A, Hart DM, Craig-Hart PA, Williams P, Simon S, Abdullaev N, Stanislawski B, Covill L (2005) Methods and motives: exploring links between transnational organized crime and international terrorism. Trends in Organized Crime 8(2). https://link.springer.com/article/10.1007/s12117-005-1024-x
55. Spich R, Grosse R (2005) How does homeland security affect U.S. firm's international competitiveness? Journal of International Management 11(4):457–478. https://www.sciencedirect.com/science/article/abs/pii/S1075425305000669
56. Stein J, Dixon R (2022) Sanctions freeze "Putin's war chest" and endanger Russian economy. Washington Post
57. Stohl MS, Lopez GA (1984) Introduction. In: Stohl MS, Lopez GA (eds) The state as terrorist: the dynamics of governmental violence and repression. Greenwood Press
58. Uniworld Database 2019 on-line. Accessed at George Mason University, 11–14 March 2019

59. Wagner RH (2007) War and the state: the theory of international politics. University of Michigan Press
60. Watkins S (2022) Russia's invasion of Ukraine highlights America's fading geopolitical influence. Oil Price. oilprice.com
61. Wolfers A (1973) National security as an ambiguous symbol. In: Art RJ, Jervis R (eds) International politics; anarchy, force, imperialism. Little, Brown and Company, pp 29–45

Chapter 2
Concepts, Methods, and Typology

2.1 Introduction

This chapter describes the theoretical foundations of this book and the methodology used for analysis of terrorist threats against commercial interests. The discussion begins with a review of findings from my first book on business related terrorism entitled, *Corporate Security Crossroads* [19]. That first book served as the foundation for this more in-depth analysis about terrorism threats to multinational corporations (MNC's) and other international enterprises.

The focus of attention is on a detailed analysis of the five host countries in the developing world with the highest number of U.S. based multinational corporations. Those five countries include India, Mexico, Brazil, South Africa, and Thailand, found in Asia, Latin America, and Africa. This monograph provides in depth analysis of specific targeting by group-type and various business targets. In the process, it extends the analysis of business security problems, "soft-line" theoretical approaches used to enhance traditional "personal security and property protection" ("P-2"), and the threat of "lone-wolf" terrorism found in my first book [63, 73–90].

The terrorist group targeting patterns illuminated in those five countries should help provide MNC leaders with the data rudiments necessary to construct more comprehensive defensive measures presented in my first book to constrain business target terrorism or reduce its effects. The goal here is to produce an empirically based country specific reference handbook for business leaders who are concerned about multinational corporation subsidiary firm security.

The framework for analysis involves: discussion of some major findings on corporate business security; description of the data sources and coding guidelines used in this book; work to craft a three-dimensional typology of terrorist and "hybrid" criminal-terrorist group-types; the set of theoretical propositions derived from that group-type typology to be tested for validity [23, 596–598, 606, 612; 79, 93–109; 80].

R. J. Chasdi, *Corporate Security Surveillance*, Advanced Sciences and Technologies for Security Applications, https://doi.org/10.1007/978-3-031-39550-5_2

The time interval examined for India and Thailand was 2013–2018 because there was ample data about terrorism events against commercial targets for bivariate analysis to uncover statistically significant and substantive relationships between explanatory variables. In the case of Mexico, Brazil, and South Africa, there were fewer events and therefore, the timeline was extended from between 2007 and 2018 to acquire a greater number of business related terrorist events. Nevertheless, there were still an insufficient number of discrete events in some of those cases to perform bivariate analysis.

For the Terrorist Assault Business Vulnerability Index (TABVI) measure and analysis, the 2013–2018 period was used because that time interval dovetailed nicely with the 2017–2018 interval of the *World Economic Forum*'s survey of business leader appraisals of the extent that terrorism poses financial costs on firms in specific countries [65, 138; 108; 109].[1] Those *World Economic Forum* country findings as assessed by business leaders in this WEF survey, comprised the denominator of the TABVI measure; thus basic consistency in the time interval for the terrorist event data base and the WEF survey dovetail well.

2.2 *Corporate Security Crossroads*—Some Major Findings

A review of my book *Corporate Security Crossroads* helps to establish a theoretical baseline for this book. It serves as a starting point for further inquiry into specific terrorism threats found in the five host countries examined. This previous book develops theoretical concepts about defensive measures that business leaders can tailor make and apply for specific business venues. It ties together different defensive measures in a system called "intervention points analysis."

In an "intervention points analysis," specific vulnerabilities in a country, city, or region, are identified. That identification process paves the way for the design of defensive "soft-line" non-kinetic policies taken by multinational corporations and other businesses. It follows that business leaders should work closely with the governments of "home" and "host" countries to develop those strategies and policies to reduce terrorism effects and sources of terrorism threat.

Those new defensive programs place focus on intelligence gathering, improvements in workplace conditions and worker living conditions, and other positive inducements that work to enhance employee loyalty to the firm. For example, human resources personnel can request descriptions about worker interests and experiences in other work environments. In certain select cases, human resource personnel could probe further for clarification from the applicant, all the while making certain that the questions posed to the applicant uphold basic incontrovertible rights such as freedom of expression, freedom of association, and freedom of assembly. To be sure,

[1] It should be noted that for Brazil, there were no GTD commercial interest target events between 2007 and 2009, and one terrorist event in the Mickolus data base against an Air France airliner in flight on July, 10, 2010 (entry # 4).

that process can also be implemented in the same carefully reasoned manner for current employees at the firm, at periodic time intervals.

Those defensive programs can be utilized in the guise of corporate security responsibility (CSR) measures. The reason why corporate social responsibility (CSR) is a useful platform to promote business security is that it is very efficient; corporate executives can tackle issues such as workplace safety, work force diversity, provision of flexible family time, conflict resolution/mediation resources, comprehensive mental health services, and environmental protections. The issue of environmental protectionism, that is an intrinsic part of CSR nowadays, also serves to promote consumer recidivism because such issues are extremely important to (potential) consumers.

Those defensive programs should dovetail well with more traditional defensive "P-2" policies already in place at firm plants. One defensive program revolves around how firms should collaborate within and across countries to achieve economies of scale in the production of counterterrorism goods and services. Those bulwarks could serve as the basis for a set of more formal business firm protections bulwarks across regions and countries.

In this book, complex systems theory serves as the basis of private sector counterterrorism efforts. It works to depict a complete terrorism system, be it a city, country, or a region. It isolates and identifies important stakeholders, explanatory factors, and political events called "stressors" [27; 76, 5–6, 10, 17–18, 20–21, 63–64, 74]. In depicting such a system, direct and indirect connections are made between stakeholders, explanatory factors, and the "stressors" that influence particular complex systems[27; 76, 5–6, 10, 17–18, 20–21, 63–64, 74].

In the first book, a complex systems depiction makes it possible for business leaders to scope out terrorism threat sources based on analysis of previous terrorist events. The analysis makes it possible to trace how threat sources grow and interact, with the underlying aim of working to provide insight into future events in specific terrorist systems [27; 76, 5–6, 10, 17–18, 20–21, 63–64, 74]. In this way, complex systems analysis moves beyond many other analytical frameworks that focus on individual aspects of threat, but which downplay how various system components are connected and interact.

Another type of defensive program template that is highlighted involves significant reinvestment of corporate revenues into the communities where MNC's or other international enterprises are located. In addition, that is coupled with reinvestment of funds into communities in close proximity. Those security driven monetary investments should be viewed as a budget necessity and as part of the fixed or variable costs required for doing business in a host country.

A portion of the revenue doled out should be allocated within the context of a government strategic framework that anticipates modernization trajectories and effects in particular geographical locales of a country. Those allocations of funds should articulate specific needs of different stakeholders in communities in short-run, middle-run, and in long-haul time intervals. A plan that takes into account and coordinates monetary distributions across different time horizons might work to prevent uneven economic development processes from unfolding in a particular country [73].

The reason why that is important is that uneven economic development creates precisely the type of political instability and social unrest that firms and governments want to avoid in the first place. This defensive program template also highlights the importance of public–private sector cooperation and how such cooperation provides "win–win" opportunities across government and business sectors and between business sectors.

2.3 The Total Security Measure Index (TSMI)

My previous book, *Corporate Security Crossroads* also introduces a quantitative measure used to appraise improvements in business security. It introduces proactive non-kinetic but still defensive security concepts that move beyond traditional "P-2" (i.e., "personal security and property protection") programs. The work conceptualizes a Total Security Measure Index (TSMI), where the TSMI reflects the equation, X2 − X1 + Y2 − Y1.

For the TSMI, ordinal measures and values are used to make that measure operational. Those ordinal values reflect the overall security condition at a facility found at the time of terrorist attack. For X2-X1, X2 is a value assigned to reflect the optimal condition of "P-2" security – X1, which is the ordinal value assigned to reflect the given security condition at the time of attack.

For example, a value of "10" for X1 is assigned to a "none-low" security condition, a value of "50" is assigned to a "medium" level security condition, while a value of "100" is assigned to a high-level of security in place at the time of a terrorist attack.[2]

The second part of the TSMI equation is Y2 − Y1. In this equation Y2 − Y1, "Y2" is the degree of non-traditional "soft-line" security measures that might have been in place at the time of attack, while "Y1" is the level of "soft-line" security measures already in place at the time attack.[3] Lastly, as indicated by the TSMI equation, X2 − X1 + Y2 − Y1, the value of the potential degree of improvement in traditional "P2" security, plus (+) the value of the potential degree of improvement in non-traditional "soft-line" security, produces a score that indicates the potential for overall security improvement [19, 56–59, 62; 63, 73–90].

---

[2] For the TSMI, the X2 − X1 equation reflects the level of traditional "P-2" (i.e., "personal security and property protection") security found at the time of attack. "P-2" security includes: defense perimeters, "lock and key" provisions, production site security plans, security protocols characterized by cross-cultural terminology, and redundancy plans. The X2 − X1 equation reflects the difference between the *normative* condition in traditional "P-2," called X2, or what augmented "P2" security might have been at the time of attack, *minus* X1, namely the value assigned for the "P-2" security provisions in place at the time of attack.

[3] Like before, conditions are appraised and ordinal measures assigned to "soft-line" conditions found. Thus, the equation Y2 − Y1 reflects the degree of potential improvement in "soft-line" security.

2.4 *Corporate Security Surveillance*—Terrorist Assault Business Vulnerability Index (TABVI)

In this section, discussion turns to a review of data sources, and coding methodologies found in this book. One new analytical tool used in this book is the Terrorist Assault Business Vulnerability Index (TABVI). The TABVI is used to examine the five countries under consideration to make a quantitative determination about terrorism threat to business related targets (and vulnerability) in each country.

The TABVI makes it possible to calculate threat (vulnerability) ranking used by "home country" C-class executives to rank host country threat (vulnerability) to terrorism and related conflict against commercial interests. Even though there is some time lag between evaluation and real time conditions in a continuously evolving environment, such "host country" evaluations that gauge threat and vulnerability to commercial interests are useful because they can, "...contribute to decisions made about where and how much businesses should invest in one country compared to others." [17; 24, 1193–1194].[4]

In addition, this TABVI index makes it possible to disaggregate numerator values according to industry/sector type, or to (re) aggregate them, to give an approximation of different risk levels to specific types of businesses found in particular or affiliated industries.[5] In this way, results from the TABV algorithm can contribute to policies intrinsic to MNC subsidiary "relocation processes" which Flores and Aguilera describe in detail. The reason why risk appraisal is crucial here is because of its intrinsic value to the "securitization" of issues in MNC policy about subsidiary location and relocation decisions [13, 164, 59, 166, 168, 171, 215, 231; 24] [45, 24, 40, 45, 49–51, 100, 125, 127, 134–135].[6]

This TABVI score is comprised of two parts. The TABVI numerator reflects the total number of terrorist assaults conducted against different types of business targets between 2013 and 2018 for a particular country. In turn, the denominator consists of a score that reflects the subjective appraisal of terrorism threat and potential terrorism cost made by business executive respondents to an "Executive Opinion Survey" conducted by the *World Economic Forum* [102, 136–137; 108; 109].[7]

The numerator of this algorithm is based on Sinai's work about terrorism as practiced against business targets. Sinai's work distinguishes between different types of business targets subject to terrorist attacks [19, 83]. For Sinai, those business target type categories include, but are not necessarily limited to, "retail," "tourism," "chemical," "energy" "transportation (aviation, ground, and maritime)," and "finance" [19, 83].

---

[4] I would like to thank Dr. Marla G. Scafe of Walsh College, Troy, Michigan for her kind assistance with this conceptualization.

[5] That TABVI appraisal holds constant the estimated cost level of terrorist threat against business, as perceived by surveyed executives in the *World Economic Forum* survey described below.

[6] Indeed, both Booth and Hendricks suggest the clarion call to respond to a high priority security issue reflects a "socially constructed" hierarchal political ranking process.

[7] Middle range ordinal scale value labels are not articulated in this WEF report.

The way the TABVI score system works is straightforward—low scores suggest low threat (vulnerability) to terrorism, while higher scores suggest higher degrees of threat (vulnerability) to terrorism. TABVI scores can be transformed into ordinal measures that indicate the extent of threat or vulnerability that business targets in specific countries confront.

In other words, when the overall TABVI score is low relative to other TABVI country scores, the threat of terrorism to commercial interests and the vulnerability of business related targets in that country is considered comparatively low. Conversely, a high TABVI score relative to other country TABVI scores indicates that the degree of terrorist threat to business targets and overall vulnerability to business interests in the country under consideration is comparatively high.

2.5 The Numerator

In this book, the TABVI numerator reflects the total number of terrorist actions against business targets in a country between 2013 and 2018. That total number of terrorist events is broken down into industry sub-categories for business targets. Those industry sub-categories include, (1) "energy/alloy firms," (2) "construction firms," (3) "hospitals/medical facilities," (4) "private establishments," such as restaurants, tea farms, cafes, liquor stores, and hotels; (5) "telecommunications firms/facilities," such as cell phone towers, television stations, radio stations, and related infrastructure; (6) "newspapers/printed media" such as targeted journalists; (7) "banking/financial institutions"; (8) "private transportation"; (9) "agriculture"; (10) NGO targets (for Mexico and Brazil) [83].[8] What follows is a more detailed description of TABVI components and how the assessment process works.

2.6 The Denominator

The *World Economic Forum* survey poses a question that captures an appraisal of domestic business executive assessments of terrorism threat for each country. The value for theTABVI denominator is determined by individual country scores produced for a *World Economic Forum* "Executive Opinion Survey" question. That question is: "in your country, to what extent does the threat of terrorism impose costs on business?" That question is associated with a Likert ordinal scale where "1" = "to a great extent – imposes huge costs," to "7" not at all—imposes no costs." [108, 109].

[8] In country cases such as Mexico where the overall number of cases was low, some non-governmental organization (NGO) terrorist assaults characterized by discernable political themes were also included in the database to make country data more robust.

2.7 The Numerator and Denominator

When the numerator is divided by the denominator, a TABVI vulnerability score is obtained. That score reflects the interaction between these two TABVI components where there is equal weighting assigned to those two components.

If the TABVI numerator is held constant, higher business cost scores (reflected by lower WEF scores) associated with terrorism for countries in the *World Economic Forum* data (the denominator), produce a lower TABVI score. That is theoretically valid because higher appraised threats should lead to higher investment in anti-terrorism measures, thus leading to a lower TABVI score.

For example, imagine a numerator of 35 in the TABVI that is held constant. The TABVI denominator (i.e., the WEF score), increased from 4.8 to 5.2 to reflect a lower threat appraisal by business executives. With a denominator at 4.8, the TABVI score is 7.29. However, with a denominator of 5.2, the TABVI score is lower at 6.73. What is significant here is the TABVI ranking system works slightly differently than the WEF ranking system. By contrast, a TABVI score of 7.29 reflects a higher degree of threat and vulnerability than a TABVI score of 6.73.

The TABVI denominator can have the same or very similar numeric value across different countries as the overall scores for countries ranked by business executives the *World Economic Forum* survey are sometimes very close. Clearly, that suggests that with the same or similar denominator values, an increase in the number of terrorist acts committed against commercial interests (the TABVI numerator) increases the score of vulnerability and/or threat index. For example, 40/4.8 equals a TABVI score of 8.33, while 45/4.8 equals a TABVI score of 9.375. This TABVI method is useful when comparisons of country vulnerability to business related terrorism are made.

In this study, examination of each country under consideration involves a TABVI analysis. This TABVI index is used to provide an approximate measure of the degree of threat (vulnerability) to business related terrorism that a country, with substantial U.S. based multinational corporation presence, has experienced between 2013 and 2018.

In its denominator, (i.e., WEF survey score under consideration) the TABVI score measure seems to take into account certain "contextual factors" linked to terrorism threat that WEF survey respondents might have implicitly identified in countries. Those "contextual factors" might have influenced *World Economic Forum* score similarities and differences across countries. Although the survey data responses do not explicitly identify what those contextual factors are, the inference is those factors might include regime-type, level of socio-economic development, political and economic inequalities, national cohesion characteristics, and certain cultural characteristics linked to business operations [21, 379–399; 46, 112–115; 49, 81–90; 61, 106–163].

To reiterate, the TABVI system makes it possible to conduct a preliminary comparative analysis of overall terrorist attack threat and vulnerability across countries and across industries found in the same region or in a different region of the world. It follows that the TABVI method might serve as a first step to compare similarities and differences across those "contextual factor" types. In this study, preliminary regional comparisons will include India and Thailand in Asia, and Mexico and Brazil in Latin America. To be sure, the TABVI analysis is not dependent on WEF survey data for its operationalization. Other similar research data that works to appraise the imputed costs of terrorism threat to business interests and operations in particular countries can be used in future research as a substitute for WEF rankings.

2.8 *Corporate Security Surveillance*—Data Sources

The data for this book are comprised primarily of terrorist event entries between 2013 and 2018 collected from the Global Terrorism Database (GTD). In addition, data entries from the multi-volume series *Terrorism: A World-Wide Chronology* published by Edward Mickolus were used in the case of Mexico, Brazil, and South Africa to augment those GTD data [65–67].[9]

In the case of Mexico, Brazil, and South Africa, the timeline for data collection was extended with GTD data and data from the Mickolus chronologies to include the years 2007–2017. The reason why was that the number of data entries for those countries was very limited in number for the 2013–2018 time interval; the increase in time range of six years for those countries made the data richer and more robust.

Hence, focus on that 2007–2018 time interval made it possible to acquire relatively new data. Further, the range of business targets in those data was sufficiently broad to make meaningful analysis possible. In the case of India and Thailand that time period was an interval rich with sufficient numbers of discrete business related terrorism events to satisfy the "law of large numbers" that is intrinsically important for empirical analysis beyond a presentation of basic descriptive statistics [84, 245].[10]

The process of data entry review involved a "contextual reading" of terrorist event scripted accounts to determine whether or not the act under consideration qualified as political terrorism. An initial review of GTD and Mickolus terrorism data focused on narratives in each of those data sources, coupled with GTD and Mickolus determinations about stakeholders involved in terrorist attacks. In the case of the GTD data, efforts were made to conform assessments to GTD guidelines and assessments about whether or not an incident qualified as terrorism, by contrast to criminal activity.

As the vast majority of the data were culled from the GTD, primary attention in this discussion revolves around that data source. During the coding process, judgement calls about whether or not a chronicled GTD event qualified as terrorism sometimes had to be made along with efforts in some cases, to extrapolate about political links to

[9] Those data are housed at the National Consortium for the Study of Terrorism and Responses to Terrorism (START) at the University of Maryland.

[10] For Sirkin, "…the law of large numbers states that if the size of the sample, n, is sufficiently large (no less than 30; preferably no less than 50) then the Central Limit Theorem will apply even if the population is not normally distributed along variable x.".

particular terrorist assaults. In many cases, secondary sources listed in primary GTD accounts were reviewed to corroborate accounts and provide additional information to fill in gaps in knowledge. Those scripted accounts were accessed primarily through Lexis-Nexis (Nexis-Uni).

In some cases, secondary sources not cited in GTD accounts were used. Those were accessed through Nexis-Uni (Lexis-Nexis) and Google. Those accounts were reviewed to corroborate the narratives in original accounts and to provide additional details about terrorism assaults. Those scripted accounts from Nexis-Uni and Google were used to access additional political and historical context about terrorist attacks to determine whether or not an event under consideration was related to a political event as defined in this study and if so, to which designated political event sub-category (e.g., religious events, commemoration of landmark events). For India, accounts included, but were not necessarily limited to, reports from *United News of India*, *The Telegraph (India)*, *Indian Express*, and *The Times of India (TOI)* [50, 96, 100].

Those secondary accounts were used to corroborate or substantiate terrorist event attributes such as numbers of dead, wounded, event location, assault-type, firm name, terrorist group-type, terrorist group involved, perpetrators, municipality, and links to political events. Many GTD scripted accounts did provide averages of deaths and injuries if a set of terrorist events was chronicled over a period of hours or at different locations or both. Such timelines were sometimes suggested by GTD accounts but in a few cases, computations about deaths and injury averages were made by hand.

A data compilation of GTD terrorist event entries was produced that conformed to standard GTD designations and keywords related to terrorism and business interests. Those keywords included: "business," "journalists & media," "utilities," "telecommunication," "tourist," "transportation" (private), "maritime," and "food or water supply." In the cases of Mexico, Brazil, and South Africa, the category "NGO" was also used [31 (entry #397); 39].[11]

In the case of business targets, small and middle size businesses (SME's) were included in the database as well as large transnational corporations found primarily in the telecommunications industry. In that way, the database produced was a more accurate and complete portrayal of the overall range of business targets subjected to terrorist assaults in each country.

One limitation of those GTD data involved gaps of in-depth knowledge about the nature of perpetrators involved in many of the terrorist assaults chronicled. In addition, certain GTD data entries did not make clear what constituted more formal terrorist group events as compared to lone operative events. It appeared that most if not all of the GTD terrorist attack events chronicled were terrorist group events.

To compound the problem, definitions of what constitute "lone operative" events were found to vary in the literature. For example, Hewitt argues that so-called "lone-wolf" events can revolve around one person and include up to three people. Hence, the small proportion of terrorist events that might have constituted the actions of lone operatives, remained speculative and indeterminate (Hewitt as found in [82, 37–38, 43–45, 128–129, 204, 251, 266]).

[11] This data entry is an example of a "food and water supply" entry.

To be sure, similar problems frequently characterized other secondary sources used to examine specific terrorist assaults. Therefore, it was not possible in an overwhelming number of cases, to distinguish between terrorist group and lone operative events, or to provide rough percentage approximations of each in this study. It was also not possible to make comparisons across countries between the business targets terrorist groups preferred and targets of choice for lone operatives. Accordingly, efforts were made to exclude lone-wolf operatives from the database.

Clearly, the distinction between terrorist groups and lone operatives is important to refine the analysis in the future. For example, access to more complete data might make it possible to increase an understanding of the range of different terrorism threat types to specific types of business found at particular geographical locales in specific countries at specific time intervals. In some cases, there are ideological and functional links between lone operatives and terrorist groups. For example, there might be a duality of effect between terrorist group and lone operatives where terrorist group agendas or target selection was somehow affected by lone operative terrorist actions, or vice versa.

What seems clear is that in the case of terrorist group influence over lone operatives, lone operatives have been frequently inspired to act based on the broader ideological themes and specific narratives about potential targets that terrorist groups espouse [19, 133–134, 145–146, 148, 225–226 n85, 158, 218–219 n50; 47; Hewitt, as found in 82, 37–38, 43–45, 128–129, 204, 251, 256; 87, 16–19, 31–33, 38–39, 48–49, 54].[12] It seems reasonable to conclude that might be especially true in cases where lone operatives had or have connections to formal terrorist group members or core constituent group leaders, or both. Plainly, the capacity to distinguish between terrorist groups and lone operatives so that data could be parsed, would contribute to a fuller, more complete analysis for each of the five countries under consideration [19, 133–134, 145–146, 148, 225–226 n85, 158, 218–219 n50; Hewitt, as found in 82, 37–38, 43–45, 128–129, 204, 251, 266; 96, 16–19, 31–23, 38–39, 48–49, 54].

2.9 Data Coding Guidelines

The bulk of the analysis in this book focuses on quantitative findings and supplemental qualitative descriptions of terrorist groups. In some cases, there are descriptions of terrorist group attacks directed against specific types of business targets. The

[12] Even though Spaaj defines a "lone wolf" as one operative, other terrorism authorities assert lone operative terrorist assaults might not be the work of lone operatives at all. For example, aside from the perpetrator, others might have an inkling about terrorist assaults to come. Those in close orbit to a lone operative might include family, close friends, and in some cases, former terrorist or political group associates. It follows that Hewitt (as found in Simon), in comparison to Spaaj, defines a "lone-wolf" more broadly, as a term inclusive of up to three people. Previous results show 70.4% of "uber-rightist" lone-operatives had terrorist or extremist group ties, while 58.3% of "nationalist" lone-operatives had such group ties. I also note that 50% of "ultra-leftist/anarchist" lone-operative terrorists chronicled had paramilitary/military experience. [19], 148, 133, 218–219 n50, 146).

notion of "political terrorism" used for definitional purposes and coding is the same jurisprudentially based definition used in previous empirical work. In this definition, terrorism is:

> the threat, practice, or promotion of force for political objectives by organizations or person(s) whose actions are designed to influence the political attitudes or policy dispositions of a third party, provided the threat, practice, or promotion of force is directed against (1) non-combatants; (2) military personnel in non-combatant or peacekeeping roles; (3) combatants, if the afore-mentioned violates juridical principles of proportionality, military necessity, and discrimination, or; (4) regimes that have not committed egregious violations of the human rights regime that approach Nuremberg category crimes. Moreover, the act itself elicits a set of images that serve to denigrate the target population while strengthening the individual or group simultaneously [8, 329–351; 9, 291–306; 10, 129–154; 12; 11; 15, 24, 50n24; 16, 9, 52, 58n58; 18, 23–25, 37 n131, 38 n132; 19, 41–43, 20, 190–191 n3, n10; 26; 52, 131–135; 75, 107–108].

In the cases of India, Mexico, and Brazil, it was sometimes difficult to distinguish between terrorism and organized or criminal activity in terrorist event scripted accounts. For example, for many Indian terrorist assaults recorded, extortion or "levies" (i.e., ransoms) remained unpaid, and the attacks that followed could not only be linked to unpaid levies, but to broader political themes.

For example, in some cases of Indian terrorism, such themes were tied into protest against government modernization efforts and the structural changes brought on by globalization. For instance, in terrorist bombing attacks against Indian construction sites paving new roads, it was sometimes difficult to separate political and monetary themes, or determine which themes were predominant in scripted accounts.

As described in Chap. 1, this conceptual overlap between traditional terrorist groups and criminal enterprises which use terrorism, seems more characteristic of the post-Cold War world. The post-Cold War world is characterized by broad, deep and increasingly thicker globalization connections that work to produce conflict. The use of "contextual analysis" helped to place terrorist events against the backdrop of broader and widely recognized conflict between terrorist groups and government, and in some cases between terrorist groups. Frequently, that process relied heavily on information gleaned from secondary sources which were pivotal to decisions made about inclusion of certain GTD events in the database.

For example, when a GTD entry suggested some uncertainty about whether or not the action under consideration qualified as terrorism, that event was reviewed more closely to determine implied political themes associated with that event and its description. In the case of Mexico for example, reliance on GTD determination about whether or not an act qualified as terrorism was relaxed in the case of certain terrorist events. That was done to take into account powerful connections between organized crime and the use of terrorism found in Mexico. These coding modifications for Mexico are described below in a chapter section devoted to additional coding guidelines for specific countries.

Terrorist assaults were coded as attacks against business targets when a business target was attacked directly. For example, if an IED was placed by a cell phone tower and only detonated when an army patrol appeared, that terrorist assault was

1. Terrorist Event ID
2. Month
3. Day
4. Year
5. Terrorist Group-Type
6. Terrorist Group-Name
7. Target-Type
8. "Structuralist-Non-Structuralist" Target
9. Firm Name
10. Target-Type-National/Foreign
11. City/Town/Village
12. State/Province
13. Country
14. Assault-Type
15. Deaths
16. Injuries
17. Business Target
18. Victim Nationality
19. Completed/Thwarted
20. Numbers of Perpetrators
21. Political Event
22. District

Fig. 2.1 Coding Sheet Data Categories

not included in the database [40] However, where bombing targets were made in error but the act involved a business target, that act was included in the database as a terrorist event.

In cases where more than one target type beyond a business target was involved, only the business involved was included as the target. That meant that other targets found nearby at the time of attack were excluded, such as such police officers close to a restaurant, for instance. In the case of deaths and injuries in specific terrorist attacks, all victims, business personnel, or non-business target personnel were included in those tallies, while terrorists were excluded from the counts.

What follows is brief description of the data coding categories relevant to the bivariate analysis and the value labels (i.e., sub-categories) associated with each data variable. The pieces of data for each terrorist event under consideration were sorted out into twenty two (22) separate data categories. For most of the data coding categories, the data were categorical/nominal data (see Fig. 2.1) [84, 34–35].

In the database, the first four categories were: (1) ID number; (2) Month; (3) Day; (4) Year. The fifth data column was "Terrorist Group-Type," where different terrorist groups and criminal syndicalist organizations that used terrorism were sorted out into six terrorist group-types, and anonymous acts. Those group-type categories included: 1 = "Maoist (Marxist/Leninist)"; 2 = "Nationalist-Irredentist;" 3 = "Anonymous"; 4 = "Religious Extremist" (e.g., Islamic); 5 = "Right-Wing Nationalism" (e.g., Hindutva ideology); 6 = "Hybrid" Terrorist-Criminal"; 7 = "Sole-Issue" (e.g., environmentalist groups, animal rights groups).

The sixth data column "Terrorist Group-Name," identified the terrorist group(s) in the event. For attribution purposes, claims of attribution by newspapers, counterterrorism authorities, government officials, scholars, or claims of responsibility by terrorist groups themselves were used to code the terrorist group involved. When two or more terrorist groups were linked to a terrorist attack, a coding decision about perpetrator was made based on claim of responsibility, account attribution, or the perpetrator emphasized most heavily in the account [16, 43–44].

In "Target-Type," the seventh data category, terrorist attack targets were coded as either civilian targets, government targets, or hybrid targets with 1 = "Civilian"; 2 = "Government"; 3 = "Mixed." When a determination about a civilian government target designation was difficult to make, additional on-line resources were used to help make coding decisions.

The eighth category was "Structuralist-Non-Structuralist" target. "Structuralist targets" included telecommunications infrastructure, energy alloy targets, and construction firms (e.g., for their role in modernization and globalization efforts in India), symbolic of the fierce struggle waged by Maoist or Marxist-Leninist terrorist groups against "world systems," such as capitalism and globalization [16, 42, 60 n101; 22; 48, 12–29].

In comparison, "non-structuralist" targets reflected terrorist group focus on targets symbolic of ethnic groups, religious groups, or particular individuals linked to such groups. Accordingly, "non structuralist targets" included private establishments, hospitals and medical facilities, newspapers and printed media infrastructure, private transportation targets, and agriculture targets. The coding categories included: 1 = "non-structuralist" target; 2 = "structuralist" target.

The ninth data coding category, "Firm-Name," identified the business attacked when information about the targeted firm was available. If there was insufficient information about the identity of a business, this coding category was left blank.

The tenth data category, "Target-Type- National/Foreign," recorded if the target was a domestic business or if the target was a subsidiary firm owned by an international enterprise. The value labels for that data category included: 1 = "National"; 2 = "Foreign"; 3 = "Mixed."

In turn, the city, town, or village where a terrorist assault happened was documented in the eleventh data category, called "City/Town/Village." A granular analysis is important because that makes it possible to identify specific geographical locales within states or provinces and in particular municipalities which experience higher and lower percentages of terrorist attacks.

In addition, granular focus is important because it illuminates where particular types of counterterrorism policies should be placed, and how to tailor make aspects of counterterrorism policy to address specific challenges when finite resources create budget limitations [18, 230, 399 n58]. For some nation-states such as India and Thailand, the number of cities, towns, and villages chronicled was extremely large.[13] When necessary, academic or newspaper Internet sources helped make determinations about how to label the venue of attack—city, town, or village.

In categories twelve and thirteen, the "Province/State" and "Country" where terrorist assaults happened were recorded. For some countries such as India and Thailand, the number of states or provinces where terrorist attacks against business

[13] In India, there were 389 cities, towns or villages articulated and 168 districts within provinces delineated,

targets happened was high. For example, terrorist assaults against commercial interests were chronicled in twenty-six states in India, while in the case of Mexico, terrorist attacks against business interests were recorded in twenty-one Mexican states and in Cuidad de Mexico (Mexico City).[14]

The fourteenth data category was "Assault-Type." That category was broken down into twenty-three sub-types to capture the range of terrorist attack methods used.[15] In the case where multiple assault types were used in an incident nearly simultaneously, efforts were made to code the most serious or predominant assault-type for each event, based on GTD or Mickolus accounts, and from the secondary sources cited in GTD accounts. In some cases, determination of the most serious (and thus predominant) assault-type used was more difficult; judgment calls were sometimes made to code that aspect of an event.

Columns fifteen and sixteen chronicled deaths and injuries caused by a terrorist assault. Those data for deaths and injuries were recorded as interval data, but recoded later, if bivariate analysis was used, into ordinal data and categories to craft a six-point Likert scale to capture intensity ranges of death and injury levels [84, 44]. The ordinal categories used included: "0 = 0" (none), "1 = 1 thru 15" (low); "2 = 16 thru 30" (moderate); "3 = 31 thru 50" (medium); 4 = "51 thru 100" (high); "5 = 101 + " (very high).

The seventeenth category "Business Target" captured the range of business targets involved in terrorist assaults linked to commercial interests. As previously mentioned, that category had ten sub-categories: (1) "Energy/Alloy firms"; (2) "Construction Firms"; (3) "Hospitals/Medical Facilities"; (4) "Private Establishments" such as (tea) farms, cafes, vineyards, liquor stores, hotels; (5) "Telecommunication" such as television infrastructure, and television reporters; (6) "Newspapers/Printed Media"; (7) "Banking/Finance"; (8) "Private Transportation"; (9) "Agriculture"; (10) NGO's (e.g., for Mexico, Brazil, and South Africa).

The eighteenth category, "Victim Nationality" identified terrorist assault victim nationality. The variable sub-categories included: 1 = "National"; 2 = "Foreign;" 3 = "Mixed" (i.e., a combination of nationals and foreign victims). One assumption made for the GTD and Mickolus data was that target nationality was stated outright or implied. The central idea was that if foreign nationals were victims, that piece of information would be conveyed in scripted accounts. To increase coding accuracy,

---

[14] For India, the "State/Province" coding category includes: (1) Assam; (2) Maharashtra; (3) Nagaland; (4) Manipur; (5) Bihar; (6) Haryana; (7) Chhattisgarh; (8) Meghalaya; (9) Odisha (Orissa); (11) Jharkhand; (12) Tamil Nadu; (13) West Bengal; (14) Jammu and Kashmir; (15) Madhya Pradesh; (16) Uttar Pradesh: (17) Tripura; (18) Andhra Pradesh; (19) Mizoram; (20) Kerala; (21) Karnataka; (22) Telangana; (23) Punjab; (24) Arunachal Pradesh; (25) Delhi; (26) Rajasthan; (27) Gujarat.

[15] Those assault-type coding categories include: (1) bombing (e.g., IED's "explosives"); (2) Shooting; (3) Bombing and Shooting; (4) Stabbing; (5) Kidnapping; (7) Threat; (8) Rape; (10) Hijacking; (11) Arson; (12) Grenade attack; (13) Vandalism; (14) Beatings; (15) Unknown; (16) Shooting and Grenade; (17) Arson and Shooting; (18) Land Mines; (19) Shooting and Stabbing; (20) Arson and Beatings; (22) Shooting and Beatings; (23) Arson and Kidnapping; (29) Kidnapping and Beatings; (30) Decapitation; (31) Arson and Stabbing. In the analysis, some assault-type outliers were recoded in the analysis to capture the predominant assault method used.

attention was paid to any additional description about victim nationality found in secondary sources.

The nineteenth data category was "Completed/Thwarted." In this study, if an explosive device was discovered through prevention or disruption efforts directed at terrorist groups for example, the act was coded as thwarted. In the coding scheme, 1 = "completed"; 2 = "thwarted."

The twentieth, twenty-first, and twenty-second categories, were "Number of Perpetrators," "Political Event," and "District." For "number of perpetrators," interval data (e.g., 1, 2, 3...) were used originally to code perpetrator numbers, and those interval data were recoded into ordinal data and ordinal categories when bivariate analysis was used [84, 44]. A six-point Likert scale was crafted for the variable "numbers of perpetrators: "0 = 0", "1 = 1 thru 15" (low); "2 = 16 thru 30" (moderate); "3 = 31 thru 50" (medium); "4 = 51 thru 100" (high); "5 = 101 + " (very high).

It is essential to link terrorism to political events because terrorism does not happen in a political vacuum. That is especially important for regions such as the Middle East and South East Asia, where religious events are frequently bound up with historical and political significance. Anderson suggests that "patrimonialism" as a style of leadership, where authority stems from one primary political or religious source, might at least be part of the reason why political/religious events are frequently so closely bound up with terrorist events [6, 1–18].

In a condition of "patrimonialism," what Anderson calls state and "societal" boundaries can be extremely permeable. In many such cases, loyalties to the group can be powerful, not necessarily corresponding completely to state allegiances, so that loyalties to the group compete with loyalties to the state. In such conditions, there are sometimes competing loyalties between religious and cultural institutions, and the state where religious actions take on political overtones [6, 1–18; 25, 94]. It follows that religious events should be coded as a type of political event in such circumstances.

In this study, "political event" has nine sub-categories: 0 = "no relation to political events"; 1 = "reaction to government policies" (e.g., visits by government officials; government policies); 2 = "reaction to ground assaults" (e.g., military or police operations); 3 = "reaction to terrorist acts"; 4 = "reaction to government assassinations"; 5 = "commemoration of landmark events (e.g., historical events/holidays)"; 6 = "commemoration of religious holidays"; 7 = "reaction to secular holidays" (e.g., Independence Day, terrorist group holidays); 8 = "reaction to private business policies" (e.g., non-payment of extortion/levies; business practices linked to environmental degradation, road construction, newspaper reports on terrorism); 9 = "reaction to elections/polls."[16]

The twenty-second data category was "District." This was another location variable to designate and define the administrative jurisdictions for cities, towns, and villages attacked. The data for district are categorical or nominal data, namely those country administrative units. Like the focus placed on cities, towns, and villages,

[16] In the coder reliability test, "0," a dash (-) or a blank in that column were interpretated as no relation to political events.

focus on "district" helps provide insight into how counterterrorism analysts can tailor make effective counterterrorism policy. That focus lends itself to additional analysis, with policy focus on even smaller administrative units such as neighborhood, or clusters of neighborhoods.

At a functional level, that granular analysis is especially important if particular clusters of neighborhoods areas are considered possible sites for foreign direct investment (FDI) by multinational corporations. Such focus also underscores the potential for intra-district cooperation, that can stimulate strategic counterterrorism planning efforts. In turn, that collaboration can lead to a condition of economies of scale, and thus a reduction in overall budget allocations for security. One recommendation made in previous work focuses on specific counterterrorism packages for clusters of neighborhoods, in much the same way as automobile manufacturers promote marketing of their products with specific clientele and neighborhood attributes in mind [18], 230, 399 n58].

Indeed, that granular approach has international ramifications for countries like India, where terrorist groups crisscross over national borders into countries such as Myanmar, Nepal, and Bhutan to establish safe-havens. It follows that counterterrorism planning should take into account those perspectives and have the capacity to plot terrorist activities such as assault and recruitment patterns, especially for districts close to international borders.

2.10 Coder Reliability Test

A coder reliability test was performed with three judges: two undergraduate students from the political science department at The George Washington University and myself. There were fourteen different terrorist events that constituted the data for this test. For each of those fourteen events, there were fourteen specific terrorist assault attributes examined, such as terrorist group-type, business-target, district, city, town, village, political event, etc. The coder reliability test formula is: (Fig. 2.2).

In this test, the specific scores for each attribute category were: (1) "Business-Target" (11.64/14); (2) "Political Event" (12.30/14); (3) "Victim Nationality" (10.94/14); (4) "District" (12.98/14); (5) "Assault Type" (13.32/14); (6) "Urban/Rural" (10.62/14); (7) "Target-Type-civilian/government" (11.66/14); (8) "Group-Type" (11.28/14); (9) "Group-Name" (10.26/14); (10) "Deaths" (12.98 /14); (11) "Injuries" (12.64/14); (12) "City/Town/Village" (13.66/14); (13) "Numbers of Perpetrators" (9.24/14); (14) "Firm-Name" (11.28/14). When these values are added, the total is 164.8. This is the numerator for ratio/fraction used to calculate *A*.

For each attribute, when judges were in full agreement, the score was "1.00." When two out of three judges were in agreement, "0.66" was recorded and with no agreement between the judges, "0.0" was awarded. In this formula, $A =$ represents the ratio of agreement in pieces of information in relation to the total number of pieces of information in the coder reliability test.

$$\frac{N(A)}{1+[(N-1)(A)]}$$

$$A = \frac{164.8}{196} = .8408$$

$$\frac{3(.8408)}{1+[3-1](.8408)} = \frac{2.5224}{1+[2(.8408)]} = \frac{2.5224}{2.6816} = .9406 = 94.1\%$$

Fig. 2.2 Coder reliability coefficient formula

The total number of bits of information was 196. That number was obtained when 14, the maximum score for each attribute category test, was multiplied 14, or the total number of terrorist event attribute categories used in this test ($14 \times 14 = 196$). This score of 196 is the denominator of the ratio/fraction used to calculate *A*. When A is calculated, $A = 0.8408$ where $A = 164.8/196$ or 0.8408. In turn, "N" in the coder reliability test represents the number of judges = 3.[17]

Therefore, the coder reliability coefficient obtained is 0.9406 or 94.1%. That 94.1% statistic is a favorable score, well above the 80% threshold score required; it is reflective of strong coding consistency across the three judges [5, 292; 16, 41–42, 60n96, 60n97; 18, 140, 172 n53, 172, n55; 19, 221, n57; 81, 56–57].

2.11 Relative Frequencies and Bivariate Crosstabulation Table Analysis

For the quantitative portion of the analysis, relative frequencies of terrorist assault attributes such as year, terrorist group-type, terrorist group-name, firm-type, and location (e.g., cities, towns, villages, municipalities, districts) are presented. In addition, cross-tabulation table analysis is used to isolate and identify statistically significant relationships between a dependent variable and an independent explanatory variable from the terrorist attack attributes articulated. Bivariate analysis is the preferred method to use to establish the parameters of terrorism in specific countries.

[17] In other words, a value of 196 is obtained by multiplying **14** (where 14 is the maximum score possible for each terrorist attribute test –e.g., for "political event," "group-type," "business target," etc.), where the "1.00's" and .66's are added together because there are 14 terrorist acts examined) **X 14** (the number of terrorist attack attribute categories). My thanks to my undergraduate students Mahima Jain and Billie Singer at The George Washington University for their coder-reliability test efforts.

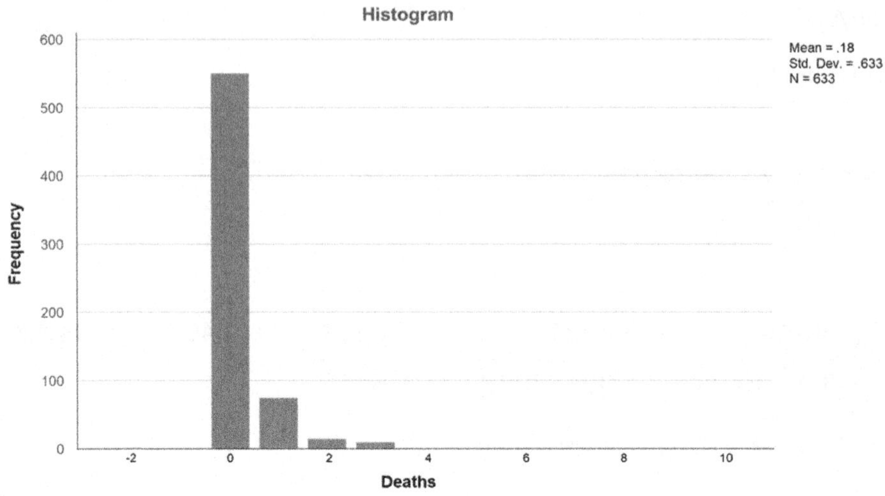

Fig. 2.3 Histogram of the variables, "Deaths"—India

The reason why is because an ordinary least squares regression (OLS) model requires that data conform to certain assumptions that the terrorism data do not meet [84, 444; 96; 107, 501–502].[18] For example, the terrorism data were skewed, characterized by a large number of zeros for terrorist assaults that do not cause any deaths or injuries. In addition, terrorist entries about deaths and injuries were by definition truncated at the zero point in a distribution—there are no negative terrorist events (or negative deaths and injuries) in the database. Therefore, it was not possible for the terrorism data distributions to conform to a normal bell-shaped distribution of events.

A histogram for "number of deaths" for Indian business related terrorist attacks revealed a data distribution skewed to the right (where the right distribution curve tail is longer than the left), with a positive "Skewness" value of 6.544—that is not a normal bell-shaped distribution. In comparison, a "skewness" factor of 0.0 would indicate a normal bell shaped distribution. While the "kurtosis" value for a normal bell-shaped distribution is 3, this histogram produced a kurtosis score of 61.989 for this sample distribution. That score indicated the sample distribution was characterized by leptokurtic kurtosis, a condition of kurtosis values of more than 3 (see Fig. 2.3) [68].

[18] Those assumptions include, but are not limited to, (1) data that conform to a normal bell-shaped distribution; (2) a condition free from multicollinearity, where independent variables regressed onto a dependent variable do not "move in the same direction" and are therefore independent and not statistically correlated; (3) a condition of homoscedasticity (the opposite of heteroscedasticity), where the assumption is the standard error (e.g., "variation") of all independent variables is the same vis a vis the dependent variable; (4) a linear, not curvilinear relationship between two variables under consideration.

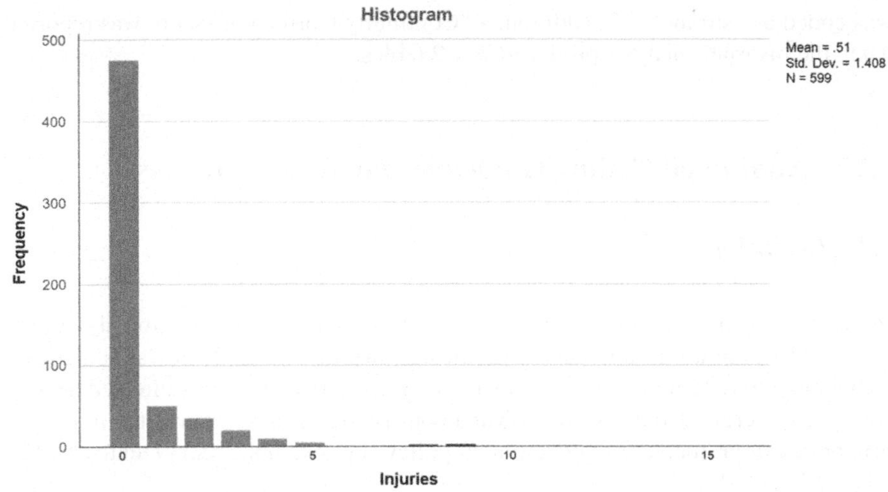

Fig. 2.4 Histogram of the variables, "Injuries"—India

Another histogram for "numbers of injuries" for business related Indian terrorist attacks revealed similar results. In that histogram, the data distribution was also skewed to the right, with a positive value for "skewness" of 4.902, by contrast to a 0.0 score indicative of a normal bell-shaped distribution. A Kurtosis value of 32.821 suggested the data distribution for "number of injuries" in this sample was also characterized by leptokurtic kurtosis, rather than a normal distribution [68] (See Fig. 2.4).

The bivariate analysis of the terrorism made use of several dependent and independent variables, such as political ideology, group-type, group-name, business target-type, province/state, district, cities towns (townships in the case of Thailand) and villages, deaths, injuries, victim nationality, and firm origin (domestic or foreign). Those crosstabulation table results made it possible to craft a composite and more complete picture of the terrorism practiced against business targets in those five developing world host countries.

In addition to a set of crosstabulation table results that included data distributions, Chi-Square values and corresponding "*p*-values," there were summary statistics presented, inclusive of measures of association to assess the strength of relationships between variables. The summary statistics and full data distributions were produced by SPSS and results are presented in bar chart format. To determine the strength of statistically significant relationships, Goodman and Kruskal tau, Phi, and Cramer's V were used and reported for categorical or nominal data, and for interval data.

In the case of ordinal data, the measures of the strength of the association used were Goodman and Kruskal's gamma and Kendall's tau b [84, 358–662, 371]. In the case of descriptors used to appraise the strength of association measures, 000 − 3.33 was coded as "weak," 0.334 − 0.666 was coded as "moderate," and 0.667 +

was coded as "strong."[19] In addition, a "Continuity Correction" score was reported when the bivariate analysis produced 2 × 2 tables.

2.12 Additional Coding Guidelines for Host Countries

2.12.1 India

In the case of India, it was sometimes difficult to make a determination about how to code pieces of information about political events. For example, it was sometimes a challenge to determine whether business related terrorist attacks directed at road construction crews from privately owned construction firms were related to private firm policy or protocol, or to government policy (For example, see 30 (entry # 143), (entry #144); 70; 99].

Most of the time, connections between Indian terrorist assaults against business targets and government policies were clear, because political manifestos or messages were left at the construction site attacked. In other cases, a coding decision was made using "contextual analysis," taking into account the Indian national and district policies that advocated road construction and other infrastructure development in specific rural areas to promote modernization and security.

The guidelines used in these circumstances was that without mention of specific business infractions, terrorist assaults were coded to reflect opposition to Indian government policies. In other words, if terrorist assault descriptions were more generic or open-ended about political context, or if terrorist messages did not identify specific infractions made by business executives in charge of targeted projects, the attack was coded as "1 = reaction government policies." However, if political messages were left at the attack scene or otherwise broadcast to highlight infractions associated with private firm policies or protocols, such as a decision to work during a "bandh" or other type of strike, the data for this data category was coded, "8 = reaction to private business policies." [32 (entry #32); 33 (entry #34); 98].

Other assumptions were made about contractor identification or firm personnel targeted. For example, when a geographical locale was described in scripted accounts as a "village panchayat" it was coded as "rural," even though other accounts might have described that same locale as a "town." In addition, a "community development block" (i.e., panchayat) in India such as Pirtend, Jharkhand, was categorized as "rural" [35 (event# 620)].[20]

An underlying problem with Indian terrorism data compilation was that in some, but certainly not all cases, it was possible terrorist event perpetrators were purposefully misidentified by security authorities for political reasons. For example, accusations directed at Indian police about irregularities in terrorist assault investigations

[19] My thanks to John Strate, Department of Political Science, Wayne State University, Detroit, MI.

[20] For example, this was the case with Sapekhati, Assam.

that involved reporters and NGOs with political views at odds with official Indian government policies, were sometimes noted in accounts [94, 10–11].

In terms of attribution, if scripted accounts described or suggested a terrorist group was actually a front or military branch of a known terrorist group, the terrorist act taken by the group described was coded as an action taken by that established terrorist organization. That procedure contrasted to when counterterrorism authorities, scholars, or newspaper accounts reported that the terrorist group was a "splinter group" or "spin-off group" of an established terrorist organization. For example, in the Indian state of Jammu and Kashmir, the terrorist assaults of the Hizbul Mujahideen "splinter group," Lashkar-e-Islam were coded as Lashkar-e-Islam events [28; 34 (entry #278), (entry #279); 71; 96].

In the case of India, the copious terrorist group splintering process made efforts to track and identify fledgling terrorist groups difficult in some cases. For example, the Communist Party of India (CPI-Maoist), that was crafted in 2004, splintered into several distinct terrorist groups such as the People's Liberation Front of India (PLFI), the Maoist Communist Party of Manipur (MKP), Jharkhand Sangharsh Jan Mukhti Morcha, and the Tritiya Prastituti Committee (TPC). In each case, each of those terrorist groups was coded as a separate terrorist organization [51; 59, 1–14; 60, 792–802; 85; 86; 97].

2.12.2 *Mexico*

In the Mickolus data chronologies, political context was almost always an intrinsic component of the qualitative accounts provided. In some cases, GTD coders were less than certain that GTD database events met their own criteria to qualify as terrorist events. A common GTD description was, "there is doubt that this incident meets terrorism-related criteria. Given the context of the drug trade in Mexico, it is unclear whether the attack was carried out by a criminal gang." (For example, see [36 (entry #6)]).

In that case, the discrete event was reviewed a second time to determine if the threat or use of force had the requisite political context necessary to include in the database. In some cases, when Mexican journalists were assaulted or radio stations attacked because of reports about government corruption or organized crime for example, I found implied political themes associated with those events, even when GTD accounts expressed reservations about inclusion in the GTD database.

Therefore, the coding assumption used was that even if perpetrators of what amounted to a terrorist act were not identified as terrorist groups or lone operatives, attacks against reporters or radio stations because of reporting on government corruption or organized crime, qualified as terrorist assaults because of political underpinnings, irrespective of perpetrator type. In a similar vein, when the threat or use of force was used to change the political dispositions of journalists in efforts to constrain reports about national/local government corruption or organized crime for example, those actions also qualified as terrorism, based on the criteria stipulated in the terrorism definition described above [15, 21–24].

That approach is robust theoretically because it conforms to more contemporary terrorism literature that points to the growth of connections between terrorism and organized crime within the post-Cold War world. For example, Makarenko describes the "crime-terror nexus," where interests and activities of organized criminal syndicalists dovetail well with terrorist group interests, especially within what she calls "black hole states." For Makarenko, "black hole states" are failed or failing states where government only exerts makeshift and incomplete political control, or is in legal or administrative control over only a few government sectors [1, 54; 29, 3–13; 56, 34–60; 62, 129–145; 78, 131–139; 79, 93–109; 80, 52–67; 106, 15–36] (Hendricks 2020, 103–104).

Indeed, Makarenko's description of "black hole" states dovetails with Gilman, Goldhammer, and Weber's description of failed or failing states as "hollowed out" to the point where cooperation is possible between terrorist groups and organized crime. Leaders of both types of illicit organizations want to exert political power and control, even though for organized criminal syndicalists, full-blown political control of a country is not the ultimate objective [29, 10].

When criminal syndicalists use terrorism as a method to procure monetary goals, the means can also become an end as both Makarenko and Kaldor suggest. Instead of control over a state or an autonomous region, the objective can be the political instability itself that can lead to reduction in state capacity to reduce or constrain illicit operations. The means involved can include efforts to increase popular mobilization against a government to exert influence over existing political organizations. The fundamental difference boils down to the pursuit of profit for organized crime, and pursuit of political goals in the case of terrorist groups [55; 62, 1–17; 101, 105–129].

As previously discussed, the alignment of common interests between terrorist groups and organized criminal elements became especially significant when the former Soviet Union's monetary support for terrorist groups dwindled. In the case of organized criminal syndicalists, a range of mutual interests materialized when the need for additional protections against government anti-drug interdiction efforts became more apparent. That need for protection was in large part due to the increased coordination and support for government anti-drug interdiction efforts made possible by the U.S. Drug Enforcement Administration (DEA).

At the same time, the world system of "intensive globalization" continuously evolved with new market opportunities; as a result, illicit drug production became more sophisticated. Weapons smuggling, human trafficking, and common criminal activity all represented new lines of cash flow opportunities beneficial to both criminal groups and terrorist organizations. For example, terrorist groups have engaged in credit card fraud or drug cultivation to raise revenues, while criminal syndicalists have employed terrorists or used terrorist tactics to intimidate judges and other local officials.

In Mexico, those interactive and synergistic relationships between drug cartels, terrorist groups, and weapons suppliers, have generated and sustained corruption within and across many sectors of Mexico's government. The effects of those activities have profound and lasting implications for the United States, and other countries in Latin America and Europe [58, 99–100, 102, 105–106, 95–98]. Therefore, it is critical that functional flexibility is introduced into terrorism definitions, and that terrorist event data coding frameworks are able to accommodate terrorist actions taken by different types of illicit organizations.

2.12.3 Brazil and South Africa

In the cases of Brazil and South Africa, the data bases used were very small. That condition limited the analysis to a presentation of basic descriptive statistics in each case. Furthermore, in the case of Brazil, terrorist assaults were anonymous events in all but one case, and there were problems in efforts to establish connections to political events, in addition to problems with terrorist event attribution.

In some cases, there were judgement calls made about whether a victim of a terrorist assault was primarily employed in the capacity of a newspaper/print company or as video or radio-blogger. That was an important distinction because as described in detail below, newspaper/print media targets were coded as "non-structuralist" targets, by contrast to telecommunication targets that were coded as "structuralist targets".

In the case of South Africa, Global Terrorism Data (GTD) accounts described terrorist assaults perpetrated by South Africans against Somali and Ethiopian shopkeepers as targets of "South African nationality." (For example, see [37 (entry #13)]). In this study, Somali and Ethiopian merchants who were victimized by other South Africans in terrorist assaults were coded as "foreign" targets ("2") rather than as "national" targets.

That scheme dovetailed well with the basic tenor of scripted accounts, even though it lacked some precision because it was not possible to determine whether or not specific Somali merchants held South African citizenship. In addition, "Woolworths" store targets in South Africa were coded as "foreign" targets because Woolworths Group Limited was located in New South Wales, Australia.

2.12.4 Thailand

In the case of Thailand, basic telephone infrastructure such as telephone booths and telephone poles were coded as "non-structuralist" targets ("1") even though they were coded as "telecommunication" business targets ("5") [38 (#12); 39 (entry #26), (entry #32)]. If however, cell phone or other telecommunications activities were linked to telephone poles, the target was coded as a "structuralist" target. In terms of "terrorist group-type," the terrorist group type category was coded as "Islamic nationalist irredentist" ("2") if there was mention of perpetrators as "separatists," "(suspected) insurgents," "southern insurgents," or "suspected Muslim rebels" [64, 3–4, 10, 12, 18, 23, 27, 50].[21] Otherwise, those acts were recorded as ("3") anonymous acts.

In terms of anonymous acts directed against ATM's, the assumption made was unless otherwise indicated, the ATM attacked was a civilian target, rather than belonging to a government owned bank such as the Krung Thai Bank in Yala Province [41 (entry # 49)] (95).[22] In addition, efforts were made to distinguish "public hospitals," such as Chulabhorn Hospital in Bangkok, from "private hospitals" and/or other medical facilities [42 (entry #141); 44 (entry #202)]. In the case specific terrorist assaults, if a scripted account(s) suggested the first part or initial purpose of a terrorist assault carried out against a "private establishment" for example, was to attract "first responders" as targets, that business target was prioritized as the target of attack [43 (entry #189)].

Lastly, for "city/township/village," attempts were made to code for those geographical locales primarily based on GTD scripted accounts. Those accounts frequently chronicled subdistricts or townships known as "tambons," "nakhon" (i.e., city), village (i.e., "muban"), or town (i.e., "mueangs"). In many cases, what was listed in GTD accounts under the designation "city" was double checked on the Internet to determine if particular designations corresponded to locations listed in other, more supplemental scripted accounts [64, 62, 80–83, 191–192, 155, 153].

2.13 A Three-Dimensional Typology of Terrorist and "Hybrid" Criminal-Terrorist Group-Types

In this study, several terrorist group-types, each with its own political ideology, goal and recruitment source, is derived from a three-dimensional terrorist group typology crafted in previous work. The delineation of terrorist group-types and what Shelley and Picarelli call "hybrid" criminal-syndicalist groups practicing terrorism, serves as the framework for a set of hypotheses about terrorism targeting patterns in "host" countries to be tested for validity [15; 16; 79, 93–109; 80, 55].

This typology draws from Starr and Most's work on conflict in the developing world. It is based on three terrorist group distinguishing characteristics that include: (1) political ideology; (2) goals; (3) terrorist group recruitment. In this rectangular cube-like structure, each dimension or plane represents one of those three distinguishing characteristics. Each characteristic works to define core differences between terrorist groups and hybrid groups that use terrorism. Those three distinguishing characteristics are different from other group attributes such as location, age, or size,

[21] This is consistent with Duncan McCargo's assertion that while Islam "frames" separatist and "new movement" terrorist attacks, "nationality" and "culture" issues are at the heart of the fierce struggle against the Buddhist regime in Thailand.

[22] Accordingly, the Islamic Bank in Thailand was originally coded as "mixed" (public/private ownership) or ("3").

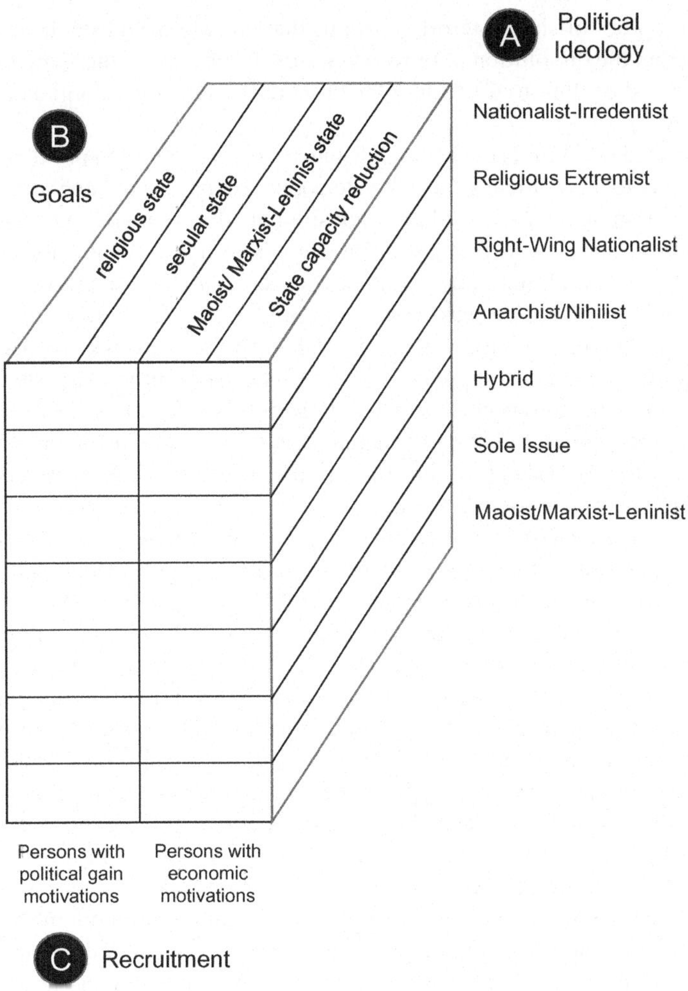

Fig. 2.5 Three-dimensional typology of terrorist and "Hybrid" criminal-terrorist group types

because the foregoing descriptors are common to all groups, and those variables fluctuate over time [72, 432–460; 88; 89, 92–117; 90, 581–620]. (see Fig. 2.5)

For political ideology, the terrorist group-type sub-categories described include: 1 = "Maoist (Marxist/Leninist)"; 2 = "Nationalist-Irredentist;" 3 = "Islamic Extremist"; 4 = "Right-Wing Nationalist" (e.g., Hindutva); 5 = "Anarchist/Nihilist"; 6 = "Hybrid" Terrorist-Criminal; 7 = "Sole Issue" [3, xiii–xiv; 7, 10–15; 15, 29–30, 52n63, 53–55n66; 23, 596–598, 606, 612; 53, 276; 54; 69, 13; 79, 93–109; 80; 105].[23] This three-dimensional typology can help catalogue the appearance of new "splinter"

[23] The category, "Hybrid" Criminal-Terrorist Group Type also draws from the Johnson typology category, "syndicalism of immaturity" and the Wilkinson typology category, "transnational gangs.".

terrorist group or "offshoot" terrorist groups that emerge from established terrorist groups or from the dissolution of terrorist groups. It can also do the same to trace the provenance and evolution offledgling "hybrid" terrorist-criminal organizations [15, 6–7, 197–201].

As discussed in Chap. 1, conceptual distance can exist between political ideology and more functional political goals when terrorist groups and criminal organizations that use terrorism are compared. For "oppositional" or "insurgent" terrorist groups, political ideology works to frame those goals within tightly woven terrorist group narratives about the reasons and rationale for fierce struggle against government, with special focus placed on mass consumption [2, 6–8, 13; 14, 163, 159, 161; 77].

Further, political ideology works to establish powerful connections between terrorist group activists or support personnel who frequently share similar motivations that drive them to become part of a terrorist organization. Likewise, political ideology and its interpretative understandings work to link constituents of terrorist organizations to one another, to families of other terrorist group members in some cases, and to terrorist group leadership.

In the case of the second typology dimension "goals," terrorist groups have particular goals that closely align with or otherwise reflect the political aims of different terrorist group types, themselves defined by ideology. In the case of each terrorist group- type, there are four articulated political goal-types: (1) a religious state or confederation; (2) a secular nation-state or state-linked autonomous area (e.g., state province, department, district); (3) a Maoist (Marxist-Leninist) nation-state or state-linked autonomous area; (4) reduction in nation-state capacity/control.

In the coding scheme, the "(end) goal" sub-category of "religious confederation" conforms to the world view of many Islamic extremists, while the sub-category, "state linked autonomous areas" reflects the emergent reality that what self-determination amounts to for many ethnic or religious groups is greater autonomy from a national government rather than full blown independence. That is the case because of harsh political and economic realities. There are international norms about the importance of ethnic diversity and state inviolability, and all too frequently, there are practical problems with the idea of an independent state that revolve around an insufficient tax base to generate revenue to support a fledgling state [57, 135–175].

In this typology, the last "(end) goal" type is "reduction in nation-state capacity and control." It is a more nebulous goal-type than the others and reflects an organization's efforts at government disruption. In this typology, "reduction in nation-state capacity and control" focuses on terrorist group or criminal syndicalist group efforts to affect the legal or policy dispositions of state and societal institutions. Those institutions include the judicial branch of government, the legislative branch (e.g., parliament), the police, media, and civil society organizations.

For example, Aum Shinrikyo's nihilist terrorist assaults or the attacks of some anarchist groups with ill-formed political goals might fall into this category. It is possible that some, but certainly not all, "new movement" terrorists in Thailand's political landscape would also qualify as terrorists seeking to reduce state capacity and control. Alternatively, the terrorism used by organized/criminal syndicalists to alter state policy and state leader political dispositions or both in their pursuit of profit would also fall into this category [62; 64, 158–159, 162, 177; 79, 93–109; 80, 55].

The notion of "reduction in nation-state capacity and control" fits well with Kaldor's point that nowadays, terrorist group chieftains have an interest in eliciting political mobilization for its own sake to maintain political instability and social unrest. Such mobilization in what Kaldor calls "new wars," reflects an "end" (i.e., a goal) in of itself, as well as a "means" for terrorist groups and organized criminal groups to enhance their power and control. What is also significant is there are oftentimes subordinate political and military goals that each type of group also strives to achieve which remain subordinate to the primary goals of political gain for terrorist groups, and monetary profit for criminal organizations [55, 1–17; 62; 64, 177, 152].

Kaldor's point about the importance of mobilization for mobilization's sake reflects another Kaldor cornerstone of "new wars." That cornerstone is her concept that "new wars" are a "mutual enterprise" where stakeholders such as governments, terrorist organizations, and criminal syndicalist organizations all benefit from sustained political instability and social unrest. Each party to a conflict promotes that "mutual enterprise" and essentially defers on endorsement of proposals to end conflict [55, 1–17; 62; 64, 177, 152].

This typology's third dimension is "recruitment." For criminal syndicalist organizations, recruitment involves efforts to persuade individuals to become part of a criminal organization to achieve economic goals, thereby in effect leading to quality of life improvements. For White, one essential difference between terrorist group and criminal recruitment is whether or not economic profit or individual or societal concerns stimulate an individual's interest and action. While some motivational overlap undoubtedly does occur, terrorist group inductees usually express strong interest in broader political goals and a desire to belong to a movement intent on structural political or economic change, or both [103, 14–15; 104, 13, 366].

In regards to leadership type, there was insufficient information available about terrorist group and criminal syndicalist leaders to make determinations about charismatic or transactional leadership [4; 16; 20, 25, 20, 22].[24] That problem might be related to the large number of terrorist groups and criminal syndicalist groups within and across the five "host" countries under consideration. It might also stem from gaps in knowledge about charismatic or transactional leadership qualities for specific leaders. In previous work on the Middle East, the total number of generally recognizable terrorist groups was fairly low; that helped make it possible to discern charismatic and transnational leadership distinctions [15, 16].

This section of Chap. 2 concludes with discussion about the structural shape of this terrorist organization and "hybrid" terrorist-criminal group-type typology. The typology is a $7 \times 4 \times 2$ rectangular cube-like structure because there are seven political-ideology types, four "end-goal" types, and two recruitment source types.

[24] Charismatic leaders, by contrast to transactional leaders, are able to capture and clearly articulate the "in-group-out-group" conflict dynamics that resonate with terrorist organization personnel and constituent groups.

It follows there are fifty-six (56) possible terrorist group and "hybrid" group-type iterations, each with different combinations of political ideology, goals, and recruitment patterns [15, 4–18, 198–201; 16, 12–14, 20–22].[25] From the fifty-six (56) different terrorist group-type and "hybrid" terrorist-criminal group iterations theoretically possible, seven group-types that appear in the larger world of action are identified.

[25] A. Ideology: 1 = Maoist (Marxist-Leninist); 2 = National-Irredentist; 3 = Religious Extremist (e.g., Islamic); 4 = Right-Wing Nationalist (e.g., Hindutva); 5 = Anarchist/Nihilist; 6 = "Hybrid" Terrorist-Criminal; 7 = Sole Issue.

B. Goals: 1 = religious state, confederation; 2 = secular state or state-linked autonomous area (e.g., state, province, department, district); 3 = Maoist (Marxist-Leninist) state or state-linked autonomous area; 4 = state capacity/control reduction.

C. Recruitment: (1) individuals with overarching political goals (e.g., ethnic group/clan and/or disenfranchised persons); (2) individuals motivated by economic gain.

This is a list of the fifty-six (56) possible terrorist group-types with different attributes derived from the typology.

1. A1 B1 C1—1, 1, 1 = a Maoist (Marxist-Leninist) terrorist group, with the goal of a religious state or confederation, recruiting from individuals with overarching political goals (i.e., an ethnic group/clan, or disenfranchised persons).

2. A1 B1 C2—1, 1, 2 = a Maoist (Marxist-Leninist) terrorist group, with the goal of a religious state or confederation, recruiting from individuals motivated by economic gain.

3. A1 B2 C1—1, 2, 1 = a Maoist (Marxist-Leninist) terrorist group, with the goal of a secular nation-state (or state- linked autonomous area), recruiting individuals with overarching political goals (i.e., an ethnic group/clan, or disenfranchised persons).

4. A1 B2 C2—1, 2, 2 = a Maoist (Marxist-Leninist) terrorist group, with the goal of a secular state (or state-linked autonomous area), recruiting from individuals motivated by economic gain.

5. A1 B3 C1—1, 3, 1 = a Maoist (Marxist-Leninist) terrorist group, with the goal of a Maoist (Marxist-Leninist) state (or state-linked autonomous area), recruiting from individuals with overarching political goals (i.e., an ethnic group/clan, or disenfranchised persons) (**e.g., Communist Party of India CPI-Maoist).**

6. A1 B3 C2—1, 3, 2 = a Maoist (Marxist-Leninist) terrorist group, with the goal of a Maoist (Marxist-Leninist) state (or state-linked autonomous area), recruiting from individuals motivated by economic gain.

7. A1 B4 C1—1, 4, 1 = a Maoist (Marxist-Leninist) terrorist group, with the goal of state capacity/control reduction, recruiting from individuals with overarching political goals (i.e., an ethnic group/clan or disenfranchised persons).

8. A1 B4 C2—1, 4, 2 = a Maoist (Marxist-Leninist) terrorist group, with the goal of state capacity/control reduction, recruiting from individuals motivated by economic gain.

9. A2 B1 C1—2, 1, 1 = a national-irredentist terrorist group, with the goal of a religious state or confederation, recruiting from individuals with overarching political goals (e.g., an ethnic group/clan or disenfranchised persons) (**i.e., Barisan Revolusi Nasional—BRN**).

10. A2 B1 C2—2, 1, 2 = a national-irredentist terrorist group, with the goal of a religious state or confederation, recruiting from individuals motivated by economic gain.

11. A2 B2 C1—2, 2, 1 = a nationalist-irredentist terrorist group, with the goal of a secular state (or state-linked autonomous area), recruiting from individuals with overarching political goals (i.e., an ethnic group/clan or disenfranchised persons) (**e.g., United Liberation Front of Assam**).

12. A2 B2 C2—2, 2, 2 = a nationalist-irredentist terrorist group, with the goal of a secular state (or state-linked autonomous area), recruiting from individuals motivated by economic gain.

2.14 The Theoretical Framework

The theoretical framework suggests that different types of terrorist and "hybrid" groups fall into three categories on a "Structuralist-Non-Structuralist" spectrum. Those categories include "structuralist" terrorist groups at the left axis of this continuum, and "non-structuralist" terrorist groups at the right axis of the continuum. In the middle of the continuum, "hybrid" criminal-terrorist groups that exhibit qualities of both "structuralist" and "non-structuralist" terrorist groups are expected to be found [15, 143, 182, 185; 79, 55; 80, 93–109]. The empirical results

---

13. A2 B3 C1—2, 3, 1 = a nationalist-irredentist terrorist group, with the goal of a Maoist (Marxist-Leninist) state (or state-linked autonomous area), recruiting from individuals with overarching political goals (i.e., an ethnic group/clan or disenfranchised persons.

14. A2 B3 C2—2, 3, 2 = a nationalist-irredentist terrorist group, with the goal of a Maoist (Marxist-Leninist) state (or state-linked autonomous area), recruiting from individuals motivated by economic gain.

15. A2 B4 C1—2, 4, 1 = a nationalist-irredentist terrorist group, with the goal state capacity/control reduction, recruiting from individuals with overarching political goals (i.e., an ethnic group/clan or disenfranchised persons). (e.g., **The "New Movement" in Thailand's southern provinces**).

16. A2 B4 C2—2, 4, 2 = a nationalist-irredentist terrorist group, with the goal of state capacity/control reduction, recruiting from individuals motivated by economic gain.

17. A3 B1 C1—3, 1, 1 = an Islamic extremist terrorist group, with the goal of a religious state or confederation, recruiting from individuals with overarching political goals (i.e., an ethnic group/clan or disenfranchised persons) (**e.g., Hizbul Mujahideen**).

18. A3 B1 C2—3, 1, 2 = an Islamic extremist terrorist group, with the goal of a religious state or confederation, recruiting from individuals motivated by economic gain.

19. A3 B2 C1—3, 2, 1 = an Islamic extremist terrorist group, with the goal of a secular state (or state-linked autonomous area), recruiting from individuals with overarching political goals (i.e., an ethnic group/clan or disenfranchised persons).

20. A3 B2 C2—3, 2, 2 = an Islamic extremist terrorist group, with the goal of a secular state (or state-linked autonomous area), recruiting from individuals motivated by economic gain.

21. A3 B3 C1—3, 3, 1 = an Islamic extremist terrorist group, with the goal of a Maoist (Marxist-Leninist state) (or state-linked autonomous area), recruiting from individuals with overarching political goals (i.e., an ethnic group/clan or disenfranchised persons).

22. A3 B3 C2—3, 3, 2 = an Islamic extremist terrorist group, with the goal of a Maoist (Marxist-Leninist) state (or state linked autonomous area), recruiting from individuals motivated by economic gain.

23. A3 B4 C1—3, 4, 1 = an Islamic extremist terrorist group, with the goal of state capacity/control reduction, recruiting from individuals with overarching political goals (i.e., an ethnic group/clan or disenfranchised persons).

24. A3 B4 C2—3, 4, 2 = an Islamic extremist terrorist group, with the goal of state capacity/control reduction, recruiting from individuals motivated by economic gain.

25. A4 B1 C1—4, 1, 1 = a right-wing nationalist terrorist group, with the goal of a religious state or confederation, recruiting from individuals with overarching political goals (i.e., an ethnic group/clan or disenfranchised persons) (**e.g., Rashtriya Sivayamsevak Sangh—RSS**).

26. A4 B1 C2—4, 1, 2 = a right-wing nationalist terrorist group, with the goal of a religious state or confederation, recruiting from individuals motivated by economic gain.

27. A4 B2 C1- 4, 2, 1 = a right-wing nationalist terrorist group, with the goal of a secular state (or state-linked autonomous area), recruiting from individuals with overarching political goals (i.e., an ethnic group/clan or disenfranchised persons).

28. A4 B2 C2—4, 2, 2 = a right-wing nationalist terrorist group, with the goal of a secular state (or state-linked autonomous area), recruiting from individuals motivated by economic gain.

are used to position different types of organizations that use terrorism on a "structuralist-non-structuralist" continuum.

That continuum of terrorist group-type and "hybrid" group-type delineates the different emphasis or mixtures that each group-type placed on those two types of terrorist assaults–structuralist types and nonstructuralist types. Terrorist assaults against "structuralist" targets are attacks against targets that represent "world systems" targets such as capitalism, globalization, and modernization, while "non-structuralist" targets include ethnic groups, individuals, or firms where ethnicity, or other facets of group solidarity such as religion are hallmarks of those types of targets.

---

29. A4 B3 C1—4, 3, 1 = a right-wing nationalist terrorist group, with the goal of a Maoist (Marxist-Leninist) state (or state-linked autonomous area), recruiting from individuals with overarching political goals (i.e., an ethnic group/clan or disenfranchised persons).

30. A4 B3 C2—4, 3, 2 = a right-wing nationalist terrorist group, with the goal of a Maoist (Marxist-Leninist) state (or state-linked autonomous area), recruiting from individuals motivated by economic gain.

31. A4 B4 C1—4, 4, 1 = a right-wing nationalist terrorist group, with the goal of state capacity/ control reduction, recruiting from an ethnic group/clan or disenfranchised persons.

32. A4 B4 C2—4, 4, 2 = a right-wing nationalist terrorist group, with the goal state capacity/ control reduction, recruiting from individuals motivated by economic gain.

33. A5 B1 C1—5, 1, 1 = an anarchist/nihilist terrorist group with the goal of a religious state or confederation, recruiting from individuals with overarching political goals (i.e., an ethnic group/ clan or disenfranchised persons).

34. A5 B1 C2—5, 1, 2 = an anarchist/nihilist terrorist group with the goal of a religious state or confederation, recruiting from individuals motivated by economic gain.

35. A5 B2 C1—5, 2, 1 = an anarchist/nihilist terrorist group with the goal of a secular state (or state-linked autonomous area) recruiting from individuals with overarching political goals (i.e., an ethnic group clan or disenfranchised persons).

36. A5 B2 C2—5, 2, 2 = an anarchist/nihilist terrorist group with the goal of a secular state (or state-linked autonomous area) recruiting from individuals motivated by economic gain.

37. A5 B3 C1—5, 3, 1 = an anarchist/nihilist terrorist group with the goal of a Maoist (Marxist-Leninist) state (or state-linked autonomous area), recruiting from individuals with overarching political goals (i.e., an ethnic group/clan or disenfranchised persons).

38. A5 B3 C2—5, 3, 2 = an anarchist/nihilist terrorist groups with the goal of a Maoist (Marxist-Leninist) state (or state-linked autonomous area), recruiting from individuals motivated by economic gain.

39. A5 B4 C1—5, 4, 1 = an anarchist/nihilist terrorist group with the goal of state capacity/ control reduction, recruiting from individuals with overarching political goals (i.e., an ethnic group/clan or disenfranchised persons) (**e.g., "Individuals Tending Towards Savagery"; "Aum Shinrikyo"**).

40. A5 B4 C2—5, 4, 2 = an anarchist/nihilist terrorist group with the goal of state capacity/ control reduction recruiting from individuals motivated by economic gain.

41. A6 B1 C1—6, 1, 1 = a "hybrid" criminal-terrorist group with the goal of a religious state or confederation, recruiting from individuals with overarching political goals (i.e., an ethnic group/ clan or disenfranchised persons.

42. A6 B1 C2—6, 1, 2 = a "hybrid" criminal-terrorist group with the goal of a religious state or confederation, recruiting from individuals motivated by economic gain.

43. A6 B2 C1—6, 2, 1 = a "hybrid" criminal-terrorist group with the goal of a secular state (or state-linked autonomous area), recruiting from individuals with overarching political goals (i.e., an ethnic group/clan or disenfranchised persons).

44. A6 B2 C2—6, 2, 2 = a "hybrid" criminal-terrorist group with the goal of a secular state (or state-linked autonomous area), recruiting from individuals motivated by economic gain.

It follows that if specific types of terrorist groups focus on targets that symbolize opposition to aspects of modernization (i.e., urbanization, industrialization) or globalization, their placement on this continuum will fall close to the "structuralist" axis.

Therefore, Maoist (Marxist-Leninist) terrorist groups are considered "structuralist" terrorist groups with its opposition to democratic capitalism. In previous work, the expected observation was that "structuralist" terrorist groups would place more focus on government targets than "non-structuralist groups," in part because governments generally favor such democratic capitalism based policies. Conversely, the expected observation was that "non-structuralist" terrorist groups would focus more on individuals and groups of individuals that in many cases are symbolic of ethnic, racial, or religious groups.

In this book, the "structuralist-non-structuralist continuum" from previous work is modified to place focus on business targets chosen by terrorists for attack. As "structuralist" terrorist groups place emphasis on "world systems" struggles, it is expected that targets of choice would include telecommunications firms and facilities, such as cell phone towers, video bloggers, and other international infrastructure. There

45. A6 B3 C1—6, 3, 1 = a "hybrid" criminal-terrorist group with the goal of a Maoist (Marxist-Leninist) state (or state-linked autonomous area), recruiting from individuals with overarching political goals (i.e., an ethnic group/clan or disenfranchised persons).

46. A6 B3 C2—6, 3, 2 = a "hybrid" criminal-terrorist group with the goal of a Maoist (Marxist-Leninist) state (or state-linked autonomous area), recruiting from individuals motivated by economic gain.

47. A6 B4 C1—6, 4, 1 = a "hybrid" criminal-terrorist group with the goal of state capacity/control reduction, recruiting from individuals with overarching political goals (i.e., an ethnic group/clan or disenfranchised persons).

48. A6 B4 C2—6, 4, 2 = a "hybrid" criminal-terrorist group with the goal of state capacity/control reduction, recruiting from individuals motivated by economic gain (**e.g., La Familia Michoaca'na, Los Caballeros Templarios, Red Commando, First Capitol Command**).

49. A7 B1 C1—7, 1, 1 = a sole-issue terrorist group with the goal of a religious state or confederation, recruiting from individuals with overarching political goals (i.e., an ethnic group or clan or disenfranchised persons).

50. A7 B1 C2—7, 1, 2 = a sole-issue terrorist group with the goal of a religious state or confederation, recruiting from individuals motivated by economic gain.

51. A7 B2 C1—7, 2, 1 = a sole-issue terrorist group with the goal of a secular state (or state-linked autonomous area), recruiting from individuals with overarching political goals (i.e., an ethnic group/clan or disenfranchised persons).

52. A7 B2 C2—7, 2, 2 = a sole-issue terrorist group with the goal of a secular state (or state-linked autonomous area), recruiting from individuals motivated by economic gain.

53. A7 B3 C1—7, 3, 1 = a sole-issue terrorist group with the goal of a Maoist (Marxist-Leninist) state (or state-linked autonomous area) from individuals with overarching political goals (i.e., an ethnic group/clan or disenfranchised persons).

54. A7 B3 C2—7, 3, 2, = a sole-issue terrorist group with the goal of a Maoist (Marxist-Leninist) state (or a state linked autonomous area) from individuals motivated by economic gain.

55. A7 B4 C1 -7, 4, 1 = a sole-issue terrorist group with the goal of state capacity control reduction, recruiting from individuals with overarching political goals (i.e., an ethnic group/clan or disenfranchised persons).

56. A7 B4 C2—7, 4, 2 = a sole-issue terrorist group with the goal of state capacity control reduction, recruiting from individuals motivated by economic gain.

should also be emphasis on "energy-alloy" firms and "banking/finance" institutions that also symbolize the global interconnections of the "world systems" standpoint.

In comparison, "non-structuralist" terrorist groups are found at the other end of the continuum. As previously mentioned, the focus of struggle is on individuals or ethnic, religious, or racial groups for "non-structuralist" groups. Nationalist-irredentist terrorist groups are considered a type of "non-structuralist" terrorist group because of the emphasis those groups place on individuals and groups as targets. It is possible to extrapolate and propose that "nationalist-irredentist" terrorist groups should also place emphasis on small business targets such as restaurants, vineyards, and farms that are representative of those interests, rather than on corporate business targets or their interests.

In between those two poles of the continuum where "structuralist" and "non-structuralist" terrorist groups are found, are where "hybrid" criminal-terrorist groups are expected to be placed. Here, "hybrid" criminal-terrorist groups encapsulate both "structuralist" and "non-structuralist" elements. The reason why is because "hybrid" terrorist group-criminal syndicalist terrorism is characterized by the goal of economic profit and more immediate, instrumental political goals to achieve profit, rather than to promote ethnic, religious, or racial group interests.

As a result, there should not be sharp distinctions between structuralist and non-structuralist targets for "hybrid" groups. For "hybrid groups," targets can include a broad array of government targets, rival organizations, newspaper or communications targets, or rival organization constituents, to help reduce the capacity and control of nation-state government, which after all is the primary instrumental goal for "hybrid groups." Therefore, the position of "hybrid" terrorist criminal groups on this continuum should fall somewhere close to the middle of the continuum.

A similar position on the continuum is expected for "religious extremist" terrorist groups. In the case of "religious extremist" terrorist groups, all "non-believers" and infrastructure, irrespective of whether or not targets are business interests, become legitimate targets. The reason why is because religious extremists view the contours of fierce struggle as an "end of times" eschatological struggle between good and evil [15, 67, 80n15, 80n16; 74, 72–88]. Therefore, the range of business target-types should be well represented, with little in terms of preference across business target-type categories.

It follows that "right-wing nationalist" terrorist groups also have an expansive choice of target-type with their focus on community leaders, ethnic, religious, or racial minority groups, political groups in opposition, and in some cases, country government infrastructure symbolic of government interests. That suggests right wing nationalist groups that target commercial interests will be found closer to the "non-structuralist" axis of this continuum.

2.15 Summary

This chapter highlights coding and methodological approaches, and theoretical approaches for this study. The discussion includes description of the TABVI measure introduced, and the bivariate analysis that serve as the basis for analysis. In terms of the coding and methodologies used, the rationale behind the coding decisions taken and the methodologies used are presented in detail. This chapter also describes the specific coding challenges and problems confronted when data were acquired from GTD sources, the Mickolus data chronologies, and other secondary accounts used.

All of the foregoing is crucial to explain the aims and underlying themes of this study. In addition, this makes it possible for other researchers to replicate this work, or incorporate parts of its research design into other studies to determine if similar results are produced.

In the process, those efforts help to standardize research about terrorism directed at commercial interests and provide first steps into the what Zinnes calls the "integrative" phase of research [110, 161–163; 111, 1–19]. This is particularly important for terrorism research, perhaps especially so in the case of efforts to study the process of commercial interest targeting, as focus is placed on parts of the world where information about stakeholders, political context, and the particular aspects of terrorist attacks often remain makeshift and incomplete.

In addition, this chapter offers a definition of terrorism that is based on jurisprudential principles showcased in previous work [15]. Almost singular focus is placed on the legal characteristics and dimensions of attack attributes, rather than on terrorist assault attributes more peripheral to terrorism definition, such as terrorist group age, size, location of attack, or organizational structure.

The reason why is that such a jurisprudentially based determination about whether or not an action qualifies as terrorism has the greatest prospect of wider acceptance because it is based on the generally recognizable and widely accepted body of international law. In the process, that approach helps to reduce the role and impact of political opinion or value judgments that contribute to "selective bias" problems associated with assessments made about the nature of forceful actions.

Furthermore, this terrorism conceptualization is flexible enough to account for terrorist actions taken by organizations and individuals other than terrorist organizations. Those include criminal syndicalist groups and so-called "lone wolf" operatives. This conceptualization of terrorism is also flexible enough to accommodate new tactical innovations such as cyberterrorism. The end result is a terrorism conceptualization that makes it possible for the analyst to distinguish between political terrorism practiced by terrorist organizations and criminal syndicalists. It also helps refine understandings about justifiable insurgency, criminal activities, and related conflict conditions such as total war, oppression, and repression [18, 74–89; 19, 134, 92].

In turn, the three-dimensional "Terrorist and 'Hybrid' Criminal-Terrorist Group-Type Typology" offered here makes it possible to derive theoretical propositions about terrorist organizations and hybrid terrorist criminal syndicalist groups that use terrorism, and to test those theoretical propositions for empirical validity.

That is important because of the robust set of interdependencies between terrorist groups and organized crime that is now a hallmark of our contemporary world. There are ten hypotheses that provide the basis of this book's organization of empirical findings; those hypotheses and empirical results are found in each of the case studies where bivariate analysis is used.

What follows is the set of five developing world "host" country case study chapters, starting with India. In those chapters, there is discussion about TABVI scores for each of the five countries under consideration, and in some cases where there was sufficient data available, a presentation of associated industry scores for particular industries for those countries. For all countries, a set of descriptive statistics about terrorist assault attributes is presented.

References

1. Abbott PK (2004) Terrorist threat in the Tri-Border area; Myth or reality? Military Review. https://smallwarsjournal.com/documents/abbott.pdf
2. Ackerman GA, Burnham M (2019) Towards a definition of terrorist ideology. Terrorism and Political Violence 33(6):1160–1190. https://www.tandfonline.com/doi/abs/10.1080/09546553.2019.1599862
3. Alexander Y, Gleason J (1981) Behavioral and quantitative perspectives on terrorism. Pergamon Press
4. Allport GW (1954) The nature of prejudice. Addison Wesley
5. Anderson SK (1998) Warnings versus alarms: terrorist threat analysis applied to the Iranian-state run media. Studies in conflict and terrorism 21(3):277–305
6. Anderson L (1987) The state in the Middle East and North Africa. Comparative Politics 20(1):1–18. https://www.jstor.org/stable/421917
7. Bell BJ (1975) Transnational terror. American Enterprise Institute for Public Policy Research
8. Beres LR (1988) Genocide law and power politics. Whitter Law Review 10(2):329–351
9. Beres LR (1988) Terrorism and international law. Florida International Law Journal 3(3):291–306
10. Beres LR (1990) Confronting nuclear terrorism. The Hastings International and Comparative Law Review 14(1):129–154
11. Blakesley CL, Lagodny O (1991) Finding harmony amidst disagreement over extradition, jurisdiction, the role of human rights and issues of extraterritoriality under international criminal law. Vanderbilt Journal of Transnational Law 24(1):1–74
12. Blakesley CL (1992) Terrorism, drugs international law and the protection of human liberty: a comparative study of international law, its nature, rule and impact in matters of terrorism, drug trafficking, war and extradition. Transnational Books
13. Booth K (2007) Theory of world security. Cambridge University Press
14. Campbell H, Hansen T (2013) Is narco-violence in Mexico terrorism? Bull Lat Am Res 33(2):158–173
15. Chasdi R (1999) Serenade of suffering: a portrait of Middle East terrorism, 1968–1993. Lexington Books
16. Chasdi RJ (2002) Tapestry of terror: a portrait of Middle East terrorism, 1994–1999. Lexington Books
17. Chasdi R (n.d.) Corporate security surveillance: an assessment of host country vulnerability to terrorism (unpublished book proposal)

18. Chasdi RJ (2010) Counterterrorism offensives for the ghost war world: the rudiments of counterterrorism policy. Lexington Books
19. Chasdi RJ (2018) Corporate security crossroads: responding to terrorism, cyberthreats, and other hazards in the global business environment. ABC-CLIO—Praeger
20. Coser L (1956) The functions of social conflict. Free Press
21. Crenshaw M (1981) The causes of terrorism. Comparative Politics. 13(4):379–399. https://www.jstor.org/stable/pdf/421717
22. Drake CJM (1998) Terrorists' target selection. Martin's Press, St
23. Fernández LM (2009) Organized crime and terrorism: from the cells towards political communication, a case study. Terrorism and Political Violence 21:595–616
24. Flores RG, Aguilera RV (2007) Globalization and location choice: analysis of US multinational firms in 1980 and 2000. Journal of International Business Studies 38(7):1187–1210. https://link.springer.com/article/10.1057/palgrave.jibs.8400307
25. Forest JJF (2006) Training camps and other centers of learning. In: Forest JJF (ed) Teaching terror: Strategic and tactical learning in the terrorist world. Rowman & Littlefield Publishers, Inc., pp 69–109
26. Fried JHE (1985) The nuclear collision course: can international law be of help? Denver Journal of International Law and Policy 14(1):97–119
27. Fuerth L, Faber EMH (2012) Anticipatory governance practical upgrades: Equipping the executive branch to cope with increasing speed and complexity of major challenges. National Defense University, Center for Technology & National Security Policy
28. Ganal N (2015) Jammu and Kashmir police blame Hizbul Mujahideen for Sopore telecom attack. India Today. https://www.indiatoday.in/mail-today/story/jammu-and-kashmir-police-sopore-telecom-sector-attacks-hizbul-mujahideen-291627-2015-05-29
29. Gilman N, Goldhammer J, Weber S (2013) Deviant globalization. In: Miklaucic M, Brewer J (eds) Convergence: illicit networks and national security in an age of globalization. National Defense University Press
30. Global Terrorism Database (GTD) "India" GTD ID: 201405280063. 28 May 2014
31. Global Terrorism Database (GTD) "India," GTD ID: 20160520043. 20 May 2016
32. Global Terrorism Database (GTD) "India," GTD ID: 201306120018. 12 June 2013
33. Global Terrorism Database (GTD) "India," GTD ID: 201306240028. 24 June 2013
34. Global Terrorism Database (GTD) "India," GTD ID: 20150724008. 24 July 2015
35. Global Terrorism Database (GTD) "India," GTD ID: 201804230019. 23 April 2018
36. Global Terrorism Database (GTD) "Mexico," GTD ID: 201304170036. 17 April 2013
37. Global Terrorism Database (GTD) "South Africa," GTD ID: 201702020022. 2 Feb 2017
38. Global Terrorism Database (GTD) "Thailand," GTD ID: 201302230006. 23 Feb 2013
39. Global Terrorism Database (GTD) "Thailand," GTD ID: 201304100043. 10 April 2013
40. Global Terrorism Database (GTD) "Thailand," GTD ID: 201306230036. 23 June 2013
41. Global Terrorism Database (GTD) "Thailand," GTD ID: 201307030033. 3 July 2013
42. Global Terrorism Database (GTD) "Thailand," GTD ID: 201405070016. 7 May 2014
43. Global Terrorism Database (GTD) "Thailand." GTD: 201503030032. 3 March 2015
44. Global Terrorism Database (GTD) "Thailand," GTD ID: 201505160085. 16 May 2015
45. Hendricks MN (2020) Manufacturing terrorism in Africa: the securitisation of South African Muslims. Palgrave Macmillan
46. Hill CWL, Hult GTM (2016) Global business today, 9th edn. McGraw Hill Education
47. Hirschi T (1969) Causes of delinquency. University of California Press
48. Hoffman B (1993) Terrorist targeting: tactics, trends, and potentialities. Terrorism and Political Violence 5(2):12–29
49. Hofstede G (1993) Cultural constraints in management theories. Acad Manag Exec 7(1):81–90
50. Indian Express (2013) Vizag engineer abducted in Assam is safe. Nexis-Uni
51. Indo-Asian News Service (2007) Maoists ask Bastar people to celebrate their anniversary
52. Intoccia GF (1985) International legal and policy implications of an American counter-terrorist strategy. Denver Journal of International Law and Policy 14(1):131–135

53. Johnson C (1978) Perspectives on terrorism. In: Laqueur W (ed) The terrorism reader: a historical anthology. New American Library
54. Johnson CA (1982) Revolutionary change, 2nd edn. Stanford University Press
55. Kaldor M (2013) In defence of new wars. Stability Journal 2(1):1–17. https://eprints.lse.ac.uk/49500/1/__lse.ac.uk_storage_LIBRARY_Secondary_libfile_shared_repository_Content_Kaldor%2CM_Kaldor_Defence_new_wars_2013_Kaldor_Defence_new_wars_2013.pdf
56. Kaplan RD ([1994] 2000) The coming anarchy. In: O'Meara P, Mehlinger HD, Krain M, Newman RM (eds) Globalization and challenges of a new century: a reader. Indiana University Press
57. Kaufman C (1996) Possible and impossible solutions to ethnic civil wars. International Security 20(4):135–175. https://www.jstor.org/stable/2539045
58. Kuhn DA, Bunker RJ (2013) Just where do Mexican cartel weapons come from? In: Bunker RJ (ed) Criminal insurgencies in Mexico and the Americas—the gangs and cartels wage war. Routledge
59. Kujur RK (2006) IPCS special report 25: left extremism in India Naxals movement in Chhattisgarh & Orissa. Institute of Peace and Conflict Studies. https://www.jstor.org/stable/resrep09325
60. Kumar S, Mishra S (2011) Naxal problem in central Bihar. The Indian Journal of Political Science 72(3):791–802. https://www.jstor.org/stable/41858853
61. Luthans F, Doh JP (2012) International management: culture, strategy, and behavior, 8th edn. McGraw-Hill Urwin
62. Makarenko T (2004) The crime-terror continuum: tracing the interplay between transnational organized crime and terrorism. Global Crime 6(1):129–145
63. Malley JA (1983) Preparing and protecting personnel and property prior to a terrorist attack. In: Montana PJ, Roukis GS (eds) Managing terrorism: strategies for the corporate executive. Quorum Books
64. McCargo D (2016) Tearing apart the land: Islam and legitimacy in southern Thailand. Cornell University Press
65. Mickolus E (2014) Terrorism 2008–2012: a worldwide chronology. McFarland & Company, Inc.
66. Mickolus E (2016) Terrorism, 2013–2015: a worldwide chronology. McFarland & Company, Inc.
67. Mickolus E (2018) Terrorism worldwide, 2016. McFarland & Company, Inc.
68. National institute of standards and technology/SEMATECH e-handbook of statistical methods (2013) 1.3.5.11. Measures of skewness and kurtosis. https://www.itl.nist.gov/div898/handbook/eda/section3/eda35b.htm
69. Nef J (1978) Some thoughts on contemporary terrorism: domestic and international perspectives. In: Carson J (ed) Terrorism in theory and practice: proceedings from a colloquium. The Atlantic Council of Canada
70. New India Express (2014) Maoists torch vehicles. Lexis-Nexis
71. Pakistan Today (2005) Hizbul Mujahideen disowns faction more attacks in IHK. Nexis-Uni
72. Pearson FS (1974) Geographic proximity and foreign military intervention. The Journal of Conflict Resolution 18(3):432–460
73. Plestina D (1992) From democratic centralism to decentralized democracy? Trials and tribulations of Yugoslavia's development. In: Allcock JB, Horton JJ, Milivojevic M (eds) Yugoslavia in transition: choices and constraints essays in honour of Fred Singleton. St. Martin's Press
74. Rapoport DC (1987) Why does religious messianism produce terror? In Paul Wilkinson and Alasdair M. Stewart (Eds.), *Contemporary research on terrorism*. Aberdeen University Press
75. Reisman M, Antoniou CT (1994) The laws of war: a comprehensive collection of primary documents on international law governing armed conflict. Vintage Books
76. Ronis SR (2007) Timelines into the future: strategic visioning methods for government, business and other organizations. Hamilton Books

77. Ross JI (1993) Structural causes of oppositional political terrorism: towards a causal model. J Peace Res 30(3):317–329
78. Shelley LI (2013) Money laundering into real estate. In: Miklaucic M, Brewer J (eds) Convergence: illicit networks and national security in an age of globalization. National Defense University Press
79. Shelley LI (2014) Identifying, counting and categorizing transnational criminal organizations. In: Sheptycki J (ed) Transnational organized crime volume II: definitional and methodological issues, constructionist and critical perspectives. Sage Publications
80. Shelley LI, Picarelli J, Irby A, Hart DM, Craig-Hart PA, Williams P, Simon S, Abdullaev N, Stanislawski B, Covill L (2005) Methods and motives: exploring links between transnational organized crime and international terrorism. Trends in Organized Crime 8(2). https://link.springer.com/article/10.1007/s12117-005-1024-x
81. Shimko KL (1991) Images and arms control: perceptions of the Soviet Union in the Reagan administration. University of Michigan Press
82. Simon JD (2013) Lone wolf terrorism: understanding the growing threat. New York Prometheus Books, 37–38, 43–45, 128–129, 204, 251, 266
83. Sinai J (2016) New trends in terrorism's targeting of the business sector. http://mackenzieinstitute.com/new-trends-in-terrorisms-targeting-of-the-business-sector/
84. Sirkin MR (1999) Statistics for the social sciences, 2nd edn. Sage Publications
85. South Asian Terrorism Portal (2001) Left-wing extremist group-people's war group (PWG). https://www.satp.org/satporgtp/countries/india/terroristoutfits/pwg.htm
86. South Asian Terrorism Portal (2001) Left-wing extremist group—Maoist Communist Centre (MCC). https://www.satp.org/satporgtp/countries/india/terroristoutfits/mcc.htm
87. Spaaj R (2012) Understanding lone wolf terrorism: global patterns, motivations, and prevention. Springer, Dordrecht
88. Starr H, Most B (1976) The substance and study of borders in international relations research. Int Stud Quart 20(4):581–620
89. Starr H, Most B (1983) Contagion and border effects on contemporary African conflict. Comp Pol Stud 16(1):92–117
90. Starr H, Most B (1985) Patterns of conflict: quantitative analysis and the comparative lessons of third world wars. In: Harkavy RE, Neumann SG (eds) Approaches and case studies vol. 1 of the lessons of recent wars in the third world. D.C. Heath
91. Statistics Solutions (2013) Homoscedasticity. https://www.statisticssolutions.com/free-resources/directory-of-statistical-analyses/homoscedasticity/
92. Stohl M, Lopez G (1984) Introduction in The state as terrorist: the dynamics of governmental repression and violence. Westview Press
93. Tangerine (2016) Hiz commander who blasted Kashmir telecom towers killed. Lexis-Nexis
94. Teltumbde A (2018) Margin speak—Umar Khalid and the hate republic. Economic and Political Weekly 53(36). https://www.epw.in/journal/2018/36/margin-speak/umar-khalid-and-hate-republic.html
95. The Bangkok Post (2013) South rebels launch wave of reprisals. Nexis Uni
96. The Telegraph (India) (2013) Four abducted from colliery-combing operation on in Tinsukia. Nexis Uni
97. The Telegraph Online (2015) Rebels torch trucks in Latehar. https://www.telegraphindia.com/jharkhand/rebels-torch-trucks-in-latehar/cid/1385563
98. The Times of India (2013) Maoists set three vehicles on fire. Nexis-Uni
99. The Times of India (2014) Maoists set five vehicles on fire in Rayagda. Lexis-Nexis
100. United News of India (2013) Press reporter shot at in Narnaund, admitted to PGI Rohtak. Nexis-Uni
101. Wagner RH (2007) War and the state: the theory of international politics. University of Michigan Press
102. Wainwright T (2017) Narconomics: how to run a drug cartel. Ebury Press
103. White JR (2002) Terrorism: an introduction, 3rd edn. Wadsworth Thomson Learning
104. White JR (2006) Terrorism and homeland security, 5th edn. Wadsworth Thomson Learning

105. Wilkinson P (1974) Political terrorism. Wiley
106. Williams P (2013) Lawlessness and disorder: an emerging paradigm for the 21st century. In: Miklaucic M, Brewer J (eds) Convergence: illicit networks and national security in an age of globalization. National Defense University Press
107. Wonnacott TH, Wonnacott RJ (1990) Introductory statistics for business and economics, 4th edn. Wiley
108. World Economic Forum (2017) Business costs of terrorism. http://reports.weforum.org/global-competitiveness-index-2017-2018/competitiveness-rankings/#series=EOSQ033
109. World Economic Forum (2017) Appendix C. http://www3.weforum.org/docs/GCR2017-2018/04Backmatter/TheGlobalCompetitivenessReport2017%E2%80%932018AppendixC.pdf
110. Zinnes D (1976) Contemporary research in international relations: a perspective and a critical appraisal. Free Press
111. Zinnes D (1976) The problem of cumulation. In: Rosenau J (ed) Search of global patterns. Free Press

Chapter 3
The Case of India

India has a political landscape liberally peppered with terrorist groups. In 2018, Khemnar reported the South Asian Terror Portal (SATP) chronicled 180 terrorist groups active in the Indian political fray over the past two decades [31]. In 2019, Sahni reported there were 136 "militant groups" in Northeast India alone, that would suggest that a high concentration of terrorist groups is found in India's Northeast Region [53, 123]. This high number of terrorist groups stems from the interplay of historical, demographic, and political explanatory factors such as the national-regional political interactions discussed below.

The geographical scope of those terrorist groups is expansive because many terrorist groups are connected to each other across several Indian states, and at least to some extent because of the close connections between political parties and terrorist groups, and the porous boundaries between them. In addition, the membership boundaries between terrorist groups can also be permeable.

In the case of India, terrorist group connections also extend across multiple nation-state borders, into in countries such as Myanmar, Bhutan, Nepal, and Bangladesh [22, 1015–1017; 37].[1] The problem is compounded even more by a set of nation-state and terrorist group connections that involve China and Pakistan, that makes it possible for particular terrorist groups opposed to Indian national and state governments to flourish.

In this study, sixty-four (64) terrorist groups targeted commercial interests between 2013 and 2018. Those terrorist groups fall into four distinguishable terrorist group-types which include: (1) Maoist (Marxist-Leninist); (2) Nationalist-Irredentist; (3) Islamic Extremist; (4) Hindu-Right Wing. The large number of terrorist groups involved in this study and the large number of criminal organizations active in India, coupled with limited information in English about those criminal

[1] For example, Gohain relates how the ULFA prepared for terrorist assaults at National Socialist Council of Nagalim (Khaplang) facilities at the Myanmar-India border, and how the UFLA was influenced by CPI-Maoist strategies and tactics.

R. J. Chasdi, *Corporate Security Surveillance*, Advanced Sciences and Technologies for Security Applications, https://doi.org/10.1007/978-3-031-39550-5_3

gangs with possible ties to terrorist organizations, limited the focus of analysis to terrorist group threat against Indian commercial interests.

In addition to the aforementioned factors, the high number of terrorist groups encountered revolved around terrorist group splintering and splinter group formation, which in turn was determined by several factors. Those factors included personal rivalries, differences of opinion about terrorist group policy, turf wars, and the demise of terrorist group leaders. In addition, it appeared terrorist group splintering and spinoff processes were associated with government policy frameworks and actions.[2]

Empirical evidence to support the existence of relationships between Indian government action and terrorist group splintering was ample. For example, the Indian national government offered to engage in peace talks with many national-irredentist terrorist groups, provided that terrorist group weapons were surrendered before peace talks commenced. In reaction, several Indian terrorist groups splintered as hardliners rejected calls for negotiations, and continued to fight.

Another example of what appears to be the interactive effect of government policy and terrorist group splintering is how government efforts to modernize dense forest areas through construction of roads and railways elicit terrorist attacks against construction firms. Some analysts argue the reason those government policies spawn terrorism is because more effective transportation translates into more effective counterterrorism policy in the short-run, while in the long-haul, those policies will contribute to the Indian national and state government's ability to exploit and control indigenous peoples and their resources.

While it is not possible to provide a complete list of major Indian terrorist groups active in the political fray, let alone a comprehensive list of splinter and spinoff groups, examples of both will be provided to supply anecdotal and impressionistic support for what drives terrorist group splintering. Descriptions of particular groups are offered so the reader can acquire a general understanding of the terrorist group splintering process and the political context behind many of the terrorist attacks aimed at Indian business targets [30, 42, 62][3]

3.1 Indian Maoist (Marxist-Leninist) Terrorist Groups

Terrorist groups that comprise the Maoist (Marxist Leninist) group-type category include, but are not limited to, the Communist Party of India CPI-Maoist ; the Maoist Communist Party of Manipur (MKP); the Popular Front for the Liberation of India

[2] For definitional purposes, splinter groups derive from terrorist groups directly in terms of personnel and ideology and in some cases organizational structure, while spinoff groups have less direct connections in those domains to parent groups.

[3] For example, the Songjibit branch of the National Democratic Front of Bodoland (NDFB-S) splintered from NDFB in 2012 and the United Democratic Liberation Army (UDLA) splintered from the United Liberation Front of Barak Valley (ULFVB) in 2008. The National Santhali Liberation Army (NSLA), is a spinoff group formed from the remnants of five Adivasi terrorist groups in Assam that relinquished their weapons to Indian government authorities.

(PFLI); CPI-ML (New Democracy). In the broader sense, the Naxalite movement is driven by economic inequality and social justice concerns [26]. It has been influenced by Marxism. Marxism was seen by Naxals as the pathway to dismantle enormous disparities of wealth based on caste and class status characteristic of Indian society from the times of the Maharaja local kingdoms, through British imperialism, and into contemporary times.

Maoist terrorist groups are motivated by fierce struggle between peasants and the landed class (the owners of capital) where peasants take on the role of the urban laborer (or proletariat) in rural, agricultural settings. The role of Marxism in Indian politics traces an arc to the Tashkent conference in Uzbekistan in 1920 where Indian Marxists articulated the goal of a Marxist Indian society, and crafted the Communist Party of India (CPI) [34, 96–97].

Spurred on by the Indo-China War (1962), an ideological split in 1964 resulted in the emergence of a new CPI faction called the Communist Party of India Marxist (M) that favored Chairman Mao Zedong and China. Soon after, leaders of the Communist Party of India Marxist (M) decided to participate in local parliamentary elections in West Bengal.

That decision to work within India's political system caused conflict with other CPI-(M) leaders who comprised a CPI-(M) sub-group called Dakshin Desh. Those Dakshin Desh leaders railed against the CPI-(M)'s sell-out of the Maoist peasant revolution to contest parliamentary elections, but in the end, CPI-(M) leadership participated in local elections. In 1966, both the CPI and the CPI-(M) crafted new political parties, and those parties formed the "United Front" coalition which won state elections to control West Bengal in 1967 [34, 97–98].

However, the United Front's new found control over West Bengal was insufficient for more extremist CPI-(M) elements who demanded a true peasant-based revolt. Isolated peasant-based violence against landholder and government interests culminated in the watershed 1967 Naxal peasant insurrection against wealthy landowners in Naxalbari, West Bengal. This Naxalite rebellion was led by Kanu Sanyal (1932–2010). The Naxal rebellion started on May 25, 1967; it was not long before the West Bengal's United Front government called for "police action" against its more ideologically oriented members.

In aftermath of the Naxalite rebellion and West Bengal's United Front government efforts to suppress it, the insouciance of the Indian national government to peasant demands and aspirations became even more profound. This was increasingly clear especially after West Bengal's state government, with the United Front (and the CPI-(M)) at the helm, used force against radical CPI-(M) "extremist cadres" who had gathered outside the halls of the West Bengal assembly on June 27, 1967 to protest against what was considered to be the West Bengal government's anti-peasant standpoint [34, 97–98].

The reaction to the full-blown suppression of the radical branch of CPI-(M) was intense. In response to those events, more extremist CPI-(M) members bent on revolution formed the All-India Coordination Committee of Revolutionaries (AICCR), originally as a core group of CPI-(M), in Calcutta in November 1967. One of AICCR's first acts was its decision to refuse to participate in all Indian elections. It was the influence of AICCR (later recast as the All-India Coordination Committee of Communist Revolutionaries) that helped consolidate the Naxalite movement [34, 97–98].

In 1969, the Communist Party of India-Marxist Leninist (ML) was crafted by its charismatic leader, Charul Mazumdar (1919–1972) to continue the political momentum produced by the Naxalbari insurrection. The Communist Party of India -Marxist Leninist (ML) remained an important source from which more contemporary Naxalite groups flowed. However, centrifugal forces within the CPI-ML were powerful from the start and led to group fragmentation. Lynch reports that between 1977 and 1994, the Communist Party of India Marxist Leninist (ML) splintered, "… into more than 40 separate small groups." [32, 5, 7, 2; 33, 791; 36, 5, 11, 7; 57, 1, 3–4].[4]

That backdrop of terrorist group splintering produced the next watershed interval for development of the Naxalite movement—the period from 1975 to 1980. In that interval, two new Naxalite organizations appeared. In 1975, Khanai Chatterjee (1933–1983) reconfigured his Dakshin Desh group to become the Maoist Communist Centre (MCC). As mentioned previously, Dakshin Desh was originally a sub-group of the Communist Party of India-Maoist (M). As it evolved, the underlying aim of Dakshin Desh was to pursue political and paramilitary objectives both through the ballot box and by means of threat and use of force.

In addition to the Maoist Communist Centre (MCC), a second new group to appear was the Communist Party of India Marxist-Leninist (ML)—People's War Group (PWG). This organization was a political party established by Kondapalli Seetharamaiah (1915–2002) around 1980, as a result of Seetharamaiah's clashes with leaders of the Communist Party of India Marxist-Leninist (ML), itself the parent organization of CPI-ML- PWG.

The Maoist Communist Centre (MCC) and the Communist Party of India Marxist-Leninist (ML)—People's War Group (PWG) remain critical political precursors to India's contemporary Naxalite threat. In addition to the direct connections those two groups had to their antecedent group, the Communist Party of India-Marxist-Leninist (ML), itself formed in 1969, both organizations left a legacy of their own. Each helped to spawn India's most formidable contemporary terrorist threat—the Communist Party of India (CPI Maoist). It is to the CPI-Maoist organization that discussion now turns [36, 5] (see Fig. 3.1).

The Communist Party of India (CPI-Maoist) is the single most predominant Maoist terrorist group in India's contemporary political fray. It was crafted on September 21, 2004 after the Maoist Communist Centre (MCC) and the Communist Party of India Marxist-Leninist (ML)—People's War Group (PWG) blended. Its armed branch is formally known as the People's Liberation Guerilla Army (PLGA) [28]. The CPI-Maoist manifesto is called STIR ("Strategy and Tactics of the Indian Revolution").

---

[4] Lynch reports that in around 2010, there were some 20,000 Naxals activists, with some 50,000 constituent group supporters.

Fig. 3.1 Historical retrospective of Indian Maoist Terrorist Groups

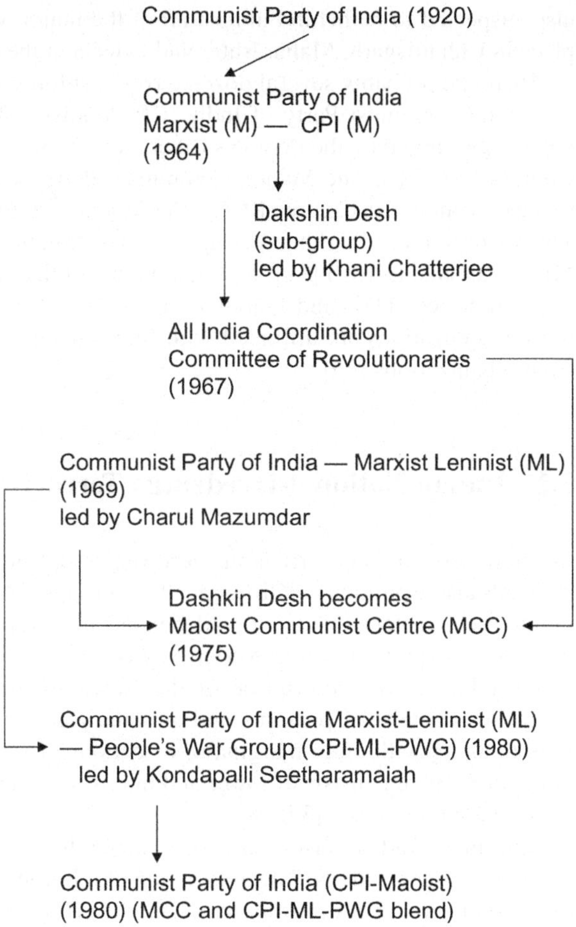

Its three strategies, "defensive," "stalemate," and "offensive" postures are framed by the STIR notion of, "seizure of political power through protracted armed struggle…." [1, 253–255, 260–261]. The CPI-Maoist political platform opposes policies to promote globalization and economic privatization. Ahlawat also reports that Naxalite activities span eighteen Indian states, from the nine states that recently experienced a Naxalite terrorism surge (i.e., about one-third of India), some 40,000 Naxalite activists operate [1, 254–255].

The CPI-Maoist group is currently led by General Secretary Nambala Keshava Rao (aka "Basavaraj"), who has provided political leadership as well as terrorist group direction in his capacity of CPI-Maoist's political committee. In 2018, Basavaraj took up the reigns of CPI—Maoist after former General Secretary Muppala Lakshmana Rao (aka "Ganapathy") resigned in poor health. Before taking full control of CPI-Maoist, Nambala Keshava Rao made a name for himself from 2004 to 2008 as an effective and combative leader of the CPI-Maoist's PGLA. Pandey reports, "he is also suspected to be behind almost all of the major Maoist attacks that have taken place in Chhattisgarh, Maharashtra and Odisha in the recent past." [45, 50].

There are probably several dozen terrorist splinter and spinoff groups that derive from the Communist Party of India (CPI-Maoist). Those terrorist groups include, but are not limited to, the People's Liberation Front India (PLFI), the Tritiya Prastuti Committee (TPC), The Maoist Communist Party of Manipur (MKP), the Revolutionary Communist Centre (RCC), the Maoists of Andhra Odisha Border Special Zonal Committee, Jharkhand Sangharsh Jan Mukhti Morcha, and Jharkhand Jana Mukti Parishad (JJMP) [59]. It should be noted that in the case of the Tritiya Prastuti Committee (TPC) and Jharkhand Jana Mukti Parishad (JJMP), there are reports those organizations are affiliated with Indian security forces or are perhaps police front organizations [25].

3.2 Indian National-Irredentist Terrorist Groups

In comparison, national-irredentist terrorist groups put special focus on the political demands and aspirations of different ethnic groups within India. The leaders of those groups seek greater autonomy or independence outright from India's national government. Kumari points to some overlap between Naxalite and national-irredentist group membership. In his description of the Naxalites, he reports, "at some places, it comprises of units of peasants and at some places of tribal. Some are the fusion of both along with other marginalized sections of society. In caste terms, the base of the movement consists of lower and intermediate castes of both Hindu as well as Muslim communities." [34, 98].

Still, many Indian terrorism experts make distinctions between these two types of terrorist organizations. The association of religion and national-separatism seems to be complex and at times inconsistent with ethnic groups of the same religion in conflict. For example, even though most Kukis (Zomi) in the states of Manipur and Mizoram are Christian, there has been fierce ethnic conflict between Christian Naga and Kuki in Manipur starting in 1992 [54, 3676–3678].[5] In addition, among many Adivasis (i.e., forest dwellers) in conflict with Indian national and state governments, a much smaller percentage of Christian Adivasis are found across India compared to most Adivasis who, in their regional "homeland," practice some form of Hinduism [1; 24, 252–253, 261, 266; 34, 98, 96].

There are some two dozen terrorist groups chronicled in this study that ostensibly operate on behalf of ethnic groups and focus attacks on business targets. Intrinsic to nationalist-irredentism is the process of self-determination for ethnic groups. The process of self-determination is inextricably bound up by what Esman calls the "ascriptive solidarities" of ethnicity that bonds people together. Those ties include

[5] Shimray also points out that the political activism of "student organizations" such as the Kuki Students organization (KSO) reflect those ethnic conflict patterns.

shared language, religion, shared visions of the future, and shared historical experiences [12]. Self-determination can take two forms: greater autonomy from a state or full-blown independence. Indeed, the depth and scope of separatism in India has made some analysts question whether or not India can continue to exist in its current form without itself splintering.

A brief description of some major Indian nationalist-irredentist groups is offered to underscore links between ethnic group grievances in Northeast India, and how Indian national government insouciance towards those claims has helped to produce calls for independence with political party and terrorist group backing. Many Indian terrorist groups illustrate the porous nature of boundaries between Indian political groups and terrorist groups. Those connections are in some cases, reflective of terrorist group splintering and spinoff effects.[6]

What follows is a brief discussion about the sources of nationalist-irredentist terrorist groups in the Northeastern region (NER) of India, with three terrorist groups examined. Those three terrorist organizations include, The United Liberation Front of Assam (ULFA), The United Democratic Liberation Army (UDLA), and The Garo National Liberation Army (GNLA).

In Northeast India, the struggles ethnic groups in pursuit of independence from India's national government experience derive from one single, most predominant nationalist-irredentist movement—the Naga nationalist movement. The Naga movement is time honored at over one hundred years old. For Sahni, Naga demands for independence began to consolidate during the First World War, when Nagas were used as medical support staff to carry wounded soldiers to field hospitals on stretchers. After the war, those veterans formed the "Naga Club" in 1918 [53, 123, 125, 120]. In "United Assam," that fledgling Naga movement waged a fierce struggle for independence, first against the British imperialists in Raj India (1858–1947) and then against the Indian national government that formed with partition in 1947.

The most predominant religion in Nagaland is Christianity. Therefore, with religion as a factor largely held constant, it is likely that economic deprivation effects, working in conjunction with ethnic and cultural identification imperatives, worked to spur on the contagion effects of the Naga insurrection. Those contagion effects increased nationalist sentiments among other ethnic groups living next to the Nagas in "United Assam" [11].

In other words, the geographical contiguity of ethnic groups in old "United Assam" translated into political contiguity, where other ethnic groups such as the Adivasi and the Kuki themselves, already politically charged with self-determination ideals, began to confront Indian national and state governments after 1947 about their own political grievances and economic demands [61].[7]

[6] One example of permeable boundaries between political and "militant" groups is Pattali Makkal Katchi (Working People's Party), that is led by Dr. S. Ramadoss. Pattali Makkal Katchi represents the political interests of a bottom rung agricultural-based Indian caste called the Vanniyers, but it also uses violence in Tamil Nadu's northern region.

[7] For example, on January 24, 2012, several core Adivasi terrorist groups that included the Santhal Tiger Force (STF), Adivasi National Liberation Army (ANLA), Adivasi People's Army, Birsa Commando Force (BCF), and the Adivasi Cobra Militants of Assam agreed to a "Suspension of

An underlying theme for many national-irredentist struggles in Northeast India remained the fear that both legal and illegal immigration of "outsiders" posed an existential threat to cultural identity because immigration worked to dilute the ethnic identities of Assam's indigenous peoples. Those fears had historical roots in British imperialist policy, as the British brought in migrant workers from other parts of India to maximize productivity in resource rich "United Assam" [53, 122–123, 120, 128; 54, 3674–3677].

As political activities and acts of violence in Assam and other Northeast Region (NER) states intensified, the Indian national government worked to impose military-style solutions to quell political unrest. Both Sahni and Baruah report that such hardline strategies and tactics, epitomized by the Armed Forces Special Powers Act (1958), while sometimes necessary for security purposes, remained insufficient as a way to resolve political and economic problems. For Sahni, the reason why is relatively straightforward as the root causes of such fears that require comprehensive but nuanced approaches, are not addressed through political/administrative and economic development initiatives [24; 53, 125–126; 54, 3674].[8]

At a political level, the Autonomous Councils designed to represent ethnic group interests and to serve as forums to articulate grievances, had limited effectiveness even though the Indian government also supplied monies and other support systems for militants, "…to rejoin society with negotiated financial support from the government for their sustenance and livelihood." [24; 53, 129]. It is probably no exaggeration to say that for some, but certainly not all, the perception was those Autonomous Councils had severe limitations in terms of what could be accomplished, and worked to perpetuate the political and economic status quo.

In addition, government outreach to specific terrorist groups produced uneven results, even though the Indian national government sponsored a set of peace negotiations with several Northeast Region (NER) based terrorist groups. One of the reasons why those results have been mixed is because government led negotiations under the banner of "Suspension of Operations (SoO)" agreements helped produce terrorist group splintering and spinoff formation—some terrorist group leaders accepted government terms by contrast to other "rejectionist" leaders who want to continue to fight.

The Naga Socialist Council of Nagaland is as good an example of such splintering effects as any, where after the Shillong Accord (1975), "rejectionist" group leaders splintered from "Naga moderates" in 1980 to form the Naga Socialist Council of Nagaland (NSCN). In turn, the Naga Socialist Council of Nagaland (NSCN)

Operations (SoO)" with the Indian government to start peace talks. On that same day, core Kuki terrorist groups such as the United Kuki Defense Army, the Kuki Revolutionary Army (KRA), and the Kuki Liberation Army (KLA) also submitted to government authorities.

[8] Sahni suggests those political/administrative and economic initiatives should be attempted in a transformed Indian federalist system.

also spawned two more spinoff groups over thirty years ago—the NSCN-IM (Isak-Muivah) and NSCN-K Khaplang that commenced operations in 1988 [53; 54, 3675, 3677]. In addition, other NSCN spinoff groups such the NSCN-NK (Nikpao Kitovi) and NSCN-R (Reformation Faction) trace an arc, albeit more indirectly, to the Shillong Accord [5, 6, 4].[9]

3.3 The United Liberation Front of Assam

The ULFA is a national-irredentist terrorist organization that has, since 1979, supported the establishment of an independent "Assamese homeland." For both Gohain and Baruah, the sources of ULFA are found in historical events and in the political, economic, and social forces that have shaped Assam. Historically, the notion of Assamese separateness stems from the Yandaboo Treaty (1826), where the British Empire is said to have illegally wrested away Assam from Burma (now Myanmar) [6, 953–954, 956–957]. In addition, permeable international borders between Burma and India, and patterns of non-indigenous people migration patterns worked to exacerbate fears that Assamese identity would become diluted if not extinguished outright.

Both authors point to the role of "foreigners," including Bengali Muslims and Indian Hindus, and their perceived threat to Assamese identity as primary drivers of the Assamese national movement. The Assamese national movement lasted from 1979 to 1985. Indeed, Baruah describes the ULFA as the extremist branch of that movement. It was seen as the protector of Assamese political rights and Assamese control over natural resources. It should be noted that unsubstantiated reports suggest UFLA is supported by Pakistan's Inter-Services Intelligence (IS) to sow discord in India [6, 970; 22, 1012–1014, 1016, 1018; 54, 3674, 3676–3677].

Gohain reports the Assamese movement (1979–1985) consisted of upper caste wealthy landowners who attempted to promote their own interests by working to manipulate widespread Assamese fears about ethnic identity and local job availability [22, 1012]. A major point of contention revolved around a shift in demographics and voter eligibility in local elections. The problem of who could vote came about because it was comparatively easy for newly arrived non-Assamese immigrants to register to vote [6, 953, 958–959, 961; 22, 1012, 1016, 1018; 27]. According to Baruah, long-standing national government's unresponsiveness to this immigrant issue worked to amplify strains and tensions. Such indifference was not new, it worked to produce Assamese calls for independence as far back as the 1930's [6, 962, 964, 973].

Hence, those local factors remained interspersed within broader tensions and "regional politics" as a whole, manifested in clusters of states like Assam, Manipur, Mizoram, and Meghalaya, and in national government policies [6, 957–958, 973; 22, 1012–1014, 1016, 1018]. Gohain argues that beyond local religious and ethnic tensions, the major issue at the heart of political instability and social unrest in

[9] Bhaattacharjee reports that in 2018, both the NSCN-NK and NSCN-R worked to extend their "suspension of operations" agreement with India's national government for an additional six months.

Assam involved the perceived indifference to Assam's socio-economic development by India's national government. That is an important observation because uneven economic development within countries has contributed to rage and similar sentiments, as it creates the perception, whether true or not, that government has favored particular groups and geographical locales over others [48, 125–168].

At first, the UFLA was accepted by much of Assam's population as its standard-bearer to articulate local political and economic grievances. However, by the 1980's, UFLA terrorism against non-Assamese "foreigners," tea estates, journalists, government officials, and others, produced one of the most significant terrorist threats in Northeast India. For many Assamese, the road to conflict resolution involves negotiation with India's national government. At the same time, that approach has been hampered by many in the Indian government and military who believed the answer to Assam's problems required military suppression of UFLA and other terrorist groups in Assam such as the Bodo Liberation Tigers [6, 953–954, 956–957].

3.4 The Garo National Liberation Army (GNLA)

The backdrop of underdevelopment in India's Northeast region compounds the effects of what Diamond describes "social fissures" in society. In the case of Meghalaya, fierce political and economic struggles happen between the Garo, who are very poor, and the Khasi, who are more affluent. The Northeast part of India includes Meghalaya, a relatively small state culled out of Assam in 1972. The predominant ethnic groups found there include the Khasi, the Garo (who favor the name "Achiks"), the Jaintia, and other minority groups [41, 121–129].

Diamond suggests that when socioeconomic characteristics that characterize different ethnic groups align with territorial boundaries where a majority ethnic group population is found (as in the case of the Garo and Khasi), ethnic conflict is frequently the result. This is an example of Diamond's "coincidental cleavages," where socioeconomic fissures coincide with ethnic and regional cleavages to produce demands for structural change, that all too frequently results in violent outcomes [11].

The idea of "coincidental cleavages" dovetails with Nayak and Singha's report that in the aftermath of sustained conflict and episodic terrorist events, "...the Garo National Council (GNC) and the Garo Students' Union (GSU) are demanding a separate state for the Garos on linguistic lines while the Hill State People's Democratic Party (HSPDP) is demanding a Khasi-Jaintia state on the other hand." [41, 121–129].

It is out of this context that the Garo National Liberation Front (GNLA) emerged. The GNLA operates in Meghalaya and in parts of Assam where other terrorist groups linked to that struggle also operate. Those other terrorist organizations include the Achik Liberation Matgrik Army (ALMA), and the Achik National Volunteer Council (ANVC).

3.5 The United Democratic Liberation Army (UDLA)

The United Democratic Liberation Army (UDLA) draws its membership from the Bengali Muslim and Bru peoples in Assam. It was crafted by Dhanyaram Reang as a splinter group of the United Liberation Front of Barak Valley (UDLF-BV), itself formed by Panchuram Reang. Dhanyaram Reang led the United Demoractic Liberation Army (UDLA) until his arrest in Mizoram in 2009. The formation of UDLA happened after the UDLF-BV, that had supported the Bru people's quest for independence since 2002, turned over 305 activists and their weapons to the Indian government in Assam in September 2008 as part of a peace agreement.

The UDLA shares the same goal as its UDLF-BV parent organization, namely to carve an independent state out of Assam's Hailakandi and Karimganj areas close to the Assam-Mizoram border. In terms of UDLA composition, one SATP reported that in 2010, the UDLA consisted of some 250 activists. (South Asian Terrorism Portal. n.d.) The UDLA has, "...engaged in kidnapping of tea officials, traders, farmers, and construction workers in the Barak Valley..." [60]. The UDLA has its base of operations in Bangladesh, and is an example of the types of ties between Maoist and nationalist-irredentist terrorist groups that can materialize, as the UDLA has shared close ties with "Naga militants" in Assam [56].

The UDLA itself splintered to form the United Democratic Liberation Front-Barak (UDLF-B). The UDLA then splintered once again to form the United Democratic Liberation Tigers (UDLT). Led by Atabur Rahman, a former aide to UDLA Chairman Dhanyaram Reang, UDLT emerged because of outrage over sustained efforts in 2009 by Bru activists within UDLA to kidnap Muslims in efforts to promote Bru group interests [30].[10] Both UDLA and UDLT have had activists who have given up to the Indian national government within the context of peace talk frameworks, and it was expected that UDLA would do the same in 2019 [23].

3.6 Indian Islamic Extremist Terrorist Groups

In 1989, the Hizb-ul-Mujahideen (HM) was crafted as a paramilitary organization to confront the Indian occupation of Kashmir. Hizb-ul-Mujahideen (HM) is led by Syed Salahuddin and estimates of its size vary—the U.S. Department of State estimated its size in 2010 to be a few hundred activists while other sources like Pike estimate numbers in the thousands [13, 261–262; 47; 51].[11] HM's founder was Muhammad

[10] UDLA official Rajeh Reang also describes "close links" to Naga extremists.

[11] In contemporary India, Kashmir is a designation that includes, but is not limited to, Indian controlled Jammu and Kashmir. For security purposes, the Indian national government under Prime Minister Narendra Modi revoked Kashmir's status as a state in 2019 and relegated it to a union territory.

Ahsan Dar (aka Master Ahsan Dar), and it is considered a spin-off group of Pakistan's predominant Islamic political party, Jammat-e-Islami (JI) [13, 262].[12]

Fair reports that Hizb-ul-Mujahideen (HM) was created either at the behest of Pakistan's Inter-Service Intelligence (ISI), or that at the very least, it works to maintain powerful connections to ISI to promote Pakistani national interests in Kashmir. Fair reports that compared to Hizb-ul-Mujahideen which recruits primarily from the broader Kasmiri population, Hizb-ul-Mujahidden activists listed as killed in action had much higher rates of educational attainment than the average educational level found for members of Hizb-ul-Mujahideen also listed as killed [13, 272, 262].

In the six year period examined in this study, Hizb-ul-Mujahideen spawned a spinoff group called Lashkar-e-Islam. Lashkar-e-Islam activists attacked business targets such cell phone towers in the Sapore area of Kashmir. According to Naqash, Abdul Qayoom Najar was the founder and chieftain of Lashkar-e-Islam. Abdul Qayoom Najar split from Hizb-ul-Mujahideen after a disagreement with HM's Amir Sayeed Salahuddin about a series of murders committed [8, 40, 46]

In comparison to Hizb-ul-Mujahideen (HM), Fair considers Lashkar-e-Taiba (LeT) the more experienced and capable of those two Islamic extremist organization. For the six year period under consideration, Lashkar-e-Taiba carried out two chronicled terrorist assaults against business targets—both were in the town of Dinanagar in India's Punjab province [20, entry #281 and entry #282]. That small number of business related targets is consistent with Fair's assertion that Lashkar-e Taiba puts special emphasis on military and police targets in Kashmir. Lashkar-e-Taiba was crafted in Muzaffarabad (Azad Kashmir) and has a broader field of operations in different parts in India. The Mumbai terrorist assaults in 2008 have probably been its most notable and successful attacks [13, 261, 263–264].

Like Hizb-ul Mujahideen, Lashkar-e-Taiba also has strong connections to Pakistan. Pakistani leaders provide monetary support for the group to promote Pakistani efforts to dislodge India from Indian controlled Kashmir. Lashkar-e Taiba also has strong connections to al-Qaeda. Osama bin Laden reportedly provided economic aid while the group itself was crafted with the assistance of Abdullah Azzam, a Jordanian-Palestinian soldier-scholar who in 1984, crafted and led al-Qaeda's antecedent group, the Office of Services (Makhtab al-Khatmat) until 1989, when he was murdered in Peshawar, Pakistan [10, 297; 14, 87].

Lashkar-e-Taiba (LeT) ("Army of the Righteous") was crafted in 1993 in Muridke, Pakistan as the para-military branch of the Pakistani religious-political institution, Markaz-ud-Dawa-wal-Irshad (MDI). In turn, Markaz-ud-Dawa-wal-Irshad was established by two academics, Hafiz Muhammad Saeed and Zulifar Iqbal, as an organization to confront American missionary activity in Pakistan [13, 262; 14, 87; 47, 1]. Both Pike and Fair report the recruitment pool for Lashkar-e-Taiba (LeT) is much

[12] The political party Jammat-e-Islami was crafted in 1946 by Abul A'la Maududi (1903–1979) to confront the British and the secularism of the Muslim League, itself led by Mohammed Ali Jinnah (1876–1948). It was Jinnah who became Pakistan's first national leader as Governor-General after British India was partitioned into India and Pakistan in 1947. It is commonplace to note that Abul A'al Maududi, and Sayyid Qutb (1906–1966) of the Muslim Brotherhood (*al-Ikhwan al-Muslimin*) are considered among the most important Islamic theoreticians of the twentieth century.

broader than is the recruitment pool for Hizb-ul-Mujahideen. While Fair reports that LeT recruits also have high levels of educational attainment, roughly comparable to their HM counterparts, an underlying difference is that LeT conscripts are found primarily in Pakistan, with Punjab as the epicenter for recruitment [13, 262; 47, 1].

Fair draws on those findings, along with similar findings about Lashkar-e-Taiba, to suggest the putative wisdom that terrorists are under-educated is probably spurious [13, 260, 270–272]. Fair goes on to assert that economic blight in general, and the "relative deprivation" effects that particular ethnic groups experience, might not be a primary reason why Kashmiri-based groups such as Hizb-ul-Mujahideen and Lashkar-e-Taiba emerged. This suggests that "soft-line" counterterrorism used by international enterprises should be tailor made to account for different political and economic contextual factors across Indian states afflicted with terrorism, where different mixtures of explanatory variable effects influence terrorist group formation and splintering [10].

3.7 Indian Right-Wing Hindutva Terrorist Groups

The Indian Hindutva movement traces an arc to the early twentieth century to both the Hindu Mahasabha (HM) organization and to the work of Vinayak Damodar Sarvarkar (1883–1946). Hindu nationalism (Hindutva) began to galvanize with the formation of the All-India-Hindu Sabha in 1915. The All-India-Hindu Sabha was a broad framework of regional Hindu nationalist groups designed to promote Hindu cultural awareness, solidarity, and nationalism [3, 589, 592].

The All-India Sabha organization renamed itself the Hindu Mahasabha (HM) in 1921. Vinayak Damodar Sarvarkar was one early leader of Hindu Mahasabha (HM); it is Vinayak Damodar who is considered to be the founding political theoretician of Hindutva. In his book, *Hindutva* (1923), Sarvarkar framed hardline Indian nationalism around the notion that India must be Hindu, where Muslims and Christians remain subordinate outsiders.

For Ramachandran, "…Sarvarkar said that Hindus are the only true Indians as their *pitrbhu* (fatherland) and *punyabhu* (holy land) are in India. Muslims and Christians however, could not be considered Indian, as their holy lands were not in India but in 'far off Arabia or Palestine.'" [3, 592; 49, 16, 16n 6] Savarkar played major roles in both Hindu Mahasabha and Rashtriya Sivayamsevak Sangh (RSS), and once again in Hindu Mahasaabha (HM) after 1937 [3, 595; 4, 679].

Hindu Mahasabha (HM) is the direct antecedent organization to Rashtriya Sivayamsevak Sangh (RSS). Former Hindu Mahasbha (HM) leader Dr. Keshav Baliram Hedgewar crafted Rashtriya Sivayamsevak Sangh (RSS) in 1925 in Nagpur, Maharashtra as an alternative to HM. As Sarsonghchalak of the RSS ("The Guide" or "Chief"), Hedgewar was virulently anti-British, but he eschewed politics. Originally, RSS was more a cultural movement to promote Hindu solidarity and the vision of "Hindu Rashtra" (i.e., a Hindu state), rather than a political party. From the start, the RSS received significant support from government workers and college age students

[4, 677] RSS remains opposed to the concept of "secularism" that in the Indian context means a condition where from a legal standpoint, "all religions are equal" [3, 593; 49, 18; 58].

In turn, Anderson suggests RSS's non-political nature was the fundamental difference between the Hindu Mahasabha (HM) and RSS organizations when he relates that, "article 4 of the RSS constitution, specifically prohibited the RSS from taking part in politics" [3, 593; 4, 678]. Hedgewar's disdain for the political fray was illuminated by his decision not to support M. K. Gandhi's anti-British "Non-Cooperation Movement" (NCM). While anti-Muslim sentiments were obviously involved, other reasons were more nuanced. Those reasons capture important Indian political process at work and are worthy of review [3, 593; 4, 678].

For Andersen, the reason behind Hedewar's decision to withhold support from the NCM was twofold. First, with an eye towards the looming conflict between Hindus and Muslims that would follow the Second World War, Hedgewar wanted to position RSS as a cultural force where it could be most effective. Hence, he worked to ensure the British did not view RSS as an acute security threat. Secondly, Hedgewar opposed Gandhi's "Non-Cooperation Movement" because the NCM provided support for the Muslim Khilafat movement in India that supported Turkish citizens who wanted to reverse Mustafa Kemal's 1924 decision to abolish the Caliphate [3, 591–592, 595].

In the 1980's the political clout of Hindutva grew apace [55, 244]. P. Gandhi reports the scope and influence of RSS in Indian politics remained enormous with more than five million adherents organized into more than forty to fifty thousand organizational units called shakhas. The strength of RSS has been bolstered by more than one hundred associated groups. [15] At a functional level, Rashtriya Sivayamsevak Sangh (RSS), is one of numerous associated Hindutva organizations and terrorist groups that belong to Sangh Parivar (i.e., the RSS family). This study includes terrorist actions taken by RSS, Shiv Sena, and Karni Sena, but it is important to recognize that numerous other organizations fall under the Sansar Parvir banner and family tree.

Those organizations include, but are not limited to, Rashtra Dal, Shri Shivpratishhthan Hindusthan (led by Sambhaji Bhide), Sri Ram Sen (led by Pramod Muthalik), and Abhinov Bharat. Plainly, the most critical Sana Parivar organization is India's predominant political party, the nationalist Bharatiya Janata Party (BJP), now led by Prime Minister Narendra Modi. What is significant is that BJP has formed the current Indian national coaltion government. For Ramachandran and other scholars, BJP's ascension to India's pinnacle of power has only worked to exacerbate Hindutva violence. [3, 595; 49, 17; 58, 11].[13]

Three RSS derivate terrorist organizations include Sanatan Sanstha, Shiv Sena, and Karni Sena. In 1999, Sanatan Sanstha was formed by Dr. Jayant Balaji Athavale in the Indian state of Goa. Sanatan Sanstha also operates in Maharashtra [58, 10]. One notable Sanatan Santha affiliated organization is called Jangsagaran Samiti [68, 63].

[13] Rashtra Dal was crafted in 1942 by the brothers Gopal and Nathuran Godse—it was Nathuran Godse who murdered MK Gandhi on January 30, 1948.

While Sanatan Sanstha is ostensibly oriented towards a "spiritual" mission to increase the scope and depth of Hinduism, Nanda points out that approach remains a zero-sum game where Hindutva groups, including Sanatan Sanstha, view other religions, particularly monotheistic religions (e.g., Christianity and Judaism) as "defective" and an overall threat to India [39, 109].

For Teltumbde, Sanatan Sanstha views "…the minorities, especially Christians and Muslims, as the biggest obstacles and speaks of the need to defeat even the police and military to build a Hindu rashtra." [39; 58, 10–11] In addition, Sanatan Sanstha views liberals and intellectuals as an acute danger to India's cultural and national ethos [39, 107–110; 55, 246].

Within the "RSS family" or Sangh Parvir, is found the organization Shiv Sena. Shiv Sena was formed in 1966 by Bal Thackery. Its original purpose was to promote the rights of indigenous Maharashtrans who perceived themselves to be vulnerable in political and economic terms to non-Maharashtran immigrants who came from other parts of India. Shiv Sena has changed its scope of operations over the years. It has continuously evolved into a broader Hindutva movement; it became a part of India's BJP ruling national coalition. As Siyech reports, Shiv Sena also engages in violence against members of minority groups [55, 244].

In comparison, the scope of Karni Sena is more limited, with its emphasis on promotion of Rajput caste rights within the context of the conflict between the Rajput and Jatt communities in Rajasthan. The first Karni Sena organization was crafted in 2006 by Ajit Singh Mamdoli, to acquire primarily economic reparations called "caste-based reservation" for the economically disadvantaged in the Raj community.

The other major theme associated with Karni Sena has been the promotion of educational reform so that text books for example, would no longer marginalize leading figures in Rajput culture [2, 38].

Nowadays, Karni Sena is perhaps best known for its forceful actions in response to the release of the film *Padmavaat*. That film depicts vanquished Hindu Queen Padmini who lived in the 1300's, in unflattering terms where she cavorts with a victorious Muslim chieftain [2, 38]. The release of the film *Padmavaat* has spawned terrorist attacks against the filmmaker of *Padmavaat*, and in addition to several attacks against movie theaters showing the film.

In terms of the "terrorist group life cycle" of Karni Sena, the first Karni Sena organization formed in 2006 by Ajit Singh Mamdoli produced two spinoff groups. It appears that at the crux of this split were personality and policy differences about the future direction of Karni Sena. Those two groups include the Shri Rajput Karni Sena (SKRS) that Lokendra Singh Kalvi has led since its formation in 2010 [35].

The second Karni Sena spinoff group is the Rashtriya Rajput Karni Sena. Rashitrya Rajput Karni Sena formed in 2015 as a result of differences of opinion between its leader, Sukhedev Singh Gogamedhi and Shri Karni Sena (SKRS) Lokendra Singh Kalvi, reportedly over the issue of Rajput reparations [2, 38].

3.8 Terrorist Assault Business Vulnerability Index (TABVI)

As described in Chapter One, conceptual links between the notions of security and vulnerability exist, where in this case business leaders experienced emotional reactions such as anxiety, abject fear, and similar sentiments about perceived inabilities to protect both the firm and themselves from terrorism threat. To capture different dimensions of vulnerability, the Terrorist Assault Business Vulnerability Index (TABVI) was used to make quantitative determinations about terrorism threat to commercial interests in the countries examined.

For the Indian TABVI numerator, the total number of terrorist attacks against commercial interests between 2013 and 2018 in India was calculated adding the total number of attacks in each sub-category of business target articulated. For the TABVI numerator, the following subcategories were summed: Energy/Alloy (111); Construction (262); Hospital/Medical facilities (8); Private Establishments (160); Telecommunications (67); Newspaper/Print (33); Banking Finance (8) Private Transportation (7); Agriculture (2); for a total of 658 acts.[14]

The TABVI denominator is based on data from the "Global Competitiveness Index 2015–2018" provided by the *World Economic Forum*. The perceived levels of terrorism threat experienced by business leaders in particular countries is captured in "business costs of terrorism" assessments in the *World Economic Forum* "Executive Opinion Survey" questionnaire.

In this survey, business leaders were asked to rate the degree that terrorism impose business costs on operations on an ordinal scale with "1" as the greatest amount of cost imposed," and "7" as the least. In the *World Executive Forum* "Executive Opinion Survey" ranking list, India ranked #117 out of the 137 countries included in this survey, with a score of "4.2". Therefore, the denominator of the TABVI is "4.2" [65, 136–137; 66, "Appendix C"].[15]

India's TABVI score is calculated by 658/4.2 = 156.7 where 658 is the total number of acts and "4.2" is that ranked assessment found in the WEF survey. That TABVI score will be compared to other TABVI scores produced for other host countries under consideration. To standardize that raw TABVI score of 156.6 for India, 156.6 is divided by 1.566 = 100.

In addition, a comparison of TABVI scores for industries for each country is provided, as well as across the five countries examined. That makes it possible to estimate threat appraisal for specific industries. A disaggregated analysis of terrorism threat by industry can be estimated for each country to compare industries across countries and regions.

In a disaggregated analysis broken down by industry, the following values are obtained: India's industry sub-category scores are: (1) Energy/Alloy (111/4.2 = 26.4); (2) Construction (262/4.2 = 62.4) (**highest** vulnerability/threat); (3) Hospitals/Medical facilities (8/4.2 = 1.9); (4) Private establishments (160/4.2 = 38.1); (5) Telecommunications (67/4.2 = 16.0); (6) Newspapers/print (33/4.2 = 7.86); (7)

[14] N = 658 with 12 missing cases.

[15] Middle range ordinal scale value labels are not articulated in this WEF report.

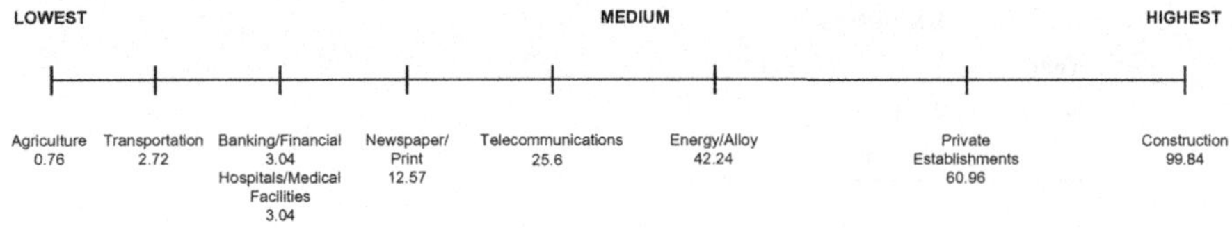

Fig. 3.2 India industry vulnerability spectrum standardized TABVI scores < 1 to 10 = Low Risk; 11 to 50 = Medium Risk; 51 to 100 = High Risk

Banking/Financial Institutions (8/4.2 = 1.9); (8) Transportation (7/4.2 = 1.7); (9) Agriculture (2/4.2 = 0.476) (**lowest** vulnerability/threat).

It is possible to craft a scale of specific Indian industries on a vulnerability spectrum that presents terrorism threat assessment by industry-type. It is necessary to standardize the scores obtained for comparison purposes to compare disaggregated industry scores across countries. That is the case because TABVI country denominator values, themselves based on WEF scores, are different. At the high end of the findings with construction targets, $62.4 \times 1.6 = 99.84$, essentially 100. Hence, multiplying each value by 1.6 provides a standardized score for each industry for the continuum of threat vulnerability from 0 to 100. Scores range from agriculture (0.76), transportation (2.72), banking and finance (3.04), hospitals/medical facilities (3.04), newspaper/print (12.57), telecommunications (25.6). At the high end of the continuum, energy/alloy (42.24), private establishments (60.96) and construction (99.84) are found (Fig. 3.2).

3.9 Some Empirical Observations About Indian Terrorism

3.9.1 Relative Frequencies and Percentages of Commercial Target Terrorist Assaults

3.9.1.1 Targets by Year

For the six-year period under consideration between 2013 and 2018, there were 670 chronicled terrorist attacks against business targets in India. The data on Indian terrorism has peaks and troughs that are characteristic of terrorism's cyclical nature [9, 148–149; 10]. The peak years were 2017, with 20.9% (140/670 acts) of the total, and 20.6% (138/670 acts) for 2015. The trough years in this sample were 2013 with 13.3% of the total (89/670 acts) and 2018, with 13.4% (90/670 acts) of the total amount of terrorism directed at commercial interests in India (see Fig. 3.3).

Statistics

Year

N	Valid	670
	Missing	0

Year

		Frequency	Percent	Valid Percent	Cumulative Percent
Valid	2013	89	13.3	13.3	13.3
	2014	107	16.0	16.0	29.3
	2015	138	20.6	20.6	49.9
	2016	106	15.8	15.8	65.7
	2017	140	20.9	20.9	86.6
	2018	90	13.4	13.4	100.0
	Total	670	100.0	100.0	

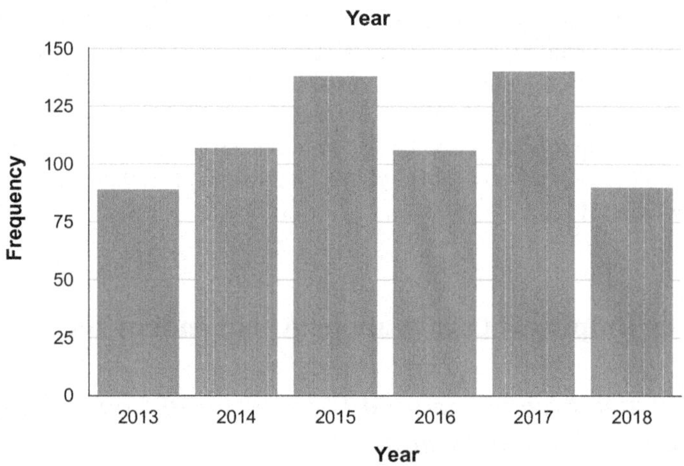

Fig. 3.3 Relative frequency of Indian terrorist attacks by year, 2013–2018

3.10 Terrorist Assault by Business Target-Type, Firm Origin, Terrorist Group-Type, and Terrorist Group

The results suggest Indian terrorism against commercial interests was primarily directed against two types of business targets. Nearly two-fifths of the total at 39.8% (262/658 acts) were directed at "construction sites." In turn, "private establishments" ranked second, with nearly one-quarter of all business target attacks at 24.3% (160/658 acts). Terrorist attacks against "energy/alloy" targets accounted for 16.9% of all attacks (111/658), "telecommunications" targets (e.g., cell phone towers), comprised 10.2% (67/658 acts), while "newspaper/print" attacks made up 5.0% (33/658 acts) of the total.

Statistics

Bus.Target

N	Valid	658
	Missing	12

Bus.Target

		Frequency	Percent	Valid Percent	Cumulative Percent
Valid	Energy/Alloy	111	16.6	16.9	16.9
	Construction	262	39.1	39.8	56.7
	Hospitals/Medical	8	1.2	1.2	57.9
	Private Establishments	160	23.9	24.3	82.2
	Telecommunications	67	10.0	10.2	92.4
	Newspapers/Print	33	4.9	5.0	97.4
	Banking/Finance	8	1.2	1.2	98.6
	Transportation	7	1.0	1.1	99.7
	Agriculture	2	0.3	0.3	100.0
	Total	658	98.2	100.0	
Missing	System	12	1.8		
Total		670	100.0		

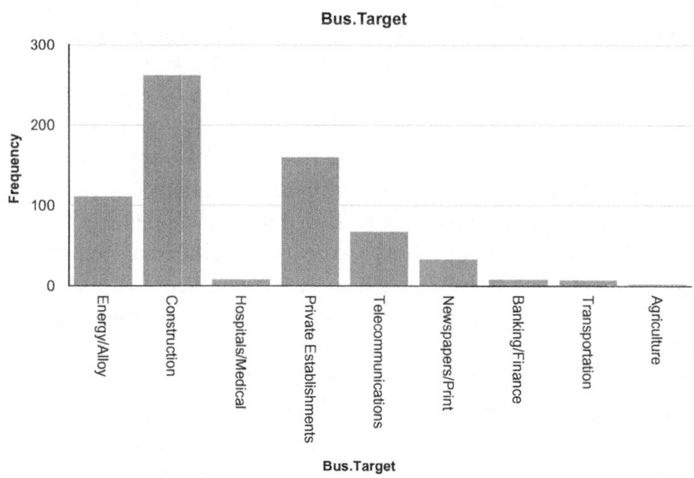

Fig. 3.4 Relative frequency of Indian terrorist attacks by business target, 2013–2018

Conversely, "hospitals and medical facilities" and "banking and finance" targets each were involved in eight acts or only 1.2% in each case, while attacks against "private transportation" accounted for seven acts or 1.1% of the total. Rounding out target types, "agriculture" targets made up under one percent (0.3%) of the total, with two acts. Those terrorist acts included two terrorist assaults in 2014 that used IED's against coffee pulping devices at the Andhra Pradesh Forest Development Corporation in Andhra Pradesh's Vishakhapatnam District [17 (entry #100 and #101)] (see Fig. 3.4).

While no authoritative interpretation for those results is available, it seems likely construction sites as terrorist targets symbolized national and state government modernization efforts. It seems reasonable to assert that symbolism played a major role in target selection because modernization policies produced threats to Indian terrorist groups which used dense forest areas as "safe-havens." In addition, "opportunity recognition" might have played a role in targeting selection because extortion and ransom threats from Indian terrorist groups at isolated construction sites involved little risk of capture.

One notable finding was the comparatively large average number of terrorist perpetrators involved in business-oriented terrorist attacks—the mean for perpetrators who carried out terrorist assaults in India against commercial interests was high, at 24.69.[16] In the case of attacks against Indian "private establishments," compelling extortion and ransom opportunities also existed. The literature points to communal conflict and its effects on terrorist targeting; it follows that at least in some cases, terrorist assaults were probably related to communal conflict where the interests of so-called "indigenous" groups were pitted against the interests of non-indigenous "foreigners" [6, 970; 22, 1012–1014, 1016, 1018; 54, 3674, 3676–3677].

In the case of firm nationality, the results indicate that between 2013 and 2018, the vast majority of terrorist assaults aimed at commercial interests in India were taken against domestic Indian firms. A full 98.3% of all terrorist attacks (635/646 acts) were directed at Indian business targets, while only 1.7% of all recorded terrorist attacks (11/646 acts) against business interests in India involved foreign firms. In turn, another bivariate analysis test revealed that terrorism against business targets in India involved civilian targets 87.5% of the time (532/608 acts), while only 12.2% (74/608 acts) focused on Indian government business targets.

Two terrorist events that amounted to less than one percent of the total (0.3%) involved hybrid business targets. Those two events included a grenade put in a rice sack in a government truck in Imphal driven by a contracted driver, and the Sikarpie, Odisha shooting of Mr. Gopal Chetty Gandhi, a contactor, who was "also a Congress worker and panchayat samiti member…." [16 (entry #92); 18 (entry #144); 43; 63].

When terrorist group-type is examined, the results show Indian Maoist (Marxist-Leninist) terrorist groups were responsible for 49.6% (331/668 acts) of all terrorism directed at business targets. Anonymous group attacks ranked second with 23.5% (157/668 acts), while nationalist-irredentist terrorist groups virtually tied that rate with 23.2% (155/668 acts). Islamic extremist attacks in India by contrast, amounted to only 2.4% (16/668), while "right-wing" Hindutva terrorism accounted for even less with only 1.3% (9/668 acts) of the total. It seems plausible a certain degree of anonymous activity is attractive to terrorists because the likelihood of capture is reduced and counterterrorism efforts become more difficult (see Fig. 3.5).

When the data are broken down by terrorist group name, the results revealed that anonymous terrorist attacks comprised the highest amount of terrorism aimed at commercial interests in India with 51.4% (341/663 acts). The Communist Party of India (CPI-Maoist) had the second highest rate at 15.5% (103/663 acts). With regards to identifiable terrorist groups, that finding about The Communist Party of India (CPI-Maoist) was consistent with former Indian Prime Minister Manmohan Singh's 2006

[16] In this test, N = 228; the mean was 24.68, with a standard deviation of 50.39.

Statistics

GroupTy

N	Valid	668
	Missing	2

GroupTy

		Frequency	Percent	Valid Percent	Cumulative Percent
Valid	Marxist-Leninist	331	49.4	49.6	49.6
	Nationalist-Irredentist	155	23.1	23.2	72.8
	Anonymous	157	23.4	23.5	96.3
	Islamic Extremist	16	2.4	2.4	98.7
	Right Wing	9	1.3	1.3	100.0
	Total	668	99.7	100.0	
Missing	System	2	.3		
Total		670	100.0		

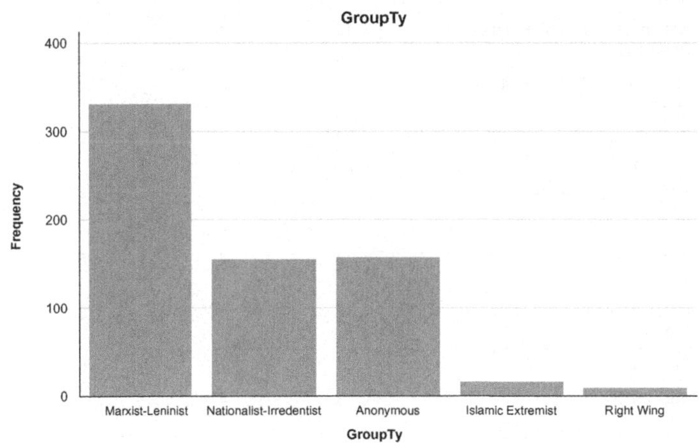

Fig. 3.5 Relative frequency of Indian terrorist attacks by group-type, 2013–2018

assessment, quoted in the Government of India Press Information Bureau, that the Naxalite movement remained, "…the single biggest internal security challenge ever faced by our country…." [1, 256–257] (see Fig. 3.6).

A second tier of business-related terrorist assaults comprised some one percent to four percent of the total number of business-related terrorist attacks. Those terrorist attacks were conducted by nationalist-irredentist, Maoist, and Islamic extremist terrorist groups. Terrorist groups with a little over two percent of the total included: the United Liberation Front of Assam (ULFA) with 3.8% (25/663 acts), the People's Liberation Front of India (PLFI) with 3.5% of the total (23/663 acts), the Garo National Liberation Army (GNLA) with 2.6% (17/663 acts), and the National Democratic Front of Bodoland (NLFB) with 2.4% (16/663 acts).

In this second tier, four Indian terrorist groups accounted for under two percent of the total number of terrorist attacks. Those were the Tritiya Prastuti Committee (TPC) with 1.5% (10/663 acts), the Kuki National Front (KNF) with 1.4% (9/663 acts), the Nationalist Socialist Council of Nagaland Khaplang (NSCN-K) with 1.4% (9/663

Statistics

GroupName

N	Valid	663
	Missing	7

Group Name

		Frequency	Percent	Valid Percent	Cumulative Percent
Valid	ULFA	25	3.7	3.8	3.8
	NSCN-K	9	1.3	1.4	5.1
	Maoist (CPI)	103	15.4	15.5	20.7
	CORCOM	1	.1	.2	20.8
	Anonymous	341	50.9	51.4	72.2
	GNLA	17	2.5	2.6	74.8
	National Democratic Front of Bodoland	16	2.4	2.4	77.2
	MKP (Maoist Communist Party of Manipur)	2	.3	.3	77.5
	PLFI (People's Liberation Front of India)	23	3.4	3.5	81.0
	Pattali Makkai Katchi	1	.1	.2	81.1
	KLO (Kamtapur Liberation Org.)	2	.3	.3	81.4
	KPLT (Karbi People's Liberation Tigers)	3	.4	.5	81.9
	UALA (United Achik Liberation Army)	2	.3	.3	82.2
	PREPAK	4	.6	.6	82.8
	Khasi Student Union	3	.4	.5	83.3
	UDLA (United Democratic Liberation Army)	2	.3	.3	83.6
	KNF (Kuki National Front)	9	1.3	1.4	84.9
	ANVC-B National Volunteer Council B	3	.4	.5	85.4
	Tamil Nadu Liberation Army	1	.1	.2	85.5
	JPC (Jharkhand Prastuti Committee)	3	.4	.5	86.0
	BVTF (Barak Valley Tiger Force)	1	.1	.2	86.1

Fig. 3.6 Relative frequency of Indian terrorist attacks by terrorist group, 2013–2018

GroupName

	Frequency	Percent	Valid Percent	Cumulative Percent
UTLA (United Tribal Liberation Army)	3	.4	.5	86.6
ASAK (A'chik Songna An'pachakgipa Kotok)	3	.4	.5	87.0
NSLA (National Santhal Liberation Army)	2	.3	.3	87.3
United Revolutionary Front	2	.3	.3	87.6
Dima Hasao National Army	1	.1	.2	87.8
MNRP (Manipur Nationalist Revolutionary Party)	1	.1	.2	87.9
NLFT (National Liberation Front of Tripura)	3	.4	.5	88.4
SIMI (Students Islamic Movement of India)	1	.1	.2	88.5
JMB (Jama'atul Mujahideen Bangladeshi)	1	.1	.2	88.7
AMEF (A'chik Matgrik Elite Force)	3	.4	.5	89.1
UGSF (United Garo Security Force)	1	.1	.2	89.3
Hindu Illaignar Sena	1	.1	.2	89.4
Jharkhand Sangharsh Jan Mukti Morcha	1	.1	.2	89.6
Hizbul Mujahideen	4	.6	.6	90.2
Lama Group	1	.1	.2	90.3
Puratchi Puligal	1	.1	.2	90.5
UNLF (United National Liberation Front)	4	.6	.6	91.1
MTF (Moran Tiger Force)	1	.1	.2	91.3
KCP (Kangleipak Communist Party)	3	.4	.5	91.7
TWA (Tiwa Liberation Army)	1	.1	.2	91.9
RCC (Revolutionary Communist Centre)	1	.1	.2	92.0
(TPDK) Thanthai Periyar Dravidar Kazhagam	1	.1	.2	92.2
Maoists of Andhra-Odisha Border Sp. Zonal Committee	2	.3	.3	92.5
Jharkhand Kranti Raksha Dal (Utari Chotanagpur)	1	.1	.2	92.6

Fig. 3.6 (continued)

GroupName

		Frequency	Percent	Valid Percent	Cumulative Percent
	Manipur Naga People's Army	1	.1	.2	92.8
	Jharkhand Janmukti	2	.3	.3	93.1
	BCF (Birsa Commando Force)	1	.1	.2	93.2
	Gorkha Janmukti Morcha	6	.9	.9	94.1
	TPC (Tritiya Prastuti Committee)	10	1.5	1.5	95.6
	Jharkhand Liberations Tigers	1	.1	.2	95.8
	Karni Sena	2	.3	.3	96.1
	LeT (Lashkar e Taiba)	2	.3	.3	96.4
	JeM (Jaish e Mohammad)	1	.1	.2	96.5
	Ghorka Liberation Army	1	.1	.2	96.7
	National Socialist Council of Nagaland IM	6	.9	.9	97.6
	Indigenous People's Front of Tripura	1	.1	.2	97.7
	People's Liberation Army of Manipur (PLA)	1	.1	.2	97.9
	CPI-ML (New Democracy)	1	.1	.2	98.0
	VIPN	2	.3	.3	98.3
	Sanatan Sanstha	2	.3	.3	98.6
	Maoist Communist Centre (MCC)	1	.1	.2	98.8
	Rashtriya Swayamsevak Sangh	1	.1	.2	98.9
	Lashkar-e-Islam	7	1.0	1.1	100.0
	Total	663	99.0	100.0	
Missing	System	7	1.0		
Total		670	100.0		

Fig. 3.6 (continued)

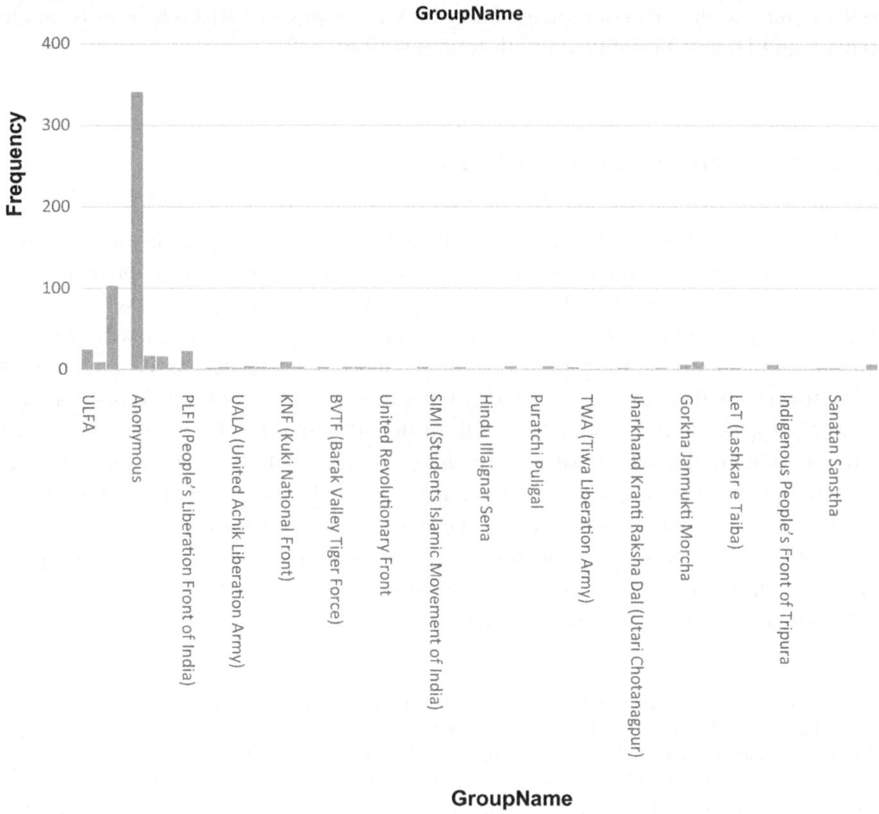

Fig. 3.6 (continued)

acts), and Lashkar-e-Islam with 1.1% of the total (7/663 acts). When all eight of those "second tier" groups are considered, it was found that 62.5% (5/8 groups) of that second tier were comprised of nationalist-irredentist terrorist groups. At 25.0%, only one-quarter were Maoist groups (2/8 groups), and only one terrorist group (12.5%) was an Islamic extremist terrorist group.[17]

A third tier of fifty-four terrorist groups accounted for less than one percent of the total amount of Indian business-related terrorist attacks. In terms of ideology, the range of terrorist groups involved was as diverse as second-tier terrorist groups. Terrorist organizations that accounted for less than one percent of the attack total included nationalist-irredentist, right-wing Hindutva, and Islamic extremist terrorist groups. Those included, but were not limited to, Gorkha Janmukti Morcha with six out of 663 acts (0.9%), the National Socialist Council of Nagaland IM with six acts

[17] Nationalist-irredentist groups included: the Garo National Liberation Army (GNLA), Kuki National Front (KNF), National Democratic Front of Bodoland (NLFB), National Socialist Council of Nagaland Khaplang (NSCN-K), the United Liberation Front of Assam (ULFA). Maoist groups included: the People's Liberation Front of India (PLFI) and the Tritiya Prastuti Committee (TPC). Lashkar-e-Islam was that one Islamic extremist terrorist group.

(0.9%), the People's Revolutionary Party of Kangleipak or PREPAK with four acts (0.6%), and Hizbul Mujahideen with four acts (0.6%).[18]

3.11 Terrorist Assaults by State

It is important for C-class executives to understand how an array of terrorist assaults against commercial interests are distributed across a country's state, provinces, or departments because past patterns of terrorist group behavior can serve as a baseline of interpretation for findings. In turn, that can assist executives with work to craft non-kinetic counterterrorism responses, and in the process, assist government policymakers with national and state counter-terrorism preparation. When terrorist assault hot zones at the state, provincial, or departmental level are aligned with hot zones at municipal levels, business executives charged with security responsibilities can obtain a more complete picture of terrorist group business target attack patterns.

The data distribution across different Indian states for terrorist attacks against commercial interests suggests clusters of terrorist assaults exist in India that comprise terrorism "hot spots" with different intensity levels. Three tiers of Indian states afflicted with commercial interest terrorism are crafted.

---

[18] Other Indian terrorist groups with less than one percent terrorist assaults included: (1) KPLT (Karbi People's Liberation Tigers) (0.5%); (2) Khasi Student Union (KSU) (0.5%); (3) ANVC-B National Volunteer Council B (0.5%); (4) JPC (Jharkhand Prastuti Committee) (0.5%); (5) United Tribal Liberation Army (UTLA) (0.5%); (6) ASAK (A'chik Songna An'pachakgipa Kotok) (0.5%); (7) NLFT (National Liberation Front of Tripura) (0.5%); (8) AMEF (A'chik Matgrik Elite Force) (0.5%); (9) UNLF (United National Liberation Front) (0.6%); (10) KCP (Kangleipak Communist Party) (0.5%); (11) MKP (Maoist Communist Party of Manipur) (0.3%); (12) NSLA (National Santhal Liberation Army) (0.3%); (13) United Revolutionary Front (0.3%); (14) Maoists of Andhra-Odisha Border Special Zonal Committee (0.3%); (15) Jharkhand Janmukti (0.3%); (16) Karni Sena (0.3%); (17) LeT (Lashkar-e-Taiba) (0.3%); (18) VIPN (The Volunteers of Innocent People of Naga) (0.3%); (19) Sanatan Sanstha (0.3%); (20) United A'chik Liberation Army (UALA) (0.3%); (21) KLO (Kamtapur Liberation Organization) (0.3%); (22) United Democratic Liberation Army (UDLA) (0.3%); (23) CORCOM (Coordination Committee) (0.2%); (24) Pattalai Makkai Katchi (0.2%); (25) Tamil Nadul Liberation Army (0.2%); (26) BVTF (Barak Valley Tiger Force) (0.2%); (27) Dima Hasao National Army (0.2%); (28) MNRP (Manipur Nationalist Revolutionary Party) (0.2%); (29) SIMI (Students' Islamic Movement of India) (0.2%); (30) JMB Jama'atul Mujahideen Bangladesh (0.2%); (31) UGSF (United Garo Security Force (0.2%); (32) Hindu Illaigner Sena (0.2%); (33) Jharkand Sangharsh Jan Mukti Morcha (0.2%); (34) Lama Group (0.2%); (35) Puratchi Puligal (0.2%); (36) MTF (Moran Tigers Force) (0.2%); (37) TWA (Tiwa Liberation Army) (0.2%); (38) RCC (Revolutionary Communist Centre) (0.2%); (39) Thanthai Periyar Dravidar Kazhagam (TPDK) (0.2%); (40) Jharkand Kranti Raksha Dal (Utari Chotanagpur) (0.2%); (41) Manipur Naga People's Army (0.2%); (42) BCF (Birsa Commando Force) (0.2%); (43) Jharkhand Liberation Tigers (0.2%); (44) JeM (Jaish-e-Mohammad) (0.2%); (45) Ghorka Liberation Army (0.2%); (46) Indigenous People's Front of Tripura (0.2%); (47) PLA (People's Liberation Army of Manipur) (0.2%); (48) CPI-ML (0.2%); (49) RSS (Rashtriya Swayamsevak Sangh) (0.2%); (50) Maoist Communist Centre (MCC) (0.2%). In turn, Jharkhand Janmukti, PREPAK, and the United Revolutionary Front are coded as nationalist-irredentist groups, while Jharkhand Prastuti Committee (JPC) and People's Liberation Front of Manipur (PLA) are coded as Maoist (Marxist-Leninist).

The first-tier includes states that experienced between 10.9% and 15.8% of all business-related terrorism chronicled. Jharkhand had the highest attack percentage with 15.8% (106/669 acts), followed by Manipur with 13.2% (88/669 acts). Bihar and Chhattisgarh, each experienced 11.2% (76/669 acts) of the total. The state of Assam accounted for 10.9% of the total (73/669 acts). Those five states accounted for close to two-thirds of the total amount of Indian terrorism directed at commercial interests between 2013 and 2018, with 62.3%.

A second-tier of Indian states with between 4.3% and 9.0% of the total amount of Indian business-related terrorist attacks recorded included three Indian states. Those states were Odisha (formerly known as Orissa) with 9.0% (60/669 acts), Meghalaya with 7.0% (47/669 acts), and Jammu and Kashmir with 4.3% (29/669 acts). Together, those second-tier Indian states accounted for one fifth (20.3%) of the total amount of business target terrorist assaults recorded.

Six Indian states experienced three percent or less of all Indian terrorist assaults aimed at business targets. That third tier of states included: Andhra Pradesh with 2.7% (18/669 acts), Maharashtra with 2.4% (16/669 acts), Uttar Pradesh with 1.9% (13/669 acts), West Bengal with 1.8% (12/669 acts), Nagaland with 1.8% (12/669 acts), and Kerala with 1.3% (9/669 acts). Together, those third-tier Indian states accounted for 11.9% of all commercial interest related terrorism in India. To summarize, the top ten Indian states most afflicted with business target terrorism are (1) Jharkhand, (2) Manipur, (3) Bihar and Chhattisgarh (tied), (4) Assam, (5) Odisha (Orissa), (6) Meghalaya, (7) Jammu and Kashmir, (8) Andhra Pradesh, (9) Maharashtra, (10) Uttar Pradesh (see Fig. 3.7).

3.12 Terrorist Assaults by District

For Indian districts, the 4.7% rate for Manipur's West Imphal district (31/659 acts) was the highest terrorist attack rate against business terrorist targets recorded for all districts in India. West Imphal district was followed closely by Chhattisgarh's Dantewada district with 4.1% (27/659 acts). Bihar's Gaya district and Latehar district in Jharkhand tied for third highest attack rate with 2.9% (19/659 acts). Tinsukia district (Assam) ranked fourth with 2.4% (16/659 acts). The districts of Baramullah (Jammu and Kashmir), East Imphal (Manipur), Koraput (Odisha), and Visakhapatnam (Andhra Pradesh), each accounted for 2.1% of the total (14/659 acts)[19] (see Fig. 3.8).

[19] It should be noted that West Imphal (4.7%) and East Imphal (2.1%) districts crisscross the city of Imphal in Manipur, and that rates for both those districts account for 6.8% of all Indian terrorism directed against commercial interests. What seems significant is those districts are found in Indian states in the northeastern part of the country, each in close proximity. For example, Chhattisgarh is west of Odisha and south of both Jharkhand and Bihar, while West Bengal and the Indian state of Sikkim, serve as a bridgehead to Assam and Manipur, found farther east. There were no terrorist assaults against commercial interests chronicled In Sikkim.

Statistics

State

N	Valid	669
	Missing	1

State

		Frequency	Percent	Valid Percent	Cumulative Percent
Valid	Assam	73	10.9	10.9	10.9
	Maharashtra	16	2.4	2.4	13.3
	Nagaland	12	1.8	1.8	15.1
	Manipur	88	13.1	13.2	28.3
	Bihar	75	11.2	11.2	39.5
	Haryana	1	.1	.1	39.6
	Chhattisgarh	75	11.2	11.2	50.8
	Meghalaya	47	7.0	7.0	57.8
	Odisha (Orissa)	60	9.0	9.0	66.8
	Jharkhand	106	15.8	15.8	82.7
	Tamil Nadu	8	1.2	1.2	83.9
	West Bengal	12	1.8	1.8	85.7
	Jammu and Kashmir	29	4.3	4.3	90.0
	Madhya Pradesh	4	.6	.6	90.6
	Uttar Pradesh	13	1.9	1.9	92.5
	Tripura	4	.6	.6	93.1
	Andhra Pradesh	18	2.7	2.7	95.8
	Mizoram	1	.1	.1	96.0
	Kerala	9	1.3	1.3	97.3
	Karnataka	4	.6	.6	97.9
	Telangana	4	.6	.6	98.5
	Punjab	3	.4	.4	99.0
	Arunachal Pradesh	3	.4	.4	99.4
	Delhi	1	.1	.1	99.6
	Rajasthan	1	.1	.1	99.7
	Gujarat	2	.3	.3	100.0
	Total	669	99.9	100.0	
Missing	System	1	.1		
Total		670	100.0		

Fig. 3.7 Relative frequency of Indian terrorist attacks by state, 2013–2018

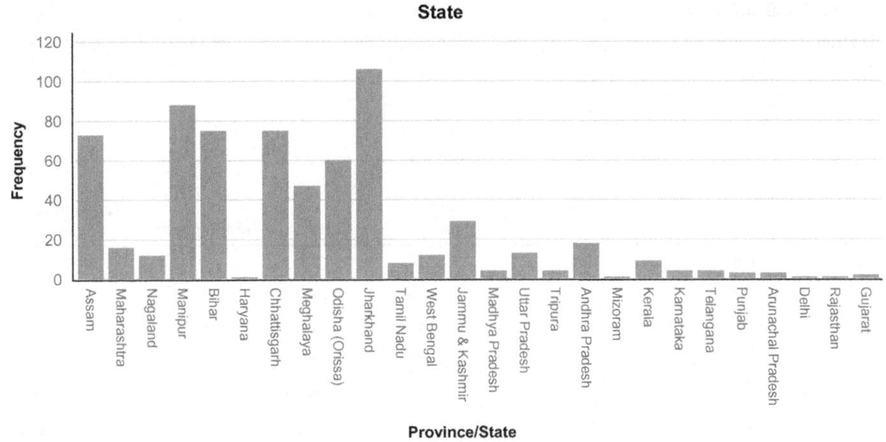

Fig. 3.7 (continued)

There were twenty (20) out of 176 districts where between 1.1 and 1.8% of Indian business linked terrorist events happened. Those districts were: Chatra in Jharkhand (1.8%), South Garo Hills in Meghalaya (1.8%), Tamenglong in Manipur (1.8%), East Garo Hills in Meghalaya (1.7%), Gumla in Jharkhand (1.7%), Hazaribaugh in Jharkhand (1.7%), Dimapur in Nagaland (1.5%), Rayagada in Odisha (1.5%), Gadchiroli in Maharashtra (1.4%), Sukma in Chhattisgarh (1.4%), West Garo Hills in Meghalaya (1.4%), Jamui in Bihar (1.2%), Malkangiri in Odisha (1.2%), East Khasi Hills in Meghalaya (1.1%), Kalahandi in Odisha (1.2%), Kanker in Chhattisgarh (1.1%), Muzaffarpur in Bihar (1.1%), Ranchi in Jharkhand (1.1%), Senapati in Manipur (1.1%), and Srinigar in Jammu and Kashmir (1.1%).[20]

[20] There were one hundred forty-five (145) districts where less than one percent of all terrorist attacks against business targets happened. There were 559 terrorist assault cases in this relative frequencies distribution by district. Those districts were: (1) Ahmednagar (Maharashtra) (0.2%), (2) Ajmer (Rajasthan) (0.2%), (3) Alipurduar (West Bengal) (0.2%), (4) Ambedkar Nagar (Uttar Pradesh) (0.2%); (5) Anantnag (Jammu and Kashmir) (0.2%), (6) Aurangabad (Bihar) (0.6%), (7) Aurangabad (Maharashtra) (0.2%), (8) Baksa (Assam) (0.5%), (9) Balaghat (Madhya Pradesh) (0.2%), (10) Balangir (Odisha) (0.6%), (11) Balrampur (Uttar Pradesh) (0.2%), (12) Bangalore Urban (Karnataka) (0.3%), (13) Banka (Bihar) (0.9%), (14) Bargarh (Odisha) (0.2%), (15) Bastar (Chhattisgarh) (0.5%), (16) Belagavi (Karnataka) (0.2%), (17) Bhadradri (Telangana) (0.2%), (18) Bhagalpur (Bihar) (0.3%), (19) Bhojpur (Bihar) (0.2%), (20) Bhopal (Madhya Pradesh) (0.3%), (21) Bokaro (Jharkhand) (0.3%), (22) Bulandshahr (Uttar Pradesh) (0.2%), (23) Chandauli (Uttar Pradesh) (0.2%), (24) Chandel (Manipur) (0.2%), (25) Changlang (Arunachal Pradesh) (0.3%), (26) Charaideo (Assam) (0.9%), (27) Chennai (Tamil Nadu) (0.3%), (28) Chirang (Assam) (0.5%), (29) Churachandpur (Manipur) (0.2%), (30) Cooch Behar (West Bengal) (0.2%), (31) Cuttack (Odisha) (0.2%), (32) Dakshina Kannada (Karnataka) (0.2%), (33) Dahod (Gujarat) (0.2%), (34) Darbhanga (Bihar) (0.2%), (35) Darjeeling (West Bengal) (0.9%), (36) Darrang (Assam) (0.3%), (37) Deoghar (Jharkhand) (0.3%), (38) Dhanbad (Jharkhand) (0.2%), (39) Dhubri (Assam) (0.2%), (40) Dibrugarh (Assam) (0.3%), (41) Dima Hasao (Assam) (0.9%), (42) Dumka (Jharkhand) (0.5%), (43) East Champaran (Bihar) (0.3%), (44) East Godavari (Andhra Pradesh) (0.2%), (45) East Singhbhum (Jharkhand) (0.6%), (46) Etawah (Uttar Pradesh) (0.2%), (47) Gajapati (Odisha)

Statistics

District

N	Valid	659
	Missing	11

District

		Frequency	Percent	Valid Percent	Cumulative Percent
Valid	Tinsukia	16	2.4	2.4	2.4
	Gadchiroli	9	1.3	1.4	3.8
	Dimapur	10	1.5	1.5	5.3
	West Imphal	31	4.6	4.7	10.0
	Jamui	8	1.2	1.2	11.2
	Jind	1	.1	.2	11.4
	Aurangabad (Maharashtra)	1	.1	.2	11.5
	East Garo Hills	11	1.6	1.7	13.2
	Baksa	3	.4	.5	13.7
	Aurangabad (Bihar)	4	.6	.6	14.3
	West Khasi Hills	1	.1	.2	14.4
	Tamenglong	12	1.8	1.8	16.2
	North Garo Hills	3	.4	.5	16.7
	Dhubri	1	.1	.2	16.8
	Chirang	3	.4	.5	17.3
	Karbi Anglong	3	.4	.5	17.8
	South Garo Hills	12	1.8	1.8	19.6
	West Garo Hills	9	1.3	1.4	20.9
	Palamu	6	.9	.9	21.9
	East Imphal	14	2.1	2.1	24.0
	Karimganj	1	.1	.2	24.1
	Chatra	12	1.8	1.8	25.9
	Etawah	1	.1	.2	26.1
	Umaria	1	.1	.2	26.3
	Bulandshahr	1	.1	.2	26.4
	Dantewada	27	4.0	4.1	30.5
	Sontipur	6	.9	.9	31.4
	East Khasi Hills	7	1.0	1.1	32.5
	Kalahandi	8	1.2	1.2	33.7
	Dhanbad	1	.1	.2	33.8

Fig. 3.8 Relative frequency of Indian terrorist attacks by district, 2013–2018

District

	Frequency	Percent	Valid Percent	Cumulative Percent
Hailakandi	3	.4	.5	34.3
Ambedkar Nagar	1	.1	.2	34.4
Koraput	14	2.1	2.1	36.6
Senapati	7	1.0	1.1	37.6
Makkangiri	8	1.2	1.2	38.8
Kokrajhar	4	.6	.6	39.5
Gaya	19	2.8	2.9	42.3
Simdega	1	.1	.2	42.5
Rayagada	10	1.5	1.5	44.0
Deoghar	2	.3	.3	44.3
Jiribam	1	.1	.2	44.5
West Tripura	2	.3	.3	44.8
Visakhapatnam	14	2.1	2.1	46.9
Khammam	2	.3	.3	47.2
Gumla	11	1.6	1.7	48.9
Madurai	3	.4	.5	49.3
Khunti	4	.6	.6	49.9
Ramgarh	5	.7	.8	50.7
Hazaribaugh	11	1.6	1.7	52.4
Muzaffarpur	7	1.0	1.1	53.4
Bastar	3	.4	.5	53.9
Pulwama	2	.3	.3	54.2
Bargarh	1	.1	.2	54.3
Krishna	1	.1	.2	54.5
West Singhbhum (Paschimi Singhbhum)	4	.6	.6	55.1
Latehar	19	2.8	2.9	58.0
Golaghat	1	.1	.2	58.1
East Singhbhum	4	.6	.6	58.7
Ganjam	2	.3	.3	59.0
Kanker	7	1.0	1.1	60.1
Garhwa	3	.4	.5	60.5
Dima Hasao	6	.9	.9	61.5
Churachandpur	1	.1	.2	61.6
Gopalganj	1	.1	.2	61.8
Nawada	4	.6	.6	62.4

Fig. 3.8 (continued)

District

	Frequency	Percent	Valid Percent	Cumulative Percent
Durrang	2	.3	.3	62.7
Ukhrul	5	.7	.8	63.4
Banka	6	.9	.9	64.3
Mamit	1	.1	.2	64.5
Madhubani	1	.1	.2	64.6
North Tripura	1	.1	.2	64.8
Nuapada	3	.4	.5	65.3
North 24 Parganas	1	.1	.2	65.4
Lakhimpur	1	.1	.2	65.6
Bhagalpur	2	.3	.3	65.9
Lohardaga	3	.4	.5	66.3
Palakkad	2	.3	.3	66.6
Jorhat	3	.4	.5	67.1
Bangalore Urban	2	.3	.3	67.4
Sivaganga	1	.1	.2	67.5
Warangal	2	.3	.3	67.8
Wayanad	2	.3	.3	68.1
Lakhisarai	1	.1	.2	68.3
Sivasagar	5	.7	.8	69.0
Nashik	1	.1	.2	69.2
Chennai	2	.3	.3	69.5
Giridih	6	.9	.9	70.4
Bhopal	2	.3	.3	70.7
Dumka	3	.4	.5	71.2
Wokha	1	.1	.2	71.3
Baramullah	14	2.1	2.1	73.4
Sukma	9	1.3	1.4	74.8
Saran (Chhapra)	3	.4	.5	75.3
Kupwara	1	.1	.2	75.4
Hojai	1	.1	.2	75.6
Srinigar	7	1.0	1.1	76.6
Balangir	4	.6	.6	77.2
Udalguri	1	.1	.2	77.4
East Godavari	1	.1	.2	77.5
Sundargarh	3	.4	.5	78.0

Fig. 3.8 (continued)

District

	Frequency	Percent	Valid Percent	Cumulative Percent
Gurdaspur	2	.3	.3	78.3
Kannauj	1	.1	.2	78.5
Ranchi	7	1.0	1.1	79.5
Alipurduar	1	.1	.2	79.7
Salem	1	.1	.2	79.8
Narayanpur	5	.7	.8	80.6
Thane	2	.3	.3	80.9
Bijapur	14	2.1	2.1	83.0
Chandauli	1	.1	.2	83.2
Seraikela Kharsawan	3	.4	.5	83.6
Dibrugarh	2	.3	.3	83.9
Gajapati	1	.1	.2	84.1
Jehanabad	3	.4	.5	84.5
Siwan	3	.4	.5	85.0
East Champaran	2	.3	.3	85.3
Rajnandgaon	4	.6	.6	85.9
Thoubal	4	.6	.6	86.5
Kaimur	2	.3	.3	86.8
Bargarh	1	.1	.2	86.9
Dakshina Kannada	1	.1	.2	87.1
Jagatsinghpur	2	.3	.3	87.4
Bhojpur	1	.1	.2	87.6
Changlang	2	.3	.3	87.9
Nagaon	1	.1	.2	88.0
Puri	1	.1	.2	88.2
Patna	1	.1	.2	88.3
Balaghat	1	.1	.2	88.5
Paschim Champaran	1	.1	.2	88.6
Ajmer	1	.1	.2	88.8
Kozhikode	1	.1	.2	88.9
Bokaro	2	.3	.3	89.2
Chandel	1	.1	.2	89.4
Sasaram	1	.1	.2	89.5
Darbhanga	1	.1	.2	89.7
Dahod	1	.1	.2	89.8

Fig. 3.8 (continued)

District

	Frequency	Percent	Valid Percent	Cumulative Percent
New Delhi	1	.1	.2	90.0
Noney	2	.3	.3	90.3
Rhotas	3	.4	.5	90.7
Vaishali	1	.1	.2	90.9
Charaideo	6	.9	.9	91.8
Kolhapur	1	.1	.2	92.0
Hathras	4	.6	.6	92.6
Kangpokpi	4	.6	.6	93.2
Kulgam	2	.3	.3	93.5
Cuttack	1	.1	.2	93.6
Umsning	1	.1	.2	93.8
Shillong	2	.3	.3	94.1
Darjeeling	6	.9	.9	95.0
Kalimpong	2	.3	.3	95.3
Kannur	3	.4	.5	95.8
Khowai	1	.1	.2	95.9
Kanpur Nagar	2	.3	.3	96.2
Jaintia Hills	1	.1	.2	96.4
Shopian	1	.1	.2	96.5
Kondagaon	1	.1	.2	96.7
Balrampur	1	.1	.2	96.8
Muzaffarnagar	2	.3	.3	97.1
Belagavi	1	.1	.2	97.3
Bhadradri	1	.1	.2	97.4
Mahabubnagar	1	.1	.2	97.6
Ahmednagar	1	.1	.2	97.7
Kandhamal	1	.1	.2	97.9
Tuensang	1	.1	.2	98.0
Malappuram	1	.1	.2	98.2
Munger	1	.1	.2	98.3
Rajkot	1	.1	.2	98.5
Jalandar	1	.1	.2	98.6
Kolkata	1	.1	.2	98.8
Mumbai City District	1	.1	.2	98.9
Anantnag	1	.1	.2	99.1

Fig. 3.8 (continued)

District

		Frequency	Percent	Valid Percent	Cumulative Percent
	Namsai	1	.1	.2	99.2
	Cooch Behar	1	.1	.2	99.4
	Raipur	1	.1	.2	99.5
	Paschim Bardhaman	1	.1	.2	99.7
	Tiruvannamalai	1	.1	.2	99.8
	Kamrup (Metropolitan)	1	.1	.2	100.0
	Total	659	98.4	100.0	
Missing	System	11	1.6		
Total		670	100.0		

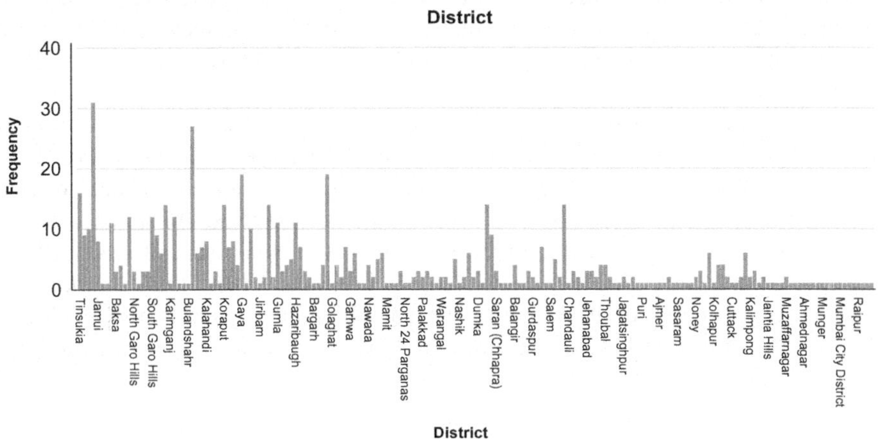

Fig. 3.8 (continued)

(0.2%), (48) Ganjam (Odisha) (0.3%), (49) Garhwa (Jharkhand) (0.5%), (50) Giridih (Jharkhand) (0.9%), (51) Golaghat (Assam) (0.2%), (52) Gopalganj (Bihar) (0.2%), (53) Gurdaspur (Punjab) (0.3%), (54) Hailakandi (Assam) (0.5%), (55) Hathras (Uttar Pradesh) (0.6%), (56) Hojai (Assam) (0.2%), (57) Jagatsinghpur (Odisha) (0.3%), (58) Jaintia Hills (Meghalaya) (0.2%), (59) Jalandar (Punjab) (0.2%), (60) Jehanabad (Bihar) (0.5%), (61) Jind (Haryana) (0.2%), (62) Jiribam (Manipur) (0.2%), (63) Jorhat (Assam) (0.5%), (64) Kaimur (Bihar) (0.3%), (65) Kalimpong (West Bengal) (0.3%), (66) Kamrup—Metropolitan (Assam) (0.2%), (67) Kandhamal (Odisha) (0.2%), (68) Kangpokpi (Manipur) (0.6%), (69) Kannauj (Uttar Pradesh) (0.2%), (70) Kannur (Kerala) (0.5%), (71) Kanpur Nagar (Uttar Pradesh) (0.3%), (72) Karbi Anglong (Assam) (0.5%), (73) Karimganj (Assam) (0.2%), (74) Khammam (Telangana) (0.3 %), (75) Khowai (Tripura) (0.2%), (76) Kokrajhar (Assam) (0.6%), (77) Kolhapur (Maharashtra) (0.2%), (78) Kozhikode (Kerala) (0.2%), (79) Khunti (Jharkhand) (0.6%), (80) Kolkata (West Bengal) (0.2%), (81) Kondagaon (Chhattisgarh) (0.2%), (82) Krishna (Andhra Pradesh) (0.2%), (83) Kulgam (Jammu and Kashmir) (0.3%), (84) Kupwara (Jammu and Kashmir) (0.2%), (85) Lakhimpur (Assam) (0.2%), (86) Lakhisarai (Bihar) (0.2%), (87) Lohardaga (Jharkhand) (0.5%), (88) Madhubani (Bihar) (0.2%), (89) Madurai (Tamil Nadu) (0.5%), (90) Mahabubnagar (Telangana) (0.2%), (91) Malappuram (Kerala)

3.13 Terrorist Assaults by Cities, Towns, and Villages

In the case of cities, towns, and villages, the data distribution suggests widespread dispersal of business-related terrorist assaults across India for the 2013–2018 time period. In the case of cities, towns, and villages where terrorism against business targets happened, the first tier of locations is comprised of four (4) cities and towns that experienced from 1.0 to 7.0% of the total.

The city of Imphal in Manipur had the highest percentage rate with 7.3% (42/575 acts). Two cities virtually tied for a very distant second place ranking: the city of Dimapur in Nagaland with 1.6% (9/575 acts) and Srinagar, the capital city of Jammu and Kashmir, with 1.2% (7/575 acts) of the total. With 1.0% (6/575 acts), the town of Sapore in Jammu and Kashmir rounded out that first tier of cities or towns.[21] In this first tier, while three-quarters of the venues (75.0%) were cities –plus the town of Sapore (25.0%)—that first tier accounted for full 11.1% percent (64/575) of all terrorist attacks, but less than one percent (0.009) of all 447 listed locations (4/447 venues).

The second venue tier is made up of fifteen (15) cities, towns, and villages that account for up to 1.0% of all business linked terrorist assaults recorded. In the city of Williamnagar in Meghalaya, 0.9% (5/575 acts) of all business related terrorism happened, while another 0.7% of the total (4/575 acts) happened in the city of Visakhapatnam in Andhra Pradesh. In the cities, towns, and villages of Bhitia (village; Bihar), Chapagedda (village; Andhra Pradesh), Chatra (city; Jharkhand), Hathras (city; Uttar Pradesh), Kambiren (village; Manipur), Kirandul (town; Chhattisgarh), Madurai (Tamil Nadu), Muzaffarpur (city; Bihar), Pattan (town; Jammu and

(0.2%), (92) Mamit (Mizoram) (0.2%), (93) Mumbai City (0.2%), (94) Munger (Bihar) (0.2%), (95) Muzaffarnagar (Uttar Pradesh) (0.3%), (96) Nagaon (Assam) (0.2%), (97) Namsai (Arunachal Pradesh) (0.2%), (98) Narayanpur (Chhattisgarh) (0.8%), (99) Nashik (Maharashtra) (0.2%), (100) Nawada (Bihar) (0.6%), (101) New Delhi (Delhi) (0.2%), (102) Noney (Manipur) (0.3%), (103) North 24 Parganas (West Bengal), (0.2%), (104) North Garo Hills (Meghalaya) (0.5%), (105) North Tripura (Tripura) (0.2%), (106) Nuapada (Odisha) (0.5%), (107) Palakkad (Kerala) (0.3%), (108) Palamu (Jharkhand) (0.9%), (109) Paschim Bardhaman (West Bengal) (0.2%), (110) Paschim Champaran (Bihar) (0.2%), (111) Patna (Bihar) (0.2%), (112) Pulwama (Jammu and Kashmir) (0.3%), (113) Puri (Odisha) (0.2%), (114) Raipur (Chhattisgarh) (0.2%), (115) Rajkot (Gujarat) (0.2%); (116) Rajnandgaon (Chhattisgarh) (0.6%), (117) Ramgarh (Jharkhand) (0.8%), (118) Rhotas (Bihar) (0.5%), (119) Salem (Tamil Nadu) (0.2%), (120) Saran (Bihar) (0.5%), (121) Sasaram (Bihar) (0.2%), (122) Seraikela Kharsawan (Jharkhand) (0.5%), (123) Shillong (Meghalaya) (0.3%), (124) Shopian (Jammu and Kashmir) (0.2%), (125) Simdega (Jharkhand) (0.2%), (126) Sivasagar (Assam) (0.8%), (127) Sivaganga (Tamil Nadu) (0.2%), (128) Siwan (Bihar) (0.5%), (129) Sontipur (Assam) (0.9%), (130) Sundargarh (Odisha) (0.5%), (131) Thane (Maharashtra) (0.3%), (132) Thoubal (Manipur) (0.6%), (133) Tiruvannamalai (Tamil Nadu) (0.2%), (134) Tuensang (Nagaland) (0.2%), (135) Udalguri (Assam) (0.2%), (136) Ukhrul (Manipur) (0.8%), (137) Umaria (Madhya Pradesh) (0.2%), (138) Umsning (Meghalaya) (0.2%), (139) Vaishali (Bihar) (0.2%), (140) Warangal (Telangana) (0.3%), (141) Wayanad (Kerala) (0.3%), (142) West Khasi Hills (Meghalaya) (0.2%), (143) West Singhbhum (or Paschimi Singhbhum) (Jharkhand) (0.6%), (144) West Tripura (Tripura) (0.3%), (145) Wokha (Nagaland) (0.2%).

[21] For the N set in this crosstabulation test, Valid = 575; Missing 95.

Kashmir), Sapekhati (village panchayat; Assam), Shillong (city; Meghalaya), Tura (Meghalaya), and Urahiloga-Jagibeel (village; Assam), the three acts of terrorism that happened in each locale made up 0.005 (3/575 acts) of the total.

In this second location tier, cities still accounted for 46.7% of venues (7/15)—that rate was down 28.3% from the 75.0% city and town rate found for the first tier of commercial interest attack locales. In addition, this second tier accounted for only 3.4% (15/447) of all listed venues. This second tier accounted for 8.3% (48/575 acts) of the total number of terrorist events.

A third venue tier of is made up of thirty-five (35) cities, towns, and villages. At each of those locations, the terrorism that occurred comprised only 0.3% (2/575 acts) of the total amount of business-related terrorism. The first sixteen locales include: Bangalore (city; Karnataka), Bhopal (city; Madya Pradesh), Bongaigaon (city; Assam), Chapi (village; Jharkhand), Chargaon (village; Chhattisgarh), Chennai (city; Tamil Nadu), Digboi (town; Assam), Dumaria ("village block"; Bihar), Gaghra ("village block"; Jharkhand), Hazaribaugh (city; Jharkhand), Kumbhariput (village; Odisha), Miangpadar (village; Odisha), Palakkad (town; Kerala), Tinsukia (town; Assam), Ukhrul (town; Manipur), Wageasi (village; Meghalaya),

The remainder include: Awangkhul (village; Manipur), Bacheli, (town; Chhattisgarh), Bhansi (village panchayat; Chhattisgarh), Bhitarokota (village; Odisha), Birbanki (village; Jharkhand), Chirand (village; Bihar), Chitrakonda (village; Odisha), Dinanagar (town; Punjab), Donaikala (village; Jharkhand), Dooru (village; Jammu and Kashmir), Gadiras (village; Chhattisgarh), Jagun (village; Assam), Kohkameta (village; Chhattisgarh), Konta (town; Chhattisgarh), Maraigude (village; Chhattisgarh), Ramgarh (town; Jharkhand), Sehjang (village; Manipur), Thane (city; Maharashtra), and Tisia (village; Jharkhand).

In this third-tier, cities comprised only 17.1% (6/35) of all locales. In addition, this third-tier accounted for 7.82% (35/447) of all "city, town, village" locations, and 12.2% (70/575 acts) of the total number of business-related terrorist attacks chronicled.[22] These results suggest that while there was a broad distribution of terrorist

[22] The fourth venue tier includes cities, towns, and villages each with 1 out of 575 acts (0.002) of the total amount of business-related terrorism. This fourth-tier, with 394/447 locations, accounted for 88.1% of all listed locations. In this fourth-tier, cities accounted for only 9.1% of all venues (36/394); those cities, towns, and villages include: (1) Aheri (town; Maharashtra), (2) Ahiapur (village; Bihar), (3) Ahmednagar (city: Maharashtra), (4) Agartala (city, Tripura), (5) Ambabhona (village; Odisha), (6) Amjharia (village; Jharkhand), (7) Amlidhar (village; Chhattisgarh), (8) Amratola (village; Bihar), (9) Anandpur (village; Bihar), (10) Andrahal (village; Odisha), (11) Annaram (village; Chhattisgarh), (12) Ara (city; Bihar), (13) Aranpur (village; Chhattisgarh), (14) Asansol-Jamuria (city; West Bengal), (15) Aulachowka (village; Assam), (16) Aurangabad (city; Bihar), (17) Badarpur (town; Assam), (18) Baddi (village; Bihar), (19) Badildeh (village; Bihar), (20) Bagabandh (village; Jharkhand), (21) Bagaha (city; Bihar), (22) Bage Bar (village, Bihar), (23) Baghmara (town; Meghalaya), (24) Balimaha (village, Odisha), (25) Balu (village; Jharkhand), (26) Balumath (village; Jharkhand), (27) Bamchuk Beel (village; Arunachal Pradesh), (28) Banapar (town, Chhattisgarh), (29) Banchatara (village; Jharkhand), (30) Bangsi Minol (village; Meghalaya), (31) Bara (village; Bihar), (32) Barabadha (village; Assam), (33) Barachatti (village panchayat; Bihar), (34) Baraua (village; Bihar), (35) Barbaspur (village, Chhattisgarh), (36) Bartola (village; Jharkhand), (37) Basaguda (village; Chhattisgarh), (38) Bautia (village; Jharkhand), (39) Bela (town; Bihar), (40) Belagavi (city; Karnataka), (41) Belkhoria (village; Bihar), (42) Bengtol

assaults across different Indian cities, towns, and villages, the highest percentage rates of terrorist assaults were concentrated primarily in Indian cities for the six-year time period under consideration.

(village panchayat; Assam), (43) Betagon (Assam), (44) Bhabua (city, Bihar), (45) Bhadrakali (village; Chhattisgarh), (46) Bhansi (village panchayat; Chhattisgarh); (47) Bharno (village—"administrative block"; Jharkhand), (48) Bhavanitola (village; Chhattisgarh), (49) Bhadrachalam (town; Andhra Pradesh), (50) Bhejji (village; Chhattisgarh), (51) Bhopalpatnam (village; Chhattisgarh), (52) Bilhaur (town; Uttar Pradesh), (53) Bishnupur (town; Meghalaya), (54) Bihubor (village panchayat; Assam), (55) Bitabari (village; Assam), (56) Bodhadih (village; Jharkhand), (57) Bomai (village, Jammu and Kashmir), (58) Borabandha (village; Odisha), (59) Borapadar (village; Odisha), (60) Borhat (village; Assam), (61) Bouserkuti (village; Assam), (62) Brakpora (village; Jammu and Kashmir), (63) Budhaniya (village; Jharkhand), (64) Budhauli (village; Bihar), (65) Bukru (village; Jharkhand), (66) Busuputtu (village; Andhra Pradesh), (67) Champijang (village; Assam), (68) Chandagre (village; Meghalaya), (69) Chandanpur (village; Odisha), (70) Charhi (town; Jharkhand), (71) Chasingre (village: Meghalaya), (72) Chawangkining (village; Manipur), (73) Chelakkad (town; Kerala), (74) Chhatarpur (village; Jharkhand), (75) Chintapalle (town; Andhra Pradesh), (76) Chirudih (village; Jharkhand), (77) Chipakur (village; Odisha), (78) Chisikgre (village; Meghalaya), (79) Chola (village; Uttar Pradesh), (80) Chouparan (town; Jharkhand), (81) Chowka (village; Jharkhand), (82) Chulabhat (village; Odisha), (83) Churchu (village "administrative block"; Jharkhand), (84) Cuttack (city; Odisha), (85) Dalgaon (town; Assam), (86) Daliakhuji (village; Odisha), (87) Dalki (village; Jharkhand), (88) Damas (village; Meghalaya), (89) Dambuk (village; Meghalaya), (90) Dangerpora (village panchayat; Jammu and Kashmir), (91) Dangia (village, Odisha), (92) Dantewada (town; Chhattisgarh), (93) Darakonda (village; Andhra Pradesh), (94) Darauli (town; Bihar), (95) Darbhanga (city; Bihar), (96) Darjeeling (town, West Bengal), (97) Darliput (village; Odisha), (98) Darna (village; Bihar), (99) Datura (village; Jharkhand), (100) Datuta (village; Jharkhand), (101) Dechlipetha (village; Maharashtra), (102) Delhi (city; National Capital Territory), (103) Demow (town; Assam), (104) Dengsupari (village; Odisha), (105) Dewaria (village, Jharkhand), (106) Dhanora (village; Maharashtra), (107) Dharampenta (village; Chhattisgarh), (108) Dhekiajuli (town, Assam), (109) Dhina (city; Uttar Pradesh), (110) Dingdinga (village; Assam), (111) Diphu (town; Assam), (112) Dogla Bathan (village; Bihar), (113) Dudheda (village; Chhattisgarh), (114) Dudhia (town; West Bengal), (115) Dudhiyatadi (village; Bihar), (116) Dugdha (village; Bihar), (117) Edira (village; Telangara), (118) Ekilsara (village; Jharkhand), (119) Era Aning (village, Meghalaya), (120) Etawah (city; Uttar Pradesh), (121) Etapalli (village; Maharashtra), (122) Fatehpura (village; Gujarat), (123) Gadchiroli (town; Maharashtra), (124) Gagaguro (village; Jharkhand), (125) Ganjeipadar (village; Odisha), (126) Ganol Apal (village; Meghalaya), (127) Garu (village; Jharkhand), (128) Gasuapara (village; Meghalaya) (129) Gatam (village; Chhattisgarh), (130) Geedam (town; Chhattisgarh), (131) Ghatampur (town; Uttar Pradesh), (132) Ghatshila (town; Jharkhand), (133) Goh (Maharashtra), (134) Goju (village panchayat; Arunachal Pradesh), (135) Golgariba (village; Bihar), (136) Gora (village; Bihar), (137) Gourapali (Odisha), (138) Guijan (town; Assam), (139) Gumda (village; Chhattisgarh), (140) Guram DatoTola (village; Jharkhand), (141) Gurua (village; Bihar), (142) Hahaladdi (village; Chhattisgarh), (143) Hajipur (city, Bihar), (144) Hajongpara (village, Meghalaya), (145) Handwara (town; Jammu and Kashmir), (146) Heirok (town; Manipur), (147) Hesakocha (village; Jharkhand), (148) Hesatu (village; Jharkhand), (149) Hisua (city; Bihar), (150) Itkhori (village; Jharkhand), (151) Jaiprakash (village "locality," Bihar), (152) Jalandhar (city; Punjab), (153) Jamakana (village; Odisha), (154) Jamgai (village; Jharkhand), (155) Jamui (town; Bihar), (156) Jangai (village; Bihar), (157) Jatatari (village; Bihar), (158) Jehanabad (town; Bihar), (159) Jiribam (town, Manipur), (160) Kadambaguda (village; Odisha), (161) Kalachand (village; Assam), (162) Kalia Atala (Odisha), (163) Kalimpong (town; West Bengal), (164) Kalyan (city; Maharashtra), (165) Kambesu (village; Odisha), (166) Kangchup (village; Manipur), (167) Kanglatongbi (village; Manipur), (168) Kangpokpi (town; Manipur), (169) Kanubari (village; Assam), (170) Kapasiya

3.14 Business Firms Attacked

The results show that 193 different identifiable businesses in India were targeted by terrorist attacks for this six-year time period between January 1, 2013 and December 31, 2018. Overall, the dispersion of terrorist assaults across different firms was

---

(village; Bihar), (171) Kasaram (village; Chhattisgarh), (172) Kashitand (village; Jharkhand), (173) Kasuguda (village; Odisha), (174) Kathapada (village; Odisha), (175) Kathupani (village; Jharkhand), (176) Keeta (village; Jharkhand), (177) Khangabok (village, Manipur), (178) Kharia (village, Bihar), (179) Khelari (town; Maharashtra), (180) Khelmati (village; Assam), (181) Kherem Mura (village; Arunachal Pradesh), (182) Kolkata (city, West Bengal), (183) Konapathar ("area"; Assam), (184) Kralchek-Keller (village; Jammu and Kashmir), (185) Kuchai (village; Jharkhand), (186) Kudag (village; Chhattisgarh), (187) Kudhni (village, Bihar); (188) Kukud (village; Jharkhand), (189) Kulgam (town; Jammu and Kashmir), (190) Kulhiamunda (village, Odisha), (191) Kulnung Khunou (Manipur), (192) Kumkumpudi (village; Andhra Pradesh), (193) Kunnoth (village; Kerala), (194) Kurseong (town; West Bengal), (195) Kusumaguda (village; Odisha), (196) Kusumba (village; Jharkand), (197) Kyang (village, Odisha), (198) Ladpur (village; Uttar Pradesh), (199) Lamlai Khullen (village; Manipur), (200) Latehar (town; Jharkhand), (201) Latrutu (village, Jharkhand), (202) Lathore (village; Odisha), (203) Laudha (village; Madhya Pradesh), (204) Ledo (town; Assam), (205) Lewadih (village; Jharkhand), (206) Lidpura (Jammu and Kashmir), (207) Lodhama (village; West Bengal), (208) Loharam (village; Odisha), (209) Lukhambi (village; Manipur), (210) Lumding (city; Assam), (211) Lumnongrim Dewlieh (village; Meghalaya), (212) Macca (village; Jharkhand), (213) Machadiha (village; Jharkhand), (214) Madded (village; Chhattisgarh), (215) Madhwapur (village; Bihar), (216) Mahuamilan (village; Jharkhand), (217) Magra (village; Bihar), (218) Mahadev Ghat (village; Chhattisgarh), (219) Mahuadanr (village; Jharkhand), (220) Majhi Gumandi (village; Odisha) (221), Majhowlia (village; Bihar), (222) Malappuram (city; Kerala), (223) Malewahi (village; Chhattisgarh), (224) Mananpur (village; Bihar), (225) Mandai ("village-block"; Tripura), (226) Manpur (town; Bihar), (227) Mandu (town; Jharkhand), (228) Mangaluru (city; Karnataka), (229) Mankelli (village; Chhattisgarh), (230) Mankidi (village; Odisha), (231) Mansai (village; West Bengal); (232) Manubothulagadda (village, Karnataka), (233) Margherita (town; Assam), (234) Mariani-Jorhat (town; Assam), (235) Mathili (village; Odisha), (236) Mawlai Nangmali (city; Meghalaya), (237) Mawlai- Mawiong (town; Meghalaya), (238) Mayyil (village panchayat; Kerala), (239) McCluskieganj (town; Jharkhand), (240) Melakajoba (village; Odisha), (241) Menda (village; Maharashtra), (242) Meppadi (village; Kerala), (243) Metoda (village; Gujarat), (244), Mirganj (town, Bihar), (245) Mirik (town; West Bengal), (246) Mirzadih (village; Jharkhand), (247) Modakpal (village; Chhattisgarh), (248) Mohanpur (village; West Bengal), (249) Mohanpur Misoroliya (village; Assam), (250) Molandubi (village, Assam), (251) Moreh (town; Manipur), (252) Motihari (city; Bihar), (253) Motphran (village; Meghalaya); (254) Mounasilli (village; Jharkhand), (255) Moyyalagummi (village; Andhra Pradesh), (256) Muchnar (village; Chhattisgarh), (257) Mumbai (city; Maharashtra), (258) Murki (village; Chhattisgarh), (259) Murki (village; Jharkhand), (260) Murumgaon (village; Maharashtra), (261) Muskel (village; Chhattisgarh), (262) Mutanpal (village; Chhattisgarh), (263) Muthbharo (village; Bihar), (264) Muzaffarnagar (city, Uttar Pradesh), (265) Naharkatia (town; Assam), (266) Namrup (town; Assam), (267) Nangalbibra (town; Meghalaya), (268) Napet Palli (village; Manipur), (269) Narnaund (town; Haryana), (270) Nashik (city, Maharashtra), (271) Nasirabad (town; Rajasthan), (272) Natun Chariali (town; Assam), (273) Navinagar (village; Bihar), (274) Navani (village; Jharkhand), (275) Nawada (city; Bihar), (276) Neema (village; Bihar), (277) Nekhavaya (village; Chhattisgarh), (278) Nender (village; Maharashtra), (279) Nepa (village, Bihar), (280) New Helipong (village, Nagaland), (281) Noonmati (city; Assam), (282) Nuadihi (village, Odisha), (283) Nuapari Khaliapur (village; Odisha), (284) Nungba (village, Manipur), (285) Nungsai Tubung (village; Manipur), (286) Nurmati (village; Andhra Pradesh), (287) Ondrungula (village; Andhra Pradesh), (288) Orchha (village; Chhattisgarh), (289) Ormanjhi (town; Jharkhand), (290) Pajibali (village, Odisha); (291) Paji Bahali (village; Odisha), (292) Pallemadi (village; Chhattisgarh), (293) Panapur (village, Bihar), (294) Pandrasali (village; Jharkhand), (295) Panhala (city; Maharashtra), (296) Papermetia

very large with 183/193 firms (94.8%) that each experienced between three out of 283 terrorist attacks (1.1% of the total), and one terrorist attack (0.4% of the total). Three state-owned firms (and one private firm) had the three highest percentage rates of terrorist attacks—Bharat Sanchar Nigam Ltd. (BSNL) with 12/283 acts or 4.2%, National Mineral Development Corporation with 8/283 acts or 2.8%, and the private MNC firm Airtel (Bharti Airtel) with eight out 283 acts (2.8%). Ranking fourth, were two state owned firms—Central Coal Fields Ltd. (CCL) (state-owned), and Pradhan Mantri Gram Sadak Yojana (PMGSY), each with 2.5% of the total (7/283 acts.). Rounding out that top tier was another state-owned firm, Indian Oil Corporation with 2.1% (6/283 acts).

(village; Odisha), (297) Paralkot (village; Chhattisgarh), (298) Parswar (village; Jharkhand), (299) Paschim Mamroni (village; Assam), (300) Patgaon (village; Assam), (301) Pathalgada (village; Jharkhand), (302) Patna (city; Bihar), (303) Pedaarlagudem (village; Andhra Pradesh), (304) Pedapadu (village; Odisha), (305) Pedakurti (village; Chhattisgarh), (306) Peeding (village; Jharkhand), (307) Piparwar (village; Jharkhand), (308) Pipghati (village; Bihar), (309) Pirtand ("community development block"; Jharkahand), (310) Pitala (village; Odisha), (311) Pombai (village; Jammu and Kashmir), (312) Pratappur (village, Jharkhand), (313) Pukhao Laipham (town; Assam), (314) Pulwama (town; Jammu and Kasmir), (315) Raghubari (village; Odisha), (316) Rajivnagar (village, Mizoram), (317) Rajpora Chowk (village; Jammu and Kashmir), (318) Rajnandgaon (city; Chhattisgarh), (319) Ramagiri (village; Odisha), (320) Rangamati (village; Assam, (321) Rankhom Gaon (village; Assam), (322) Rayagada (city; Odisha), (323) Rekhabat (village; Chhattisgarh), (324) Ritu Kathalguri (village, Assam), (325) Roam (village; Jharkhand), (326) Rodo (village; Jharkhand), (327) Rompalli (village; Maharashtra), (328) Rongara (village, Meghalaya), (329) Rongrikimgre (village; Meghalaya), (330) Rupai Siding (town; Assam); (331) Samanda (village; Meghalaya), (332) Samri (village; Chhattisgarh), (333) Sandengleli (village; Odisha), (334) Sangkini Dabgre (village; Meghalaya), (335) Sarivella (village; Andhra Pradesh), (336) (52) Sasatgre (village, Meghalaya), (337) Saun (village; Bihar), (338) Savalvahi (village; Chhattisgarh), (339) Sawombung (village; Manipur), (340) Sahyara (village Bihar), (341) Selenghat ("community development block"; Assam), (342) Senduwar (village; Jharkhand), (343) Sevanan (village; Bihar), (344) Sheikhbigh (village; Bihar), (345) Shivpur (village; Bihar), (346) Shuwa (village; Jammu and Kashmir), (347) Sikandra (village; Bihar); (348) Sikarpai (village; Odisha), (349) Siladon (village; Jharkhand), (350) Simaluguri (town, Assam), (351) Simdega (city, Jharkhand), (352) Sirigidi (village; Odisha), (353) Sivaganga (town; Tamil Nadu), (354) Sivasagar (city; Assam), (355) Sohra/Cherrapunji (town; Meghalaya), (356) Somrei (village; Manipur), (357), Sorodo (village; Odisha), (358) Sudikona (village; Jharkhand), (359) Sukma (town; Chhattisgarh), (360) Sumandi (village; Jharkhand), (361) Suriya (village; Jharkhand), (362) Swangre (village; Meghalaya), (363) Tanda (town; Uttar Prasdesh), Tandwa (village; Jharkhand), (364) Tarkhola (village; West Bengal), (365) Tarlaguda (village; Chhattisgarh), (366) Tarwadih (village; Jharkhand), (367) Taupadar (village, Odisha), (368) Tekulagudem (village; Telangana), (369) Teokghat (village; Assam), (370) Telenpali (village; Odisha), (371) Tikhali (village; Odisha), (372) Tiskopi (village; Jharkhand), (373) Thingou (village, Manipur), (374) Thoubal (town; Manipur), (375) Thoubal Khunou (village; Manipur), (376) Tikak (town, Assam), (377) Tilaparal-Bakenang (village; Meghalaya); (378) Tirtol (village panchayat; Odisha), (379) Tiruvanna Malai (city; Tamil Nadu); (380) Tori (village, Jharkhand), (381) Toylanka (village; Chhattisgarh), (382) Tuisenphai (village, Manipur), (383) Turki (village; Bihar), (384) Umpling (village, "locality"; Meghalaya), (385) Umrangso (town; Assam), (386) Upampalli (village; Chhattisgarh), (387) Upar Pakhi (village; Odisha), (388) Uripok (town; Manipur, (389) Vangaichungpao (village; Manpur), (390) Vardeltong (village; Chhattisgarh), (391) Vijayawada (city; Andhra Pradesh), (392) Woka (town; Nagaland), (393) Yukharia (village; Bihar), (394) Zalembung (village; Manipur).

Next, four firms in India experienced terrorist attacks that accounted for between 1.8 and 1.4% of the total. Those firms included, Vodofone with 1.8% (5/283 acts, Coastal Projects Limited with 1.4% (4/283 acts), Essar Steel with 1.4% (4/283 acts), and the state-owned firm, Andhra Pradesh Mineral Development Corporation (APMDC). In turn, seven firms suffered three terrorist attacks apiece (1.1%). Those firms included: the BSC-C&C JV Construction Co. (1.1%), Andhra Pradesh Forest Development Corporation (1.1%), Numaligarh Refinery Ltd. (NRL) (1.1%), Simplex Infrastructure Ltd. (1.1%), Jayaswal Neco Industries Ltd. (1.1%), Reliance Communications (1.1%), and Hindalco Industries (1.1%).[23]

---

[23] Firms in India that experienced two out of 283 terrorist attacks (**0.7% of the total**) included: Dainik Bhaskar, the Regional Institute of Medical Science & Hospital (state-owned), Hi-Tech Co., Virgo Cement Co., the government-owned State Bank of India (SBI), ECI Co., Bharti Airtel Ltd., ABCI Infrastructure Pvt. Ltd., RSB Co., Tamil Nadu State Markets Corp. (TNSMC), Aircel Telecom, S.P. Singla Co., J.C. Bamford Excavators Ltd. (JCB), Gas India Ltd. (GAIL) (state-owned), Jammu and Kashmir Bank (state-owned), Hindustan Construction Company, Oil India Ltd. (state-owned), Chandra Talkies, Jyoti Cinema, and Kanubari Tea Estate.

By contrast, firms in India that suffered one out of 283 terrorist attacks apiece (**0.4% of the total**) included: Brahmaputra Infrastructure Ltd., Ingole Patil Co., Oak Tasar Farm, K.C. Sharma, St. Mixer Bakery, U.C. Consultation, Lloyds Metal & Energy Ltd., Primary Agriculture Credit Society (PACS), Kulgam District Hospital, Imphal Urban Cooperative Bank (IUCB), M/S Sudhir Iron & Steel, R.M. Sinha & Co., Barak Valley Cement, Ltd., Sita Jewelers, Rhino Railways, Corp., Rt. 39 Restaurant, Nagrijuli Tea Estate Hospital, Hindi Daily, Naven Store Cinema, the state-owned National Hydroelectric Power Corp. (NHPC), Meghalaya Machineries, Hero Motorcycle, Deshbandhu, RSS Co., KK Builder, Power Grid Corporation of India Ltd., Pabhoi Tea Estate, Meghalaya Electricity Corp. Ltd., JKM Infrastructure, Reliance Retail, Sidhhartha Construction Co., Imphal Free Press, Shirdi Sai Construction Co., Adhunik Group, Cacher Paper Mill (CPM), Janusa Oil (state-owned), Uranium Corp. of India (state-owned), Kanak TV, Vashishta Constructions, Muzaffarpur Road Construction Development (state-owned), Prudhi Construction, Triveni Construction, Bagara Tea Estate, Nitu Glass Hardware Shop, Midwest Granite Pvt. Ltd, National Buildings Construction Corporation. (NBCC), KFC, McDonalds, Coconut Grove, New Bharat Stone Crusher, Kerala Tourism Development Corporation (KTDC), Sripur Colliery, Puthiya Thalaimurai TV, Kwality Hotel, Shivam Road & Infrastructure Pvt. Ltd., Shell Oil Company, Balaji Transport, Bhardwaj Constructions, Pammi Travels, Mahabir Trade Agency, Indergope Construction Co., Gayatri ECI, Eastern Motors, Gammon India, Asomiya Pratidan, Christian Institute of Health Services & Research, Chaubatiya Construction, Kiran Hospital, Smaridhi (United India), Uttarbanga Sangbod, Kalyan Hotel, Patil Construction, Indian Railways (state-owned), Sky Golden Café, Ashiyana Hotel, Hahaladdi Mining Co., Manipur Golden Travels (MGT) Tata Motors, Shirram Power and Steel Pvt. Ltd., GIIS Ltd, All India Radio (AIR) (state-owned), Sarda Energy & Minerals Ltd., Punya Motors Pvt. Ltd., Canchi Indane Service, Hari Construction Co., M/S Sorojini Oil, Padumani Tea Estate, NS Mall, Kherem Tea Estate, Taaza News, Hindustan Daily, Spica Projects & Infrastructure Pvt. Ltd., New Woodlands Hotel, NKC Projects Pvt. Ltd., Jawarhalal Nehru Institute of Medical Sciences, ANA Mining Pvt. Ltd., Surjagod Lloyds Metals & Energy Ltd., Pandam Daily, Ram Kripal Singh Construction, Nagarjuna Construction Co., A-One Bicycle Co., Ramie Construction Co., Nissan Motor Co., Puja Enterprises, Disam Tea Estate, Nutan Construction Co., Singjamei Supermarket, Viacom 18 Motion Pictures, Bihar State Bridge Construction Corp. (state-owned), SPR Construction Co., Dimapur Gas Agency, Cuttack Central Cooperative Bank, Meghalaya Power Distribution Corporation (state-owned), Meg Mini Tea Co., Mornoi Tea Estate, Mahavir Medicos, Manipur Motors, West Bengal State Electricity Distribution Co. Ltd. (state-owned), DGR Velocity, Lankesh Patrike, Hindustan Construction Co., Wellson Energy C. Pvt. Ltd., Dinraat News Channel, Dehingiya Tea Estate, Kopli Tea Estate, Rani Beauty Parlor, Rajdhar Coal Siding, Hyundai, Baba Hans Construction Co., Tripura Garmin Bank (state-owned), North Eastern Coalfields Coal India

One notable observation is the number of state-owned enterprises targeted with more than one terrorist attack; five out of six firms in that first tier of firms were state owned. This focus on state-owned firms in the top tier of firms targeted, is consistent with the central idea that firms associated with India's government and modernization efforts by government are of special interest to some terrorist groups in India as a reaction to modernization and overall globalization conditions that encourage modernization. At the same time, some widely recognized Western, Japanese, and South Korean firms such KFC (0.4%), McDonalds (0.4%), Shell Oil Company (0.4%), Nissan Motor Company (0.4%), and Hyundai (0.4%), were not targets of multiple terrorist group attacks in India (see Fig. 3.9).

3.15 Variable Analysis

The theoretical framework for this study is introduced in Chap. 2, where a continuum of "structuralist" and "non-structuralist" terrorist group-types are placed between two poles. To reiterate, on that continuum's left axis, are "structuralist" terrorist groups that view conflict as a function of fierce struggle against "world systems" such as capitalism or globalization. On that continuum's right axis are "non-structuralist" terrorist groups, whose chieftains view fierce struggle as a function of conflict with ethnic or racial groups, or individuals, or a combination thereof.

It follows that "structuralist" terrorist groups (i.e., Maoist or Marxist-Leninist terrorist groups) are expected to place more emphasis on business related targets perceived by perpetrators to symbolize links to capitalism, modernization, and globalization. Those targets can also include government owned business targets as governments are symbolic of and have ties to capitalism, modernization, and globalization. In comparison, "non-structuralist" terrorist groups (i.e., nationalist-irredentist terrorist groups, and right-wing terrorist groups) are expected to put more emphasis on business targets with civilian emphasis, such as private establishments owned by a proprietor(s) from a particular ethnic, religious, or racial group, or targets that symbolize or provide narratives for ethnic conflict [9, 180–186; 10, 15, 24, 35–37, 133–134, 382–385].[24]

In between those two poles, are "hybrid" terrorist groups that share both "structuralist" and "non-structuralist" dimensions. For "hybrid" groups, conflict is perceived as a fierce struggle against both a particular system such as Western style

Ltd. (state-owned), MKB Tea Garden, Amar Agency, Prakash Cinema, Bhanu Sagar Cinema Hall, Shyam Cinema Hall, M/S Puna & Hunda Construction, Sarhad, The Shillong Times, Reasonable Enterprises, Brahmaputra Fuel Centre (state-owned), RS Agency, Chandrika Malayalam Daily, Phaneng Tea Garden, Kolkata-Basa Enterprises, Rising Kashmir, Emerald Estate, Seleng Tea Estate, Go Rakisha Samti, Redding Construction Co., Times Now, Daily Aaj, Sai Construction, Sati Tea Estate, Shau Mahamaya Jt. Venture, Jindal Co., Visah Mega Mart.

[24] The variable "Group-Type" was recoded into the "same variable" with 1 → 1; 2 → 2; ELSE → SYSMIS. The variable "Business Target" was recoded into the same variable with 2 → 2; 4 → 4; ELSE → SYSMIS. 415–416.

Statistics

FirmName

N	Valid	283
	Missing	387

FirmName

		Frequency	Percent	Valid Percent	Cumulative Percent
Valid	Nagajan Oil Collection Centre	2	.3	.7	.7
	Brahmaputra Infrastructure Ltd.	1	.1	.4	1.1
	Ingole Patil Co.	1	.1	.4	1.4
	Oak Tasar Farm	1	.1	.4	1.8
	Indian Oil Corp. Ltd.	6	.9	2.1	3.9
	Dainik Bhaskar	2	.3	.7	4.6
	K.C. Sharma	1	.1	.4	4.9
	BSC-C&C JV Construction Co.	3	.4	1.1	6.0
	Regional Institute of Medical Science & Hospital	2	.3	.7	6.7
	Coastal Projects Ltd.	4	.6	1.4	8.1
	St Mixer Bakery	1	.1	.4	8.5
	Hi-Tech Co.	2	.3	.7	9.2
	UC Consultation	1	.1	.4	9.5
	Lloyds Metal & Energy Ltd.	1	.1	.4	9.9
	Primary Agriculture Credit Society (PACS)	1	.1	.4	10.2
	Kulgam District Hospital	1	.1	.4	10.6
	Virgo Cement Co.	2	.3	.7	11.3
	Imphal Urban Cooperative Bank (IUCB)	1	.1	.4	11.7
	M/S Sudhir Iron & Steel	1	.1	.4	12.0
	State Bank of India (SBI)	2	.3	.7	12.7
	R.M. Sinha & Co.	1	.1	.4	13.1
	Barak Valley Cement Ltd.	1	.1	.4	13.4
	Sita Jewelers	1	.1	.4	13.8
	Rhino Railways Corp.	1	.1	.4	14.1
	Rt. 39 Restaurant	1	.1	.4	14.5

Fig. 3.9 Relative frequency of Indian terrorist attacks by firm, 2013–2018

FirmName

	Frequency	Percent	Valid Percent	Cumulative Percent
Nagrijuli Tea Estate Hospital	1	.1	.4	14.8
Hindi Daily	1	.1	.4	15.2
Naven Store Cinema	1	.1	.4	15.5
Nat. Mineral Development Corp. (NMDC)	8	1.2	2.8	18.4
Nat. Hydroelectric Power Corp. (NHPC)	1	.1	.4	18.7
Bharat Sanchar Nigam Ltd. (BSNL)	12	1.8	4.2	23.0
Meghalaya Machineries	1	.1	.4	23.3
Hero Motorcycle	1	.1	.4	23.7
Deshbandhu	1	.1	.4	24.0
RSS Co.	1	.1	.4	24.4
ECI Co.	2	.3	.7	25.1
Bharti Airtel Ltd.	2	.3	.7	25.8
KK Builder	1	.1	.4	26.1
Power Grid Corp. of India Ltd.	1	.1	.4	26.5
Pabhoi Tea Estate	1	.1	.4	26.9
Andhra Pradesh Forest Devel. Corp. Ltd.	3	.4	1.1	27.9
Meghalaya Electricity Corp. Ltd.	1	.1	.4	28.3
JKM Infrastructure	1	.1	.4	28.6
Numaligarh Refinery Ltd. (NRL)	3	.4	1.1	29.7
Reliance Retail	1	.1	.4	30.0
Sidhhartha Construction Co.	1	.1	.4	30.4
Imphal Free Press	1	.1	.4	30.7
Central Coal Field Ltd. (CCL)	7	1.0	2.5	33.2
Shirdi Sai Construction Co.	1	.1	.4	33.6
ABCI Infrastructure Pvt. Ltd.	2	.3	.7	34.3
Essar Steel	4	.6	1.4	35.7
Pradhan Mantri Gram Sadak Yojana (PMGSY)	7	1.0	2.5	38.2
Adhunik Group	1	.1	.4	38.5
Cacher Paper Mill (CPM)	1	.1	.4	38.9
Janusa Oil	1	.1	.4	39.2
Uranium Corp. of India	1	.1	.4	39.6
Kanak TV	1	.1	.4	39.9
RSB Co.	2	.3	.7	40.6

Fig. 3.9 (continued)

FirmName

	Frequency	Percent	Valid Percent	Cumulative Percent
Vashishta Constructions	1	.1	.4	41.0
Muzaffarpur Road Construction Development	1	.1	.4	41.3
Prudhi Construction	1	.1	.4	41.7
Simplex Infrastructure Ltd.	3	.4	1.1	42.8
Triveni Construction	1	.1	.4	43.1
Bargara Tea Estate	1	.1	.4	43.5
Nitu Glass Hardware Shop	1	.1	.4	43.8
Midwest Granite Pvt. Ltd.	1	.1	.4	44.2
Nat. Buildings Construction Corp. (NBCC)	1	.1	.4	44.5
KFC	1	.1	.4	44.9
McDonalds	1	.1	.4	45.2
Coconut Grove	1	.1	.4	45.6
Tamil Nadu State Markets Corp. (TNSMC)	2	.3	.7	46.3
New Bharat Stone Crusher	1	.1	.4	46.6
Kerala Tourism Devel. Corp. (KTDC)	1	.1	.4	47.0
Sripur Colliery	1	.1	.4	47.3
Puthiya Thalaimurai TV	1	.1	.4	47.7
Kwality Hotel	1	.1	.4	48.1
Shivam Road & Infrastructure Pvt. Ltd.	1	.1	.4	48.4
Shell Oil Co.	1	.1	.4	48.8
Jayaswal Neco Industries Ltd. (JNIL)	3	.4	1.1	49.8
Balaji Transport	1	.1	.4	50.2
Bhardwaj Constructions	1	.1	.4	50.5
Airtel Telecom	8	1.2	2.8	53.4
Aircel Telecom	2	.3	.7	54.1
Vodofone	5	.7	1.8	55.8
Pammi Travels	1	.1	.4	56.2
Mahabir Trade Agency	1	.1	.4	56.5
Indergope Construction Co.	1	.1	.4	56.9
Gayatri ECI	1	.1	.4	57.2
Eastern Motors	1	.1	.4	57.6
Gammon India	1	.1	.4	58.0

Fig. 3.9 (continued)

FirmName

	Frequency	Percent	Valid Percent	Cumulative Percent
Asomiya Pratidan	1	.1	.4	58.3
Christian Institute of Health Services & Research	1	.1	.4	58.7
Chaubatiya Construction	1	.1	.4	59.0
Kiran Hospital	1	.1	.4	59.4
Smaridhi (United India)	1	.1	.4	59.7
Uttarbanga Sangbod	1	.1	.4	60.1
Reliance Communications	3	.4	1.1	61.1
Andhra Pradesh Mineral Devel. Corp. (APMDC)	4	.6	1.4	62.5
Kalyan Hotel	1	.1	.4	62.9
Patil Construction	1	.1	.4	63.3
Indian Railways	1	.1	.4	63.6
Sky Golden Café	1	.1	.4	64.0
Ashiyana Hotel	1	.1	.4	64.3
Hahaladdi Mining Co.	1	.1	.4	64.7
Manipur Golden Travels (MGT) Tata Motors	1	.1	.4	65.0
Shirram Power and Steel Pvt. Ltd.	1	.1	.4	65.4
SP Singla Co.	2	.3	.7	66.1
GIIS Ltd.	1	.1	.4	66.4
All India Radio (AIR)	1	.1	.4	66.8
Sarda Energy & Minerals Ltd.	1	.1	.4	67.1
Punya Motors Pvt. Ltd.	1	.1	.4	67.5
Canchi Indane Service	1	.1	.4	67.8
Hari Construction Co.	1	.1	.4	68.2
M/S Sorojini Oil	1	.1	.4	68.6
Padumani Tea Estate	1	.1	.4	68.9
NS Mall	1	.1	.4	69.3
Kherem Tea Estate	1	.1	.4	69.6
Taaza News	1	.1	.4	70.0
Hindustan Daily	1	.1	.4	70.3
Spica Projects & Infrastructures Pvt. Ltd.	1	.1	.4	70.7
New Woodlands Hotel	1	.1	.4	71.0
J.C. Bamford Excavators Ltd. (JCB)	2	.3	.7	71.7

Fig. 3.9 (continued)

	Frequency	Percent	Valid Percent	Cumulative Percent
NKC Projects Pvt. Ltd.	1	.1	.4	72.1
Jawarhalal Nehru Inst. of Medical Sciences	1	.1	.4	72.4
ANA Mining Pvt. Ltd.	1	.1	.4	72.8
Surjagod Lloyds Metals & Energy Ltd.	1	.1	.4	73.1
Pandam Daily	1	.1	.4	73.5
Ram Kripal Singh Construction	1	.1	.4	73.9
Nagarjuna Construction Co,	1	.1	.4	74.2
A-One Bicycle Co.	1	.1	.4	74.6
Ramie Construction Co.	1	.1	.4	74.9
Nissan Motor Co.	1	.1	.4	75.3
Puja Enterprises	1	.1	.4	75.6
Hindalco Industries	3	.4	1.1	76.7
Disam Tea Estate	1	.1	.4	77.0
Nutan Construction Co.	1	.1	.4	77.4
Singjamei Supermarket	1	.1	.4	77.7
Viacom 18 Motion Pictures	1	.1	.4	78.1
Gas (India) Ltd. (GAIL)	2	.3	.7	78.8
Bihar State Bridge Construction Corp. (BSBCCO)	1	.1	.4	79.2
Jammu and Kashmir Bank	2	.3	.7	79.9
SPR Construction Co.	1	.1	.4	80.2
Dimapur Gas Agency	1	.1	.4	80.6
Cuttack Central Cooperative Bank	1	.1	.4	80.9
Meghalaya Power Dist. Corp. Ltd.	1	.1	.4	81.3
Meg Mini Tea Co.	1	.1	.4	81.6
Mornoi Tea Estate	1	.1	.4	82.0
Mahavir Medicos	1	.1	.4	82.3
Manipur Motors	1	.1	.4	82.7
West Bengal State Electricity Distribution Co. Ltd.	1	.1	.4	83.0
DGR Velocity	1	.1	.4	83.4
Lankesh Patrike	1	.1	.4	83.7
Hindustan Construction Co.	2	.3	.7	84.5
Wellson Energy Co. Pvt. Ltd.	1	.1	.4	84.8
Dinraat News Channel	1	.1	.4	85.2

Fig. 3.9 (continued)

	Frequency	Percent	Valid Percent	Cumulative Percent
Dehingiya Tea Estate	1	.1	.4	85.5
Kopli Tea Estate	1	.1	.4	85.9
Rani Beauty Parlor	1	.1	.4	86.2
Rajdhar Coal Siding	1	.1	.4	86.6
Hyundai	1	.1	.4	86.9
Baba Hans Construction Co.	1	.1	.4	87.3
Tripura Gramin Bank	1	.1	.4	87.6
North Eastern Coalfield Coal India Ltd.	1	.1	.4	88.0
MKB Tea Garden	1	.1	.4	88.3
Oil India Ltd.	2	.3	.7	89.0
Chandra Talkies	2	.3	.7	89.8
Jyoti Cinema	2	.3	.7	90.5
Amar Agency	1	.1	.4	90.8
Prakash Cinema	1	.1	.4	91.2
Bhanu Sagar Cinema Hall	1	.1	.4	91.5
Shyam Cinema Hall	1	.1	.4	91.9
Kanubari Tea Estate	2	.3	.7	92.6
M/S Puna & Hunda Construction	1	.1	.4	92.9
Sarhad	1	.1	.4	93.3
The Shillong Times	1	.1	.4	93.6
Reasonable Enterprises	1	.1	.4	94.0
Brahmaputra Fuel Centre	1	.1	.4	94.3
RS Agency	1	.1	.4	94.7
Chandrika Malayalam Daily	1	.1	.4	95.1
Phaneng Tea Garden	1	.1	.4	95.4
Kolkata-Basa Enterprises	1	.1	.4	95.8
Rising Kashmir	1	.1	.4	96.1
Emerald Estate	1	.1	.4	96.5
Seleng Tea Estate	1	.1	.4	96.8
Go Rakisha Samiti	1	.1	.4	97.2
Redding Construction Co,	1	.1	.4	97.5
Times Now	1	.1	.4	97.9
Daily Aaj	1	.1	.4	98.2
Sai Construction	1	.1	.4	98.6

Fig. 3.9 (continued)

		Frequency	Percent	Valid Percent	Cumulative Percent
	Sati Tea Estate	1	.1	.4	98.9
	Shau Mahamaya Jt. Venture	1	.1	.4	99.3
	Jindal Co.	1	.1	.4	99.6
	Visah Mega Mart	1	.1	.4	100.0
	Total	283	42.2	100.0	
Missing	System	387	57.8		
Total		670	100.0		

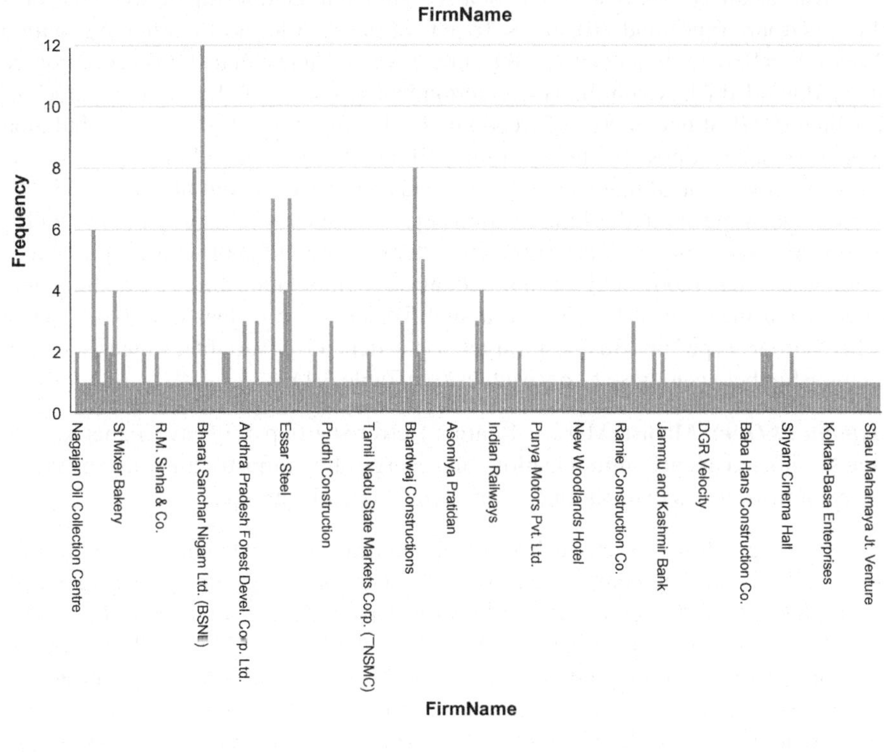

Fig. 3.9 (continued)

capitalism, Western liberalism's cultural norms and values, and against ethnic or religious groups, and individuals from those groups. Accordingly, Islamic extremist groups are considered "hybrid" terrorist organizations.

At a more granular level, business targets are sorted out to reflect those "structuralist" and "non-structuralist" characteristics. The "structuralist" category is comprised of business targets symbolic of links to capitalism, modernization, or globalization, such as (1) "energy/alloy" targets, (2) "construction sites," (3) "telecommunications" infrastructure, and (3) "banking/financial institutions".[25] In contrast, the "non structuralist category is comprised of targets that symbolize terrorist group emphasis on individuals or groups of people. Those targets include: (1) "hospitals/medical facilities," (2) "private establishments," (3) newspaper/print," (4) "private transportation," and (5) "agriculture".

3.16 Political Ideology X Business Target-Type

The bivariate analysis reveals a statistically significant relationship between the variables, "Group-Type" and "Business Target" at the 0.05 level of confidence, with a Pearson Chi Square statistic of 75.789 and a "p-value" of less than 0.001 at one degree of freedom (1 d.f.). A continuity correction measure of 73.534 with a "p-value" of less than 0.001 at one degree of freedom (1 d.f.) used for a 2×2 cross-tabulation table also makes it possible to reject the null hypothesis of no relation between the variables. It was found that 0 cells (0.0%) had an expected count of less than 5.[26]

In terms of the strength of the relationship, a "Cramer's V" score of 0.484 with a significance score of less than 0.001 and a "Phi" score of 0.484 with a significance score of less than 0.001 suggests a moderate strength relationship. A Goodman and Kruskal *tau* measure of 0.235 with a significance score of less than 0.001 when either "Group Type" or "Business Target" is the dependent variable, suggests a weak relationship between those two variables (see Table 3.1).

Hypothesis One: Maoist (Marxist-Leninist) terrorist groups will have higher rates of attacks directed at telecommunications and energy alloy infrastructure, and banking/ financial institutions than nationalist-irredentist terrorist groups.

For "energy/alloy" targets such as mines and firms involved in the mineral extraction and the ore refinement process, nationalist-irredentist groups placed first with a full 28.9% (44/152 acts). Indian Maoist groups ranked second with 16.0% (52/ 326 acts). Anonymous terrorist assaults ranked third with 9.2% of all anonymous incidents (14/153 acts) aimed at "energy/alloy" targets. There was one chronicled Islamic extremist attack, out of sixteen Islamic extremist acts recorded, that was directed at an "energy/alloy" target (6.3%). There were no recorded attacks against "energy alloy" targets by "right-wing" Hindutva groups. Energy/alloy targets made up 16.9% (111/656 acts) of the total number of terrorist assaults [34, 98].[27]

---

[25] This category includes "construction sites" because work to pave roads is linked to anti-government modernization and anti-globalization sentiments expressed by Maoist terrorist group leaders who believe new roads will decrease their security that forests in rural areas provide.

[26] N = 323 with 347 missing cases.

[27] There is no authoritative interpretation to explain the results for Maoist terrorist groups, but it is possible those patterns might be somehow linked to the notion that "energy and alloy" targets are tied to indigenous peoples, their rights to natural resources, and perceived resource exploitation by India's national and state governments. Kumari points to constituent group support overlap

Table 3.1 Relative frequency of Indian business targets by group-type, 2013–2018 (summary statistics)

Case processing summary

	Valid		Cases missing		Total	
	N	Percent	N	Percent	N	Percent
GroupTy * Bus.Target	323	48.2%	347	51.8%	670	100.0%

GroupTy * Bus.Target Crosstabulation

			Bus.Target		
			Construction	Private establishments	Total
GroupTy	Marxist-Leninist	Count	188	35	223
		% within GroupTy	84.3%	15.7%	100.0%
		% within Bus.Target	83.9%	35.4%	69.0%
		% of Total	58.2%	10.8%	69.0%
	Nationalist-Irredentist	Count	36	64	100
		% within GroupTy	36.0%	64.0%	100.0%
		% within Bus.Target	16.1%	64.6%	31.0%
		% of total	11.1%	19.8%	31.0%
Total		Count	224	99	323
		% within GroupTy	69.3%	30.7%	100.0%
		% within Bus.Target	100.0%	100.0%	100.0%
		% of total	69.3%	30.7%	100.0%

Chi-square tests

	Value	df	Asymptotic significance (2-sided)	Exact significance (2-sided)	Exact significance (1-sided)
Pearson chi-square	75.789[a]	1	< 0.001		
Continuity correction[b]	73.534	1	< 0.001		
Likelihood ratio	73.607	1	< 0.001		
Fisher's exact test				< 0.001	< 0.001
Linear-by-linear association	75.555	1	< 0.001		
N of valid cases	323				

(continued)

Table 3.1 (continued)

Directional measures

			Value	Asymptotic standard error[c]
Nominal by nominal	Lambda	Symmetric	0.286	0.079
		GroupTy dependent	0.290	0.084
		Bus.Target dependent	0.283	0.086
	Goodman and Kruskal tau	GroupTy dependent	0.235	0.051
		Bus.Target dependent	0.235	0.051

Directional measures

			Approximate T[d]	Approximate Significance
Nominal by nominal	Lambda	Symmetric	3.202	0.001
		GroupTy dependent	2.954	0.003
		Bus.Target dependent	2.835	0.005
	Goodman and Kruskal tau	GroupTy dependent		< 0.001[e]
		Bus.Target dependent		< 0.001[e]

Symmetric measures

		Value	Approximate significance
Nominal by nominal	Phi	0.484	< 0.001
	Cramer's V	0.484	< 0.001
N of valid cases		323	

[a]0 cells (0.0%) have expected count less than 5. The minimum expected count is 30.65
[b]Computed only for a 2 × 2 table
[c]Not assuming the null hypothesis
[d]Using the asymptotic standard error assuming the null hypothesis
[e]Based on chi-square approximation

In comparison, for "construction sites," Indian Maoist (Marxist-Leninist) groups had the highest rate of attack with a full 57.7% (188/326 acts) of all Maoist attacks, while "anonymous" terrorist groups ranked second with 24.2% (37/153 acts). In

---

between Maoist and nationalist-irredentist groups across group lines such as peasants and Adavasi, and across "intermediate" and "lower" caste lines; that might also have influenced targeting patterns. The extremely low rate for Maoist terrorist group attacks against "banking/financial institutions" was also at odds with the expected results.

turn, it was found that "national-irredentist" terrorist groups followed one half a percentage point behind with 23.7% (36/152 acts) of the total. There were no recorded terrorist attacks against construction sites, either by Islamic extremist terrorist groups or "right-wing" Hindutva terrorist outfits. Terrorist assaults aimed at "construction sites" made up 39.8% (261/656 acts) of the total number of terrorist incidents.

When compared to other types of terrorist groups, Islamic extremist terrorist groups had the highest attack rate against "telecommunications" targets with 50.0% (8/16 acts).[28] In turn, the rates for anonymous attacks, Maoist terrorist group attacks, and "right-wing" Hindutva attacks were clustered together very closely, with 12.4% for anonymous attacks (19/153 acts), 11.3% for Maoist terrorist attacks (37/326 acts), and 11.1% for "right-wing" Hindutva attacks (1/9 acts). Indian "nationalist-irredentist" groups" followed very far behind with only 1.3% (2/152 acts) directed against telecommunications infrastructure. Telecommunications targets comprised 10.2% (67/656 acts) of the total.

At 12.5%, Islamic extremist groups also had the highest rate of "banking/financial institutions" attacks (2/16 acts). Anonymous group attacks followed very far behind at 2.0% (3/153 acts), while Indian "nationalist-irredentist" groups placed third at 1.3% (2/152 acts). Interestingly enough, Maoist terrorist groups had the lowest rate of "banking/financial institutions" attacks with under one percent at 0.3% (1/326 acts). There were no "banking/financial" target attacks by "right-wing" Hindutva terrorist organizations. Overall, "banking/financial institutions" terrorist attacks made up only 1.2% of the total, with a paltry eight out of 656 events. The results were not supportive of Hypothesis One and it is rejected[29] (see Table 3.2).

Hypothesis Two: As "non-structuralist" Indian terrorist groups, nationalist-irredentist terrorist groups will have higher rates of attacks against hospitals/medical facilities, private establishments, newspaper/print, private transportation and agricultural targets than Maoist (Marxist-Leninist) terrorist groups.

The results demonstrate there was little focus overall on "hospitals/medical facilities" by the different types of Indian terrorist groups examined. Islamic extremists again had the highest percentage rate of attacks with 6.3% (1/16 acts) against this business target type, followed by anonymous attacks with 3.3% (5/153 acts).

In comparison, the focus of Maoist terrorist groups in India on hospitals and medical facilities was extremely low at less than one percent with 0.6% (2/326 acts). There were no terrorist attacks against "hospitals/medical facilities" recorded either for nationalist-irredentist terrorist groups or for "right-wing" Hindutva terrorist groups. Terrorist assaults against "hospital/medical facilities" only comprised 1.2% (8/656 acts) of the total.

---

[28] Some scripted accounts also point to terrorist group security concerns as a reason why at least some telecommunications infrastructure, such as cell phone towers, were attacked.

[29] It is possible to trim the tail of the terrorist event data distribution curve to account for extreme outliers and remove them from the analysis. Accordingly, if the business target categories "agriculture" (0.06% or 4/656 acts), "transportation" (1.1% or 7/656 acts), "banking/financial institutions" (1.2% or 8/656 acts), are trimmed, it is still necessary to reject Hypothesis One.

Table 3.2 Relative frequency of Indian business targets by group-type, 2013–2018

Case processing summary

	Valid		Cases missing		Total	
	N	Percent	N	Percent	N	Percent
GroupTy * Bus.Target	656	97.9%	14	2.1%	670	100.0%

GroupTy * Bus.Target Crosstabulation

			Bus.Target		
			Energy/ Alloy	Construction	Hospitals/ Medical
GroupTy	Marxist-Leninist	Count	52	188	2
		% within GroupTy	16.0%	57.7%	0.6%
		% within Bus.Target	46.8%	72.0%	25.0%
		% of total	7.9%	28.7%	0.3%
	Nationalist-Irredentist	Count	44	36	0
		% within GroupTy	28.9%	23.7%	0.0%
		% within Bus.Target	39.6%	13.8%	0.0%
		% of total	6.7%	5.5%	0.0%
	Anonymous	Count	14	37	5
		% within GroupTy	9.2%	24.2%	3.3%
		% within Bus.Target	12.6%	14.2%	62.5%
		% of total	2.1%	5.6%	0.8%
	Islamic extremist	Count	1	0	1
		% within GroupTy	6.3%	0.0%	6.3%
		% within Bus.Target	0.9%	0.0%	12.5%
		% of total	0.2%	0.0%	0.2%
	Right wing	Count	0	0	0
		% within GroupTy	0.0%	0.0%	0.0%
		% within Bus.Target	0.0%	0.0%	0.0%
		% of total	0.0%	0.0%	0.0%
Total		Count	111	261	8
		% within GroupTy	16.9%	39.8%	1.2%

(continued)

Table 3.2 (continued)

GroupTy * Bus.Target Crosstabulation

			Bus.Target		
			Energy/ Alloy	Construction	Hospitals/ Medical
		% within Bus.sTarget	100.0%	100.0%	100.0%
		% of Total	16.9%	39.8%	1.2%

GroupTy * Bus.Target Crosstabulation

			Bus.Target		
			Private establishments	Tele-communications	Newspaper/ Print
GroupTy	Marxist-Leninist	Count	35	37	4
		% within GroupTy	10.7%	11.3%	1.2%
		% within Bus.Target	21.9%	55.2%	12.5%
		% of total	5.3%	5.6%	0.6%
	Nationalist-Irredentist	Count	64	2	2
		% within GroupTy	42.1%	1.3%	1.3%
		% within Bus.Target	40.0%	3.0%	6.3%
		% of total	9.8%	0.3%	0.3%
	Anonymous	Count	51	19	24
		% within GroupTy	33.3%	12.4%	15.7%
		% within Bus.Target	31.9%	28.4%	75.0%
		% of total	7.8%	2.9%	3.7%
	Islamic extremist	Count	3	8	1
		% within GroupTy	18.8%	50.0%	6.3%
		% within Bus.Target	1.9%	11.9%	3.1%
		% of total	0.5%	1.2%	0.2%
	Right wing	Count	7	1	1
		% within GroupTy	77.8%	11.1%	11.1%
		% within Bus.Target	4.4%	1.5%	3.1%

(continued)

Table 3.2 (continued)

GroupTy * Bus.Target Crosstabulation

			Bus.Target		
			Private establishments	Tele-communications	Newspaper/ Print
		% of total	1.1%	0.2%	0.2%
Total		Count	160	67	32
		% within GroupTy	24.4%	10.2%	4.9%
		% within Bus.Target	100.0%	100.0%	100.0%
		% of total	24.4%	10.2%	4.9%

GroupTy * Bus.Target Crosstabulation

			Bus.Target		
			Banking/ Finance	Transportation	Agriculture
GroupTy	Marxist-Leninist	Count	1	5	2
		% within GroupTy	0.3%	1.5%	0.6%
		% within Bus.Target	12.5%	71.4%	100.0%
		% of total	0.2%	0.8%	0.3%
	Nationalist-Irredentist	Count	2	2	0
		% within GroupTy	1.3%	1.3%	0.0%
		% within Bus.Target	25.0%	28.6%	0.0%
		% of total	0.3%	0.3%	0.0%
	Anonymous	Count	3	0	0
		% within GroupTy	2.0%	0.0%	0.0%
		% within Bus.Target	37.5%	0.0%	0.0%
		% of total	0.5%	0.0%	0.0%
	Islamic extremist	Count	2	0	0
		% within GroupTy	12.5%	0.0%	0.0%
		% within Bus.Target	25.0%	0.0%	0.0%
		% of total	0.3%	0.0%	0.0%
	Right wing	Count	0	0	0

(continued)

Table 3.2 (continued)

GroupTy * Bus.Target Crosstabulation

			Bus.Target		
			Banking/ Finance	Transportation	Agriculture
		% within GroupTy	0.0%	0.0%	0.0%
		% within Bus.Target	0.0%	0.0%	0.0%
		% of total	0.0%	0.0%	0.0%
Total		Count	8	7	2
		% within GroupTy	1.2%	1.1%	0.3%
		% within Bus.Target	100.0%	100.0%	100.0%
		% of total	1.2%	1.1%	0.3%

GroupTy * Bus.Target Crosstabulation

			Total
GroupTy	Marxist-Leninist	Count	326
		% within GroupTy	100.0%
		% within Bus.Target	49.7%
		% of total	49.7%
	Nationalist-Irredentist	Count	152
		% within GroupTy	100.0%
		% within Bus.Target	23.2%
		% of total	23.2%
	Anonymous	Count	153
		% within GroupTy	100.0%
		% within Bus.Target	23.3%
		% of total	23.3%
	Islamic extremist	Count	16
		% within GroupTy	100.0%
		% within Bus.Target	2.4%
		% of total	2.4%
	Right wing	Count	9
		% within GroupTy	100.0%
		% within Bus.Target	1.4%
		% of total	1.4%
Total		Count	656

(continued)

Table 3.2 (continued)

GroupTy * Bus.Target Crosstabulation

			Total
		% within GroupTy	100.0%
		% within Bus.Target	100.0%
		% of total	100.0%

In sharp contrast to the low interest found for attacks against hospitals and medical facilities, the results revealed that terrorist group interest in attacks against private enterprises was much higher. In fact, the percentage rate of attacks directed at "private establishments" was very high across several terrorist group-types. For example, over three-quarters of all "right-wing" Hindutva terrorist attacks at 77.8% (7/9 acts) were directed at "private establishments," while nationalist-irredentist groups devoted 42.1% of their attacks (64/152 acts) at "private establishment" targets.

That pattern of high "private establishment" focus continued when anonymous acts were scrutinized. Anonymous terrorist attacks focused on "private establishment" targets 33.3% of the time (51/153 acts). Islamic extremist terrorist group attacks, by contrast, staked out the middle ground with 18.8% (3/16 acts) aimed at "private establishments." At the opposite end of the spectrum, Maoist groups attacked "private establishments" only about one-tenth of the time at 10.7% (35/326 acts). In total, "private establishment" terrorist attacks made up a full 24.4% of the total (160/656 acts).

Overall, the 4.9% rate found for newspaper/print target terrorist attacks (32/656 acts) was very low. When terrorist assaults against newspaper reporters or other printed media targets were examined, it was found that anonymous terrorist attacks ranked first with 15.7% (24/153 acts). A "right-wing" Hindutva terrorist assault against a "newspaper/print" target accounted for 11.1% of all Hindutva attacks (1/9 acts).

One unexpected finding was Islamic extremist terrorist groups in India placed little emphasis on terrorist assaults against newspaper/printed media targets with only 6.3% (1/16 acts) of Islamic extremist attacks aimed at those targets. Nationalist-irredentist terrorist groups paid even less attention to newspaper/printed media targets than Islamic extremist terrorist groups did with only 1.3% of nationalist-irredentist attacks (2/152 acts). Maoist terrorist groups accounted for the smallest share of attacks directed against newspaper/printed media targets with only 1.2% (4/326 acts).

There was even less interest demonstrated by Indian terrorist groups for "private transportation" and "agricultural" targets. For "private transportation" targets, Maoist terrorist group attacks comprised 1.5% of the total (5/326 acts), while the focus of "nationalist-irredentist" terrorist groups was about the same at 1.3% (2/152 acts). There were no chronicled "private transportation" attacks for anonymous actors, Islamic extremist groups, and "right-wing" Hindutva terrorist groups. "Private transportation" attacks comprised 1.1% of the total (7/656 acts), about the same rate as found for "hospital medical/facilities (1.2%) and "banking and financial institutions" (1.2%).

Still, the results suggest that "agricultural" targets were of least interest to Indian terrorist groups and anonymous stakeholders. Maoist groups in India attacked "agriculture" targets 0.6% of the time (2/326 acts); there were no terrorist attacks against agriculture targets recorded for any other type of terrorist group. In fact, the percentage of terrorist assaults devoted to "agricultural" targets made up even less of the total than did "private transportation" attacks, with only 0.3% (2/656 acts). The results were not supportive of Hypothesis Two and it is rejected.

3.17 Political Ideology X Numbers of Deaths

In the theoretical framework, "structuralist" terrorist groups such as Maoist (Marxist-Leninist) groups are expected to target business interests more closely associated with world systems conflict, such as the fierce struggle against capitalism, modernization, or globalization, and government targets symbolic of that ideology and those contemporary processes.

In comparison, "non-structuralist" terrorist groups, with their emphasis on specific ethnic groups and individuals, including those from ethnic groups targeted, are expected to place more emphasis on civilian targets. The underlying struggle against world systems such as capitalism is perceived here to be more abstract than struggle against particular, ethnic, religious, or racial groups or individuals from those groups, with less emphasis on efforts to inflict personal injury or death. It follows that "non-structuralist" terrorist assaults, with their greater focus on civilian business targets, should have a comparatively higher number of terrorist attacks with at least one fatality.

Hypothesis Three: Nationalist-Irredentist terrorist groups will have a higher rate of attacks that caused between one and fifteen deaths than Maoist (Marxist-Leninist) terrorist groups.

Hypothesis Four: Islamic extremist terrorist groups, with their broad range of targets, will have a higher rate of attacks that caused between one and fifteen deaths than Maoist (Marxist-Leninist) terrorist groups and nationalist-irredentist terrorist groups.

A cross-tabulation table analysis with the variables, "Group-Type" and "Deaths" suggests there is a statistically significant relationship between the two variables. With a Pearson Chi Square statistic of 21.082 and a "p-value" of less than 0.001 at 2 degrees of freedom (2 d.f.), it is possible to reject the null hypothesis of no relation between the variables at the 0.5 level of confidence. It was found that 16.7% cells (1 cell) had an expected count of less than 5. The mean for numbers of dead in terrorist attacks was low at 0.18.[30]

[30] N = 479 with 191 missing cases. Recode (the same variable) commands: "Group-Type": 1 → 1; 2 → 2; 4 → 4; ELSE → SYSMIS; "Deaths": 0 = 0; 1 = 1–15; 2 = 16–30; ELSE → SYSMIS. The

A Goodman and Kruskal *tau* diagnostic of 0.008 with a significance score of 0.024 when "Group-Type" is the dependent variable suggests a weak relationship between the variables. A Goodman and Kruskal *tau* diagnostic of 0.044 with a significance score of less than 0.001 when "Deaths" is the dependent variable suggests a weak relationship. In addition, a "Cramer's V" score of 0.210 with a significance score of less than 0.001 and a "Phi" value of 0.210 with a significance score of less than 0.001 also suggest a weak relationship between the variables (see Table 3.3).

The data distributions suggest that with 50.0% (8/16 acts), Islamic extremist groups had the highest rate of terrorist assaults in India that killed between one and fifteen people. Nationalist-Irredentist terrorist attacks with 14.0% (19/136 acts) and anonymous attacks with 14.0% (20/143) ranked second. In turn, thirty-five Maoist (Marxist-Leninist) group terrorist attacks in India resulted in the death of one to fifteen people 10.7% of the time (35/327 acts). There were no recorded lethal "right-wing" Hindutva terrorist assaults. Those data findings were supportive of Hypotheses Three and Hypothesis Four, and both were accepted as valid (see Table 3.4).

3.18 Political Ideology X Numbers of Injuries

Trends for number of injuries mirrored patterns for numbers of deaths, with structuralist terrorist groups having a lower number of terrorist assaults that caused between one and fifteen injuries, as compared to non-structuralist terrorist groups that were expected to put special focus on civilians. The following hypotheses about terrorist group-type and injury rates are tested for validity.

Hypothesis Five: Nationalist-irredentist terrorist groups will have a higher rate of attacks that caused between one and fifteen injuries than Maoist (Marxist-Leninist) terrorist groups.

Hypothesis Six: Islamic extremist terrorist groups, with their broad range of targets, will have a higher rate of attacks that caused between one and fifteen injuries than Maoist (Marxist-Leninist) terrorist groups and nationalist-irredentist terrorist groups.

A Pearson Chi Square statistic of 27.540 with a "*p*-value" of less than 0.001 at 1 degree of freedom (1 d.f.) makes it possible to reject the null hypothesis of no relation between the variables "Political Ideology" (i.e., "Group-Type") and "Injuries" at the 0.05 level of confidence. A continuity correction score of 26.128 with a significance score of less than 0.001 at 1 degree of freedom (1 d.f.) also indicates a significant and substantive relationship. It was found that 0 cells (0.0%) had an expected count of less than 5. The mean for number of injuries in terrorist assaults was low at 0.51.[31]

---

mean number of deaths (0.18) involved a test with 633 cases. In the crosstabulation test, the total breakdown of death free terrorist assaults was 87.1% (417/479 acts); 12.9% (62.419 acts) caused between one and fifteen deaths.

[31] N = 432 with 238 missing cases. Recode (the same variable) commands: "Group-Type": 1 → 1; 2 → 2; ELSE → SYSMIS; "Injuries": 0 = 0; 1 = 1–15; 2 = 16–30. For the mean number of

Table 3.3 Relative frequency of group-type by numbers of dead in Indian terrorist attacks 2013–2018 (0 = 0; 1=1 through 15) (summary statistics)

Case processing summary

	Valid		Cases missing		Total	
	N	Percent	N	Percent	N	Percent
GroupTy * Deaths	479	71.5%	191	28.5%	670	100.0%

GroupTy * Deaths Crosstabulation

			Deaths		
			0	1	Total
GroupTy	Marxist-Leninist	Count	292	35	327
		% within GroupTy	89.3%	10.7%	100.0%
		% within deaths	70.0%	56.5%	68.3%
		% of total	61.0%	7.3%	68.3%
	Nationalist-Irredentist	Count	117	19	136
		% within GroupTy	86.0%	14.0%	100.0%
		% within deaths	28.1%	30.6%	28.4%
		% of total	24.4%	4.0%	28.4%
	Islamic extremist	Count	8	8	16
		% within GroupTy	50.0%	50.0%	100.0%
		% within deaths	1.9%	12.9%	3.3%
		% of total	1.7%	1.7%	3.3%
Total		Count	417	62	479
		% within GroupTy	87.1%	12.9%	100.0%
		% within deaths	100.0%	100.0%	100.0%
		% of total	87.1%	12.9%	100.0%

Chi-square tests

	Value	Df	Asymptotic significance (2-sided)
Pearson chi-square	21.082[a]	2	< 0.001
Likelihood ratio	14.410	2	< 0.001
Linear-by-linear association	15.570	1	< 0.001
N of valid cases	479		

Directional measure

			Value	Asymptotic standard error[b]
Nominal by nominal	Lambda	Symmetric	0.000	0.000
		GroupTy dependent	0.000	0.000
		Deaths dependent	0.000	0.000
	Goodman and Kruskal tau	GroupTy dependent	0.008	0.006
		Deaths dependent	0.044	0.027

(continued)

Table 3.3 (continued)

Directional measures

			Approximate T	Approximate significance
Nominal by nominal	Lambda	Symmetric	.[c]	.[c]
		GroupTy dependent	.[c]	.[c]
		Deaths dependent	.[c]	.[c]
	Goodman and Kruskal tau	GroupTy dependent		0.024[d]
		Deaths dependent		< 0.001[d]

Symmetric measures

		Value	Approximate Significance
Nominal by nominal	Phi	0.210	< 0.001
	Cramer's V	0.210	< 0.001
N of valid cases		479	

[a]1 cells (16.7%) have expected count less than 5. The minimum expected count is 2.07
[b]Not assuming the null hypothesis
[c]Cannot be computed because the asymptotic standard error equals zero
[d]Based on chi-square approximation

The relationship between the variables, "Political Ideology" and "Injuries," appears weak as a Goodman and Kruskal *tau* value of 0.064 with a significance score of less than 0.001 when "Group-Type" is the dependent variable, indicates a weak relationship. A "Cramer's V" value of 0.252 with a significance score of less than 0.001 and a "Phi" value of 0.252 with a significance score of less than 0.001 also indicates a weak relationship (see Table 3.5).

The data distribution suggests that Indian nationalist-irredentist terrorist groups and anonymous acts had the highest rates of terrorist assaults that injured between one and fifteen people. Nationalist-Irredentist terrorist attacks involved one to fifteen injuries 31.9% (43/135 acts) of the time, while anonymous terrorist acts caused injuries 31.4% of the time (44/140 acts). Islamic extremist terrorist attacks ranked third with 31.3% (5/16 acts). At the other extreme, Maoist terrorist groups (33/297) and "right wing" Hindutva terrorist groups (1/9 acts) both caused injuries to between one and fifteen people 11.1% of the time. Those data findings are supportive of Hypothesis Five but not supportive of Hypothesis Six, and Hypothesis Five is accepted as valid (see Table 3.6).

---

injuries (0.51) test, N = 599. The total breakdown for numbers of injuries: 471/597 acts (78.9%) were injury-free events; 126/597 acts caused between one and fifteen injuries.

Table 3.4 Relative frequency of group-type by numbers of dead in Indian terrorist attacks, 2013–2018 (0 = 0; 1=1 through 15)

Case processing summary

	Valid		Cases missing		Total	
	N	Percent	N	Percent	N	Percent
GroupTy * Deaths	631	94.2%	39	5.8%	670	100.0%

GroupTy * Deaths Crosstabulation

			Deaths		
			0	1	Total
GroupTy	Marxist-Leninist	Count	292	35	327
		% within GroupTy	89.3%	10.7%	100.0%
		% within deaths	53.2%	42.7%	51.8%
		% of total	46.3%	5.5%	51.8%
	Nationalist-Irredentist	Count	117	19	136
		% within GroupTy	86.0%	14.0%	100.0%
		% within deaths	21.3%	23.2%	21.6%
		% of total	18.5%	3.0%	21.6%
	Anonymous	Count	123	20	143
		% within GroupTy	86.0%	14.0%	100.0%
		% within deaths	22.4%	24.4%	22.7%
		% of total	19.5%	3.2%	22.7%
	Islamic extremist	Count	8	8	16
		% within GroupTy	50.0%	50.0%	100.0%
		% within deaths	1.5%	9.8%	2.5%
		% of total	1.3%	1.3%	2.5%
	Right wing	Count	9	0	9
		% within GroupTy	100.0%	0.0%	100.0%
		% within deaths	1.6%	0.0%	1.4%
		% of total	1.4%	0.0%	1.4%
Total		Count	549	82	631
		% within GroupTy	87.0%	13.0%	100.0%
		% within deaths	100.0%	100.0%	100.0%
		% of total	87.0%	13.0%	100.0%

3.19 Business Target-Type X Deaths

It follows from how "structuralist" terrorist groups are defined that business targets symbolic of "world systems ideologies" and processes (i.e., capitalism, globalism, modernization) should have a lower rate of terrorist attacks that killed between one

Table 3.5 Relative frequency of group-type by numbers of injuries in Indian terrorist attacks (0 = 0; 1=1 through 15) (summary statistics)

Case processing summary

	Valid		Cases missing		Total	
	N	Percent	N	Percent	N	Percent
GroupTy * Injuries	432	64.5%	238	35.5%	670	100.0%

GroupTy * Injuries Crosstabulation

			Injuries		
			0	1	Total
GroupTy	Marxist-Leninist	Count	264	33	297
		% within GroupTy	88.9%	11.1%	100.0%
		% within injuries	74.2%	43.4%	68.8%
		% of total	61.1%	7.6%	68.8%
	Nationalist-Irredentist	Count	92	43	135
		% within GroupTy	68.1%	31.9%	100.0%
		% within injuries	25.8%	56.6%	31.3%
		% of total	21.3%	10.0%	31.3%
Total		Count	356	76	432
		% within GroupTy	82.4%	17.6%	100.0%
		% within injuries	100.0%	100.0%	100.0%
		% of total	82.4%	17.6%	100.0%

Chi-square tests

	Value	df	Asymptotic significance (2-sided)	Exact significance (2-sided)	Exact significance (1-sided)
Pearson chi-square	27.540[a]	1	< 0.001		
Continuity correction[b]	26.128	1	< 0.001		
Likelihood ratio	25.739	1	< 0.001		
Fisher's exact test				< 0.001	< 0.001
Linear-by-linear association	27.476	1	< 0.001		
N of valid cases	432				

Directional measures

			Value	Asymptotic standard error[c]
Nominal by nominal	Lambda	Symmetric	0.047	0.040
		GroupTy dependent	0.074	0.062
		Injuries dependent	0.000	0.000
	Goodman and Kruskal tau	GroupTy dependent	0.064	0.025

(continued)

Table 3.5 (continued)

Directional measures

			Value	Asymptotic standard error[c]
		Injuries dependent	0.064	0.026

Directional measures

			Approximate T[d]	Approximate significance
Nominal by nominal	Lambda	Symmetric	1.149	0.251
		GroupTy dependent	1.149	0.251
		Injuries dependent	.[e]	.[e]
	Goodman and Kruskal tau	GroupTy dependent		< 0.001[f]
		Injuries dependent		< 0.001[f]

Symmetric measures

		Value	Approximate significance
Nominal by nominal	Phi	0.252	< 0.001
	Cramer's V	0.252	< 0.001
N of valid cases		432	

[a]0 cells (0.0%) have expected count less than 5. The minimum expected count is 23.75
[b]Computed only for a 2 × 2 table
[c]Not assuming the null hypothesis
[d]Using the asymptotic standard error assuming the null hypothesis
[e]Cannot be computed because the asymptotic standard error equals zero
[f]Based on chi-square approximation

and fifteen people than "non-structuralist" terrorist attacks that killed between one and fifteen people.

As previously mentioned, the idea is that "structuralist" group struggles, which highlight political grievances and economic inequalities linked to the international political system, are more abstract and symbolic compared to the flesh and bone struggles that "non-structuralist" terrorist groups wage against ethnic, religious, or racial groups and individuals from those groups. Accordingly, terrorist attacks carried out by "non-structuralist" groups should be more lethal.

Hypothesis Seven: Terrorist attacks against business targets that symbolize ethnic group or individuals (i.e., "non-structuralist" targets) will have a higher rate of terrorist attacks that caused between one and fifteen deaths than business related terrorist attacks linked to "world systems" effects and processes (i.e., "structuralist" targets).

Table 3.6 Relative frequency of group-type by numbers of injuries in Indian terrorist attacks, 2013–2018 (0 = 0; 1=1 through 15)

Case processing summary

	Valid		Cases missing		Total	
	N	Percent	N	Percent	N	Percent
GroupTy * Injuries	597	89.1%	73	10.9%	670	100.0%

GroupTy * Injuries Crosstabulation

			Injuries		
			0	1	Total
GroupTy	Marxist-Leninist	Count	264	33	297
		% within GroupTy	88.9%	11.1%	100.0%
		% within injuries	56.1%	26.2%	49.7%
		% of total	44.2%	5.5%	49.7%
	Nationalist-Irredentist	Count	92	43	135
		% within GroupTy	68.1%	31.9%	100.0%
		% within injuries	19.5%	34.1%	22.6%
		% of total	15.4%	7.2%	22.6%
	Anonymous	Count	96	44	140
		% within GroupTy	68.6%	31.4%	100.0%
		% within injuries	20.4%	34.9%	23.5%
		% of total	16.1%	7.4%	23.5%
	Islamic extremist	Count	11	5	16
		% within GroupTy	68.8%	31.3%	100.0%
		% within injuries	2.3%	4.0%	2.7%
		% of Total	1.8%	0.8%	2.7%
	Right Wing	Count	8	1	9
		% within GroupTy	88.9%	11.1%	100.0%
		% within injuries	1.7%	0.8%	1.5%
		% of total	1.3%	0.2%	1.5%
Total		Count	471	126	597
		% within GroupTy	78.9%	21.1%	100.0%
		% within injuries	100.0%	100.0%	100.0%
		% of total	78.9%	21.1%	100.0%

A Pearson Chi Square statistic of 25.175 with a "*p*-value" of less than 0.001 at 1 degree of freedom (1 d.f.) makes it possible to reject the null hypothesis of no relation between the variables, "Business Target" and "Deaths." A Continuity Correction measure of 22.462 with a "*p*-value" of less than 0.001 at 1 degree of freedom (1 d.f.) also makes it possible to reject the null hypothesis (see Table 3.7).

Table 3.7 Relative frequency of business-type target by deaths in Indian terrorist attacks (0 = 0; 1 = 1 through 15) (summary statistics)

Case processing summary

	Valid		Cases missing		Total	
	N	Percent	N	Percent	N	Percent
Bus.Target * Deaths	137	20.4%	533	79.6%	670	100.0%

Bus.Target * Deaths Crosstabulation

			Deaths		
			0	1	Total
Bus.Target	Energy/Alloy	Count	98	8	106
		% within Bus.Target	92.5%	7.5%	100.0%
		% within deaths	85.2%	36.4%	77.4%
		% of total	71.5%	5.8%	77.4%
	Newspapers/Print	Count	17	14	31
		% within Bus.Target	54.8%	45.2%	100.0%
		% within deaths	14.8%	63.6%	22.6%
		% of total	12.4%	10.2%	22.6%
Total		Count	115	22	137
		% within Bus.Target	83.9%	16.1%	100.0%
		% within deaths	100.0%	100.0%	100.0%
		% of total	83.9%	16.1%	100.0%

Chi-square tests

	Value	df	Asymptotic significance (2-sided)	Exact significance (2-sided)	Exact significance (1-sided)
Pearson chi-square	25.175[a]	1	< 0.001		
Continuity correction[b]	22.462	1	< 0.001		
Likelihood ratio	21.326	1	< 0.001		
Fisher's exact test				< 0.001	< 0.001
Linear-by-linear association	24.991	1	< 0.001		
N of valid cases	137				

Directional measures

			Value	Asymptotic Standard Error[c]
Nominal by nominal	Lambda	Symmetric	0.113	0.081
		Bus.Target dependent	0.194	0.136
		Deaths dependent	0.000	0.000

(continued)

Table 3.7 (continued)

Directional measures

			Value	Asymptotic Standard Error[c]
	Goodman and Kruskal tau	Bus.Target dependent	0.184	0.079
		Deaths dependent	0.184	0.081

Directional measures

			Approximate T[d]	Approximate significance
Nominal by nominal	Lambda	Symmetric	1.287	0.198
		Bus.Target dependent	1.287	0.198
		Deaths dependent	.[e]	.[e]
	Goodman and Kruskal tau	Bus.Target dependent		< 0.001[f]
		Deaths dependent		< 0.001[f]

Symmetric measures

		Value	Approximate significance
Nominal by nominal	Phi	0.429	< 0.001
	Cramer's V	0.429	< 0.001
N of valid cases		137	

[a]1 cells (25.0%) have expected count less than 5. The minimum expected count is 4.98
[b]Computed only for a 2 × 2 table
[c]Not assuming the null hypothesis
[d]Using the asymptotic standard error assuming the null hypothesis
[e]Cannot be computed because the asymptotic standard error equals zero
[f]Based on chi-square approximation

There was 1 cell (25.0%) that had an expected count of less than 5; the results were reported because the chance of making a "Type II" or "beta" error, where the null hypothesis was not rejected when it should be rejected, was high. This relationship was found to be weak to moderate, with a Goodman and Kruskal *tau* score of 0.184 with a significance score of less than 0.001 when "Business Target was the dependent variable, and with a "Cramer's V" value and a "Phi" value of 0.429, both with a significance score of less than 0.001.[32]

To reiterate, telecommunications targets, and energy/alloy firms, banking/finance, and construction site targets were classified as targets favored by "structuralist"

[32] N = 137 with 533 missing cases. Recode (the same variable) commands: "Business Target": 1 → 1; 6 → 6; ELSE → SYSMIS; "Deaths": 0 = 0; 1 = 1–15; ELSE → SYSMIS.

terrorist groups. It was found that terrorist assaults against "Energy/Alloy" targets killed between one and fifteen people 7.5% of the time (8/106 acts). In a similar vein, it was found terrorist assaults against "telecommunications" targets killed between one and fifteen people 10.4% of the time (7/67 acts). For "banking/finance institution" targets, the rate was a full 25.0% (2/8 acts) and the rate for construction site targets was 9.6% (23/239 acts).

For "non-structuralist" targets, the terrorist assault rate for "hospitals/medical facilities" that killed between one and fifteen people was also 25.0% (2/8 acts). In turn, "private establishments" followed with a rate of 15.6% (24/154 acts), while a full 45.2% of all terrorist attacks (14/31 acts) directed at newspaper print targets killed between one and fifteen people. There were no recorded terrorist assaults that caused at least one death for acts against "private transportation" and "agriculture" targets. (See Table 3.8).

In the analysis, the 25.0% rates for terrorist acts that killed between one and fifteen people found for "banking/financial" institutions targets and "hospitals/medical facilities" can be cancelled out across "structuralist" and" non-structuralist" target categories. Having done that, the terrorist attack rates that resulted in one to fifteen deaths were found to be much higher for "non-structuralist" business targets than for "structuralist" business targets.

Thus, for "structuralist" targets, the rate for assaults that caused between one and fifteen deaths was 27.5% (where 7.5% + 10.4% + 9.6% = 27.5%), while for "non-structuralist" related targets, the rate for terrorist assaults that caused at least one death was 60.8% (45.2% + 15.6% = 60.8%) when the rates for "banking/finance" (25.0%) and "hospitals/medical facilities" (25.0%) are removed. Hence, the results suggest there is empirical support for Hypothesis Seven; it is accepted as valid.

3.20 Business Target X Number of Perpetrators

If "non structuralist" business targets are associated with a higher rate of attacks that killed between one and fifteen people, it follows that a statistically significant and substantive relationship might exist between the number of perpetrators involved in terrorist attacks and different types of business targets. That is the case because "non-structuralist" target assaults with more intensive death and injury focus might involve more perpetrators. The following hypotheses are based on previous results that suggest terrorist attacks in India aimed at "non-structuralist" targets were linked to higher rates for attacks that killed between one and fifteen people.

Hypothesis Eight: For "non-structuralist" terrorist groups, the rates of perpetrator terrorist attacks with between 1 to 15 terrorists will be higher than corresponding rates for "structuralist" terrorist groups.

Hypothesis Nine For "non-structuralist" terrorist groups, the rates of perpetrator terrorist attacks with between 16 to 30 terrorists will be higher than corresponding rates for "structuralist" terrorist groups.

Table 3.8 Relative frequency of business-type target by numbers of dead in Indian terrorist attacks, 2013–2018 (0 = 0; 1 = 1 through 15)

Case processing summary

	Valid		Cases missing		Total	
	N	Percent	N	Percent	N	Percent
Bus.Target * Deaths	622	92.8%	48	7.2%	670	100.0%

Bus. Target * Deaths Crosstabulation

			Deaths		
			0	1	Total
Bus.Target	Energy/Alloy	Count	98	8	106
		% within Bus.Target	92.5%	7.5%	100.0%
		% within deaths	18.1%	10.0%	17.0%
		% of total	15.8%	1.3%	17.0%
	Construction	Count	216	23	239
		% within Bus.Target	90.4%	9.6%	100.0%
		% within deaths	39.9%	28.7%	38.4%
		% of total	34.7%	3.7%	38.4%
	Hospitals/Medical	Count	6	2	8
		% within Bus.Target	75.0%	25.0%	100.0%
		% within deaths	1.1%	2.5%	1.3%
		% of total	1.0%	0.3%	1.3%
	Private establishments	Count	130	24	154
		% within Bus.Target	84.4%	15.6%	100.0%
		% within deaths	24.0%	30.0%	24.8%
		% of total	20.9%	3.9%	24.8%
	Telecommunications	Count	60	7	67
		% within Bus.Target	89.6%	10.4%	100.0%
		% within deaths	11.1%	8.8%	10.8%
		% of total	9.6%	1.1%	10.8%
	Newspapers/Print	Count	17	14	31
		% within Bus.Target	54.8%	45.2%	100.0%
		% within deaths	3.1%	17.5%	5.0%
		% of total	2.7%	2.3%	5.0%
	Banking/Finance	Count	6	2	8
		% within Bus.Target	75.0%	25.0%	100.0%
		% within deaths	1.1%	2.5%	1.3%
		% of total	1.0%	0.3%	1.3%

(continued)

Table 3.8 (continued)

Bus. Target * Deaths Crosstabulation

			Deaths		
			0	1	Total
	Transportation	Count	7	0	7
		% within Bus.Target	100.0%	0.0%	100.0%
		% within deaths	1.3%	0.0%	1.1%
		% of total	1.1%	0.0%	1.1%
	Agriculture	Count	2	0	2
		% within Bus.Target	100.0%	0.0%	100.0%
		% within deaths	0.4%	0.0%	0.3%
		% of total	0.3%	0.0%	0.3%
Total		Count	542	80	622
		% within Bus.Target	87.1%	12.9%	100.0%
		% within deaths	100.0%	100.0%	100.0%
		% of total	87.1%	12.9%	100.0%

A Pearson Chi Square statistic of 8.501 with a "*p*-value" of 0.014 at 2 degrees of freedom (2 d.f.) makes it possible to reject the null hypothesis of no relation between the two variables, "Business Target" and "Number of Perpetrators." One cell or 16.7% of the total number of cells has an expected count of less than 5 (see Table 3.9).

The relationship between the variables is very weak with a Goodman and Kruskal *tau* score of 0.014 with a significance score of 0.114 when "Business Target" was the dependent variable, and a "Cramer's V" value of 0.234 with a significance score of 0.014, and a "Phi" value of 0.234 with a significance score of 0.014.[33]

When "low" numbers of perpetrators of between 1 and 15 were examined across business target-type, no discernable patterns were illuminated. Because of the sharper focus on ethnic groups and individuals that characterized "non-structuralist terrorist groups," between 2013 and 2018, the expected results were that "non-structuralist" terrorist groups would also favor attacks with large numbers of perpetrators.

Overall, the results did not conform to expectations. For example, while 100.0% (14/14 acts) of terrorist attacks against "non-structuralist" newspaper/print targets involved between one and fifteen perpetrators, there were none that involved a "moderate" number of perpetrators of between 16 and 30 people. The same pattern was found for non-structuralist "private transportation" where 100.0% of all attacks were comprised of between one and fifteen people. In addition, there were no terrorist assaults that clearly involved between 1 and 15 or 16 and 30 terrorists chronicled for the "non-structural" target-type "agriculture."

[33] N = 154 with 516 missing cases. Recode (the same variable) commands "Business Target": 1 → 1; 2 → 2; 5 → 5; ELSE → SYSMIS; "No. of Perpetrators": 1 → 1–15; 2 → 16–30; ELSE → SYSMIS.

Table 3.9 Relative frequency of business-type target by number of perpetrators (1 = 1–15, 2 = 16–30) (summary statistics)

Case processing summary

	Valid		Cases missing		Total	
	N	Percent	N	Percent	N	Percent
Bus.Target * No. Perps	155	23.1%	515	76.9%	670	100.0%

Bus.Target * No. Perps Crosstabulation

			No. Perps		
			1	2	Total
Bus.Target	Energy/Alloy	Count	29	8	37
		% within Bus.Target	78.4%	21.6%	100.0%
		% within no. Perps	27.6%	16.0%	23.9%
		% of total	18.7%	5.2%	23.9%
	Construction	Count	71	33	104
		% within Bus.Target	68.3%	31.7%	100.0%
		% within no. Perps	67.6%	66.0%	67.1%
		% of total	45.8%	21.3%	67.1%
	Telecommunications	Count	5	9	14
		% within Bus.Target	35.7%	64.3%	100.0%
		% within no. Perps	4.8%	18.0%	9.0%
		% of total	3.2%	5.8%	9.0%
Total		Count	105	50	155
		% within Bus.Target	67.7%	32.3%	100.0%
		% within no. Perps	100.0%	100.0%	100.0%
		% of total	67.7%	32.3%	100.0%

Chi-square tests

	Value	df	Asymptotic significance (2-sided)
Pearson chi-square	8.501[a]	2	0.014
Likelihood ratio	8.082	2	0.018
Linear-by-linear association	8.441	1	0.004
N of valid cases	155		

Directional measures

			Value	Asymptotic standard error[b]
Nominal by nominal	Lambda	Symmetric	0.040	0.036
		Bus.Target dependent	0.000	0.000
		No. Perps dependent	0.080	0.072

(continued)

Table 3.9 (continued)

Directional measures

			Value	Asymptotic standard error[b]
	Goodman and Kruskal tau	Bus.Target dependent	0.014	0.010
		No. Perps dependent	0.055	0.037

Directional measures

			Approximate T[c]	Approximate significance
Nominal by nominal	Lambda	Symmetric	1.073	0.283
		Bus.Target dependent	.[d]	.[d]
		No. Perps dependent	1.073	0.283
	Goodman and Kruskal tau	Bus.Target dependent		0.114[e]
		No. Perps dependent		0.015[e]

Symmetric measures

		Value	Approximate significance
Nominal by nominal	Phi	0.234	0.014
	Cramer's V	0.234	0.014
N of valid cases		155	

[a]1 cells (16.7%) have expected count less than 5. The minimum expected count is 4.52
[b]Not assuming the null hypothesis
[c]Using the asymptotic standard error assuming the null hypothesis
[d]Cannot be computed because the asymptotic standard error equals zero
[e]Based on chi-square approximation

Likewise, while 100.0% of terrorist attacks against "hospital/medical facilities" (2/2 acts) involved one to fifteen perpetrators, there were none that involved between 16 and 30 persons. However, while "telecommunications" targets, also considered "structuralist," had a relatively low rate of attacks at 35.7% (5/14 acts) that involved one to fifteen people, nearly two-thirds of its attacks at 64.3% (9/14 acts) involved a "moderate" number of terrorists of between 16 and thirty perpetrators. Those results undercut Hypothesis Nine. Even though a full 68.9% of all "construction site" attacks involved one to fifteen people, nearly one-third at 31.7% (33/104 acts) also involved between 16 and 30 terrorists; that tally ranked second highest in this "structuralist" category, behind the rate for "telecommunications" targets.

Some results were mixed or in some cases were a better fit with the expected observations. For example, 100% of terrorist attacks against "banking and finance" targets involved between one and fifteen terrorists—a finding at odds with Hypothesis Eight—there were none that involved between 16 and 30 persons, which is consistent with expectations about "structuralist" targets. In the broadest senses, the data results do not support Hypothesis Eight and Hypothesis Nine and those theoretical propositions are rejected (Table 3.10).

3.21 Business Target X State

It is important for business executives to understand the sharp focus of terrorist assaults directed at commercial interests in India, especially in Indian states noted for profound and lasting ethnic conflict. The central notion is that in India's seven-sister state region there should be higher rates of attacks against private establishments [6, 34]. The seven-sister state region is known for its deep ethnic divisions exacerbated further by national government policies in Delhi and Indian state governments.

The business category "private establishment" was analyzed because it captures terrorist group focus on people as legitimate targets distinguished along ethnic or religious lines. That contrasts with terrorist attacks taken by "non-structuralist" terrorist groups with their symbolic emphasis on capitalism, globalization, or modernization. It is also the largest target category of commercial interest targets with 160/655 (24.4%) as presented in Table 3.2. The Northeast of India, India's "seven-sister state" region is comprised of Arunachal Pradesh, Assam, Manipur, Meghalaya, Mizoram, and Nagaland, along with Tripura.

Hypothesis Ten: Several "seven sister states" will have higher rates of terrorist attacks against "private establishments" than attack rates for "private establishment" terrorist assaults in other Indian states.

The bivariate analysis suggests that a statistically significant association with moderate strength exists between the variables, "Business Target," and "Province/State." With a Pearson Chi Square statistic of 31.84 and a "*p*-value" of less than 0.001 at 2 degrees of freedom (2 d.f.), it is necessary to reject the null hypothesis of no relation between these variables. It is found 0 cells (0.0%) have an expected count of less than 5. The testing indicates a moderate relationship with a Goodman and Kruskal *tau* value of 0.577 and a significance score of less than 0.001, when "Business Target" is the dependent variable. However, a "Cramer's V" score of 0.760 with a significance score of less than 0.001 and a "Phi" score of 0.760 with a significance score of less than 0.001 indicates a strong relationship (see Table 3.11).

In regards to terrorist attacks that involved "private establishment" targets, the data distribution is consistent with expected findings for the seven-sister state region. Assam had the highest rate of "private establishment" attacks across all Indian states examined with 23.1% (37/160 acts). Manipur had the second highest rate of "private establishment" attacks across all "seven-sister" states examined with 20.0% (32/160 acts). Another "seven-sister state," Meghalaya, ranked third with 8.1% (13/160 acts)

Table 3.10 Relative frequency of business-type target by number of perpetrators, 2013–2018 (1 = 1–15, 2 = 16–30)

Case processing summary

	Valid		Cases missing		Total	
	N	Percent	N	Percent	N	Percent
Bus.Target * No. Perps	238	35.5%	432	64.5%	670	100.0%

Bus.Target * No. Perps Crosstabulation

			No. Perps		
			1	2	Total
Bus.Target	Energy/Alloy	Count	29	8	37
		% within Bus.Target	78.4%	21.6%	100.0%
		% within no. Perps	16.3%	13.3%	15.5%
		% of total	12.2%	3.4%	15.5%
	Construction	Count	71	33	104
		% within Bus.Target	68.3%	31.7%	100.0%
		% within no. Perps	39.9%	55.0%	43.7%
		% of total	29.8%	13.9%	43.7%
	Hospitals/Medical	Count	2	0	2
		% within Bus.Target	100.0%	0.0%	100.0%
		% within no. Perps	1.1%	0.0%	0.8%
		% of total	0.8%	0.0%	0.8%
	Private establishments	Count	52	10	62
		% within Bus.Target	83.9%	16.1%	100.0%
		% within no. Perps	29.2%	16.7%	26.1%
		% of total	21.8%	4.2%	26.1%
	Telecommunications	Count	5	9	14
		% within Bus.Target	35.7%	64.3%	100.0%
		% within no. Perps	2.8%	15.0%	5.9%
		% of total	2.1%	3.8%	5.9%
	Newspapers/Print	Count	14	0	14
		% within Bus.Target	100.0%	0.0%	100.0%
		% within no. Perps	7.9%	0.0%	5.9%
		% of total	5.9%	0.0%	5.9%

(continued)

Table 3.10 (continued)

Bus. Target * No. Perps Crosstabulation

			No. Perps		
			1	2	Total
	Banking/Finance	Count	4	0	4
		% within Bus.Target	100.0%	0.0%	100.0%
		% within no. Perps	2.2%	0.0%	1.7%
		% of total	1.7%	0.0%	1.7%
	Transportation	Count	1	0	1
		% within Bus.Target	100.0%	0.0%	100.0%
		% within no. Perps	0.6%	0.0%	0.4%
		% of total	0.4%	0.0%	0.4%
Total		Count	178	60	238
		% within Bus.Target	74.8%	25.2%	100.0%
		% within no. Perps	100.0%	100.0%	100.0%
		% of total	74.8%	25.2%	100.0%

of all commercial interest terrorist attacks directed at "private establishments" (see Methodological Appendix).

In turn, both Jharkhand and Bihar, two Indian states outside of this region, ranked fourth, each with 6.9% (11/160 acts). Odisha ranked a close fifth with 6.3% (10/160 acts), while Nagaland ranked sixth, with 5.0% (8/160 acts). In Arunachal Pradesh, only 0.6% of all "private establishment" attacks (1/160 acts) happened. There were no recorded "private establishment" incidents for Tripura and Mizoram. The top three ranked states in this test—all "sister-state region" states—accounted for a full 51.2% of all "private establishments" attacks. The data were supportive of Hypothesis Ten and it was accepted as valid.

3.22 Group-Type X Political Events

It is critical for business leaders to understand the extent that business related terrorist assaults in India were linked to political events. The reason why is because data about links between political events and business related terrorist assaults can provide subtlety and nuance to the analysis, thereby in effect working to assist C-class executives with proactive counterterrorism preparation in anticipation of those political events.

In previous work, results indicated that in Algeria, Egypt, and in Israel and the Occupied Territories, there was evidence of linkage between some, but certainly not all, terrorism events and political events for the 1994–1999 interval. For example, in the case of Israeli-Palestinian-Arab terrorist attacks from 1968 to 1999, most attacks

Table 3.11 Relative frequency of business target-type by Indian state, 2013–2018 (summary statistics)

Case processing summary

	Valid		Cases missing		Total	
	N	Percent	N	Percent	N	Percent
Bus.Target * State	54	8.1%	616	91.9%	670	100.0%

Bus. Target * State Crosstabulation

			State			
			Manipur	Meghalaya	Jammu and Kashmir	Total
Bus.Target	Energy/Alloy	Count	11	17	1	29
		% within Bus.Target	37.9%	58.6%	3.4%	100.0%
		% within State	73.3%	89.5%	5.0%	53.7%
		% of total	20.4%	31.5%	1.9%	53.7%
	Telecommunications	Count	4	2	19	25
		% within Bus.Target	16.0%	8.0%	76.0%	100.0%
		% within State	26.7%	10.5%	95.0%	46.3%
		% of total	7.4%	3.7%	35.2%	46.3%
Total		Count	15	19	20	54
		% within Bus.Target	27.8%	35.2%	37.0%	100.0%
		% within State	100.0%	100.0%	100.0%	100.0%
		% of total	27.8%	35.2%	37.0%	100.0%

Chi-square tests

	Value	df	Asymptotic significance (2-sided)
Pearson chi-square	31.184[a]	2	< 0.001
Likelihood ratio	36.438	2	< 0.001
Linear-by-linear association	21.791	1	< 0.001
N of valid cases	54		

Directional measures

			Value	Asymptotic standard error[b]
Nominal by nominal	Lambda	Symmetric	0.576	0.080
		Bus.Target dependent	0.720	0.095

(continued)

Table 3.11 (continued)

Directional measures

			Value	Asymptotic standard error[b]
		State dependent	0.471	0.091
	Goodman and Kruskal tau	Bus.Target dependent	0.577	0.116
		State dependent	0.312	0.078

Directional measures

			Approximate T[c]	Approximate significance
Nominal by nominal	Lambda	Symmetric	7.885	< 0.001
		Bus.Target dependent	4.811	< 0.001
		State dependent	4.394	< 0.001
	Goodman and Kruskal tau	Bus.Target dependent		< 0.001[d]
		State dependent		< 0.001[d]

Symmetric measures

		Value	Approximate significance
Nominal by nominal	Phi	0.760	< 0.001
	Cramer's V	0.760	< 0.001
N of valid cases		54	

[a]0 cells (0.0%) have expected count less than 5. The minimum expected count is 6.94
[b]Not assuming the null hypothesis
[c]Using the asymptotic standard error assuming the null hypothesis
[d]Based on chi-square approximation

were "proactive," that is, not linked to political events. For those "reactive" terrorist events that were, there were differences in the degree of focus Middle East terrorist groups placed on civilian and government targets [7].[34]

As in the Middle East, political events in India and Pakistan should include religious events as political events from a theoretical point of view. In the Indian context, business practices are frequently politicized largely because of the nature of ethnic conflict between groups and the fear many Indian terrorists have that modernization,

[34] In previous work, I based my approach on Brecher and James's notion of conflict as a "servo-mechanism" where violent actions elicit more peaceful actions and vice versa, to keep conflict within an established range, similar to a thermostat.

such as the building of new roads, will decrease terrorist group security. Therefore, political events in this study included religious events such as Janmashtami or Christmas, and business practices of firms linked to government directives (i.e., road construction firms) [19 (entry #161); 21 (entry #331); 29; 64].

Hypothesis Eleven: Most business related terrorist assaults in India will not be linked to political events in the region, such as diplomatic initiatives, the commemoration of religious or secular events, or counterterrorism activity [9, 175].[35]

Hypothesis Twelve: Maoist terrorist groups in India will have the highest rate of business related terrorist attacks linked to government policies and elections or polls.

A bivariate correlations test with the variables "Group-Type" and "Reaction to Political Event" determined a statistically significant relationship between those variables. With a Pearson Chi Square statistic of 5.080 and a "*p*-value" of 0.024 at 1 degree of freedom (1 d.f.), it is possible to reject the null hypothesis of no relation at the 0.05 level of confidence. It was found that 1 cell (25.0%) had an expected count of less than 5, but the results were reported for fear of making a "Type II" error, where the null hypothesis should be rejected, but is not rejected [44, 270].

The statistically significant relationship was found to be weak, indicated by a Goodman and Kruskal tau value of 0.051 with a significance score of 0.025 when "Group Type" is the dependent variable. Likewise, a Cramer V's score of 0.225 with a significance score of 0.024, and "Phi" score of 0.225 with a significance score of 0.024 also indicate a weak relationship (see Table 3.12).

To begin with, the total amount of Indian terrorism directed at commercial targets linked to political events was high with 82.8% (309/373 acts). The data distribution suggests when the data were parsed by political event type, terrorist attacks in reaction to business practices linked to broader government directives such as modernization efforts, comprised the largest portion of terrorist acts tied to political events with 41.8% (156/373 acts).[36] That dovetailed with the empirical finding that terrorist attacks with direct links to Indian government policies ranked second with 25.7% (96/373 acts). In comparison, terrorist assaults with no discernable ties to political events ranked third with only 17.2% (64/373 acts).

Terrorist attacks taken in reaction to ground assaults (e.g., counterterrorism actions) comprised 5.4% of all terrorist events (20/373 acts) In contrast, attacks to commemorate secular holidays comprised 4.0% of the total (15/373 acts). Terrorist assaults linked to elections or polls made up only 2.9% of the total (11/373 acts). Only 1.9% (7/373 acts) were tied to commemoration of landmark events, and less than half that amount at 0.5% (2/373 acts, was linked to commemoration of religious

---

[35] The notion that Maoist targeting preferences devote special attention to government targets serves as the basis for this theoretical proposition. The variable "Group-Type" was recoded into the same variable: 1 → 1; 2 → 2; ELSE → SYSMIS, while the variable "Reaction to Political Event" was recoded into the same variable: 1 → 1; 7 → 7; ELSE → SYSMIS.

[36] It is important to mention that "opportunity recognition" might have also played a role decisions to target these firms because construction of roads, bridges, and railways for example, happens in isolated areas.

Table 3.12 Relative frequency of group-type by political event, 2013–2018 (summary statistics)

Case processing summary

	Valid		Cases missing		Total	
	N	Percent	N	Percent	N	Percent
GroupTy * ReacPol.Evnt	100	14.9%	570	85.1%	670	100.0%

GroupTy * ReacPol.Evnt Crosstabulation

			ReacPol.Evnt		
			Govt. policies	Secular holidays	Total
GroupTy	Marxist-Leninist	Count	71	7	78
		% within GroupTy	91.0%	9.0%	100.0%
		% within ReacPol.Evnt	81.6%	53.8%	78.0%
		% of total	71.0%	7.0%	78.0%
	Nationalist-Irredentist	Count	16	6	22
		% within GroupTy	72.7%	27.3%	100.0%
		% within ReacPol.Evnt	18.4%	46.2%	22.0%
		% of total	16.0%	6.0%	22.0%
Total		Count	87	13	100
		% within GroupTy	87.0%	13.0%	100.0%
		% within ReacPol.Evnt	100.0%	100.0%	100.0%
		% of total	87.0%	13.0%	100.0%

Chi-square tests

	Value	df	Asymptotic significance (2-sided)	Exact significance (2-sided)	Exact significance (1-sided)
Pearson chi-square	5.080[a]	1	0.024		
Continuity correction[b]	3.591	1	0.058		
Likelihood ratio	4.392	1	0.036		
Fisher's exact test				0.035	0.035
Linear-by-linear association	5.029	1	0.025		
N of valid cases	100				

(continued)

Table 3.12 (continued)

Directional measures

			Value	Asymptotic standard error[c]
Nominal by nominal	Lambda	Symmetric	0.000	0.000
		GroupTy dependent	0.000	0.000
		ReacPol.Evnt dependent	0.000	0.000
	Goodman and Kruskal tau	GroupTy dependent	0.051	0.052
		ReacPol.Evnt dependent	0.051	0.053

Directional measures

			Approximate T
Nominal by nominal	Lambda	Symmetric	.[d]
		GroupTy dependent	.[d]
		ReacPol.Evnt dependent	.[d]
	Goodman and Kruskal tau	GroupTy dependent	
		ReacPol.Evnt dependent	

Directional measures

			Approximate significance
Nominal by nominal	Lambda	Symmetric	.[d]
		GroupTy dependent	.[d]
		ReacPol.Evnt dependent	.[d]
	Goodman and Kruskal tau	GroupTy dependent	0.025[e]
		ReacPol.Evnt dependent	0.025[e]

Symmetric measures

		Value	Approximate significance
Nominal by nominal	Phi	0.225	0.024
	Cramer's V	0.225	0.024
N of valid cases		100	

[a]1 cells (25.0%) have expected count less than 5. The minimum expected count is 2.86
[b]Computed only for a 2 × 2 table
[c]Not assuming the null hypothesis
[d]Cannot be computed because the asymptotic standard error equals zero
[e]Based on chi-square approximation

holidays Terrorist assaults tied to government assassinations (1 act or 0.3%) were extreme outlier cases (see Table 3.13).

Parenthetically, a full 50.0% (4/8 acts) of Hindutva attacks were taken in reaction to government policies. That result might reflect the deep ties between the national government to "right wing" Hindutva groups. In turn, nationalist-irredentist terrorist attacks were linked to government policies 16.3% of the time (16/98 acts). Anonymous acts ranked fourth with 10.4% of all anonymous attacks (5/48 acts) linked to government policies. There were no recorded Islamic extremist group attacks linked to government policies.

One standout finding is that with 4.2% (2/48 acts), anonymous actors carried out the highest rate of terrorist attacks linked to elections or polls. Maoist terrorist acts followed with 3.7% (8/218 acts). Only one business related nationalist-irredentist terrorist act (1/98 acts) was linked to elections or polls. Both "right-wing" Hindutva terrorist organizations and Islamic extremist groups abstained from business related terrorist assaults with ties to elections or polls. The data results were not supportive of Hypothesis Eleven and it was rejected.

When links between Maoist business related terrorism in India and political events were analyzed, it was found that Maoist attacks against "business practices" linked to government directives and broader modernization efforts had at 39.9% (87/218 acts), the second highest rate across terrorist groups considered. It trailed behind nationalist irredentist terrorist groups that had a 49.0% (48/98 acts) rate. However, with nearly one-third of all Maoist terrorist attacks at 32.6% (71/218 acts), in reaction to government policies, Maoist groups ranked first. If we relax the assumptions of hypothesis twelve and discard anonymous acts from the analysis, as it is not a formal group-type, it appears there is empirical support for Hypothesis Twelve.

3.23 The "Structuralist—Non-structuralist" Terrorist Group-Type Continuum—Indian Terrorist Group Placement

As in previous work on Middle East terrorism, it was found the variable "political ideology" was critically important. In this work, it was found to influence what type of business target was attacked. An ordering of targets according to targets more representative of a structuralist standpoint to conflict and targets more reflective of a non-structuralist standpoint, made it possible to isolate and identify the types of business targets of primary interest to different types of terrorist groups, themselves distinguished by political ideology.

The expected findings were that "structuralist" Maoist (Marxist-Leninist) terrorist groups would emphasize targets linked in a symbolic or functional sense or both, to capitalism, globalization, or modernization. Accordingly, their placement on the continuum was expected to be close to its structuralist axis. In turn, the expected findings were that "non-structuralist" nationalist-irredentist and right-wing Hindutva

Table 3.13 Relative frequency of group-type by political event, 2013–2018

Case processing summary

	Valid		Cases missing		Total	
	N	Percent	N	Percent	N	Percent
GroupTy * ReacPol.Evnt	373	55.7%	297	44.3%	670	100.0%

GroupTy * ReacPol.Evnt Crosstabulation

			ReacPol.Evnt		
			No Relation	Govt. Policies	Ground Assaults
GroupTy	Marxist-Leninist	Count	25	71	16
		% within GroupTy	11.5%	32.6%	7.3%
		% within ReacPol.Evnt	39.1%	74.0%	80.0%
		% of total	6.7%	19.0%	4.3%
	Nationalist-Irredentist	Count	19	16	3
		% within GroupTy	19.4%	16.3%	3.1%
		% within ReacPol.Evnt	29.7%	16.7%	15.0%
		% of total	5.1%	4.3%	0.8%
	Anonymous	Count	20	5	1
		% within GroupTy	41.7%	10.4%	2.1%
		% within ReacPol.Evnt	31.3%	5.2%	5.0%
		% of total	5.4%	1.3%	0.3%
	Islamic extremist	Count	0	0	0
		% within GroupTy	0.0%	0.0%	0.0%
		% within ReacPol.Evnt	0.0%	0.0%	0.0%
		% of total	0.0%	0.0%	0.0%
	Right wing	Count	0	4	0
		% within GroupTy	0.0%	50.0%	0.0%
		% within ReacPol.Evnt	0.0%	4.2%	0.0%
		% of total	0.0%	1.1%	0.0%
Total		Count	64	96	20
		% within GroupTy	17.2%	25.7%	5.4%

(continued)

Table 3.13 (continued)

GroupTy * ReacPol.Evnt Crosstabulation

			ReacPol.Evnt		
			No Relation	Govt. Policies	Ground Assaults
		% within ReacPol.Evnt	100.0%	100.0%	100.0%
		% of total	17.2%	25.7%	5.4%

GroupTy * ReacPol.Evnt Crosstabulation

			ReacPol.Evnt		
			Terrorist Acts	Govt. Assassinations	Landmark Events
GroupTy	Marxist-Leninist	Count	0	0	4
		% within GroupTy	0.0%	0.0%	1.8%
		% within ReacPol.Evnt	0.0%	0.0%	57.1%
		% of total	0.0%	0.0%	1.1%
	Nationalist-Irredentist	Count	1	1	2
		% within GroupTy	1.0%	1.0%	2.0%
		% within ReacPol.Evnt	100.0%	100.0%	28.6%
		% of total	0.3%	0.3%	0.5%
	Anonymous	Count	0	0	1
		% within GroupTy	0.0%	0.0%	2.1%
		% within ReacPol.Evnt	0.0%	0.0%	14.3%
		% of total	0.0%	0.0%	0.3%
	Islamic extremist	Count	0	0	0
		% within GroupTy	0.0%	0.0%	0.0%
		% within ReacPol.Evnt	0.0%	0.0%	0.0%
		% of total	0.0%	0.0%	0.0%
	Right wing	Count	0	0	0
		% within GroupTy	0.0%	0.0%	0.0%
		% within ReacPol.Evnt	0.0%	0.0%	0.0%

(continued)

Table 3.13 (continued)

GroupTy * ReacPol.Evnt Crosstabulation

			ReacPol.Evnt		
			Terrorist Acts	Govt. Assassinations	Landmark Events
		% of total	0.0%	0.0%	0.0%
Total		Count	1	1	7
		% within GroupTy	0.3%	0.3%	1.9%
		% within ReacPol.Evnt	100.0%	100.0%	100.0%
		% of total	0.3%	0.3%	1.9%

GroupTy * ReacPol.Evnt Crosstabulation

			ReacPol.Evnt	
			Religious holidays	Secular holidays
GroupTy	Marxist-Leninist	Count	0	7
		% within GroupTy	0.0%	3.2%
		% within ReacPol.Evnt	0.0%	46.7%
		% of total	0.0%	1.9%
	Nationalist-Irredentist	Count	1	6
		% within GroupTy	1.0%	6.1%
		% within ReacPol.Evnt	50.0%	40.0%
		% of total	0.3%	1.6%
	Anonymous	Count	1	1
		% within GroupTy	2.1%	2.1%
		% within ReacPol.Evnt	50.0%	6.7%
		% of total	0.3%	0.3%
	Islamic extremist	Count	0	1
		% within GroupTy	0.0%	100.0%
		% within ReacPol.Evnt	0.0%	6.7%
		% of total	0.0%	0.3%
	Right wing	Count	0	0
		% within GroupTy	0.0%	0.0%
		% within ReacPol.Evnt	0.0%	0.0%

(continued)

Table 3.13 (continued)

GroupTy * ReacPol.Evnt Crosstabulation

			ReacPol.Evnt	
			Religious holidays	Secular holidays
		% of total	0.0%	0.0%
Total		Count	2	15
		% within GroupTy	0.5%	4.0%
		% within ReacPol.Evnt	100.0%	100.0%
		% of total	0.5%	4.0%

GroupTy * ReacPol.Evnt Crosstabulation

			ReacPol.Evnt		
			Business policies	Elections/ Polls	Total
GroupTy	Marxist-Leninist	Count	87	8	218
		% within GroupTy	39.9%	3.7%	100.0%
		% within ReacPol.Evnt	55.8%	72.7%	58.4%
		% of total	23.3%	2.1%	58.4%
	Nationalist-Irredentist	Count	48	1	98
		% within GroupTy	49.0%	1.0%	100.0%
		% within ReacPol.Evnt	30.8%	9.1%	26.3%
		% of total	12.9%	0.3%	26.3%
	Anonymous	Count	17	2	48
		% within GroupTy	35.4%	4.2%	100.0%
		% within ReacPol.Evnt	10.9%	18.2%	12.9%
		% of total	4.6%	0.5%	12.9%
	Islamic extremist	Count	0	0	1
		% within GroupTy	0.0%	0.0%	100.0%
		% within ReacPol.Evnt	0.0%	0.0%	0.3%
		% of total	0.0%	0.0%	0.3%
	Right wing	Count	4	0	8

(continued)

Table 3.13 (continued)

GroupTy * ReacPol.Evnt Crosstabulation

			ReacPol.Evnt		
			Business policies	Elections/ Polls	Total
		% within GroupTy	50.0%	0.0%	100.0%
		% within ReacPol.Evnt	2.6%	0.0%	2.1%
		% of total	1.1%	0.0%	2.1%
Total		Count	156	11	373
		% within GroupTy	41.8%	2.9%	100.0%
		% within ReacPol.Evnt	100.0%	100.0%	100.0%
		% of total	41.8%	2.9%	100.0%

terrorist groups would emphasize ethnic groups and individuals heavily as targets; those terrorist group-types were expected to lie close to the "non-structuralist" axis of this continuum.

The analysis sorted out and tallied the total amount of "structuralist" and "non-structuralist" related terrorist targets chosen by the different types of terrorist groups under consideration. In the case of Indian Maoist (Marxist-Leninist) terrorist groups, "structuralist" related targets were tallied accordingly in Table 3.2: "energy alloy" targets (16.0% = 52/326 acts) + "construction sites" (57.7% = 188/326 acts) + "telecommunications" (11.3% = 37/326 acts) + "banking/financial" institutions (0.3% = 1/326 acts), for a total of 85.3%.

In comparison, the target breakdown for Maoist group terrorist assaults against "non-structuralist" related targets were: "hospitals/medical" sites (0.6% = 2/326 acts) + "private establishments" (10.7% = 35/326 acts) + "newspaper/print" (1.2% = 4/326 acts) + "private transportation" (1.5% = 5/326 acts) + "agriculture" targets (0.6% = 2/326 acts) for a total of 13.4%. With a ratio of 13.4% to 85.3% in favor of structuralist targets, Maoist terrorist groups in India were placed towards the left of the continuum, near the "structuralist" axis, as expected.

For nationalist-irredentist terrorist groups, "structuralist" related targets were attacked 55.2% of the time. The target breakdown was: "energy/alloy" targets (28.9% = 44/152 acts) + "construction sites" (23.7% = 36/152 acts) + "telecommunication" (1.3%% = 2/152 acts) + "banking/financial" institutions (1.3% = 2/152 acts) = 55.2%.

In comparison, "non-structuralist" related targets were attacked 44.7% of the time by nationalist-irredentist terrorist groups: "hospitals/medical" sites (0.0%) + "private establishments" (42.1% = 64/152 acts) + "newspaper/print" (1.3% = 2/152 acts) + "private transportation" (1.3% = 2/152 acts) + "agriculture" targets (0.0%).

Hence, nationalist-irredentist groups, expected to place very heavy emphasis on "non-structuralist" type targets with emphasis on ethnic groups and people, did not conform to expected observations. They were positioned slightly over the continuum center line towards its "structuralist" axis.

For "right-wing" Hindutva terrorist groups, the mixture of attack rates for "structuralist" related targets were: "energy alloy" targets (0.0%) + "construction sites" (0.0%) "telecommunications" (11.1% = 1/9 acts) + "banking/financial" institutions (0.0%), for a total of 11.1%. When Hindutva target choice for "non-structuralist" type targets was examined, the tallies found were: "hospitals/medical" sites (0.0%) + "private establishments" (77.8% = 7/9 acts) + "newspaper/print" (11.1% = 1/9 acts) + "private transportation" (0.0%) + "agriculture" targets (0.0%), for a total of 88.9%. With a ratio of 11.1% to 88.9% in favor of "non-structuralist" targets, right-wing Hindutva groups were found very close to the right hand "non-structuralist" axis of the continuum, as expected.

For Islamic extremists, the percentage rates found for "structuralist" related targets were: "energy alloy" targets" (6.3% = 1/16 acts) + "construction sites" (0.0%) + "telecommunications" (50.0% = 8/16 acts) + "banking and financial" institutions (12.5% = 2/16 acts) for total of 68.8%. When "non-structuralist" rates were examined, the breakdown for Islamic extremist terrorist groups was: "hospitals/medical" sites (6.3% = 1/16 acts) + "private establishments" (18.8% = 3/16 acts) + "newspaper/print" (6.3% = 1/9 acts) + "private transportation (0.0%) + "agriculture" targets (0.0%) for a total of 31.4%. The expected finding was that Islamic extremist groups would be found at the midpoint of the continuum. While Islamic extremist groups were positioned in that general area, placement of that group-type was unexpected, over the continuum center line in the direction of the "structuralist" axis.

It was found that placement of Indian terrorist group-type categories on the continuum largely conformed to expectations, albeit with some exceptions. Maoist terrorist groups were found closest to the "structuralist" axis, while "right-wing" Hindutva groups were positioned closest to the "non-structuralist" axis, as expected.

In comparison, Islamic extremist terrorist groups were found farther to the left on the continuum centerline than anticipated. However, it was Indian nationalist-irredentist terrorist groups that comprised the predominant deviant case, with placement of that group-type slightly to the left of the spectrum centerline. What accounts for that result remains unclear, but there are some possible interpretations available.

One possible interpretation to help to explain why nationalist-irredentist terrorist groups were found so far from their expected position, close to the "non-structuralist" axis, is the condition of overlap recruitment between Maoist and nationalist-irredentist groups that Kumari describes [34, 96–98]. An overlap in recruitment suggests an overlap in target preference to satisfy core demands of leader and constituent support interests. In the broader sense, those results suggest contextual factors in different operational environments provide results that in some cases do not conform fully to the basic assumptions behind the "non-structuralist-structuralist" continuum, this theme will be explored in chapters to come (see Fig. 3.10).

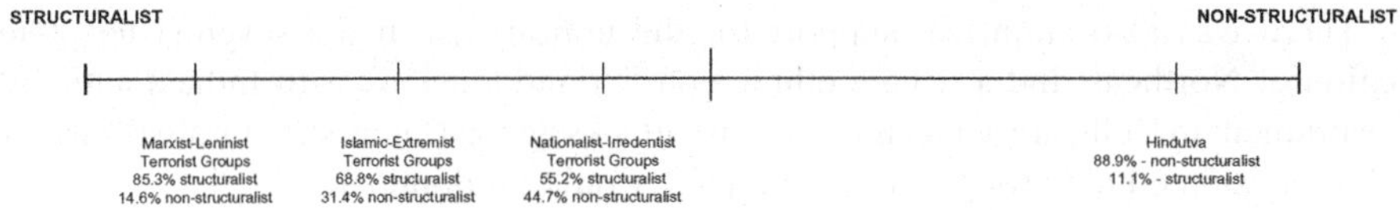

Fig. 3.10 Structuralist—non-structuralist continuum for Indian terrorist group-type

3.24 Conclusions

This chapter describes the basic contours of terrorism directed at commercial interests in India. What is evident is the size and complexity of this terrorism system, with its very large number of terrorist groups, a broad range of locations, and terrorist group splintering and spinoff group formation complexities. There were 64 identifiable terrorist groups chronicled that conducted terrorist assaults against commercial interests across 26 states in 176 districts.

The rates of terrorism in India by year comprise a pattern of cyclical activity that is commonplace to note in other countries when broad categories of terrorism are examined. At the same time, the peaks and troughs observed were not especially pronounced. There were four types of terrorist organizations identified. Those included Maoist (Marxist Leninist) groups, nationalist-irredentist groups, Islamic extremist groups, and "right-wing" Hindutva terrorist organizations.

With respect to business targets, construction sites and related infrastructure (e.g., vehicles) constituted the largest portion of all terrorist attacks aimed at commercial interests, followed by private establishments. At the other extreme, terrorist assaults against private transportation, banking and financial institutions, and agriculture targets were outlier cases.

While anonymous attacks comprised the largest portion of business-related terrorist attacks the single most predominant terrorist group in the Indian political fray was the Communist Party of India (CPI-Maoist). The United Liberation Front of Assam (ULFA), a nationalist-irredentist terrorist group, followed far behind, while another Maoist terrorist organization, the People's Liberation Front of India (PLFI), ranked third.

The results from tests to appraise the validity of the theoretical propositions offered were mixed. In terms of support for the structuralist- non-structuralist continuum, there was solid support for the notion that Maoist terrorist groups favored target-types associated with a structuralist standpoint towards conflict. Those targets included telecommunication infrastructure, construction sites, and energy/alloy targets. Hence, Maoist terrorist groups were placed close to the "structuralist" axis of the continuum as expected.

There was also support for the expected findings that "right-wing" Hindutva terrorist groups would primarily focus on "non-structuralist" targets, targets that reflected emphasis on individuals and ethnic groups. As a result, those Hindutva terrorist groups were positioned close to the "non-structuralist" axis of the continuum, as expected.

There was also empirical support for the notion that in the seven-sister state region of Northeast India, where ethnic conflict and tensions with India's national government in Delhi are acute, that terrorist attacks against "non-structuralist" targets with focus on ethnic groups and individuals, would predominate.

However, Islamic extremist groups were positioned closer to the structuralist pole of the continuum than expected. That result deviated from the expected observation that Islamic extremist groups would be found around the midpoint of the "structuralist-non structuralist" continuum. One possible reason why is because while "hybrid" terrorist groups put emphasis on targets symbolic of globalization and modernization, those groups also focus on individual and small groups as targets. The stand-out deviant case was "nationalist-irredentist" terrorist groups. Nationalist-irredentist groups were positioned much closer to the "structuralist" axis of the continuum than predicted.

Plainly, there is no authoritative interpretation for those results, but one possible interpretation about why nationalist irredentist terrorist groups were found so far from its expected place near the "structuralist" axis involves the overlap in recruitment patterns between Maoist and nationalist-irredentist groups [34, 96–98]. Other political and economic explanatory factors that contributed to this unexpected result remained unknown.

These mixed results probably reflect the major role that contextual factors in each terrorism system play to influence target selection choice. Those data findings also provide fertile ground for future work on terrorist group splintering and spinoff formation processes. The reason why is because of the high number of active terrorist groups found in many Indian states, districts, and cities, towns, and villages.

The results also point to the continued relevance, at least at the sub-national actor level, for Marxist-Leninism and Maoism, as guiding principles to frame and interpret the political demands and aspirations of a significant part of India's population. That undercurrent of non-state actor support for Marxist-Leninism (or Maoism) in India's political system is significant because Maoist terrorist group actions help shape the domestic policies of a state increasingly receptive to international business and important to the international liberal economic order [52, 81–82–98].

The Terrorist Assault Vulnerability Index (TABVI) scores produced and the broader set of empirical findings for business related terrorism in India beg the question of what conclusions can be made based on cross-national comparisons. One issue is whether or not the TABVI scores for business executive appraisals of specific country vulnerability to terrorism share similarities with the results for India.

India received a TABVI score of 156.6. The industry sub-category raw scores for India were: (1) Energy/Alloy = 26.4; (2) Construction = 62.4 (**highest** vulnerability threat); (3) Hospitals/Medical facilities = 1.9; (4) Private establishments = 38.1; (5) Telecommunications = 16.0; (6) Newspapers/Print = 7.86; (7) Banking/Financial Institutions = 1.9; (8) Transportation = 1.7; (9) Agriculture = 0.476 (**lowest** vulnerability/threat).

In closing, this book chapter serves as a baseline of expectations for anticipated findings and for unanticipated findings about different types of terrorist groups and their behavior in the other nation-states under consideration. This book will delve into the empirical results that share similarities and differences not only across countries, but by extrapolation, across regions. It is to those issues that this book now turns, with the presentation of four additional case studies, starting with Mexico.

References

1. Ahlawat D (2018) Maoist insurgency in India: Grievances, security threats and counter-strategies. Journal of Policing, Intelligence, and Counter-Terrorism 13(2):252–266. https://doi.org/10.1080/18335330.2018.1478114
2. Ahmad S (2018) Rajput pride, moustachioed men and legacy: what drives the Kari Sena protests against Padmaavat. Hindustan Times. https://www.hindustantimes.com/jaipur/in-many-faces-of-karni-sena-lokendra-kalvi-the-pivot/story-tUwFTXtyxczOAkhizitV1H.html
3. Andersen W (1972) The Rashtriya Sivayamsevak Sangh I: early concerns. Economic and Political Weekly 7(11):589–597. https://www.jstor.org/stable/4361126
4. Andersen W (1972) The Rashtriya Sivayamsevak Sangh III: Participation in politics. Econ Pol Wkly 7(13):589–597
5. Bhattacharjee G (2017) India: Mizoram: managing irritants. South Asia Intelligence Review Weekly Assessments & Briefings 15(43):1–7
6. Baruah S (2009) Separatist militants and contentious politics in Assam, India: the limits of counterinsurgency. Asian Survey 49(6):951–974. https://www.jstor.org/stable/10.1525/as.2009.49.6.951
7. Brecher M, James P (1987) Crisis management in the Arab-Israeli conflict. In: Dor GB, DeWitt D (eds) Conflict management in the Middle East. Heath
8. Business Standard (2016) Hizb commander who blasted Kashmir telecom towers killed (Roundup). Business Standard. https://www.business-standard.com/article/news/-lans/hizb-commande-who-blasted-kashmir-telecom-towers-killed-roundup-116062801196_1.html
9. Chasdi RJ (1999) Serenade of suffering: a portrait of Middle East terrorism, 1968–1993. Lexington Books
10. Chasdi RJ (2002) Tapestry of terror: a portrait of Middle East terrorism, 1994–1999. Lexington Books
11. Diamond L (1990) Nigeria: pluralism, statism and the struggle for democracy. In: Diamond L, Linz JL, Lipset SM (eds) Politics in developing countries: comparing experiences with democracy. Lynne Rienner
12. Esman MJ (1994) Ethnic politics. Cornell University Press
13. Fair CC (2014) Insights from a database of Lashkar-e-Taiba and Hizb-ul-Mujahidden militants. Journal of Strategic Studies 37(2):259–290. https://www.tandfonline.com/doi/abs/10.1080/01402390.2013.811647
14. Forest JJF (2006) Training camps and other centers of learning. In: Forest JJF (ed) Teaching terror: Strategic and tactical learning in the terrorist world. Rowman & Littlefield Publishers, Inc., pp 69–109
15. Gandhi P (2014) Rashtriya Sivayamsevak Sangh: how the world's largest NGO has changed the face of Indian democracy. DNA India. https://www.dnaindia.com/analysis/standpoint-rashtriya-swayamsewak-sangh-how-the-world-s-largest-ngo-has-changed-the-face-of-indian-democracy-1988636
16. Global Terrorism Database (GTD) "India," GTD ID: 201401110011. 11 Jan 2014
17. Global Terrorism Database (GTD) India. GTD ID: 201401280061. 28 Jan 2014
18. Global Terrorism Database (GTD) India. GTD ID: 201406030072. 3 June 2014
19. Global Terrorism Database (GTD) India. GTD ID: 201408190069. 19 Aug 2014
20. Global Terrorism Database (GTD) India. GTD ID: 201507270014. 27 July 2015
21. Global Terrorism Database (GTD) India. GTD ID: 201512170031. 17 Dec 2015

22. Gohain H (2007) Chronicles of violence and terror: rise of the united liberation front of Asom. Economic and Political Weekly 42(12):1012–1018. https://www.jstor.org/stable/4419382
23. Goswani BB (2019) 22 militants of two Bru rebel outfits lay down arms, more to follow suit. The Times of India
24. Haokip T (2011) Paradoxes within the Kuki Nation. Voices of the Hill 2(3):25–29. https://papers.ssrn.com/sol3/papers.cfm?abstract_id=1808676
25. Hindustan Times (2016) Maoists blow up Panchayat building, torch cell tower
26. Holsti KJ (1985) The dividing discipline: hegemony and diversity in international theory. Allen & Unwin
27. Indo-Asian News Service (2004) Fear and panic in Assam after serial blasts
28. Indo-Asian News Service (2007) Maoists ask Bastar people to celebrate their anniversary
29. Khan S (2015) Grenade attack in Garo Hills. The Telegraph (India)
30. Khangchain, V (2011) Assam: trouble at the margins. South Asia Intelligence/IBNS
31. Khemnar S (2018) Causes and effects of terrorism in India: an overview. International Journal of Applied Information Systems 12(15):29–32. https://www.ijais.org/archives/volume12/number15/khemnar-2018-ijais-451772.pdf
32. Kujur RK (2006) Left extremism in India: Naxal movement in Chhattisgarh & Orissa. Institute of Peace and Conflict Studies, IPCS Special Report 25:1–14
33. Kumar S, Mishra S (2011) Naxal problem in central Bihar. The Indian Journal of Political Science 72(3):791–802. https://www.jstor.org/stable/41858853
34. Kumari A (2018) Dynamics of internal security in India: special reference to Naxalism. Impact: International Journal of Research in Humanities, Arts and Literature 6(8):91–100
35. Lasswell HD (1978) Terrorism and the political process. Terrorism: An International Journal 1(3/4):255–263
36. Lynch TF (2016) India's Naxalite insurgency: history, trajectory, and implications for U.S.-India security cooperation on domestic counterinsurgency, strategic perspectives. Institute for National Strategic Studies (INSS) 22:1–41. https://css.ethz.ch/content/dam/ethz/special-interest/gess/cis/center-for-securities-studies/resources/docs/INSS-India's%20Naxalite%20Insurgency.pdf
37. Meghalaya Times (India) (2013) Trader escapes unhurt in militant firing
38. Mehta A, Purohit D (2018) Padmavati: the rise & rise of Karni Sena. India News—Times of India. https://timesofindia.indiatimes.com/india/the-rise-rise-of-karni-sena/articleshow/62626854.cms
39. Nanda M (2009) Hindu triumphalism and the clash of civilizations. Economic and Political Weekly 44(28):106–114. https://www.jstor.org/stable/40279263
40. Naqash AA (2015) Hizbul Mujahideen disowns splinter faction in Kashmir. Reuters https://www.reuters.com/article/pakistan-india-kashmir-hizbul/hizbul-mujahideen-disowns-splinter-faction-n-kashmir-idUSKCN0PX26V20150723
41. Nayak P, Singha K (2015) Identity, deprivation and demand for bifurcation of meghalaya. In: Singha K, Singh MA (eds) Identity, contestation and development in northeast India, 1st edn. Routledge. http://dspace.cus.ac.in/jspui/bitstream/1/4366/1/Identity%2C%20deprivation%20and%20demand.pdf
42. Nepali Current Affairs (2016) National Santhali Liberation Army (NSLA). https://nepalicurrentaffairs.blogspot.com/2016/05/national-santhali-liberation-army-nsla.html
43. New Indian Express (2014) Maoists kill Cong worker in Rayagada
44. Noursis M (1991) The SPSS guide to data analysis, 2nd edn. SPSS
45. Pandey A (2018) CPI (Maoist) gets a new leader. India Today. https://www.indiatoday.in/india/story/cpi-maoist-gets-a-new-leader-1383395-2018-11-06
46. Pakistan Today (2015) Hizbul Mujahideen disowns faction more attacks in IHK
47. Pike J (2004) Lashkar-e-Taiba-Lashkar-e-Taayiba (Army of the Righteous). FAS Intelligence Resource Program. https://fas.org/irp/world/para/lashkar.htm
48. Plestina D (1992) From democratic centralism to decentralized democracy? Trials and tribulations of Yugoslavia's development. In: Allcock JB, Horton JJ, Milivojevic M (eds) Yugoslavia in transition: choices and constraints essays in honour of Fred Singleton. St. Martin's Press

49. Ramachandran S (2020) Hindutva violence in India. Counterterror Trends and Analyses 12(4):15–20. https://www.jstor.org/stable/10.2307/26918077
50. Real Estate Monitor Worldwide (2016) Maoists attack road construction co-office
51. Regan H, Suri M (2019) India downgrades Kashmir's status and takes greater control over contested region. CNN World. https://www.cnn.com/2019/10/31/asia/jammu-kashmir-union-territory-intl-hnk/index.html
52. Rogers P (2001) Losing control: global security in the twenty-first century. Pluto Press
53. Sahni A (2019) A peaceful northeast is imperative for India's act easy policy. World Affairs: The Journal of International Issues 23(3):118–135. https://www.jstor.org/stable/48531055
54. Shimray UA (2001) Ethnicity and socio-political assertion: the Manipur experience. Economic and Political Weekly 36(39):3674–3677. https://www.jstor.org/stable/4411161
55. Siyech MS (2018) A typology of insurgent, terrorist and extremist threats in India. Journal of Policing, Intelligence and Counter-Terrorism 13(2):231–251. https://www.tandfonline.com/doi/abs/10.1080/18335330.2018.1473629?journalCode=rpic20
56. South Asian Terrorism Portal (ND) United Liberation Front of Barak-Valley (ULFBV)—terrorism group of Assam. https://www.satp.org/satporgtp/countries/india/states/assam/terrorist_outfits/ULFBV.htm
57. Srivastava D (2009) Terrorism & armed violence in India: an analysis of events in 2008. Institute of Peace and Conflict Studies, IPCS Special Report 71:1–21
58. Teltumbde A (2018) Margin speak—Umar Khalid and the hate republic. Economic and Political Weekly. https://www.epw.in/journal/2018/36/margin-speak/umar-khalid-and-hate-republic.html
59. The Telegraph (India) (2020) Rebels torch trucks in Latehar
60. The Times of India (2011) Udla militant gives police the slip
61. The Times of India (2012) Surrendered Adivasi rebels seek interlocutor to start talks
62. The Times of India (2013) Trader killed, 3 hurt in NDFB-S attack
63. The Times of India (2014) Grenade found inside Imphal truck
64. The Times of India (2014) One injured in Imphal blast
65. Wainwright T (2017) Narconomics: how to run a drug cartel. Ebury Press
66. World Economic Forum (2017) Business costs of terrorism. http://reports.weforum.org/global-competitiveness-index-2017-2018/competitiveness-rankings/#series=EOSQ033
67. World Economic Forum (2017) Appendix C, the executive opinion survey: the voice of the business community. http://www3.weforum.org/docs/GCR2017-2018/04Backmatter/TheGlobalCompetitivenessReport2017%E2%80%932018AppendixC.pdf
68. Zafar S, Wasi AB (2010) Terrorism in India: method in madness. Policy Perspectives 7(2):51–74. https://jstor.org/stable/42909276

Chapter 4
The Case of Mexico

4.1 Introduction

In this chapter, the scope of terrorist groups active in the Mexican political fray that have attacked commercial interests is much narrower than in India. Mexican terrorist organizations chronicled between 2007 and 2018 conducted a very few terrorist events against business targets. Those ranged from anti-government terrorist groups such as the Popular Revolutionary Army (EPR), to "single issue" terrorist organizations, such as the Earth Liberation Front (ELF) and the Animal Liberation Front (ALF). Two incidents conducted by Choi and Tzeltol Indians were also recorded.

In comparison, a comparatively large number of anonymous terrorist acts directed at business targets were recorded, most of which were probably carried out by drug trafficking organizations. It appears most terrorist acts conducted by those criminal syndicalists remained anonymous, but a few terrorist events were attributed by the government or the media or both, to well established drug trafficking organizations such as Los Caballeros Templarios (Knights Templar) and Los Zetas.

Accordingly, Mexico presents an important case study for terrorism analysis in countries where complex connections exist between the use of terrorism and organized crime. In such situations, terrorism threat analysis can become difficult and convoluted from a theoretical point of view because while terrorist organizations or loosely formed terrorist proto-groups conduct terrorism to address political and economic grievances, criminal syndicalist organizations practice terrorism primarily to increase economic profits [20, 91–111; 21; 64, 138; 85, 52–67].

At a theoretical level, the use of terrorism across terrorist and criminal syndicalist groups is reminiscent of the theoretical overlap between different conflict conditions described in Chap. 1 and in previous work [16, 84–89; 87, 8]. For example, in the Second World War, the bombings of Hiroshima and Nagasaki, the London Blitz, and the bombing of Dresden can be considered examples of the overlap between "total war" "oppression," "repression," and "state terrorism" [16, 84–89].

R. J. Chasdi, *Corporate Security Surveillance*, Advanced Sciences and Technologies for Security Applications, https://doi.org/10.1007/978-3-031-39550-5_4

In a similar vein, there can be overlap between organizations that theoretically fall in the domain of terrorist groups, and drug cartels which fall in the domain of organized crime. Clearly, organized criminal enterprises can also use terrorism as I define it in Chap. 2 in the ways that terrorist groups do, oftentimes to acquire similar objectives.

For example, in that terrorism definition, I describe, "the threat, practice, or promotion of force for political objectives …to influence the political attitudes or policy dispositions of a third party…." such judges, politicians, police, and other state officials. However, a basic difference is that in the case of criminal syndicalists, the primary goal is the pursuit of profit [14, 24, 50n24; 15, 9, 52, 58n58]. Hence, those overlap conditions sometimes make binary and mutually exclusive classification of a violent group as either an example of a terrorist group or an example of a criminal syndicalist group, theoretically problematic and therefore a challenge for researchers.

4.2 Mexico—The Political Context of Criminal Syndicalism

A substantive discussion about terrorism requires a basic understanding of the political context where terrorism is practiced. Mexico's political framework is a federal system of government where Mexican states are broken down into municipalities, with the exception of Mexico City (Ciudad de Mexico). In comparison, districts in Mexico are administrative units, primarily used for election purposes.

Mexico is a country characterized by a set of seemingly intractable political contradictions. It is commonplace to note that scholars do not consider Mexico to be a "failed" or "failing state" on a par with states like Somalia, Afghanistan, Sierra Leone, Liberia, Yemen, Tajikistan, or Myanmar for example. However, Mexico has many national characteristics that resemble those found in "failed" or "failing states". Those include makeshift or incomplete government control over certain areas, such as in Mexico's northwest region, and wide-spread corruption, found at national and state levels, and within the ranks of local police and municipal officials.

The scope of corruption in Mexico has contributed to the inability of Mexico's national government to monopolize control over the use of force. This is similar to conditions found in most failed and failing states; it is at odds with Max Weber's notion of a fully functional and strong "rational-legal state" [3, 1–18; 6, 35, 43, 51; 9, 34–35, 32–33, 41–43; 10; 11, 163, 159, 161; 64, 138; 68, 196–198, 204–206; 93, 123]. Nowadays, what Bunker and Sullivan call "third phase cartels" operate in Mexico as formidable competitors to the Mexican government. Those drug cartels "…rule parallel polities or criminal enclaves, acting much like warlords." [9, 34–35, 32–33, 42–43; 68, 198; 90, 92].

At the same time, Mexico's democracy has continued to evolve, with the election of President Vincente Fox Quesada in 2000. President Fox Quesada, who succeeded President Ernesto Zedillo Ponce de León was affiliated with the National Action Party (PAN). What is significant about the election of Fox is that this election signaled the end of the complete political dominance of Mexico's Partido Revolucionario Institucional (Institutional Revolutionary Party).

In the narrower sense, that is important because of PRI's long-standing involvement with Mexico's drug trade, and that trade's historical focus on American markets. That relationship served as the blueprint for ties between certain officials in Mexico's national government, and both state and local Mexican government support and collusion with drug traffickers—both remain basic hallmarks of the contemporary Mexican drug trade [7, 787–789, 791–792; 23, 308, 314; 68, 196–198, 204–206].[1]

In addition to the development of Mexico's democracy, Mexico's economy has flourished since the introduction of substantial economic sector privatization and business deregulation policies that started in the 1980s. Those economic liberalization and reform policies allowed for greater international private sector investment into formerly government regulated industries. Accordingly, Mexico has developed a large and vibrant economy with international impact, not only within NAFTA, now known as the United States, Mexico, Canada, Agreement (USMCA), but throughout the world [6; 46, 28–29; 47, 271–273; 79, 81–82].

While the foregoing are positive developments, what stands out is how those changes in Mexican democracy and the growth of Mexico's economy contrasts to other more troubling political conditions that, as previously mentioned, resemble conditions in many failed and failing states. An important source of those political conditions in Mexico derive from what Huntington calls the "praetorian state" [29, 68, 72; 42; 49, 63, 192–196, 209].

For Huntington, the "praetorian state" is a condition where religious clergy, paramilitary leaders, or warlords for example, make political decisions of national significance outside of legitimate political institutions. For instance, the powerful ISI (Inter-Services Intelligence) in Pakistan, or certain rogue ISI members, has made some largely independent political decisions outside the scope of Islamabad's national government that essentially fit the requirements of Huntington's "praetorian state".

In the case of Mexico, that internal or parallel state is run by networks of drug cartel chieftains, corrupt political officials at both national and state levels, police officials, and judges who form complex and, in some cases, highly unstable alliances. In Mexico, the one governmental institution largely untainted by full-blown corruption is Mexico's navy; some Mexican officials have relied heavily on the navy to implement anti-drug policies.

Invariably, those alliances between drug cartels and some state officials work to promote political instability, social unrest, and violence. That is the case because the alliances that drug cartels create with certain government officials pit the interests of drug cartels against each other. To begin with, some of that instability stems from the inherent instability of the cartel structure, as cartel factions have potential to promote factional interests at the expense of the interests of a cartel. Such drug cartel dynamics are similar to the processes of the Organization of Petroleum Exporting

[1] For example, Medel and Thoumi point to Mexico's Federal Directorate of Security (DFS) that was dissolved in 1985 because of its links to drug traffickers.

Countries (OPEC) where there is incentive for individual states to pump oil beyond their official allotments [12, 165–166; 79, 83].

In addition, another source of instability in Mexico and other countries with similar problems derives from the interaction between the drug cartels themselves. Much like the nation-states that Wolfers describes in his analysis of how countries interact, drug cartels pursue their best interests; this is a game that other nation states and drug cartels also play. Therefore, it inevitable that cartels will bump into each other in the way that nation-states do for Wolfers, "like billiards on a billiard table" [97, 29–45].

It follows that with Mexico's problem with weak political institutionalization, drug cartels have made enormous strides in controlling areas critical to drug trafficking [62, 27, 7, 11–12]. For example, Campbell and Hansen report that by 2013, Mexican drug cartels were in charge of nearly three quarters of all municipalities (71.5%) in Mexico, locales that successive Mexican governments have called "zones of impunity" [11].

4.3 Terrorist Groups Operative in the Political Landscape

In the case of anti-government terrorist organizations active between 2007 and 2018, the Popular Revolutionary Army (EPR) emerged in 1996. It was led by Comandante Francisco who received support from several other comandantes, including Comandante Oscar, Comandante Victoria, and Comandate José Arturo [43, 210–212; 94, 280, 283, 226, 174]. The EPR is considered a terrorist group by the Mexican government and is the second armed movement to take up the cause of economic inequality and social justice issues in Mexico. Its creation in 1996 followed on the heels of the formation of the Zapatista National Liberation Army (EZLN) in 1994.

For Weinberg, the EPR is an example of a more traditional Marxist-Leninist terrorist group with a vanguard at the helm of fierce struggle to emancipate indigenous people and mestizos in Mexico [94, 225, 281, 194]. That struggle revolved around systemic political discrimination, government policies which favored international corporate interests and wealthy Mexican landowners, and economic blight conditions.

In comparison, the leadership of the EZLN placed a premium on a "bottoms-up" collectivist approach to policy decision-making. That emphasis was based on the past practices and experiences of political associations in the 1980s, such as OCEZ (Emiliano Zapata Peasant Organization), that were devoted to efforts to reclaim or provide restitution for land belonging to indigenous peoples seized by the Mexican government [43, 108–109].

The sources and origins of EPR remain somewhat murky. While it was probably formed in Sierra Madre del Sur, in the state of Guerrero, some argue the EPR was either a drug trafficking group or a PRI party artifact, crafted to carry out "false flag" activities against state interests. The idea was those actions would create a pretext for Mexican government action against Mexican communities supportive of the EZLN [43, 279–280].

Sole issue or "single issue" terrorist groups have had an important role in Mexico's terrorism landscape. Both the Earth Liberation Front (ELF) and the Animal Liberation Front (ALF) have conducted terrorist actions, for the most part against ATM machines at established banks in Mexico. One Global Terrorism Data (GTD) scripted account suggests ties between those two organizations, with a report that an ELF terrorist assault against an ATM in Mexico City was claimed by ELF on a website called "Biteback," run by the Animal Liberation Front [33].

There is not much publicly available information about the Mexican terrorist group, "Individuals Tending Towards Savagery." As described below, the "Individuals Tending Towards Savagery" remained a terrorist group oriented towards environmental protectionism. It also appears to embrace a somewhat Luddite standpoint in regards to the role that technology plays in contemporary society [6; 71, 135–136; 76, 561; 77, 576–579].

4.4 Mexico's War Against Drug Traffickers

The contemporary drug war in Mexico against the cartels began in 2006. It traces an arc to "Operation Condor" in 1977, where for the first time, there was significant involvement of Mexico's military in sustained efforts to dismantle drug organizations. The introduction of the military in that fierce political struggle reflected the hardline view of President Felipe Calderón (Partido Acción Nacional—PAN) who argued that reliance on the military was the best approach to Mexico's burgeoning drug problem.

Sometimes known as the "kingpin strategy," there has been debate in academic and policy circles about whether or not, and if so to what degree, this Calderón sponsored hardline military strategy has contributed to the high degree of internecine conflict between Mexican drug organizations. That anti-drug cartel "kingpin" strategy continued under President Enrique Peña Nieto, and was a hallmark of the current Andrés Manuel López Obrador administration, at least in early years [17, 273; 65, pptx; 67].

In the broader sense, President Calderón's war against Mexican drug lords also corresponded with a 1990s shift in the international cocaine trade route epicenter in the Western Hemisphere. That drug network originally started in Colombia, but with U.S. supported drug interdiction efforts in Colombia, that locus of international drug activity began to shift to Mexico. Those U.S. supported interdiction efforts focused against FARC and drug organizations [6, 1, 60, 65, 42, 37, 39, 58–59; 11, 158–159, 170; 13, 12; 23, 308, 324; 41, 29–30; 67] (Wainwright 2007, 237–238). In addition, the easy access that Mexico afforded to nearby American drug markets helped compel drug cartel leaders to move the bulk of cocaine trafficking operations to Mexico [6, 43; 13, 12, 16–17]. It should be noted FARC is a Columbian based Marxist insurgent group and not usually classified as a "drug organization" even though it has colluded with Mexican drug cartels [65].

In fact, that American supported anti-drug war in Colombia against FARC, Pablo Escobar's Medellín Cartel, and other drug cartels was the basic template for President

Calderón's hardline policies. American supported Colombian anti-drug campaigns such as "Operation Stopgap," "Plan Colombia," "Plan Patriota," and the "Mérida Initiative," almost always reflected the American preference for proactive attacks against the supply-side part of the drug problem. Unfortunately, that supply side focus of anti-drug cartel campaigns overshadowed the importance of emphasis on the demand-side of the problem, largely found in the United States [6, 67–68; 9, 47; 52, 2; 67; 93, 7, 13–14, 20].

4.5 Globalization Links to Terrorism and Criminal Syndicalism

The functional overlap between terrorist groups and organized crime is a comparatively recent development, spurred on by the end of the Cold War, the subsequent spread of capitalism, and the continuously evolving system of globalization. In the case of Mexico, what Gilman et al. call "deviant globalization" includes not only drug organization activities, but weapons and munitions procurement. Kuhn and Bunker report that in addition to illegal weapons that traverse the U.S.-Mexico border and the weapons supplied by corrupted Mexican army and police officials, "...a clear connection to the weapons (acquired and currently within the inventories of the cartels) and governments/arms trafficking in Central America, South America, Eastern and Northern Europe exits." [31, 3–13; 54, 99–100, 102, 105–106, 95–98].[2]

Equally important, new theoretical problems for terrorism research appeared in conjunction with those developments. One source of new theoretical problems for terrorism research emanated from a set of new globalization dimensions or characteristics that emerged in the late twentieth century. This new phase of "intensive globalization" is both a cause and effect of new technological innovation, and creates an ever-expanding system that is a hallmark of the post-Cold War world. That is the case even though globalization is an age-old phenomenon that traces an arc back at least to the sea faring Phoenicians and to Ancient Hellas.

Hence, what I describe as "intensive globalization" is really a new dimension of a condition that dates back to antiquity. As previously mentioned, in its present form, globalization is inextricably bound up with new technological innovation. The synthesis of globalization and late twentieth century computer technology helped to create an augmented globalization system characterized by both physical and virtual network connections [17, 1, 183n1; 52; 73, 17; 93, 133–134].[3]

That condition of "intensive globalization" has increased economic opportunities and the prospect of sustained economic growth for many but not all developing world states. That is the case largely because multi-national corporation (MNC) offshoring

---

[2] For Kuhn and Bunker, the notion that U.S. guns which traverse the U.S. border to Mexico somehow account for 90% of guns belonging to Mexican drug organizations is spurious.

[3] My term "intensive globalization" largely corresponds with Nayar's idea of "deep globalization".

to developing world countries and MNC outsourcing activities for specific services have allowed firms to reduce their fixed and variable costs and expand profit margins.

However, contemporary globalization is no panacea for much of the developing world's economic backwater condition as it is certainly not able to provide benefits for all developing countries [63, A-1, A-12]. In many cases, the developing world states left outside the scope of globalization effects are "failed" states with profound and lasting political control and economic infrastructure problems. Indeed, investors will avoid investment in those states because of the acute risk to foreign direct investment (FDI) and to the personal safety of employees.

In other cases, nation-states outside of the scope of globalization's effects have continued on their trajectory to "failed" nation-state status. In those cases, FDI flows end or are severely curtailed by international investors as the stability of political and economic conditions deteriorate. Hence, the often-quoted axiom associated with globalization, namely that "a rising tide will lift all ships," does not apply to all developing world countries.

There has been noticeable growth in the number of "failed" and "failing" states that has corresponded with the increased impact of what Kegley calls the "North–South Divide." In this "North–South Divide," political inequalities and economic disparities have created strains and tensions between those two blocs where in the "North," political institutions usually work well, and in the "South," where these "hollowed out" states are usually found, political institutions work poorly or not at all [31, 3–13; 93, 123].

In "failed" and some "failing" states, what most people assume to be basic government services that are provided in exchange for taxation are not readily available to the general population. Those services include reliable police protection, clean water provision at affordable prices, educational infrastructure, medicines, and effective sanitation services; their absence is indicative of acute "political dysfunction."

As previously mentioned, conflict is often endemic in "failed" and "failing" states and as a result, leaders of international firms who are risk averse, will not commit to FDI or other forms of investment. Thus, such political dysfunction and economic backwater conditions are factors characterized by cross-fertilization effects, making each of those conditions more powerful in states afflicted with political instability.

Within the context of those problems, both Makarenko and Shelley and Picarelli point out that "failed" and "failing" states provide fertile grounds for the growth and development of terrorist organizations and organized criminal groups. Equally important, there is growth in the potential for both of these types of organizations to cooperate and collude, with "win–win" results [9, 42; 27, 596–598, 600–602, 612; 64; 83, 131–146; 84, 93–109; 85, 52–67; 89, 30, 32, 3]. In the larger world of action, examples of that type of symbiotic relationship abound. Those include Hezbollah in Venezuela, Sendero Luminoso ("the Shining Path") in Peru, and the Taliban in Afghanistan, whose leaders were supportive of poppy cultivation and opium production prior to the fall of Kabul in 2021 [18; 19; 45; 96, 133].

For terrorism specialists, all of the foregoing creates conditions where it is sometimes difficult to distinguish between political and criminal behavior, at least without more detailed knowledge about the contextual factors associated with the environments where specific forceful actions take place. Oftentimes, specific information about perpetrator motivations and original intensions in such attacks is extremely difficult to acquire. Structural changes in the international political system such as "intensive globalization," where new opportunities materialize for both terrorist groups and syndicalists, oftentimes make it even more difficult for researchers to make informed conjecture about perpetrator motivation and intention.

For example, take the case of the Somali pirates that raid international shipping targets. Somali pirates can be viewed as organized criminal elements (to a greater or lesser degree) if the primary goal of attacks is to increase pirate wealth. Conversely, if some of the actions taken by Somali pirates are politically driven expressions of despair about Somalia's political and economic conditions, those actions against ships in the Red Sea might qualify as terrorism. In fact, certain Somali pirate attacks might qualify as organized criminal activity and terrorism, consistent with the discussion of conflict overlap conditions described above and in Chap. 1.

4.6 The Theoretical Dimensions of Terrorism

The changes in the relationships between terrorist groups and organized crime documented here have theoretical implications. The point is that convergence of terrorist group and criminal enterprise interests is now commonplace to note and a hallmark of our contemporary world. As previously mentioned, that emergent condition poses new theoretical challenges which require new modifications to many existing definitions of terrorism penned during an era when distinctions between organized crime and terrorism were much less opaque.

The most robust terrorism definitions have conceptual fundamentals that remain immutable across time and spatial dimensions (i.e., geographical locale). Nevertheless, those definitions should also have the inherent flexibility to accommodate evidence of terrorist group structural change, such as movement away from hierarchal organizational structures, to "flat" or horizontal organizational structures. Such terrorism definitions also are able to accommodate stakeholders with new significance, such as lone operatives and cyberterrorists [9, 32–34; 52, 148–149].

Terrorist group organizational change mirrors the structural organizational changes found in the legitimate business world. In the business world, "flat" organizations are more characteristic of many start-up companies in the United States in places like Silicon Valley. At the same time, structural changes in organizational format involves new, more complex models of organization used both by terrorist organizations and criminal groups. As both types of organizations mature and grow, both types of organizations will require product portfolio diversification and specialization, to take advantage of new opportunities afforded by globalization.

For terrorist groups, complex organizational structures take into account the need of terrorist groups to raise funds by means of narcotics trafficking and other organized criminal activities, such as prostitution, money laundering, and credit card fraud. In the larger world of action, aspects of hierarchal and horizontal frameworks can be found in many terrorist and criminal organizations [6, 61, 64–65; 26, 237–253; 44, 6–18]. In addition, horizontal organizational structures have become more popular in the criminal enterprise netherworld because, as in the case of terrorist groups, horizontal organizational structures pose greater problems for law enforcement infiltration efforts than do hierarchal organizations.

Related to the embrace of horizontal frameworks characteristic of illicit organizations is the adaptation of the "leaderless resistance" model. The notion of "leaderless resistance" was first advocated by Ulius Louis Amoss, an American government intelligence specialist, and later by Ku Klux Klan leader Louis Beam who called for "leaderless resistance" within the context of FBI efforts to infiltrate into the Ku Klux Klan to snare its top leadership. The notion of "leaderless resistance" has been embraced by many criminal syndicalists involved with illicit trade and almost by definition, by "lone-wolf" operatives.

The need for theoretical flexibility in terrorism definition is neither new nor original. For example, the most useful "insurgent" or "oppositional" terrorism conceptualizations were crafted to distinguish between non-state actor terrorism and the use of illegitimate force by nation-states to pursue political objectives. For example, the invasion of Ukraine by President Vladimir Putin that began on February 24, 2022, is a conflict condition where state terrorism happens when the "laws of war" are violated by a country [80, 317–329; 81, 76–107; 82, 76–107].

Furthermore, terrorism definitions should be crafted to dovetail well with other state terrorism characteristics such as mobilization of the private sector, including research institutions. Such was the case in Nazi Germany when for example Volkswagen Daimler-Benz produced vehicles for Nazi military forces, and when the Bayer company, as part of IG Farben group, produced the Zyclon B poison pellets used in Nazi gas chambers.

In addition to the capacity to account for cyberterrorism, useful terrorism definitions should be able to distinguish between cyber-terrorism and cyber-crime, and other forms of cyber intrusion such as cyber-politicking, or the use of cyber-protest that some scholars call "hactivism" [9, 43; 17, 134; 25, 24–25]. One example of cyber-politicking would be the efforts made by the on-line group "Anonymous" to offset the Russian government's coverage of the War in Ukraine by hacking into Russian television and "streaming" sources, and into Russian Internet service sites [53].

The broader issue to address is whether or not there is theoretical equivalence between terrorist groups and what Phillips describes as the "terrorist tactics" used by organized criminal syndicalists primarily to enhance profits [27, 596–599, 612; 75, 56, 48, 46; 93, 270]. In other words, the issue is whether or not it is theoretically correct to call organizations that use terrorism terrorist groups, beyond the term as applied to traditional terrorist groups.

It follows that a related research area to be explored in the future is the definition of the threshold(s) where a non-terrorist organization that uses political terrorism, namely the illegitimate use of force to influence others politically, becomes a terrorist group and what constitutes crossing that threshold beyond a one-off use of terrorism.

As Flanigan reports in her work on syndicalists and terrorism, "to the extent that the activities of these two types of entities overlap, perhaps one key element in determining which label to apply is a matter of proportion." [28, 291].

Even though a comprehensive treatment of those issue areas is beyond the scope of this book, there are other possible metrics to approach that research topic that might be useful. Instead of reliance on quantitative thresholds of terrorist attacks to signal transition to a terrorist group, some scholars have focused on ideological transformation. Akerman and Burnham's perspective is one such example where efforts are made to mark, "...qualitative changes in an actor's ideology, by demarcating the point at which a violent actor's ideology takes on a terrorist character." [1, 6]. Although the authors' reasoning seems somewhat tautological because social, economic, or religious ideology is inherently political and "a terrorist character" is by nature political, the idea of qualitative benchmarks to mark the transition into a terrorist group is worthy of consideration.

4.7 Should "Terrorist Group" Describe Criminal Syndicalists and Gangs?

The extant literature suggests two standpoints about the theoretical equivalence between terrorist groups and criminal syndicalists who use terrorism. The first standpoint asserts the term terrorism is accurate to use, if qualified by such terms as "narco," to describe organized criminal activities if certain actions carried out by organized criminal elements meet at least some of terrorism's definitional criteria.

The second standpoint is that it is flawed outright from a theoretical point of view to label organized criminal syndicalists as terrorist groups. The reason why is that such a broad use of the term terrorism conflates two distinct types of organizations. For those who embrace that approach, each type of organization has different purposes and aims, differences in recruitment patterns, and different types of constituent groups, in ways that reflect overall differences in orientation and purpose. For some scholars, work that conflates these two types of organizations muddles analytical efforts at more meticulous comparisons about ideological and organizational similarities and differences between terrorist groups and criminal enterprises [27, 596–599; 90, 83–84, 93n23].[4]

For example, Campbell and Hansen's work falls in the first standpoint's domain, where the authors assert that syndicalists should qualify as terrorists because many of their actions conform to themes found in several terrorism definitions. Campbell and Hanson report that, "narco-terrorists (which may include corrupt police and military officials, as well as direct cartel members) are thus able to accrue power and obtain tight de facto control of specific locales that goes beyond mere regulation of drug trafficking routes." [11, 161, 160, 163, 170].

[4] Teiner presents Alex Schmid's important take on this point.

The authors go on to describe the importance of "...calculated symbolic language...." that criminal syndicalist groups use in communications to rival organizations and underlying efforts made to generate and sustain abject fear in the population [11, 161, 160, 163, 170; 75, 48]. The aforementioned is consistent with aspects of Rapoport's seemingly more open-ended definition of terrorism in this context that emphasizes "...extra-normal or extra-moral violence...." [28, 280, 283; 78, 73].

At one level, Campbell and Hansen's work points to actions or instrumentalities that capture some secondary goals such as population control in specific geographical locales to make the case that those two types of organizations should both be described as terrorist groups. Those shared instrumentalities include the need for population control and effective communications to various stakeholders to produce abject fear. But therein lies the problem as Campbell and Hansen's work is useful, but does not drill down further to illuminate sufficiently the nature of instrumentality differences that are found when terrorist groups and criminal syndicalist organizations are compared.

Campbell and Hansen's work is useful because it works to focus attention on what constitutes broader political goals and the ideologies behind them that are fully articulated in the case of terrorist organizations, but not for criminal syndicalist groups. That is important because for terrorist groups, political objectives are framed and contextualized within tightly woven narratives. That stands in contrast to the discourse of criminal organizations.

While criminal organization messages sent to rivals and other audiences might have some political elements attached, they are for the most part, narrower in scope, designed to facilitate illicit business operations. That contrasts sharply with terrorist group narratives that characterize manifestos and many other communications which re transmitted to broad audiences. It is that political backdrop which helps to distinguish terrorism from organized criminal activity and by extrapolation, terrorist groups from criminal enterprises that use terrorism.

Another example of work from this first standpoint is Longmire and Longmire's work in Teiner's discussion about the nature of those two types of organizations that the author frames within the context of his ("narco") terrorism and "criminal insurgency" debate [90, 92, 85].[5] Longmire and Longmire draw on observable similarities between terrorist organizations and criminal syndicalists to make the case that Mexican criminal syndicalist groups can be called terrorist groups. The authors report that, "tactics, strategy, organization, and even (to a limited extent) the goals of the Mexican drug cartels are perfectly consistent with those of recognized terrorist organizations." [90].

The first problem with Longmire and Longmire's argument is that "strategies," "tactics," and "organization" are not characteristics that distinguish terrorist groups from syndicalist organizations in the same way that political ideology, goals, and

[5] For Teiner, Haupt makes an argument similar to Campbell and Hansen to assert that both terrorist groups and criminal syndicalists work with similar aims, namely to undercut the ultimate decision-making power of the state and its capacities.

recruitment patterns are distinguishing characteristics used to sort out different terrorist groups into categories of terrorist group-types. [14, 68–70, 80n25, 26; 81n33, 204n56; 30, 4–5, 146, 149, 157, 161; 59, 24; 74, 63, 65].

It follows those efforts to distinguish terrorist groups from criminal syndicalist organizations should be consistent with methodologies used to distinguish between different types of terrorist groups. Instead, in ways that resemble Campbell and Hansen's work, what Longmire and Longmire describe are descriptive attributes rather than a set of distinguishing characteristics.

Longmire and Longmire's focus on those three descriptive attributes has limited utility for classification efforts and resemble other descriptive attributes such as age and size that themselves do not amount to distinguishing characteristics [14, 68–70, 80n25, 26, 81n33, 204n56; 30, 4–5, 146, 149, 157, 161; 59, 24; 74, 63, 65]. For example, it is known that irrespective of political ideology, recruitment patterns, or leadership, all terrorist organizations become larger or smaller, as they mature and inevitably decline. Therefore, age and size are not useful distinguishing characteristics to differentiate terrorist groups from each other, or terrorist groups from criminal syndicalist groups.

In a similar vein, "strategies," "tactics," and "organization" are descriptive attributes of all terrorist and criminal organizations. In each case, particular outfits at particular moments in time, are subject to strategic, tactical and organizational change. It follows that whether or not a terrorist organization is hierarchal or horizontal or its strategies are X and Y at particular times is irrelevant to making meaningful comparisons between terrorist groups, and between terrorist groups and organized criminal outfits.

In a similar vein, there is a problem with the basic logic behind the notion that observable similarities somehow make it possible to conclude terrorist groups and criminal syndicalists which use terrorism amount to the same type of entity. An example might serve to illustrate the problem. Imagine a situation where an exotic car can travel at excessive speed in a straight line much like an airplane, where speed is analogous to the tactics used by both organizations.

In this example, the aircraft and automobile each have the same goal, to arrive at a destination as quickly as possible. However, that does not make them the same or even similar modes of transportation. If terrorist groups and organized criminal enterprises each have the same tactics analogous to speed and the same goal analogous to destination arrival, that does not make them identical modes of transportation.

To reiterate, some scholars use broad brush strokes to make the case that drug cartels which use terrorism amount to terrorist groups. In many cases, the conclusion those scholars reach is largely based on some set of superficial similarities found between these different types of organizations.

Oftentimes, those similarities focus on methodologies used in the context of achieving secondary goals like population control that are subordinate to the primary goal involved, which is to make money. The problem is that such observations are just visual notation and description. While those observations probably indicate some conceptual overlap between these two types of organizations, free association observations do not constitute rigorous efforts at typology construction for classification purposes.

Conversely, many scholars embrace a second standpoint, namely that terrorism is not an appropriate term to describe criminal enterprises. From this standpoint, what constitutes a fundamental difference between terrorist organizations and criminal syndicalist groups is that to qualify as a terrorist group, political goals must predominate over economic goals. While work to underscore the overriding difference in goals (and thus ideology) is the correct conceptualization, at least as far as it goes, it is worth noting from the start that distinction in and of itself has some limitations because it does not take time passage into account.

For example, it is reasonable to assume that in some criminal organizations, acute political needs such as alliance building, wars with rivals, or the capacity to weather the storm of an anti-drug government campaign might rank of equal importance or near equal importance to profit accumulation at particular time intervals. In other words, in such crisis situations, existential political necessities might even temporarily outrank profit maximization as a goal.

It follows that the problem with this hard and fast distinction between political and economic goals is that this approach remains stagnant, without the flexibility required to take into account shifting priorities, given the reality that political or economic shocks to both types of organizations in specific operational environments can and do happen; both terrorist groups and criminal enterprises experience external political and economic set-backs and relapses, that in turn might lead to internal problems.

In work that embraces this second standpoint, Phillips cautions against wholesale application of the term terrorism to criminal organizations. At the same time, Phillips helps to continue our exploration of the boundaries of the political dimensions associated with terrorism because his argument places emphasis on how politics, what Lasswell describes as "who gets what when and how," is intrinsically bound up with thinking about terrorism [57].

It appears Phillips' discussion mirrors Weinberg, Pedahzur, and Hirsch-Hoefler's take on political terrorism, with its emphasis on "disruption" of government control and capacities to provide services, or the goal of outright government replacement, or both. In the process, Phillips suggests a set of firm boundaries around what should constitute political goals. He cites Williams, who himself draws on Clausewitz, to suggest that in contrast to political terrorism, syndicalist terrorism constitutes the, "continuation of business by other means." [75, 46–47]. It follows that if profit is the primary goal of perpetrators, an act should be classified as organized criminal activity or common criminal activity, falling short of terrorism.

What amounts to a dichotomous approach to the relationship between political goals and economic goals here also has limitations with the central notion that motivations which drive behavior to achieve goals are either profit oriented or political. As Collier and Hoeffler demonstrate with their "greed and grievance" model of terrorism, the goal of terrorism can be a mixture of both, found along a "greed and grievance" continuum.

Hence from this perspective, the relationship between political and economic goals is a continuous rather than a dichotomous relationship, which means greed or grievance motivations are not an either-or proposition [20, 91–111; 21]. It follows that if motivations are mixed or have the potential to be mixed, goals should also have the potential to be mixed.

What is significant here is Collier and Hoeffler's point about "greed and grievance" illustrates the potential for convoluted political goals or competing goals with cross purposes, even for terrorists. For criminal enterprises, the concept of convoluted or mixed political goals is also relevant. The reason why is because the communications of criminal syndicalist groups that use terrorism have some similarities to terrorist group communications.

That is the case even though the political component to their communications and activities is narrower, and more makeshift and incomplete. That, coupled with the importance of economic gain for criminal groups overall, makes it very likely the sources of syndicalist group terrorist event motivations are also determined by different mixtures of political and economic factors.

In addition, what is known is that amorphous or ill-defined political aims can span across the ideological gamut of different terrorist group-types. For example, the experiences of some religious extremist terrorist groups, nationalist-irredentist terrorist groups, and the nihilist group Aum Shinrikyo for instance, demonstrate that what constitutes goals, even in the realm of the more purely political, can be amorphous or ill-defined. That contributes to a condition where sometimes the line between crime and terrorism is permeable or otherwise hard to discern.

The notion of "disruption" that Weinberg, Pedahzur, and Hirsch-Hoefler raise is useful because it describes drug cartel leader interest in efforts to control cities or regions to promote drug cultivation and distribution. However, the authors' focus on efforts to oust government or "disruption" as goals somehow does not appear to underscore the idea that more mundane political processes and events such as killing police officers or influencing the judicial system also characterize most criminal organization activities, even though such processes are in most cases secondary and subordinate to profit maximization.

An important characteristic of the political dimensions associated with criminal syndicalism is those dimensions are smaller in scope than the political objectives associated with terrorist groups. However, those dimensions are still political in nature, and critical for understanding the context for drug smuggling, human trafficking, and other illegal cartel activities [9, 41; 93, 215].

A related issue with the Weinberg, Pedahzur, and Hirsch-Hoefler argument revolves around its focus on "disruption" as a goal, without more rigorous efforts to distinguish between types of "disruption," and possible implications for government and business policies. In fact, terrorist "disruption" activities can be either a means or an end (i.e., a goal) or a means and a goal at the same time.

There are additional problems with focus on "disruption" to help define political terrorism. For example, "disruption" as a means or a goal or both, is not the exclusive domain of either terrorist groups or criminal enterprises, as political protestors for example also have a vested interest in disruption strategies and tactics. Therefore, an emphasis on "disruption" is not especially useful in scholarly efforts to make theoretical distinctions between terrorism and organized crime.

What that all suggests is that the range or tenor of the political goals scoped out by Weinberg, Pedahzur, and Hirsch-Hoefler could be expanded beyond "disruption," and "government replacement" [75]. For example, propaganda victories, or efforts to facilitate two- or three-party negotiations, and what Kydd and Walter call the promotion of "social control" could be pursued by both terrorist groups and governments [55; 75, 52, 56, 58–59, 64, 67]. Plainly, such efforts move beyond efforts to "disrupt" or undermine government stability, function, and overall durability.

Therefore, it follows the essential difference between drug cartels and terrorist groups involves the nature of the political dimension and pursuits at hand, namely the difference between political goals for criminal syndicalists and political ideology for terrorist organizations. Put another way, the issue revolves around the relationship between political objectives and the presence or absence of solid political context. Such political context itself consists of what Ackerman and Burnham call a "belief system" about normative societal goals [1, 7–8, 13; 27, 598]. As a result, those who eschew the use of the term terrorist group to describe drug cartels are correct in broader theoretical terms because of these basic conceptual differences.

This critical distinction between the tightly interwoven political themes characteristic of the terrorist narrative, and the more makeshift and functional narrative characteristic of criminal syndicalist messages when terrorism is used, is worthy of additional discussion. It follows the terrorism used by criminal syndicalists might be more reactive than terrorist group terrorist assaults. It also follows those criminal syndicalist communications might be more oriented towards the short-run interval across issue areas in comparison to terrorist group narratives. Plainly, those topics deserve the increased attention of researchers [1, 11–13; 27].

In the broadest sense, what seems clear is that political goals for criminal organizations are not ideologically driven with clearly articulated political platforms in the mainstream political system that shape political support. That is the case even though criminal enterprises such as the Sinaloa and Knights Templar cartels for example, provide community benefits such as education, hospitals, and protection, to help generate and sustain political loyalties in communities. Clearly, the provision of such social services can bind constituents and supporters to criminal syndicalists in the ways that resemble how terrorist groups help galvanize constituent support with the provision of constituent services [9, 45; 41, 79; 89, 35, 42; 90, 90–91].

However, the provision of social services by criminal gangs to meet the demands and aspirations of people whose needs are not addressed by government, is not the same as the promotion of a well-articulated political agenda. By contrast to social services and communiques about them, the political agendas of terrorist groups propose structural political and economic change to benefit broader segments of society within a broader, established, and legitimate political system.

In essence, Teiner's work acknowledges the basics of that difference in perspective when he reports that for some scholars, "…the cartels were lacking any form of ideology or political motivation, thus excluding them from being considered terrorists." [1, 16; 90, 92]. In addition, while the audience scope as well as the structure of those political goals are usually different for criminal syndicalists and terrorist groups, what helps establish conceptual overlap between terrorist groups and criminal organizations is the political nature of those goals.

As previously mentioned, some scholars who support the use of the term terrorism to describe criminal enterprises craft arguments with logic gap problems. It is also the case that some scholars opposed to that approach do the same. For example, some scholars make distinctions between terrorist groups and criminal enterprises based on the political objective of land control, acquisition, or both.

The crux of that argument is that terrorist groups are interested in land control, while criminal enterprises do not pursue that goal [75, 49–51; 90, 86, 90]. The reason why that argument is flawed is because criminal enterprises do acquire land to control or facilitate illicit drug activities that in the case of Mexico are known as "zones of impunity." Those "zones of impunity" or "drug corridors" serve to facilitate other criminal activities like human trafficking. In addition, the argument is flawed because lone operatives who are regarded as terrorists if their actions have political dimensions, also have no interest in land control or acquisition.

To reiterate, what is significant is that most terrorist groups have well-articulated manifestos or political agendas or at least parts thereof which advocate for structural political and economic change in the legitimate political arena. Indeed, that is consistent with the widely shared and generally recognizable political role terrorist groups play to influence event outcomes.

Indeed, Hoffman reports terrorist groups work as illicit "pressure groups" within a political system [48, 10–15]. Hoffman's inference is that terrorist groups draw on ideologically based conversations with government officials, constituent groups, and rival terrorist organizations to influence those outcomes [48, 10–15]. In comparison, most criminal enterprises issue political messages that lack that overarching political or religious ideological framework where communications are directed broadly at government and the population writ large.

Nevertheless, there are exceptions to this observation as Ackerman and Burnham report. For example, the Mexican cartel La Familia Michoacána is a "quasi-religious" drug cartel with religious underpinnings and its own set of moral imperatives for people to follow in states like Jalisco, Guerrero, and Michoacán. Likewise, Bunker and Sullivan point to the influence of the "narco-saints," such as Santa Muerte and Jesús Malverde on certain Los Zetas and other cartel activists, and their actions as another example of "quasi-religious" thinking associated with some, but certainly not all, cartel members [1, 10, 11–13; 6; 9, 44–46; 28, 286, 288, 290; 89, 35, 42–44].

In other words, the trend is for syndicalists to engage in political acts without well-articulated or formal ideological context to influence a population or government over and beyond what is necessary to manipulate processes associated with the legitimate political system for business activities. In most cases, syndicalists work in "low profile" capacities to influence judges, police, other state officials, or rival gangs.

The central idea that criminal enterprises communicate without well-articulated political agendas outside or beyond the parameters of legitimate political systems is augmented by Ackerman and Burnham's notion that terrorist groups have an underlying political morality tale to tell linked to prominent societal concerns. In comparison, criminal enterprise criminal goals do not embrace a political morality tale, but instead constitute, "...decidedly amoral concerns such as procedural prescriptions or desired properties of the natural world." [1, 9, 14].

In addition, there are other important differences between terrorist groups and criminal syndicalist groups that conduct terrorism. White's solid description of the differences between criminals (i.e., syndicalist groups), and terrorists and terrorist groups, puts focus on the different motivational factors associated with people who gravitate towards the orbit of each type of organization [27, 597–599, 612; 95, 14–15, 22–23].

Generally speaking, people who gravitate towards organized crime highly value economic interests and do not express much if any in the way of political motivations as drivers to join criminal organizations. As previously mentioned, the political messages of criminal syndicalist groups are frequently characterized by narrower functionality issues designed to promote effective economic operations, such as control and subordination of populations and rivals.

For White and many other scholars, the reverse is true for the recruitment pool of terrorist organizations where candidates are imbued with the notion of making a large and significant political impact [27, 597–599, 612; 95, 14–15, 22–23]. Terrorist groups appeal to broad based political notions of independence or greater autonomy for particular ethnic or religious groups distinguished from others by race. To be more specific, terrorist group chieftains attach themselves to broad political demands and aspirations of specific populations.

It follows that similar dynamics influence differences in terrorist organization leadership standpoints in regards to their roles and the objectives scoped out to pursue. In comparison, the norms and values of terrorist group chieftains contrast sharply with corresponding norms and values that leaders of criminal syndicalist organizations embrace.

At the same time, White and other scholars suggest there are some important similarities between terrorist groups and criminal enterprises that contribute to the debate about the appropriateness of the terms terrorist group and terrorism to describe some criminal organizations and their activities. For instance, both the leaders of terrorist groups and criminal enterprises are rational actors.

In addition, both types of organizations are able to threaten or use force in pursuit of political objectives, although as mentioned previously, the nature of political objectives pursued is different. For terrorist groups and for criminal syndicalists, at least in some cases, the purpose of those forceful actions is to generate abject fear in the population. Further, both types of organizations can and do use similar criminal methods to generate wealth, such as credit card fraud and money laundering schemes [52, 28, 75; 55, 67–69].

There are other similarities between terrorist groups and criminal syndicalist organizations worthy of note. According to Kydd and Walter, terrorist group chieftains make carefully reasoned appraisals about different "cost tolerances" to terrorism that characterize different types governments. For terrorists, those appraisals illuminate which governments provide the best rate of return for terrorism use. For Kydd and Walter, "dovish" governments have lower "cost tolerances" vis a vis terrorism, and "hawkish" governments have higher "cost tolerances." In turn, the authors report that, "the dove-hawk dimension may correlate with the left–right dimension in domestic politics, leading left-wing parties to be more likely to grant terrorist demands." [55, 62, 70, 74, 79–80].

It follows that Kydd and Water's "cost tolerances" matrix also extends to regime-type. Western style liberal democracies might have lower "cost tolerances" than authoritarian systems, and where, in the case of democratic regimes, differences in individual leader sensitivities to death and casualties might also affect "cost tolerances." [55, 62, 70, 74, 79–80].

As the rationality assumption in decision-making presumably holds for cartel leaders at least in most cases, similar processes are likely found in the criminal enterprise leadership calculus about when to use or threaten to use force. This brings us full circle, back to the Phillips argument that organized crime sometimes uses "terrorism tactics." It might be prudent to think about a certain select set of actions a criminal organization can take as "terrorist tactics," and it follows criminal organizations that use terrorism methods are "hybrid groups," to use Shelley and Picarelli's phrase [28, 287, 298, 291; 75, 49; 84, 93–109; 85, 54; 89, 30–31].

4.8 Conceptual Placement of "Hybrid" Criminal-Terrorist Groups

That overall condition of "hybrid" criminal-terrorist organizations and efforts to position them within a related conflict condition conceptualization in previous work can be illustrated with a Venn Diagram. In that Venn Diagram, those activities fall within the intersection of two circles that represent terrorism and organized criminal activity, as illustrated in Chap. 1.

As previously discussed, previous work showcased terrorism and terrorism related conflict conditions with conceptual and functional overlap in the larger world of action. Those conflict conditions marked by conceptual overlap include "total war," "oppression," and "terrorism," where a small sliver of each type of action qualifies as an example of each of the other conflict conditions [16, 84–89; 27, 597–598, 606, 612; 60; 87, 8; 88].

In Mexico, such conflict condition overlap between oppression, terrorism, and total war was plain to see within the context of federal and state government efforts to dismantle the Zapatista National Liberation Army (EZLN) and quell support for the broader Zapatista movement [70, 79]. To illustrate those overlapping conditions, the case of the EZLN, that for the most part qualifies as a "justifiable insurgency" rather than a terrorist group in my judgement, is worthy of further discussion.

Many analysts do not consider the EZLN to be a terrorist group, but rather an example of justifiable insurgency, even though there are some incidents of terrorism documented [79, 78].[6] It began operations after it became clear the path to substantive negotiations with the Mexican government had been irrevocably blocked and that all non-violent conflict alternatives had been exhausted without success. It was also careful to marshal its forces only against Mexican security forces for the brief time it engaged in armed struggle.

The EZLN began to galvanize in the Chiapas part of the Lacandon Forest in 1983 in reaction to decades of unfulfilled promises by Mexico's governments. Those promises revolved around efforts to redress fundamental political demands and grievances of indigenous peoples like the Tzeltal, Tzotzil, and the Chol [43, 195, 79–85, 89–90, 147–168; 72, 20, 22, 24–25].

The specific issues in contention included, but were not limited to, economic blight conditions, infant mortality, government land seizure, devolution of government to the community level, problems with credit union loan opportunities for indigenous people, corruption problems linked coffee retail operations, and exorbitant interest rates [2, 680–682; 43, 81, 84, 86, 89–90, 156, 162; 72, 20–21, 23; 94, 191, 233].

The EZLN led Chiapas rebellion, with sub-comandante Marcos-Rafael Sebastián Gullén Vincente at the helm, began operations on January 1, 1994; as Al points out, that date corresponded with the establishment of the North American Free Trade Agreement (NAFTA) [2, 679, 682–685; 79, 78, 87; 94, 198].[7] For EZLN officials, NAFTA as a free trade area (FTA) symbolized how intensive globalization in particular, and the international liberal economic order in general, worked to undercut the interests of poor and marginalized people world-wide, and increase the enormous political and economic distance between the world's "have's" and "have-nots." [2, 679, 682–685; 66; 79, 79, 81–82, 98; 94, 192].

Early on in its struggle against the Mexican government, EZLN in 1994 stopped its armed campaign and worked to promote social justice and economic equity issues. In the process, as both Al and Rogers report, the EZLN gained an international reputation as a champion of such causes [2, 680, 683–685, 688–689, 691; 72, 20; 79, 78–79]. Sad to say, the same carefully reasoned approach used by EZLN to place limits on the threat or use of force in accordance with international law did not characterize the PRI government's tough and heavy handed response to the Zapatistas, implemented by PRI President Ernesto Zedillo.

In fact, police murders of protestors, beatings, and arrests signaled the use of state terrorism in the context of state oppression against Chiapas communities sympathetic to the Zapatistas. In addition, those state actions constituted repression efforts aimed at Zapatista movement leaders. Those activities happened in systematic and sustained ways prior to the Acteal massacre in 1997 in Chenalhó municipality, where a Mexican

[6] There are three EZLN business related terrorist events for 1994 and one for 1996 chronicled in the GTD data base. Those include: Global Terrorism Database (GTD) "Mexico" GTD ID: 199401050001, Date: January 5, 1994; Global Terrorism Database (GTD) "Mexico" GTD ID: 199401060001, Date: January 6, 1994; Global Terrorism Database "Mexico" GTD ID: 199401060002, Date: January 6, 1994; Global Terrorism Database (GTD) "Mexico" GTD ID: 199604290001, Date: April 29, 1996.

[7] Weinberg reports the possibility that "sub-comandante Marcos" might constitute more than one person.

paramilitary unit known as "Máscara Roja" (Red Mask) murdered 45 people camped on a roadside near Acteal [16, 84–89, 108, n199, 108, n201, 108, n202; 43, 155–156; 60; 61; 72, 20–22, 24; 79, 97; 87, 3–5, 8–9; 88, ix-v; 94, 169, 171].

The EZLN case highlights the conceptual overlap of state terrorism, oppression, and repression. Based on that, it is possible to add to the depiction of conceptual overlap in conflict conditions because certain criminal enterprise activities directed at populations or specific communities also fall into the domains of "oppression" and "terrorism" [16, 84–89, 108, n199, 108, n201, 108, n202].

Moreover, it might even be possible to include the conflict condition "total war" into this related conflict condition conceptualization to take into account criminal syndicalist organizations and some governments, such as the Putin regime in Russia, that use terrorism. That is the case because civilians are legitimate targets for drug cartels and for some militaries or paramilitary groups. In the case of both cartel drug activities, and government anti-drug campaigns, some people are hurt or killed purposefully. That approach dovetails nicely with a hallmark of "total war," namely private sector mobilization, in this case to support either cartel or government efforts to irradicate the other.

To summarize, this section presents a brief discussion about some of the theoretical complexities associated with the use of the term terrorism to describe drug cartels. Those theoretical complexities have increased to the point where coding decisions can sometimes be particularly vexing for terrorism analysts. For coding purposes, this study embraces the notion, found in Chaps. 1 and 2, that what constitutes terrorism is a judgement decision taking into account the event itself; whether or not it conforms to jurisprudential standards of the "laws of war."

To reiterate, what that means is the jurisprudential principles of *jus ad bellum* ("justice of war") and *jus in bello* ("justice in war") served as the essential guideposts for data interpretation and coding. Those juridicial standards were the basis for the coding process, irrespective of who, where, or what kind of organization practiced actions that qualified as terrorism [14; 15, 12–15, 20–22]. As the terrorism definition used in this study is jurisprudentially based and events driven, the actions of non-terrorist group organizations whose actions meet the terrorism criteria presented in Chap. 2 were included in this study.

4.9 Terrorist Group-Types and Terrorist Groups in Mexico

It is incumbent to note that in many cases, specific information about Mexican terrorist group and drug cartel actions that qualified as terrorism against commercial targets often remained makeshift and incomplete. While more general descriptive information about Mexican drug cartels is readily available, the GTD data and Micklous data used in this study suggest a large portion of Mexican drug cartel events which qualified as terrorism remained anonymous between 2007 and 2018.

Consequently, the large number of anonymous terrorist attacks directed against commercial interests in Mexico posed some analysis problems. It put limitations on attempts to describe the scope of specific drug cartel business target preferences for media targets or energy/alloy targets, for example. That condition did not make it possible to rank what the preferences were for business target types such as energy/alloy, or private establishments, across a range of Mexican drug cartels and terrorist groups.

Notwithstanding that, it is probably no exaggeration to say that a significant portion of anonymous terrorism against Mexican business targets was linked in some way to identifiable drug cartels in that controlled "drug corridors" or other Mexican locales that qualified as "plazas" or "zones of impunity" [9, 31, 45–46]. Even solid information about particular geographical locales that drug cartels controlled did not provide much if any insight into how to make informed conjecture about the perpetrators of anonymous terrorism in Mexico directed at commercial interests.

Aside from the lack of solid data, there appeared to be other related reasons why being able to identify the syndicalist organization in charge of specific geographical locales was of little help for perpetrator identification with respect to terrorist assaults. The first is what Bunker and Sullivan describe as the fledgling "third phase of drug cartel development" in Mexico. A hallmark of Bunker and Sullivan's "third phase of drug cartel development" is collaboration between drug cartels and subordinate criminal gangs that remain less sophisticated than the drug cartels which employ them, at least in most cases [9, 30–32, 34, 36–37, 42, 50; 50, 127; 89, 33]. Clearly, that condition increases difficulties in terrorist assault perpetrator identification.

While most Mexican criminal gangs put emphasis on more parochial or pedestrian interests such as "turf control," turf wars to facilitate control, and on profit made through drug sales in markets close to where those gangs are based, there remained some important exceptions. For example, organizations such as the "18th Street" outfit, and Mara Salvatrucha (MS-13), while operative in Mexico also crafted transnational connections in several parts of the United States [9, 30–32, 34, 36–37, 42, 50; 50, 127; 89, 33].

It follows that certain drug cartel terrorist acts were at least in some cases outsourced to criminal gangs to reduce risk of capture—to obscure the origins of attacks, and to impede government anti drug cartel efforts. The potential for temporary alliances of convenience, even across syndicalist groups under certain select conditions, and perhaps between particular gang members within subordinate gangs, further work to muddle attribution efforts.

Second, there is the issue of time passage and its effects. Over time drug cartels splinter and new splinter groups with many of the same individuals or spinoff groups, characterized by looser connections to parent organizations can emerge [16]. Nowadays, most drug cartel networks are characterized by independent or loosely connected nodes that continuously evolve.

For example, the control that specific criminal syndicalist groups wielded over particular locales in Mexico ebbed and flowed in large part because of inter-cartel conflict. Examples of such conflict include struggles between the Tijuana and Sinaloa cartels in the 1990s, and between the Sinaloa and Beltrán-Leyva Organization (BLO), following the decision BLO leaders made to side with Los Zetas, and the conflict between the Juárez and Sinaloa cartels in 2008 [5, 253, 255–256; 23, 313, 315, 316–317, 322; 41, 68, 72, 74–75; 50, 100, 105, 128; 69, 123].

The processes of group splintering or spinoff formation are characteristic of "horizontal" divisions between criminal syndicalist organizations. It follows that "vertical" interpenetration effects between criminal syndicalist groups and subordinate criminal gangs can also happen. In those cases, attachments form between especially talented criminal gang members and criminal syndicalist organizations. Those internal processes also contribute the dynamic nature of group composition and organizational control issues that can be volatile and hard to track.

Indeed, some authorities report those intra-group and intergroup processes have been exacerbated by President Calderón's proactive use of military force in anti-drug cartel efforts. Thus, any depiction or description of control that drug cartel groups have over particular areas is essentially a snap-shot in time. It is not necessarily reflective of drug cartel control conditions in place in particular locales at the time of attack, nor is it reflective of current realities [6, 43–44, 60, 65, 68; 9, 35; 13, 17] (Campbell and Hansen 2014, 166).

The problems with attempts to identify "criminal/terrorist hybrid groups" in the anonymous terrorism events data are consistent with [92] study of North American terrorism and its evolution over fifty-one years. The authors assert that for drug cartels or criminal gangs, "the only known perpetrators are the Jalisco New Generation Cartel, and the Pumba and Tata Cartel, and even then, they have only been put on record for one attack each—the Jalisco New Generation Cartel bombed a government embassy in Jalisco, and the Pumba and Tata Cartel bombed a business in Quintana Roo." [69, 123; 92, 7].[8] Clearly, Tibbet and Bankole's remarks mirror underlying problems with the data used in this study.

Between 2007 and 2018 there were five identifiable terrorist groups and three identifiable drug cartels or their affiliates that conducted terrorist assaults against commercial interests. There were two terrorist group-types crafted for the Mexico data—Marxist-Leninist terrorist organizations, and "sole issue" terrorist organizations. In turn, there was a third category articulated for anonymous terrorist events, and a fourth category, "criminal/terrorist hybrid groups."

This "criminal/terrorist hybrid groups" category captures the "hybrid" nature of criminal enterprises that caused political terrorism, but whose primary focus was on profit maximization [9; 75, 49; 84, 93–109; 85, 54, 43]. The Pumba and Tata Cartel (Pumba y Tata), Los Zetas, the Sinaloa gang (affiliate) identified, and Los Pelenos Gang fall into the category of the "hybrid-terrorist/criminal" group-type.

Not much information is publicly available about the Pumba and Tata Cartel. However, it appears to be a criminal organization associated with either the Sinaloa Cartel or Los Zetas [4, 8].[9] With its probable connections to either the Sinaloa Cartel or Los Zetas, the Pumba and Tata Cartel has put emphasis on terrorist attacks against

[8] At the same time, Mickolus chronicles the killing of Lesley Ann Enriquez, a U.S. Consulate staffer in Juárez, Chihuahua by the Juárez cartel affiliate Barrio Azteca on March 14, 2010.

[9] These conflicting accounts report that the drug lords "Pumba" and "Tata" have established connections to the Sinaloa Cartel or Los Zetas.

maritime commercial interests, ferries, and other related targets in Mexico in efforts to apply political pressure on Mexico's national government and the state government in Quintana Ro.

What is also significant is that the Pumba and Tata Cartel relationship, either to the Sinaloa Cartel or its rival Los Zetas, illustrates two important processes. The first is how more sophisticated and developed drug cartels can make use of criminal outfits to enhance their profit-making abilities. The second is how criminal gangs and their resources can be used by predominant criminal syndicalist groups to offset other criminal gangs or even criminal syndicalist group rivals who might employ them [9, 31, 50].

4.10 The Pumba and Tata Cartel: Possible Links Los Zetas, La Familia Michoacána, or the Sinaloa Cartel

In the absence of more authoritative information that is publicly available, the discussion now turns to a description of some major Mexican criminal enterprise organizations with possible connections to the Pumba and Tata Cartel. Those organizations include Los Zetas, La Familia Michoacána, and the Sinaloa Cartel.

From a security point of view, Los Zetas stands out in significance because of its military-like prowess. The introduction of former Mexican army and ex-Guatemalan Special Forces personnel into its ranks led to a substantial upgrade in paramilitary capabilities, compared to other Mexican organizations across the drug cartel spectrum. The scope of that upgrade was so extensive that Bunker and Sullivan describe Los Zetas as "…true specialized mercenaries." [6, 48; 9, 34, 43; 28, 285; 41, 30–31, 33; 50, 107; 54, 105–106, 94–95].

Los Zetas, with its array of international connections in its drug running operations, started out as a personal security detail to protect Osiel Cárdenas Guillén, once the chieftain of the Gulf Cartel (El Golfo). The Gulf Cartel is the parent organization of Los Zetas [5, 243–244, 246, 6, 45–46, 23, 313, 315, 321, 323]. Even with their shared history, the relationship between the Gulf Cartel and Los Zetas was marked by fierce conflict that culminated in a formal split between Los Zetas and the Gulf Cartel in 2010. As of 2010, Los Zetas had an estimated size between 1500 and 3000 activists [6, 49–50, 54; 23, 313; 28, 284; 50, 126].

Los Zetas began to evolve from its original role as the Gulf Cartel's premier security team and into a formidable drug cartel in its own right. That process began after the arrest of Gulf Cartel chieftain Osiel Cárdenas Guillén by Mexican authorities in 2003. Osiel Cárdenas Guillén's arrest and subsequent extradition to Texas in 2007 was a major set-back for the Gulf Cartel, whose operations became disjointed.

In comparison to the operational difficulties the Gulf Cartel experienced, Los Zetas operations continued largely uninterrupted under the direction of two leaders: Jorge Castilla Sánchez, an ex-policeman from the Mexican state of Tamaulipas, and Antonio Ezequiel Cárdenas Guillén, who was Osiel Cárdenas Guillén's older brother.

This organizational structure was maintained until Antonio Ezequel Cárdenas Guillén crafted a Los Zetas splinter group known as Los Escorpines (The Scorpions) [6, 54, 46–48; 23, 314].

A watershed event for the development of Los Zetas was the attempt by the Sinaloa Cartel organization to take control of the Nuevo Laredo region from the Gulf Cartel [6, 46–48; 23]. The Nuevo Laredo affair was a major shock to the Mexican drug cartel system. During that drug war, Gulf Cartel leaders had to recruit Los Zetas fighters into their battle against the Sinaloa Cartel to defeat powerful Sinaloa Cartel forces.

The end result was the emergence of Los Zetas as a drug organization with predominant paramilitary strength. In fact, some authorities note the Nuevo Laredo affair propelled Los Zetas into a position of increased power, comparable to that wielded by a cartel. It had control over both the city of Nuevo Laredo and the Gulf Cartel elements allowed to remain in Nuevo Laredo, when Los Zetas led paramilitary forces prevailed [6, 46–48; 23].

A second watershed event for Los Zetas development involved paramilitary training and support that Los Zetas provided to the fledgling La Familia Michoacána organization in the Mexican state of Michoacán in 2008. Those training programs enhanced Los Zetas' influence and its reputation for having extremely effective paramilitary capabilities. In 2010, Barria-Issa estimated that La Familia Michoacána had some 300 activists [5, 244; 6, 51–52, 54; 23, 32].

As discussed previously, basic underlying differences exist between terrorist group political ideological composition and narrative, and the narrower, more functional political goals of criminal syndicalist groups. At the same time, there are exceptions to this general trend. The drug cartels La Familia Michoacána and its splinter group, Los Caballeros Templarios (Knights Templar) are two examples of such exceptions found in Mexico.

For Flanigan, La Familia Michoacána is the criminal syndicate involved in the drug trade that comes closest to espousing the type of political ideology characteristic of terrorist groups. In terms of leadership, Nazaro Moreno González was one of several La Familia Michoacána organizers who led the cartel and spearheaded its operations until he was killed by the Mexican Federal Police in 2014 [50, 114–116].

While its sources and origins trace back to the 1980s, La Familia Michoacána rose to national prominence in 2006 when activists deposited five decapitated heads into a dance hall crowd in Uruapan, Michoacán. Reportedly, those five men had raped and murdered a woman who was in an intimate relationship with a La Familia Michoacána activist [5, 244–246, 250, 253; 28, 287; 29, 68–69, 74–76; 41, 68, 70–71; 89, 42]. In terms of its overall size, Beith reports in 2011 that La Familia Michoacána has some 4000 activists [7, 795, 797].

Unlike the overwhelming number of Mexican drug cartels that have no political/religious ideology, La Familia Michoacána (and some elements of Los Zetas), present a tantalizing case because its chieftains claim adherence to Christian theology. For Bunker and Sullivan, La Familia Michoacána espouses, "Christian evangelical beliefs," where a strict code of morality is enforced in communities under its control. In that context, Flanigan reports La Familia offered "social services" to poor Mexican citizens such as financial aid to pursue education, medicines, and monies for reconstruction of buildings. In turn, La Familia collected taxes, and compelled local farmers to dedicate some of their land to poppy and marijuana production [5, 244–246, 250, 253; 28, 287; 29, 68–69, 74–76; 41, 68, 70–71; 89, 42].

By contrast, the Knights Templar (Los Caballeros Templarios) is a La Familia Michoacána spinoff group that materialized under the aegis of Servando Gómez in 2011. Gómez, a former teacher and one of the founding members of La Familia Michoacána, probably led La Familia at one point until his imprisonment in 2015. It appears the boundaries between La Familia Michoacána and the Knights Templar remained permeable, with occasional alliances as well as underlying competition between those two groups as hallmarks of their relationship.

Both La Familia Michoacána and the Los Caballeros Templarios (Knights Templar) have engaged in extortion to raise funds from firms involved in the Mexican mining industry and from firms in other economic sectors. In terms of "cooptation" efforts aimed against the state, both the Knights Templar and its parent organization La Familia Michoacána have placed heavy emphasis on efforts to corrupt Mexican bureaucrats at local and state government levels [7; 23, 796; 50, 105, 115–116]. That contrasts to the powerful connections between the Sinaloa Cartel and many Mexican national political officials, such as former President Vincente Fox Quesada [7, 788–789; 50, 115–116].

In comparison, the Sinaloa Cartel remains the single, most predominant drug cartel in Mexico because of the diversity and extent of its activities, and because of its extensive international connections that include ties to the Medellín Cartel in Colombia. For Atuesta and Pérez-Dávila, the Sinaloa Cartel traces its origins through the Juárez Cartel to the Guadalajara Cartel, that was run by Miguel Félix Gallardo. The fledgling Sinaloa Cartel evolved in the Mexican state of Sinaloa as a powerful force under Félix Gallardo's influence [5, 241–243; 7, 793–794, 799].

Miguel Félix Gallardo, who once was a member of the State Judicial Police and who would eventually become known as El-Padrino (Godfather), ascended through the local Sinaloa drug organization ranks that had become powerful because of its links to the PRI government [23, 309–311; 41, 23, 25–27]. After years at the helm of the Sinaloa syndicate, Félix Gallardo was arrested in April 1989 for the unprecedented murder of an American DEA official working undercover in Mexico—Mr. Enrique Camarena.

The Camarena murder was a bellwether event in the fierce struggle that Mexico and the United States waged against Mexican drug trafficking operations. It followed Camarena's report to Mexican and American authorities about "el-Bufalo," a massive homestead devoted to marijuana cultivation in the Mexican state of Chihuahua.

Faced with life imprisonment, Félix Gallardo broke down Sinaloa cartel operations into new geographical locales (i.e., "plazas"), each to be led by one of his top associates. One of those associates was Joaquín "El Chapo" Guzmán Lorea, "...who...received Mexicali and San Luis Rio Colorado, Sonora, which lies along the U.S. border at the intersection of Sonora, Baja California, Arizona and California." [7, 788, 796–798, 800; 23, 312; 41, 67–68, 32–33].

These brief descriptions of major drug cartel operations showcase some of the important events associated with the growth, maturity, and in some cases, decline in drug cartels. Those descriptions highlight the importance of splintering and spinoff formation processes, the relationship between those processes and threat development, and the importance of organization rivalries with respect to the growth, development, and maturity cycles of criminal syndicalist groups [14, 204n65; 56, 37, 107, 110, 252–253; 58, 261–263].

Indeed, what amounts to a criminal syndicalist development process mirrors the "terrorist group life-cycle" that Lasswell describes for terrorist groups which was first discussed in Chap. 1 and previous work [14, 204n65; 56, 37, 107, 110; 252–253; 58, 261–263]. In the case of terrorist groups in India and elsewhere, the "terrorist group life cycle" unfolds with terrorist group splintering and splinter group formation.

To reiterate, those fragmentation processes stem from rivalries between terrorist group leader personalities marked by high-risk tolerance and a preference for industrious and ambitious activities, and differences of opinion between those leaders about terrorist group strategies and tactics [14, 204n65; 56, 37, 107, 110, 252–253; 58, 261–263]. It is probably no exaggeration to say that similar dynamics are found in the evolution of criminal syndicalist organizations.

At the same time, what is significant for both types of organizations are their set of connections to other similar groups, and increasingly across criminal syndicalist groups and terrorist organizations. That makes it possible to create conditions where mutual gain as well as well as win-lose conditions materialize. In the narrower sense, criminal syndicalists can earn rent from "drug corridors" leases made with other syndicalist organizations, or conceivably work to collude with other syndicalist groups or criminal gangs for short run gains.

In the broader sense, the evolution of criminal organizations that produce and sell drugs in Mexico reflect such "win–win conditions." Examples include the emergence of Los Zetas as an independent organization from the Gulf Cartel, the provision of arms and training by Los Zetas to La Familia Michoacána, and to the relationships drug cartels and subordinate criminal gangs have, such as that between the Pumba and Tata criminal gang and predominant Mexican drug lords who in many cases, guide or otherwise influence their actions.

4.11 The Individuals Tending Towards Savagery (ITS)

The "Individuals Tending Towards Savagery" is coded in this study as a "sole issue" environmentalist-oriented terrorist organization. It is categorized as a "sole-issue" terrorist group with "anarchist/nihilist" tendencies. In addition to its primary emphasis on environmental concerns, it opposes the efforts of the Mexican government to promote modernization and technology [71, 135–136; 76, 561; 77, 576–579].

That coding decision is consistent with Phillips' description of ITS as an "eco-anarchist" organization. Phillips goes on to report eco-terrorism gained an increasingly significant foothold in Mexico around 2002 where the targets of Mexican "eco-terrorists" were primarily limited to ATM machines [71, 135–136; 76, 561; 77, 576–579].

In essence, ITS embraces a Luddite perspective and reflects the underlying theme that for some terrorist group chieftains and lone operatives like Dr. Theodore Kaczynski (The Unabomber), environmental concerns and anti-modernization standpoints are inextricably bound up. In terms of its scope, Phillips reports that ITS is transnational in nature with ties to the "Olga Cell" of the Italian anarchist group known as the Informal Anarchist Federation International Revolutionary Front [71, 135–136; 76, 561; 77, 576–579].

ITS has put a premium on terrorist assaults directed at the Mexican nanotechnology sector. Phillips suggests that is the case for two reasons. First, nanotechnology, with its blending of new and innovative technology and its focus on genetic modification, makes that sector an attractive one for eco-terrorists. What also makes the nanotechnology sector alluring for eco-terrorists is that it is viewed by many Mexican government and business officials as critical to promote continued socio-economic development in Mexico [71, 135–136; 76, 561; 77, 576–579].

4.12 Terrorist Assault Business Vulnerability Index (TABVI)

As in the case of India, the denominator for Mexico's Terrorist Assault Business Vulnerability Index (TABVI) derives from data presented in the "Global Competitiveness Index 2017–2018" published by *World Economic Forum.* A sub-field of this study is entitled, "Business Costs of Terrorism" [98; 99, Appendix C].[10] As mentioned in Chap. 2, this nation-state ranking associated with "Business Costs of Terrorism" is based on business leader appraisals about the cost of terrorism for business operations [98].

In this WEF survey, the question asked was, "in your country, to what extent does the threat of terrorism impose coasts on business?" The ordinal scale used ranged from " "1" = to a great extent—imposes huge costs" to "7 = not at all—imposes no costs" [98]. In this *World Economic Forum* index where lower scores indicate greater business costs associated with terrorism, Mexico ranked higher at #87th place, with a score of "4.8," as compared to India which ranked 117th place, with a score of "4.2."

In the case of the TABVI numerator, the numerator value is calculated by adding the total number of business-related terrorist attacks in Mexico in each sub-category of business target found between 2013 and 2018. As mentioned in Chap. 2, the reason data from 2013 to 2018 are used to calculate the TABVI score instead of the full

[10] Middle range ordinal scale value labels are not articulated in this WEF report.

range of data starting from 2007 to 2018 is to ensure the TABVI analysis remains consistent with *World Economic Forum* business leaders survey data. Therefore, the TABVI sub-component numbers and the business target frequencies presented in Fig. 4.3 are different.

For the TABVI numerator, the following sub-categories for the 2013–2018 interval were summed: (1) Energy/Alloy (1); (2) Private Establishments (2); (3) Telecommunications (16); (4) Newspaper/Print (24); (5) NGO (2) for a total of 45 acts.[11] In this analysis, the TABVI value for Mexico is 9.375. The TABVI is calculated by 45/4.8 where 45 represents the total number of terrorist acts chronicled and "4.8" is the assigned score for Mexico as determined by World Economic Forum data.

As previously mentioned, lower scores on the TABVI index suggest lower degrees of vulnerability/threat and vice versa. In comparison to India with a TABVI score of 156.6, this TABVI score of 9.375 for Mexico suggests that the overall assessed threat of terrorism/vulnerability in Mexico was much lower than the TABVI assessment of terrorism/vulnerability estimated for India.

What is significant is those raw TABVI findings in this study are consistent with the rankings found in the *World Economic Forum* "Global Competitiveness Index 2015–2018." In those rankings, Mexico ranked #87 and India ranked #117. Those rankings were out of a total of 137 ranked countries, were Yemen ranked last at 2.4—where business costs associated with terrorism were highest [98]. To obtain a standardized aggregate TABVI score for Mexico, 9.375/1.566 = 5.98 because the highest raw TABVI score 156.6 (India) is divided by 1.566 = 100.0.

As in the case of India, a comparison of threat/vulnerability scores for specific industries in Mexico can be obtained as a basis to compare vulnerability/threat in those industries across countries and regions. The raw sub-category TABVI industry scores for Mexico are: (1) Energy/Alloy (1/4.8 = 0.208) (**lowest** vulnerability/threat); (2) Private Establishments (2/4.8 = 0.416); (3) Telecommunications (16/4.8 = 3.33); (4) Newspaper/Print (24/4.8 = 5.00 (**highest** vulnerability/threat); NGO's (2/4.8 = 0.416). What follows is a scale with standardized scores of specific Mexican industries found on a spectrum that presents vulnerability/threat to terrorism assessment by industry type.

As in all the case studies, it is critical to standardize the TABVI scores obtained for cross-country comparison purposes. The highest raw TABVI score obtained for newspaper print is 5.00, so 5.00 is multiplied by 20 = 100.00. Accordingly the following scores are obtained: Energy/Alloy (4.16), NGO's (8.32), private establishments (8.33), telecommunications (66.6), and newspaper/print (100.00). What follows is a depiction of the Mexican industries continuum with those standardized TABVI measures used to appraise terrorism threat/vulnerability (see Fig. 4.1).

---

[11] N = 45; those results are produced by hand-count for data between 2013 and 2018.

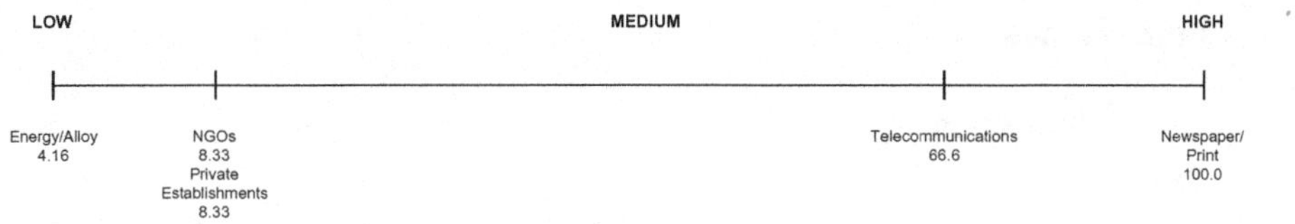

Fig. 4.1 Mexico industry vulnerability spectrum standardized TABVI scores < 1 to 10 = Low Risk; 11 to 50 = Medium Risk; 51 to 100 = High Risk

4.13 Relative Frequencies and Percentages of Commercial Target Terrorist Assaults

Unlike the case of India, the small number of Mexican terrorist acts directed at commercial interests created some difficulties for acquiring a more complete description of Mexican terrorism based on variables such as (identifiable) group-name and other terrorist assault characteristics. Accordingly, in the descriptive statistics and bivariate analysis sections of this chapter on Mexico, the 2013–2018 database was enriched by including GTD accounts for the 2007–2012 time interval. That did not affect the TABVI calculations, where the original 2013–2018 time interval examined remained congruent with the 2017–2018 data from the WEF survey responses.

4.14 Targets by Year

For the twelve-year interval (January 2007–December 2018) considered, the data exhibited a common trait found in terrorism assault patterns. Cyclical patterns of attacks were illuminated, characterized by peaks years and troughs. The peak year for this time interval was 2012, a year marked by 17/81 terrorist attacks that comprised a little over one-fifth (21.0%) of all attacks documented. For 2017 and 2018, that were also peak years, each year was marked by 12/81 terrorist attacks (14.8%). Together, those two years accounted for 29.6% of the total. At the other extreme, four terrorist events (4.9%) took place in the trough year 2014, and four terrorist events (4.9%) happened in the trough year 2016 (see Fig. 4.2).

4.15 Terrorist Assault by Business Target

In Mexico, the bulk of terrorist attacks against commercial interests were focused on newspaper/print targets and telecommunications targets for the twelve-year time period under consideration between January 1, 2007 and December 31, 2017.

Frequencies

Statistics

Year

N	Valid	81
	Missing	0

Year

		Frequency	Percent	Valid Percent	Cumulative Percent
Valid	2013	8	9.9	9.9	9.9
	2014	4	4.9	4.9	14.8
	2015	9	11.1	11.1	25.9
	2016	4	4.9	4.9	30.9
	2017	12	14.8	14.8	45.7
	2018	12	14.8	14.8	60.5
	2007	8	9.9	9.9	70.4
	2010	4	4.9	4.9	75.3
	2011	3	3.7	3.7	79.0
	2012	17	21.0	21.0	100.0
	Total	81	100.0	100.0	

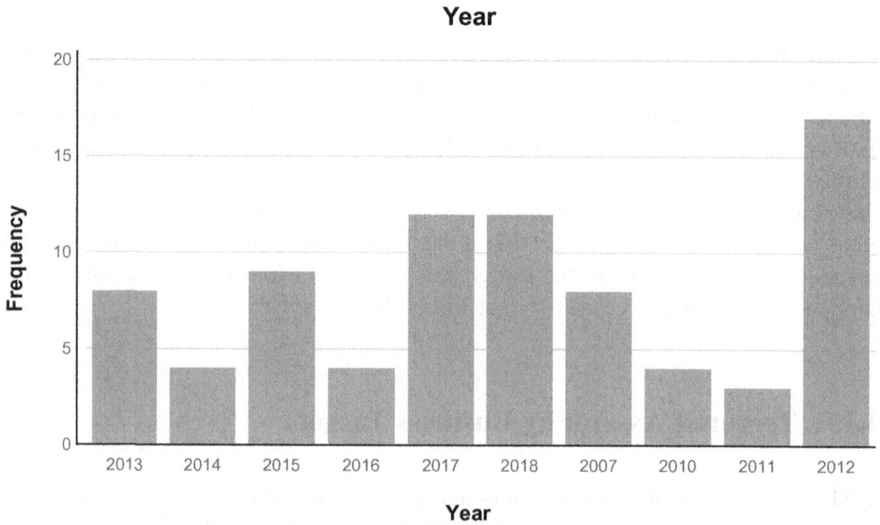

Fig. 4.2 Relative frequency of Mexico terrorist attacks by year, 2007–2018

Telecommunications targets accounted for 25.0% of the total (20/80 acts). Newspaper/print targets, including hard-copy newspaper reporters and associated infrastructure such as newspaper office buildings, accounted for 43.8% of the total (35/80 acts). Together, those two target categories accounted for 68.8% of the business type target total.

In comparison, telecommunications targets, including radio television hosts, broadcast infrastructure, and on-line bloggers, accounted for 25.0% of the total (20/80 acts). In turn, fourteen out of eighty terrorist attacks were directed against "private establishments" 17.5% of the time. Those included two attacks by the Pumba and Tata Cartel against tourism boats owned by Baracos Caribe in Playa del Carmen, Mexico. In one case, an IED detonated on board a boat, while in the other, an explosion on another boat was thwarted when an IED was discovered [37, 38] (Mickolus 2019, 133).

At the other extreme, there were five terrorist attacks or 6.3% of the total that involved one "energy-alloy" target, Mexico's state-owned Pemex oil company (Petróleos Mexicanos) [32, 34]. There were also two terrorist assaults or 2.5% of the total directed against non-governmental organizations (NGO's). The two 2014 attacks against NGO's included the abduction of a Natura Y Ecosistemas Mexicanos A.C. worker, and the abduction of four Na Bolom Cultural Association workers and two tourists [35, 36, 86] (see Fig. 4.3).

One notable finding was that the overwhelming number of businesses targeted in Mexico were Mexican owned business. The results revealed that 92.6% of all Mexican terrorist assaults directed at commercial interests involved Mexican owned businesses. In contrast, only while only 7.4% (6/81 acts) involved foreign owned businesses. Those terrorist attacks against foreign owned businesses included one attack against a Kentucky Fried Chicken outlet in 2010, and one attack against Coca-Cola in 2014 (see Fig. 4.4).

In turn, when group-type and anonymous acts are analyzed, the results revealed that at 66.7% (54/81 acts), anonymous terrorist events at two thirds of the total, comprised the largest portion of business-related terrorism in Mexico. The rate for "hybrid groups," defined as criminal syndicalist groups that use terrorism followed, was a little over three times less at 19.8%, with sixteen out of 81 acts [27, 597–598, 606, 612; 28, 287, 298, 291; 75, 49; 84, 93–109; 85, 54; 89, 30–31]. Lastly, "sole issue" terrorist groups with primary focus on environment, technology or globalization or a combination thereof, carried out seven terrorist attacks that made up 8.6% of the total (see Fig. 4.5).

4.16 Business Related Terrorist Assaults by Organization

A breakdown of the data by terrorist group, revealed Los Zetas had six events or 7.4% of the total, while the Pumba and Tata Cartel, and a terrorist proto-group of "Choi and Tzeltol Indians" that appeared to coalesce to carry out terrorism, each had two events or 2.5% of the total. In contrast, the percentage rate for the terrorist group,

Frequencies

Statistics

Bus.Target

N	Valid	80
	Missing	1

Bus.Target

		Frequency	Percent	Valid Percent	Cumulative Percent
Valid	Energy/Alloy	5	6.2	6.3	6.3
	Private Establishments	14	17.3	17.5	23.8
	Telecommunications	20	24.7	25.0	48.8
	Newspapers/Print	35	43.2	43.8	92.5
	Banking/Finance	4	4.9	5.0	97.5
	NGO	2	2.5	2.5	100.0
	Total	80	98.8	100.0	
Missing	System	1	1.2		
Total		81	100.0		

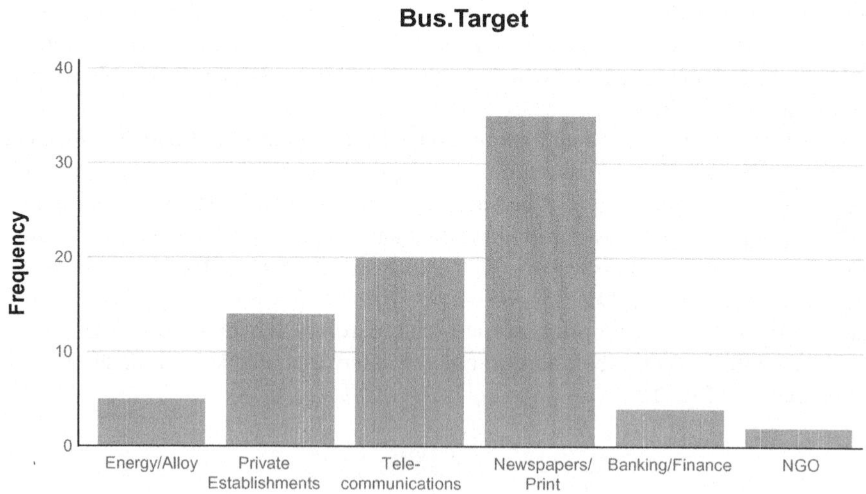

Fig. 4.3 Relative frequency of Mexico terrorist attacks by business target, 2007–2018

Frequencies

Statistics

TargNatForei

N	Valid	81
	Missing	0

Bus.Target

		Frequency	Percent	Valid Percent	Cumulative Percent
Valid	National	75	92.6	92.6	92.6
	Foreign	6	7.4	7.4	100.0
	Total	81	100.0	100.0	

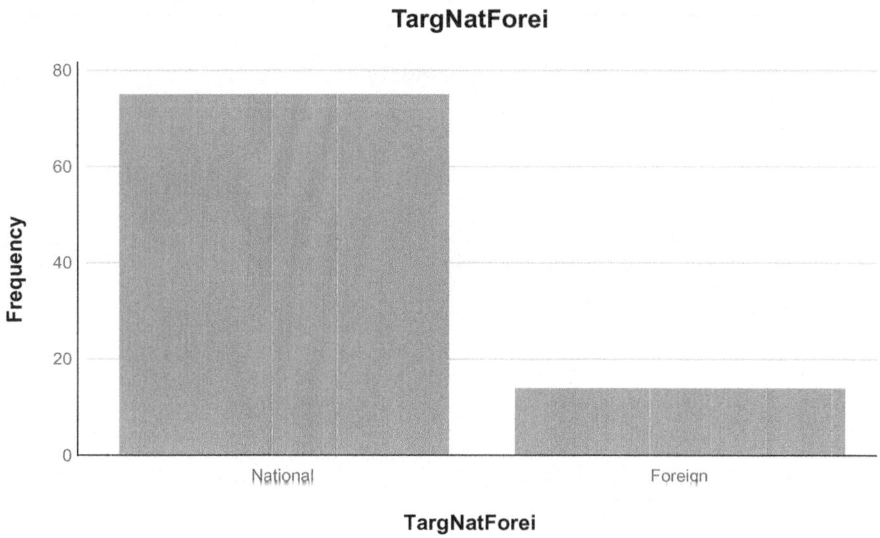

Fig. 4.4 Relative frequency of Mexico business target by nationality, 2007–2018

Individuals Tending Towards Savagery had about one-half that rate with 1.2% (1/81 acts). In terms of "hybrid" groups, the terrorist acts conducted by a Sinaloa gang affiliate and the Los Pelones Gang each comprised 1.2% of the total (see Fig. 4.6).

Frequencies

Statistics

GroupTy

N	Valid	81
	Missing	0

GroupTy

		Frequency	Percent	Valid Percent	Cumulative Percent
Valid	Marxist-Leninist	4	4.9	4.9	4.9
	Anonymous	54	66.7	66.7	71.6
	Hybrid-Terrorist/Criminal	16	19.8	19.8	91.4
	Sole Issue	7	8.6	8.6	100.0
	Total	81	100.0	100.0	

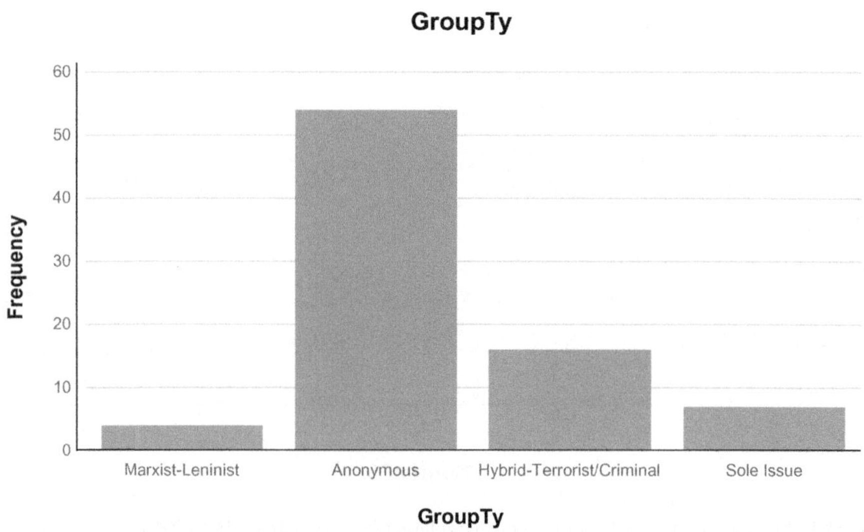

Fig. 4.5 Relative frequency of Mexico terrorist attacks by group-type, 2007–2018

4.17 Business Related Terrorist Assaults by State

A relative frequencies count by state reveals that between 2007 and 2018, Veracruz had the highest rate of terrorist attacks against commercial interests with 14.7% (11/75 acts). Tamaulipas had the second highest rate of such terrorist attacks with 12.0% (9/75 acts). At 8.0% (6/75 acts) the rates for Chihuahua and Ciudad de Mexico both

Frequencies

Statistics

GroupName

N	Valid	81
	Missing	0

GroupName

		Frequency	Percent	Valid Percent	Cumulative Percent
Valid	Ind. Tending Towards Savagery	1	1.2	1.2	1.2
	Pumba and Tata Cartel	2	2.5	2.5	3.7
	Choi and Tzeltol Indians	2	2.5	2.5	6.2
	Los Zetas	6	7.4	7.4	13.6
	Anonymous	54	66.7	66.7	80.2
	Sinaloa Gang Affiliate	1	1.2	1.2	81.5
	Los Pelones Gang	1	1.2	1.2	82.7
	People's Revolutionary Army	4	4.9	4.9	87.7
	Animal Liberation Front	2	2.5	2.5	90.1
	Earth Liberation Front	2	2.5	2.5	92.6
	Caballeros Templarios	6	7.4	7.4	100.0
	Total	81	100.0	100.0	

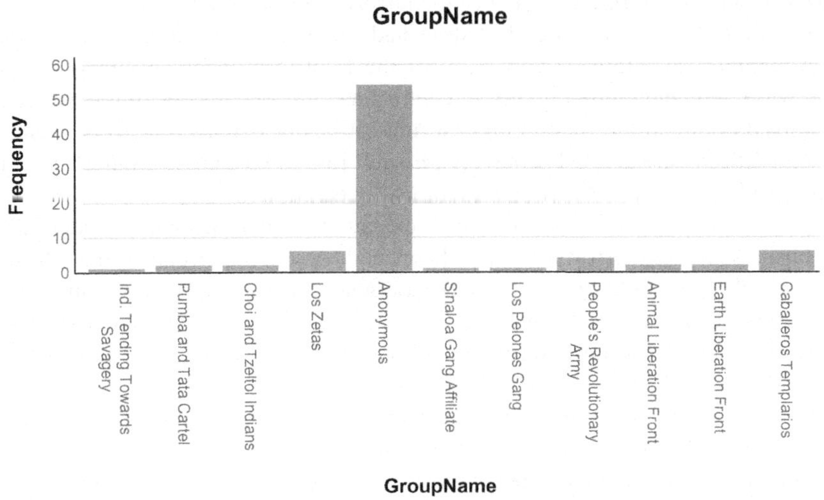

Fig. 4.6 Relative frequency of Mexico terrorist attacks by organization, 2007–2018

ranked third. The state of Guerrero ranked fourth with 6.7% (5/75 acts). Two Mexican states followed with 5.3% of the total (4/75 acts)—Michoacán, and Quintana Roo.

In turn, the Mexican states of Jalisco (4.0%) Chiapas (4.0%), Oaxaca (4.0%), Guanajuato (4.0%), and Sonora (4.0%) with three acts apiece, ranked in sixth place. At the other extreme, were a cluster of Mexican states with terrorist attacks against business targets that accounted for less than four percent of the total.

The Mexican states of Coahuila (2.7%), Baja California Sur (2.7%), Morelos (2.7%), Querétaro (2.7%), and Tabasco (2.7%) each experienced two terrorist assaults. Rounding out the results, five states scored lowest with only 1.3% of the total (1/75 acts). Those states included Sinaloa (1.3%), Nayarit (1.3%), Tlaxcala (1.3%), Nuevo León (1.3%) and Hidalgo (1.3%). The low result for Sinaloa was somewhat unexpected because it is home to the Sinaloa Cartel. At the same time, that result might reflect very tight drug cartel control where threats of force were largely unnecessary (see Fig. 4.7).

4.18 Business Related Terrorist Assaults by Municipality

A more granular analysis of business-related terrorist attacks by municipality suggests two trends. There were two discernable clusters of municipalities in Mexico that experienced business related terrorist attacks noted. One cluster ranged from those municipalities that experienced little over 4.0% to a little under 10.0% of all attacks, while the other cluster of municipalities was comprised of municipalities that experienced about three percent of the terrorist attack total or less.

In this first cluster, the Federal District had the highest rate of terrorist attacks against commercial interests with 7.2% of the total (5/69 acts). Following close behind was Chihuahua municipality in Chihuahua, and Matamoros municipality in Tamaulipas; both had the second highest rates of business-related terrorist attacks, each with 5.8% (4/69 acts). The terrorist assault rate in Ocosingo municipality (in Chiapas) followed with 4.3% of the total (3/69 acts).

The second cluster was comprised of Mexican municipalities where under 4.0% of all business-related terrorist assaults happened. At the upper end of that cluster, Miahuatlán de Porfirio Diaz (in Oaxaca) experienced 2.9% (2/69 acts), Solidaridad (in Quintana Roo) had 2.9% (2/69 acts), Felipe Carrillo Puerto (in Quintana Roo) had 2.9% (2/69 acts), Nuevo Laredo (in Tamaulipas) had 2.9% (2/69 acts), and Victoria (in Tamaulipas) had a rate of 2.9% (2/69 acts).

In turn, there were forty-three (43) Mexican municipalities where terrorist assault rates against commercial interests each amounted to 1.4% of the total (1/69 acts). Those municipalities included, but were not limited to: Ojinaga (in Chihuahua), Zapopan (in Jalisco), Santiago Juxtlahuaca (in Oaxaca), Guanajuato (in Guanajuato), Orizaba (in Veracruz), Taxco de Alarcón (in Guerrero), Guachochi (in Chihuahua), Yanga (in Veracruz), Los Cabos (in Baja California Sur), Poza Rica de Hidalgo (in Veracruz), Culiacán (in Sinaloa), Autlán de Navarro (in Jalisco), Múgica (in Michoacán), Ometepec (in Guerrero), Acayucan (in Veracruz), Centro (in Tabasco),

Frequencies

Statistics

State

N	Valid	75
	Missing	6

State

		Frequency	Percent	Valid Percent	Cumulative Percent
Valid	Ciudad de Mexico	6	7.4	8.0	8.0
	Coahuila	2	2.5	2.7	10.7
	Chihuahua	6	7.4	8.0	18.7
	Jalisco	3	3.7	4.0	22.7
	Veracruz	11	13.6	14.7	37.3
	Chiapas	3	3.7	4.0	41.3
	Tamaulipas	9	11.1	12.0	53.3
	Oaxaca	3	3.7	4.0	57.3
	Guanajuato	3	3.7	4.0	61.3
	Guerrero	5	6.2	6.7	68.0
	Baja California Sur	2	2.5	2.7	70.7
	Sinaloa	1	1.2	1.3	72.0
	Michoacan	4	4.9	5.3	77.3
	Quintana Roo	4	4.9	5.3	82.7
	Tabasco	2	2.5	2.7	85.3
	Morelos	2	2.5	2.7	88.0
	Nayarit	1	1.2	1.3	89.3
	Sonora	3	3.7	4.0	93.3
	Queretaro	2	2.5	2.7	96.0
	Tlaxcala	1	1.2	1.3	97.3
	Nuevo Leon	1	1.2	1.3	98.7
	Hidalgo	1	1.2	1.3	100.0
	Total	75	92.6	100.0	
Missing	System	6	7.4		
Total		81	100.0		

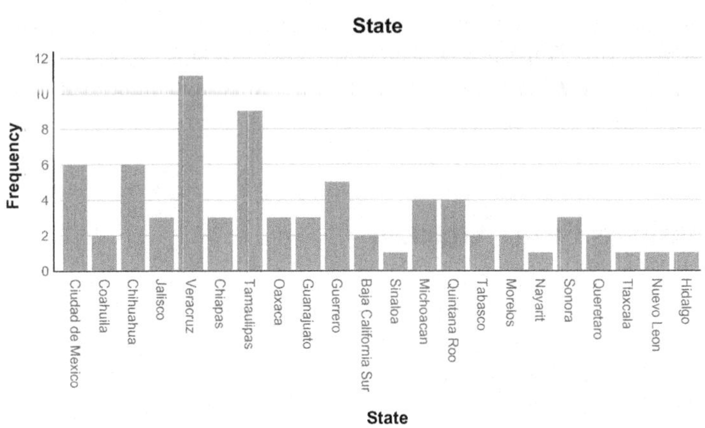

Fig. 4.7 Relative frequency of Mexico terrorist attacks by state, 2007–2018

Torreón (in Coahuila), Saltillo (in Coahuila), and Las Choapas (in Veracruz) (See Fig. 4.8).

4.19 Terrorist Assault by City and Town

There were forty-nine (49) cities or towns chronicled where business related terrorist assaults in Mexico happened. The highest concentration of business-related terrorist assaults happened in three cities. In Mexico City, Chihuahua, and Matamoros (Tamaulipas) each city experienced 6.3% of the total (4/64 acts).

The terrorist assault rate in the town of Playa del Carmen (in Quintana Roo) ranked second with 4.7% of the total (3/64 acts). In the city of Victoria, 3.1% of all business related terrorist attacks happened (2/64 acts). The city of Nuevo Laredo and the two towns of Medellín de Bravo (in Veracruz) and Miahuatlán de Porfirio Diaz (in Oaxaca) each also accounted for 3.1% (2/64 acts) of the total.

There were forty-one (41) cities and towns that each experienced 1.6% of the total (1/64 acts). Those cities include: Torreón (in Coahuila), Zapopan (in Jalisco), Guanajuato (in Guanajuato), Orizaba (in Veracruz), Taxco (in Guerrero), Guachochi (in Chihuahua), Altamirano (in Guerrero), Yanga (in Veracruz), San José del Cabo (in Baja California Sur), Poza Rica de Hidalgo (in Veracruz), Culiacán-Rosales (in Sinaloa), Autlán de Navarro (in Jalisco), Nueva Italia de Ruiz (in Michoacán), Ometepec (in Guerrero), Acayucan (in Veracruz), Villahermosa (in Tabasco), Saltillo (in Coahuila), Las Choapas (in Veracruz), Tlaquiltenango (in Morelos), La Paz (in Baha California Sur), Felipe Carrillo Puerto (in Quintana Roo), Valle de Santiago (in Guanajuato), Yajalón (in Chiapas), Tepec (Jalisco), Uruapan (Michoacán), Acapulco (in Guerrero), Camargo (in Chihuahua), León (in Guanajuato), Guadalajara (Jalisco), Tlalpan (in CDMX), Caderyta Jiménez (in Neuvo León), Veracruz (in Veracruz), Hermosillo (in Sonora), Cuernavaca (in Morelos), Ciudad Obregón (in Sonora), Xalapa (in Veracruz), Tepojaco (in Hidalgo), and Cárednas (in Tabasco). The towns include: Ojinaga (in Chihuahua), Agua Prieta (in Sonora), and Tultitlán (Federal District) (see Fig. 4.9).

4.20 Business Firms Attacked

The results from a relative frequencies test revealed that at 8.7% (6/69 acts) the soft-drink company Sabritas, (a Pepsi Cola affiliate) was the focus of most terrorist attacks against a single firm. The state owned Pemex Oil Company (Petróleos Mexicanos) was targeted 7.2% of the time (5/69 acts), while the television studio Televisa was targeted 4.3% of the time with three out of 69 acts recorded.

In turn, there were six firms, each with 2.9% of the total number of terrorist acts (2/69 acts) that comprised 17.4% of the total. Those firms included Barcos Caribe, a ferry boat service company with 2.9% (2/69 acts), El Mañana Matamoros newspaper

Frequencies

Statistics

Municipality

N	Valid	69
	Missing	12

Municipality

		Frequency	Percent	Valid Percent	Cumulative Percent
Valid	Federal District	5	6.2	7.2	7.2
	Ojinaga	1	1.2	1.4	8.7
	Chihuahua	4	4.9	5.8	14.5
	Zapopan	1	1.2	1.4	15.9
	Matamoros	4	4.9	5.8	21.7
	Santiago Juxtlahuaca	1	1.2	1.4	23.2
	Miahuatlan de Porfirio Diaz	2	2.5	2.9	26.1
	Guananjuato	1	1.2	1.4	27.5
	Orizaba	1	1.2	1.4	29.0
	Taxaco de Alarcon	1	1.2	1.4	30.4
	Guachochi	1	1.2	1.4	31.9
	Yanga	1	1.2	1.4	33.3
	Los Cabos	1	1.2	1.4	34.8
	Poza Rica de Hildago	1	1.2	1.4	36.2
	Culiacan	1	1.2	1.4	37.7
	Autlan de Navarro	1	1.2	1.4	39.1
	Mugica	1	1.2	1.4	40.6
	Ometepec	1	1.2	1.4	42.0
	Acayucan	1	1.2	1.4	43.5
	Nuevo Laredo	2	2.5	2.9	46.4
	Solidaridad	2	2.5	2.9	49.3
	Centro	1	1.2	1.4	50.7
	Torreon	1	1.2	1.4	52.2
	Saltillo	1	1.2	1.4	53.6
	Las Choapas	1	1.2	1.4	55.1
	Ocosingo	3	3.7	4.3	59.4
	Medellin	1	1.2	1.4	60.9
	Altamirano	1	1.2	1.4	62.3
	Tlaquiltenango	1	1.2	1.4	63.8
	La Paz	1	1.2	1.4	65.2
	Felipe Carrillo Puerto	2	2.5	2.9	68.1
	Valle de Santiago	1	1.2	1.4	69.6
	Yajalon	1	1.2	1.4	71.0
	Tepec	1	1.2	1.4	72.5
	Victoria	2	2.5	2.9	75.4

Fig. 4.8 Relative frequency of Mexico terrorist attacks by municipality, 2007–2018

		Frequency	Percent	Valid Percent	Cumulative Percent
	Agua Prieta	1	1.2	1.4	76.8
	Uruapan	1	1.2	1.4	78.3
	Acapulco de Juarez	1	1.2	1.4	79.7
	Camargo	1	1.2	1.4	81.2
	Leon	1	1.2	1.4	82.6
	Guadalajara	1	1.2	1.4	84.1
	Aguililla	1	1.2	1.4	85.5
	Tultitlan	1	1.2	1.4	87.0
	Cadereyta	1	1.2	1.4	88.4
	Veracruz	1	1.2	1.4	89.9
	Hermosillo	1	1.2	1.4	91.3
	Cuernavaca	1	1.2	1.4	92.8
	Cajeme	1	1.2	1.4	94.2
	Xalapa	1	1.2	1.4	95.7
	Tizayuca	1	1.2	1.4	97.1
	Arcelia	1	1.2	1.4	98.6
	Cardenas	1	1.2	1.4	100.0
	Total	69	85.2	100.0	
Missing	System	12	14.8		
Total		81	100.0		

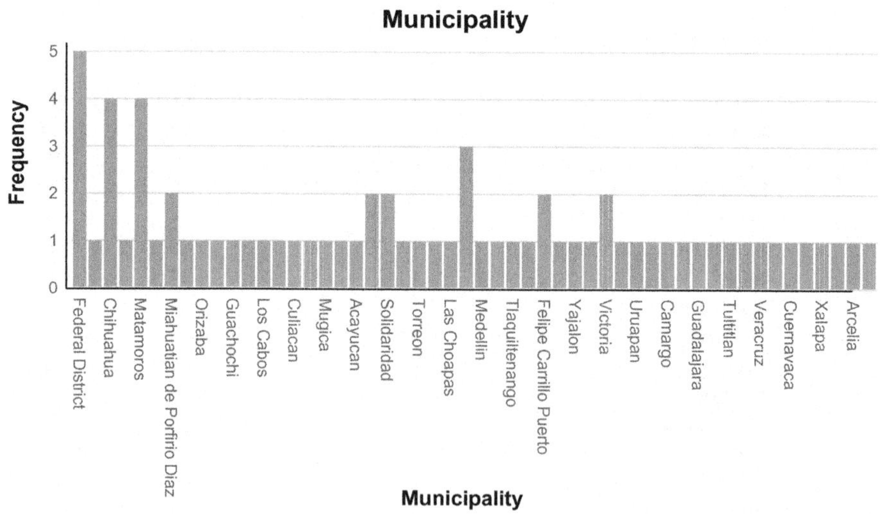

Fig. 4.8 (continued)

Frequencies

Statistics

CityVillage

N	Valid	64
	Missing	17

CityVillage

		Frequency	Percent	Valid Percent	Cumulative Percent
Valid	Mexico City	4	4.9	6.3	6.3
	Torreon	1	1.2	1.6	7.8
	Ojinaga	1	1.2	1.6	9.4
	Chihuahua	4	4.9	6.3	15.6
	Zapopan	1	1.2	1.6	17.2
	Medellin de Bravo	2	2.5	3.1	20.3
	Matamoros	4	4.9	6.3	26.6
	Miahuatlan de Porfirio Diaz	2	2.5	3.1	29.7
	Guanajuato	1	1.2	1.6	31.3
	Orizaba	1	1.2	1.6	32.8
	Taxco	1	1.2	1.6	34.4
	Guachochi	1	1.2	1.6	35.9
	Altamirano	1	1.2	1.6	37.5
	Yanga	1	1.2	1.6	39.1
	San Jose del Cabo	1	1.2	1.6	40.6
	Poza Rica de Hildago	1	1.2	1.6	42.2
	Culiacan (Rosales)	1	1.2	1.6	43.8
	Autlan de Navarro	1	1.2	1.6	45.3
	Nueva Italia de Ruiz	1	1.2	1.6	46.9
	Ometepec	1	1.2	1.6	48.4
	Acayucan	1	1.2	1.6	50.0
	Nuevo Laredo	2	2.5	3.1	53.1
	Playa del Carmen	3	3.7	4.7	57.8
	Villahermosa	1	1.2	1.6	59.4
	Saltillo	1	1.2	1.6	60.9
	Las Choapas	1	1.2	1.6	62.5
	Tlaquiltenango	1	1.2	1.6	64.1
	La Paz	1	1.2	1.6	65.6
	Felipe Carrillo Puerto	1	1.2	1.6	67.2
	Valle de Santiago	1	1.2	1.6	68.8
	Yajalon	1	1.2	1.6	70.3
	Tepec	1	1.2	1.6	71.9

Fig. 4.9 Relative frequency of Mexico terrorist attacks by city, town, and village, 2007–2018

		Frequency	Percent	Valid Percent	Cumulative Percent
	Victoria	2	2.5	3.1	75.0
	Aqua Prieta	1	1.2	1.6	76.6
	Uruapan	1	1.2	1.6	78.1
	Acapulco	1	1.2	1.6	79.7
	Camargo	1	1.2	1.6	81.3
	Leon	1	1.2	1.6	82.8
	Guadalajara	1	1.2	1.6	84.4
	Tultitlan	1	1.2	1.6	85.9
	Tlalpan	1	1.2	1.6	87.5
	Caderyta Jimenez	1	1.2	1.6	89.1
	Veracruz	1	1.2	1.6	90.6
	Hermosillo	1	1.2	1.6	92.2
	Cuernavaca	1	1.2	1.6	93.8
	Ciudad Obregon	1	1.2	1.6	95.3
	Xalapa	1	1.2	1.6	96.9
	Tepojaco	1	1.2	1.6	98.4
	Cardenas	1	1.2	1.6	100.0
	Total	64	79.0	100.0	
Missing	System	17	21.0		
Total		81	100.0		

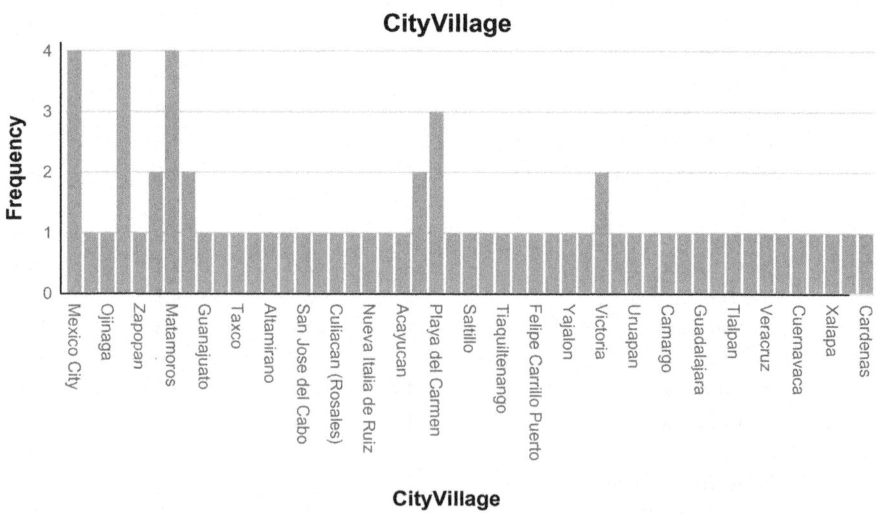

Fig. 4.9 (continued)

with 2.9% (2/69 acts), a radio station called La Voz de la Tierra Caliente with 2.9% (2/69 acts), Semanario Playa News with 2.9% (2/69 acts), Expresso newspaper with 2.9% (2/69 acts), and Santander Bank, which is a foreign owned bank headquartered in Spain with 2.9% (2/69 acts).

There were forty-three (43) business firms in Mexico that each experienced one terrorist attack (1.4%). Those included: El Foro de Taxaco, El Politico, Norte, La Opinión de Poza Rica, Riodoce, Semanario Costeño magazine, 6 TV, Guerrero Radio and TV, La Voz de Sur, El Siglio de Torreón, Ojinaga Noticias, Diaro de Juárez, Channel 44 News, Mural Newspaper, Vanguardia, Liberal del Sur, Natura Y Ecosistemas Mexicanos (NGO), Na Bolom Cultural Association (NGO), La Unión, Radio Espacio, El Tábano, Escribiendo La Verdad, La Favorito 103.3 FM Radio, Antena 102.5 Radio, Norawa, Veracruz City Press Department, Colectivo Pericú, Encuesta Hoy, Enlace Informativo Regional, El Heraldo de Chiapas, Orion Informativo, Diario de Agua Prieta, La Opinión Michoacán, Diario de Mexico, Kentucky Fried Chicken, Norvatis Pharmaceuticals, El Dia de Michoacán, Bancomer Bank, La Última Palabra, Marquesina Politica, El Regional de Sonora, Milenio newspaper, and Coca-Cola (see Fig. 4.10).

4.21 Reaction to Political Events

A relative frequencies distribution shows that at 87.8% (43/49 acts), the vast majority of business-related terrorist attacks were not associated with political events, but were likely independent events. In comparison, terrorist attacks were linked to "landmark events" such as holidays 4.1% of the time (2/49 acts), while two out of the 49 terrorist attacks in this test (4.1%) were linked to "elections or polls." In turn, "secular" holidays such as World Press Freedom Day, accounted for 2.0% of the total (1/49 acts). In 2018, there was one terrorist act (2.0%) taken on the anniversary of another terrorist act where journalist Javier Valdez was killed the previous year [22, 39, 40, 91] (see Fig. 4.11).

4.22 Variable Analysis

This bivariate analysis should be considered preliminary findings, that constitute a first pass at analysis and a first pass at presenting results. In large part, that is the case because only one terrorist group, the Popular Revolutionary Army (EPR), constitutes the Marxist-Leninist category.

In comparison, six criminal organizations/gangs made up the "hybrid group" category where criminal syndicalists used terrorism—Los Zetas, Los Caballeros Templarios (Knights Templar), a Sinaloa "affiliate," the Pumba and Tata Cartel, and Los Pelones. There were four "single issue" groups or proto-groups: The Individuals

Frequencies

Statistics

FirmName

N	Valid	69
	Missing	12

FirmName

		Frequency	Percent	Valid Percent	Cumulative Percent
Valid	El Foro de Taxaco	1	1.2	1.4	1.4
	El Politico	1	1.2	1.4	2.9
	Norte	1	1.2	1.4	4.3
	La Opinion de Poza Rica	1	1.2	1.4	5.8
	Riodoce	1	1.2	1.4	7.2
	Semanario Costeno Magazine	1	1.2	1.4	8.7
	6 TV	1	1.2	1.4	10.1
	Guerrero Radio & TV	1	1.2	1.4	11.6
	La Voz del Sur	1	1.2	1.4	13.0
	Barcos Caribe	2	2.5	2.9	15.9
	Pemex State Co.	5	6.2	7.2	23.2
	El Siglio de Torreon	1	1.2	1.4	24.6
	Ojinaga Noticias	1	1.2	1.4	26.1
	Diaro de Juarez	1	1.2	1.4	27.5
	Channel 44 News	1	1.2	1.4	29.0
	Mural Newspaper	1	1.2	1.4	30.4
	Vanguardia	1	1.2	1.4	31.9
	Liberal del Sur	1	1.2	1.4	33.3
	Natura Y Ecosistemas Mexicanos	1	1.2	1.4	34.8
	Na Bolom Cultural Association	1	1.2	1.4	36.2
	La Union	1	1.2	1.4	37.7
	El Manana Matamoros	2	2.5	2.9	40.6
	Radio Espacio	1	1.2	1.4	42.0
	El Tabano	1	1.2	1.4	43.5
	Escrbiendo La Verdad	1	1.2	1.4	44.9
	La Favorito 103.3 FM Radio	1	1.2	1.4	46.4
	La Voz de la Tierra Caliente	2	2.5	2.9	49.3
	Antena 102.5 Radio	1	1.2	1.4	50.7
	Norawa	1	1.2	1.4	52.2
	Veracruz City Press Dept.	1	1.2	1.4	53.6
	Colectivo Pericu	1	1.2	1.4	55.1
	Encuesta Hoy	1	1.2	1.4	56.5
	Enlace Informativo Regional	1	1.2	1.4	58.0

Fig. 4.10 Relative frequency of Mexico terrorist attacks by firm, 2007–2018

		Frequency	Percent	Valid Percent	Cumulative Percent
	Semanario Playa News	2	2.5	2.9	60.9
	El Heraldo de Chiapas	1	1.2	1.4	62.3
	Orion Informativo	1	1.2	1.4	63.8
	Expreso Newspaper	2	2.5	2.9	66.7
	Diario de Agua Prieta	1	1.2	1.4	68.1
	La Opinion Michoacan	1	1.2	1.4	69.6
	Televisa	3	3.7	4.3	73.9
	Diario de Mexico	1	1.2	1.4	75.4
	Kentucky Fried Chicken	1	1.2	1.4	76.8
	Norvatis Phamaceuticals	1	1.2	1.4	78.3
	Ed Dia de Michoacan	1	1.2	1.4	79.7
	Bancomer Bank	1	1.2	1.4	81.2
	Santander Bank	2	2.5	2.9	84.1
	La Ultima Palabra	1	1.2	1.4	85.5
	Marquesina Politica	1	1.2	1.4	87.0
	El Regional de Sonora	1	1.2	1.4	88.4
	Sabritas	6	7.4	8.7	97.1
	Milenio Newspaper	1	1.2	1.4	98.6
	Coca-Cola	1	1.2	1.4	100.0
	Total	69	85.2	100.0	
Missing	System	12	14.8		
Total		81	100.0		

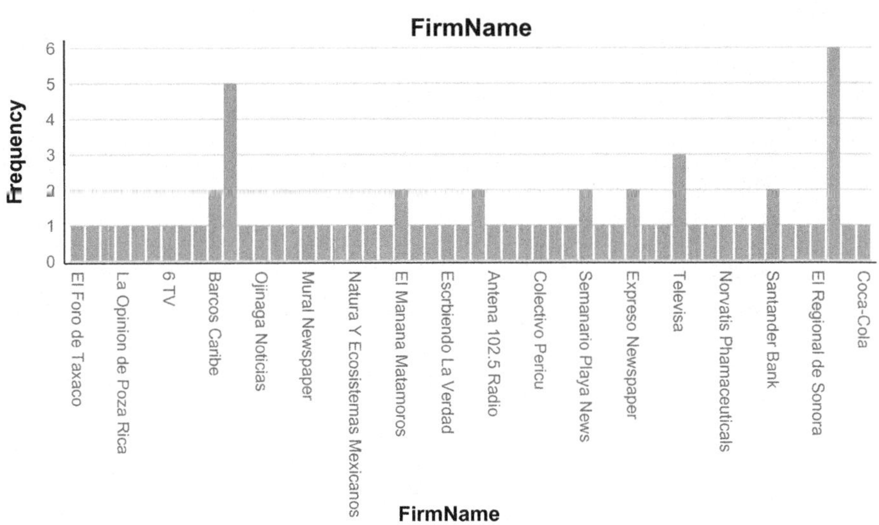

Fig. 4.10 (continued)

Frequencies

Statistics

ReacPolEvnt

N	Valid	49
	Missing	32

ReacPolEvnt

		Frequency	Percent	Valid Percent	Cumulative Percent
Valid	No Relation	43	53.1	87.8	87.8
	Terrorist Acts	1	1.2	2.0	89.8
	Landmark Events	2	2.5	4.1	93.9
	Secular Holidays	1	1.2	2.0	95.9
	Elections/Polls	2	2.5	4.1	100.0
	Total	49	60.5	100.0	
Missing	System	32	39.5		
Total		81	100.0		

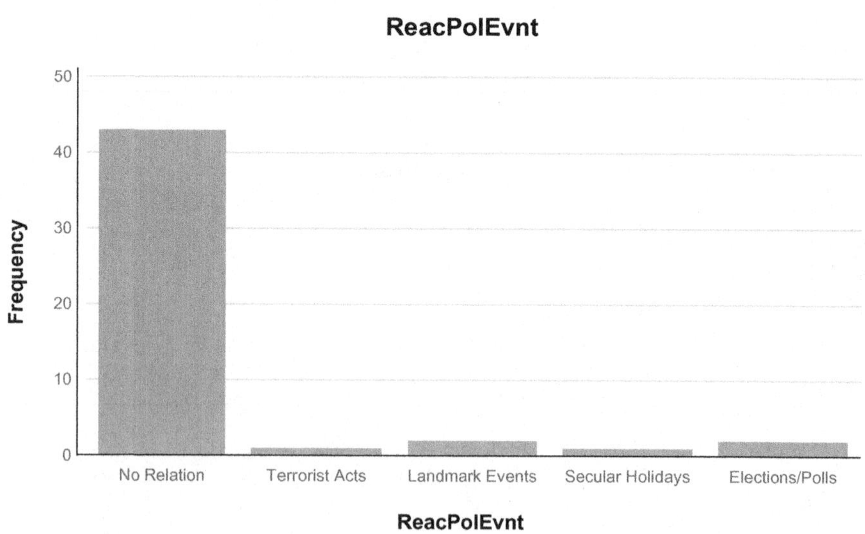

Fig. 4.11 Relative frequency of Mexico terrorist attacks by political event, 2007–2018

Tending Towards Savagery, the Animal Liberation Front (ALF), the Earth Liberation Front (ELF) and Tzeltol and Choi Indians.

The notion is that Marxist-Leninist terrorist groups are oriented towards terrorist attacks reflective of their focus on the world system of capitalism and on the processes of globalization and modernization. In the case of "sole issue" terrorist groups, the corresponding notion is that "sole issue" terrorist groups in the Mexican political context are primarily focused on environmental concerns that can include animal rights. The basic intent of these hypotheses is to compare death rates for both types of terrorist groups with "hybrid" criminal syndicalist organizations that use terrorism. The following hypotheses capture those dynamics:

Hypothesis One: "Hybrid" criminal groups that use terrorism will have a higher rate of terrorist attacks that result in the deaths of between one and fifteen persons than Marxist-Leninist terrorist groups.

Hypothesis Two: "Hybrid" criminal groups that use terrorism will have a higher rate of terrorist attacks that result in the deaths of between one and fifteen persons than "sole issue" terrorist groups.

4.23 Political Ideology X Numbers of Deaths

The bivariate tests conducted illuminated only one statistically significant relationship between the terrorist assault attributes, "Group-Type" and "Numbers of Deaths" [15, 99–102, 105–107].[12] With a Pearson Chi Square statistic of 8.875 and a "*p*-value" of 0.003 at one degree of freedom (1 d.f.), it is possible to reject the null hypothesis of no relation between the variables at the 0.05 level of confidence.[13] A Continuity Correction score of 7.207 with a "*p*-value" of 0.007 was produced for this 2 × 2 matrix (Table 4.1).

A breakdown of the data distributions revealed that with a full 72.2% (39/54 acts), the highest percentage of terrorist attacks that killed between one and fifteen persons were anonymous terrorist acts. Conversely, only 27.8% (15/54 acts) of anonymous acts were non-lethal events. In comparison, "hybrid groups," namely criminal syndicalists or their affiliate gangs that used terrorism, ranked second with 31.3% (5/16 acts). A full 68.8% of those hybrid group attacks (11/16 acts) were non-lethal events.

[12] While no authoritative reason is available, it is possible some statistical relationships were difficult to discern because of the large number of anonymous terrorism events, the overwhelming preference for terrorist acts against civilian business targets rather than government or "mixed" targets, and the lopsided attack percentages across industry sub-categories that favored journalists and other media targets. The assumption of specific terrorist group-type was relaxed to include anonymous acts in the bivariate analysis.

[13] N = 70 with 11 missing cases. Recode (the same variable) "Group-Type": 3 → 3; 6 → 6; ELSE → SYSMIS; "Deaths" 0 = 0; 1 = 1 → 15; ELSE → SYSMIS.

Table 4.1 Relative frequency of group-type by deaths in Mexico terrorist attacks, (0 = 0; 1 = 1 through 15) (summary statistics)

Case processing summary

	Valid		Cases missing		Total	
	N	Percent	N	Percent	N	Percent
GroupTy* Deaths	70	86.4%	11	13.6%	81	100.0%

Bus. Target * Deaths Crosstabulation

			Deaths		
			0	1	Total
GroupTy	Anonymous	Count	15	39	54
		% within GroupTy	27.8%	72.2%	100.0%
		% within deaths	57.7%	88.6%	77.1%
		% of total	21.4%	55.7%	77.1%
	Hybrid-terrorist/Criminal	Count	11	5	16
		% within GroupTy	68.8%	31.3%	100.0%
		% within deaths	42.3%	11.4%	22.9%
		% of total	15.7%	7.1%	22.9%
Total		Count	26	44	70
		% within GroupTy	37.1%	62.9%	100.0%
		% within deaths	100.0%	100.0%	100.0%
		% of total	37.1%	62.9%	100.0%

Chi-square tests

	Value	df	Asymptotic significance (2-sided)	Exact significance (2-sided)	Exact significance (1-sided)
Pearson chi-square	8.875[a]	1	0.003		
Continuity correction[b]	7.207	1	0.007		
Likelihood ratio	8.674	1	0.003		
Fisher's exact test				0.007	0.004
Linear-by-linear association	8.748	1	0.003		
N of valid cases	70				

(continued)

Table 4.1 (continued)

Directional measures

			Value	Asymptotic standard error[c]
Nominal by nominal	Lambda	Symmetric	0.143	0.084
		GroupTy dependent	0.000	0.000
		Deaths dependent	0.231	0.135
	Goodman and Kruskal tau	GroupTy dependent	0.127	0.083
		Deaths dependent	0.127	0.081

Directional measures

			Approximate T[d]	Approximate Significance
Nominal by nominal	Lambda	Symmetric	1.525	0.127
		GroupTy dependent	.[e]	.[e]
		Deaths dependent	1.525	0.127
	Goodman and Kruskal tau	GroupTy dependent		0.003[f]
		Deaths dependent		0.003[f]

Symmetric measures

		Value	Approximate significance
Nominal by nominal	Phi	– 0.356	0.003
	Cramer's V	0.356	0.003
N of valid cases		70	

[a]0 cells (0.0%) have expected count less than 5. The minimum expected count is 5.94
[b]Computed only for a 2 × 2 table
[c]Not assuming the null hypothesis
[d]Using the asymptotic standard error assuming the null hypotheses
[e]Cannot be computed because the asymptotic standard error equals zero
[f]Based on chi-square approximation

It was found there no fatalities of between one and fifteen people associated with the terrorist attacks for Marxist Leninist terrorist groups, where the assumption was that target preference would favor "structuralist targets." There was one "sole issue" terrorist attack chronicled between 2007 and 2018 taken by the Individuals Tending for Savagery on March 31, 2013 in Mexico City that resulted in 37 fatalities at Pemex State Oil Company headquarters, but that was one outlier case over a twelve year period [34]. The findings are basically supportive of Hypothesis One and Hypothesis Two (see Table 4.2).

Table 4.2 Relative frequency of group-type by deaths in Mexico terrorist attacks, 2007–2018 (0 = 0; 1 = 1 through 15)

Case processing summary

	Valid		Cases missing		Total	
	N	Percent	N	Percent	N	Percent
GroupTy* Deaths	80	98.8%	1	1.2%	81	100.0%

GroupTy * Deaths Crosstabulation

			Deaths		
			0	1	Total
GroupTy	Marxist-Leninist	Count	4	0	4
		% within GroupTy	100.0%	0.0%	100.0%
		% within deaths	11.1%	0.0%	5.0%
		% of total	5.0%	0.0%	5.0%
	Anonymous	Count	15	39	54
		% within GroupTy	27.8%	72.2%	100.0%
		% within deaths	41.7%	88.6%	67.5%
		% of total	18.8%	48.8%	67.5%
	Hybrid-terrorist/Criminal	Count	11	5	16
		% within GroupTy	68.8%	31.3%	100.0%
		% within deaths	30.6%	11.4%	20.0%
		% of total	13.8%	6.3%	20.0%
	Sole issue	Count	6	0	6
		% within GroupTy	100.0	0.0%	100.0%
		% within deaths	16.7%	0.0%	7.5%
		% of total	7.5%	0.0%	7.5%
Total		Count	36	44	80
		% within GroupTy	45.0%	55.0%	100.0%
		% within deaths	100.0%	100.0%	100.0%
		% of total	45.0%	55.0%	100.0%

4.24 Conclusions

This chapter describes the basic empirical parameters of terrorism use in Mexico based on sketchy data, particularly in the case of perpetrator identification. It is probably fair to say that for the 2007–2018 time interval analyzed, criminal syndicalist organizations made use of terrorism in the majority of anonymous acts, rather than terrorist groups, whose hallmark is the pursuit of ideologically based political objectives with a clear articulation of broad political goals.

At the same time, this convoluted condition about terrorist event attribution compels business executives and analysts to confront a key issue of contemporary terrorism research and efforts to craft non-kinetic, "soft-line" private sector counterterrorism policy. At a theoretical level, this issue is about whether or not criminal syndicalist groups with economic profit as their primary objective, qualify as terrorist groups.

The many differences in political context, narrative, and scope and composition of audiences that characterize those two types of organizations suggest criminal syndicalists are not terrorist groups, even though there are some superficial similarities primarily in methods used. In other words, tactics might be similar in some cases, but strategies to achieve strategic goals differ in profound and lasting ways.

The fundamental difference between those two types of organizations is relatively straightforward. Terrorist groups place almost singular emphasis on the threat or use of illegal force to produce broader abject fear in populations, but this is done to achieve structural political change. That stands in sharp contrast to the terrorism used that is bound up with political infighting among criminal gangs whose primary purpose is to make illicit profits or to ensure political control over regions.

Therefore, Schmid is correct when he asserts that to equate criminal syndicalist groups which use terrorism to traditional terrorist groups is to conflate two mostly distinct theoretical concepts about organization type, central for effective and sustained research efforts. To do so, diminishes from the ability to make robust comparisons; in other words, to conflate those two organizational types results in work that diminishes or ignores outright the fundamental attributes that help distinguish between those two types of organizations. In fact, Shelley and Picarelli's term "hybrid-group" is as good as any description for criminal organizations that use terrorism in certain select circumstances basically in pursuit of monetary gain [27, 597–598, 606, 612; 84, 93–109; 85].

Mexico received a TABVI score of 9.375, which is a much lower threat/vulnerability score than India received with its score of 156.6 when only the years 2013–2018 were included in the calculations. In other words, the assessed level of threat/vulnerability to terrorism in India was much higher than it was in Mexico.

Nevertheless, those raw TABVI scores for Mexico and for India were consistent with the rankings of terrorism threat appraisal produced by *World Economic Forum*, based on data produced from a survey of business leaders in 137 countries. In terms of a breakdown of industry type for Mexico, the following raw TABVI industry subcategory scores were produced: (1) Energy/Alloy = 0.208 (**lowest** vulnerability/threat); (2) Private Establishments = 0.416; (3) Telecommunications = 3.33; (4) Newspapers/Print = 5.00 (**highest** vulnerability/threat); (5) NGO's = 0.416.

The implications of Mexico's political condition are profound, both for U.S. foreign policy and for higher echelon U.S. business executives based in Mexico. For some scholars, the evolution of drug cartel influence and control in Mexico, is both a cause and effect of new drug cartel paramilitary capabilities, and the broader process of globalization. The emergent realities might lead U.S. policymakers to craft informal, but generally recognizable, conflict parameters or boundaries with Mexican drug syndicalists about the scope and intensity of national and international collaborate anti-drug efforts for instance, to ensure Mexico's political stability and American influence in Mexico.

On the other hand, some analysts appear to be more hopeful about the continued growth of political institutionalization and democracy that Mexico has experienced since the election of President Vincente Fox Quesada in 2000. Those analysts point to the influence of those "nation-state" level factors and the "hurting stalemate" that syndicalist drug organizations have produced, as a bellwether for change that, coupled with the positive influence of "intensive globalization," could produce more positive political developments in Mexico's future.

Those processes, both endogenous to Mexico in the case of democracy and political institution development, and exogenous in the case of globalization, however those unfold, will undoubtedly affect how multinational corporations conduct business in Mexico. Even though it is not possible to predict exactly how either set of processes and conditions could translate into specific directives or guideposts for international enterprise business transactions, what is known is that this political crossroads for Mexico will have significant effects on multinational corporation investment decisions since, as previously mentioned in Chap. 1, investment decisions are based on cost benefit analysis and continuously evolving "strengths, weaknesses, opportunities, and threat" analysis (SWOT) of specific business environments [24, 298–200].

In this chapter, the case of Brazil will be examined and attempts made to illuminate some of the basic parameters of terrorist assaults directed at commercial interests in that country. As with India and Mexico, qualitative description of some of the perpetrators of terrorism in Brazil between 2007 and 2018 will be provided. The qualitative and quantitative analysis will help to establish a baseline of expectations for the reader that will make it possible to make a preliminary cross-national comparison of business related terrorist attacks in parts of Latin America.

References

1. Ackerman GA, Burnham M (2019) Towards a definition of terrorist ideology. Terrorism and Political Violence 33(6):1160–1190. https://www.tandfonline.com/doi/abs/10.1080/09546553.2019.1599862
2. Al S (2015) Local armed uprisings and the transnational image of claim making: the Kurds of Turkey and the Zapatistas of Mexico in comparative perspective. Globalizations 12(5):677–694. https://doi.org/10.1080/14747731.2014.991541
3. Anderson L (1987) The state in the Middle East and North Africa. Comparative Politics 20(1):1–18. https://www.jstor.org/stable/421917
4. Arce R (2018) More alleged cartel bombings discovered on another tourist ferry in Mexico. Breitbart News. https://www.breitbart.com/border/2018/03/03/alleged-cartel-bombs-discovered-another-tourist-ferry-mexico/
5. Atuesta LH, Pérez-Dávila YS (2018) Fragmentation and cooperation: the evolution of organized crime in Mexico. Trends in Organized Crime 21:235–261. https://link.springer.com/article/10.1007/s12117-017-9301-z
6. Barria-Issa CA (2010) The use of terrorism by drug trafficking organizations' paramilitary groups in Mexico. Master's thesis, Naval Postgraduate School. https://calhoun.nps.edu/handle/10945/5048

7. Beith M (2011) A broken Mexico: allegations of collusion between the Sinaloa cartel and Mexican political parties. Small Wars & Insurgencies 22(5):787–806. https://www.tandfonline.com/doi/abs/10.1080/09592318.2011.620813
8. Bolyard P (2018) Cruise lines cancel Mexican shores excursion after ferry explosion in Playa del Carmen. PJ Media. https://pjmedia.com/culture/paula-bolyard/2018/03/08/cruise-lines-cancel-mexican-shore-excursions-ferry-explosion-playa-del-carmen-n171226
9. Bunker RJ, Sullivan JP (2010) Cartel evolution revisited: third phase cartel potentials and alternative futures in Mexico. Small Wars & Insurgencies 21(1):30–54. https://doi.org/10.1080/09592310903561379
10. Campbell H, Hansen T (2012) Extreme violence and terrorism in Mexico. Small Wars Journal. http://citeseerx.ist.psu.edu/viewdoc/download?doi=10.1.1.259.6432&rep=rep1&type=pdf
11. Campbell H, Hansen T (2013) Is narco-violence in Mexico terrorism? Bull Lat Am Res 33(2):158–173
12. Carbaugh RJ (1989) International economics, 3rd edn. Wadsworth Thomson Learning
13. Cardash SL, Cilluffo FJ, Tussing BB (2011) HPSI issue brief: Mexico and the triple threat. The hybrid threat: crime, terrorism and insurgency in Mexico. Center for Cyber and Homeland Security at Auburn University
14. Chasdi R (1999) Serenade of suffering: a portrait of Middle East terrorism, 1968–1993. Lexington Books
15. Chasdi RJ (2002) Tapestry of terrorism: a portrait of Middle East terrorism, 1994–1999. Lexington Books
16. Chasdi RJ (2010) Counterterror offensives for the ghost war world: the rudiments of counterterrorism policy. Lexington Books
17. Chasdi RJ (2018) Corporate security crossroads: responding to terrorism, cyberthreats, and other hazards in the global business environment. ABC CLIO-Praeger
18. Chasdi RJ (2021) Implications of the new Taliban government for the Biden administration. The International Journal of Intelligence, Security, and Public Affairs 22. https://doi.org/10.1080/23800992.2021.2011071
19. Clarke CP (2019) Hezbollah is in Venezuela to stay. The RAND Blog. https://www.rand.org/blog/2019/02/hezbollah-is-in-venezuela-to-stay.html
20. Collier P (2000) Doing well out of war: an economic perspective. In: Berdal M, Malone DM (eds) Greed & grievance: economic agendas in civil wars. Lynne Rienner Publishers
21. Collier P, Hoeffler A (2000) Greed and grievance in civil war. Policy Research Working Paper, No. 2355. World Bank
22. Committee to Protect Journalists. (2018) Jose Guadaluoe Chan Dzib. https://cpj.org/data/people/jose-guadalupe-chan-dzib/
23. Corcoran P (2013) Mexico's shifting criminal landscape: changes in gang operation and structure during the past century. Trends in Organized Crime 16:306–328. https://link.springer.com/article/10.1007/s12117-013-9190-8
24. Cullen J, Parboteeah KP (2014) Multinational management: a strategic approach, 6E. South-Western Cengage Learning
25. Denning D (2000) Activism, hacktivism, and cyberterrorism: the internet as a tool for influencing foreign policy. Computer Security Journal 16(3):239–288. http://www.scinapse.io/papers/2256947274
26. Dishman C (2005) The leaderless nexus: when crime and terror converge. Studies in Conflict & Terrorism 28(3):237–252. https://doi.org/10.1080/10576100590928124
27. Fernandez LM (2009) Organized crimes and terrorism: from the cells towards political communication, a case study. Terrorism and Political Violence
28. Flanigan ST (2012) Terrorists next door? A comparison of Mexican drug cartels and Middle Eastern terrorist organizations. Terrorism and Political Violence 24(2):279–294. https://doi.org/10.1080/09546553.2011.648351
29. Flanigan ST (2014) Motivations and implications of community service provision by La Familia Michoacána/Knights Templar and other Mexican drug cartels. Journal of Strategic Security 7(3):63–83. https://www.jstor.org/stable/10.2307/26465194

30. Flemming PA (1992) Patterns of transnational terrorism in Western Europe, 1968–1987: a quantitative perspective. Ph.D. dissertation, Purdue University
31. Gilman N, Goldhammer J, Weber S (2013) Deviant globalization. In: Miklaucic M, Brewer J (eds) Convergence: illicit networks and national security in an age of globalization. National Defense University Press
32. Global Terrorism Database (GTD) "Mexico" GTD ID:200709100002. 10 Sept 2007
33. Global Terrorism Database (GTD) "Mexico." GTD ID: 201012070019. 7 Dec 2010
34. Global Terrorism Database (GTD) "Mexico" GTD ID: 201301310030. 31 Jan 2013
35. Global Terrorism Database (GTD) "Mexico," GTD ID: 201404290085. 27 April 2014
36. Global Terrorism Database (GTD) "Mexico," GTD ID: 201405250056. 25 May 2014
37. Global Terrorism Database (GTD) "Mexico," GTD ID: 201803011034. 3 Feb 2018
38. Global Terrorism Database (GTD) "Mexico," GTD ID: 201802210044. 21 Feb 2018
39. Global Terrorism Database (GTD) "Mexico" GTD ID: 201805150056. 15 May 2018
40. Global Terrorism Database (GTD) "Mexico" GTD ID: 201806300015. 30 June 2018
41. Grayson GW (2014) The cartels: the story of Mexico's most dangerous criminal organizations and their impact on U.S. security. Praeger
42. Harris P, Reilly B (eds) (1998) Democracy and deep rooted conflict options for negotiators. IDEA
43. Harvey N (1998) The Chiapas rebellion: the struggle for land and democracy. Duke University Press
44. Helbardt S (2015) Deciphering south Thailand's violence: organization and insurgent practices of BRN-Coordinate. ISEAS Publishing
45. Hennigan WJ (2019) The U.S. sent its most advanced fighter jets to blow up cheap opium labs now it's cancelling the program. Time
46. Hill CWL (2014) Global business today, 8th edn. McGraw Hill Irwin
47. Hill CWI, Hult GTM (2016) Global business today, 9th edn. McGraw Hill Education
48. Hoffman B (1984) The Jewish defense league. Terrorism, Violence, Insurgency Journal 5(1):10–15
49. Huntington SP (1968) Political order in changing societies. Yale University Press
50. Jones NP (2016) Mexico's elicit drug networks and the state reaction. Georgetown University Press
51. Kaldor M (2013) In defence of new wars. Stability: International Journal of Security and Development 2(1):1–34
52. Kinney M (2007) From Pablo to Osama: trafficking and terrorist networks, government bureaucracies and competitive adaptation. Pennsylvania State University Press
53. Klein R (2022) Anonymous releases 364,000 files about Russia's censorship of invasion. UPI
54. Kuhn DA, Bunker RJ (2013) Just where do Mexican cartel weapons come from? In: Bunker RJ (ed) Criminal insurgencies in Mexico and the Americas—the gangs and cartels wage war. Routledge
55. Kydd AH, Walter BF (2006) The strategies of terrorism. Int Secur 31(1):49–79
56. Lasswell HD (1935) World politics and personal insecurity. McGraw Hill, Whittlesey House
57. Lasswell HD (1958) Politics: who gets what, when, how—with postscript. Meridian Books
58. Lasswell HD (1978) Terrorism and the political process. Terrorism: An International Journal 1(3/4):261–263
59. Long DE (1990) The anatomy of terrorism. Free Press
60. Lopez GA (1984) A scheme for the analysis of government as terrorist. In: Stohl M, Lopez GA (eds) The state as terrorist: the dynamics of governmental violence and repression. Greenwood Press
61. Lopez GA, Stohl M (1989) Introduction: the development and dependence factors of state repression. In: Lopez GA, Stohl M (eds) Dependence, development, and state repression. Greenwood Press
62. Loveman B, Davies TM (1997) The politics of antipolitics. A Scholarly Resources, Inc.
63. Lynch DJ (2022) War could be a global economic "game changer," not just for now. The Washington Post

64. Makarenko T (2004) The crime terror continuum: tracing the interplay between transnational organized crime and terrorism. Global crime 6(1):129–145
65. McClintock C (2022) Department of Political Science, George Washington University. e-mail
66. McClintock C (2022) Mexico 2022, pptx Power Point slides
67. McClintock C (2022) drugcontrol2022withColandMex, pptx Power Point slides
68. Medel M, Thoumi FE (2014) Mexican "drug cartels", Chapter 9. In: Paolo L (ed) The Oxford handbook on organized crime. Oxford University Press
69. Mickolus E (2014) Terrorism, 2008–2012: a worldwide chronology. McFarland and Company, Inc.
70. Mickolus E (2016) Terrorism, 2013–2015: a worldwide chronology. McFarland and Company, Inc.
71. Mickolus E (2018) Terrorism worldwide, 2016. McFarland and Company, Inc.
72. Nadal A (1998) Terrorism in Chiapas. Bulletin of the Atomic Scientists 54(2):18–25
73. Nayar BR (2014) Globalization and India's economic integration. Georgetown University Press
74. Oots KL (1984) Transnational terrorism: a political organization approach. Ph.D. dissertation. Northern Illinois University
75. Phillips BJ (2018) Terrorist tactics by criminal organizations: the Mexican case in context. Perspectives on terrorism 12(1):46–63
76. Phillips L (2012) Anarchists attack science: armed extremists are targeting nuclear and nanotechnology workers. Nature
77. Phillips L (2012) Armed resistance—nature assesses the aftermath of a series of nanotechnology-lab bombings in Mexico—and asks how the country became a target of eco-anarchists. Nature 576–579. https://www.nature.com/articles/488576a
78. Rapoport DC (1987) Why does religious messianism produce terror? In: Wilkinson P, Stewart AM (eds) Contemporary research on terrorism. Aberdeen University Press
79. Rogers P (2001) Losing control global security in the twenty-first century. Pluto Press
80. Ross JI (1993) Structural causes of oppositional political terrorism: towards a causal model. J Peace Res 30(3):317–329
81. Ross JI, Miller RR (1997) The effects of oppositional political terrorism: five actor base models. Low Intensity Conflict and Law Enforcement 6(3):76–107
82. Ross JI, Gurr TR (1989) Why terrorism subsides: a comparative study of Canada and the United States. Comp Polit 21(4):76–107
83. Shelley LI (2013) Money laundering into real estate. In: Miklaucic M, Brewer J (eds) Convergence: illicit networks and national security in the age of globalization. Center for Complex Operations, Institute for National Strategic Studies, National Defense University
84. Shelley LI (2014) Identifying, counting and categorizing transnational criminal organizations. In: Sheptycki J (ed) Transnational organized crime volume II definitional and methodological issues, constructionist and critical perspectives. Sage Publications
85. Shelley LI, Picarelli J, Irby A, Hart DM, Craig-Hart PA, Williams P, Simon S, Abdullaev N, Stanislawski B, Covill L (2005) Methods and motives: exploring links between transnational organized crime and international terrorism. Trends in Organized Crime 8(2). https://link.springer.com/article/10.1007/s12117-005-1024-x
86. Stevenson M (2014) Environmentalists kidnapped, freed in Mexico. AP News
87. Stohl M, Lopez GA (1984) Introduction. In: Stohl M, Lopez GA (eds) The state as terrorist: the dynamics of governmental violence and repression. Greenwood Press
88. Stohl M (1984) International dimensions of state terrorism. In: Stohl M, Lopez GA (eds) The state as terrorist: the dynamics of governmental violence and repression. Greenwood Press
89. Sullivan JP, Bunker RJ (2013) Rethinking insurgency: criminality, spirituality, and societal warfare in the Americas. In: Bunker RJ (ed) Criminal insurgencies in Mexico and the Americas: the gangs and cartels wage war. Routledge
90. Teiner D (2020) Cartel related violence in Mexico as narco-terrorism or criminal insurgency. Perspectives on Terrorism 14(4):83–98. https://www.jstor.org/stable/pdf/26927665.pdf
91. Telesur E (2017) Mexican indigenous radio host murdered in Guerrero. https://www.telesurenglish.net/news/Mexican-Indigenous-Radio-Host-Murdered-in-Guerrero--20170603-0014.html

92. Tibbet I, Bankole N (2021) Terrorism: how have terrorist attacks changed in North America from 1970 to 2018? Story Maps. https://storymaps.arcgis.com/stories/67a79c8d56e94b699ba0dcca06bc3742
93. Wainwright T (2017) Narconomics: How to run a drug cartel. Ebury Press
94. Weinberg B (2000) Homage to Chiapas: the new indigenous struggles in Mexico. Verso
95. White JR (2002) Terrorism: an introduction, 3rd edn. Wadsworth Thomson Learning
96. Wilkinson P (2003) Why modern terrorism? Differentiating types and distinguishing ideological motivations. In: Kegley CW (Ed) The new global terrorism: characteristics, causes, controls. Prentice Hall, pp 106–138
97. Wolfers A (1973) "National security" as an ambiguous symbol. In: Art RJ, Jervis R (eds) International politics: anarchy, force, imperialism. Little, Brown and Company
98. World Economic Forum (2017) Global competitiveness index 2017–2018 reports
99. World Economic Forum (2017) Appendix C: the executive opinion survey: the voice of the business community. http://www3.weforum.org/docs/GCR2017-2018/04Backmatter/TheGlobalCompetitivenessReport2017%E2%80%932018AppendixC.pdf

Chapter 5
The Case of Brazil

5.1 Introduction

The experience with "insurgent" terrorism in Brazil traces an arc to the 1960s. At that time, the Brazilian military and Brazilian "left-wing" terrorist groups began to clash over Brazil's political policies and direction [59, 317–329; 63, 36–37]. In the time interval between the 1964 military coup and the end of military rule in 1984, "oppositional" terrorist assaults against business targets, including banks, were commonplace to note.

An underlying notion in the field of comparative politics is that political processes and political factors that affect events in one time interval, are sourced and nestled in pervious historical periods [34, 7–8, 19–20, 29, 178–179, 184; 35, 6–9, 13]. Indeed, several scholars point to the importance of such historical continuity and the sequence of historical events as especially important in the Brazilian context. That is because the basic Brazilian political themes of emancipation from Western domination and the importance of socioeconomic development for nation-state security have exerted powerful influence throughout different historical eras [40, 3, 10–11, 8; 44, 737, 759, 761, 765, 743; 58, 245–246].

The foregoing suggests that more contemporary Brazilian terrorism use, both traditional political terrorism, and the terrorism used by criminal syndicalists, has been influenced by explanatory factors from previous historical eras embedded in Brazilian society and in the international political system. Nowadays, terrorism is used in Brazil primarily by criminal syndicalists groups and other types of criminal gangs selling drugs and in some cases other illicit goods, against targets that include several types of business targets.

Those explanatory factors stem from the political standpoints of major political stakeholders, political processes, and specific events with potential to influence terrorist group and criminal syndicalist formation and behavior. To be more specific, those explanatory factor sources include political and economic inequalities, slavery in Brazil as an institution, corruption, and broader "social cohesion" problems in the

R. J. Chasdi, *Corporate Security Surveillance*, Advanced Sciences and Technologies for Security Applications, https://doi.org/10.1007/978-3-031-39550-5_5

Brazilian context [5, 308; 29, 38; 40, 10, 8; 44, 756; 45, 45; 58, 245–246; 79, 323, 325, 333–334, 337].

For example, in the case of political and economic inequalities, Abbott explains that many of the poor in contemporary Brazil are represented by the political group, Movement of Those Without Land ("Movimento Sem Terra"). For Abbott, the Movement of Those Without Land is one of several political groups in South America, "...whose leaders are gaining political prominence, and who could be susceptible to terrorism's appeals." [1, 55; 5, 307–308, 313–314, 319].

In addition, other nation-state level factors such as the makeshift incomplete government control likely contribute to the potential growth of organizations that use terrorism. In contemporary Brazil, such incomplete government control is found, in the case of geographical location, primarily in Brazil's Amazon region, its tri-border areas, and in several favelas in urban settings [5, 309, 311; 66, 115–116; 79, 334, 337]. This theme of historical continuity and the importance of nation-state and explanatory factors at the international political systems level, such as globalization, served as a template and set of guideposts for this analysis.

One criminal group with a significant capacity for terrorism is the First Capitol Command (PCC). The PCC has used terrorist assaults inside and outside of Brazil's prison system to advocate for prison reform and prisoners' rights. In the process, PCC targets of terrorist assaults have included commercial interests such as private establishments, newspaper/print, and telecommunications targets, as was the case in the PCC's 2006 terrorist campaign, carried out largely in response to Brazilian government policies to regulate and secure the prison system [11; 20, 600–603, 606, 596–599, 612; 29, 95, 53; 79, 332, 337; 80, 283–284].

Those data on Brazilian terrorist assaults were also makeshift and incomplete in another sense. That was the case because in many scripted accounts of terrorist assaults, substantive ties to political events, a fuller qualitative description of terrorist threat for the eleven year time period under consideration, and examples of direct terrorist event attribution were sometimes difficult to find. The foregoing data limitations added to the importance of a careful description of Brazilian political context for this analysis, in part to cull out important background information about anonymous terrorist assaults that themselves made up a full 85.0% (17/20 acts) of the total.

The underlying aim of this chapter is to acquire a deeper appreciation about how the threat of terrorism in Brazil has evolved since the end of the Cold War and the onset of "intensive" globalization. That was done with work to establish connections with past historical processes and events in Brazil. In the narrower sense, that approach helped shaped appraisals of more contemporary threats of terrorism against commercial interests [22, 23].

One focus of this qualitative discussion of "insurgent" terrorism in Brazil is on the political context of terrorism in the 1960s and 1970s. In addition, special attention is put on description of the activities of foreign terrorist organizations active in Brazil's "tri-border area" between the countries of Paraguay, Argentina, and Brazil (in addition to Brazil's shared border with Uruguay). Many of those foreign terrorist organizations were sourced in the Middle East. Those Middle East based terrorist groups include, but are not necessarily limited to, Hezbollah, its affiliate organization al-Muqawamah, Hamas, al-Jihad, al-Qaeda, and al-Jama'a al-Islamiya [5, 320; 31, 12, 17–18, 20; 36, 103; 55, 154–155, 157].

Many scripted accounts suggest those terrorist groups operate for the most part in narrower organizational capacities—to recruit, indoctrinate, raise funds and acquire weapons. For Rabasa et. al., "these groups engage in black market operations, arms purchases, and planning for terrorist attacks on U.S., Israeli, and Jewish targets." [1, 51; 31, 14–15, 27–30; 36, 24–26; 55, 154, 157]. At the same time, those terrorist groups have the potential to conduct terrorist assaults inside Brazil.

The primary geographical locale examined is Brazil's "tri-border area" where the contiguous borders of Argentina, Paraguay, and Brazil meet, and where episodic and inconsistent law enforcement is the norm [55, 153; 59, 317–329; 60, 76–107; 80, 281–284]. In addition to problems with law enforcement in this "tri-border area," there are other terrorism risk factor influences with potential cascade effects that pose threats to national and international security. Moreover, another fledgling Brazilian "tri-border area" near Peru, Bolivia, and Brazil, also poses potential national and international security problems [1, 55; 5, 307; 31, 35; 36, 103; 80, 281–282].

Those other terrorism explanatory risk factor effects are largely a function of the convergence of terrorist group and syndicalist criminal interests and activities [80, 281–284]. For example, Hudson describes broader linkages in the TBA between different international criminal gangs linked to Chinese and Russian organized crime and al-Qaeda, in addition to more specific linkages between international gangs and terrorist groups such as the "Hong Kong Mafia" with its ties to both Hezbollah and al-Jama'a al-Islamiya. [7, 165–166; 31, 16–17, 43–44, 35, 20, 24, 31, 46; 55, 155–156].[1]

Zúquete delves deeper to describe a specific set of relationships between Hezbollah and the First Capitol Command (PCC) when he makes mention of a scripted *O Globo* account in 2014 that describes ties between Hezbollah and PCC. As Zúquete reports, that agreement reportedly stipulated that "... in exchange for protection inside the Brazilian prison system for Hezbollah operatives, PCC would have at its disposal contraband arms and explosives...." [29, 93–95; 54, 3–4; 80, 283].

For some scholars and government analysts, the potential for terrorist groups in contemporary Brazil to move away from primary emphasis on organizational and administrative activities to carrying out terrorist assaults is significant. Some potential terrorist targets in contemporary Brazil might include international sports event venues, should terrorist group leaders or criminal syndicalist groups calculate that the net benefits which accrue from such attacks will outweigh the (potential) costs. For example, Brazil has a storied history of hosting international soccer events. Past appraisals of potential terrorist targets have included, but were not limited to, sports arenas associated with such international tournaments such as FIFA soccer events [63, 2–3; 80, 284].

[1] In essence, al-Jama'a al-Islamiya was a designation for several Islamic extremist sub-groups such as Dr. Ayman Rabi al-Zawahri's group, Jama'at al Jihad.

It is beyond the scope of this chapter to discuss the broader number of Brazilian criminal syndicalist groups active in Brazil's drug trade. In fact, it was extremely difficult to find much information in English about links between syndicalist groups and the Brazilian terrorist assaults chronicled.[2] Still, there is some valuable information available about those organizational ties that can be presented. For example, the Brazilian drug lord, "Commander" João Arcanjo Ribeiro in the Brazilian state of Mato Grasso and the drug kingpin Luiz Fernando da Costa ("Seaside Freddy") from the Red Commando syndicate, will be mentioned within the context of criminal organization descriptions [20, 604; 29, 71, 81, 85; 79, 331–332, 337].

5.2 The Political Context of Business Related Terrorism in Brazil

This chapter section focuses on description of Brazilian "left wing" terrorist groups in the 1960s and early 1970s. Many of the terrorist assaults conducted involved business related terrorist assaults. In some cases, those terrorist assaults were very high profile events. One such high profile terrorist assault was the 1971 São Paulo murder of Mr. Henning Albert Boilsen, who was the President of the Brazilian energy firm Ultragas [63, 68, 74, 27–28, 91]. Boilsen was a prominent supporter of the Brazilian government who served as a "leading fundraiser" for the Brazilian security services DOI-CODI (Operations of Internal Defense). He was killed by the National Liberating Alliance (ALN), a terrorist organization founded by Carlos Marighella [30, 29; 58, 250, 143, 250–251; 63, 37, 27–28, 143, 91, 76, 31, 53; 46].[3]

As previously mentioned, a more complete appreciation of terrorism requires a close examination of relevant political context, and that is where this chapter begins. On March 31, 1964, a military coup led by General Humberto Castello Branco and backed by U.S. President Lyndon B. Johnson, overthrew the left of center civilian government of Brazilian João President Goulart (1961–1964) [29, 51; 44, 765; 58, 241–243; 63, 1, 4–5, 36–37, 27, 49–50]. That military coup against President Goulart helped spawn some forty left-wing terrorist groups in opposition to the country's now militarily controlled state. Those terrorist groups protested against the military's authoritarian rule, its egregious human rights violations, and the military's half-hearted promises to help promote return to civilian rule [63, 116, 2; 64, 741, 744].

What is significant is that aspects of that struggle between the military government and those terrorist groups seem to be sourced in a set of broader political tensions from the early and middle twentieth century [44, 765; 63, 37, 27; 64, 743, 738]. Time honored political tensions between Brazilian army leadership and civilian

[2] Likewise, neither the Global Terrorism Database (GTD) nor the Mickolus data chronologies had an in depth account of the business targets that were assaulted during the PCC terrorist campaign of 2012.

[3] For Serbin, there is no evidence that "left-wing" terrorist groups and Brazilian drug dealers collaborated in the 1960s or 1970s.

politicians, and later between the military officer corps, characterized much of the political discourse during the period of the First Republic of Brazil (1899–1930). This discourse revolved around questions about Brazil's global standing, how to spur on Brazil's socio-economic development, and Brazil's security standpoint, with its emphasis on domestic threats, and ties to economic development. [40, 10, 8; 44, 737, 759, 761, 743; 58, 245–246].

At the heart of the matter, was underlying debate about whether Brazilian politicians or the Brazilian military were best suited to promote Brazilian national interests [62, 76–77]. In the early twentieth century, those tensions played out as Brazilian civilian governments engaged in fierce struggle with a dissatisfied military. The Brazilian military was extremely scornful of the civilian politicians in charge of government who were both supported by the landed aristocracy and seen as corrupt and ineffective [40, 3–4; 44, 753, 747; 45, 42–43].

Overall, the military's antipathy towards Brazil's civilian leadership stemmed from how poorly the military was treated by successive civilian governments. For McCann, the ruling elite, "...ignored the officer corps, keeping salaries low, promotions slow, and arms scarce, while seeking to minimize the army's political power...." [44, 753, 747; 45, 42]. In addition to the corruption endemic to Brazil's political system dominated by "oligarchs" and "bosses," this antipathy towards Brazil's civilian leaders was driven by the perception of Brazil's subservience to the United States.

The central idea was that Brazil's civilian politicians had succumbed to Western interests inherent to the international liberal economic order, an "international political systems" factor that stressed Western political and economic dominance, and the exploitation of Brazil and other Latin American countries. It also was identified by the Brazilian military leadership as the source of Brazilian corruption [40, 3, 11; 53; 62, 80–81; 64, 722; 73]. Equally important, there were a set of divisions within the military officer corps itself about the proper relationship between the Brazilian military and Brazil's civilian politicians.

One set of divisions traced an arc to the Paraguayan War (1865–1870) and revolved around two different standpoints in Brazil's military officer corps about the reasoning behind the involvement of the armed forces in politics. The "tarimbeiros" embraced a pragmatic standpoint, where the military's political involvement was designed to enhance the military's power with respect to civilian politicians.

In comparison, the "doutores" embraced a more normative notion of what McCann calls the "citizen-soldier" concept [44, 750; 45, 41–46, 49–50]. This notion of "citizen-soldier" advocated that, "the distinction between the concept of citizen and soldier should be extinguished in favor of a broadened view of citizenship." [44, 750; 45, 41–46, 49–50]. The "citizen-soldier" concept held that the military as an institution would pass into eclipse as Brazil's socio-economic development continued to unfold.

At a functional level, those basic divisions in the military officer corps reflected philosophical differences and generational cleavages, at least to some degree, where many younger officers viewed the military as the principal vehicle for societal cohesion and socio-economic development. The end result was that those divisions worked to generate and sustain political instability, especially when coupled with the machinations of outside political factions within Brazil's political elite, in fierce competition with one another.

Those philosophical divisions were not the only set of fissures that rend apart the military. A second set of strains and tensions involved Brazil's old guard military and reform minded junior military corps officers known as the "tenentes," or the "lieutenants." The "tenentes" comprised the "tenentismo movement," a reformer movement that would increasingly influence the trajectory of Brazilian politics well into the middle twentieth century [62, 80–81]. The early "tenentismo movement" was particularly active between 1922 and 1930; it reflected the reform interests of those junior military corps officer leaders and their belief that effective political reform was an urgent imperative.

In the early twentieth century, many of those young military corps officers were eager to confront the older military generation that had powerful ties to Brazil's civilian leaders, and therefore, to the oligarchs who backed civilian leadership at both federal and state levels. Still, it is important not to overestimate differences between the tenentes and other Brazilian officer corps members. For McCann, "...there was little difference between the tenente rebels and the rest of the officer corps; where they differed was in their patience and choice of means to effect solutions." [44, 764].

The rise of tenentismo in the 1920s and its raison d'etre reflected powerful connections to time honored and unresolved tensions in Brazilian politics. As previously mentioned, those tensions revolved around the role of the military in politics, and the types of strategies to use to attain political goals and strengthen Brazil. In his work, Schneider alludes to the importance of historical continuities in shaping more contemporary events when he suggests the underlying tenentes theme of "reform," itself to be spearheaded by Brazil's military, dovetailed well with the central notion of "Florianismo." [40, 11; 44, 765; 45, 51; 62, 77]. It is also important to note the concept of "Florianismo" stemmed from the belief held by former Brazilian President Marshal Floriano Vieira Peixoto (1839–1895) that "state consolidation," was the elixir required for Brazil's development [44, 743, 750; 61, 74, 132, 166–167; 62, 77; 64, 733].

In their quest for reform, the "tenentes" initially embraced western style liberal democracy and promoted efforts to replicate western style political institutions. That was the case even though support for "right-wing politics," by means of the National Democratic Union of Brazil (UDN) for example, became the hallmark of "tenentes" politics in years to come [44, 753–754; 56, 47, 49–51, 41, 43, 53; 61, 131; 64, 725; 79, 326, 336, 338].[4]

As a group, the "tenentes" lacked cohesion, and at first were broken down into two broader political sub-groups. [56, 49; 64, 735]. One sub-group led by Juarez Távora embraced what Rachum calls a "moralistic approach." It advocated what amounted to authoritarian democracy where the officer corps viewed themselves as morally superior and well equipped to act as guardians of the state.

[4] Both Rachum and Schneider suggest Benito Mussolini's fascism influenced aspects of the Tenentes movement.

In this way, that "moralistic approach" seems somewhat consistent with certain aspects of both the "doutores" and "tarimbeiros" approaches, as previously mentioned. That is precisely because the Brazilian military was viewed by many military officers as the vehicle for social and political change, albeit with a high dose of pragmatism injected into the political system. For example, one distinguishing characteristic of this "moralistic" strand of "tenente" where the military saw itself as morally predominant, was that its leader, Juarez Távora, refused to confront Brazil's oligarchs, with their political and economic clout [44, 739, 743–744, 749–750, 763; 56, 47–48, 52].

A second "tenentes" sub-group was essentially Marxist-Leninist in its orientation. This sub-group was led by Luis Carlos Prestes, who advocated for broader structural political and economic change in Brazil in the guise of socialism. Later in 1945, after his imprisonment in Brazil, Prestes would become the General Secretary of the Brazilian Communist Party (PCB). Notwithstanding that, what unified these two sub-groups at the time was their ardent belief that it was the military that should essentially act as guardians of the state, tasked with the responsibility to propel Brazil into the future [18; 40, 3; 44, 740, 743–744, 750; 56, 52; 63, 10–11; 64, 735].

In time, the "right of center" Távora faction of the "tenentes" would predominate over the Prestes "leftists." For Rachum, that was in large part because of broader political support the Távora faction elicited, support which was linked to tactical mistakes made by Luis Carlos Prestes [56, 51; 64, 735].[5] The end result was that Távora's middle of the road politics made it possible for the "tenentes," now under Távora's control, to acquire new influence and simultaneously embarrass the old military guard. That happened when the 1930 Revolution ousted President Washington Luis, dissolved the First Republic, and installed President Getúilo Vargas, a civilian politician, as the leader of a new "provisional government," known as the Second Republic (1930–1937) [44, 718; 56, 41, 48–49, 52, 58; 64, 725, 740].

To be sure, that fierce competition between the "tenentes" and the old guard military continued to play out with the 1937 establishment of the Estado Novo ("New State") or Third Republic. For Rachum, the Estado Novo pitted the interests of the old guard military, that helped craft the Estado Novo, against those of the "tenentes," who wanted to exert full control over the state's political apparatus. What is significant here is that the Estado Novo leadership embraced full blown authoritarian government, where the fascist "Integralist" movement, which eschewed Brazil's old constitution (1934), gained political sway, perhaps even with some "tenentes" support [56, 51; 61, 167; 64, 740, 738, 726, 743].

Even after the fall of the Estado Novo (New State), many of those old political fissures continued to influence Brazilian politics. The interplay between the "tenentes" and the old guard military continued, where each side jockeyed for political position under successive governments. Ironically, those conflict dynamics changed as the increasingly older group of original "tenentes," which continued to confront

[5] One such mistake was Prestes' almost singular focus on publication of his Marxist-style manifesto; that worked to alienate potential supporters.

Brazilian generals less interested in reform, transformed into Brazil's current military establishment.

The ineluctable conclusion was that a new junior officers corps in Brazil began to articulate new political demands and aspirations vis a vis the "tenentes," now firmly entrenched in Brazil's military. When those new political demands were overlaid onto old political demands and aspirations made by the tenentes and other military leaders, political instability and unrest increased. That process in Brazil seems as good an example as any of "government overload," where a multiplicity of demands made simultaneously on government elicits political instability and social unrest because government is unable to respond fully to many of those demands [9, 168–169, 176n26; 69, 19; 77, 10–11, 5–7, 17n4].

As Rachum reports, national policy differences that corresponded to generational cleavages within the military involved efforts to craft Brazil's national oil policy in the early 1950s. Those national policy differences were both a cause and effect of competing sets of demands previously mentioned. The issue revolved around whether Brazil's oil exploration efforts should include American participation, or whether a more "nationalist" policy where Brazil would work more independently, would prevail.

The latter position was associated with the Military Club with its strong "tenentes" component, as well as with former Estado Nuvo President Vargas, who himself was dependent on military support in his bid to become Brazil's constitutionally elected President. After his election, President Vargas did endorse this nationalist position. For Serbin, "Vargas veered to the left, carrying out a nationalistic platform that included the nationalization of the country's oil and the creation of Petrobras, a state owned petroleum firm, in 1953." [56, 54–55; 61, 167–168; 63, 2; 64, 744; 66, 112–113].

Another example of deep divisions over national policy revolved around Brazil's "Superior War School" (Escola Superior de Guerra or ESG) that was crafted in 1949. The ESG was characterized by competing national security perspectives which reflected differences in foreign policy standpoints. The "tenentes" had a preference for a military perspective. That military perspective stressed fundamental linkages between national security and socioeconomic development, and sustained the role of military officer political engagement in the political and diplomatic system [40, 10–11, 3, 5–6, 8; 44, 765; 45, 51; 56, 51, 54–55; 58, 245–247; 61, 167; 66][6]

That military perspective amounted to a political posture which was also highly anti-Soviet and pro-American. At the same time, that posture was still highly nationalistic when it came to oil exploration and production. That was the case even though its basic pro-American stance was reflective of Távora's early perspective as a fledgling "tenente," when he stood in opposition to the Marxism of tenentes led by Prestes [40, 10–11, 3, 5–6, 8; 44, 765; 45, 51; 56, 51, 54–55; 58, 245–247; 61, 167; 66].

What is significant here is those different sets of political, generational, and factional divisions within Brazil's political system, and the frenetic competition that

[6] For Loveman and Davies, that link between the military and the requisite of Brazilian economic development is a hallmark of their "anti-politics" concept.

ensued, had middle-run to long-haul effects on future Brazilian political developments [44, 765; 45, 51; 58, 245–247]. That notion is consistent with Johnson's notion that it is impossible to divorce political, societal, or cultural elements of a "post-revolutionary regime" from such characteristics associated with the "ancient regime" that came before [35; 44, 765; 64, 743, 738].

Those historical continuities, reflected in the political hardship conditions elicited by the political system from the 1930s through the 1950s, worked to spur on terrorist action to confront military governments in place after 1964. It follows that similar types of political and "social cohesion" problems found in earlier historical eras of Brazilian politics probably have had some influence on conflicts between different types of criminal syndicalist organizations which use terrorism in contemporary Brazil.

To delve deeper, those types of societal problems reflected what Diamond calls "coincidental cleavages," where political and economic inequalities for example, aligned closely with specific and clearly discernable ethnic or racial groups. In response, terrorist assaults were designed to strike back against broader government oppression of Brazilians, and the narrower government repression directed at Brazilian reformist leaders, and some in Catholic ecumenical circles, opposed to military control [16; 39, ix–xv; 65, 8].

In addition, those political fissures were reflected in competing perspectives about the importance of human rights, perceived links between economic development and Brazilian national security, the relationships between military and civilian leadership, and critical political and economic inequalities that afflicted Brazilian society [63, 164, 172, 178]. Those hallmark divisions in Brazilian politics remained largely intractable until the end of military rule in 1984 and Brazil's return to civilian rule and democracy with the election of Jose Ribamar Ferriera Araujo, (Jose Sarney).

In addition to the historical links between pre-1964 military coup conditions and what followed, other linkages between historical epochs in Brazil seem discernable. For instance, the state terrorism or "police terror" as Skidmore puts it, that was characteristic of Brazilian military rule in the 1960s and 1970s, had precedent, and derived from the political and philosophical standpoints and experiences found in the earlier Estado Novo era of Brazilian history [44, 765; 63, 3; 64, 743].

Nowadays, similar political issues and dynamics reverberate in Brazil's political system. For instance, the First Capitol Command (PCC) has conducted terrorist campaigns with the aim to improve human rights conditions in Brazil's prisons; that resonates with terrorist group struggles in the 1960s to oppose egregious human rights violations in Brazilian prisons and in Brazilian society writ large.

The contemporary condition of "intensive globalization" and its effects on Brazil serve as another example of historical continuity in Brazil. The international liberal economic order, that for some scholars spawned "intensive globalization," was seen by many Brazilian generals in the middle twentieth century as the source of Western predominance, domestic corruption, and Brazil's overall national security problems [40, 3, 11]. However, it was precisely that condition of "intensive globalization," with the international liberal economic order squarely behind it, that elicited the type of socioeconomic development in Brazil so craved by the military as a way to help ensure national security and propel Brazil into the future.

Still, those Brazilian generals were not completely wide of the mark in their assessment that globalization would cause increased national security dangers; those generals were only wrong about the particulars of threat. That was the case because contemporary Brazil's primary national security threat is not the more traditional military oriented nation-state security threat probably envisioned. In fact, the socioeconomic development in Brazil, with its intrinsic linkages to global markets, has increased the allure of illicit drug trafficking and worked to facilitate the rise of Brazilian drug cartels. Plainly, criminal syndicalist groups that sell drugs and use terrorism have become a major national security threat for Brazil [5, 309; 20, 598; 54, 2; 66, 106, 116; 79, 323, 327, 337–338].

5.3 The 1964 Military Coup and Terrorist Groups Spawned

The 1964 military coup that installed President Humberto Castello Branco, and the successive military governments that followed, helped spawn some forty "left-wing" insurgent terrorist organizations. For Serbin, the total number of activists across those terrorist groups was about 800, in or around 1973 [29, 51; 63, 116]. While it is beyond scope of this chapter to provide a complete description of those terrorist groups, focus is placed on several high profile terrorist groups active in the Brazilian political fray of the 1960s and early 1970s to highlight some basic themes those terrorist groups shared.

This chapter examines the National Liberating Alliance (ALN), the 8th October Revolutionary Movement (MR-8), and the Popular Revolutionary Vanguard (VPR). It also examines the Armed Revolutionary Vanguard Palmares (VAR-Palmares), and the Communist Party of Brazil (PC do B)'s Red Wing" unit, also known as Ala Vermelha. It explores the origins of those terrorist groups, and helps shed light on the broader issues of contention that pitted those groups primarily against Brazil's military government. The analysis also illuminates terrorist group growth and development processes.

As in the case of India and Mexico, terrorist group splintering and offshoot formation were influenced by government policies such as counterterrorism measures. That set of underlying connections between government anti-terrorism efforts and group splintering processes helped shape the trajectory of Brazilian terrorist group evolution, as it has in the case of other terrorist groups in other nation-states.

5.4 The National Liberation Alliance (ALN)

The National Liberation Alliance (ALN) was the most high-profile Brazilian terrorist group active at that time. Its sources trace back to the Brazilian Communist Party (PCB), that was rend apart by political divisions. The PCB constituted one branch of a broader Brazilian Marxist-Maoist political front. That front also included Brazilian Trotskyites, known as the Revolutionary Workers' Party, the Marxist Revolutionary Movement (ORM), that became known as POLP, and the Communist Party of Brazil or PC do B.

The Communist Party of Brazil (PC do B) claimed ideological affinity to Beijing and to Maoism. In contrast, the PCB was distinguished from other coalition members by its close ideological ties to the U.S.S.R. [58, 250; 61, 256; 63, 10–11, 33–34; 46, 375–376]. What Schneider describes as a "Cuban-influenced" component of the PCB was led by Carlos Marighella, Joquim Camara Ferreira, and Mario Alves.

In the late 1960s, those PCB officials were cast out of the PCB, presumably because of ideological and personal differences, in addition to specific differences of opinion about PCB policy direction. At the heart of the matter, was a rift between more militant PCB officials and more mainstream, non-violent PCB leadership about the usefulness of forceful operations to confront Brazil's military government [58, 250; 61, 256; 63, 10–11, 33–34; 46, 375–376].

Out of this group of former PCB officials, several Brazilian terrorist groups were established. In many cases, terrorist group activists came from what Serbin calls, "privileged families." [63, 3]. The National Liberation Alliance (ALN) was one of those groups, crafted in 1967 by Marxist revolutionary Carlos Marighella (1911–1969). Marighella is perhaps best known for his treatise, the *Mini-Manual of the Urban Guerilla* [12, 153; 43; 80, 277].

Marighella was born in the Brazilian state of Bahia; his father was an Italian national while his mother was a product of Brazil's slave trade, a Brazilian institution that only ended in 1888 [61, 256, 263–264, 62; 62, 250; 63, 33]. As a result, Marighella experienced Brazil's profound and lasting social, political, and economic inequalities first hand [61, 256, 263–264; 62, 250; 63, 33]. Marighella was killed on November 4, 1969 in a shootout in São Paulo with Brazilian security forces. In turn, former Brazilian Captain Carlos Lamarca, led the ALN until his own death on September 17, 1971 at the hands of Brazilian security forces [58, 250–251].

For some, Marighella eschewed strict Leninism in the Brazilian context, because he did not believe that a formal urban proletariat should work as a vanguard for Brazilian revolutionary activity. His approach was influenced by both Maoism and by the Cuban Revolution (1959), spearheaded by Fidel Castro and Che Guevera.

Marighella favored the underlying notion of the "urban guerilla" who would assist the "rural guerilla" with the practice of revolutionary social and political structure with the armed people in power. As such, Marighella plainly advocated for urban venues as his primary emphasis for revolutionary activities [14, 97; 33, 21; 43, 21, 10; 57, 78].

In its halcyon days, the ALN was comprised of about 200 activists [12, 153; 15; 63, 11, 33–34; 67, 323, 314; 46, 375–376].[7] In many cases, Brazilian terrorist groups and their factions emanated from distinct geographical locales in Brazil. For example, the paramilitary branch of the Communist Party of Brazil (PC do B) that was called the "Red Wing" or Ala Vermelha was originally based in the Amazon region of Brazil as was its parent organization, the PC do B [63].

Likewise, the National Liberation Action (ALN) was structured with different sub-groups based in different urban areas. There were two ALN sub-groups, one based in São Paulo, and the other in Rio de Janeiro. In addition, those two ALN factions were characterized by cohort differences in activist membership. ALN activists based in Rio de Janeiro were usually in their middle and late teens, while in São Paulo, ALN members were slightly older undergraduate student age types for the most part, who worked in São Paulo with what Serbin calls the, "...older members of the working class." [63, 37, 82].

5.5 The 8 October Revolutionary Movement (MR-8)

The 8 October Revolutionary Movement (MR-8) was an ALN affiliate group primarily based in Rio de Janeiro. Its location in Rio de Janiero probably helped MR-8 retain and sharpen its own independence and identity [29, 54]. Like ALN, the MR-8 organization was a splinter group from the Communist Party of Brazil (PCB) It was formed by PCB dissidents dissatisfied with the non-violent approach to political reform in Brazil that was a hallmark of PCB party politics.

As Teló reports, there were actually two MR-8 organizations that operated over the Brazilian political landscape. The original MR-8 was operational in Brazil for a relatively short time, from around 1964 to 1969, before it was demolished by Brazilian security forces. In its aftermath, a new MR-8 materialized where the MR-8 name was appropriated by student revolutionary leader Vladimir Palmeira and his followers. For Teló, that acquisition of the MR-8 nameplate was done largely to offset the political propaganda benefits acquired by Brazil's government after it defeated the original MR-8 group [67, 316, 333; 75].

A major part of MR-8 consisted of university students from Brazilian families with middle class and small merchant or shopkeeper "petit bourgeoise" backgrounds.Early on, MR-8 discarded as impractical the central notion of an "outside in" revolution for Brazil [67, 316, 333; 75]. Under the leadership of Palmeira and others MR-8 chieftains, MR-8 activities unfolded both in Brazilian cities and in the countryside.

For example, in Brotas de Macaubas, in the state of Bahia, Jose Campos Barretto ("Zequinah"), his brother Olderico, and former Brazilian Captain Carlos Lamarca, worked with peasants to illuminate the policies that caused social injustice and economic inequality problems, such as Brazil's regressive taxation system, and to

[7] Serbin reports the ALN was comprised of some 300 activists, in contrast to McHugh who estimates 200 activists.

isolate and identify the political institutions responsible [67, 321–322, 326, 332, 336].

However, MR-8 efforts lurched to a halt in 1969 after a watershed terrorist event conducted by both the ALN and MR-8. That terrorist assault was the September 1969 ALN—MR-8 abduction of U.S. Ambassador Charles Burke Elbrick in Rio de Janeiro. Ambassador Elbrick was abducted after a joint ALN-MR-8 squad intercepted his automobile [12, 154; 63, 27–32, 37–50]. Shortly after that landmark terrorist assault, local MR-8 chieftain Olderico Baretto was shot and wounded by Brazilian authorities, while Luiz Antonio Santa Barbara was killed in August 1971. The next month, while on the run, Carlos Lamarca, who became ALN leader after Marighella's death in 1969, and Jose Campos Barreto ("Zequinah"), were both killed in or around Brotus de Macaubas, Bahia [29, 54–56; 63, 321–322, 326–327, 329–332].[8]

The abduction of Ambassador Elbrick was an extraordinarily high-profile terrorist event that focused almost singular attention on ALN and MR-8 activities. Unequivocally, that attention by counterterrorism authorities worked to shorten the terrorist "life cycle" for both terrorist organizations. Ambassador Elbrick was held by the ALN for a little over five days before he was released in Rio de Janeiro. His release came on the heels of extensive negotiations, where Elbrick's freedom was ensured in exchange for the Brazilian government's release of then MR-8 leader Vladimir Palmeira and other activists.

That ALN and MR-8 terrorist assault against Elbrick was noteworthy for several reasons. One was because it illuminated how terrorist groups can, at least temporarily, put personal differences aside to cooperate when mutual interests converge. It also hints at the permeability of terrorist group membership and leadership. Further, this terrorist assault remains as good an example as any of how poor communications between or within terrorist groups can lead to uncontrollable and unpredictable results. Marighella never authorized the Elbrick plan, but the assault happened because of compelling opportunity recognition [29, 54–56; 63, 321–322, 326–327, 329–332].

5.6 Other Brazilian Terrorist Groups

In addition to the National Liberating Action (ALN) and the MR-8, Schneider reports that the splintering of the Communist Party of Brazil (PCB) in the late 1960s produced at least two other terrorist groups. One terrorist group was the Revolutionary Brazilian Communist Party (PCBR) that was led by Mario Alves [58, 250–251; 61, 256, 263, 226; 63, 290].

Other Brazilian splinter or spinoff terrorist groups that formed in the late 1960s included the Popular Revolutionary Vanguard (VPR), which evolved from the POLOP party. It was led by former Brazilian Captain Carlos Lamarca, the same

[8] Grillo relates the Elbrick abduction story somewhat differently when he suggests MR-8 was the single, most predominant terrorist group involved in this event.

Brazilian militant who supported MR-8 activities in Bahia. Another terrorist group linked to POLOP was the National Liberation Command (COLINA). In 1969, both VPR and COLINA blended to become the Armed Revolutionary Vanguard-Palmares (VAR-Palmares) [61, 256].

Around 1967, another possible path for former ex-PCB members to take was to join an already well established and time honored PCB splinter political party called the Communist Party of Brazil (PC do B). Some ten years earlier, the PC do B was formed by Mauricio Grabois, Pedro Pomar, and João Amazonas, who brought many of their followers into the PC do B with them. The formation of the PC do B was the result of similar political processes—another earlier splintering event within the PCB, this time in 1957. That earlier split within the PCB also pitted the interests of certain PCB hard-liners and those more content with actions relegated to the traditional political sphere.

As a political group, PC do B advocated violence in the cities and the countryside to combat the political economic, and social status quo in Brazil. In essence, the PC do B straddled the line between non-violent political activities and terrorism. However, its paramilitary unit known as the Ala Vermelha (Red Wing), engaged in terrorist assaults, primarily against rural targets. As previously mentioned, the PC do B, Ala Vermelha (Red Wing) were both centered in the Amazon region of Brazil. In terms of membership, Ala Vermelha most likely shared permeable boundaries with its parent organization, the PC do B [61, 226].

5.7 The Role of Historical Continuities—Brazil's "Tri-border Area (TBA)"—Paraguay, Argentina, Brazil

This underlying theme of historical continuity in Brazil's political system carries over into contemporary times where much of the Brazilian terrorism threat emanates. The "tri-border area" of Paraguay, Argentina, and Brazil (an area that also borders Uruguay), is a multi-cultural, multi-racial, and multi-religious political landscape, and an epicenter for terrorist groups and criminal syndicalist gangs. In addition to its prominent Chinese and Muslim communities, many in the "tri-border area" population have direct ties to those three countries.

The "tri-border area" or "triple frontier" as it is sometimes called, has become a significant financial center and tourist attraction in no small part to the downside effects of "intensive globalization." For example, the duty free area established in the "tri border area" provides shoppers with high quality good and is in high demand. At the same time, consumer demands of other shoppers, more interested in rock bottom prices are also met, as inexpensive, counterfeit "knock-off" products such as stolen computer software and CDs are manufactured in the TBA for purchase and transnational shipment [1, 52; 70, 4, 6–9, 11–12, 22].

The "tri-border area" is also liberally peppered with organizations willing and able to use terrorism. Here, Middle Eastern terrorist groups and a wealth of international criminal syndicalist gangs predominate. For example, the TBA hosts Hezbollah, its affiliate group al-Muqawamah, Jama'a al Islamiya, Hamas, and al-Qaeda [1, 51; 3, 14–15, 17; 5, 320; 31, 15; 70, 3].[9] Those groups have focused primarily on organizational activities such as revenue acquisition, but those endeavors have spin-off effects that include illicit drug trade involvement, weapons sales, and participation in illegal immigration networks [5, 322; 36, 103; 51; 70, 3, 12–13].

What is significant for terrorist organizations and syndicalist groups that use terrorism is to consider the continuity and change of the Brazilian military's role in the political system across historical epochs. Such appraisals can expose vulnerabilities such as changes in contemporary government response to threat that might for example, involve links between political decision-making and time lags in rapid military response time. A significant driver of change to limit the military's role has been popular reaction to Brazil's human rights violations under military control, and the political infighting within and across military and political factions. The continuity of the Brazilian military's role in state security operations remains, but the scope of the Brazilian military's responsibilities has changed dramatically with the end of military rule in 1985.

That watershed transition formalized removal of the military from Brazil's political sphere. Nowadays, the Brazilian military has a much narrower but more focused role on traditional security affairs [61, 376; 71]. Nonetheless, that security role is likely to be constrained overall because, "...memories of the military dictatorships of the 1970s and 1980s have not been forgotten, and the people are afraid such dictatorships might return if the military's role expands." [1, 53]. In addition, Brafman Kittner points to organizational problems, corruption, and budget shortfalls that contribute to a condition in the TBA where Brazilian counterterrorism services can be ineffective [5, 316–317].

In essence, Schneider suggests that security emphasis for the military in his discussion about the security condition of Brazil's northern border. For Schneider, there is a security imperative, "...the need to establish an effective military presence on the vast reaches of the country's northern frontier....particularly salient in light of the present inability to control drug smugglers or the estimated half million gold prospectors spread across the inaccessible border regions...." [31, 48; 61, 376]. It follows that Schneider's description of the security imperative for the Northern part of Brazil and its borders with Peru, Colombia, Venezuela (and by extension Suriname and Guyana), also should also resonate with the "tri-border area."

That notion seems borne out by security developments in the "tri-border area" which unfolded in the early twenty first century. Undoubtedly spurred on and influenced by 9/11 effects, the Brazilian government helped to shape and improve further the TBA security condition, presumably with some military input into policy directives. For example, a Brazilian Federal Police (PF) headquarters was crafted in the

[9] Trevisi also points to the activities of the Moroccan Islamic Combatant Group and the Jihad Media Battalion in the TBA.

TBA in 2005, while the Secretariat of Federal Revenues (Secretaria de Receita Federal), was crafted in 2006, tasked with its mission to resolve customs related matters [1, 52; 3, 15, 3–4; 31, 24; 36, 105; 79, 329].

A second historical factor important for an appreciation of contemporary terrorism is the legacy of "social cohesion" or national integration problems in Brazil and the continuity of those issues across historical periods [32]. The demographic composition of the "triple frontier" is certainly reflective of broader national integration problems in Brazil because within a comparatively small area, there are important social fissures along ethnic, racial, religious, and nationality lines between TBA communities.

The multiplicity of ethnic, racial, and nationality characteristics intrinsic to the TBA probably helps to increase complexities associated with effective law enforcement control. For example, if there are cultural and communications problems between police and community members, coupled with long-standing and unresolved political demands and aspirations linked to specific communities, it follows that terrorist groups or syndicalist organizations have windows of opportunity to exploit those conditions [78].

As previously mentioned, "social cohesion" problems have the potential to resonate in "tri-border area" society; that is the case because society in the TBA is defined by a set of religious, ethnic, and racial fissures. For example, Chinese and Middle Eastern communities make up a significant part of the TBA population; the latter have ties to both the Chinese mainland and Taiwan. Hence, national origin also contributes to important community divisions.

In the case of the Middle Eastern population, Rabasa et al. report in 2006 that some 630,000 people lived in the tri-border area with 25,000 from Palestinian, Lebanese, or Syrian families [55, 153; 70, 6, 8]. Many Middle Eastern residents trace an arc to flows of Palestinian, Lebanese, Syrian, Jordanian, Egyptian, and Iraqi migrants who made their way to the TBA in the middle twentieth century. Meanwhile, broader immigration flows to Brazil from the Middle East date back to the 1800s [3, 16; 17, 4].

Hudson reports those twentieth century migration flows began around 1956 and were augmented by a spike in migration influxes linked to Lebanon's civil war in 1976. Both Abbott and Trevisi state most Arabs in the TBA are Shia Muslims, not Sunni Muslims [1, 51; 3, 16; 31; 55, 153; 71, 8–10]. Therefore, many TBA inhabitants have discernable links to old world communities and to conflicts associated with unresolved political issues. For Abbott, "the TBA offers terrorists…a sympathetic population from which to recruit new members and spread global messages." [1, 51; 5, 316].

At the same time, Trevesi suggests that what Diamond calls "cross-cutting cleavages" are at work in the TBA to serve as a balm of sorts to reduce political instability and social unrest [16, 19, 28]. For Trevisi, "religious beliefs, ethnic origins, political affiliations or commercial activities are all elements that can lead an individual to identify himself with one or several communities. Therefore, individuals develop local ties and a feeling of belonging to communities that cannot be circumscribed by a specific territory." [5, 316–317; 70, 7].

Every society has societal fault lines that work to create divisions which can have enormous socio-economic and political impact. In essence, cross-cutting conditions exist when social fissures or "fault lines" in society such as ethnic, racial, religious, and regional divisions are found across political parties or political institutions, or across working class, middle class, and upper class in society that amount to socioeconomic fissures [16].

For example, different societal fissures are found across political parties, political institutions such as the U.S. Congress, and the U.S. military, and across socio-economic fissures (i.e., upper class, middle class and working class divisions) in the United States. Those are as good a set of examples as any of "cross-cutting cleavage" or "crisscrossing cleavage" conditions [16, 32]. What is significant is that the presence of certain "cross cutting cleavages" in the "tri-border area" are conditions that Trevisi suggests works to offset, at least to some degree, inherent "social cohesion" problems in the region [70, 7].

In summation, linkages across historical time periods and specific issue areas such as lack of "social cohesion" helps to provide the basis of a useful framework for analysis. Those linkages make it possible to consider how political processes and problems found in pervious eras of Brazilian history work to provide contextual backdrop to more contemporary events. In turn, such contextual backdrop illuminates explanatory factors and possible connections between them that remain critical for an appreciation of contemporary Brazilian terrorism and its evolution.

The central notion that historical continuities impact terrorism threat development in Brazil is perhaps best illuminated by the experiences of the criminal syndicalist group Red Commando. The formation of Red Commando serves as a bellwether for continuously evolving sets of connections between terrorist groups and criminal gangs in Brazil. Moreover, a description of Red Commando serves as a useful segue for discussion about more contemporary terrorism in the Argentina, Paraguay, and Brazil "tri-border region," precisely because it helps illustrate the role of explanatory factors such as socioeconomic, ethnic, racial and religious fissures.

The criminal enterprise that is Red Commando coalesced in 1979–1980 around William Da Silva Lima, a serial bank robber who had experienced favela life hardships first hand. The deeper sources and origins of Red Commando trace back to the 1964 military coup when "left-wing" political prisoners, primarily from middle class background, were housed in the Ilha Grande prison in the same cell blocks as hardened criminals who were mostly from Brazil's favelas and villages [29, 42, 44, 59–63, 66, 69, 80; 79, 331].

However, the mix of those two prison populations was a lurking catastrophe for the Brazilian government. As Grillo reports, instead of this tactic working to break the spirit of those "left wing" prisoners, the demands and aspirations of the criminals, which stemmed from economic blight experienced, dovetailed perfectly with the "left-wing" prisoners' Marxist-Leninist standpoint and set of political agendas.

What reverberated powerfully was the Marxist-Leninist idea about the imperative for structural political and economic change. That set of ideological and functional relationships between the criminal gang Red Commando and many Marxist-Leninist revolutionary terrorist groups only dissolved in 1985, when military rule passed into eclipse and former terrorist chieftains ran for political office [12, 124; 29, 42, 44, 59–63, 66, 69, 80; 79, 331].

As a result, the criminal syndicalist group Red Commando was, as Grillo reports, imbued with a certain Marxist-Leninist hue that would stress the importance of social services provision. In addition to that ideological goodness of fit, such social service provision would work to promote Red Commando interests and the interests of favela constituents who lived in areas of Brazil where government was only able to exert makeshift or incomplete control [29, 42, 70–72, 82, 69, 66, 84, 88; 41, 129–145; 79, 331–332, 334, 336–337].[10]

Instead of the bank robberies that served as cash flow sources in the 1980s, the Red Commando has turned to its current cash cow—cocaine. At a functional level, Red Commando is a top-down hierarchal organization. At the top of this pyramid structure are its incarcerated chieftains, followed mid-level organizational heads in favelas called "donos." In turn, there are "drug mouth bosses" ("gerentes de boca") who sell drugs at kiosks on favela streets, armed enforcers ("soldados"), and "lookouts" known as "the vapors," who watch out for police [20, 606; 29, 82, 92; 79, 335–336, 331].[11]

In time, the Red Commando organization spawned a splinter group in the 1990s known as the "Third Commando," and both organizations became fierce rivals [29, 26, 42, 75, 82, 84, 86–87, 91–92]. A second Red Commando splinter group known as Amigos dos Amigos ("Friends of Friends") also galvanized around that time [29, 26, 42, 75, 82, 84, 86–87, 91–92]. This developmental phase is similar to what Lasswell calls the "terrorism life-cycle" and is reminiscent of intra-group processes encountered previously in the Indian and Mexican terrorist group formation context; it is applicable to both political terrorist and syndicalists who use terrorism to achieve objectives [37, 1935; 38, 255–263].

It is here we come full circle, to the formation of the First Capitol Command (PCC). The PCC is a Red Commando spinoff group that galvanized in 1992. A Phillip Morris International scripted account, suggests PCC had some "11,000 members" in 2019 [54, 3]. The Red Commando served as the motivational source, and functional and ideological template for the First Capitol Command, which itself set up shop in São Paulo, rather than in Rio de Janeiro. The PCC also has a socialist hue much like its antecedent group the Red Commando and it is involved in the drug trade, in addition to other illicit activities.

As previously mentioned, the PCC was designed to promote the interests of prisoners where systematic abuse in the prison system was the norm. Like the Red Commando, it is characterized by an "inside out" structure and process, where top

---

[10] That point by Grillo underscores Makarenko's point that unmanageable or poorly managed geographical locales, perhaps compounded by "social cohesion" problems, can serve as a seedbed for terrorist groups and criminal enterprise activities.

[11] By the same token, Zorovich's generic hierarchal structure for Red Commando includes: incarcerated chieftains → "gerentes de boca" ("mid-level administrators") → "soldados" ("armed enforcers") → "vaporeiros" ("drug dealers") → "fogueterios" ("lookouts").

incarcerated PCC leaders issue policy driven directives to activists. For example, the PCC terrorist campaign of 2006 probably revolved around PCC demands for changes in prisoner transfer policies and manufactured goods prisoners could obtain. Once those demands were met, that terrorism campaign, which included multiple terrorist assaults against business targets, ended [29, 93–95, 97–99, 42, 72, 82, 69, 89–90; 79, 327, 336; 20, 607, 596].

5.8 Terrorist Groups and Criminal Syndicalists in TBA

Many analysts suggest the terrorism threat in Brazil's TBA has grown since 2001 [55, 153–157; 52]. Moreover, there has now been the dissemination of terrorist group activities well beyond the confines of the time honored operations originally found in the four major "tri-border area" cities: the cities of Chuí and Foz do Iguaçu in Brazil, Chuy in Uruguay, and Ciudad de Este in Paraguay [31, 12, 15–16, 23, 35–36, 45; 52].

That wide-ranging dissemination of terrorists throughout the region happened largely in response to increased pressure from Brazilian and American counterterrorism authorities. As a result, some terrorist group elements moved into the Brazilian and Paraguayan countryside. In addition, Hudson reports that al-Qaeda expanded its narrower presence found at the border of Uruguay into the interior of that country [5, 316; 31, 12, 15–16, 23–36, 45; 80, 282].

It should be clear that the threat of actual terrorism is at issue here, rather than only the indirect threat associated with ancillary but still essential terrorist group organizational activities used to strengthen Middle terrorist groups. After all, the 1994 watershed terrorist assault that demolished the Argentine-Israel Mutual Association (AIMA) Jewish community center in Buenos Aries, was a Hezbollah attack carried out in conjunction with a local, Argentinian based syndicalist group called "Local Connection."

In the AMIA terrorist assault, Hezbollah terrorists were assisted by their "Local Connection" compatriots, taking a sea route to land on the coast of Argentina in striking range of Buenos Aries [5, 323, 320; 36, 104; 51; 55, 154–155]. Plainly, the AIMA terrorist assault illustrated the continuously evolving problem of terrorist group criminal syndicalist collaboration. Still, this was not the first time Hezbollah conducted a watershed terrorist event from the "tri-border area"—in 1992, a Hezbollah explosive device detonated at the Israeli Embassy in Buenos Aries [1, 51; 5, 321; 17, 5, 9; 31, 13–14, 24, 38–39; 36, 104; 51; 70, 3].

In addition to terrorism, the "Local Connection" also has been active at the other end of what Makarenko calls the "crime-terror continuum," with its involvement in organized crime. Those activities have involved participation in the drug trade and other forms of organized criminal activity. The "Local Connection" has been known to act as a conduit to supply illegal weapons to illicit organizations in Brazil [5, 307, 309–310, 314, 319; 41].

Presumably, those illicit organizations included other Brazilian drug trafficking organizations or groups linked to them. An important Brazilian drug lord who might have had ties to this network was "Commander" João Arcanjo Ribeiro, the leader of organized crime in the state of Mato Grasso [31, 48, 24]. In addition, one confirmed and significant set of ties that the "Local Connection" had was to the Brazilian drug kingpin Luiz Fernando da Costa, who himself was associated with Red Commando [5, 316; 29, 75, 81, 85; 31, 38–39, 28].

What seems significant here is that when Luiz Fernando da Costa was captured by Columbian security forces in April 2001, he was with associates from the Colombian Marxist-Leninist terrorist group, FARC (Revolutionary Armed Forces of Colombia). It follows the "Local Connection" and its ties to Hezbollah, FARC, and to international drug organization networks like Red Commando through da Costa for example demonstrate that such organizations, are in some cases, permeable. Those constitute the type of hybrid-terrorist and drug organizational network that can thrive in effective and sustained ways in a globalized world [1, 52; 5, 316; 17, 5–6; 31, 46].

In addition to the Argentinian based "Local Connection," Hudson points to other Latin American based criminal syndicalist groups active in the "tri-border area" with links to terrorist groups. For example, Hudson reports that Columbian as well as Russian drug organizations have also had links to the Colombian terrorist group FARC. Grillo reports that Red Commando provides FARC with weapons acquired from corrupted soldiers in countries at the Brazilian northern border in exchange for Colombian cocaine [1, 52; 5, 312; 29, 75; 31, 35; 79, 328–330].

In addition to Latin American syndicalist groups, the "triple fronter" is inhabited by other criminal organizations with roots in Asia, the Middle East, Russia, and Africa. Chinese criminal groups with sources in both the mainland and in Taiwan, have played major roles in the "tri-border area" underworld. In addition, the Japanese organized crime ring known as the Yakuza, and certain Korean criminal syndicalist group elements, have also been active in the TBA criminal fray [31, 41–43; 79, 330].

In the broader sense, Chinese syndicalists active in the TBA trace their origins to the 1990s, when criminal "Triad" groups extorted monies from local Chinese business owners. In exchange for their "protection" services, businesses and business owners remained free from threats of attack, attacks that would amount to "criminal terrorism." [4, 10–15; 6, 55 n66; 48, 1317–1318].[12] Simultaneously, those Chinese criminal groups would compel business owners to purchase particular types of products and pay so-called "taxes." [31].

Hudson tells us the Chinese syndicalist groups active in the TBA underworld included groups such as the "Continental Group," the Pac Lun Fu, the "Tai Chen Saninh," and the "Fuk Ching." [31, 42]. Other notable Chinese criminal groups that have been active in the TBA include "The Flying Dragons" and The Big Circle Boys (BCB or Dai Huen Jai). The "Flying Dragons" is described by Hudson as a strongman outfit linked to the New York based "Flying Dragons," that itself has had powerful ties to the Hip Sing Triad [31, 42–43].

[12] For example, see the both the Edward Mickolus typology and the Boyer Bell typology that articulate "criminal terrorism" as one form of terrorism.

In turn, the Big Circle Boys was a "non-Triad" organization that also engaged in illegal criminal activities. Unlike many more tightly-knit Chinese criminal groups, the Big Circle Boys consisted of a set of somewhat atomized but still interconnected sub-groups. The illicit activities conducted by the Big Circle Boys included, but were not necessarily limited to, bogus credit card production and illegal immigration schemes, and those activities were oftentimes carried out in conjunction with criminal syndicalist groups from Central Europe and Russia [31, 42–43].

It follows that the type of ethnic divisions between communities in the TBA which were previously described could be exacerbated by international criminal syndicalist demands for "protection monies" and other extortion payments. Those demands are oftentimes levied against local merchants and community leaders.

It is probably no exaggeration to say that in many cases, demands have been framed, at least implicitly, with cultural and political motivations and expectations in mind [17, 4–5; 31, 32]. For example, one demand might be to support a Chinese or Middle Eastern political cause or organization. That is the case because as described, many "tri-border area" international criminal gangs are linked to ethnic communities by nationality, or ethnicity, or both.

Hudson also reports that some Chinese syndicalist groups in the "tri-border area" have also worked closely with Middle Eastern terrorist groups such as al-Islamiya and Jama'a al-Islamiya. The Chinese syndicalist groups with such links include the "Ming families" and "Sung-I families." Those families were based in Ciudad del Este, Paraguay, and in Hernandásias, Brazil, respectively. Hudson provides description of such events when he reports that, "in December 2000, Sung-I sold a shipment of munitions to the Islamic Group, sending it to Egypt by ship as 'medical equipment.'" [31, 43].

In comparison, TBA syndicalist groups sourced in the Middle East include the so-called "Lebanese Mafia," a criminal syndicalist group with very strong ties to Hezbollah's leadership in the TBA. Those powerful familial ties between the "Lebanese Mafia" and Hezbollah were illuminated by the Assad Ahmad Barakat organization known as "the clan." In essence, the "Lebanese Mafia" in the TBA was led by Assad Ahmed Barakat who was Hezbollah chieftain in the TBA and Hezbollah's lead financer for that region [5, 320–321; 31; 36, 106; 51; 79, 330].

The cross-fertilization between Hezbollah and the "Lebanese Mafia" became apparent to analysts when the rosters of both organizations were cross-referenced. For example, Assad Ahmad Barakat's two cousins, Hassan Abdallah Dayoub and Hassan Naboulsi, were both inextricably bound up with the "Lebanese Mafia." At a functional level, the cities of Ciudad del Este, Paraguay, and Foz do Iguaçu, Brazil have served as twin hubs for the "Lebanese Mafia" to expedite shipments of cocaine from Colombia to destinations such as São Paulo, Brazil, Europe, and the Middle East [31, 13, 22, 25–26, 29, 31; 51; 55, 159].

Those types of family relationships are not uncommon in many Islamic extremist organizations. For example, one al-Dawa-17 member imprisoned in Kuwait, was Imad Mughniyah's cousin and brother in law. It should be noted that Imad Mughniyah, who was Hezbollah's top chief of military operations was heavily involved in Hezbollah affairs in the TBA—it was he who planned the Buenos Aries terrorist assaults [1, 8, 52]. Another terrorist group with similar familial and personal interconnections was the al-Qaeda affiliate group, al-Ittihad al-Islamiya. In 2002, al-Ittihad al Islamiya carried out the Mombasa and Kikambala, Kenya attacks against the Paradise Hotel and an Arkia jet at Moi international airport [8, 93; 31, 35, 26, 16, 13, 19, 23].

In a similar vein, the so-called "Russian Mafia" has also made forays into the TBA with its infiltration into the cities of Foz do Inguaçu, Brazil and Pedro Juan Caballero-Ponta in Paraguay. The idea was to craft connections with other criminal groups from Mercosur member countries to facilitate cocaine shipments from the Andes to Europe.

For Abbott, at least part of the reason why those links were forged was that the leadership of Mercosur put priorities associated with short-term political and economic benefits ahead of effective and sustained counterterrorism policies [1, 53, 55; 66, 107–108]. Hudson also reports that Chechen rebel groups based in Argentina have become involved in the international drug trade, and also ship illegal weapons to underworld clients in Colombia, and Brazil [31, 46–47, 24].

5.9 Terrorist Assault Business Vulnerability Index (TABVI)

For the TABVI numerator the following business target types are summed. For newspaper/print targets, there are 4 acts (2 in 2013; 1 in 2014; 1 in 2018). For "private establishments" there was 1 act (1 in 2016). There was 1 act against an NGO (1 in 2015) and there were 10 acts against telecommunications targets (3 in 2015; 2 in 2016; 2 in 2017; 3 in 2018) for a total of 16 acts between 2013 and 2018. The numerator 16 is divided by "6.2," that is the *World Economic Forum* score for Brazil. It also constitutes the denominator of the TABVI score produced here.

To reiterate that "6.2" score is the WEF assigned value, which represents the costs to Brazilian business that the threat of terrorism imposed. Presumably, it is a function, at least for the most part, of costs imposed by the threat of terrorism for "P-2" ("personal security and property protection"), that in turn might overlap with more intangible costs that are harder to measure such as potential psychological costs to workers and their families [8, 49, 187n33, 57–59, 62, 86, 89–91; 42, 73–90].[13]

To interpret TABVI scores, recall the lower the TABVI score, the lower the ranking a country has with respect to the degree of business target vulnerability/threat to terrorism threat. To be sure, the reverse holds true, where the higher the TABVI score, the higher the TABVI ranking, reflective of a higher degree of vulnerability and threat.

The TABVI score for Brazil is "2.58" (16/6.2 = 2.58). This TABVI score of 2.58 suggests the appraised threat of terrorist attack to business targets in Brazil is much lower than the corresponding TABVI score for India. It is almost four times less

[13] As previously mentioned, that cost was appraised by Brazilian business leaders from responses to a WEF survey. In the WEF index crafted, a score of "6.2," that corresponds to a country rank of #8, is very high, reflective of terrorism's of very low impact on business costs.

than the business target threat in Mexico, based on a TABVI appraisal of "9.375." In turn, the raw aggregate TABVI score of "2.58" for Brazil is standardized, where 2.58/1.566 = 1.64. The reason why is because the highest raw TABVI score of 156.6 (India) is divided by 1.566 = 100.0. The considerable difference between the eighth place WEF survey ranking of Brazil in the *World Economic Forum* index and the comparatively low TABVI score assessment of terrorism/vulnerability threat is notable.

There are no authoritative interpretations to explain that discrepancy in results but that difference might reflect the very low number of Brazilian business related terrorist attacks (16) conducted between 2013 and 2018. In addition, what the difference between that very high WEF index ranking for Brazil and the low TABVI score produced suggests is that high amounts of funds might have been marshalled by Brazilian business into anti-terrorism security preparations in comparison to the relatively few terrorist actions chronicled to produce that TABVI score.

A breakdown of the data across Brazilian industry type revealed that with a TABVI industry score of 1.61 (10/6.2), "telecommunications" targets had the highest threat/vulnerability rate to business related terrorist assaults. In turn, "newspaper/print targets" followed with a score of 0.806 (5/6.2 = 0.806). With TABVI scores of 0.161, "private establishments" (1/6.2 = 0.161), "NGO's" (1/6.2 = 0.161), and "transportation" (1/6.2 = 0.161) appeared to be the least vulnerable industry type targets in Brazil between 2013 and 2018. There were no reported attacks against "energy/alloy" targets (0/6,2 = 0) in this six year period.

At this juncture, the raw TABVI scores are standardized so that meaningful comparisons of industry type terrorism threat/vulnerability appraisals across countries can be made. In the case of Brazil, "telecommunications" targets, the industry with the highest raw TABVI score of 1.61 is multiplied by 62.1 = 99.98. In turn, the standardized TABVI scores are: "private establishments" (9.99); "NGO's" (9.99); "transportation" (9.99); "newspaper/print" (50.0); and "telecommunications" (99.98). The placement of those Brazilian industries are found on the Brazil Industry Vulnerability Spectrum (see Fig. 5.1).

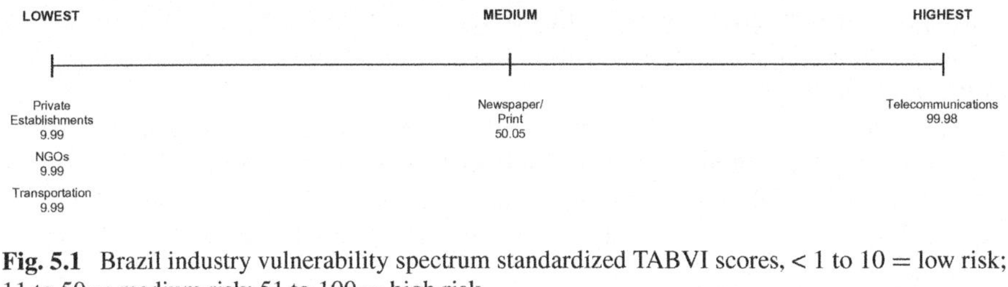

Fig. 5.1 Brazil industry vulnerability spectrum standardized TABVI scores, < 1 to 10 = low risk; 11 to 50 = medium risk; 51 to 100 = high risk

5.10 Relative Frequencies of Commercial Target Terrorist Assaults

There was a very small number of business target terrorist assaults over the Brazilian landscape for the 2007–2018 time interval. That condition only makes it possible to provide basic descriptive statistics about terrorist assault patterns. What was significant was that neither the Global Terrorism Database (GTD) nor the Mickolus data chronology for that time period, had in depth description about specific commercial interest terrorist attacks for the First Capitol Command (PCC) terrorist campaign of 2012 [21, 46, 68].[14]

5.11 Targets by Year

When the Brazilian data were broken down by year, a cyclical pattern in the data was illuminated; that is similar to what was found in the cases of India and Mexico. The three years with the highest number of terrorist assaults were 2015, 2016, and 2018, each with one-fifth of the total with four events (20.0%).

The two trough years were 2010 and 2012, each with one act or 5.0% of the total. Together, those three peak years accounted for 60.0% of the total (12/20 acts). In contrast, the two trough years accounted for 10.0% of the total (2/20 acts). There were no Brazilian terrorist attacks recorded against commercial interests between 2007 and 2009 (see Fig. 5.2).

5.12 Terrorist Assault by Business Target

It was found that telecommunications targets were the commercial target of choice over the Brazilian landscape for this time interval. Telecommunications targets, considered "structuralist targets" in this study, were attacked 55.6% of the time (10/18 acts). In comparison, newspaper/print targets placed a distant second with 27.8% of the total (5/18 acts).

At the other extreme, one terrorist attack against a "private establishment" happened in the Conjunto Nacional Mall in Brasila in 2016 [13, 24]. There was also a terrorist assault against a transportation target—a threat made against an Air France jetliner that departed from Rio de Janeiro in 2010 [46, 138; 74].[15] There

[14] For example, the only First Capitol Command (PCC) terrorist attack included in the 2022 GTD database on-line is a 2006 terrorist assault "near Sáo Paulo." Likewise, scripted accounts in English about the 2006 PCC terrorist campaign I could access did not provide in-depth descriptions about specific commercial targets of PCC terrorist assaults.

[15] The French government owns a minority share of Air France, while the bulk of the airline is owned by private investors.

Frequencies

Statistics

Year

N	Valid	20
	Missing	0

Year

		Frequency	Percent	Valid Percent	Cumulative Percent
Valid	2012	1	5.0	5.0	5.0
	2013	2	10.0	10.0	15.0
	2014	2	10.0	10.0	25.0
	2015	4	20.0	20.0	45.0
	2016	4	20.0	20.0	65.0
	2017	2	10.0	10.0	75.0
	2018	4	20.0	20.0	95.0
	2010	1	5.0	5.0	100.0
	Total	20	100.0	100.0	

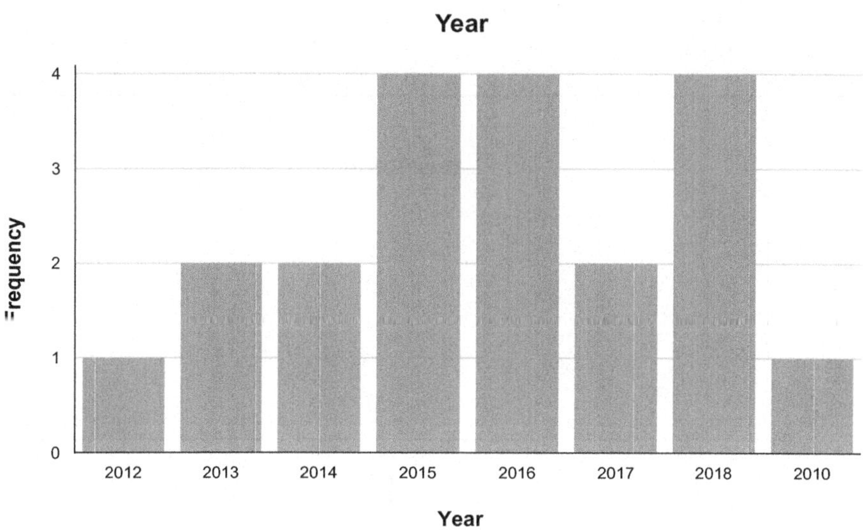

Fig. 5.2 Relative frequency of Brazil terrorist attacks by year, 2007–2018

was one improvised explosive device (IED) attack in 2015 directed at an NGO—the Lula Institute in Sao Paulo. It seems likely that NGO attack had political underpinnings, although the exact nature of those political dimensions remained unclear (see Fig. 5.3).

Frequencies

Statistics

Bus.Target

N	Valid	18
	Missing	2

Bus.Target

		Frequency	Percent	Valid Percent	Cumulative Percent
Valid	Private Establishments	1	5.0	5.6	5.6
	Telecommunications	10	50.0	55.6	61.1
	Newspapers/Print	5	25.0	27.8	88.9
	Transportation	1	5.0	5.6	94.4
	NGO	1	5.0	5.6	100.0
	Total	18	90.0	100.0	
Missing	System	2	10.0		
Total		20	100.0		

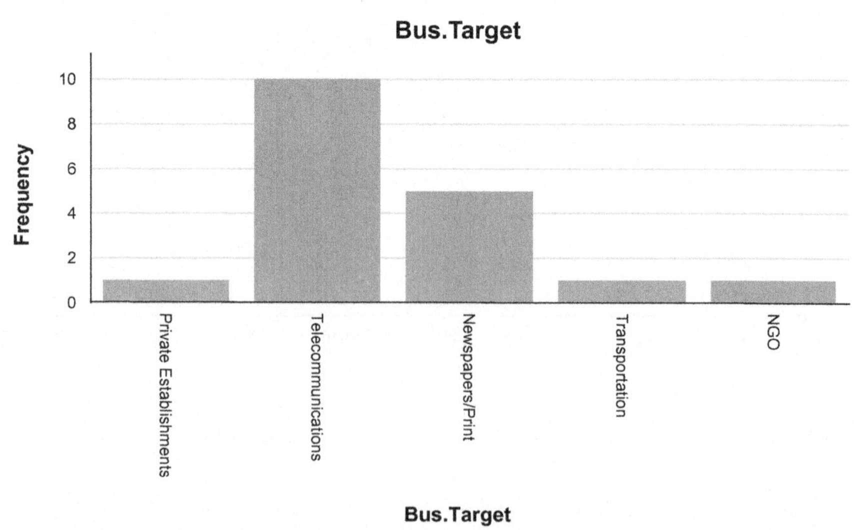

Fig. 5.3 Relative frequency of Brazil terrorist attacks by Business Target, 2007–2018

When the data were broken down based on "Group-Type," it was found that one out of 20 acts (5.0%) was carried out by an Islamic extremist organization, while a "hybrid-terrorist/criminal" group carried out another terrorist act (5.0%) within the context of struggles between "rival gangs in Mossoro." [49, 269]. The remainder of Brazilian business related terrorist acts recorded at 85.0% (17/20 acts) were anonymous events (see Fig. 5.4).

Frequencies

Statistics

GroupTy

N	Valid	20
	Missing	0

GroupTy

		Frequency	Percent	Valid Percent	Cumulative Percent
Valid	Anonymous	17	85.0	85.0	85.0
	Islamic Extremist	1	5.0	5.0	90.0
	Hybrid Terrorist/Criminal	1	5.0	5.0	95.0
	Sole Issue	1	5.0	5.0	100.0
	Total	20	100.0	100.0	

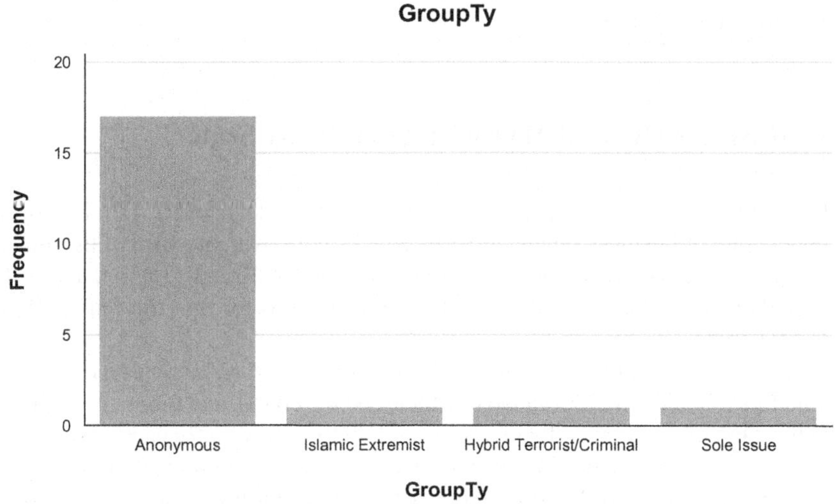

Fig. 5.4 Relative frequency of Brazil terrorist attacks by Group-Type, 2007–2018

5.13 Business Related Terrorist Assaults by Organization

There were two identifiable Brazilian terrorist organizations chronicled in this study. The first is Jundallah ("Soldiers of God")—a Sunni Muslim terrorist organization opposed to the Khamene'i regime in the Islamic Republic of Iran. It was crafted by Abdul Malik Rigi in 2002, with its sources and origins in the "southeastern province of Sistan-Baluchistan" in Iran. One *al-Jazeera* scripted account reports Jundallah has less than 1000 activists [2, 52].

In Brazil, members from a "…part of Jundallah…." as Mickolus puts it, were arrested by Brazilian authorities in a series of three "disruption" counterterrorism actions after on-line plans threatening to attack the 2016 Olympic Games in Rio de Janeiro were discovered [50, 130–131; 71; 72, 175, 178–179].[16] This Jundallah threat comprised 5.0% (1/20 acts) of the total, while anonymous terrorist assaults comprised 90% (18/20) of the total (see Fig. 5.5). When Brazilian business targets were broken down by national and foreign based commercial targets, it was found that a full 94.7% (18/19 acts) of all Brazilian business related terrorist attacks were directed against national targets. In comparison, only 5.3% (1/19 acts) involved a foreign target (see Fig. 5.6).

The second identifiable terrorist organization that assaulted a commercial interest target is Sociedade Secreta Silvestre (SSS), otherwise known as the Sivestre Secret Society. The SSS has been described as the Brazilian branch of the Mexican "eco-terrorist organization," Individuals Tending Towards Savagery (ITS). Presumably, the Sivestre Secret Society had also marked Brazilian President Jair Bolsonaro for death because of Bolsonaro's problematic environmental policies that adversely affected the Amazon rain forest [13].

5.14 Business Related Terrorist Assaults by State

A relative frequencies count by Brazilian state reveals the state of Rio de Janeiro had the highest rate of business related terrorist attacks with over one-fifth of the total at 21.1% (4/19 acts). The Brazilian state of Goiás, found in Brazil's region, above the states of Paraná and São Paulo, tied with Rio de Janeiro for that top ranking with 21.1% (4/19 acts).

There were three states that followed suit with 10.5% (2/19 acts) each. Those states included São Paulo, Maranhão (northeast on the coast), and the state of Paraná, where the TBA city of Foz do Igauçu is located. In turn, four states each experienced 5.3% of the total (1/19 acts). Those states were Rôndonia, (in mid-western Brazil), Rio Grande do Norte (northeast on the coast), Ceará (northwest and contiguous to Rio Grande do Norte), Bahia, (north of Rio de Janeiro), and Minas Gerais, a state contiguous to Rio de Janeiro and close to the coast (see Fig. 5.7).

---

[16] Beside "opportunity recognition," accounts I read offered no definitive motivation for such plans; it could have amounted to an ISIS attack or an attack in solidarity with ISIS, since, as Mickolus reports, some arrested Jundallah members had sworn allegiance to ISIS.

Frequencies

Statistics

GroupName

N	Valid	20
	Missing	0

GroupName

		Frequency	Percent	Valid Percent	Cumulative Percent
Valid	Jundailah	1	5.0	5.0	5.0
	Anonymous	18	90.0	90.0	95.0
	Sociedade Secreta Silvestre	1	5.0	5.0	100.0
	Total	20	100.0	100.0	

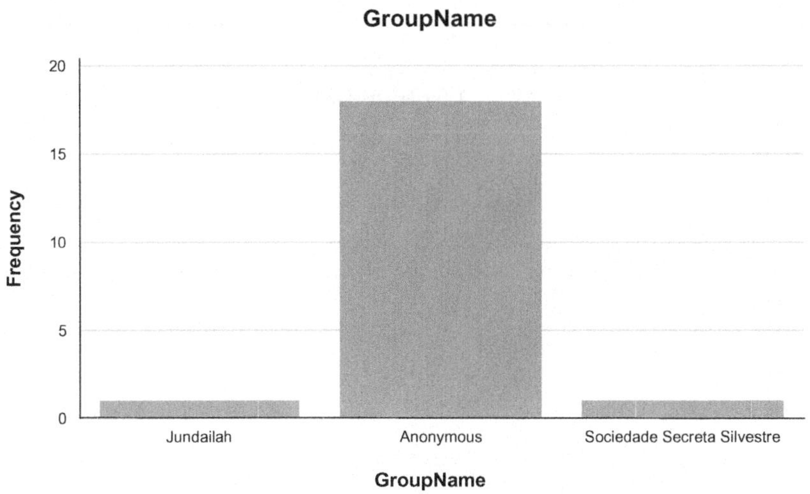

Fig. 5.5 Relative frequency of Brazil terrorist attacks by Group-Name, 2007–2018

5.15 Business Related Terrorist Assaults by Municipality

In terms of the highest concentration of business related terrorist assaults, Grajáu municipality in the state of Maranhão, and Goiás municipality in Goiás each accounted for 11.1% of the total (2/18 acts). In comparison, the remainder of business related terrorist attacks were dispersed rather widely across thirteen municipalities, four of which were in the state of Rio de Janeiro, two in the state of São Paulo, two in the state of Paraná, one in the state of Rôndonia, one in Maranháo, one in Rio Grande do Norte, one in Ceará, and one in Bahia.

Each of the following municipalities experienced one terrorist assault or 5.6% of the total: São João da Barra (Rio de Janeiro), Nova Iguaçu (Rio de Janeiro), Miguel Pereira (Rio de Janeiro), São Paulo (São Paulo), São José do Rio Preto

Frequencies

Statistics

TargNatForei

N	Valid	19
	Missing	1

TargNatForei

		Frequency	Percent	Valid Percent	Cumulative Percent
Valid	National	18	90.0	94.7	94.7
	Foreign	1	5.0	5.3	100.0
	Total	19	95.0	100.0	
Missing	System	1	5.0		
Total		20	100.0		

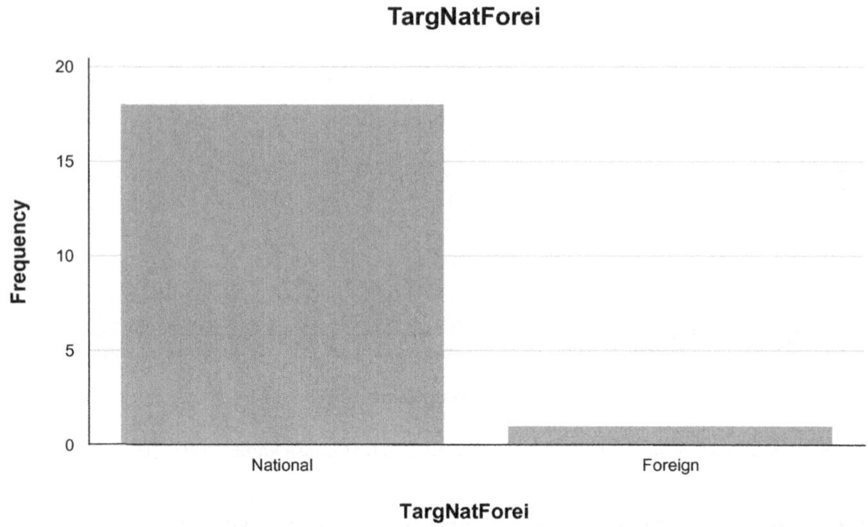

Fig. 5.6 Relative frequency of Brazil terrorist attacks by Foreign Business Target and National Business Target, 2007–2018

(São Paulo), Cacoal (Rôndonia), Curtiba (Paraná), Paranaguá (Paraná), São Luis do Maranhão (Maranhão), Rio de Janeiro (Rio de Janeiro), Mossoró (Rio Grande do Norte), Camocim (Ceará), and Conceição da Feira (Bahia). The Federal District, which is a stand-alone federal area without municipalities also experienced 5.6% of the total, with one terrorist assault (see Fig. 5.8).

Even though the Brazilian municipalities with the highest concentrations of business related terrorist attacks were outside of the state of Rio de Janeiro, this strong

Frequencies

Statistics

State

N	Valid	19
	Missing	1

State

		Frequency	Percent	Valid Percent	Cumulative Percent
Valid	Rio de Janeiro	4	20.0	21.1	21.1
	Sao Paulo	2	10.0	10.5	31.6
	Maranhao	2	10.0	10.5	42.1
	Goias	4	20.0	21.1	63.2
	Rondonia	1	5.0	5.3	68.4
	Parana	2	10.0	10.5	78.9
	Rio Grande do Norta	1	5.0	5.3	84.2
	Ceara	1	5.0	5.3	89.5
	Bahia	1	5.0	5.3	94.7
	Minas Gerais	1	5.0	5.3	100.0
	Total	19	95.0	100.0	
Missing	System	1	5.0		
Total		20	100.0		

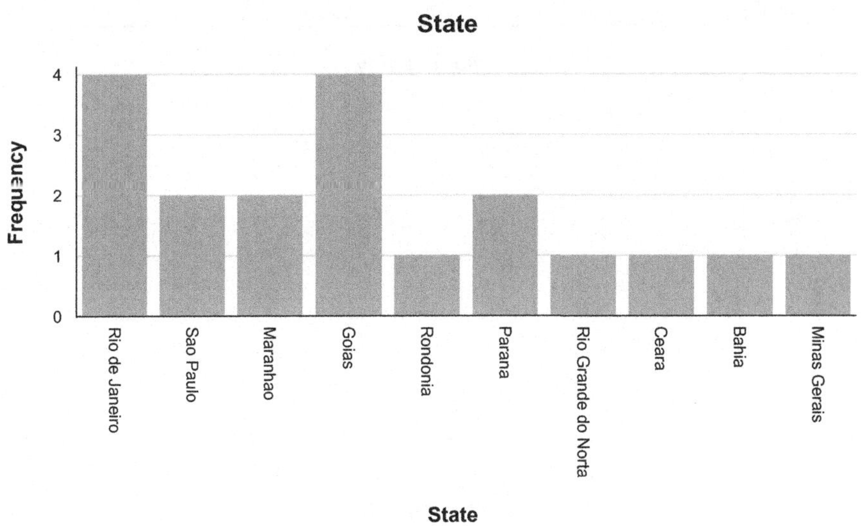

Fig. 5.7 Relative frequency of Brazil terrorist attacks by State, 2007–2018

Frequencies

Statistics

Municipality

N	Valid	18
	Missing	2

Municipality

		Frequency	Percent	Valid Percent	Cumulative Percent
Valid	Sao Joa da Barra	1	5.0	5.6	5.6
	Nova Iguacu	1	5.0	5.6	11.1
	Miguel Pereira	1	5.0	5.6	16.7
	Sao Paulo	1	5.0	5.6	22.2
	Grajau	2	10.0	11.1	33.3
	Goias	2	10.0	11.1	44.4
	Sao Jose do Rio Preto	1	5.0	5.6	50.0
	Cacoal	1	5.0	5.6	55.6
	Curtiba	1	5.0	5.6	61.1
	Paranagua	1	5.0	5.6	66.7
	Sao Luis do Maranhao	1	5.0	5.6	72.2
	Rio de Janeiro	1	5.0	5.6	77.8
	Mossoro	1	5.0	5.6	83.3
	Camocim	1	5.0	5.6	88.9
	Conceicao da Feira	1	5.0	5.6	94.4
	Federal District	1	5.0	5.6	100.0
	Total	18	90.0	100.0	
Missing	System	2	10.0		
Total		20	100.0		

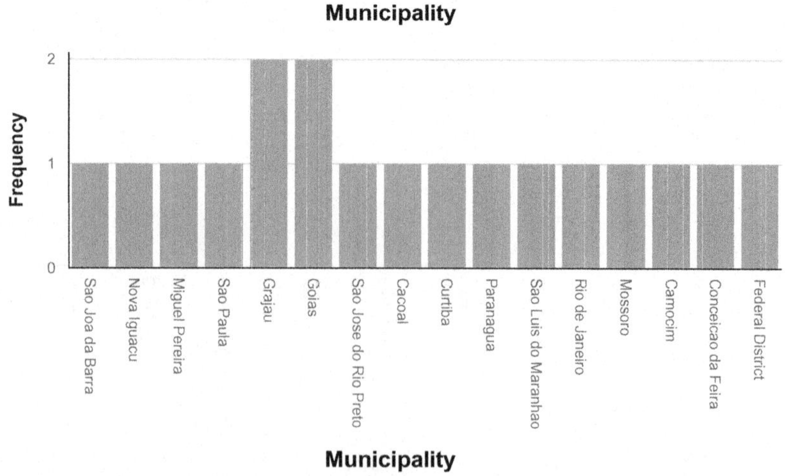

Fig. 5.8 Relative frequency of Brazil terrorist attacks by Municipality, 2007–2018

showing for Rio de Janeiro municipalities is consistent with Rio de Janeiro's first place standing among Brazilian states that experienced business related terrorism. Equally important, those findings underscore the significance of the state of Rio de Janeiro for business related terrorism in Brazil.

5.16 Terrorist Assault by City and Town

There were fifteen (15) cities or towns where chronicled Brazilian terrorist attacks against commercial interests happened. In all cases, Brazilian terrorist assaults against commercial interests happened in cities or towns and not in rural areas.

The city with the highest concentration of terrorist attacks was Edealina (in Goiás), with nearly one-fifth of the total at 16.7% (3/18 acts). The city of Rio de Janeiro followed suit rather closely behind with 11.1% (2/18 acts). As was the case for the findings about municipality, the remainder of business related terrorist assaults were widely dispersed, this time across thirteen different cities and towns (see Fig. 5.9).

Each of those thirteen different cities or towns experienced 5.6% of the total (1/18 acts). Those cities and towns included: Brasilia (The Federal District), Nova Iguaçu (Rio de Janeiro), Miguel Pereira (Rio de Janeiro), São Paulo (São Paulo), Grajaú (Maranháo), Cacoal (Rôndonia), Curtiba (Paraná), Paranaguá (Paraná), São Luis (Maranháo), Mossoró (Rio Grande do Norte), Camocim (Ceará), Conceição da Feira (Bahia), and Padre Paraiso (Minas Gerais).

5.17 Business Firms Targeted and Reaction to Political Events

A relative frequencies distribution revealed that Rádio Beira Rio FM, in Edealina Goiás, had the highest set of clustered attacks, with three out of 16 attacks or nearly one-fifth of the total at 18.8%. In two of the three cases which spanned some 14 months, the assault type was arson, while in the third case, a Rádio Beira Rio FM radio reporter, Mr. Jefferson Pureza Lopes was murdered [25–27].

That 18.8% rate was nearly three times higher than the rates found for other identifiable business firms attacked. In those cases, each firm experienced one terrorist attack (1/16 acts) or 6.3% of the total. Those thirteen other firms included, Hora H (newspaper/journal), Panorama Regional (newspaper), Air France, the Lula Institute (NGO), Diário de Região, Jornal de Rondônia (newspaper/journal), Bandeirantes TV, Jornol dos Bairros Litoral, O Estado do Moranhão, Rádio Liberdade, RCA-FM, Coruja do Vale/O Globo, and the Conjunto Nacional mall in Brasilia (24; 48) (see Fig. 5.10).

Frequencies

Statistics

CityVillage

N	Valid	18
	Missing	2

CityVillage

		Frequency	Percent	Valid Percent	Cumulative Percent
Valid	Rio de Janeiro	2	10.0	11.1	11.1
	Nova Iguacu	1	5.0	5.6	16.7
	Miguel Pereira	1	5.0	5.6	22.2
	Brasila	1	5.0	5.6	27.8
	Sao Paulo	1	5.0	5.6	33.3
	Grajau	1	5.0	5.6	38.9
	Edealina	3	15.0	16.7	55.6
	Cacoal	1	5.0	5.6	61.1
	Curtiba	1	5.0	5.6	66.7
	Paranagua	1	5.0	5.6	72.2
	Sao Luis	1	5.0	5.6	77.8
	Mossoro	1	5.0	5.6	83.3
	Camocim	1	5.0	5.6	88.9
	Conceicao da Feira	1	5.0	5.6	94.4
	Padre Paraiso	1	5.0	5.6	100.0
	Total	18	90.0	100.0	
Missing	System	2	10.0		
Total		20	100.0		

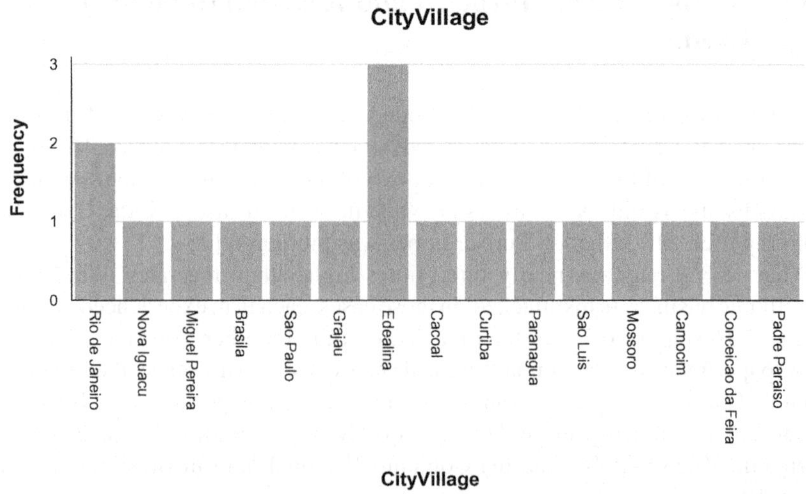

Fig. 5.9 Relative frequency of Brazil terrorist attacks by City, Town, and Village, 2007–2018

Frequencies

Statistics

FirmName

N	Valid	16
	Missing	4

FirmName

		Frequency	Percent	Valid Percent	Cumulative Percent
Valid	Hora H Newspaper	1	5.0	6.3	6.3
	Panorama Regional Newspaper	1	5.0	6.3	12.5
	Air France	1	5.0	6.3	18.8
	Lula Institute	1	5.0	6.3	25.0
	Beira Radio FM	3	15.0	18.8	43.8
	Diario de Regiao	1	5.0	6.3	50.0
	Jornal de Rondonia (newspaper)	1	5.0	6.3	56.3
	Bandeirantes TV	1	5.0	6.3	62.5
	Jornal dos Bairros Litoral	1	5.0	6.3	68.8
	O Estado do Moranhao	1	5.0	6.3	75.0
	Radio Liberdade	1	5.0	6.3	81.3
	RCA-FM	1	5.0	6.3	87.5
	Coruja do Vale	1	5.0	6.3	93.8
	Conjunto Nacional Mall	1	5.0	6.3	100.0
	Total	16	80.0	100.0	
Missing	System	4	20.0		
Total		20	100.0		

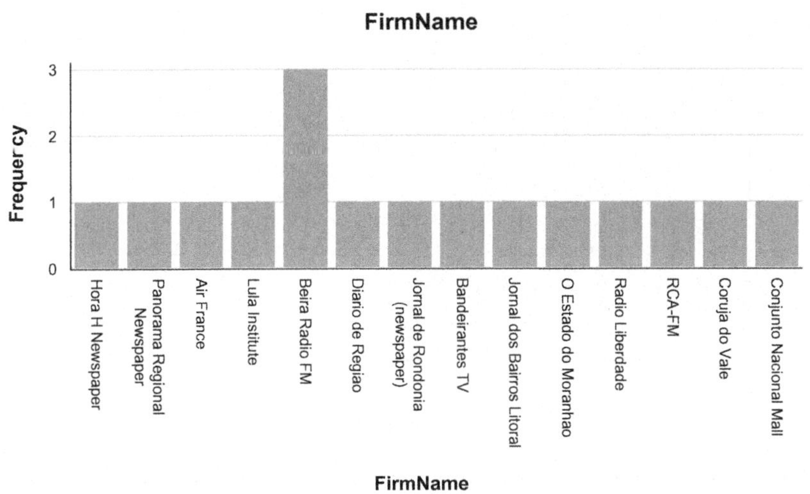

Fig. 5.10 Relative frequency of Brazil terrorist attacks by Firm, 2007–2018

Turning to the link between Brazilian business related terrorist attacks and to political events, it was found the majority of terrorist assaults chronicled were unrelated to political events. There were 19/20 terrorist assaults characterized by no relation political events—that comprised 95.0% of the total amount. In turn, only one Brazilian terrorist assault against commercial interests was linked to a landmark political event. That terrorist assault was Jundallah's threat to attack the Olympic Games in Rio de Janeiro in 2016 [50, 130–131] (see Fig. 5.11).

Frequencies

Statistics

ReacPolEvnt

N	Valid	20
	Missing	0

ReacPolEvnt

		Frequency	Percent	Valid Percent	Cumulative Percent
Valid	No Relation	19	95.0	95.0	95.0
	Landmark Events	1	5.0	5.0	100.0
	Total	20	100.0	100.0	

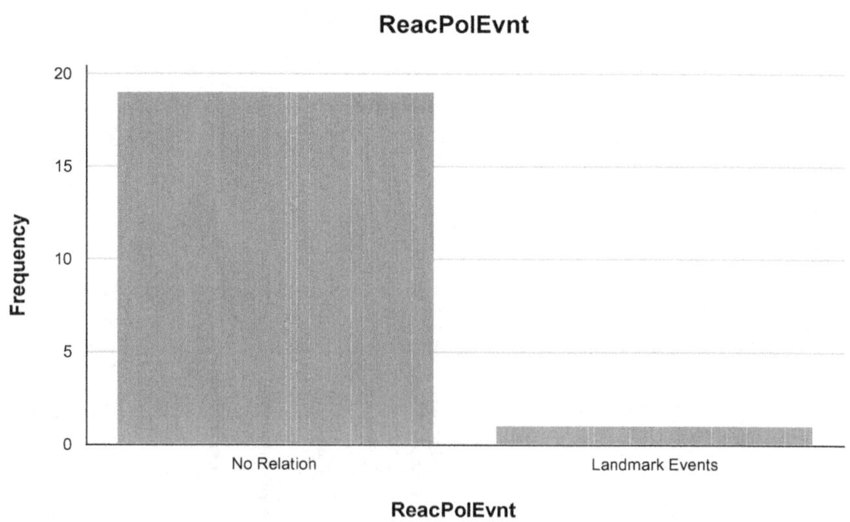

Fig. 5.11 Relative frequency of Brazil terrorist attacks by Political Event, 2007–2018

5.18 Final Reflections

This chapter works to make the case that there are examples of historical continuity and change over the Brazilian political landscape that span over different times intervals to influence how terrorism has evolved and been used in Brazil. The historical continuities highlighted were nestled primarily in the previous time intervals of the 1920s, and in the 1930s through the 1950s. Those historical continuities and changes were also marked by the watershed events of Brazil's military coup (1964) and Brazil's return to civilian rule in 1985.

The analysis focused primarily on what Diamond calls "social fissures" in society, with specific emphasis on ethnic, religious, and socioeconomic divisions. The use of Diamond's framework makes it possible to focus on earlier eras of Brazilian history, twentieth century terrorism, and on the more contemporary threat of terrorism. It appears the contemporary threat is sourced in the "tri-border area" (TBA) of Argentina, Paraguay, and Brazil, at least for now. The analysis used Diamond's notion of "cross-cutting cleavages" to make the case that "coincidental cleavage effects" have contributed to political instability and social unrest in Brazil, both across broader historical epochs, and within specific areas such as the TBA [16].

The analysis also underscored the importance of the illicit organizational "life cycle" process where terrorist organizations and criminal syndicalist group splinter or form spin-off groups. Those processes happen as a result of several interconnected explanatory factors. Splinter or spin-off groups can appear as a function of government counterterrorism policy or effective and sustained law enforcement actions, or by contrast, ineffective or sporadic police actions. In the case of terrorist group—criminal enterprise collaboration and synthesis (i.e., spinoff group formation), the two case studies presented are useful and instructive—the collusion between Hezbollah and the First Capitol Command (PCC), and the origins of Red Commando in Ilha Grande prison, against the backdrop of government prison policy where hardened criminal gang members from favelas and poor villages were incarcerated in the 1960s and 1970s with "leftist" revolutionary terrorists.

In addition to internal strife within terrorist groups, terrorist group splintering or spin-off group formation can involve positive processes as well as internal processes, themselves frequently associated with the clash of personalities, conflicting personal ambition, and divergent opinions about policy. What the analysis suggests is that this notion of cooperative or collaborative relationship effect pertains to Brazil, with for instance, the emergence of Sociedade Secreta Silvestre as a military branch of Mexico's Individuals Tending Towards Savagery.

Those positive evolutionary steps are showcased for criminal groups by the relationship the syndicalist organization Third Command, had with its antecedent organization, Red Commando. In that case, the formation of Third Command presupposed and derived from positive connections and shared interests between criminal syndicalist leaders—it was linked to the dissemination of Red Commando ideology throughout the Brazilian prison system.

What is significant in the case of the Third Command is that "spinoff group" was not produced by criminal kingpin animosity, differences of opinion, or differences in policy direction between the criminal chieftains as found to be the case in India with terrorist groups, and in Mexico, primarily with criminal syndicalist drug organizations. Instead, Red Commando's "spinoff" group the Third Commando, was elicited by admiration for Red Commando founder, William da Silva Lima.

The sources and origins of those differences in terrorist group and criminal enterprise formation and development most likely involved different "contextual factors" within environments that spawned those two types of groups. Indeed, some of those contextual factors, at the nation-state level of analysis for instance, could be similar or even the same. In the case of Brazil, the presence of favelas and the social fissures that characterize Brazilian society might be fruitful areas to explore in future research that examines terrorist group and criminal enterprise growth and fragmentation processes.

In addition, the controlled environment of the Brazilian prison system, itself characterized by extreme brutality, might be an important component to criminal syndicalist development. That begs the question of whether prison systems in general across countries are linked or have potential to become linked to criminal group or terrorist organization splinter group or spin-off group formation and if so, under what circumstances and to what degree.

Moreover, that issue seems significant for Brazil's business community because of the First Capital Command (PCC) terrorist campaigns which focused on commercial interests as part of the target selection strategy. Since the PCC leadership's calculus to respond to prison policies involved commercial interests, Brazilian C-class executives ought to seriously consider working to support prison reform, if present or future research suggests a link between prison systems and such organizational fragmentation processes.

One reason why is Brazilian executives should be concerned about prison reform is intrinsic to nature of globalization. Nowadays, CEO and other C class executives from original equipment manufacturers (OEM's) must ensure security for "Tier 1," "Tier 2," and "Tier 3" companies to preserve supply chain integrity, as those types of firms supply assembled structures or individual parts or both, for the finished OEM commodity [10]. If criminal syndicalists are able to infiltrate into the heart of those business manufacturing processes to leverage government or business concessions, a new dimension of criminal syndicalist threat or terrorist group-criminal syndicalist collusion or both, might materialize.

The chapter analysis also illuminated close links between terrorist groups such as Hezbollah and FARC, and criminal syndicalist groups that oftentimes collaborated with those groups and sometimes with each other, presumably in one or a combination of illicit activities such as drug trafficking, money laundering, credit card fraud, and perhaps the darkest foreboding of all, illegal weapons shipments. What was also significant was that many state actors were found to be inextricably bound up with terrorist groups, themselves tied to criminal syndicalists, with the "tri-border area" as a primary epicenter. Those states included, but were not necessarily limited to, Iran and Lebanon.

At the same time, regional nation-state governments to the north and northwest of Brazil, such as Suriname and Guyana, and states to Brazil's south-west such as Paraguay, have also been implicated in underworld activities. That appeared to be the case in no small part because the border security efforts needed to interdict illegal shipments of goods were less than robust in some of those countries.

A common theme across the case studies of India, Mexico, and Brazil is the deleterious role of "intensive globalization" and its potential to contribute to political and economic instability and social unrest. Several analysts note that globalization's continuously evolving condition presents new opportunities, such as new markets and new transit points for illegal drugs, that work to expand underground markets in illicit goods and services. At the same time, as drug use is primarily a demand side affliction, it is imperative for policymakers to tackle problems related to economic blight and related conditions that create incentives for drug use and in some cases, send individuals into the orbit of drug kingpins.

Finally, it follows that multilateral efforts to tackle threats of terrorism from terrorist groups and from criminal syndicalists, rather than heavy reliance on the unilateral efforts of any specific nation-state, becomes the imperative approach to take. To be sure, that approach must also be coupled with a variety of domestic security counterterrorism and anti-crime policies tailor made to confront the effects of "contextual factors" at hand. In the twenty-first century multilateralism is required to combat what Williams calls "wicked challenges" such as terrorism, organized crime, and their overlapping domains, that confront policymakers, and government officials, including law enforcement personnel [76, 15–36].

References

1. Abbott PK (2004, September–October) Terrorist threat in the tri-border area: myth or reality? Military Rev. https://smallwarsjournal.com/documents/abbott.pdf
2. Al-Jazeera (2010, 20 June) Jundallah: Iran's Sunni rebels. https://www.aljazeera.com/news/2010/6/20/jundallah-irans-sunni-rebels
3. Barbosa AM (2007) Combating terrorism in the Brazilian tri border area: a necessary law enforcement strategic approach. Master's degree thesis, Naval Post Graduate School. https://apps.dtic.mil/sti/pdfs/ADA469908.pdf
4. Bell BJ (1975) Transnational terror. American Enterprise Institute for Public Policy Research
5. Brafman Kittner CC (2007) The role of safe havens in Islamist terrorism. Terrorism Polit Violence 19(3):307–329. https://doi.org/10.1080/09546550701246791
6. Chasdi RJ (1999) Serenade of suffering: a portrait of Middle East terrorism, 1968–1993. Lexington Books
7. Chasdi RJ (2002) Tapestry of terror: a portrait of Middle East terrorism, 1994–1999. Lexington Books
8. Chasdi RJ (2018) Corporate security crossroads: responding to terrorism, cyberthreats, and other hazards in the global business environment. Praeger
9. Chasdi RJ (2022) Enhanced terrorism and the prospect of its use in the United States: an update. In: Gunaratna RK, Aslam MM (eds) Covid 19 pandemic: the threat and response. Routledge
10. Chasdi RJ (2019, 16 May) Tackling horizontal and vertical supply chain vulnerabilities: risk from interstate conflict and terrorism. J Counterterrorism Homel Secur Int 24(4):10–14. https://issuu.com/fusteros/docs/iacsp_magazine_v24n4_issuu/12

11. Clendenning A (2006, August 8) Attacks in São Paulo target police, government buildings. The Associated Press
12. Clutterbuck R (1994) Terrorism in an unstable world. Routledge
13. Correlo Braziliense (2019, July 19) Member of the Sivestre secret society has a plan to kill Bolsonaro. https://www.correiobraziliense.com.br/app/noticia/politica/2019/07/19/interna_politica,772202/atentado-a-bolsonaro.shtml
14. Crenshaw M (2003) The causes of terrorism. In: Kegley Jr CW (ed) The new global terrorism: characteristics, causes, controls. Prentice Hall, pp 92–105
15. Debray R, Ortiz B (1967) Revolution in the revolution? Armed struggle and political struggle in Latin America. Grove Press, Inc
16. Diamond L (1990) Nigeria: pluralism, statism and the struggle for democracy. In: Diamond L, Linz JL, Lipset SM (eds) Politics in developing countries: comparing experiences with democracy. Lynne Rienner
17. Ellis RE (2015) Radical Islam in Latin America and the Caribbean: implications for U.S. national strategy. Air Space Power J. https://apps.dtic.mil/sti/pdfs/ADA618995.pdf
18. Encyclopedia.com. Prestes, Luis Carlos (1998–1990). https://www.encyclopedia.com/humanities/encyclopedias-almanacs-transcripts-and-maps/prestes-luis-carlos-1898-1990
19. Esman MJ (1994) Ethnic politics. Cornell University Press
20. Fernández LM (2009) Organized crime and terrorism: from the cells towards political communication, a case study. Terrorism Polit Violence 21(4):595–616
21. Global Terrorism Database (GTD). First capitol command. GTD ID: 200608300002; Date: August 30, 2006
22. Global Terrorism Database (GTD) Brazil. GTD ID: 201301080025; Date: January 8, 2013
23. Global Terrorism Database (GTD). Brazil. GTD ID: 201507300031; Date: July 30, 2015
24. Global Terrorism Database (GTD). Brazil. GTD ID: 201608010063; Date August 1, 2016
25. Global Terrorism Database. Brazil. GTD ID: 201611150061; Date: November 15, 2016
26. Global Terrorism Database. Brazil. GTD ID: 201711160033; Date: November 18, 2017
27. Global Terrorism Database. Brazil. GTD ID: 201801170052; Date: January 17, 2018
28. Gordon M (1964) Assimilation in American life: the role of race, religion and national origins. Oxford University Press
29. Grillo I (2016) Gangster warlords, drug dollars, killing fields, and the new politics of Latin America. Bloomsbury Press
30. Hoffman B (1998) Inside terrorism. Columbia University Press
31. Hudson R (2003, July) Terrorist and organized crime groups in the Tri-Border Area (TBA) of South America. Library of Congress Federal Research Division. https://apps.dtic.mil/sti/pdfs/ADA439846.pdf
32. Huntington SP (1968) Political order in changing societies. Yale University Press
33. Jenkins BM (2003) International terrorism: the other world war. In: Kegley Jr CW (ed) The new global terrorism: characteristics, causes, controls. Prentice Hall, pp 15–26
34. Johnson CA (1962) Peasant nationalism and communist power: the emergence of Revolutionary China, 1937–1945. Stanford University Press
35. Johnson CA (1982) Revolutionary change, 2nd edn. Stanford University Press
36. Klidev AV (ed) (2006) Terrorism country by country. Nova Scotia Publishers Inc.
37. Lasswell HD (1935) World politics and personal insecurity. Whittlesey House McGraw Hill
38. Lasswell HD (1978) Terrorism and the political process. Terrorism: Int J 1(3–4):255–263
39. Lopez GA, Stohl M (1989) Introduction: the development and dependence factors of state repression. In: Lopez GA, Stohl M (eds) Dependence, development, and state repression. Greenwood Press
40. Loveman B, Davies Jr T (1997) The politics of antipolitics. In: Loveman B, Davies Jr TM (eds) The politics of antipolitics: the military in Latin America—revised and updated. Scholarly Resources Inc
41. Makarenko T (2004) The crime-terror continuum: tracing the interplay between transnational organized crime and terrorism. Global Crime 6(1):129–145

42. Malley JA (1983) Preparing and protecting personnel and property prior to a terrorist attack. In Montana PJ, Roukis GS (eds) Managing terrorism: strategies for the corporate executive. Quorum Books
43. Marighella C (1969.1972) A definition of the urban guerilla. In: Minimanual of the urban guerilla. Red and Black Publishers. Translation: American Revolutionary Movement
44. McCann FD (1984) The formative period of twentieth-century Brazilian Army thought, 1900–1922. Hisp Am Hist Rev 64(4):737–765
45. McCann FD (1997) Origins of the "new professionalism" of the Brazilian military. In: Loveman B, Davies Jr TM (eds) The politics of antipolitics: The military in Latin America—revised and updated. Scholarly Resources Inc.
46. McHugh R (2011) Marighella, Carlos (1911–1969). In: Martin G (ed) The Sage encyclopedia of terrorism. Sage Publications
47. Mickolus EF (1976) Negotiating for hostages: a policy dilemma. Orbis: J World Affairs 19(4):1309–1325
48. Mickolus EF (2014) Terrorism, 2008–2012: a worldwide chronology. McFarland & Company, Inc.
49. Mickolus EF (2016) Terrorism, 2013–2015: a worldwide chronology. McFarland & Company, Inc.
50. Mickolus EF (2018) Terrorism, worldwide, 2016. McFarland & Company, Inc.
51. Nielsen S (2019, 9 December) Fighting terror in the tri-border area: Q&A with Alison August Treppel. Wilson Center, Latin American Program. https://www.wilsoncenter.org/article/fighting-terror-the-tri-border-area
52. Notezai MA (2016, 7 January) Can ISIS gain a foothold in Balochistan? There is growing evidence it is trying to do just that. The Diplomat. https://thediplomat.com/2016/01/can-isis-gain-a-foothold-in-balochistan/
53. Nye Jr JS (1993) Understanding international conflict: an introduction to theory and history. HarperCollins College Publishers
54. Phillip Morris International (2019, 13 December). https://www.pmi.com/illicit-trade-prevention/blog/the-growing-threat-of-organized-crime-groups-in-the-tri-border-area-of-south-america
55. Rabasa A, Chalk P, Cragin K, Daly SA, Gregg HS, Karasik TW, O'Brien KA, Rosenau W (2006) Beyond al-Qaeda: Part 2, the outer rings of the terrorist universe. RAND Corporation, pp 101–160. https://doi.org/10.7249/mg430af.14
56. Rachum I (1977) From young rebels to brokers of national politics: The tenentes of Brazil. Bol Estud Latinoam Caribe 23:41–60
57. Raymond GA (2003) The evolving strategies of political terrorism. In: Kegley Jr CW (ed) The new global terrorism: characteristics, causes, controls. Prentice Hall, 71–83
58. Roett R (1997) The post-1964 military republic in Brazil. In: Loveman B, Davies Jr TM (eds) The politics of antipolitics: the military in Latin America—revised and updated. Scholarly Resources Inc.
59. Ross JI (1993) Structural causes of oppositional political terrorism: towards a causal model. J Peace Res 30(3):317–329
60. Ross JI, Miller RR (1997, Winter) The effects of oppositional political terrorism: five actor-based models. Low Intensity Conflict Law Enforcement 6(3):76–107
61. Schneider RM (1991) Order and progress: a political history of Brazil. Westview Press
62. Schneider RM (1997) The military and Brazilian politics to World War II. In: Loveman B, Davies Jr TM (eds) The politics of antipolitics: the military in Latin America—revised and updated. Scholarly Resources Inc.
63. Serbin KP (2019) From revolution to power in Brazil: how radical leftists embraced capitalism and struggled with leadership. University of Notre Dame Press
64. Skidmore TE (1975) The historiography of Brazil, 1899–1964: part 1. Hisp Am Hist Rev 55(4):716–748
65. Stohl M, Lopez GA (1984) Introduction. In: Stohl MS, Lopez GA (eds) The state as terrorist: the dynamics of governmental repression and violence. Greenwood Press

66. Stuenkel O (2010, October) Strategic threats surrounding Brazil. Konrad Adenauer Stiftung (KAS) International Reports. http://www.jstor.com/stable/resrep10025
67. Teló F (2020) Communication between the militants and the "8 October" revolutionary movement and the peasants of Brotas de Macaubas, Bahia, Brazil (1969–71). J Lat Am Stud 54(2):313–335. https://doi.org/10.1017/S0022216X22000220
68. The Associated Press (NBC) (2006, May 13) At least 30 killed in rampages by Brazilian gang. https://www.nbcnews.com/id/wbna12776214
69. Theen RHW, Wilson FL (1986) Comparative politics: an introduction to six countries. Prentice Hall
70. Trevisi AF (2013, October) Assessing the terrorist threat in the tri-border area of Brazil, Paraguay and Argentina. IDC Herzliya: International Institute for Counter-Terrorism. https://i-hls.com/wp-content/uploads/2014/01/Assessing-the-Terrorist-Threat-in-the-Tri-Border-Area.pdf
71. U.S. Department of State (2017) Chapter 2: country reports Western Hemisphere. Country Reports on Terrorism 2016 (July). https://www.state.gov/reports/country-reports-on-terrorism-2016/#:~:text=Country%20Reports%20on%20Terrorism%202016%20is%20submitted%20in%20compl
72. U.S. Department of State (2019) Country Reports on Terrorism 2019. https://www.state.gov/wp-content/uploads/2020/06/Country-Reports-on-Terrorism-2019-2.pdf
73. Waltz KN (1959) Man, the state and war—a theoretical analysis. Columbia University Press
74. Wikipedia. Air France-KLM. https://en.wikipedia.org/wiki/Air_France%E2%80%93KLM
75. Wikiwand (n.d.) 8th October revolutionary movement. https://www.wikiwand.com/en/8th_October_Revolutionary_Movement
76. Williams P (2013) Lawlessness and disorder: an emerging paradigm for the 21st century. In: Miklaucic M, Brewer J (eds) Convergence: illicit networks and national security in an age of globalization. National Defense University Press
77. Wilson FL (1990) European politics today: the democratic experience. Prentice Hall
78. Wright A (2002) Policing: an introduction to concepts and practice. Willan Publishing
79. Zorovich MRS (2015) The power of organized crime in Brazil. In: Bagley BM, Rosen JD (eds) Drug trafficking, organized crime, and violence in the Americas today. University of Florida Press
80. Zúquete J (2017) Counterterrorism in Brazil: from dictatorship to democratic times. In Romaniuk S, Grice F, Irrera D, Webb S (eds) The Palgrave handbook of global counterterrorism policy. Palgrave Macmillan

Chapter 6
The Case of South Africa

6.1 Introduction

This chapter on terrorism in South Africa begins with a discussion about "insurgent" terrorism conducted under the system of apartheid (1950–1994). It provides a contextual backdrop to political events and to the threat and practice of terrorism in more contemporary South Africa. As such, the central idea of historical change in South Africa predominates, by contrast to still important examples of historical continuity, such as who controls top echelon economic wealth. The chapter continues with description of particular terrorist groups that operate in South Africa, and certain South African criminal syndicalist groups also capable of terrorist assaults.

In addition to the systematic state terrorism carried out by apartheid era South African security services, there were certain select forceful actions taken by anti-regime activists against civilian or other non-combatant targets that qualified as terrorism. In some cases, those targets of terrorist assaults were commercial targets. For example, Lodge lists a host of different non-combatant civilian and government targets that include, "recreational facilities," "crowded business districts," "economic infrastructure," and "hotels or restaurants." [8, 9, 19n50, 19n52; 39, 56, 140, 165–166, 186; 51, 3, 22, 18].[1] Plainly, what made those actions so troubling were their ties to the broader political campaign against apartheid in South Africa, a campaign

[1] In this book, Chapter One's discussion about the "laws of war" works to showcase how forceful acts against the apartheid state qualified as justifiable insurgency rather than terrorism, provided the notions of "proportionality" and "discrimination" under the jurisprudential standard of *jus in bello* ("justice in war") were upheld. Plainly, the third *jus in bello* criterion of "military necessity" was met when all non-violent measures to end apartheid, a system characterized by egregious human rights violations that approached Nuremberg category crimes, were exhausted without the prospect of success. Hence, legitimate use of force could be directed at certain South African National Party (NP) government or government supported targets that included, but were not necessarily limited to, law enforcement, other security services, (para) military targets, and government support infrastructure with military or police operational capacity such as state intelligence networks.

R. J. Chasdi, *Corporate Security Surveillance*, Advanced Sciences and Technologies for Security Applications, https://doi.org/10.1007/978-3-031-39550-5_6

that unequivocally qualified as justifiable insurgency from an international law point of view.

The framework of discussion for "insurgent" terrorism in South Africa involves the African National Congress (ANC), its military branch Umkhonto we Sizwe ("Spear of the Nation"), and the ANC's primary rival, the Pan-Africanist Congress (PAC). Like the ANC, the Pan-Africanist Congress (PAC) had its own paramilitary group known as Poqo. The description of each of those major organizations include certain watershed events such as the dismemberment of Sophiatown (1955), the Sharpsville massacre (1960), and the Soweto uprising (1976), to provide historical and political context and examples of political processes lined to those groups.

In addition to this primary focus, brief description of certain lesser known South African organizations that have used or threatened to use force against non-combatants is provided. Those lesser known South African organizations include the African Resistance Movement (ARM), formerly known as the National Committee of Liberation (NCL), and two Muslim groups, namely the Call to Combat (1961–1962) and Qiblah [39, 63–64, 69, 101, 164–165, 182–183, 185; 63, 317–329; 64, 76–107; 65, 76–107].[2]

For South Africa in the post 1994 era, some analysts have put almost singular focus on the potential threat that Islamic extremists pose to South Africa, both from outside and inside South Africa [38].[3] The central notion here is the threat of terrorism in South Africa is most likely broader than that, notwithstanding the sources and identities of perpetrators commonplace to note. Also of interest in this chapter is the terrorism threat that contemporary South African criminal syndicalists pose, either as stand-alone actors, or within the context of criminal syndicalist collaboration with terrorist organizations.

To be sure, those types of linkages across terrorist group and criminal syndicalist organization types were illuminated in the previous case studies of threats to business in Mexico and Brazil, even though those ties appeared more discernable in the case of Brazil. In the case of India, it seems likely that similar connections between those two types of organizations existed for the time periods examined, although the literature and data findings in this study suggest that ties might have been weaker, more sporadic or both at least in the broader sense, as compared to such relationships in the Argentina, Paraguay, Brazil "tri-border area" for example.

What is also significant here is the contemporary South African political landscape provides an example of a criminal vigilante group in the People Against Gangsterism and Drugs (PAGAD), that has evolved from a criminal group into a terrorist organization [36; 55, 136–137, 133]. The PAGAD experience is extremely insightful because it illuminates a critical part of the Lasswell terrorist "life cycle" not often seen where the practice of terrorism committed by what amounts to a terrorist group, remains

[2] Regrettably, this book's focus on "insurgent" or "oppositional" terrorism does not allow for treatment of the systemic, sustained state terrorism practiced by South Africa's National Party Government (1948–1994).

[3] In contrast, Hendricks supplies a critical theory based approach to terrorist threat appraisals in South Africa, with his focus on the "socially constructed" threat Islamic extremists pose, a perspective propagated by the West especially after 9/11.

at odds with its official statement of purpose and de facto role as a vigilante group designed to confront illegal drug operations [49, 2–3].

Equally important, PAGAD's evolution from criminal vigilante gang to terrorist organization is extremely significant because the reverse process, with devolution from terrorist group status to a criminal enterprise, appears to be more common in the larger world of action. Examples of that more common devolution process from terrorist organization to organized criminal group include Abu Sayyaf in the Philippines, and al-Mourabitoun and the Battalion of Blood (Muwaqi'un Bil Dima) in the Sahel [10; 47; 48, 253–263].

The People Against Gangsterism and Drugs (PAGAD) is examined in preliminary efforts to isolate and identify certain conditions that might help spur on criminal enterprise development across a watershed threshold into a terrorist organization. The idea is that identification of key developmental phases, the influence and intersection of domestic politics, and overarching globalization effects at the international political system level might provide bits of significant information and some insight into whether or not, and if so under what conditions, such transformations are possible.

6.2 African National Congress (ANC)

The African National Congress is a political organization that traces an arc to a January 1, 1912 conference held at Wesleyan Church in Waaihoek, Bloemfontein, where the South African Native National Congress (SANNC) was crafted. In 1923, the SANNC would rebrand itself to become the African National Congress (ANC) [36, 126, 128; 45, 187, 189; 77, 156]. The SANNC-ANC was crafted to confront the systemic racism found in early twentieth century South Africa, a full thirty six years before South Africa's formal system of apartheid galvanized in 1948.

The SANNC originated in a codified racial system of segregation in South Africa where the so-called color bar made legal and political distinctions between Caucasians and people of color. In addition to "whites," those color bar distinctions included, "Coloureds," "Africans (blacks)," and "Indians." In South Africa's segregation system, the term "Coloureds" was the racial category used to classify people who were biracial or multiracial, irrespective of the combination of Indian (Asian), African (black), or "European" background under consideration [39, 108, 133, 137–138, 185; 45, 183, 185; 52, 1102–1103; 73].

Early leaders of the SANNC-ANC included, but were not limited to, John Langalibalele Dube who became SANNC's first General President, James S. Thaele, and SANNC-ANC Secretary Sol Plaatje [3, 45, 39, 44; 36, 126, 126 n1; 39, 318–319; 44, 4; 77, 165, 156].[4] Two hallmarks of the ANC were its emphasis on nonviolence as a

[4] Three other ANC General Presidents included: Dr. Aldred Bitni Zuma (1940–1949), Chief Albert Latuli (1952–1967), and Oliver Tambo (1967–1991). Parenthetically, Sol Plaatje is also known for his mentorship of Z.K. Matthews, a future ANC leader and anthropologist.

vehicle for political change in South Africa, and its willingness to involve whites as well as people of color in its ranks.

The sources and origins of the fledgling African National Congress (ANC) were rooted in the context of events that culminated in the creation of the Union of South Africa in 1910. In their quest to form the Union of South Africa, Britain's leaders backtracked on promises made to "Africans" about a condition of improved civil rights. Indeed, realpolitik considerations and the racism inextricably bound up with imperialism compelled British officials to break those promises and to promote more harmonious relations with the Dutch Boers following Britain's victory in the Boer War (1899–1902) [3, 42, 44; 36, 127–128, 80; 77, 143–144].

For British officials, what spurred on this acute interest in work to craft the Union of South Africa were the twin strategic and economic roles the Union of South Africa would play to strengthen the British Empire. When British leadership produced a draft of the civil rights afforded to "Africans" under the Union of South Africa's proposed constitution, the hollowness of British promises to "Africans" and the political concessions made to the Dutch Boers were fully exposed.

In response, several SANNC antecedent groups were crafted by black political leadership to promote "African" civil rights. Those political organization antecedent groups included the Transvaal Native Union, the Orange River Colony Native Vigilance Association, and the African People's Organization (1902) [3, 42, 46; 36, 128; 38, 80; 77, 157–158].

As Hirson points out, that edifice of racial segregation was reinforced by sharp economic distinctions between peoples, where "whites" who were more affluent as a distinct legal and political grouping in that system, contrasted in profound and lasting ways with the abject poverty most of South Africa's other populations experienced. Such environmental characteristics amounted to a landscape where racial and economic fissures in society aligned to produce what Diamond calls "coincidental cleavage" effects, that caused political instability and social unrest [15].

Hirson also suggests that basic condition of political instability was exacerbated when capitalism became more firmly entrenched in South Africa. The consolidation of capitalism in South Africa happened against the backdrop of increasing recognition of South Africa's vast gold and diamond reserves. That remains a dramatic example globalization's power, as a "systems level" factor, to influence intra-national conflict in this case, in the days of imperialism [80].

Hirson makes clear early ANC leaders were aware of links between the politics of white domination and economic empowerment in South Africa, and indeed throughout the British Empire. Still, ANC public pronouncements at the time placed almost singular focus on the political dimension of "African nationalism." For Hirson, "the men who emerged as leaders.... preferred to couch their statements in terms of colour and race, but more often than not they used this to conceal their class interests." [39, 318–320, 6].

Presumably, that focus by black South African leaders reflected at least in part, more proximate political expediency and mobilization issues and concerns, which were bound up with efforts to confront the emergent political, legal, and economic realities in the Union of South Africa. Another possible reason why public discourse about class distinctions were eschewed at that time, was that only some, but certainly not all, ANC leaders embraced Marxist-Leninism (51, 20, 22–23).

The ANC's continuously evolving role in South African politics came to full blown prominence with the rise of South Africa's National Party (NP) government in 1948. The National Party government was linked to the passage of several racist laws that restricted educational opportunities for Africans, as well as the geographical locales where "Africans" could live. In the broader sense, those laws violated some of the single, most incontrovertible rights under international law that include freedom from the threat or use of force, freedom of movement, and freedom of assembly [6, 59–86; 12, 417; 39, 42, 50; 45, 183, 185; 55, 135].[5]

To be more specific, educational opportunities were severely restricted for Africans with the Bantu Education Act (1953) that was put into force under the Daniël F. Malan government. In 1959, the Hendrik F. Verwoerd government broadened the scope of those original restrictions by means of the Extension of University Education Act to include high schools and institutions of higher learning [16, 46; 39, 40, 50; 77, 181]. In practice, the Department of Native Affairs was tasked with implementation of "native education", Hirson makes it clear from the start that all of the foregoing in South Africa's educational system comprised a vehicle to exert "social control" by the apartheid government [39, 42–43, 45, 62, 54, 93; 52, 1104; 77, 190, 181].[6]

Mariotti points to another facet of Hirson's notion of "social control." What is significant is that the enormous difference in educational levels between South Africans of English stock and many Dutch Afrikaners, as compared to the lower levels of education for most black South Africans, had profound and lasting consequences for South Africa's stratified labor market. Those different educational levels were both a cause and effect of South Africa's political framework as they dovetailed nicely with the labor market's "job reservation" system. In apartheid South Africa's continuously evolving "job reservation system," the most coveted employment opportunities were given to white workers [39, 92, 94–95, 66; 52, 1105–1107, 1110, 1112–1114, 1116–1117, 1120; 77].

Likewise, the Group Areas Act (1950) codified South Africa's time honored system of racial segregation into an even more intractable system. For one thing, the Group Area Act made underlying control over black labor by the National Party government even more entrenched. From the apartheid government's perspective, it was crucial to control black labor because in a labor intensive economy, sufficient black labor on the docks, in the mines, and even in the clothing industry for

[5] These are considered *jus cogens* rights, defined as the single most basic incontrovertible rights human beings possess under international law. Under international law, all *jus cogens* rights are examples of natural law, but not all natural law qualifies as *jus cogens* rights. For many legal scholars, the United States Constitution is a source of international law as it elucidates fundamental *jus cogens* preemptory norms.

[6] At the most basic level, Thompson reports the twin pillars of apartheid revolved around the Immorality Act (1950) and the Prohibition of Mixed Marriages Act (1949).

example, was seen as necessary to ensure South African socio-economic development and thereby in effect, white predominance [4, 33; 39, 122–123, 125, 318; 52, 1104, 1106, 1110–1111; 73, 3, 4, 6, 7].

Prior to that, more "provisional" racist laws throughout South Africa, to use Katz and Tuschaus' term, were sometimes less comprehensive, makeshift or incomplete. For example, in 1913, the Natives Land Act crafted the reserve system where a paltry 7.0% of all South African lands were apportioned to black South Africans to live—in the 1930s, that land amount was increased, but only to some 11.7% [45, 184–186; 77, 165]. Equally important, the Group Areas Act (1950) culled out a "Reserve" system comprised of nine "Homeland" geographical locales controlled by South African National Party government sanctioned administrative bodies [39, 107–109, 70, 115; 45, 200, 184; 73, 3; 77, 190–191].[7]

In this legislation, stipulations afforded the right of South Africa's National Party government to exercise what amounted to American style "eminent domain" powers, as Katz and Tuschaus put it, to acquire land without proper restitution made to black property owners. Overall, that "reserve" system stipulated the geographical locales where South African blacks could live and what types of carefully regulated political activities were permitted within those "Homeland" jurisdictions [39, 107–108, 70; 45, 186].

In the narrower sense, one result of the Group Areas Act (1950) was the dismemberment of Sophiatown (1955) and later on, Cape Town's "District 6" (1966). In close proximity to Johannesburg, Sophiatown was a suburban locale generally recognizable for its more integrated residential areas and its corresponding political, social, and cultural attributes, found even after passage of the 1923 Urban Act. In essence, the Group Areas Act made it possible for the apartheid government to remove and relocate Sophiatown's black population by means of overt threats or use of force in what essentially amounted to "ethnic cleansing" operations [39, 107–108, 70; 45, 184–186; 78].[8]

Katz and Tushaus suggest that in addition to the Bantu Education Act (1952), the emergent reality of Sophiatown's demise became a second clarion call to increase ANC action against the apartheid government. In turn, the third issue of contention that precipitated more direct ANC actions against the South African National Party government was the notorious system of pass document laws. That system required "Africans" to have documentation in the form of pass books on their person at all times [39, 47, 49, 54; 45, 186, 188]. The culmination of effects from these and other watershed political and legal issues and events, led to the 1954 ANC "Resist Apartheid Campaign." [39, 47, 54, 66, 101, 49; 45, 186].

The use of pass books to monitor blacks en route traces an arc to Cape Colony in the late eighteenth century, where "free blacks" were forced to use pass documents to travel between urban and rural locales [77, 37, 103, 117–118, 121, 166]. It continued to be used by British officials to monitor and regulate, based on race, who would

[7] In this context, Thompson describes the Natives Land Act (1936–1937).

[8] In this United Nations document, U.N. "ethnic cleansing" descriptors include, but are not limited to, "displacement and deportation of civilian population," and "forcible removal."

work in the fledgling gold and diamond industries as capitalism took hold in South Africa in the late 1880s. That pass book practice continued to evolve with the Union of South Africa (1910) and well beyond with enhanced pass laws promulgated in the 1930s [45, 183–184, 187; 73, 3–4].

The emergence of the Republic of South Africa in 1960 was designed to supersede the Union of South Africa. With that, the intensity of "pass law" enforcement increased even more. Thompson reports that, "…the government intensified its predecessors' attempts to limit the influx of rural Africans by prohibiting them from visiting an urban area for more than seventy- two hours without a special permit…. Every year, more than 100,000 Africans were arrested under the pass laws; the number peaked at 381,858 in the year 1975–76." [3, 46; 39, 101; 77, 193]. The pass law system only passed into eclipse under the regime of President P.W. Botha (1984–1989) [45, 190, 187].

Indeed, the "pass law" framework was the catalyst issue that led to the Sharpsville massacre outside of South African police headquarters in 1960. In response to Pan Africanist Congress (PAC) organized protests against the pass system mandate that were peaceful, 69 demonstrators were shot dead by Sharpsville police while 180 demonstrators were wounded. The Sharpsville massacre remains a watershed event in the history of South Africa because it transformed the basic nature of the political struggle for black emancipation [77, 210–211].

6.3 The Umkhonto We Sizwe ("Spear of the Nation")

Shortly after the Sharpsville massacre, both the ANC and its "splinter group," the Pan-Africanist Congress (PAC), were criminalized by the apartheid government [3, 46, 48; 4, 33; 36, 130; 38, 89; 39, 6, 334, 101; 45, 188]. In the case of the African National Congress (ANC), the Sharpsville massacre was a pivotal turning point in the emancipation struggle—it led to the emergence of the Umkhonto we Sizwe ("Spear of the Nation") paramilitary branch of the ANC in 1960.

The Umkhonto we Sizwe (MK) was crafted by Nelson Mandela and other ANC officials, who now endorsed movement away from ANC's time honored approach of non-violent political struggle in pursuit of black emancipation in South Africa. While the Umkhonto we Sizwe or MK (and the ANC) eschewed violence against civilians, it instead endorsed what was called "sabotage" against a wide ranging set of government targets. As previously mentioned, this study considers the selection of non-combatant targets, inclusive of many government targets, as intrinsic to what events qualify as acts of terrorism [7, 24, 51n26; 8, 6–9, 19n 52; 68, 3; 77, 229].

Lodge reports the Umkhonto we Sizwe (MK) was the single, most predominant institution within the ANC. The Umkhonto we Sizwe operational framework was a traditional top-down hierarchal structure, a structure that was common for terrorist groups during the Cold War. As the paramilitary branch of the African National Congress (ANC), the Umkhonto we Sizwe was not an ANC "splinter" group where ANC members of the parent organization branched out to form a new group. Neither was the Umkhonto we Sizwe an ANC "spin-off" group, where new membership served as the basis for "spinoff" group composition [11, 48; 51, 6].

South Africa's apartheid government criminalized the ANC and Pan-African Congress (PAC) in 1960 after the Sharpsville massacre and in reaction to the social unrest almost certain to follow after those killings. As a result, the Umkhonto we Sizwe (MK) joined the ANC and PAC in exile in countries in close proximity to South Africa such as Angola, Tanzania, Mozambique, Swaziland, Botswana, and Zambia (Northern Rhodesia) [3, 53; 11, 48; 14, xvi, 140–141; 38, 89; 51, 6, 13, 15; 77, 213].

In terms of Umkhonto we Sizwe's numerical size, assessments by experts vary based on source and time period. Lodge estimates there were some 400 MK activists in South Africa, while some 10,000 MK activists lived in exile, finding safe-haven in those neighboring countries [51, 5, 15]. The size of Umkhonto we Sizwe grew apace after the student led Soweto riots in 1976, another watershed event in South African history described below. For Lodge, the total number of MK terrorist attacks was small, with less than 500 acts in total [51, 8].

After the Sharpsville massacre, the initial Umkhonto we Sizwe terrorism campaign began to unfold in 1961 and lasted until 1965. Jukes reports the first round of terrorist assaults happened at several locales on December 16, 1961. *The New York Times* describes one set of early MK terrorist assaults where, "among the places hit were a suburban post-office, several African-affairs offices and an electric power station. The sites were mainly around Johannesburg and Port Elizabeth." [7, 4, 240, 16 n17; 11, 46–47, 200 n23; 43, 102–103; 75, 3]. It was during that early phase of the initial Umkhonto we Sizwe terrorist campaign that Nelson Mandela, leader of the "Spear of the Nation" was arrested, convicted at the Rivonia trial in 1963–1964, and imprisoned until his release in 1990 by F.W. de Klerk [3, 47; 45, 191; 77, 211].

After this initial campaign, Umkhonto we Sizwe leaders put terrorist operations on hold for some twelve years between 1965 and 1977. Thompson suggests the incarceration of Mandela and ANC stalwart Walter Sisulu caused some organizational disruptions that appear to have been overcome by 1977, when ANC terrorist assault campaigns resumed [51, 8; 55, 133; 77, 211].

Notwithstanding that, singular focus on MK terrorist assaults would represent only a makeshift and incomplete picture of Umkhonto we Sizwe activities. In fact, the scope of MK activities was much broader and spanned several different countries. For example, in addition to focus on armed struggle against the South African regime, Umkhonto we Sizwe played an important role in work to provide basic social services to broader groups of people who would ordinarily be underserved or not served at all by state government policies.

The United Democratic Front (UDA) was a parallel political organization or ANC "affiliate" that emerged in South Africa in 1983 [22, 59, 63–65, 68; 45]. It was established close to the tail end of the 1960–1990 period when ANC was criminalized and forced to operate in exile from Zambia. The United Democratic Front echoed ANC in its support for the Freedom Charter that *inter-alia* called for "collaboration" between "liberals" and other opponents of the South African regime, and in its clarion call for multiracial diversity within its ranks. Like the ANC, the ranks of the United

Democratic Front were comprised of an ideologically eclectic group of political activists [20, 490, 494; 22, 59, 63–65, 68; 77, 210].

In exile, Umkhonto we Sizwe also had capacities to provide a variety of social services to its activists and constituents; those social services originated from its main offices in Lusaka Zambia. As was seen in the cases of India, Mexico, and Brazil, part of the reason why terrorist organizations and criminal syndicalists do this is to generate and sustain loyalty and other similar sentiments. For example, Lodge reports Umkhonto we Sizwe offered critically important educational services, ranging from pre-school to high school programs, crafted at MK's educational hub in Morogoro, Tanzania. At the same time, medical services and social activities to serve "cultural" needs were provided [51, 5, 11–13].

6.4 The Pan-Africanist Congress (PAC)

The Pan-Africanist Congress (PAC) was a "splinter group" of the African National Congress that emerged in 1959. It is reported that a significant number of activists who become top echelon PAC leaders had origins in the ANC's Congress Youth League (CYL), that itself was crafted in 1944 [3, 45; 60, 2]. One issue of contention between ANC leaders and fledgling PAC officials revolved around the Freedom Charter (1955) with its basic interplay between whites and "Africans" within the context of political institutions designed to promote black emancipation.

In the broader sense, a prevailing notion among some, but certainly not all black activists at the time, was that a significant role for whites in political institutions devoted to black emancipation failed to capture or somehow diluted the basic nature and premise of what black emancipation was all about. From the start, the ANC endorsed racial diversity within its ranks; that underlying notion was reflected in ANC alliances with like-minded South African organizations. In a nutshell, the scope of those who participated in ANC activities was broad, to include what Hirson calls white "progressives," "liberals," and "democrats." [3, 45–46, 42; 22, 64; 39, 54, 65, 67, 113–114; 45, 188–190; 60, 2].

In comparison, most ANC leaders who comprised the core of the future PAC, were skeptical about ANC's racial diversity perspective. The strains and tensions between those opposing points of view would soon produce volcanic-like political eruptions. Boesak reports how a stipulation in the Freedom Charter of the South African Congress (of which the ANC was a dominant part), elicited fierce debate between leaders. That stipulation read, "South Africa belongs to all who live in it, black and white, and that no government can justly claim authority unless it is based on the will of the people." [3, 45–47; 45, 188–189; 77, 208; 60, 4-6; 19, 1–2].

This difference in opinion about racial diversity in the ranks and the overall policy direction of the black emancipation movement were at the heart of those debates. In turn, those debates spurred on political actions which ultimately led to the creation of the Pan-Africanist Congress (PAC). The main group of dissident ANC leaders involved included Peter Raboroko, Zeph Mothopeng, Potlake Leballo, and A.P. Mda. Out of that political fray, Robert Mongaliso Sobukwe emerged as the first President of the PAC [3, 45–47; 45, 188–189; 77, 208].

6.5 Pan-Africanist Congress (PAC) Influence: SASO, SASM, and Soweto

While the Sharpsville protests were the handiwork of the Pan-Africanist Congress, the political tenor of the Soweto riots (1976) was also inextricably bound up in political and ideological terms with the Pan-Africanist Congress. Those ties involved the Pan-Africanist Congress (PAC) imperative and broader "Black Consciousness Movement" (i.e., Black People's Convention—BPC) standpoint that South Africa's emancipation from apartheid had to be led exclusively by "Africans." [39, 7, 65–71–72, 82].[9]

In the case of the Soweto uprising, it was the South African Student Association (SASO) led by Stephen Biko that helped breathe life into that black emancipation standpoint to inspire the South African Student Movement (SASM), the organization at the heart of the uprising in Soweto. In fact, SASO leaders did so in ways that reflected Banton's definition of race in social and political terms, rather than anthropological terms.

For Banton, "race as a role sign" or what political scientists call a "social signifier" is what is significant here, so that people victimized by white dominated political and social institutions regard themselves and are regarded by others as people of color. In essence the SASO leadership put that notion into practice because the SASO leadership's racial framework included South African "Indians" and "Coloureds" as members of the black population [2, 4–5, 55–76, 142, 66; 39, 71–73; 53, 95].

There are clear connections between SASO and SASM, even though the exact nature of those ties remains the subject of debate. The South African Student Association (SASO) was crafted in 1969 as an emancipation movement to work within South Africa's extensive education system. Its leader was student activist Stephen Biko, who would later be mortally wounded in prison in 1977 by police officials as retribution for the Soweto Revolt. It is probably no exaggeration to say that at least in functional terms, SASM probably had broader social and political disruptive effects than SASO.

The racial constraints put on SASO membership contrasted sharply with, and served as a counterpoint to, the racial diversity approach embraced by the Union of South African Students (NUSAS). Like many other black emancipation organizations, SASO had powerful ties to the Church; it espoused "Black theology," a doctrine that put emphasis on Christianity's role to free people of color in South Africa. For Stephen Biko it worked," …to relate God and Christ once more to the black man and

[9] The Black People's Convention was crafted in 1972.

his daily problems. It wants to describe Christ as a fighting god, not a passive god who allows a lie to rest unchallenged...." [Biko as found in 39, 78, 81; 16, 57].

As in-depth discussion of the Soweto Revolt (1976–1977) is beyond the scope of this chapter, only the basics of that fierce struggle can be described. Still, that description is essential to provide political context to acts taken that qualified as (state) terrorist assaults. As previously mentioned, the single, most predominant actor in the Soweto Revolt was the South African Student Movement (SASM), itself crafted in 1972. SASM might be described as a parallel organization to SASO, or as some authorities claim, as an SASO "affiliate." [16, 41–42, 62, 44; 39, 103].

For those who argue that SASM was a distinct organization separate from SASO, the sources and origins of SASM were independent of SASO involvement or influence. The argument is that SASM was self-contained, characterized by its operational independence. Furthermore, SASM was distinct and different from SASO because, as both Hirson and Diseko report, SASM did not galvanize out of opposition to NUSAS's embrace of racial diversity, as did SASO. Moreover, as Diseko informs us, SASMO had no link to the "Black Consciousness Movement." [16, 41–42, 62, 44; 39, 103].

Be that as it may, the ANC allied with SASM with what both Diseko and Hirson describe as a set of "informal" interconnections between those two black emancipation organizations [16, 61, 42; 39, 201–202]. What also seems significant here is that the broader struggles of the ANC and PAC informed and gave structural shape to the direction of more proximate events planned and led by SASM in Soweto.

The first wide-ranging event that sparked the Soweto revolt was a 15,000 student strong protest in Soweto on June 16, 1976 against the government's the use of Afrikaans as the language of choice for educational purposes. That initial protest and others like it were met by extremely disproportionate police responses that amounted to state terrorism. Those police responses included beatings and shootings at unarmed civilians, including children. For Hirson, is important to note the start of the Soweto revolt was more spontaneous, rather than the product of extensive SASM plans [39, 180–182].

Once word of the egregious human rights violations taken by the South African police in Soweto spread, the crisis accelerated as other groups of young people began to assault government buildings and commercial targets such as Barclay's Bank, bars, business vehicles, and automobiles. What is also significant is the Soweto revolt worked to elicit profound and lasting cascade effects, where violence soon broke out in other parts of South Africa, in rural areas and in or around cities such as Pretoria [39, 186, 182, 188–189].

At the same time, Hirson points out that the contentious issue of Afrikaans as the language of choice for education must be understood against the backdrop of other critical issues that plagued Soweto residents. Those included low wage rates, high transportation costs, problems with "worker rights," and exorbitant rents [39, 199, 175–177]. When thinking about what led to the outbreak of violence and terrorism in Soweto, the use of Afrikaans to teach children rather than English for example, can be understood as an issue that qualified as what Reiss and Roth call a short-run "precipitating factor" or "activating factor." [62, 296–298, 304, 209–210].

To be more specific, the Reiss and Roth conceptualization that is used to explain violent outcomes also has bearing on the low wage rates, high transportation costs, high rents, and "worker rights" issues that Hirson describes. Those four explanatory factors intrinsic to the Soweto revolt are found at what Reiss and Roth would call the "situational factor" level of analysis. In essence, those are, for Reiss and Roth, the "middle-run" factors bound up with the outbreak of violence that culminated in the Soweto revolt [62, 296–298, 304, 209–210].

In turn, the broader contours or parameters of the black emancipation movement, as articulated and operationalized by the African National Congress (ANC), the Pan-Africanist Congress (PAC), and other black emancipation organizations, are crucial parts of this analysis based on Reiss and Roth's work. In turn, articulated demands and aspirations for black emancipation, that itself traces an arc to at least the late nineteenth century, highlight what Reiss and Roth call long-haul "predisposing" factors. Those "predisposing factors" are "deep" factors that include the apartheid system and its effects, and the time honored codification of segregation in South Africa prior to apartheid [39, 201].

6.6 Poqo—The Azanian People's Liberation Army (APLA)

The paramilitary branch of the Pan-Africanist Congress (PAC) was originally known as Poqo. The translation of Poqo into English is uncertain—some translate it to mean "Pure," or "To Go One's Own Way," or "for blacks only." Poqo was crafted sometime after both the Pan-Africanist Congress (PAC) and the African National Congress (ANC) were criminalized by the South African government in 1960. In South Africa, Poqo's constituents were primarily from the Western Cape and the Vaal Triangle [19, 1, 2; 60, 4, 6; 71, 2; 77, 211].

In exile, the Pan-Africanist Congress set up shop in Mesaru, Lesotho (formerly Basotholand). In 1968, as the political strength of the Pan-Africanist Congress (ANC) in South Africa began to pass into eclipse, Poqo was rebranded as the Azanian People's Liberation Army (APLA). In its new incarnation as the APLA, Poqo continued to operate until 1994, mainly from outside South Africa, before it was skillfully dismantled by South Africa's new post-apartheid government [19, 2; 38, 84; 60, 4–5, 7; 77, 259, 268].[10]

As early as 1962, Poqo leaders conducted terrorist assaults against civilian targets outright. That target selection calculus stood in sharp contrast to how terrorism was practiced by Umkhonto we Sizwe (MK). While the Umkhonto we Sizwe primarily scoped out civilian government infrastructure targets in "sabotage" campaigns and officially eschewed acts of violence against civilians, Poqo moved beyond that stated MK position to target civilians such as policemen, white farmers, and "government collaborators." [22, 60; 39, 64; 60, 4; 71, 1; 72, 1].

[10] O'Malley describes another PAC spinoff group, the Azanian People's Revolutionary Party (APRP) crafted around 1979 as a distinct "competitive organization" to the Pan-Africanist Congress.

APLA's paramilitary capacities were probably diminished because of its inability to galvanize broad based support, no doubt influenced by its use of terrorism against civilians, and because of the political infighting that rend apart the Pan-Africanist Congress (PAC). Indeed, South Africa's post-apartheid Truth and Reconciliation Commission (1996) would lambast the APLA for its use of unbridled terrorism [60, 4; 72]. The APLA was also hamstrung early on by effective and sustained South African counterterrorism measures that accelerated in the early to middle 1960s. Still, the threat of APLA terrorist assaults remained potent as APLA continued to operate into the 1990s.

Those APLA attacks culminated in the early 1990s with what Thompson calls the "spectacular" set of terrorist assaults that included attacks taken against white South African churches in 1993. At the same time, there did not seem to be special focus placed by APLA on commercial interests in that time period. For example, the Global Terrorism Database (GTD) only chronicled one non-lethal APLA terrorist assault against a business target in the early 1990s—a "steakhouse" in Queenstown, Eastern Cape Province, where 18 people were wounded [9, 48, 100 n49; 29; 72, 1; 77, 248].[11]

It is incumbent to note that this chapter's focus on Umkhonto we Sizwe and the Azanian People's Liberation Army (APLA), as the primary stakeholders in South Africa that used terrorism under apartheid, is certainly not an exhaustive discussion of the subject. In particular, two other South African organizations that used what amounts to "oppositional" terrorism under the apartheid government are noteworthy, even though more in-depth discussion about the range of smaller or less well known organizations is beyond the scope of this chapter [64, 76–107; 65 76–107].

One group was the National Committee of Liberation (NCL) that was crafted around 1963; it evolved into the African Resistance Movement (ARM) [39, 64]. Like the ANC, the African Resistance Movement (ARM) embraced the underlying theme of racial diversity within the context black emancipation efforts. For Thompson, the ARM was, "...(a multiracial organization consisting mainly of young white professionals and students)...." [77, 211]. In his work, du Toit reports how Ethel Rhys was killed and twenty two other passengers wounded when an ARM bomb detonated at a South African railways station after repeated ARM warnings to authorities were ignored outright [18, 1].

In contrast, the Azanian People's Organization (AZAPO) was formed in April, 1978, some fifteen years later than the African Resistance Movement (ARM). Thompson suggests that in terms of composition, AZAPO paralleled APLA (i.e., Poqo) recruitment patterns with an underlying focus on some of South Africa's black intelligentsia and fledgling occupational elite [39, 64–66, 69; 77, 236, 252, 248]. Moreover, AZAPO embodied many underlying themes of the "Black Consciousness" and "Black Theology" movements described above.

[11] Terrorist experts sometimes make distinctions between "spectacular" terrorist assaults and what one British expert calls "boilerplate" terrorist assaults.

In this way, AZAPO closely paralleled the Pan-Africanist Congress (PAC) and its standpoint to black emancipation. Indeed, Stephen Biko of both SASO and SASM, was an early leader and human capital cornerstone of the AZAPO edifice. Examples of AZAPO business related terrorist assaults included, but are not limited to, the 1992 attacks on the PA Sound Corporation in Johannesburg, and a bar in King William's Town in Eastern Cape Province [27, 28].

6.7 The Threat of Terrorism Post-apartheid (1994–)

In the broader sense, the threat of terrorism in South Africa has shifted in dramatic fashion after apartheid ended in 1994. This shift is reflective of structural political change from a condition where the apartheid national government faced internal threats and external threats from several black emancipation organizations in exile, to a condition where the threat of terrorism in contemporary South Africa is comparatively low, but with potential to increase.

One aspect of South Africa's contemporary terrorism threat revolves around systemic economic pressures and what amounts to continued coincidental cleavage effects [15]. For some, much of that terrorism threat stems from prevailing economic conditions where abject economic blight and related issues still afflict much of the population. For Hendricks, "...socio-economic threats are the main security concerns which confront the majority of South Africans..." [38, 84].

In a similar vein, some South African specialists argue that condition of economic tensions, at least in part, is linked to the sources and origins of large scale economic wealth in South Africa, which is still heavily controlled by the white minority population. Be that as it may, it is important to recall most terrorism analysts point only to an indirect relationship between socioeconomic status (e.g., economic blight conditions) and terrorism [11, 135, 221 n58; 33; 38, 87; 74].

A second aspect of South Africa's terrorism threat involves domestic "right-wing" terrorism and the potential threat that regional, and international terrorist organizations pose. The historical legacy of "right-wing" terrorism in South Africa is profound and tortuous; it provides the basis for concern about racially motivated terrorist attacks in the post-apartheid era. For example, South African "right-wing" white supremacist organizations active in the late 1980s and 1990s included, but were not limited to, the Nazi Boerestat Party, the Afrikaner Resistance Movement (AWB), and the White Wolves [23–26; 57, 119].[12]

For some, but certainly not all analysts, the primary threat of terrorism to South Africa presupposes and derives from South Africa's role as a "safe-haven" for several foreign sourced terrorist groups [46, 9–10, 14]. Those terrorist groups include al-Shabaab, Hezbollah, al-Qaeda, and other Islamic extremist organizations. Still, as McFarlane points out, it is incumbent to note that, "...the vast majority of Muslims

[12] One more contemporary South African "right-wing" terrorist group chronicled by Mickolus in 2013 is, "Boeremag (white farmer force)".

in South Africa live amicably with their co-citizens and are not supportive of fundamentalist terrorism." [38; 41, 17; 55, 137].

With that caveat in mind, Hussein Solomon reports the presence of al-Shabaab facilities to train activists in South Africa. For instance, what analysts labeled as an al-Shabaab "scout" unit was found near Cape Town. Solomon also reports that in response to a U.S. Navy Seal strike in 2009 that killed al-Qaeda chieftain, Mr. Saleh Ali Saleh Nabhan in Somalia, al-Shabaab issued threats which forced the offices of the United States Agency for International Development (USAID), the U.S. Embassy, and several American consulates in South Africa to shut down temporarily [11, 93–115; 21, 67; 56, 85; 68, 5, 2–3; 69, 153–157].

Solomon also reports that as far back as 1996, Israeli authorities found five Hezbollah camps in South Africa used to train recruits and other more experienced terrorists. The author also chronicles what appears to be a 2003 notification from Israel's Mossad or Shin Bet about "recognizable Hamas activity" in South Africa. Furthermore, the presence of another "Jihadi facility" located near Port Elizabeth was illuminated in the South African publication *Molotov Cocktail* in March 2007. Solomon reports that South African security services also detected a Hezbollah contingent located near or in Johannesburg [69, 152, 159–160].

Plainly, strenuous efforts by foreign sourced terrorists to mask those facilities remained intrinsic to continued terrorist group success. Accordingly, Hezbollah set up camps to train recruits and presumably other more seasoned terrorists at secluded farms and other rural locales in South Africa. In the broader sense, Islamic extremists have also set up shop in countries close to South Africa. For example, Botswana has been known as a safe-haven for al-Qaeda, Mozambique has sheltered al-Shabaab, and the Democratic Republic of Congo (DRC) has provided sanctuary to Hezbollah [21, 52, 54; 69, 152–154, 164n 63, 144, 157–159; 70, 1].[13]

Equally important, Hezbollah and presumably other international terrorist groups with ties to South Africa such as Hamas, have worked to exploit South Africa's financial system. In a 2007 *Jamestown Foundation* report, John Solomon describes how the ex-coordinator of South Africa's National Intelligence Coordinating Committee, Mr. Barry Gilder, has focused on, "…the terrorist use of the country's banks, and a pattern of illegally obtained South African passports ending up in the hands of al-Qaeda suspects or their associates in Europe…." [70, 1].

In some cases, there are terrorist organizational links to South African criminal groups that work to compound South Africa's security problems. Recall that such links are established so terrorist organizations and criminal syndicalists can benefit from collaboration that results in win–win outcomes (i.e., positive sum solutions). In the case of South Africa, Solomon reports, "…organized crime syndicates (especially those involved in narco-trafficking) were already regional in character by the 1990s, and that these had a working relationship with Islamists, syndicates could piggyback on criminal networks already operating in the region." [69, 153].

---

[13] That *Molotov Cocktail* report was cited in John Solomon's scripted account and in turn by Hussein Solomon.

6.8 People Against Gangsterism and Drugs (PAGAD)

The People Against Gangsterism and Drugs (PAGAD) is crucial to study because it showcases how a criminal group that uses terrorism and all but qualifies as a terrorist organization, can evolve into a terrorist organization. PAGAD qualified as a criminal "vigilante" organization that used terrorism well before it detonated an explosive device at Cape Town's Planet Hollywood restaurant in 1998. In that terrorist assault, two people were killed and twenty six people were wounded [49, 1–6].

The sources and origins of PAGAD are found within the immediate aftermath of the apartheid system. It was crafted in December 1995 in South Africa's Western Cape Province at Cape Flats, after several grass roots "civic organizations" merged [1, 187, 198, 195–196, 190]. Even though it lacked a formal political ideology, PAGAD's mission was clear- to combat illegal drug proliferation and other organized criminal activities in the Cape Flats and Woodstock areas of Cape Town [1, 198; 17, 24–26, 30–31]. That provenance is consistent with Theen and Wilson's notion that the use of violence based political frameworks to solve state problems such as South Africa's apartheid system, elicits violence and violent organizations [1, 187; 17, 25–26; 76].

An examination of PAGAD's early organizational structure illuminates some of the internal dynamics in terrorist and criminal organizations previously mentioned. At first, PAGAD embraced a "troika" style leadership where Farouk Jaffer, Nadthme Edries, and Ali Parker were at the helm of a loosely organized group of Cape Town's citizens, comprised mostly of Muslims. As Dixon and Johns report, that "troika" continued until September 29, 1996, when it was dissolved at proceedings held at the Habiba Mosque. For Dixon and Johns, the strains and tensions caused by competing personal ambition, and the allure of public recognition, led to the collapse of that troika [17, 25–26].

At PAGAD's inception, there were also external ties between PAGAD and a pro-Iranian South African Islamic extremist organization known as Qiblah. Qiblah was established in 1979–1980 by Achmat Cassiem, after the Iranian revolution in 1979 [1, 198–201, 205; 20, 477–479, 482, 484]. Achmat Cassiem is a Shi'a Muslim, with deep personal attachment to Iran and Ayatollah Khomeini. At first, PAGAD membership was not limited to Muslims, but having said that, the majority of Qiblah membership with ties to PAGAD remained adherents to Sunni Islam, rather than to Shia Islam, in no small part because Sunnis predominated in Cape Town [1, 193, 198 200–202, 204–205, 208; 20, 485, 491].

Qiblah had a close set of connections to the Pan-Africanist Congress (PAC). Both organizations were supportive of efforts to craft PAGAD and its mission to eradicate drug trafficking in Cape Town. Qiblah leaders have continued to provide support for the establishment of an Islamic state in South Africa, even though that likelihood is practically nil. For Esack, "the idea of an Islamic revolution *á la* Iran in South Africa is essentially that of Qiblah." [1, 200; 20, 485, 475, 479].

All of the foregoing makes it is difficult to come to a clear-cut determination about whether or not Qiblah qualifies as a direct antecedent group to PAGAD [49, 2–3]. On one hand, Bangstad reports PAGAD's leadership cadre was infiltrated by

Qiblah leaders in the 1990s. For some analysts, that serves as the basis of claims that PAGAD is part of Qiblah [1, 201]. At the same time, PAGAD has not issued statements that amount to a political ideology consistent with an anti-Western and anti-Israel Islamic extremist agenda, nor has it called for an Islamic state in South Africa.

If Qiblah served in some sense as an inspirational source for PAGAD, it did not provide PAGAD with an aspirational template, at least not initially. The only political objectives articulated by PAGAD leaders were demands that South African police dismantle organized crime networks. It follows that PAGAD's relationship with "Islamism" and "Islamist rhetoric" was, at least in its early years, complex, nuanced, and ultimately indeterminate. Bangstad describes two ways to think about PAGAD in its early years and its relationship to "Islamist rhetoric," in addition to one approach that views "Islamism"as intrinsic to PAGAD's development [1, 189].[14]

In the case of "Islamist rhetoric," one approach is that "Islamist rhetoric" helped PAGAD cope with existing leadership problems in South Africa's Muslim community where there was a "...crisis of secular and religious leadership among South African Muslims." [1, 189, 195–196, 198, 205]. A second approach suggests PAGAD used "Islamist rhetoric," rather than "Islamism" to capture and appeal to what Pillay describes as the multi-dimensionality of South African identity. That national identity, as mirrored in South African youth, had multiple sources, "...produced within colonialism, globalization and the post-apartheid era." [1, 189, 189 n, 13,188 n5; Sureen Pillay as quoted and cited in Bangstad) In contrast, Bangstad's third approach stresses the political religiosity of "Islamism" as an intrinsic part of PAGAD's development [1, 189, 195–196, 198, 204–205; 20, 204, 207, 198–199].

The early activities of PAGAD consisted of organized "march-and-confront" protests that were non-violent. Those protests were directed against known drug dealers in various Cape Town locales. Initially, PAGAD found a niche and high degree of acceptance from citizens, in large part due to that organization's intolerance of crime and drug use. PAGAD's unequivocal position about drugs and organized crime resonated with its constituents because of the South African police were perceived as either indifferent or unable to mount an effective challenge to organized crime in Cape Town [1, 204, 207, 198–199; 17, 30].

What is critical to note is that in its first phase, PAGAD had a set of positive interactions with the Cape Town police who supported PAGAD's anti-drug efforts. As Dixon and Johns report, "...Western Cape Attorney-General Frank Kahn suggested that if PAGAD wanted to do something about drugs it should focus its attention on entry points such as Cape Town International [airport]." [1, 198; 17, 27–28].

However, in the late 1990s, PAGAD moved away from its original emphasis on peaceful protest and into a second phase of its development that was marked by terrorist assaults against criminal syndicalists [1, 187]. In this second phase of its

[14] For Bangstad, "Islamism" involves non-violent pursuit of an Islamic state or a state where Sharia is a significant part of the state apparatus. In comparison, "militant Islamism" accepts violence as a means to pursue either of those goals. The author suggests "Islamist rhetoric" can be used to promote either "Islamism" or "militant Islamism," but can also be used for instrumental purposes such as organizational goals.

"life-cycle," PAGAD was clearly a criminal organization that used terrorism. It seems likely that the event which ushered PAGAD into this second phase of development was the 1996 murder of Cape Town drug kingpin Rashaad Staggie [1, 199, 187, 208, 201; 47; 48, 253–263].

PAGAD's transformation into a criminal group that used terrorism happened in response to criminal syndicalist violence against Cape Town citizens. In the 1990s, syndicalist assassins murdered several people somehow perceived to be connected to PAGAD. For example, one victim was only an anti-drug protestor seen marching at a PAGAD demonstration [1, 202–203; 20]. What is important to reiterate is that all of the foregoing happened within the context of the wide-ranging perception in Cape Town that Cape Town police were unable to or unwilling to constrain and control organized crime due to outright indifference.

In response to PAGAD's use of criminal terrorism, there was a volt-face in the Cape Town police approach to that group. At the same time, there also seemed to be a mixed response from Cape Town citizens to this shift in PAGAD tactics. That is significant because in its first phase of non-violent opposition to drug kingpins, there was a high degree of public support for PAGAD and its mission to irradicate drug networks. It was around that time Cape Town police began to crack down hard on PAGAD and refer to its leaders as criminals and terrorists [1, 198; 17, 27–28].

It is also important to note that top echelon South African government leaders also contributed to the confusion that characterized the PAGAD relationship with the police during PAGAD's first phase of operations. For example, at the time when PAGAD activists began to organize peaceful operations at Cape Town International Airport, actions that were sanctioned by Attorney-General Frank Kahn, President Nelson Mandela and former Minister of Transportation Mac Maharaj took the opposite position and informed PAGAD leaders, "...not to go near the place." [17, 27–28].

Those "mixed messages" from South African officials about behavioral expectations might have worked to shape the "middle-run" trajectory of PAGAD's development. It is possible that "cognitive dissonance" effects were at work in PAGAD-Cape Town police meetings held soon after PAGAD materialized. The processes associated with "cognitive dissonance" might have been experienced by one or both sides, leading to interpretation problems in those information exchanges [1, 198; 17, 26–27; 42]. However, while that interpretation is possible and intriguing, further discussion about "cognitive dissonance" as an explanatory factor in PAGAD's evolution into a full blown terrorist group awaits future research.

In the broader sense, the transition PAGAD made into its second phase most likely happened because of the confluence in effects of several explanatory variables. In addition to the possibility that "cognitive dissonance" effects were at work, there are two other possible explanatory factors, in addition to other unspecified ones, that deserve the attention of future research to determine possible explanatory factor effects on the evolution of PAGAD.

One possible explanatory factor found at the "nation state level" of analysis is "ineffective political institutionalization." [1, 195–196; 17, 26–27; 29–30; 40].[15] Hence, the ineffective Cape Town police response to organized crime and drug kingpins commonplace to note in accounts, might have derived from government agency disruptions intrinsic to the end of apartheid that Skocpol might call South Africa's "social revolution." [50, 47; 59; 67; 80, 159–186][16]

The central idea is that in South Africa, political institutionalization problems intrinsic to the transition from the de Klerk regime to a post-apartheid South Africa under President Nelson Mandela, created "political space" where organized crime could flourish and where PAGAD could materialize [1, 190]. It is important to recall that PAGAD galvanized only about a year after the end of apartheid, after President Mandela and the African National Congress (ANC) came to power in 1994.

There seems to be some empirical support for this interpretation events that surround PAGAD's development. For example, in Indonesia, cliques in different government departments engaged in fierce competition for a limited number of political positions and finite political resources after President Suharto's resignation in 1998 [1, 190–191; 13, 990]. At that time, the new Indonesian government had problems with effective and sustained police control over areas of the country as several political stakeholders jockeyed for political control over the country [13, 990].

PAGAD's experience vis à vis the South African police came at a similar historical juncture in nation-state historical development. In the case of Indonesia with the fall of Suharto, there was also transition from a highly authoritarian system to a democratic system. It is probably no exaggeration to say that at least some of the political processes in the South African experience might have been similar to processes that contributed to the Indonesian government's functionality and security problems after Suharto's resignation in 1998 [13, 990].

A second possible explanatory factor to help explain PAGAD's transition from a political pressure group to a "vigilante group" comfortable with the use of terrorism involves South Africa's "hyper-politicized" population. Found at the "nation-state" level of analysis, that possible explanatory variable was also a characteristic of the Indonesian political landscape at the time of Suharto's resignation. In the case of South Africa, it is important to note that "hyper-politicized population" as an explanatory factor for formation of violent groups represents an example of political continuity across almost the entire spectrum of South African history, from the era of apartheid and before, to South Africa's post-apartheid democratic government [20, 495; 80, 159–186].

In that vein, Thompson suggests that South African society has been "hyper-politicized" at least from the early to middle twentieth century onwards. From the beginning of the apartheid system in 1950 until its end in 1994, the predominant

[15] In this case, some degree of (police) corruption might have also served as a source of ineffective political institutionalization.

[16] For Skocpol, the fundamental rules of governance are changed in a "social revolution".

set of political divisions in South Africa that mobilized its citizens revolved around support or opposition to apartheid.[17]

For example, there were unified efforts on the part organizations such as the United Democratic Front (UDF) and the ANC to confront apartheid in conjunction with The Call to Combat (1961–1962), their ally in South Africa's Muslim community. The Call to Combat was a short-lived Muslim anti-apartheid organization formed by Imam Abdullah Haroon that worked to overthrow the apartheid government. It was crafted in response to the expulsion of Muslims from communities around Cape Town that was made possible under the Group Areas Act (1950) [1, 200; 20, 483, 475–477, 478n20, 478 n18, 489–490, 494].[18]

The "life-cycle" of the Call to Combat organization was short and grim [47; 48, 253–263]. In 1969, Imam Abdullah Haroon was murdered in prison by South African police after a brief period of incarceration. Nonetheless, Esack reports that The Call to Combat (1962–1962) was a watershed political group because it was the first Muslim organization to contextualize Muslim principles and teachings within the secular fray of political demands and aspirations to end apartheid [20, 475, 489, 491].

In addition, the notion of South Africa's "hyper-politicized" population as a possible explanatory variable for PAGAD's continued development, dovetails well with the realities of "economic blight" and related conditions that all too many South Africans experienced. While there is no direct link between socioeconomic status (SES) and terrorism established in the terrorism literature, political context in operational environments is critical.

In the case of PAGAD, the legacy of an apartheid system, and a "hyper-politicized" population was coupled with economic blight conditions, and subsequent opportunities for citizen political involvement precisely because issues between drug dealers and society were clear-cut, and because of the perception the police were indifferent to crime in parts of Cape Town. It seems likely that at least some of those variables might have been at work, and at least in some cases interconnected, in ways that could have contributed to PAGAD's eventual embrace of violence [7; 8, 104; 37; 54, 10–12].

Indeed, what Gurr might call those "relative deprivation" effects had profound and lasting economic and political influences on much of the South African population. In the post 1994 era, South Africa's government tried to emphasize a "human security" approach in South Africa with mixed results. Nowadays, the dominant pieces of the political discourse have revolved around "ethnic identifications," housing, education, and economic blight, and by extrapolation, related conflict conditions such as crime [1, 190; 34; 35, 82–95; 38; 64, 176; 77, 245].

---

[17] In Brazil, unresolved political tensions within top echelon political circles contributed to "hyper-politicized" political and military factions engaged in elite struggles about who would rule the state. By contrast, South Africa's "hyper-politicized" struggle involved fierce grassroots struggles inclusive of "civic organizations" to end apartheid.

[18] The Call to Combat organization (1961–1962) should not be confused with another group of the same name that emerged in 1983. For Esack, there is no linkage between those two groups.

To be sure, Thompson's remarks about criminal actions taking on political overtones captures the impact of economic blight and its connection to a "hyper-politicized" populace. For Thompson, "...with so many Africans trapped in penury and suffering from family disruption, and with an unemployment rate of more than 50%, the African townships were riddled with crime; and criminal violence shaded into political violence as people sided with rival factions." [1, 190–191; 77, 245–246].

If economic blight is one explanatory factor associated with a "hyper-politicized" population, and a "hyper-politicized" population condition has been associated with the formation of groups with potential to use force, PAGAD, with its early experience working to tackle the social political problem of crime, should be considered a criminal "vigilante group," at least until around 1998. That is important for future research because economic blight's capacity to generate and sustain crime such as vigilantism, and its potential to interface with deeply divided political groups in society, seems to skirt around the issue that scholars have found no direct link between socio-economic status (SES) and terrorism [11, 135, 221 n58].

It follows that if broad based evidence can be produced that both explanatory factors are associated, perhaps in a "feedback loop" where each make the other more powerful, that might help to explain conditions where links between "hyper-politicized populations" and the formation of groups that use of terrorism become more discernable. In other words, "socio-economic status" (SES) might in certain select and acute circumstances, act as an intervening variable between "hyper-politicized society" and the formation of groups that use terrorism.

PAGAD entered into its third phase of its "lifecycle" around 1998. The watershed event for PAGAD's transformation from a criminal group that used terrorism, to a full-fledged terrorist organization, was the 1998 terrorist assault against the Planet Hollywood complex in Cape Town [79]. Interestingly enough, PAGAD denies responsibility for that terrorist assault. As Lefkowitz reports, that situation presents analysts with an unusual case where a fledgling terrorist group professes to act only within the narrower scope of its previous phase of development, as a "vigilante" group, with what was its singular focus on drug lords and organized crime.

In early parts of this book, emphasis has been placed on the presence of political ideology, rather than a set of narrower political objectives, as a critical characteristic to distinguish terrorist groups from criminal organizations that use terrorism. That PAGAD appears to have embraced the political ideology of Islamic extremists sometime around the time of the Plant Hollywood restaurant terrorist assault in 1998 is very close to the implicit embrace of an Islamic extremist political ideology, even if that is not articulated explicitly by PAGAD.

PAGAD's fledgling and virulent anti-Western posture, if not indicative of a full blown political ideology, certainly appears to comport with the political ideology and goals of many Islamic extremist organizations. Indeed, Lefkowitz points out that PAGAD's leaders have started to use standard Islamic extremist terminology such as Shaheed ("martyrs") and "Mujahideen" ("holy warriors") to describe its activists, at least since 2004 [49]. Lefkowitz also reports that one possible reason for the Plant Hollywood terrorist attack was that it served as retribution for American operations in Afghanistan and Sudan [49].

At the same time, it is not clear exactly when and even if PAGAD has adopted a formal political platform indicative of a political ideology that would be congruent with its actions. Nonetheless, whether or not there has been a formal transition into the domain of political ideology almost seems tangential or beside the point. In this case, PAGAD's behavior makes the case on its own for a determination that PAGAD has evolved into a terrorist group in the first phase of its development [47; 48, 253–263].

Lastly, it is important to note there is no clear consensus about whether or not PAGAD has had significant international ties to terrorist organizations such as al-Qaeda. Likewise, the fundamental nature of PAGAD's links to Middle Eastern states remains opaque. For example, there some scholars assert that PAGAD has ties to Algeria, or Iran or both, but definitive proof of those connections is hard to find [1, 187 n1]. Likewise, some scholars mention that PAGAD might have had ties to Colonel Muamaar Qaddafi in Libya [20, 497–498].

6.9 Terrorist Assault Business Vulnerability Index (TABVI)

As in the cases of India, Mexico, and Brazil, a TABVI score is calculated for South Africa. The TABVI score for South Africa is "5.96" (28/4.7 = 5.96) [81, 82].[19]

That TABVI score provides an overall estimate of business related terrorism threat to commercial interests in South Africa. A TABV score of "5.96" placed South Africa at the lower end of the range of raw TABVI scores produced for India (156.6), Thailand (83.7), Mexico (9.375), and Brazil (2.58). That result suggests the overall terrorism threat to South African commercial interests was comparatively low between 2013 and 2018. Next, that raw TABVI score of 5.96 is divided by1.566 to obtain a standardized TABVI score of 3.80 for South Africa.

The TABVI numerator was obtained when the number of business target attacks were summed for the 2013–2018 time interval. As in the case of Mexico, the TABVI sub-component frequencies and percentages presented will differ from those presented in Fig. 6.3. For the TABVI numerator, two (2) terrorist assaults against "private establishments" and one (1) on a "telecommunications" target happened in 2013. In 2014, three terrorist assaults (3) happened at "private establishments." In 2015, one (1) terrorist assault involved a "transportation" target, while one (1) "private establishment" was targeted. In 2017, there were four (4) private establishment attacks and one (1) telecommunications" attack.

The numerator of South Africa's TABVI score was also broken down by industry type to assess the threat of terrorism to specific South African industries under consideration. The breakdown of results suggested "private establishments" had the **highest** level of threat/vulnerability with a score of 4.89 (23/4.7). That was followed by a "telecommunications" target rate of 0.426 (2/4.7). In comparison, the South

[19] Recall the TABVI denominator is the *World Economic Forum*'s "business costs of terrorism" survey score of "4.7" for South Africa.

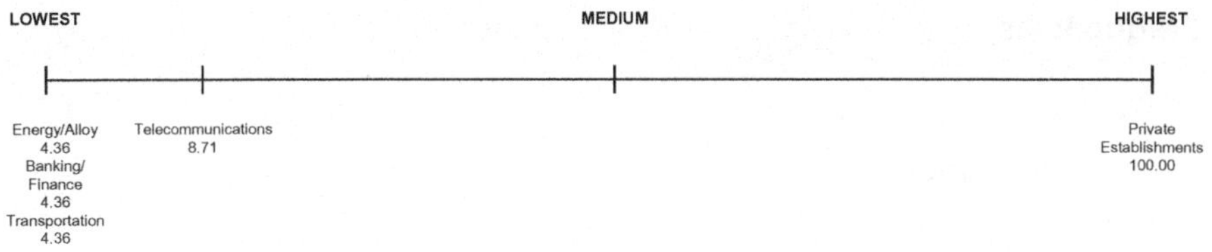

Fig. 6.1 South Africa industry vulnerability spectrum standardized TABVI scores < 1 to 10 = low risk; 11–50 = medium risk; 51–100 = high risk

African industries that experienced the **lowest** level of terrorism threat/vulnerability in that time interval included: "Energy/Alloy" with a score of 0.213 (1/4.7 = 0.213), "banking finance" with 0.213 (1/4.7 = 0.213), and "transportation" targets with 0.213 (1/4.7 = 0.213).

At this juncture, the raw TABVI scores for South Africa are transformed into standardized TABVI scores. As "private establishments" had the highest raw TABVI score for any South African industry with "4.89," so "4.89" is multiplied by 20.45 = 100.00 for standardization purposes. Hence, the standardized TABVI scores for industries in South Africa are: Energy Alloy (4.36); banking/finance (4.36); transportation (4.36); telecommunications (8.71); private establishments (100.00). (See Fig. 6.1).

6.10 Some Empirical Observations About South African Terrorism

6.10.1 Relative Frequencies of Commercial Target Terrorist Assaults by Year

As in the case of Mexico, the range of data collection was extended six years to include South African terrorist assaults between 2007 and 2018. The reason why was because for South Africa, there were only twenty-six (26) business related terrorist assaults chronicled by GTD and Mickolus between 2013 and 2018.

When those data were broken down by year, it was found that 2018 was the peak year with 13 terrorist assaults or 46.4% of the total directed at commercial interests. In turn, 2017 had the second highest amount of business related terrorism documented with 17.9% (5/28 acts). The years 2013 and 2014 ranked third, each with 10.7% of the total (3/28 acts), followed by 2015, where 7.1% of the total amount (2/28 acts) happened. The years 2007 and 2008 were trough years, each with 3.6% of the total or one terrorist assault a piece. The year 2018 had the highest concentration of terrorist assaults in South Africa between 2007 and 2018, with thirteen (13) terrorist attacks. (see Fig. 6.2).

Frequencies

Statistics

Year

N	Valid	28
	Missing	0

Year

		Frequency	Percent	Valid Percent	Cumulative Percent
Valid	2007	1	3.6	3.6	3.6
	2008	1	3.6	3.6	7.1
	2013	3	10.7	10.7	17.9
	2014	3	10.7	10.7	28.6
	2015	2	7.1	7.1	35.7
	2017	5	17.9	17.9	53.6
	2018	13	46.4	46.4	100.0
	Total	28	100.0	100.0	

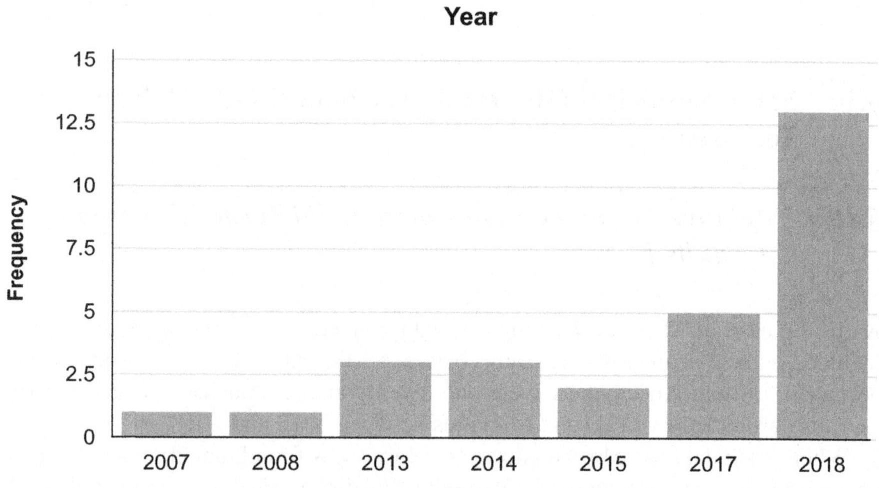

Fig. 6.2 Relative frequency of South Africa terrorist attacks by Year, 2007–2018

6.11 Terrorist Assaults by Business Target-Type, Firm Origin, Terrorist Group Type, and Terrorist Group

When attack rates against South African business targets were compared, it was found that at 82.1% (23/28 acts), the highest percentage of business related terrorist attacks between 2007 and 2018 were directed against "private establishments." Attacks against "telecommunications" targets placed a very distant second with 7.1% (2/28 acts). Ranking third, "energy/alloy," "banking/finance," and "transportation" targets in South Africa each accounted for only 3.6% of the total number with one terrorist assault a piece (see Fig. 6.3).

When the South Africa data were broken down by "Firm Origin," the results revealed that with 71.4% (20/28 acts), nearly three-fourths of all targets attacked were "foreign" firms. In contrast, 28.6% of commercial interest targets attacked were national targets. That 71.4% foreign firms rate reflected the spate of terrorist attacks against Somali and Nigerian establishments that took place primarily from 2017 to 2018, and that several terrorist assault targets were tied to Woolworths Group Limited headquarters, based in New South Wales, Australia [53, 89–94, 96–98, 103–107, 111].[20]

In the case of "foreign" business targets owned by Somali or Nigerian merchants, five attacks involved stores owned by Somali merchants, while nine attacks were directed at Nigerian owned small businesses. There was one terrorist attack where specific victim nationality was not noted in the Mickolus data chronology. It appeared those anonymous terrorist assaults sometimes occurred in clusters as indicated below (see Fig. 6.4) [57, 124].[21]

---

[20] For GTD, while the term "Nationality of Target South Africa" was used to describe Woolworths Group Limited stores, that failed to capture the foreign source of Woolworth Group Limited. At the same time, it was unclear whether or not some of those Somali and Nigerian small business owners were South African citizens, so the coding scheme for "Target: National/Foreign" in this study followed GTD data descriptions of "Nationality of Target Somalia" or "Nationality of Target Nigeria" to code those events.

[21] ***For Somali establishments***, see Global Terrorism Database (GTD) "South Africa" GTD ID: 201412110082, Date: December 11, 2014, (entry #7); Global Terrorism Database (GTD) "South Africa" GTD ID: 201701240031, Date: January 24, 2017, (entry #10); Global Terrorism Database (GTD) "South Africa" GTD ID: 201702020020, Date: February 2, 2017 (entry #11); Global Terrorism Database (GTD) "South Africa" GTD ID: 201702020021, Date: February 2, 2017 (entry #12); Global Terrorism Database (GTD) "South Africa" GTD ID; Global Terrorism Database (GTD) "South Africa" GTD ID: 201702020022, Date: February 2, 2017 (entry #13). ***For Nigerian establishments***, see Global Terrorism Database (GTD) "South Africa" GTD ID: 201810210008, Date: October 21, 2018 (entry #18); Global Terrorism Database "South Africa" GTD ID: 201810210009, Date: October 21, 2018 (entry #19); Global Terrorism Database (GTD) "South Africa" GTD ID: 201810210010, Date: October 21, 2018 (entry #20); Global Terrorism Database (GTD) "South Africa" GTD ID: 201810210011, Date: October 21, 2018 (entry#21); Global Terrorism Database (GTD) "South Africa" GTD ID: 201810210012, Date: October 21, 2018 (entry #22); Global Terrorism Database (GTD) "South Africa" GTD ID: 201810210013, Date: October 21, 2018 (entry #23); Global Terrorism Database (GTD)"South Africa" GTD ID: 201810210014, Date: October 21, 2018 (entry #24); Global Terrorism Database (GTD)"South Africa" GTD ID: 201810210015, Date: October 21, 2018 (entry #25); Global Terrorism Database (GTD) "South Africa" GTD ID:

Frequencies

Statistics

Bus.Target

N	Valid	28
	Missing	0

Bus.Target

		Frequency	Percent	Valid Percent	Cumulative Percent
Valid	Energy/Alloy	1	3.6	3.6	3.6
	Private Establishments	23	82.1	82.1	85.7
	Telecommunications	2	7.1	7.1	92.9
	Banking/Finance	1	3.6	3.6	96.4
	Transportation	1	3.6	3.6	100.0
	Total	28	100.0	100.0	

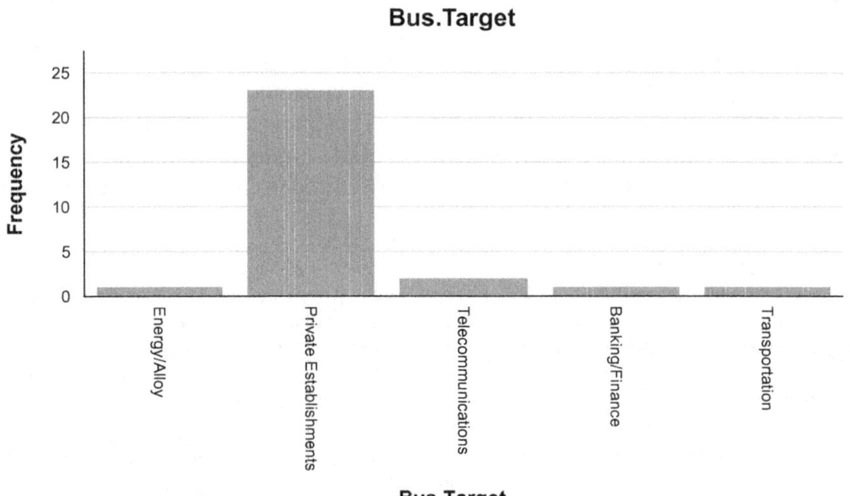

Fig. 6.3 Relative frequency of South Africa terrorist attacks by Business Targets, 2007–2018

When "Group-Type" was examined for this twelve year time interval between January 1, 2007 and December 31, 2018, an "Islamic extremist" group or groups comprised the one identifiable group-type involved in South African commercial target attacks in that time interval. Attacks by "Islamic extremist" groups, proto-groups or "Islamic elements" accounted for five acts or 17.9% of the total. In turn,

201810210016, Date: October 21, 2018 (entry #26). In addition, Mickolus chronicles one terrorist assault on February 26, 2015 (entry #27) without specific reference to victim nationality.

Frequencies

Statistics

TargNatForei

N	Valid	28
	Missing	0

TargNatForei

		Frequency	Percent	Valid Percent	Cumulative Percent
Valid	National	8	28.6	28.6	28.6
	Foreign	20	71.4	71.4	100.0
	Total	28	100.0	100.0	

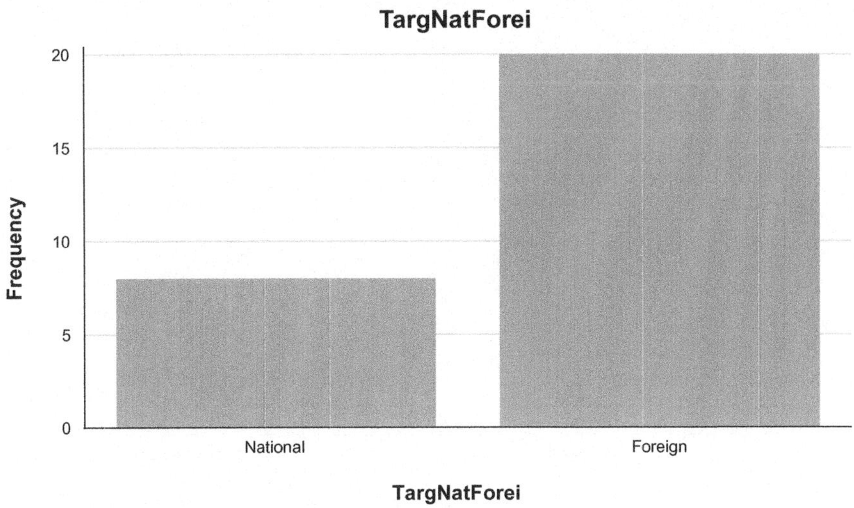

Fig. 6.4 Relative frequency of South Africa terrorist attacks by Foreign Business Target and National Business Target, 2007–2018

the vast majority of business related terrorist assaults chronicled were anonymous terrorist assaults. With 23/28 acts, "anonymous" terrorist assaults accounted for a full 82.1% of the total amount (see Fig. 6.5).

There was only one terrorist group generally recognized as having attacked a business target during this time interval. That terrorist group was the People Against Gangsterism and Drugs (PAGAD), and even in that case, PAGAD denied responsibility. In this non-lethal and injury free terrorist assault, a bomb exploded at the Velocity Cars dealership in Cape Town's Athlone section in the City of Cape Town Metropolitan Municipality [30] (see Fig. 6.6).

Frequencies

Statistics

GroupTy

N	Valid	28
	Missing	0

GroupTy

		Frequency	Percent	Valid Percent	Cumulative Percent
Valid	Anonymous	23	82.1	82.1	82.1
	Islamic Extremist	5	17.9	17.9	100.0
	Total	28	100.0	100.0	

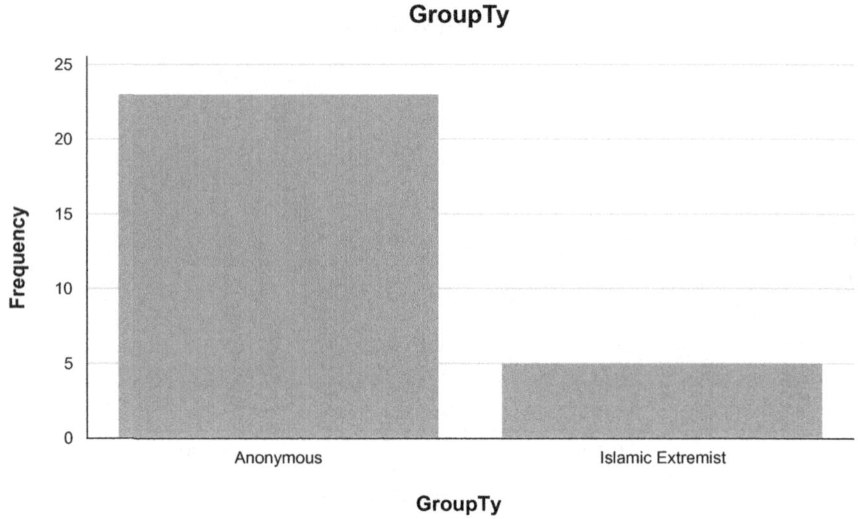

Fig. 6.5 Relative frequency of South Africa terrorist attacks by Group-Type, 2007–2018

6.12 Business Related Terrorist Assaults by Province

A frequencies distribution of business related terrorist assaults by province suggested that Gauteng Province, with 44.4% or twelve attacks (12/27 acts) had the highest rate of business related terrorist assaults in the eleven year period under consideration. In turn, 29.6% of all business related terrorist assaults (8/27 acts) happened in Western Cape Province. The remainder of all chronicled terrorist assaults against commercial interests were distributed across three provinces: KwaZulu-Natal with 18.5% (5/27 acts), North West Province with 3.7% (1/27 acts), and Free State Province with 3.7% (1/27 acts) (see Fig. 6.7).

Frequencies

Statistics

GroupName

N	Valid	28
	Missing	0

GroupName

		Frequency	Percent	Valid Percent	Cumulative Percent
Valid	PAGAD	1	3.6	3.6	3.6
	Anonymous	27	96.4	96.4	100.0
	Total	28	100.0	100.0	

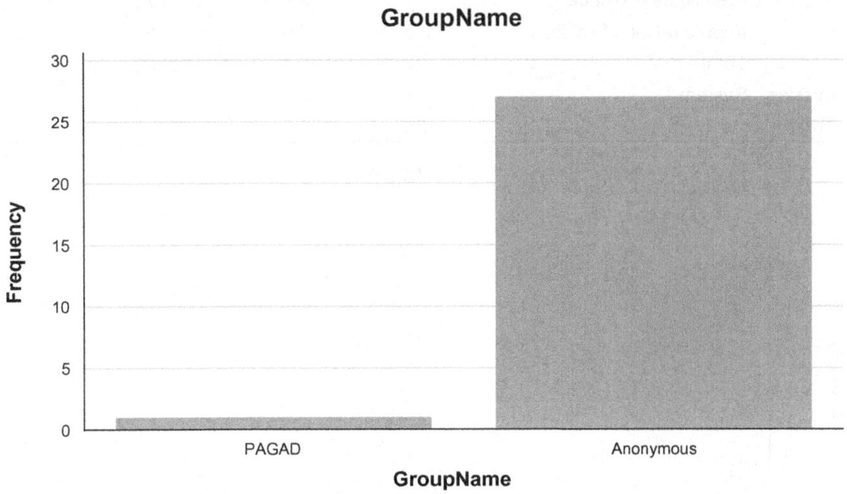

Fig. 6.6 Relative frequency of South Africa terrorist attacks by Terrorist Group, 2007–2018

6.13 Business Related Terrorist Assault by Municipality

When business related terrorist attacks in South Africa were broken down based on South African municipality, the results suggested at a full 40.7%, the City of Johannesburg Metropolitan Municipality with 11/27 acts, had the highest rate of business related attacks. In contrast, terrorist attacks against commercial interests in City of Cape Town Metropolitan Municipality accounted for 29.6% of the total (8/27 acts).

In turn, eThekwini Metropolitan Municipality in KwaZulu-Natal Province experienced 18.5% (5/27 acts) of the total. At the other extreme, Bojanala Platinum District Municipality in Gauteng Province accounted for less than one-tenth of the total at

Frequencies

Statistics

Province

N	Valid	27
	Missing	1

Province

		Frequency	Percent	Valid Percent	Cumulative Percent
Valid	Gauteng Province	12	42.9	44.4	44.4
	North West Province	1	3.6	3.7	48.1
	Western Cape Province	8	28.6	29.6	77.8
	Free State Province	1	3.6	3.7	81.5
	KwaZulu-Natal Province	5	17.9	18.5	100.0
	Total	27	96.4	100.0	
Missing	System	1	3.6		
Total		28	100.0		

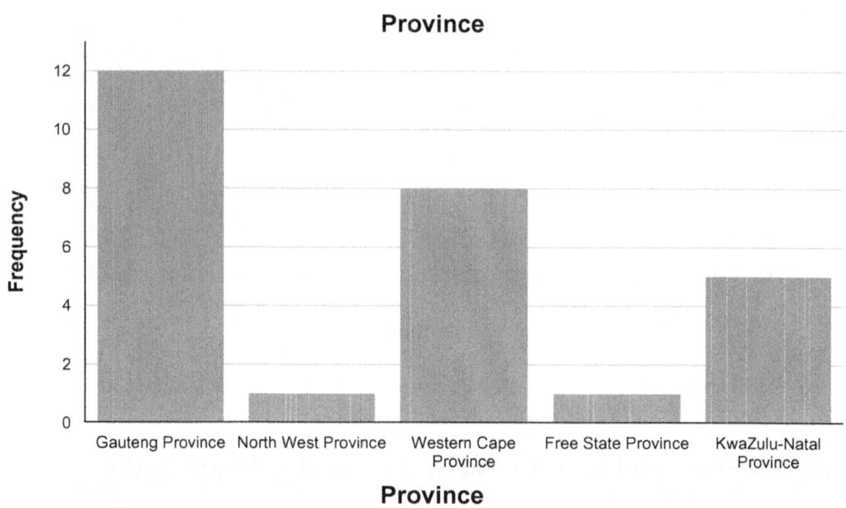

Fig. 6.7 Relative frequency of South Africa terrorist attacks by Province, 2007–2018

7.4% (2/27 acts), while only 3.7% of the total (1/27 acts) took place in Fezile Dabi District Municipality in Free State Province (see Fig. 6.8).

Frequencies

Statistics

Municipality

N	Valid	27
	Missing	1

Municipality

		Frequency	Percent	Valid Percent	Cumulative Percent
Valid	Bojanala Platinum District Municipality	2	7.1	7.4	7.4
	City of Cape Town Metropolitan Munici	8	28.6	29.6	37.0
	Fezile Dabi District Municipality	1	3.6	3.7	40.7
	eThekwini Metropolitan Municipality	5	17.9	18.5	59.3
	City of Johannesburg Metropolitan Munici	11	39.3	40.7	100.0
	Total	27	96.4	100.0	
Missing	System	1	3.6		
Total		28	100.0		

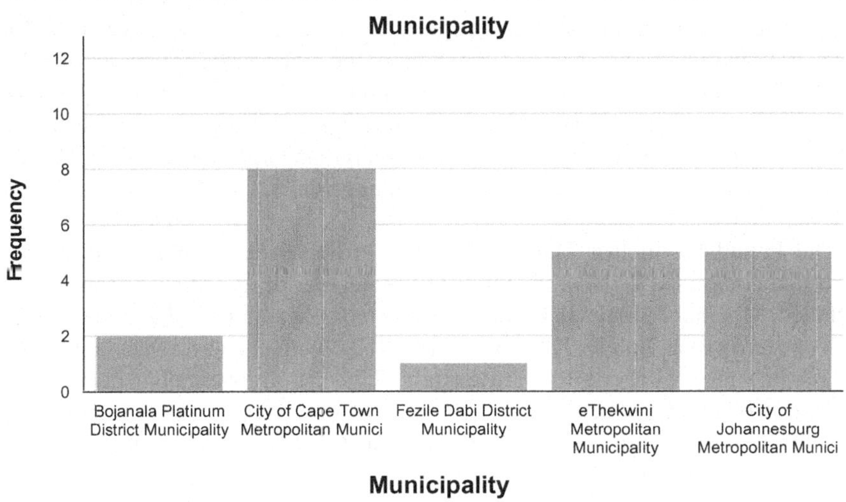

Fig. 6.8 Relative frequency of South Africa terrorist attacks by Municipality, 2007–2018

6.14 Terrorist Assault by City, Town, Township

A more granular analysis showed that terrorist assaults against South African commercial interests happened in cities, towns, and in one South African township between 2007 and 2018. The city of Johannesburg (Guateng Province) had the highest concentration of terrorist attacks against commercial interests (11/27 acts) with 40.7% or some two-fifths of the total. The city of Cape Town (Western Cape Province) ranked second, with about one-fourth of the total at 25.9% (7/27 acts).

In turn, the city of Durban (KwaZulu-Natal Province) had the third highest amount of business related terrorist assaults with 14.8% (4/27 acts). The remainder of commercial interest terrorist assaults in South Africa were distributed across five geographical locales, each with 3.7% of the total (1/27 acts). Those included the "tiny town" of Pelindaba (Gauteng Province), the towns of Mooinooi (North West Province), Strand (Western Cape Province), the township of Kwa Mashu (KwaZulu-Natal Province), and the city of Sasolburg (Free State Province) [66] (see Fig. 6.9).

6.15 Business Firms Attacked, Assault Type, and Reaction to Political Events

There were nine identifiable business target attacks in South Africa between 2007 and 2018. Woolworths' Group Limited experienced the highest rate of terrorist attacks at 38.5% (5/13 acts). There was one government owned energy facility (i.e., Pelindaba nuclear plant), one other government owned target and six other identifiable business firms that experienced terrorist attacks. In fact, civilian targets made up 92.9% of the total (26/28 acts) while government targets comprised 7.1% of the total (2/28 acts) (see Fig. 6.10).

The Pelindaba nuclear plant in Guateng Province experienced one attack in 2015 that comprised 7.7% of the total. The remainder of identifiable firms attacked included, Mooinooi Shopping Center with one terrorist assault (7.7%), Velocity Cars with one terrorist assault (7.7%), Karabo FM Radio with one terrorist assault (7.7%), Belgravia Autos with one terrorist assault (7.7%), the government owned South African Broadcasting Corporation with one terrorist assault (7.7%), Intercape Bus with one terrorist assault (7.7%), and Moneypoint Gold and Jewelry with one terrorist attack (7.7%) (see Fig. 6.11).

In the case of terrorist assault-type, different types of bombs (i.e., improvised explosive devices) were the method of choice to attack commercial interests. A full 42.9% or over two fifths of all attacks against commercial interests (12/28) involved explosive devices, while a little over one-third of all business related terrorist attacks at 35.7% (10/28 acts) involved arson. In turn, shootings accounted for the remainder of the terrorist acts under consideration with 21.4% (6/28 acts) or a little over one-fifth of the total (see Fig. 6.12).

Frequencies

Statistics

CityVillage

N	Valid	27
	Missing	1

CityVillage

		Frequency	Percent	Valid Percent	Cumulative Percent
Valid	Pelindaba	1	3.6	3.7	3.7
	Mooinooi	1	3.6	3.7	7.4
	Cape Town	7	25.0	25.9	33.3
	Sasolburg	1	3.6	3.7	37.0
	Kwa Mashu	1	3.6	3.7	40.7
	Strand	1	3.6	3.7	44.4
	Durban	4	14.3	14.8	59.3
	Johannesburg	11	39.3	40.7	100.0
	Total	27	96.4	100.0	
Missing	System	1	3.6		
Total		28	100.0		

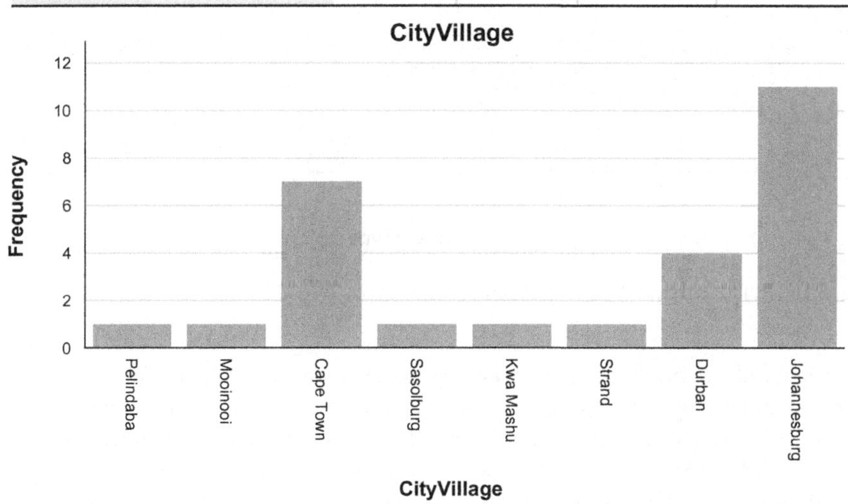

Fig. 6.9 Relative frequency of South Africa terrorist attacks by City, Town, and Village, 2007–2018

Frequencies

Statistics

TargetType

N	Valid	28
	Missing	0

TargetType

		Frequency	Percent	Valid Percent	Cumulative Percent
Valid	Civilian	26	92.9	92.9	92.9
	Government	2	7.1	7.1	100.0
	Total	28	100.0	100.0	

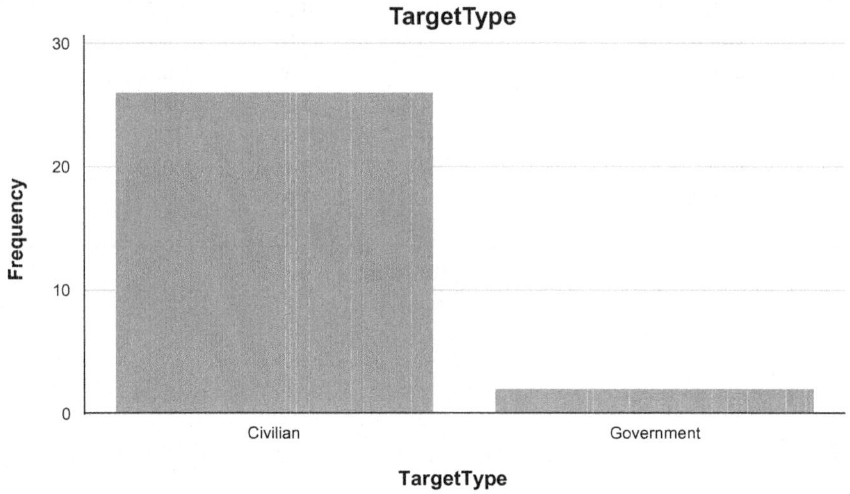

Fig. 6.10 Relative frequency of South Africa target-type, 2007–2018

When links to political events were analyzed, it was found that a full 92.9% of all terrorist attacks against commercial interests (26/28 acts) were unrelated to political events. There were two terrorist acts linked to political events. One terrorist assault against Karbo FM Radio in 2013 was linked to government policies, namely the abandonment of attempts to blend two municipalities in the Free State [31, 61]. The other terrorist assault tied to "business practices" happened in 2017, when a South African Broadcasting Corporation (SABC) journalist who protested against SABC policy not to broadcast violent demonstrations, was attacked [32, 58] (see Fig. 6.13).

Frequencies

Statistics

FirmName

N	Valid	13
	Missing	15

FirmName

		Frequency	Percent	Valid Percent	Cumulative Percent
Valid	Pelindaba Nuclear Plant	1	3.6	7.7	7.7
	Mooinooi Shopping Center	1	3.6	7.7	15.4
	Velocity Cars	1	3.6	7.7	23.1
	Karabo FM Radio	1	3.6	7.7	30.8
	Belgravia Autos	1	3.6	7.7	38.5
	Woolworths	5	17.9	38.5	76.9
	South African Broadcasting Corp.	1	3.6	7.7	84.6
	Intercape Bus	1	3.6	7.7	92.3
	Moneypoint Gold & Jewelry	1	3.6	7.7	100.0
	Total	13	46.4	100.0	
Missing	System	15	53.6		
Total		28	100.0		

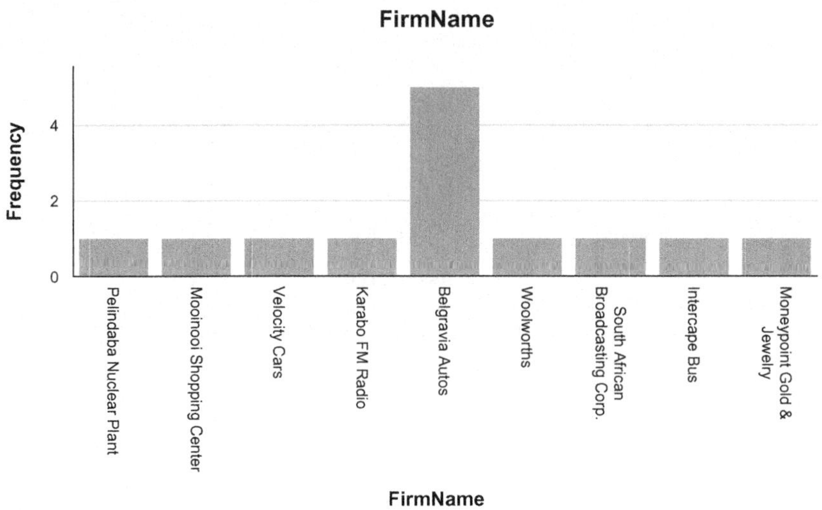

Fig. 6.11 Relative frequency of South Africa terrorist attacks by Firm, 2007–2018

Frequencies

Statistics

AssaultType

N	Valid	28
	Missing	0

AssaultType

		Frequency	Percent	Valid Percent	Cumulative Percent
Valid	Bombing	12	42.9	42.9	42.9
	Shooting	6	21.4	21.4	64.3
	Arson	10	35.7	35.7	100.0
	Total	28	100.0	100.0	

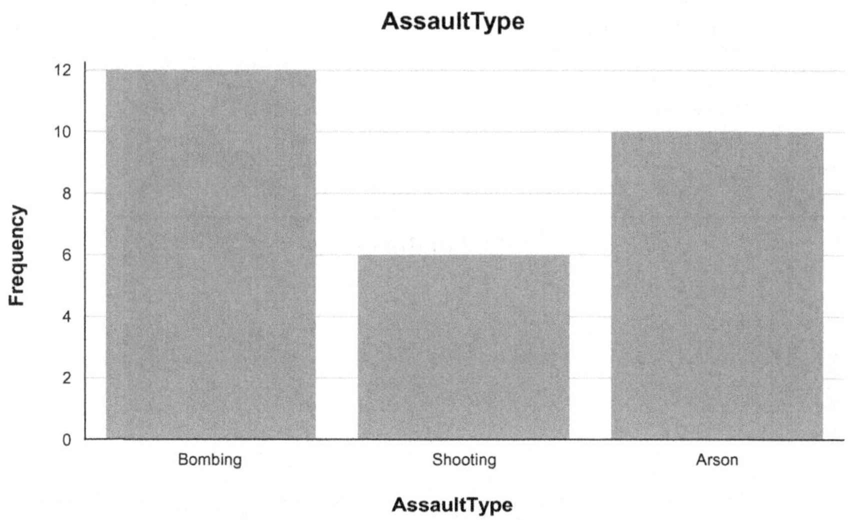

Fig. 6.12 Relative frequency of South Africa terrorist attacks by Assault-Type, 2007–2018

Frequencies

Statistics

ReacPolEvnt

N	Valid	28
	Missing	0

ReacPolEvnt

		Frequency	Percent	Valid Percent	Cumulative Percent
Valid	No Relation	26	92.9	92.9	92.9
	Govt. Policies	1	3.6	3.6	96.4
	Business Practices	1	3.6	3.6	100.0
	Total	28	100.0	100.0	

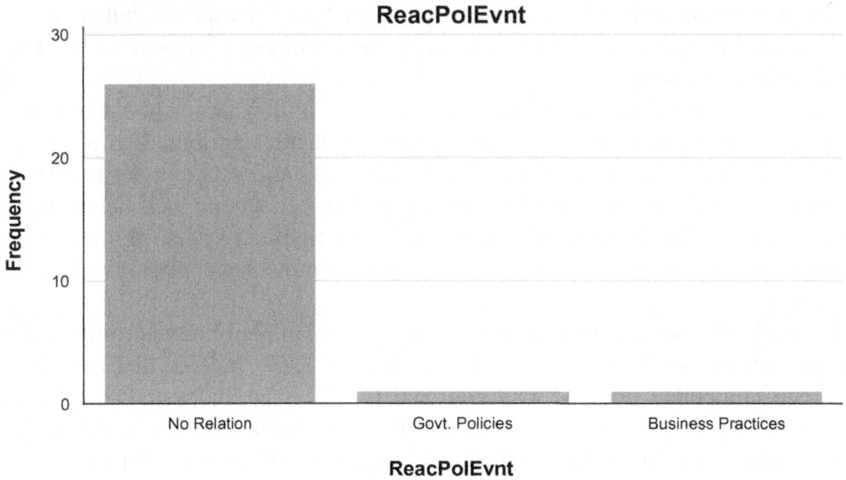

Fig. 6.13 Relative frequency of South Africa terrorist attacks by Political Event, 2007–2018

6.16 Conclusions

This chapter provides political context to track the direction of political protest in South Africa and the eventual use of terrorism by certain select organizations. Those included, but were not necessarily limited to, ANC's Umkhonto we Sizwe, and Poqo, itself the military branch of the Pan-Africanist Congress. The first part of this chapter puts primary focus on "oppositional" terrorism within the formal system of apartheid (1950–1994) in addition to political opposition and conflict in South Africa's segregation system that was codified in law under the Union of South Africa (1919).

South Africa's black emancipation movement qualifies as "justifiable insurgency" from an international law point of view, but terrorism has also left its mark. That leaves the reader with critical and unresolved theoretical questions about thresholds between "justifiable insurgency" and terrorism, issues raised in Chapter One and Chapter Two of this book. It compels us to think about how to square conditions in the larger world of action that by necessity require forceful response, but at the same time, create nuances and subtleties to complicate operationalization of the notion of "justifiable insurgency."

One observation that stems from this analysis is how watershed racist South African government policy decisions under apartheid contributed to a chain of events that ultimately undercut broad and long-haul nation-state interests, not only in regards to the physical security, and political and economic well-being of most South Africans, but in regional and international political system terms, because of the transnational nature of black emancipation movements after 1960 [5, 3–5, 302–303].

For example, the pass law system with its draconian punishments resulted in the Sharpstown massacre by South African police in 1960. Indeed, that act of state terrorism compelled both African National Congress (ANC) and Pan-Africanist Congress (PAC) leaders to resort to the use of force, which in some cases for the MK and in many cases for the Pan-Africanist Congress, qualified as terrorism.

Another example of how watershed South African government policy ultimately spawned acts of terrorism against the backdrop of systemic and sustained state terrorism, was the decision by the South African government to use Afrikanns as the language of instruction in schools. For Hirson, that bureaucratic decision was designed as a method of "social control" but it ultimately undercut that objective as it served as the primary impetus for the Soweto uprising in 1976 [39, 92, 94–95, 66]. In the Soweto rebellion, for example, systemic state terrorism that included brutal beatings of children was conducted by the police, while more sporadic acts of "insurgent terrorism" happened.

This chapter also surveys the use of terrorism by anonymous stakeholders and the People Against Gangsterism and Drugs (PAGAD) in South Africa's post 1994 era. What is significant here is the PAGAD experience, as PAGAD evolved from a criminal "vigilante" group devoted to attacks on criminal syndicalists, to a terrorist organization. PAGAD began as a criminal organization that embraced aspects of

Islamic theology, in ways reminiscent of how La Familia Michoacán in Mexico embraced its own notion Christianity, but apparently evolved past the point that La Familia Michoacán had reached in its "life-cycle" history.

Prior to 1998 before its attack on the Planet Hollywood restaurant, PAGAD could still be classified as a criminal "vigilante" group as it straddled the threshold between criminal group and terrorist organization. It was able to do that even more than La Familia Michoacán could because PAGAD satisfied another terrorist organization criterion—it had legitimate constituent supporters by contrast to La Familia Michoacán, whose constituents were and remain coerced to support La Familia Michoacán by means of the threat or use of force. Those relationships between criminal gangs and terrorist groups and the continuously evolving nature of PAGAD can be depicted on a continuum with "criminal gangs" towards the left axis and "terrorist groups" towards the right axis (see Fig. 6.14).

Before 1998, what appeared to be the case was that PAGAD lacked a clearly articulated political ideology to qualify as a terrorist organization. However, PAGAD has achieved what amounts to that stage of developmental growth precisely because of its de-facto political ideology, if not a publicly disseminated one, showcased with its attack on the Planet Hollywood restaurant and its implicit embrace of an Islamic extremist political ideology that targets the West (Fig. 6.13).

In other words, the PAGAD case demonstrates that a continuously evolving criminal group does not, in some circumstances, necessarily have to craft and disseminate a coherent political ideology to qualify as a terrorist group. In the case of PAGAD, that criminal "vigilante" group crossed the criminal-terrorist organization threshold to became a terrorist organization when it began to frame its actions, including its terrorist assault against the Planet Hollywood restaurant, within the context of the Islamic extremist discourse.

That observation is an important addition to the beginnings of a conceptualization of criminal group evolution into a terrorist group. For one thing, PAGAD's "silent evolution" is one strand of evolution from criminal group to terrorist organization that has not ordinarily been considered by some analysts in the terrorist group development process. In ways reminiscent of the term "quiet revolution" used to describe the incremental changes in U.S. policy associated with President Franklin Delano Roosevelt's "New Deal," "silent evolution" in this context can happen without public communication or declarative statements and actions that signal the emergence of a new terrorist group.

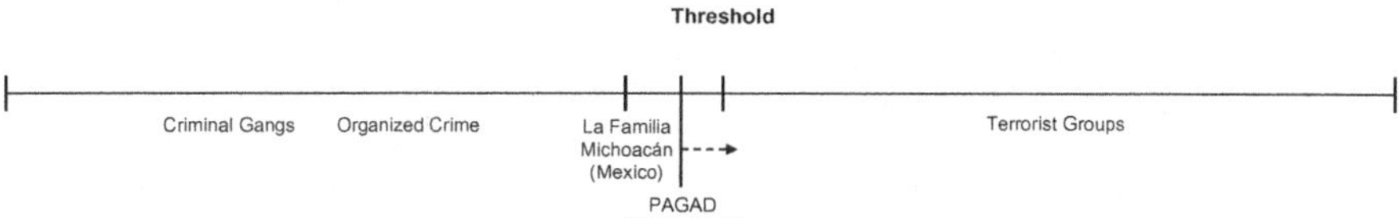

Fig. 6.14 Criminal enterprise to terrorist group development the case of PAGAD

In addition PAGAD's "silent evolution" demonstrates the importance of world events in the context of "intensive globalization" that interact with "nation-state" and "individual level" explanatory factors associated with that evolution process [59, 80]. For example, there is the continued influence of the 1979 Iranian revolution on many terrorist and criminal groups that sometimes frame opposition and actions vis a vis governments in Islamic terms, narrative, or context.

In terms of the statistical analysis, the small number of business related terrorist assaults South Africa experienced between the 2007 and 2018 time period under consideration (N = 28) limited the statistical analysis to a presentation of relative frequencies results. In terms of its aggregate TABVI score, South Africa scored a "5.96." That "5.96" score and the standardized TABVI score of 3.80 for South Africa, placed the threat to South African business at the lower end of the threat spectrum when compared to the threat commercial interests experienced in India, Thailand, Mexico, and Brazil.

References

1. Bangstad S (2005) Hydra's heads: PAGAD and responses to the PAGAD phenomenon in a cape Muslim community. J S Afr Stud 31(1):187–208. https://doi.org/10.1080/03057070500035919
2. Banton M (1967) Race relations. Tavistock Publications
3. Boesak WA (1993) God's wrathful children toward an ethic of vengeance, retribution, and renewal for a post-apartheid nation. Ph.D. Dissertation, University of Cape Town. https://open.uct.ac.za/bitstream/handle/11427/17354/thesis_hum_1993_boesak_willem_andreas.pdf
4. Brown J (2010) The DurbaSoweto strikes of 1973: political identities and the management of protest. In: Beinart W, Dawson MC (eds) Popular politics and resistance movements in South Africa. Wits University Press
5. Brown S (1994) Faces of power: United States foreign policy from Truman to Clinton, 2nd edn. Columbia University Press
6. Chasdi RJ (1994) Terrorism: stratagems for remediation from an international law perspective. Shofar 12(4):59–86
7. Chasdi RJ (1999) Serenade of suffering: a portrait of Middle East terrorism, 1968–1993. Lexington Books
8. Chasdi RJ (2002) Tapestry of terror: a portrait of Middle East terrorism, 1994–1999. Lexington Books
9. Chasdi RJ (2010) Counterterror offensives for the ghost war world: the rudiments of counterterrorism policy. Lexington Books
10. Chasdi RJ (2013) Terrorist group dynamics through the lens of the Tigantourine assault in Algeria. Stability 2(2):1–10. http://www.stabilityjournal.org/article/view/sta.bw/106
11. Chasdi RJ (2018) Corporate security crossroads responding to terrorism, cyberthreats, and other hazards in the global business environment. Praeger Publishers–ABC-CLIO
12. Chasdi RJ (2020) A typology of public private partnerships and its implications for counterterrorism and cyber-security. In: Vacca JR (ed) Online terrorist propaganda, recruitment, and radicalization. CRC Press
13. Chasdi RJ (2021) Prevention of major economic disruptions following acts of terrorism: the case of the Bali bombings of 2002 and 2005. In: Schmid AP (ed) Handbook of terrorism prevention and preparedness. ICCT
14. Clutterbuck R (1994) Terrorism in an unstable world. Routledge

15. Diamond L (1990) Nigeria: pluralism, statism and the struggle for democracy. In: Diamond L, Linz JL, Lipset SM (eds) Politics in developing countries: comparing experiences with democracy. Lynne Rienner
16. Diseko NJ (1992) The origins and development of the South African Student's Movement (SASM): 1968–1976. J S Afr Stud 18(1):40–62. https://www.jstor.org/stable/pdf/2637181
17. Dixon B, Johns L-M (2001, May) Gangs, Pagad & the state: vigilantism and revenge violence in the Western Cape. Violence and transition series. https://help.csvr.org.za/wp-content/uploads/2001/05/gangspagadstate.pdf
18. Du Toit A (1991) The National Committee for Liberation ("ARM") 1960–1964: sabotage and the question of the ideological subject. MA thesis, University of Cape Town
19. Encyclopedia Britannica (n.d.) Pan-Africanist congress of Azania South African organization. https://britannica.com/topic/Pan-Africanist-Congress-of-Azania#ref1046983
20. Esack F (1988) Three Islamic strands in the South African struggle for justice. Third World Quart 10(2):473–498. http://www.jstor.org/stable/3992653
21. Fox T (2016) War without end? Terrorism, policy and conflict management in Africa. In: Marongwe N, Mawere M (eds) Violence, politics and conflict management in Africa: envisioning transformation, peace and unity in the twenty-first century. Langaa Research & Publishing Common Initiative Group
22. Friedman S (1987) The struggle within the struggle: South African resistance strategies. Transformation (3). https://scholar.google.com/scholar?hl=en&as_sdt=0%2C21&q=The+Struggle+within+the+Struggle+Steven+Friedman&btnG=
23. Global Terrorism Database South Africa. GTD ID: 198911020008. 2 Nov 1989
24. Global Terrorism Database South Africa. GTD ID:199005230001. 23 May 1990
25. Global Terrorism Database South Africa. GTD ID: 199007040002. 4 July 1990
26. Global Terrorism Database South Africa. GTD ID: 199108090021. 9 Aug 1991
27. Global Terrorism Database South Africa. GTD ID:19920107007. 7 Jan 1992
28. Global Terrorism Database South Africa. GTD ID: 1992211280003. 28 Nov 1992
29. Global Terrorism Database South Africa. GTD ID:199212030004. 3 Dec 1992
30. Global Terrorism Database (GTD) South Africa. GTD ID: 201307250042. 24 July 2013
31. Global Terrorism Database (GTD) South Africa. GTD ID: 2013309070017. 7 Sept 2013
32. Global Terrorism Database (GTD) South Africa. GTD ID: 201701150018. 15 Jan 2017
33. Goodman PS (2017, 24 October) End of apartheid in South Africa? Not in economic terms. The New York Times. https://www.nytimes.com/2017/10/24/business/south-africa-economy-apartheid.html
34. Gurr TR (1988) Some characteristics of political terrorism in the 1960s. In: Stohl M (ed) The politics of terrorism third edition, revised and expanded. Marcel Dekker
35. Gurr TR, Harff B (1994) Ethnic conflict in world politics. Westview Press
36. Haasbroek J (n.d.) Founding venue of the African National Congress (1912), Wesleyan School, Fort Street, Waaihoek, Bloemfontein: Conclusion. Navors Nas Mus Bloemfontein 18(7). https://doi.org/10.10520/AJA00679208_840
37. Hafez MM (2003) Why Muslims rebel: repression and resistance in the Islamic world. Lynne Rienner
38. Hendricks MN (2020) Manufacturing terrorism in Africa: the securitisation of South African Muslims. Palgrave MacMillan
39. Hirson B (1979) Year of fire, year of ash: the Soweto Revolt: roots of revolution? Zed Press
40. Huntington SP (1968) Political order in changing societies. Yale University Press
41. Institute for Economics & Peace (2020) Al-Shabaab. In: Global terrorism index 2020: Measuring the impact of terrorism. https://www.economicsandpeace.org/wp-content/uploads/2020/11/GTI-2020-web-2.pdf
42. Jervis R (1976) Perception and misperception in international politics. Princeton University Press
43. Jukes JJ (1995) Opposition in South Africa: the leadership of Z.K. Matthews, Nelson Mandela and Stephen Biko. Praeger

44. Ka Plaatjie T (2012, 20 January) ANC has been home to many intellectuals. SowetanLive. https://www.sowetanlive.co.za/opinion/columnists/2012-01-20-anc-has-been-home-to-many-intellectuals/
45. Katz J, Tushaus D (2008) Terrorism and human rights: The South Africa and Northern Ireland experience. J Inst Justice Int Stud 8:182–199
46. KlidevAV (2006) Africa overview. In: Terrorism country by country. Nova Science Publishers
47. Lasswell HD (1935) World politics and personal insecurity. McGraw Hill, Whittlesey House
48. Lasswell H (1978) Terrorism and the political process. Terrorism 1(3/4):253–263
49. Lefkowitz J (2004, August 18) Terror's South African front. The National Interest. https://nationalinterest.org/article/terrors-south-african-front-2742
50. Lindblom CE (1980) The policy-making process, 2nd edn. Prentice Hall
51. Lodge T (1987) State of exile: The African National Congress of South Africa, 1976–1986. Third World Quart 9(1):1–27. https://www.jstor.org/stable/3991845
52. Mariotti M (2012) Labour markets during apartheid in South Africa. Econ History Rev 65(3):1100–1122. https://doi.org/10.1111/j.1468-0289.2011.00621.x?casa_token=8ZJa0Th-5UEAAAAA:Sep9ZGo_jvns3ejCDWBcdvhfFb5IztLYfi8wao_-2wHFwfJm8ZPl99fG8E6VsahImRPOkAjv-ij6lHg
53. Marongwe N, Mawere M (2016) Violence, identity and politics of belonging: The April 2015 Afrophobic attacks in South Africa and the emergence of some discourses. In: Marongwe N, Mawere M (eds) Violence, politics and conflict management in Africa: envisioning transformation, peace and unity in the twenty-first century. Langaa Research & Publishing Common Initiative Group
54. McCargo D (2008) Tearing apart the land: Islam and legitimacy in southern Thailand. Cornell University Press
55. McFarlane C (2003) Special report: terrorism in South Africa. Prehosp Disaster Med 18(2):133–139
56. Mickolus E (2014) Terrorism, 2008–2012: a world chronology. McFarland Company Inc
57. Mickolus E (2016) Terrorism, 2013–2015: a worldwide chronology. McFarland Company Inc
58. News 24 (2017, 27 January) SABC 8 journalist shot in face with pellet gun. https://www.news24.com/news24/sabc-8-journalist-shot-in-face-with-pellet-gun-20170127
59. Nye Jr JS (1993) Understanding international conflicts: an introduction to theory and history. Harper Collins College Publishers
60. O'Malley P (2022) Pan Africanist Congress (PAC). In: The O'Malley archives. Nelson Mandela Foundation, pp 1–8
61. Patel K (2013, 12 September) South Africa: burn it up—a Zamdela community radio station feels the political heat. Daily Maverick. https://www.dailymaverick.co.za/article/2013-09-12-burn-it-up-a-zamdela-community-radio-station-feels-the-political-heat/
62. Reiss Jr AJ, Roth JA (eds) (1993) Understanding and preventing violence. National Academy Press
63. Ross JI (1993) Structural causes of oppositional political terrorism: towards a causal model. J Peace Res 30(3):317–329
64. Ross JI, Gurr TR (1989) Why terrorism subsides: a comparative study of Canada and the United States. Comp Polit 21(4):76–107
65. Ross JI, Miller RR (1997) The effects of oppositional political terrorism: five actor base models. Low Intensity Conflict Law Enforcement 6(3):76–107
66. SA Venues.com (1999–2022) About Pelindaba. https://www.sa-venues.com/attractionsnwp/pelindaba.php
67. Skocpol T (1979) States and social revolutions: a comparative analysis of France, Russia and China. Cambridge University Press
68. Solomon H (2011) Playing ostrich: lessons learned from South Africa's response to terrorism. Africa Security Brief. https://apps.dtic.mil/sti/pdfs/ADA546781.pdf
69. Solomon H (2012) Researching terrorism in South Africa, more questions than answers. Sci Mil 4(2):153–157. https://scientiamilitaria.journals.ac.za/pub/article/view/1000

70. Solomon J (2007, 7 May) New report of terrorist camp in South Africa. Terrorism Focus 4(12). https://jamestown.org/program/new-report-of-terrorist-camp-in-south-africa/
71. South African History Online (n.d.) Poqo. https://www.sahistory.org.za/article/poqo
72. South African History Online (1999, 20 March) The Azanian People's Liberation Army disbands. https://www.sahistory.org.za/dated-event/azanian-peoples-liberation-army-apla-disbands
73. South African History Online (2021) The Group Act of 1950. https://www.sahistory.org.za/article/group-areas-act-1950
74. Swarns RL (2000, 20 April) For South African whites, money has no color. The New York Times. https://www.nytimes.com/2000/04/20/world/for-south-african-whites-money-has-no-color.html
75. The New York Times (1961, 18 December) South Africa blasts protest apartheid
76. Theen R, Wilson FL (1996) Comparative politics: an introduction to six countries. Prentice Hall
77. Thompson L (1995) The history of South Africa, Revised. Yale University Press
78. United Nations (n.d.) Ethnic cleansing—background. United Nations Office on Genocide Prevention and the Responsibility to Protect. https://www.un.org/en/genocideprevention/ethnic-cleansing.shtml
79. United States Department of State (1999) Patterns of global terrorism 1998 Africa review. https://1997-2001.state.gov/global/terrorism/1998Report/africa.html
80. Waltz KN (1959) Man, the state and war: a theoretical analysis. Columbia University Press
81. World Economic Forum (2017a) Global competitiveness index 2017–2018 reports. https://www.weforum.org/reports/the-global-competitiveness-report-2017-2018/#series=EOSQ033
82. World Economic Forum (2017b) Appendix C, The executive opinion survey: the voice of the business community. http://www3.weforum.org/docs/GCR2017-2018/04Backmatter/TheGlobalCompetitivenessReport2017%E2%80%932018AppendixC.pdf

Chapter 7
The Case of Thailand

7.1 Introduction

In the case of Thailand, the issue that elicits the most terrorism is the unresolved final status of the "deep south" or "far south" provinces, namely, Yala, Pattani, and Narathiwat. Both the historical sources of this fierce struggle and what generates and sustains it nowadays, involves the independence of Pattani and those surrounding areas in close proximity, from the control of Bangkok's ruling elite [22, 22–23; 35, 28, 40].[1]

This struggle is especially complex; there is debate among scholars and government officials even about its contemporary sources and origins. For example, McCargo reports there are several points of view about the sources of continued conflict. Those viewpoints range from the struggle as one waged by criminal elements in conjunction with corrupt Thai officials, to one waged by Salafists, to conflict reflective of broader struggle between monarchists and Thai officials, to perspectives that place emphasis on a nationalist-irredentist struggle with Islamic trappings [14, 307; 33, 154–155; 40, 10, 32, 26–27, 52, 6, 12–13].[2]

McCargo reports the nature of terrorism in Thailand has changed from the late twentieth century, to one now marked by terrorist group decentralization into cells and clusters of cells, and an increase in anonymous terrorist assaults [40, 142]. He suggests contemporary terrorism is elicited, at least in part, by Thai political inertia about its "deep south" problem. Hence, the 2004 Krue-Se mosque incident was "…a spectacular display of wild fury on the part of profoundly disenchanted Malay-Muslim youth. That latent fury signaled serious dangers ahead for Thailand's

---

[1] Thailand's fourteen "southern provinces" include, but are not limited to, Narathiwat, Yala, Phuket, Satun, Krabi, Phatthalung, Phang Naga, Surat Thani, and Nakhon Si Thammarat. In turn, the "Deep South" refers to Satun, Yala, Pattani, and Narathiwat, and twenty-five percent of Songkhla province (4/16 districts). Those four districts are: Channa, Nathawi, Sabai Yoi, and Thepa.

[2] That wide-ranging set of opinions reflect Allison's notion of "Miles Law," namely that "where you stand (on an issue) depends on where you sit.".

R. J. Chasdi, *Corporate Security Surveillance*, Advanced Sciences and Technologies for Security Applications, https://doi.org/10.1007/978-3-031-39550-5_7

legitimacy and authority in the Southern border provinces." [22, 21; 35, 11; 40, 146, 57; 65, 55, 43].[3]

As Poocharoen relates, that political inertia stems primarily from "bureaucratic politics" effects, where various stakeholders within and across Thailand's state and society apparatus compete to control the national security agenda, and implementation of counterterrorism policies [14, 307; 41, 14, 26; 47, 194–195, 201, 191, 187]. That condition of fierce competition between stakeholders at national, provincial, and local levels, is both a cause and effect of Thailand's highly centralized government [21, 274, 271; 22, 22, 33; 32, 11, 20; 33; 47, 194–195, 201–202].

In turn, that continuously evolving competition helps to create a political landscape in Thailand's "deep south" where both political conflict and perennial violence are the ineluctable conclusions. At a theoretical level, that condition is consistent with Kaldor's notion of "new wars," where mobilization and conflict become goals rather than just a means to acquire political objectives. In this case, political objectives and benefits accrue to "political entrepreneurs" on both the government and terrorist sides [34; 8, 1–34; 40; 47, 185].

The framework for discussion includes a conflict framework, a historical brief about the struggle for autonomy that is itself interspersed with religious, cultural, regional, and political/administrative dimensions; description of major terrorist groups active in the contemporary political fray, and religious-cultural "micro-fissures" that continue to fracture Thailand's political landscape. The Islamic tenor of the conflict is explored, and with it, discussion about the national-irredentist sources that lie at the heart of the conflict [32, 32; 35, 34; 40, 3, 26–27, 31–32; 65, 43–44].

7.2 A Conflict Framework

Like all countries, Thailand is characterized by what Diamond calls "social fissures" that amount to "fault lines" which help give structural shape and character to a country. In addition to broad ethnic, religious, and regional cleavages, there are socio-economic fissures at play because the "deep South" is generally recognizable as having lower levels of socio-economic development than northern Thailand [17, 3, 9; 27, 242, 246; 32, 18, 24–25; 33, 14; 35, 11; 40, 12].

Most of Thailand's regions are Buddhist; a little below one-half of all Muslims in the country live in the "far South" provinces [40, 25]. Thailand's Muslims are overwhelmingly Sunni and can be broken down into two broad groups: Northern Muslims who Yusuf states are "integrated" into Thailand's political system, and Muslims in the deep southern provinces, who have embraced "separatist" sentiments. In Yala, Pattani, and Narathiwat, "These southern Muslims make up about 44% of the total Thai Muslim population (which currently is between 5 and 7 million)." [21, 267; 22, 22, 30; 32, 7; 40, 3, 26–27, 31–32, 12; 65, 44–45].

---

[3] For McCargo, the "upper southern" provinces include Patthalung, Nakhon Si Thsmmarat, and Songkhla.

In other words, Thailand has, as other countries do, a particular set or configuration of "social fissures" that can contribute to conflict potential. As Diamond points out, when societal fault lines based on region, socio-economic status, religion, ethnicity, or race align or "coincide" where, for example, a majority of people in one ethnic group who are poor also live in a particular part of the country, the prospect of intra-national conflict will increase [23; 32, 18, 24–25; 33, 115, 14; 40, 12; 65, 55].

At the same time, this analysis highlights what can be called "micro-fissures" which also appear to have the potential to contribute to additional terrorism or transform the extant nature of terrorism in Thailand. As previously mentioned, the terrorism observed nowadays can perhaps best be described as "nationalist irredentist" terrorism with Islamic underpinnings. Still, the nature of terrorist ideology might be prone to transformation or structural shifts because of international Jihadist or Salafi influences [17, vii, 1,12; 5; 32, 66; 40, 12].[4]

Those "micro-social" fissures are a set of narrower social fissures with connections that traverse within and across religious and cultural boundaries. Those "micro-fissures" might include differences in religious cultural orientation within Islam and Muslim society in the far Southern provinces. For example, "micro-fissures" are found between traditional "pondoks" (i.e., "Islamic boarding schools") and the system of "private Islamic schools" in Thailand, that themselves blend Western educational curriculum agendas and teaching methods with more traditional training in Islamic studies.

A second set of "micro-fissures" in Thailand's Islamic society might revolve around differences with respect to other aspects of Islamic outlook that overlap into cultural and political domains. Those include the "traditionalist" Khana Khao and the Khana Mai or "modernist" orientations to Islam in Thailand's southern provinces [21, 268; 22, 31; 40, 23, 20, 25–26, 28–29]. Even though the Khana Mai "modernists" are considered more stringent in their Islamic interpretations, McCargo asserts that as a whole, Khana Mai "modernists" are less prone to nationalist rhetoric and might be inclined to favor some "accommodation" with the Bangkok government [22, 31; 35, 44; 40, 23, 20–21, 26–29].

Still, both of these sets of "micro" fissures are delicate and as previously mentioned, might be vulnerable to outside influence and manipulation by foreign based Salafi groups, where one side might be supported by an outside party, that in turn, creates demand for outside support from the other side. Those foreign based Jihadist groups include, but are not limited to, al-Qaeda, ISIS, Jema'ah Islamiyah (JI) remnants or Tanzim Qaedat al-Jihad (al Qaeda in the Malay Archipelago) remnants from Indonesia [20, 1001–1003; 21, 268–269; 32, 29–31, 33, 53, 68; 40, 12].

When considered together, those two-fold set of "micro-fissures" have the potential to contribute to an especially fractured political landscape in Thailand. Those terrorism related "micro-fissures" in Thailand and the prospect of manipulation by

---

[4] The Thai terrorism under consideration could be described as nationalist-irredentist with Islamic underpinnings. It falls under the "nationalist-irredentist" heading, even though some contemporary Thai terrorist groups might not (in some cases) have the goal of a specific Islamic state in mind, but rather government disruption.

international terrorist groups from the Middle East, Indonesia, or the Philippines for example, might generate a newer dimension of conflict with potential to deepen the crisis for self-determination in the "Far-South." [32, 89, 29–31, 33, 68].

7.3 Historical Prelude to Conflict

The tradition of resistance in Pattani to centralized rule is a time- honored phenomenon, worthy of a brief historical overview. Up until the time that Siam's Rama II consolidated control over Patani in 1786, there was an independent Malay kingdom; an Islamic Sultanate basically unfettered from Buddhist and Siamese control. In reference to the Kingdom of Patani, Patani is spelled with one "t," to offset the Kingdom from the contemporary state of Pattani [32, 8–9; 35, 28; 40, 2].

In 1808, King Rama II divided Patani into eight sultanates and that loose confederation-like system prevailed until the early twentieth century, when those sultanates were more fully incorporated into Siam through a system of taxation [17, 2; 22, 22; 32, 7; 33, 154–155; 45, 99–100, 93, 93 n14, n15; 47, 184–185; 65, 45; 41, 7]. The broader political landscape was crafted when the Anglo-Siam Treaty (1909) demarcated boundaries between Siam's "deep South" and the "states" of Kelantan, Pertis, Perak, and Kedah in Malay, in what is now Malaysia [27, 235; 65, 46]. Indeed, Chalk suggests one of the reasons behind the high degree of centralization in Thailand's government presupposed and derived from efforts, "…to forestall the steady expansion of British colonial influence throughout the Malay peninsula." [17, 2; 32, 8; 37, 2, 6].

In the contemporary world, the time-honored struggle over the status of "deep south" or "far south" provinces has resonated throughout Thailand and the region, especially in terms of national integration and national security concerns. While the conflict is sourced in domestic factors in Thailand, what is significant is that it also has an international dimension to it, primarily because of support from the long-standing Malay-Thai community found in Kelantan province in Malaysia, and because of Malay-Muslim sympathizers found within Indonesia [27, 243; 32, 19, 68; 40, 12].

From a historical perspective, the early part of the twentieth century was a time when a number of Muslims from South East Asia, from the ethnic group known collectively as the "Jawi community," travelled to Mecca for religious study. Indeed, several important religious figures from Pattani made the Haj to Mecca, after their focus on completing a set of more localized pilgrimages to holy shrines in Siam and areas in close proximity. Those local and regional pilgrimages were known collectively as Ziarah [26; 45, 89, 92].

Those persons who made the Haj included scholar Mohammad Nur Fatani, active in Pattani in the 1920s, and Daud ibn Abd Allah al-Fatani who preceded him. Daud ibn Abd Allah al Fatani became Pattani's most distinguished Islamic scholar in the early 1800s, after he completed his Haj to Mecca in the middle to late 1700s. Ockey reports that by the turn of the twentieth century, the number of pilgrims making the

Haj and those who stayed on for religious study had increased as a result of improved transportation services. That trend continued until a precipitous drop in Haj numbers happened with the onset of the First World War [45, 97, 99–100, 89].

What is significant here for Ockey is that the First World War, and especially the volcanic-like political events in the Middle East leading up to the Great War, affected Hajis from South East Asia in profound and lasting ways beyond religious significance. For many, what started out as a sojourn for religious study became a journey that was also highly politicized within the context of world events. Later on, those experiences would contribute to increased nationalist sentiments and shape demands for structural political change [45, 89, 99–100, 102–106].

For example, those pilgrims making the Haj were exposed to Arab nationalism, and experienced first-hand, the results of misplaced trust in the British. What was clear to Muslims who chafed under Ottoman and Young Turk control was that Ottoman governor Sharif Hussein of Mecca and his son Prince Faisal, who led the Arab Revolt (1916) against the Turks in exchange for an independent Arab state described in the Hussein-McMahon correspondence (1915–1916), were betrayed [45, 89, 99–100, 102–106].

7.4 Haji Sulong Abdulkadir Al-Fatani

One Malay-Muslim who studied in Mecca, who became an exceptional Malay-Muslim leader was Haji Sulong (1895–1954). He was one of several Islamic leaders who stoked nationalist sentiments in the "deep South" provinces after his religious study was completed in Mecca. He was ideologically akin to other southern province political nationalist leaders such as Tengku Abdulqadir and his son, Tengku Mahayidden [40, 61; 45, 109, 111; 65, 46].

It is important to recall all of this happened in an era where nationalism was as Nye explains, an explanatory factor for conflict at both the "nation-state" level and at the "international system" level. In other words, nationalism was "in the air" on a stage of world-wide proportions [44, 48, 59–64]. For example, nationalism and similar sentiments were captured by President Woodrow Wilson's declaration of his "fourteen points." At a functional level, it was equally important—it had for example, mobilization effects throughout the Austro-Hungarian Empire, and the Ottoman Empire, as well as in parts of Indo-China [44, 48, 59–64].

In many cases, religious leaders in Pattani and surrounding locales were able to acquire political power because of their family connections, wealth, or religious authority [45]. Those leaders were unhappy with the set of patronizing and ineffective efforts to promote Buddhist culture practiced by Bangkok authorities in southern Thailand [40, 18; 45, 103, 107; 65, 50]. Those community leaders generated and sustained nationalist and other similar sentiments, and captured the political support of much of the "deep-south" population.

The Haji Sulong's story is one worth telling precisely because it illuminates several underlying themes common to those with self-determination goals in mind in those heavily Muslim southern provinces. Haji Sulong was a resident of Pattani who travelled to Saudi Arabia for religious study and returned to Pattani after the First World War.

Haji Sulong was an Islamic reformer and modernist, who as Ockey reports, was cut from the same cloth as his intellectual mentor, Islamic Egyptian scholar Mohammad Abduh (1849–1905), who himself stressed the importance of education reform. It was Abduh and his mentor Jamal al-Din al-Afghani (1838–1897) who himself promoted the idea of Pan-Islamism, who were two Islamic luminaries who promoted the central notion that Islam and modernity could dovetail well [2, 153, 168, 148–149; 39, 180–181; 40, 21; 45, 92, 103–104, 107, 112, 114, 10, 16; 48, 44–48].

Haji Sulong's underlying interest in educational reform and in judicial reform to empower Islamic jurists probably intensified after Thailand's absolute monarchy passed into eclipse in 1932 in favor of a constitutional monarchy. After one year, the existing government of Pharaya Manopakorn Nitifhada (1932–1933) was overthrown and replaced by the Phraya Phahon government (1933–1938). In this brief interval of more accommodationist thought, certain government officials were more supportive than others for greater autonomy in local affairs within the southern provinces [32, 12; 45, 108, 111; 47, 185; 65, 47].

One such government official who would later become Prime Minister of Thailand was Pridi Phanomyong. At the time, Pridi Phanomyong served as the Minister of Interior (1934–1935) in the government of Prime Minister Phraya Phahon, until 1935. What is significant here is that Minister of Interior Pridi Phanomyong (also known as Pridi Banothyong) shared Haji Sulong's reformist and modernist mindset. Pridi Phanomyongho had an outlook about and affinity towards western style liberal democracy not widely shared by many other Thai leaders in government [22, 23; 32,13; 45, 107–111, 92].[5]

The Thai national government would shift to a more hardline stance when Prime Minister Phibun Songkhran came to power for his first term as Prime Minister (1938–1944). Prime Minster Phibun was a Field Marshal and hardliner who implemented sweeping new assimilationist policies in 1938. Those assimilation policies resulted in further political marginalization for Islamic leaders and their communities in the "deep south" who had to confront what amounted to intensified "Buddhist chauvinism," to use Helbardt's phrase [17, 2; 27, 235; 32, 12, 20–21; 33, 9–13; 35, 36; 40, 2–4; 65, 47].

That hardline system of assimilation was highly endorsed by the Siamese monarchy and Buddhist government officials. It was a priority of those Bangkok officials to keep upper-level control over basic functions of the southern provinces out of the hands of Malay-Muslim leadership, except for those Malay-Muslim leaders

[5] Thailand's Prime Ministers after the overthrow of Siam's "absolute monarchy" (1932) and the establishment of Thailand (1932), include: Phaya Manopakorn Nitithada (1932–1933); Phraya Phahon (i.e., Phahonphonphayuhasena) (1933–1938); Phibun Songkhram (i.e., Plaek Phibunsongkhram) (1938–1944), (April 1948–Sept 1957); Khuang Aphaiwong (Aug 1944–Aug 1945), (Jan–May 1946), (Nov 1947–April 1948); Pridi Phanomyong (i.e., Pridi Banomyong; Luang Praditmanutham) (Mar 1946–Aug. 1946); Pote Sarasin (Sept 1957–Jan 1958) [40, 60; 45, 108–111; 61].

who were corrupt or otherwise vulnerable to cooptation by the Thai government [17, 2; 33, 9–13, 14–15, 154; 40, 16–17].

It is probably fair to say those new policies were watershed events in the consolidation of a critical mass of support for self-determination and similar separatist sentiments. In conjunction with those "assimilationist" approaches and policies, Bangkok government officials used a system of political control and cooptation known as "virtuous rule." That system of "virtuous rule" with its reinforcing impact on the prevailing assimilationist approach in Bangkok is discussed below.

As previously mentioned, Haji Sulong was originally involved in efforts to strengthen the Islamic religious educational system in the "deep South" provinces. This focus on educational reform was especially significant as he was the founder of the "private Islamic" school system in Thailand, an educational system designed to offset traditional "pondok" religious boarding school education. From the point of view of Bangkok's leadership, the problem was that the Pondok system was characterized by a free-wheeling religious instruction system and overall leadership resistance to government regulation.

Paradoxically, Haji Sulong's efforts to create the "private Islamic school" system to offer aspects of secular training for students, had a duality of effect that undercut some of Haji Sulong's political goals. While work to craft that "private Islamic" school system was an accomplishment which appealed to some of Haji Sulong's modernist and reformist sensibilities, it also served to undercut his goal of greater independence for the provinces, as that "private Islamic school" system, itself supported by Thailand's government, made even greater national political involvement in provincial affairs possible [40, 39–40].

Notwithstanding that, it was Haji Sulong's involvement with broader politics, with his specific focus on greater independence for Islamic administrative infrastructure, that ultimately led the Thai government to brand him as a fundamental threat to the state. In 1937, Haji Sulong issued a "seven point" set of political demands that captured the essence of Malay-Muslim political dissent, and articulated demands and aspirations for self-determination. In that agenda, Haji Sulong called for a wide ranging set of political and legal reforms.

To be more specific, Haji Sulong called for: (1) a new political framework "unit" for the provinces; (2) educational curricula where Malay would be used to teach youth in elementary school; (3) a commitment for tax revenues raised in the "deep south" to be distributed there for projects; (4) an 80–85% province quota for Malay bureaucratic officials; (5) the use of Malay and Thai as languages in government transactions; (6) full blown Islamic provincial committee control over Islamic provincial government functions; (7) an independent Muslim court system parallel to the Thai court system found in the provinces [40, 17, 21, 40; 45, 113; 47, 199; 65, 47–50].[6]

It was that clarion call for fundamental political reform and empowerment, coupled with an effective and sustained program now rebranded as the "seven requests," that was initiated and nurtured by Haji Sulong. The central notion was to ensure national government compliance with his "seven points" agenda otherwise

[6] In comparison to Ockey, McCargo provides a figure of 80%.

now broadly known as the "seven requests." With that political agenda as backdrop, Haji Sulong led an unsuccessful insurrection in 1947; it was that campaign which ultimately led Haji Sulong to run afoul of the law, and to his incarceration by Thai authorities. He and his son Ahmad, who reportedly served as a translator for his father, were killed while in police custody in 1954 [1, 125; 32, 14; 40, 63; 45, 103, 107; 65, 31].

7.5 Bangkok's Twin Systems of Political Control

Beyond the experiences of individual leaders and communities, it is critically important to understand the basic nature of the two systems taken by the Bangkok government to assert political and bureaucratic control in the South. These two systems were overlaid against the set of assimilationist policies that emanated from the Bangkok governments as previously described.

The first of those systems was the system of "virtuous rule" and the second was the system of "representative politics." From the point of view of Bangkok officials, both systems were a natural extension of a highly centralized government [40, 15–18, 83, 163; 47, 191]. At a theoretical level, the system of "virtuous rule" dovetailed well with long-standing assimilationist policies while in practice, the "representative politics" system was designed to do the same. However, both "virtuous rule" and "representative politics" systems were ineffective in practice.

The "virtuous rule" approach traces an arc to the early twentieth century and King Vajiravudh (1910–1925) (Rama VI) of the Chakri Royal House. It was popular with the Thai monarchy and extended into the reign of King Bhumibol (1946–2016) (Rama IX). For example, as far back as the 1940s, the central notion was that "virtuous bureaucracy" would prevail, where "good" and "honorable" administrative staff primarily from Bangkok's elite, would work in conjunction with others at provisional and local levels to administer political and economic affairs in the "Deep South." [17, 2–3; 40, 7, 15–16, 18].

For McCargo, the notion of "virtuous rule" was twofold. First, it consisted of "virtuous politics," characterized by centralized bureaucratic control by "good" and "honorable" politicians who presumably had "deep south" population interests at heart. That system included government sanctioned members of local Islamic political councils loyal to those politicians, thereby in effect loyal to the Bangkok regime. Second, "virtuous rule" involved "virtuous bureaucracy" practiced by Thai bureaucrats more often than not from outside of the "deep" southern provinces.

The overall objective was to achieve what McCargo calls "virtuous legitimacy" among "deep south" province populations, but in practice that approach produced results that were makeshift and incomplete at best [32, 21–23, 25; 40, 59–60, 57]. Part of the problem stemmed Bangkok's perspective's because all too frequently, the "southern provinces" were considered by some in northern Thailand as a more of a monolithic block even though at an administrative level, that was not the case [32, 21–23, 25; 40, 59–60, 57].

Hence, time-honored ethnic tensions continued to exist between "deep southerners" from the provinces of Yala, Pattani and Narathiwat, and "upper southerners" about the use of "upper southerners" to staff "deep South" bureaucratic positions. In fact, Yusuf describes the importance of the ethnic component of Malay-Muslim nationalism with his term, "ethnoreligious nationalism," to describe the continuously evolving nationalist-irredentist terrorism movement in Thailand's "deep south." [17, 2–3, 8; 32, 19–20, 33, 55–57; 40, 59–60; 65, 46–47].

The reality of "virtuous rule" was much different for "Deep-South" populations than what its proponents in Bangkok touted as its strengths through beneficence. The reason why was because "virtuous rule" was unequivocal in its demand for cultural assimilation or "Thaification." As far back as the Education Reform Act of 1921, government assimilation efforts were promoted in educational programs, where teaching Islam and promotion of religious culture were heavily regulated by government agencies [21, 272–273; 27, 237; 32, 9, 10–11, 21, 70–71; 33, 4, 46, 156; 35, 28–29, 34; 40, 10, 18–19, 26, 52, 39–45].[7]

One stated reason for this proactive regulatory approach by government vis a vis the pondoks was that individual "pondoks" (i.e., "Islamic boarding schools") lacked a set of uniform teaching standards to follow. Still, the security component of assimilationism framed by "virtuous rule" was not lost on the Bangkok government as "pondoks" would be required under the regime Prime Minister Field Marshal Sarit Thanarat (1957–1963), to register with the government, thereby in effect working to enhance government scrutiny and surveillance capabilities [21, 272–273; 27, 237; 32, 9, 10–11, 21, 70–71; 33, 4, 46, 156; 35, 28–29, 34; 40, 10, 18–19, 26, 52, 39–45].

That "virtuous rule" approach to governance failed in large part because of the absence of trust that "outside" political officials could generate within "deep south" populations. It also failed because of the underlying suspicions most "deep south" province populations had that the penultimate goal of the Thai government was to dilute or eliminate the relevance of critical political, religious, and cultural, and economic institutions [22, 29; 32, 57; 33, 9–11; 35, 19; 40, 37, 58–60].

To be fair, Poocharoen [47], reports there have been substantive efforts by the national government in Bangkok to change the composition of "Deep-South" bureaucrats largely because of those strains and tensions between "upper southerners" and "Deep South" populations. These national efforts, primarily carried out after 2009, have alleviated some of the tensions and stress, even though there remain some outstanding questions about certain "deep south" bureaucrat educational attainment levels and competency [40, 58; 47, 198, 202–203, 200].

In comparison, the South's system of "representative politics" was part of a broader system of Thai bureaucratic rule that traces an arc to King Chulalongkorn in the 1890s [22, 22; 40, 54, 16, 83, 163]. In the case of the south provinces, that system was also deeply flawed but for reasons that probably had more to do with wide ranging and deep intense corruption, in addition to the absence of trust about "outsiders" who staffed political and bureaucratic positions [32, 21–23, 25; 40, 59; 47, 196, 198–199; 65, 50]. In the "representative politics" system, personal loyalties

[7] For Helbardt, his term is "Islamo-nationalism".

between local officials, coupled with different expectations about the role and goal of conflict, resolution compounded that system's problems.

As a result, those competing goals and personal rivalries created conditions ripe for corruption or "buy-offs" by the Thai government. In effect, those political dynamics helped to create a peculiar condition where the emergent reality was that the promotion of "representative politics" was undermined almost from the start. The end result was to make local religious and political officials illegitimate in the eyes of the populace in Yala, Pattani, and Narathiwat, and largely ineffective for Thailand's ruling elite to use as a vehicle to exert authority [40; 45; 47, 184–185].

In the broader sense, this system of "representative politics" was identified with attempts to create political and economic opportunity structures for "deep south" populations that would, as the argument went, take the wind out of the sails of nationalist sentiments. In addition to socio-economic development, part of what was hoped for in the South was an increase in higher level Malay-Muslim government positions for workers in the army and police, and in bureaucratic positions [40, 17]. It was also hoped that economic development would help secure some of the broader political control objectives envisioned by Bangkok leadership.

In summation, this emphasis by the Thai national government on "representative politics" resulted in political outcomes that were much different than anticipated. In fact, McCargo suggests the function of the institution of "representative politics" as implemented, actually helped craft "political space" for terrorist groups. As previously mentioned, failure in that "representative politics" system was in large part because of wide ranging corruption, where the loyalty of politicians was bought and sold. Populations are not oblivious to such matters—that produced an electorate with wide spread dissatisfaction with the political system [32, 20; 40, 14–15, 11, 80, 87, 183–184, 8–9, 84, 36, 42].[8]

In a nutshell, the political approaches of "virtual rule" and "representative politics" both failed the populations of the Southern province populations. For McCargo, "virtuous rule" remained a prevailing political approach even up until the 1980s for some in government, such as former Prime Minister Prem Tinsulanond (1980–1988), who continued to try to breathe life into "virtuous politics" principles with national government apparatus such as the Southern Border Province Administrative Centre (SBPAC). The original SBPAC was crafted by Perm Tinsulanond in 1981 but it was dissolved by Prime Minister Thaksin Shinawatra in 2002 [17, 9; 22, 2, 33; 32, 16, 18, 22; 35, 229 n37; 40, 2, 16; 41, 16, 13, 9, 6, 26, 53].

[8] In this sense, Thailand's experience with "representative politics" and corruption is reminiscent of the wide ranging and deep corruption that led Nigeria's "Second Republic" to fail.

7.6 Thailand's Labyrinth Bureaucracy

Be that as it may, the 1980s were a time when the national government's approach towards "virtuous rule" began to pass into eclipse in favor of more emphasis on "representative politics." [40, 2, 83, 163]. For Poocharoen, an assessment of the problems with "representative politics" must also include problems that stemmed from the sordid condition of Thailand's bureaucracy. It is not only hampered by "red tape" and inefficiencies for bureaucrats working to tackle problems, but it has been characterized by "bureaucratic politics" effects.

As Poochareon reports, Thailand's bureaucracy is characterized by competing stakeholders, turf wars, personal rivalries, and interests. The stakeholders involved include, but are not limited to, officials at the provincial level of government, Thailand's Fourth Army, National Security Council, and the Southern Border Province Administrative Centre (SBPAC), that was itself resurrected by Prime Minister Surayud Chulanont after it was dissolved by Prime Minister Thaksin Shinawatra in May 2002 [17, 9; 27, 247–250; 35, 229n37; 37, 8; 47, 188, 190–191; 65, 49–50]. There are also a host of community leaders, including religious leaders, who interact with bureaucrats who staff those institutions.

For Poocharoen, the dynamics between those stakeholders, coupled with that system's emphasis on "bureaucratic function" (i.e., budget allocations) rather than on "area specialization," makes the likelihood of significant bureaucratic reform for the "far south" almost practically nil. For Poocharoen and other scholars, that is largely the case because in Thailand's bureaucratic system, there is not the emphasis on tailor made approaches fit to the contextual factors in each province that address the needs of people in specific geographical locale like those in the "deep south." [32, 27–28; 47, 196–198-199, 192–193].

In addition, Poocharoen suggests the extensive efforts at structural bureaucratic change made by the Bangkok government, and the volatility that has resulted because of those ineffective efforts, have in fact contributed to the violence. In addition to makeshift and incomplete policy implementation, a series of bureaucratic reshuffling decisions by the Thai government has put the military in charge of some government apparatus whose functions are much more conducive to civilian control [47, 187–188].

For example, the reconstituted SBPAC, an apparatus that has served as an interlocutor for government and society, was for a time placed under the aegis of Thailand's Fourth Army, itself an institution with time-honored significance in the Thai political system [22, 33; 32, 16; 35, 229 n 37; 47, 33]. Another example Poocharoen provides are the training programs for bureaucrats run by the Thai military. There were performance deficiencies that stemmed from having different government institutions run different training programs, that process led to gaps in knowledge for Thailand's bureaucrats as they were not exposed to a standardized training curriculum [22, 33; 32, 16; 35, 229 n 37; 47].

As Poocharoen points out, these are but a few examples of a trend where the Thai military has, for significant time intervals, been in charge of broader government apparatus designed to confront issues beyond national security [22, 33; 32, 16; 35, 229n37; 47]. On the ground, the Royal Thai Army's visibility in the Southern provinces is unmistakable. In 2005, Croissant reported, "...the government has enforced martial law in Narathiwat, Yala, and Pattani, giving troops the right to make arrests without a court warrant, and more than 12,000 Royal Thai Army troops are now deployed in the region...." [22, 24].

It appears the transition from military to civilian rule after the 2006 military coup d'état that deposed Prime Minister Thaksin Shinawatra, did precious little if anything to change those patterns of military involvement. After the 2006 military coup, Prime Minister General Surayud Chulanont, who Funston suggests was open to accommodation, remained in power for about a year [27, 247–250; 32, 56; 41, 7].

In turn, the PPP (Palang Prachachon Party or People's Power Party) under Samak Sundaravej (2008–2008) came to power after Thailand's national election in 2007. Yusuf points to Prime Minister Samak Sundaravej's uncompromising PPP government as one government during this period that was heavily invested in the military's involvement in "deep south" affairs [17, 1, ix; 27, 247–250; 40, 59, 54–55; 65, 51].

Interestingly enough, it appears former Interior Minister Chalerm Yubamrung in Prime Minister Samak Sundaravej's government floated a trial balloon of sorts—the notion of greater political autonomy for the "deep south." In response, Prime Minister Samak Sundarvej did a volte face on that proposal in the midst of fierce political infighting with PPP's arch-rival, the People's Alliance for Democracy (PAD).

That specific example from the Samak Sundarvej regime is a particular example of how political machinations have contributed to political instability and social unrest in the southern provinces. Indeed, all of the foregoing illuminates how in Thailand, a powerful set of connections exist between intensive political infighting and bureaucratic problems that exacerbate bureaucratic politics effects and conflict in the broader sense [65, 49–52].

In this section of the analysis, there has been discussion about the multiple sources of Thailand's political inertia and the set of ineffective and episodic responses to clarion calls for self-determination, either in the form of national independence outright, or greater autonomy within Thailand. Those sources involve a series of historical events, political processes, and a set of close and thick links between politics and bureaucracies that seem to be a hallmark of Thailand's contemporary political landscape.

The analysis also showcases how broader "virtuous rule" and "representative politics" approaches to political control, that amount to time honored historical processes in each case, have contributed to conflict. What is also significant is those approaches have been taken against the backdrop of hardline Buddhist assimilationist political and cultural policies in a country with deep social divisions along regional, religious, socio-economic, and ethnic lines [22, 22; 23, 55; 32, 7–8, 14, 17; 35, 11; 40, 21, 27–28; 65, 46–47, 54–55, 44][9]. Such assimilationist policies have only exacerbated the conflict potential that stems from what Diamond calls the "coincidental cleavages" effects which derive from those social fissure alignments [23, 55; 32, 101].

Furthermore, the results of those assimilationist policies are precisely the opposite of what carefully reasoned policies crafted to reduce the effects "coincidental cleavages" might achieve. For example, under the Second Republic, the Nigerian government expanded the number of Nigerian states to reduce the political instability and social unrest produced by a majority of one ethnic or religious group living in particular regions of the country, itself defined by socio-economic status as either affluent or poor [23, 55; 32, 101].

In addition, it seems clear that bureaucratic inefficiencies and malfunction have become basic sources of conflict. As both Poocheroen and McDermott point out, "bureaucratic politics" is a hallmark of the political landscape in Thailand [41, 26; 47]. It is to a description of Thailand's separatist terrorism, that started in the middle twentieth century within the context of a highly centralized state and highly assimilationist policies, this discussion now turns [32, 11, 20; 33, 33–35]. In this section, several major separatist terrorist organizations in Thailand and some of their splinter groups, are examined.

7.7 Two Terrorism Phases in Thailand

7.7.1 Phase One

In the broader sense, it is possible to break down the historical legacy of highly effective and sustained "separatist" terrorism in Thailand into two broad time periods. As Croissant suggests, the first phase of terrorism in Thailand started up in about the middle of the twentieth century and lasted into the 1980s and early 1990s [13, 53–93; 17, 1, 5; 22, 21].[10] This was an era characterized by the formation of well-known terrorist groups such as Barisan Revolusi Nasional (BRN) and the Pattani United Liberation Organization (PULO).

To be sure, terrorist assaults in Thailand from the 1960s through the 1980s focused primarily on government targets [32, 60, 68–69; 40, 2, 4; 41, 7]. In the case of the

[9] There are what Yusuf calls "well integrated" Muslims outside of the south who live in Northern Thailand, so religious fissures might not be as distinct in that case.

[10] For Croissant, a first phase ranges from the 1940s to the 1980s. In contrast, Chalk breaks down Thailand's terrorism struggle into three distinct time periods. The first period is 1960–1998, the second period is from 1998 to 2004, and the third period is from 2008 onwards. Be that as it may, 2004 remains a watershed year for the intensification of struggle. In essence, Abuza skillfully breaks down what can be called the "second phase" of terrorism in Thailand, into "five waves."

Barisan Revolusi Nasional, BRN leadership put almost singular focus on "government targets" and "informants" until 1993 [33, 166–167; 41, 7]. That emphasis on government targets was also found to be true for PULO.

In the case of both the BRN and PULO, terrorist splintering and spinoff formation began to happen in the 1980s and 1990s with deleterious effects for both terrorist organizations. In terms of operational capacity, leadership of both the BRN and PULO understood the underlying value of constituent group support; those terrorist group leaders worked to craft a set of ties to a myriad of Thai villages. At the same time, Helbardt reports those ties were makeshift and incomplete, and oftentimes did not function in effective and sustained ways [35, 41–42, 28–29; 40, 160, 163].

7.7.2 Phase Two

A second phase of terrorism in Thailand was ushered in around 1980. It followed a lull in terrorism that had lasted for several decades. For McCargo, this new phase of terrorism started in earnest around 2003 and it accelerated in intensity in the early 2000s [37, 1–2; 40, 146, 4]. McCargo suggests that second phase of the struggle has been distinguished by an uptick in violence that itself might have stemmed at least in part from the military coup that brought Thaksin Shinawatra to power [40, 55–56]. For Yusuf, much of that second phase of terrorism has been characterized by terrorist assaults conducted by "faceless insurgents." [65, 52; 35, 2, 3, 18, 20].

What that suggests is that terrorist chieftains of major terrorist organizations, as well as the chieftains of less well known terrorist groups, have largely come to the conclusion that most terrorist assaults should be anonymous, to decrease the chance terrorists will be captured by Thai security services. In a similar vein, terrorist group conglomerates, with formal collaboration and coordination between groups, have been the exception rather than the rule in Thailand nowadays. The two terrorist conglomerate groups of note are Bersatu and MARA Pattani.

In the case of Bersatu, the separatist groups PULO, New PULO, and BRN comprised that overarching organization, while in the case of Wan Kadir Che Man's MARA Pattani organization, that conglomerate was made up of BNPP/BIPP and PULO. Both of these terrorist group conglomerates had limited effectiveness and were not especially impactful over the Thai political landscape [13, 129–130; 32, 64, 80, 105–106, 15; 37, 2].

It seems likely that condition might have also contributed to the high degree of anonymous terrorist assaults found in contemporary Thailand. There is also a permeability or interoperability to these second phase separatist organizations in Thailand that is relatively new which might affect the heavy use of anonymous terrorist assaults. Perhaps the single most dominant example of this phenomenon is Masae Useng, who has been a terrorist group chieftain or member of GMIP, BRN, and PULO nearly simultaneously [32, 117–118, 112, 76, 117; 35, 30].

At both a theoretical and a functional level, terrorist group leader emphasis on anonymous terrorist assaults is also consistent with a notion associated with prior work on Middle East terrorism. What I found in the case of some Middle East terrorism was that if the political issues of contention were sufficiently articulated and well known by both sides in a terrorist campaign, it seemed beneficial for a terrorist organization not to claim responsibility for at least some terrorist actions, to decrease the risk of capture by state security services [5, 188; 6, 270–271; 19].

What several scholars have noted is this second phase of terrorism in Thailand has also been marked by an increase in focus on civilian targets, as well as a spate of watershed terrorism and counterterrorism events. Those watershed events include two heavy handed government responses to terrorist events in 2006 [32, 76, 71, 58]. Both of these pivotal events helped to revitalize separatist terrorism in Thailand and point to the role that blunt and sometimes crude counterterrorism measures practiced by government play to exacerbate conflict.

The first of those watershed events was the Krue-Se mosque assault in 2004 in Mueang District, Pattani, and the second, the Tak Bai incident in 2006 in Tak Bai District, Narathiwat [40, 1, 16, 3, 50, 141–143, 148, 163; 35, 3, 36].[11] The related violence that preceded the Kru-Se mosque siege and the counterterrorist assault at the mosque itself happened on April 28, 2004. Yusuf identifies the Brotherhood of the Eternal Judgement of God (or Hikmat Allah Abadan) with Ustaz Soh at the helm, as the group that carried out the Krue-Se mosque incident. Yusuf reports that Hikmat Allah Abadan was "a radical religious cell," with an almost singular hatred for Buddhists [17, 10; 27, 242, 251; 40, 135–136, 143, 146, 148; 65, 48–49].

Those Hikam Allah Abadan activists first carried out forceful assaults primarily against police and military targets in the provinces of Songkhla, Yala, and Pattani; then retreated into the Krue-Se mosque for sanctuary as Thailand's security services pursued them. In turn, other separatist activists pursued the security services. All of the foregoing resulted in copious bloodletting where 107 activists died, including thirty-seven Hikam Allah Abadan activists in the Kru-Se mosque itself, and between five to seven Thai security forces personnel [17, 10; 27, 242, 251; 40, 135–136, 143, 146, 148; 65, 48–49].

In the case of the Tak Bai incident on October 25, 2004, the arrest of six local separatist political activists and their subsequent incarceration in Tak Bai sparked a public protest, demonstration, and a police massacre. This small town in Thailand is nestled on or in close proximity to the border between Thailand and Malaysia.

Faced with what amounted to a very large and mostly peaceful demonstration where some 1300 people were detained, "heavy-handed" Tak Bai police and Fourth Army troops made a series of arrests to break up that demonstration [32, 39, 48–50, 58–59; 65, 50].[12] When preparations were made to transfer those arrested protestors to jail, overly zealous Thai police and Thai military packed too many protestors into prison bound vehicles at once.

---

[11] The Global Terrorism Data (GTD) data base records between zero and under fifty terrorist attacks for five year intervals between 1970 and 2000.

[12] This event unfolded in ways reminiscent of how the 1960 Sharpsville protest and police massacre further radicalized the Pan Africanist Congress (PAC) in South Africa.

All of the foregoing led to seven protestors left dead at the scene, and some seventy-five to eighty protestors who suffocated to death en route to incarceration at Thai military facilities [27, 241–243; 41, 7; 65, 50]. As if that was not enough of a problem, McDermott [41] reports the Thai security personnel implicated in the Tak Bai affair were never prosecuted or otherwise held accountable for their crimes, at least within the ten years that followed the event [41, 7–8].

In addition to political blow back in Thailand, the Tak Bai incident caused volcanic-like repercussions in Malaysia. Indeed, Funston reports the Tak Bai debacle caused more political instability and social unrest that emanated largely from Malaysia's "Muslim NGO's" and "opposition parties" than what was elicited by the Krue Se incident [27, 242–243, 251; 32, 42, 45; 40, 1, 50,141–143, 148, 168; 35, 3, 36]. What is also significant here is that Funston's important observation is consistent with Starr and Most's notion that cross border "contagion effects" can replicate or intensify conflict potential with increased proximity to national borders [27, 241–43; 32, 10, 34, 16; 11, 432–460; 12, 581–620; 52, 33–52].

Overall, what is also significant for this second phase of separatist conflict in Thailand is what seems to be a closer set of relationships between terrorist groups and criminal elements. For example, Croissant points to a "grey zone" between organized criminal syndicalists, common criminality, and terrorist organizations, similar to Hoffman's conceptualization of the term [22, 24–26; 25, 1–35; 32, 21–22, 66; 7, 27–28, 210 n32; 41, 10]. For Croissant, "Thailand is a hot spot for the small arms trade, with the military itself involved in the black market for arms. Given the ubiquity of organized and petty crime, small arms trade, smuggling, and drug trafficking in the south, it would be naïve to assume criminals and terrorists can be clearly distinguished." [22, 26].

In turn, Funston describes effective and sustained smuggling operations over the Thailand-Malaysia border even in the aftermath of top-down elite efforts to stem the tide of contraband that terrorists could utilize to their advantage [27; 32, 16]. It also follows that in certain select circumstances even low-level criminals can and have been selected by terrorist organization chieftains to conduct terrorist assaults against targets [19, 233, 399 n60; 22, 26; 40, 158–159; 46, 49–50, 53; 60, 42–43, 232].

Lastly, this second phase of separatist terrorism in Thailand has been marked by generally recognizable shifts in terrorist group organizational structures, from top down bureaucratic hierarchal frameworks, to "flatter" more horizonal cell structures. In some cases, as Helbardt reports, those terrorist group organizational structures probably amount to "hybrid" structures, with characteristics from both organizational types [32, 47–48; 35, 6, 18; 36, 56–60, 68–72, 99–100, 131].

There are several possible reasons for this general shift in organizational structure that are most likely linked to specific "contextual factors" in Thailand. For example, one explanatory factor might be the improved condition of counterterrorism coordination after 9/11 between the Malaysian and Thai governments, that built upon previous efforts in 1998 by the governments of Thailand and Malaysia to improve border security.

In addition, a second possible explanatory factor for this structural shift to a "flatter" or more "hybrid" structure is the increased recognition of certain benefits associated with a horizontal organizational structure where terrorist group cells and clusters of cells can collude if required. There has been increased recognition that concepts of "leaderless resistance," espoused by both American intelligence specialist Ulius Louis Amoss and Louis Beam, when writ large in practice, are more resilient than top down bureaucratic organization frameworks because "leaderless resistance" infrastructure is less vulnerable to infiltration by counterterrorism authorities [35, 6, 14–15, 17- 20, 25; 40, 164, 142; 59, 116].

In this, the "new terrorism" template scoped out by Lesser, Hoffman, Arquilla, Ronfeldt, and Zanini, there is emphasis on horizontal organizational structure and alternative funding sources for terrorists in a post-Cold War world where the Soviet Union and most of its Marxist-Leninist client states do not exist [38, 85–144]. In a similar vein, it is it seems possible there was a decline in cohesiveness and overall relevance in the post-Cold War world for old-style nationalist-irredentist groups like BRN, that were originally fitted with Marxist-Leninist trappings.

What we know is that era of plentiful monetary support from nation-states to terrorist groups passed into eclipse with the tail end of the Cold War, the demise of the Soviet Union in 1991, and most of the Soviet Union's client states. What we also know is that underlying condition has facilitated terrorist organization and criminal syndicalist group collaboration [10, 138; 49, 131–146; 50, 93–109; 51, 52–67]. What we do not know about with a high dose of certainty is if, and if so to what degree, international political and economic structural effects linked to the Cold War's end influenced significant Thai nationalist-irredentist groups with a Marxist-Leninist hue [13, 26–27; 33, 34; 35, 8, 13]. In turn, those political and economic disruptions might have contributed to instances of terrorist group splintering or spinoff formation.

7.8 First Phase Terrorist Organizations in Thailand

7.8.1 Gabungan Melayu Pattani Raya—GAMPAR

The Gabungan Melayu Pattani Raya—GAMPAR or Union of Malay for an Independent Patani, was one of the first political groups to work for Pattani's independence after the Second World War. It was crafted in 1945 or 1948; its leaders waged a political campaign from its headquarters in Kelantan, Malaya to compel British and American officials to recognize Pattani as independent from Thailand [13, 14, 17; 22, 23; 32, 14].[13]

For Abuza, the political goal for GAMPAR was independence outright, or Pattani's seamless integration into the Federation of Malaya. Invariably, British and American officials sided with Bangkok's ruling elite and with Cold War interests in mind,

[13] Croissant provides a date of 1948 for GAMPAR's inception, while Abuza suggests the date is 1945.

refused to endorse any of GAMPAR's political demands. Indeed, Gunaratna and Acharya point to the threat for Mao Ze Dong and the Chinese Communist Party in particular [13, 14, 16–17; 22, 22–23; 27, 237; 32, 13–14].

7.9 Barisan Nasional Pemebasan Pattani (BNPP)

The post Second World War struggle for Pattani began to galvanize even further with efforts by Malay-Muslim leader, Tengku Abdul Jalaal to craft what would become the Barisan Nasional Pembebasan Pattani (BNPP) or Pattani National Liberation Front. Tengku Abdul Jalal was a GAMPAR ex-deputy whose father, Tanku Abdul Kader, was a prominent Malay-Muslim activist from the 1930s [13, 16–17].

In the literature, there are differences in some authoritative accounts about the sources and origins of BNPP with respect to its provenance and the time frame for Tengku Abdul Jalal's work to craft the BNPP. One difference revolves around whether BNPP was a terrorist organization that was a contemporary of the Barisan Revolusi Nasional (BRN) or whether Barisan Nasional Pembebasan Pattani (BNPP) was formed much later, in effect as a BRN splinter group.

For Abuza, "the BNPP was established in 1959–1960 by Tengku Abdul Jalal, the former deputy of GAMPAR who was jailed following World War II for his activism in demanding regional autonomy…." [13, 16–17; 1, 125; 22, 23].[14] Tengku Abdul Jalal was at the helm of BNPP at least for the best part of those eighteen years, until 1977 [13, 16–17; 33, 158, 33–34]. The BNNP marshalled much of its strength from what Croissant calls Malay-Muslim "traditional aristocrats" and "religious elites," and for Abuza, that relatively narrow support base contributed to a reduction in BNPP's robust nature with the passage of time [13, 16–17; 1, 125; 22, 23, 25; 32, 14].

In contrast, Gunaratna, Acharya, and Chua's account reports that the BNPP was crafted in 1972, essentially as a "splinter group" of the Barisan Revolusi Nasional (BRN). For Gunaratna, Acharya, and Chua, "in 1972, another [BRN] founding member—Tengku Jalal Nasir—also quit from BRN and declared his own Pattani National Liberation Front (BNPP). He took Pak Ye and more than half of the 600 strong ABREP with him. Idris also joined the new formation as BNPP's Commander-in Chief." [32, 73; 33, 158, 34–35]. The foregoing suggests one estimate of BNPP front-line activists is between 306 and 390 members around 1972.[15] Both the Barisan Revolusi Nasional (BRN) and its "military" branch, Angkatan (ABREP) are discussed below.

From the start, BNPP had a narrower political goal in mind than did Gabungan Melayu Pattani Raya (GAMPAR). That political goal was a fledgling Islamic state in

[14] Alternately, Croissant states BNPP was crafted in 1963.

[15] BNPP activist estimates for around 1972 are based on Gunaratna, Acharya, and Chua's work and range from: 600 X **0.51** = ***306*** (low BNPP estimate); 600 X **0.60** = ***360*** (average BNPP estimate); 600 X **0.65** = ***390*** (high BNPP estimate).

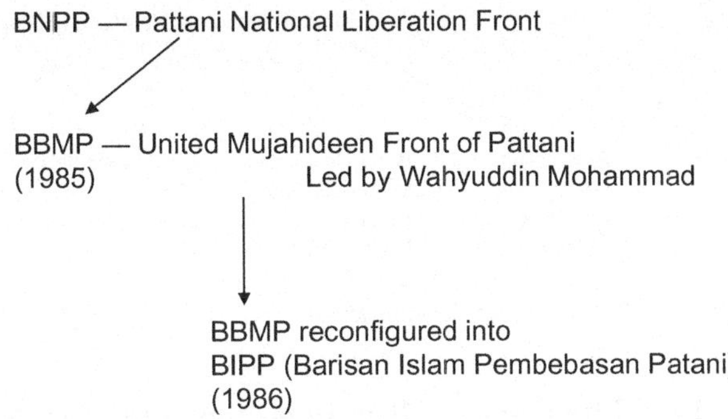

Fig. 7.1 BNPP fragmentation process

Thailand. For Croissant, "…its objective was neither mere autonomy or integration of Patani with Malaysia but complete independence and the establishment of an Islamic state, dar-al-Islam." [22, 25].

Indeed, Abuza asserts, "the BNPP was the most religiously motivated of the Thai organizations and, by 1986, ten of thirteen central committee members were Middle East-trained *ustadz* (Islamic teachers)." [13, 17, 17 n26, 1; 22, 23; 33, 33–35, 157].[16] Abuza also points out that BNPP crafted basic links to the fledgling PLO (1964), and significant ties to several Saudi madrassah, as well as to certain Egyptian Islamic scholars.

7.10 BNPP Demise and Spinoff Group: From BNPP to BBMP to BIPP

The decade of the 1980s was a lurking calamity for the BNPP. Abuza asserts the BNPP (Barisan Nasional Pembebasan Pattani or the Pattani National Liberation Front), began to pass into eclipse around 1982. Some three years later, remnants of the BNPP crafted a new BNPP "spinoff group" in 1985 called the BBMP or Barisan Bersata Mujahideen Pattani—the United Mujahideen Front of Pattani. At the helm of BBMP was its new leader, Wahyuddin Mohammad (see Fig. 7.1) [13, 17–18, 112; 32, 15].

Still, the fledgling BBMP transformed itself about a year later in 1986 into the BIPP (Barisan Islam Pembebasan Patani) or Islamic Liberation Front of Patani. Some authors suggest that was done at least in part for ideological reasons, to align more closely with the surge in world-wide popularity for the Jihadist movement. Be that as it may, the BBMP-BIPP organization became marginal to the political-military fray in Thailand and was moribund by the middle or late 1980s [13, 17–18, 112; 32, 15] (see Fig. 7.2).

[16] By contrast, Croissant provides 1963 as the inception date for BNPP.

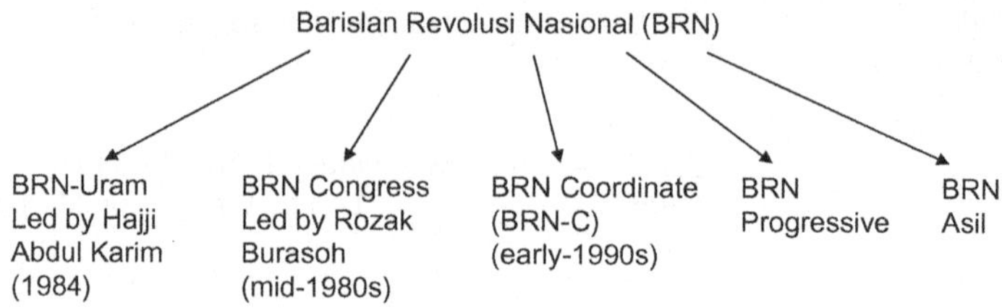

Fig. 7.2 BRN fragmentation process

7.11 The Barisan Revolusi Nasional (BRN)

Aside from Haji Sulong's short-lived Pattani People's Movement (PPM) in 1947, the Barisan Revolusi Nasional (BRN) represents perhaps the strongest historical ties to Thailand's early twentieth century history of resistance to Thai rule. A powerful set of ideological and familial connections existed between Haji Sulong Abdulkadir al-Fatani and the Barison Revolusi Nasional (BRN), primarily through his two sons, Amin Tohmeena and Den Tohmeena [13, 15; 32, 72; 41, 6]. In 1968, the original "military branch" of the BRN, known as the Angkatan Bersenjath Revolusi Pattani (ABREP), was culled out from the BRN [33, 33–34, 166, 163, 158–159].

McCargo reports Amin Tohmeena was one of four primary BRN founders who crafted that organization in 1960 [17, 8, 5, 8 n10; 31, 65; 32, 72, 76; 29, 29; 33, 33–35 157–158; 40, 63].[17] In addition to Amin, the other primary founders of BRN included Tenku Jalal Nasir, Dr. Haji Harun Sulong, Yasof Chapakiya, and Abdul Karim Hassan [17, 8, 5, 8 n10; 31, 65; 32, 72, 76; 33, 33–35 157–158; 35, 29; 40, 63]. A testament to those powerful family connections was that after Amin Tohmeena's death, Haji Sulong's other son, Den Tohmeena, took his brother's place as "President" of the BRN organization.

Den Tohmeena's replacement of his brother as BRN "President" followed a series of tortuous historical episodes for BRN around 1980. At that time, fierce political infighting between Amin Tohmeena and BRN chieftain Lukman Iskander on the one hand, and BRN's Supreme Council on the other, compelled Amin Tohmeena to exile himself to Malaysia in Kelantan province, and for a time in Sweden [32, 74–75; 33, 33–35, 157, 159; 35, 16; 40, 80, 67–69, 63].[18]

The Barisan Revolusi Nasional (BRN) is probably Thailand's most time-honored and widely recognizable terrorist organization. Its ideological perspective has been national-irredentism, originally augmented by Marxist-Leninist underpinnings. For some analysts, the BRN remains representative of older, top-down hierarchal terrorist groups in Thailand [17, vii, 1, 12; 32, 76; 33, 163, 159; 35, 28, 38; 40, 80].

---

[17] Helbardt reports that original BRN incarnation dissolved in 1981.

[18] Gunaratna, Acharya, and Chua report much of the problem revolved around Amin Tohmeena's collusion with elements of Malaysia's military to overthrow Malaysia's government, thereby in effect promoting Pattani's eventual liberation from Thailand.

That ideological perspective was one reason why the BRN maintained a close affiliation with the Communist Party of Malaya. Moreover, BRN had close ties to the PLO, Syria, Libya, and the FLN in Algeria [13, 26–27; 17, 7 n7, 8; 33, 34]. Indeed, the BRN remains as good an example as any of what Lesser, Hoffman, Arquilla, Ronfeldt, and Zanini label the "old terrorism." The notion of the "old terrorism" at least in part, refers to top-down bureaucratic, hierarchal frameworks characteristic of most terrorist groups in the Cold War [35, 6, 14–15, 17–20; 38, 85–144].

Prior to Malaysia's Prime Minister Mahathir bin Mohamad's decision in 1998 to tighten security at the Thailand-Malaysia border, members of BRN leadership and many BRN activists had significant access to safe-havens and resources in Malaysia's Kelantan province, and beyond [17, 8, 5, 8n10; 32, 100, 102; 33, 33–35, 157; 40, 63]. That still seems to be the case even though joint military efforts by Thailand and Malaysia to craft the Thai-Malaysia General Border Committee started in 1977 [13, 27; 1, 125; 27, 236–237, 242, 246; 33, 168–170, 164, 85, 108; 37, 5]. These cross-border effects also involved effective and sustained financial flows from sources in Malaysia that bolstered the coffers of BRN.

In the case of terrorist group size, Gunaratana, Acharya, and Chua report that BRN size levels have fluctuated over several decades. The authors suggest those fluctuations presuppose and derive from two sets of dynamics: first, political infighting that has led to terrorist group splintering or "spinoff formation," and second, enhanced Thai counterterrorism actions, that include examples of what Baldwin would call "positive sanctions," where economic and political "development programs" were used to disrupt or otherwise help dismantle terrorist organizations [3; 4; 21, 273–274; 33, 106; 35, 7–8].

McDermott suggests a third reason for BRN size fluctuation, namely the Thai government's amnesty program offered to Malay-Muslim separatist activists in the 1980s [41, 7]. In essence, Gunaratna, Acharya, and Chua divide BRN activist recruitment and retention levels into two phases. The authors report that between 1974 and 1977, BRN had some 600 front line activists, that number grew apace to some 1000 activists by 1981. A second phase of BRN recruitment, from around 1989, was marked by Thai government "development projects," and hardline Thai military and police actions; both those "hardline" and "soft-line" policies led to an atrophied BRN [33, 166–167; 35, 53].

For instance, we are told that, "in mid-1987, BRN and PULO were said to number between 350 to 400 fighters combined. In 1998, BRN was reported to have 100 active fighters. In 2000, BRN was estimated to have between 60 and 80 fighters. In 2001, authorities said BRN only had about 60 members left. By July 2002, the group is said to operate with just 30 members." [33, 166–167; 35, 53]. At the same time, estimates about more contemporary BRN membership numbers remain makeshift and incomplete [17; 33, 158, 33–35].

Chalk reports that from its earliest days, the primary political goal for BRN was twofold: first to craft an independent Pattani, and second, to craft what Chalk calls "...a wider pan-Southeast Asian Malay-Muslim socialist nation." [13, 20; 17, 5–6;

33, 157].[19] Around the time the Cold War began to pass into eclipse, BRN began to deemphasize its Marxist-Leninist rhetoric. It showcased more of what Yusuf calls its "ethno-religious nationalism," based on a fusion of Malay-Muslim ethnic identity and Islam [35, 28–29; 65, 45–47, 54–55].

Hence, the "new movement" of terrorists in Thailand McCargo describes has embraced Islam, and its language and symbols, to frame its core message of nationalist-irredentism [17, 2–3, 5–6; 6, 273–274; 37; 65, 46–47, 54–55].[20] The official political program of BRN now calls for the establishment of an Islamic state in Pattani and other geographical locales in close proximity Gunaratna et al. [33] report that in more recent years, BRN has put more emphasis on greater autonomy rather than on independence outright [33, 33–35, 157].

In addition, more current accounts also suggest that the path to take for Malay-Muslim self-determination is an issue still unresolved. For example, one International Crisis Group account states, "it is not clear that members and supporters have relinquished their maximalist goal of full-fledged independence, even if some leaders concede that autonomy or special administration may be a necessary waypoint." [37, 6].

At the same time, Chalk points to several factors that might have contributed to why BRN, at least in its original incarnation, has lost much of its significance for the contemporary struggle for self-determination in Thailand. Chalk points to the end of the Cold War and as mentioned above, to stringent cross border efforts in 1998 by Thai and Malaysian authorities to confront terrorism, as two watershed events that affected BRN adversely. Chalk also suggests that generational differences might have pitted the interests of older BRN activists, with a clearer Marxist-Leninist political agenda and world outlook, against the interests of younger generations of Malay-Muslims in the "deep south." [17, 1, 5–6; 32, 15].

Undoubtedly, less seasoned BRN terrorists have experienced political and economic frustrations similar to those which afflicted BRN terrorists of an earlier generation. Still, world events such as the end of the Cold War, the Iranian Revolution (1979), and the system of "intensive globalization" have largely outstripped the relevance of a Marxist-Leninist framework for the BRN struggle, where it is no longer bridled by a Cold War framework of "anti-imperialism" and "anti-capitalism." [17, 1, 5–6; 32, 15].

At the same time, the BRN might have also lost some of its relevance precisely because it seems possible the range of motivations to spur on terrorism in Thailand might have expanded. The central notion is that the expansion in the range of motivation to engage in terrorism might have happened within the context of Bangkok's political inertia about conflict resolution. Motivations might now include personal

---

[19] For Gunaratna, Acharya, and Chua the single, most predominant goal was to craft "an Islamic Republic".

[20] This seems reminiscent of the Kurdistan Workers Party (PKK) historical trajectory where Marxist-Leninist terminology was eventually eschewed in favor of Islamic phraseology to frame political statements in the post-Cold War world.

(e.g., retribution for Thai government oppression against family members), criminal, secular, and religious motivations, all within the context of Bangkok's political inertia over conflict resolution [8, 1–34; 40, 16].

What seems significant is that many of those explanatory factor effects linked to motivation and watershed world events dovetail nicely with Kaldor's notion of "new wars." In Kaldor's "new wars" conceptualization, mobilization for mobilization's sake is crucial in contemporary conflict where it becomes a political goal in and of itself, beyond a means to acquire other political goals [8, 1–34; 40, 16]. In other words conflict becomes what Kaldor calls "a mutual enterprise" where both sides profit from the continuation of the conflict. As of 2022, BRN continues to experience strains and tensions, BRN's political and military branches continue to wrestle over whether or not to participate in official peace negotiations with the Thai government, sponsored by the Malaysian government [37, 4, 6, 2–3, 9].

7.12 The Pattani United Liberation Organization (PULO)

The Pattani United Liberation Organization (PULO) is considered by some authorities to be the largest and most extensive terrorist organization that is operational in Thailand. Its sources and origins trace back to 1967 or 1968, when it was crafted and led by Tungku Bira Kotoniro and Kabir Abdul Rahman [13, 18; 33, 36–37; 40, 2, 168, 170, 143, 153; 41, 21, 8].[21] Gunaratna, Acharya, and Chua report that Kabir Abdul Rahman served as PULO "president" and was succeeded by Dr. Haji Harun Moleng in 1988 [32, 85; 33, 36–37]. Other important PULO chieftains included, Haji Sam-ae Thanam otherwise known as Haji Ismail Ghaddafi, Haji Had Mindosali, Dato Thanon, and Haji Mae Yala [13, 16; 1, 125].

The PULO was characterized primarily by its ethnocentric nationalist-irredentist ideology or as Abuza puts it, its "nationalist agenda." [13, 16, 18, 112]. As Gunaratna, Acharya, and Chua state, "moreover, during the 1980s, separatist groups such as (Pattani United Liberation Organization PULO) were largely secular." [33, 9, 36–37]. The penultimate goal for PULO has been political independence for Thailand's Southern states.Nevertheless, the foregoing authors report that prior to the Tak Bai incident in 2006, PULO had been largely inactive since the 1980s [17, 9; 33, 29–30].

Chalk describes the PULO mission as twofold: first to place emphasis on political indoctrination and the provision of educational services to the Malay Muslim population; second, to engage in terrorist actions against Thai government targets and civilians [17, 6]. In 2010, Poocharoen reported that what amounted to Thai government decentralization of control over the southern provinces, with the use of new apparatus, was an approach that PULO seemed to accept. In this plan, emphasis was placed, "…on shifting powers to new bureaucratic entities or to actors outside of the central government." [47, 193].

[21] Conversely, McDermott reports that PULO is "…the second largest…." terrorist organization in Thailand's southern provinces [41, 8, 21].

In terms of international connections, PULO had significant international ties to Iran, Syria, Egypt, and Libya. PULO also had a complex web of connections to Saudi Arabia, up until 1984. In 1984, Saudi authorities closed the offices of PULO permanently because of PULO's relationships to those aforementioned countries, and because of illicit PULO efforts to bring Malay-Muslims from Thailand into the Kingdom of Saudi Arabia [13, 26–27; 1, 126; 17, 7, 7 n7, 8; 32, 79, 90–91; 33, 38]. In addition to political connections to those state actors, PULO had also forged interconnections to Hezbollah [32, 34, 89, 9].

Both Funston and McDermott report that PULO began to splinter in the 1980s and into the 1990s [27, 248; 41, 21]. At least in part, that might account for why PULO has remained largely incommunicado with state authorities from the 1980's up until recently [32, 50, 61, 63, 67]. In fact, McDermott notes little BRN communication with both its constituents and the Thai government for about a ten year period [35, 3; 41, 23].

The current number of front-line activists PULO has at its disposal is hard to discern; what seems clear is those rates, like BRN rates, have fluctuated over time. Gunaratna, Acharya, and Chua report in 2005 that, "in the 1970s, at its peak of its popularity, PULO had 1000 members. That number is now reduced to about 30–50 active armed cadres." [33, 38, 33–35, 158; 35, 7]. Conversely, Chalk [17], who called PULO "...the largest and most prominent..." terrorist organization in Thailand from 1960 through 2000, estimated that at its height PULO numbered approximately 350 hard-core cadres [17, 6; 33, 36, 38, 33–35, 158; 41, 21, 8]. Clearly, Chalk's appraisal of PULO strength is different from Gunaratna, Acharya, and Chua's estimate, but both estimates are useful because it is possible to establish a range of PULO membership.

7.13 Second Phase Terrorist Organizations in Thailand

7.13.1 Barisan Revolusi Nasional (BRN) Splinter Organizations

In the middle 1980s, the Barisan Revolusi Nasional (BRN) essentially splintered into three or four terrorist groups or "factions" that were distinguishable from one another. For Abuza, these "factions" included the BRN Coordinate (BRN-C) that Helbardt reports went public in 2013, the BRN-Congress, and the BRN-Uram. In contrast, Gunaratna, Acharya, and Chua (2005) add two other BRN "splinter" group factions to the mix—the BRN Progressive, and BRN Asli [13, 20; 27, 238, 248; 32, 75; 33, 35, 161–162; 35, 3, 5].[22]

[22] Abuza also tells us several less significant terrorist groups or proto-groups materialized at that time that included, but were not limited to, Dawlaw Taloh, Tantra Jihad Islam and Sabil-illah. In turn, Gunaratna, Acharya, and Chua report that Tantra Jihad Islam was crafted from a group of "disgruntled" BRN and PULO activists [13, 20; 33, 161].

There seems to be more agreement about the severe political infighting that started in the 1980s or 1990s that rend apart BRN leadership. Gunaratna, Acharya, and Chua's emphasis on "...conflict of interest" between group leaders reflects the same type of fierce political infighting showcased in previous case studies that stemmed from personal rivalries and animosities, and differences of opinion in this case about how to frame and promote the struggle for an independent Pattani. For Abuza, "the groups were highly fractious, and divided on issues of ideology, tactics, and goals." [13, 20; 27, 238, 248; 32, 75; 33, 35, 161–162; 35, 3, 5].

Those authors also seem to suggest that international systems structural factor effects were at work, with the end of the Cold War and the Iranian revolution (1979) that itself can be positioned both at the "international systems" level and the "nation-state" level of analysis [32, 43, 59, 69; 33, 6; 44, 48, 59–64; 58, 12, 159–186]. Those two watershed events influenced many terrorist groups such as the Kurdistan Workers Party (PKK) in Turkey, as previously mentioned, terrorist groups in Thailand have also embraced Islamic symbols and language to frame the nationalist-irredentist nature of their struggle for Pattani. The focus of attention in this brief section is on the major BRN splinter groups that many experts assert have played major roles in the contemporary conflict in Thailand.

The sources of BRN Coordinate (BRN-C) trace their origins back to the early 1990s; in the case of the BRN "strategic" template, its origin dates to 1984 [35, 32]. The top echelon BRN-C leadership structure is the Dewan Pimpinan Parti (DPP), itself comprised of some thirty five top BRN-Coordinate chieftains. In addition, Helbardt reports the BRN-Coordinate had some 3000 front-line activists around 2004, against the backdrop of some 30,000 others, for whom there appears to be some variation in scope and degree of BRN-Coordinate involvement [35, 32, 36, 38–40, 53].

The BRN-Coordinate has traditionally placed an emphasis on political activity, but Gunaratna, Acharya, and Chua assert that with the uptick in violence in 2004, the BRN-C evolved to become "...the vanguard of separatist groups in the south." For example, we are told of several pondok instructors who were tied into BRN-C and implicated in the watershed January 4, 2004 arms heist in Narathiwat, as well as to other terrorist assaults on schools. According to authoritative sources, that arms heist was reportedly led by pondok teacher Loh Supeh, also known as Waeyusoh Waedeuramae, who himself had substantive ties to the BRN-Coordinate [15, 20; 17, 9; 32, 77, 43, 51, 64, 60, 68–69; 33, 163, 31, 104; 35, 2–3, 5, 13, 31; 37, 1–2; 40, 4, 146, 148; 65, 47–48, 54; 27, 241, 247, 238].

In that arms heist, which in my judgement does not qualify as a terrorist assault based on the juridical criteria used in this study because it was designed only to steal weapons, a sizeable number of M-16 assault rifles, grenade launchers, and other weapons were seized from a Thai military installation in Narathiwat [13, 20; 32, 76, 78, 43; 33, 156, 162–163; 35, 2]. In terms of terrorist group funding, BRN-Coordinate has imposed its own "tax" as Helbardt puts it, on its membership that initially started at 30 Bhat each month. In turn, as BRN-C activists become more seasoned, those monthly "tax rates" increased in kind [35, 43–44].

BRN-Coordinate has also acquired revenue from voluntary donations (zakat) from pondoks and individuals, as well as from extortion [35, 43–44]. For Helbardt, it remains unclear if BRN-Coordinate is involved in organized criminal activities beyond the extortion practiced against large-scale private establishments owned or run by Buddhists [35, 43–44, 50]. Nowadays, although many of the separatist terrorist groups that perpetrate terrorist assaults in Thailand remain shrouded in obscurity, experts agree BRN-C is a major terrorist group stakeholder in Thailand's southern provinces [13, 20; 32, 76, 78, 43; 33, 156, 162–163; 35, 2, 41, 43, 44, 50, 55].

In contrast, the BRN-Congress has had a much more singular approach to military action in Thailand's southern provinces. Its chieftain, Rosa Buraka, otherwise known as Abdul Razakk Rahaman or Rozak Burasoh, has been at the helm of the BRN-Congress, presumably since its inception in the middle 1980s. In fact, the BRN-Congress is considered by some scholars to be the most hardline and aggressive of those BRN splinter groups. In the early 2000s, the BRN-Congress remained active in the southern provinces of Yala and Narathiwat under the aegis of one of its chief terrorist tacticians, Masu-ngai Badu [13, 20; 32, 76, 78, 43; 33, 156, 162–163; 35, 2, 41, 44, 50].

In turn, the BRN-Uram was a BRN splinter group formed by Hajji Abdul Karim. Hajji Abdul Karim led that organization from around 1984, until his death. The primary activities of BRN-Uram included work to write and publish documents about political matters and religious affairs, and engage activists in political canvassing. As Gunaratna, Acharya, and Chua point out, that focus was rather far removed from the military fray. Lastly, the BRN-Progressive was another BRN appendage with primarily a military orientation. It is described as a "paramilitary" branch that galvanized decades after the establishment of BRN's Angkatan Bersenjath Revolusi Pattani (ABREP) [13, 20; 32, 76, 78, 43; 33, 156, 162–163; 35, 2, 41, 44, 50] (see Fig. 7.2).

7.14 New PULO—A PULO Splinter Group

The basic contours of New PULO emerged in 1995 within the context of political disagreements in PULO in 1993. Gunaratna and Acharya report the primary issue that led to the splintering of the group was how to proceed with a 1993 government offer of cessation of hostilities, to be followed up by new and presumably more serious efforts at conflict resolution. While that offer must have pulled parts of the PULO leadership in different directions, both McDermott and Funston point to strains and tensions within PULO leadership circles that date back as far as the 1980s.

In contrast to other PULO leaders who were inclined to accept that confidence building measure (CBM) in pursuit of peace talks, Haji Abdul Rohman and A-rong Muleng split from PULO in 1995 to craft two new paramilitary branches that gave structural shape to the fledgling New PULO organization [32, 95–97, 100; 35, 3, 16]. To be more specific, Haji Abdul Rohman formed the Cadden Army, while A-rong Muleng, who appeared to some to be the more militant of the two, crafted PULO

88. In comparison to PULO, these two New PULO branches were distinguished from each other by their different orientation and emphasis on political or military activities [32, 95–97, 100; 35, 3, 16].

In essence, New PULO was nationalist-irredentist in nature, tinged with an Islamic hue. New PULO leaders issued a clarion call for either an independent Islamic nation-state, or for a return to an Islamic Sultanate. In addition to differences with PULO about the prospect of a ceasefire and peace talks in 1993, Gunaratna and Acharya point out that broader differences between the New PULO and PULO also revolved around a preference by New PULO chieftains to carry out less intensive terrorist assaults directed at civilians, with more emphasis placed on the symbolic significance of terrorist attacks [32, 95–97, 100; 35, 3, 16].

PULO's base of operations was found in Kelantan Province, Malaysia. At its peak in the 1980s, New PULO had some 1000 front line activists. In 1998, the New PULO leadership was hampered severely by a series of arrests by Malaysian authorities that decimated the operational effectiveness of New PULO and its ideological orientation for the future. In those arrests, Abdul Rohman bin Kadir, Haji Da-oh Thanam, and Haji Bueda, were incarcerated [32, 95–97, 100; 35, 3, 16]. For Gunaratna and Acharya, "the arrests left New PULO's rank and file in a state of confusion. Morale was very low and some of its members, who lost faith in the group, gave themselves up to the Thai government." [32, 97].

Gunaratna and Acharya report that by 2013, the number of New PULO activists had diminished by some ninety percent or more, to about 100 front-line activists or even less. At the same time, the authors report that New PULO was characterized by sharp divisions between its military branch, led by A-rong and its political branch, led by Haji Abdul Rohman [32, 97–98, 33]. The foregoing has led some analysts to conclude that New PULO has ceased to play a significant role in the contemporary political fray.

7.15 Gerakan Mujahideen Islam Pattani (GMIP)

Authoritative accounts about the sources and origins Gerakan Mujahideen Islam Pattani (GMIP) also appear to diverge at least to some degree. For Abuza, Gerakan Mujahideen Islam Pattani (GMIP) was originally crafted as a Thai separatist organization by Vae-Hama Vae-Yuso in 1986 [13, 106–108; 32, 101].[23] In comparison, Gunaratna and Acharya suggest GMIP coalesced as a spinoff group from a localized Malay-Muslim separatist organization called Gerakan Mujahideen Pattani (GMI), itself crafted in 1986. The Gerakan Mujahidden Pattani (GMI), as GMIP's antecedent organization, operated in Yangi District in Narathiwat, and in Mayo, Ruesoh, and Ra-ngae districts in Pattani [32, 101–102].

[23] Gunaratna and Acharya provide at date of 1995.

According to Gunaratna and Acharya's account, it was Nasorae Saesaeng, otherwise known as Haji Wae or Awae Keleh Poh Wa, who crafted GMIP in 1995. Nevertheless, both accounts describe the important roles that Nasae Saning, and particularly Jaekumae Kutae, played in the galvanization of Gerakan Mujahideen Islam Pattani (GMIP). With the passage of time, it was Jackmae Kutae who emerged as "President" of GMIP, presumably after some political infighting between Vae-Hama Vae Youso and other GMIP chieftains [13, 106–108; 32, 100–104; 33, 33, 40–41]. Abuza reports GMIP's base of operations, like several other Thai separatists groups, was found across the border in Malaysia's Kelantan province [13, 108].

Still, both accounts converge in their assessment that GMIP has been the closest of all of Thailand's separatist groups in the "deep south" to the basic ideological orientation of Salafism, and to Jihadism's international networks. In similar vein, authorities point to the exposure that (future) chieftains of GMIP had to Jihadist ideas when serving in Afghanistan [13, 108]. For Abuza, GMIP straddles the line between terrorist group and criminal syndicalist organization in ways that are reminiscent of the Abu Sayyaf Group (ASG) in the Philippines. For example, Abuza reports powerful ties between GMIP and the Aceh Free Movement (GAM) in Indonesia that have included collaborative illegal arms transfers [13, 106–108; 32, 100–104; 33, 33, 40–41].

The GMIP has been a significant stakeholder in the separatist struggle against the Thai government for Pattani's political independence since at least 2005. In his report on the absence of BRN-C in the 2005 "peace talks" between Thai separatist groups and the Thaksin Shinawatra government, Funston relates that, "…the GMIP is assumed to conduct some on the ground activities…." [27, 247]. As some scholars suggest, the strong GMIP ideological affinity to Salafism as GMIP helps to spearhead what McCargo calls the "new movement" of terrorism might provide the portal to greater Jihadi influence in Thailand's separatist struggle that itself might come from Indonesia, the Philippines, the Middle East, or a combination thereof.

7.16 Runda Kumulan Kecil (RKK)—Small Patrol Groups

There is comparatively little information available about the sources and origins of the Runda Kumulam Kecil (RKK), otherwise known as the "Small Patrol Groups". Some scholars such as Gunaratna and Acharya suggest that Runda Kumulan Kecil (RKK) could actually be a BRN- Coordinate front group or a BRN-C "splinter group." [17, 11; 32, 113, 118; 35, 46–47, 49, 51, 54; 40, 172]. In fact, Abuza's account about RKK lends weight to that central notion about RKK as a BRN-C front group. The author states, "…the RKK is not an independent group per se, but rather a name for BRN-C militants who had received some training in Indonesia—mostly, it seems, while studying there." [13, 117, 114, 119; 35, 46–47, 49, 51, 54].

What scholars do know is that BRN-C (Coordinate) and RKK, which almost certainly have some type of close links, both have been extremely active in Thailand's contemporary political and military fray [32, 114, 47–48; 35, 6, 14–15, 19–20, 25, 27;

40, 142; 1, 119].[24] In fact, Runda Kumulan Keceil (RKK) is perhaps the most prolific terrorist organization in what McCargo calls the "new movement" of terrorism in contemporary Thailand [32, 113; 40, 172, 174]. What has also been established is that like many other Thai separatist groups such as GMIP, RKK's base of operations is in Malaysia's Kelantan province.

According to Gunaratna and Acharya, RKK is led by Ustaz Rohring Ahsong, while another RKK chieftain of note is Zulkifli Bin Hir. Even though there is very little information to report about Ustaz Rohring Ahsong, what is known is that Zulkifli Bin Hir, who was thought to be in the Philippines in 2013, has had strong ties to Jema'ah Islamiyah (JI) and JI activities in Indonesia [13, 113–114, 117; 32, 114, 116–117]. In addition, other notable RKK chieftains have included Sapee-aree Jehkar, Udeeman Samoh, and Ma-ae Aphibalbabe (32, 116; 1, 94).

To be sure, not much is known about the nature of RKK leadership. In turn, there are similar information problems with respect to RKK size, where estimates are wide-ranging. According to Gunaratna and Acharya, RKK has between some 300–1000 activists [13, 117; 32, 115]. In comparison, Abuza's estimate is that RKK is comprised of some 500 front-line activists [13, 117]. Notwithstanding that, the geographical scope of RKK operations appears narrower than for some other Thai separatist groups. One authoritative account asserts that in 2013, RKK had put almost singular emphasis on activities in parts of Yala province, specifically in Than To, Pinang, Krong, Muang, and Banang Sata districts [32, 115].

7.17 Terrorist Assault Business Vulnerability Index (TABVI)

As in the cases of India, Mexico, Brazil, and South Africa, a TABVI index score is calculated to provide an overall assessment of the threat to business targets in Thailand and the susceptibilities of different types of business targets in Thailand to terrorism between 2013 and 2018. Thailand's TABVI score was calculated by dividing the total number of business-related terrorist assaults chronicled (343 acts) by the *World Executive Forum* ranking score for Thailand—"4.1"—that itself reflected the degree that terrorism threat exacted costs on business operations in Thailand ([62, 63], Business costs of terrorism; Methodological Appendix—Thailand). The TABVI score obtained is 83.7 where 343 acts is divided by the TABVI "Executive Opinion Survey" score of "4.1".

Recall that in terms of the TABVI scale, a higher score reflects a higher degree of risk and perceived vulnerability, while a lower TABVI score indicates lower degrees of risk and perceived vulnerability. In terms of Thailand's 83.7 TABVI score, that

---

[24] In contrast, Helbardt contends that the BRN-C organizational structure is a "hybrid" of both the top-down hierarchal bureaucratic model and the "horizontal" or "flat" model of organization [35, 6, 17–18].

score for Thailand compares favorably to India's very high TABVI score of 156.6, which in turn, reflects very high rates of threat and vulnerability.

In turn, Thailand's raw aggregate TABVI score of 83.7 reflects a condition of terrorism threat that based on this measure, is greater than the degree of risk and perceived vulnerability found for business targets in Mexico (TABVI = 9.375), South Africa (TABVI = 5.96) and Brazil (TABVI = 2.58), but less than for business targets in India.

Overall, that TABVI ranking for terrorism threat for Thailand differs to some degree from the *World Economic Forum* "Business costs of terrorism" rankings. In the *World Economic Forum* survey, those rankings suggest that the influence that terrorism threat exerts over business costs India (ranked #117/137 countries) is less than for Thailand (ranked #121/137) as assessed by business leaders of a particular country, where the higher rankings reflect higher terrorism costs imputed.

It should be noted that lower TABVI scores, such as Mexico (TABVI = 9.375) and South Africa (TABVI = 5.96) for example, indicated lesser amounts of risk and/ or perceived vulnerability. As previously mentioned in Chapter Two, the TABVI ranking system is the reverse of the *World Economic Forum* survey results. For instance, those *WEF* results ranked business costs in Mexico as slightly less affected by the threat of terrorism (Mexico was ranked #87/137) compared to South Africa (#92/137 countries).

In turn, in the cases of India and Thailand, there was a similar pattern of divergence in ranking between TABVI scores and the *World Economic Forum* rankings of perceived costs of terrorism on business operations. In contrast to TABV findings, business executives in India in those *WEF* data perceived the threat of terrorism on business costs of operations in India as lower (India #117/137 countries) than corresponding Thai executives did for Thailand (Thailand #121/137 countries).

Notwithstanding that, there was convergence between TABVI scores and WEF rankings for Brazil. In the case of Brazil, the TABVI score of 2.58 suggested that commercial interests in Brazil were not at risk to the same degree as commercial interests in the other four host countries under consideration for the 2013–2108 time period. In a similar vein, Brazil was ranked very highly in the WEF survey results with a ranking of #8/13 countries [62, 63].

It is now possible to craft a continuum of aggregate country TABVI measures with standardized scores. Each of those raw TABVI scores is divided by 1.566 (or multiplied by 0.638) to correspond with how the highest raw score of 156.6 (India) was divided by 1.566 to obtain 100.0. The standardized TABVI aggregate scores for the five developing world host countries under consideration are: Brazil with 1.65; South Africa with 3.80; Mexico with 5.99; Thailand with 53.4, and India with 100.0.

In this continuum, a three-point Likert ordinal scale with a range to correspond to those standardized scores is articulated. On this continuum, what amounts to a "low level" of terrorism threat and vulnerability is the range between 1 and 10, while "medium level" terrorist threat and vulnerability levels range from TABVI scores of between 11 and 50. In turn, "host states" with TABVI scores between 51 and 100 fall on points in the "high" level rage of the terrorism threat and vulnerability continuum.

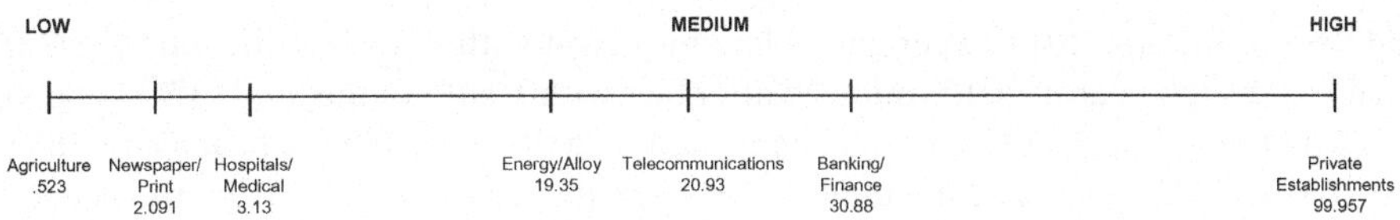

Fig. 7.3 Thailand industry vulnerability spectrum standardized TABVI scores < 1 to 10 = low risk; 11 to 50 = medium risk; 51 to 100 = high risk

It follows that in the business related terrorism threat appraisal for the 2013–2018 period, Brazil, South Africa, and Mexico were all found at the "low risk" part of the continuum, while Thailand was found at the medium–high range of the continuum. The TABVI measure suggests India exhibited the highest threat/vulnerability level to business related terrorist assaults for this six year period of between January 2013 and December 31, 2018.

In the case of specific industries in Thailand, it is possible generate threat/vulnerability scores to make ranking comparisons of industries across Thailand's economic sectors and across countries. The industry scores for Thailand are: Agriculture (1/4.1 = 0.244); Newspaper (print) (4/4.1 = 0.976); Hospitals/Medical (6/4.1 = 1.46), Energy/Alloy (37/4.1 = 9.02), Telecommunications (40/4.1 = 9.76); Banking/Finance (59/4.1 = 14.4); Private Establishments (191/4.1 = 46.6).

As in the case of "host country," it is possible to craft a continuum of Thai industry threat/vulnerability with standardized TABVI scores. At the high end of results, 46.6 × 2.145 = 99.957 Thus, multiplying each TABVI score obtained by 2.145 provides standardized scores for a continuum of threat/vulnerability from 0 to 100. In the case of "Agriculture," the standardized score is 5.22; "Newspaper (print)" is ***2.091***; "Hospitals/Medical" is ***3.13***; "Energy/Alloy" is ***19.34***; "Telecommunications" is ***20.93***; "Banking and Finance" is 30.88; Private Establishments is 99.957.

In turn, it is possible to craft this continuum of Thai industry threat/vulnerability with ordinal values to designate degrees of risk. For the purposes of this study about Thailand's industry, 0.522–10.0 is "low risk," while 11.0–50.0 is "medium level risk" and 51–100.00 is "high risk." (see Fig. 7.3).

7.18 Empirical Observations About Terrorism in Thailand

7.18.1 Relative Frequencies and Percentages of Commercial Target Terrorist Assaults

7.18.1.1 Targets by Year

Those data for the 2013–2018 interval were marked by cyclical peaks and troughs commonplace to note in data breakdown by year. In this sample, 2013 was the highest peak year for commercial terrorist targets in Thailand with 31.5% of the total (108/

343 acts). In turn, 2014 experienced less terrorism with 21.9% of the total (75/343 acts). A trough year in 2015 followed after that with 10.8% of the total (37/343 acts). Two additional peaks in those data happened in 2016 and 2018, that each amounted to 16.0% (55/343 acts) of the total. In between those peaks was 2017—the deepest trough year with 3.8% (13/343 acts) of the total (see Fig. 7.4).

7.19 Terrorist Assault by Business Target-Type, Firm Origin, Terrorist Group-Type, and Terrorist Group

For business terrorist assault type, a breakdown of data reveals that a full 56.5% of all commercial target based terrorism in Thailand (191/338 acts) was directed at "private establishments." Terrorism aimed at "banking and finance" institutions placed a very distant second place at 17.5% (59/338 acts) while attacks against "telecommunications" targets ranked third with 11.8% (40/338 acts). In turn, "energy/ alloy" targets ranked fourth with 10.9% (37/338 acts), while "hospitals/medical facilities" placed fifth with 1.8% (6/338 acts) of the total. The types of business targets with the lowest rates of attack in Thailand were newspaper/print targets with 1.2% (4/338 acts) and agricultural targets with one act or 0.3% of the total (see Fig. 7.5).

The top rate for terrorist assaults against commercial targets in Thailand is compared to corresponding rates across the four other "host countries" under consideration. That 56.5% rate for "private establishments" in Thailand is over twice as high as the 24.3% (160/658 acts) rate for "private establishments" in India. In addition, that 56.5% "private establishments" rate for Thailand dwarfs "private establishments" rates for Mexico (4.4%), and Brazil (5.6%). However, it falls well short of the 82.1% mark set by South African "private establishments."

In the case of firm nationality of the business targets selected for attack, those data show a full 87.7% (249/284 acts) were aimed at Thai targets, while only 12.3% of all commercial based terrorist attacks (35/284 acts) in Thailand were directed against foreign based firms. Indeed, the findings for India, Mexico, and Brazil had foreign based and domestic business target data breakdowns that were similar to those ratios found for Thailand.

For example, India had a 98.3% rate for national targets and a 1.7% for foreign based targets; Brazil had a 94.7% rate for national targets and a 5.3% for foreign based targets; Mexico had a 92.6% for national targets and a 7.4% for foreign based targets. The exception was South Africa—it was found that South Africa was characterized by almost mirror like findings to all of the foregoing; 71.4% involved foreign based targets, but only a little over one-fourth at 28.6% involved targets with national South African origins (see Fig. 7.6).

In the case of terrorist group-type, Thailand's political landscape was marked by terrorist assaults against commercial targets carried out by nationalist-irredentist terrorist groups with Islamic trappings, and by anonymous attacks. It was anonymous attacks at 52.0% (178/342 acts) that comprised the largest portion of terrorism

Frequencies

Statistics

Year

N	Valid	343
	Missing	0

Year

		Frequency	Percent	Valid Percent	Cumulative Percent
Valid	2013	108	31.5	31.5	31.5
	2014	75	21.9	21.9	53.4
	2015	37	10.8	10.8	64.1
	2016	55	16.0	16.0	80.2
	2017	13	3.8	3.8	84.0
	2018	55	16.0	16.0	100.0
	Total	343	100.0	100.0	

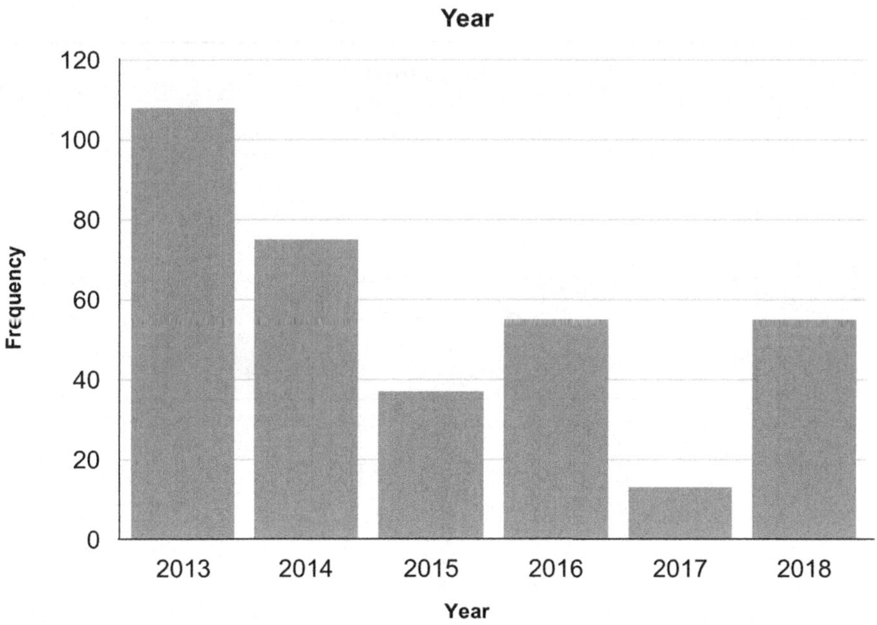

Fig. 7.4 Relative frequency of Thailand terrorist attacks by Year, 2013–2018

Frequencies

Statistics

Bus.Target

N	Valid	338
	Missing	5

Bus.Target

		Frequency	Percent	Valid Percent	Cumulative Percent
Valid	Energy/Alloy	37	10.8	10.9	10.9
	Hospitals/Medical	6	1.7	1.8	12.7
	Private Establishments	191	55.7	56.5	69.2
	Telecommunications	40	11.7	11.8	81.1
	Newspaper/Print	4	1.2	1.2	82.2
	Banking/Finance	59	17.2	17.5	99.7
	Agriculture	1	.3	.3	100.0
	Total	338	98.5	100.0	
Missing	System	5	1.5		
Total		343	100.0		

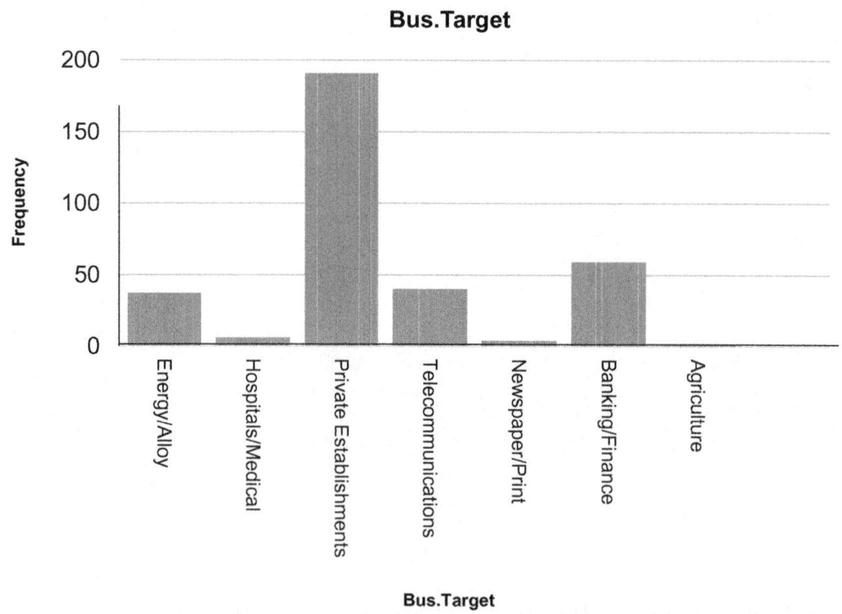

Fig. 7.5 Relative frequency of Thailand terrorist attacks by Business Target, 2013–2018

Frequencies

Statistics

Target

N	Valid	284
	Missing	59

Target

		Frequency	Percent	Valid Percent	Cumulative Percent
Valid	National	249	72.6	87.7	87.7
	Foreign	35	10.2	12.3	100.0
	Total	284	82.8	100.0	
Missing	System	59	17.2		
Total		343	100.0		

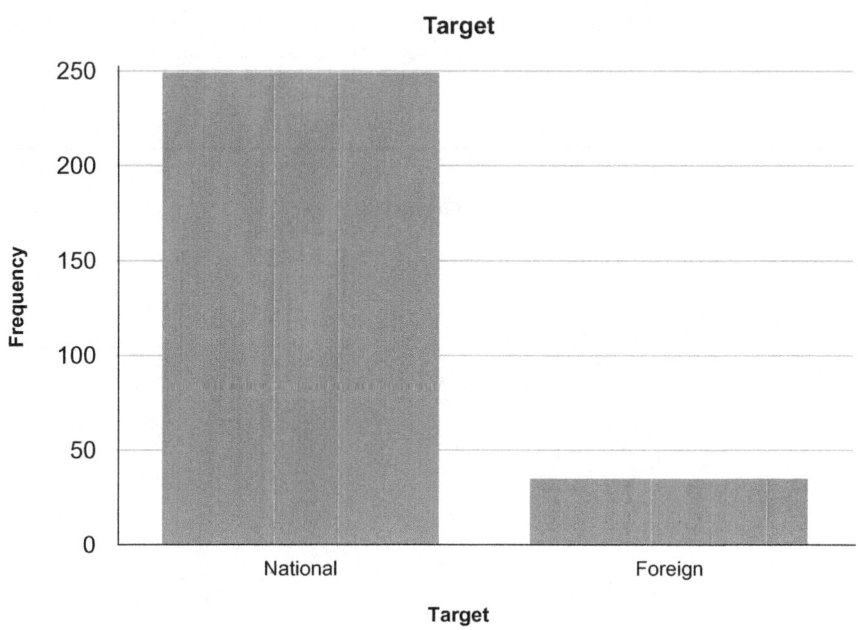

Fig. 7.6 Relative frequency of Thailand terrorist attacks by Foreign Business Target and National Business Target, 2013–2018

against commercial targets, followed closely behind by Islamic nationalist-irredentist terrorist groups with 48.0% (164/342 acts) (35, 5, 9, 18, 20). Those findings for group-type largely conformed to the literature that described anonymous terrorism as a hallmark of contemporary Thai terrorism, but the high rate of attributable terrorist assaults by group-type was somewhat unexpected [40, 165, 168] (see Fig. 7.7).

Frequencies

Statistics

GroupTy

N	Valid	342
	Missing	1

GroupTy

		Frequency	Percent	Valid Percent	Cumulative Percent
Valid	Anonymous	178	51.9	52.0	52.0
	Islamic Nationalist-Irredentist	164	47.8	48.0	100.0
	Total	342	99.7	100.0	
Missing	System	1	.3		
Total		343	100.0		

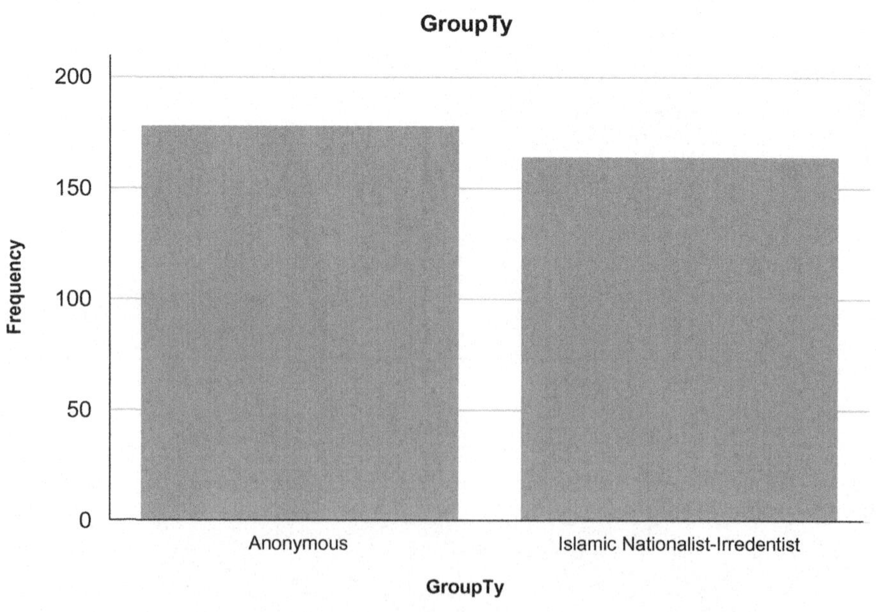

Fig. 7.7 Relative frequency of Thailand terrorist attacks by Group-Type, 2013–2018

For identifiable Thai terrorist groups, the results show that with 9.9% of the total (34/343 acts), Barisan Revolusi Nasional (BRN) had the highest percentage of terrorist assaults with attribution. The rate for Runda Kumpulan Kecil (RKK) followed with 5.0% (17/343 acts) of the total. In turn, the Masorae Duerama Group, the Hundum Musordee Group, and the Mayakoh Lateh Group each carried out one terrorist assault for 0.3% of the total[25] (see Fig. 7.8).

7.20 Terrorist Assaults by Province (Changwat)

A breakdown of data by province revealed two tiers of empirical results. The first tier included provinces in Thailand that experienced more than one percent of the total amount of commercial based terrorism chronicled. The second tier of provinces was comprised of provinces in Thailand that experienced less than one percent of the total amount of business related terrorism chronicled (see Fig. 7.9).

For provinces with much more than one percent of the total, the "deep south" provinces stood out in sharp relief. For example, Pattani had the highest rate with 34.7% (118/340 acts), followed by Narathiwat province with 25.3% (86/340 acts). Yala province followed very closely behind with 23.5% (80/340 acts). In turn, Songkhla accounted for 9.7% (33/340 acts) of all chronicled commercial based terrorism, while 2.6% of the total (9/340 acts) took place in "Bangkok Metropolitan Region." [29, 30]. Hence, Pattani, Narathiwat, and Yala accounted for a full 83.5% (284/340 acts) of all business related terrorism in Thailand from 2013 to 2018.

The second tier of findings was comprised of Thai provinces with less than one percent of the total amount of chronicled commercial based terrorism in Thailand—there were nine provinces in all. Those nine provinces included: the northern province of Chiang Mai with 0.9% (3/340 acts), and three provinces each with 0.6% a piece—Pathum Thani province in central Thailand (2/340 acts), Prachuap Khiri Khan province in west Thailand (2/340 acts), and Chachoengsao province in the central part of Thailand (2/340 acts).

In turn, five Thai provinces each experienced 1/340 acts or only 0.3% of the total. Those provinces included Nonthaburi (0.3%); Tak (0.3%), Surat Thani (0.3%), Krabi (0.3%), and Nakhon Si Thammarat (0.3%) in the northern-central part of Thailand. Those empirical findings suggest that at least for business related terrorism between 2013 and 2018, terrorism seepage from the south into parts of the central and northern areas of Thailand was very small.

25 What is significant here is that even though many terrorist assaults could be attributed as carried out by nationalist-irredentist with Islamic trappings, there could be no further identification based on specific terrorist group- name. That might help to explain the foregoing results where for terrorist group-type, the percentage rate for anonymous nationalist-irredentist groups (with Islamic trappings) almost matched the percentage of anonymous terrorist acts, but where with the terrorist group-name findings, there was a very large difference between the percentage of identifiable terrorist groups and anonymous groups.

Frequencies

Statistics

GroupName

N	Valid	343
	Missing	0

GroupName

		Frequency	Percent	Valid Percent	Cumulative Percent
Valid	Masorae Duerama Group	1	.3	.3	.3
	Runda Kumpulan Kecil (RKK)	17	5.0	5.0	5.2
	Hundum Musordee Group	1	.3	.3	5.5
	Barisan Revolusi Nasional (BRN)	34	9.9	9.9	15.5
	Anonymous	289	84.3	84.3	99.7
	Mayakoh Lateh Group	1	.3	.3	100.0
	Total	343	100.0	100.0	

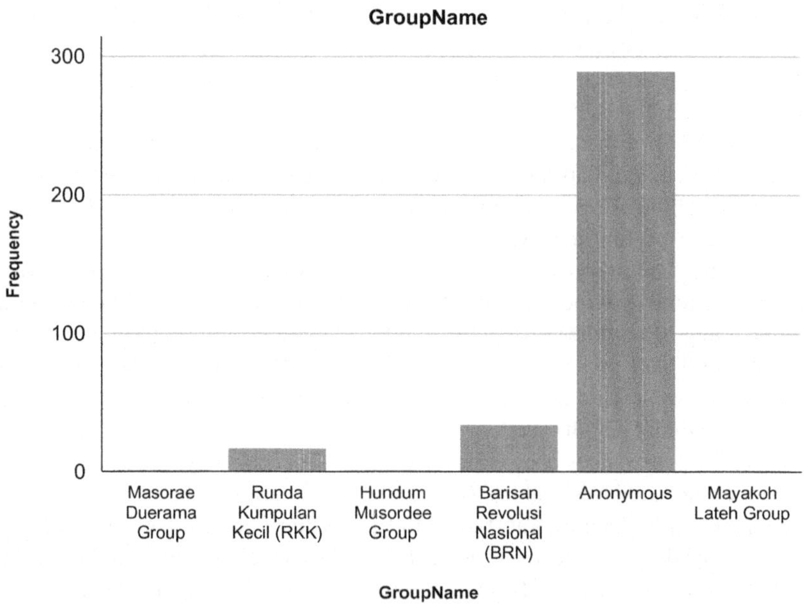

Fig. 7.8 Relative frequency of Thailand terrorist attacks by Terrorist Group, 2013–2018

Frequencies

Statistics

ProvState

N	Valid	340
	Missing	3

ProvState

		Frequency	Percent	Valid Percent	Cumulative Percent
Valid	Narathiwat Province	86	25.1	25.3	25.3
	Pattani Province	118	34.4	34.7	60.0
	Yala Province	80	23.3	23.5	83.5
	Bangkok Metropolis	9	2.6	2.6	86.2
	Songkhla Province	33	9.6	9.7	95.9
	Nonthaburi Province	1	.3	.3	96.2
	Chiang Mai Province	3	.9	.9	97.1
	Tak Province	1	.3	.3	97.4
	Pathum Thani Province	2	.6	.6	97.9
	Surat Thani Province	1	.3	.3	98.2
	Prachuap Khiri Khan Province	2	.6	.6	98.8
	Krabi Province	1	.3	.3	99.1
	Nakhon Si Thammarat Province	1	.3	.3	99.4
	Chachoengsao Province	2	.6	.6	100.0
	Total	340	99.1	100.0	
Missing	System	3	.9		
Total		343	100.0		

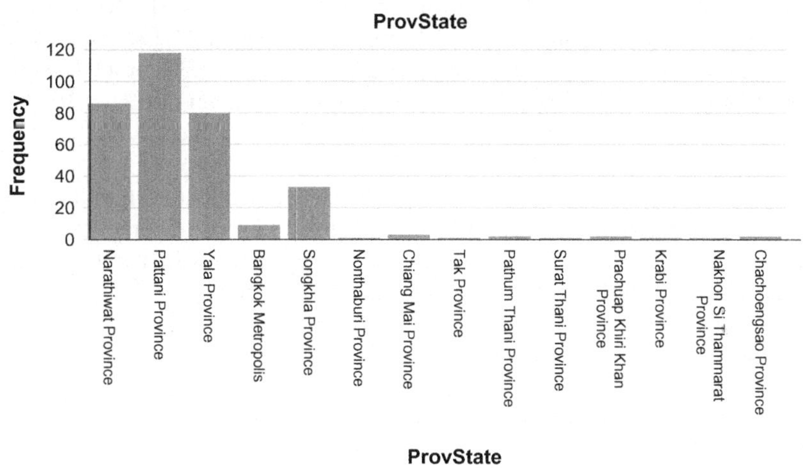

Fig. 7.9 Relative frequency of Thailand terrorist attacks by Province (Changwat), 2013–2018

7.21 Terrorist Assaults by District

When data were broken down based on district, the results show relative frequencies clustered into three groupings. The first grouping was comprised of districts in Thailand where more than 10.0% of all commercial based terrorism happened. That first grouping was comprised of Mueang Pattani district in Pattani province where a full 18.5% of all commercial based terrorism (58/314 acts) happened and Mueang Yala district in Yala province, where 11.5% of the total amount (36/314 acts) took place. In sum, those two Thai districts accounted for 30.0% (94/314 acts) or nearly one-third of all commercial based terrorism chronicled in this sample (see Fig. 7.10).

A second grouping of Thai districts had rates of between some 6.0 and 1.0% of the total. For example, Yarang district (in Pattani) experienced 6.1% of the total (19/314 acts), while Mueang Narathiwat district (in Narathiwat) and Su-ngai Kolok district (in Narathiwat) each experienced 4.8% (15/314 acts) of the total. In turn, Khok Pho District (in Pattani) accounted for 4.1% the total (13/314 acts). There were three Thai districts that each experienced 3.8% of the total—Ra-ngae district (12/314 acts) in Narathiwat province, Bannang Sata district in Yala province (12/314 acts,) and Yaha district, also in Yala province. Thepa district in Songkhla province accounted for 3.5% of the total (11/314 acts), as compared to Yi-ngo district in Narathiwat with 10/314 acts (3.2%).

Six districts followed: Ruseo district in Narathiwat (2.9% or 9/314 acts), Mayo district in Pattani (2.2% or 7/314 acts), Nong Chik district in Pattani (2.2% or 7/314 acts) Tak Bai district in Narathiwat (1.9% or 6/314 acts), Sai Buri district in Pattani (1.6% or 5/314 acts), and Kabang district in Yala province (1.6%) or 5/314 acts). In turn, nine Thai districts were afflicted with some one percent of the commercial based terrorism chronicled.

Those districts included: Saba Yoi in Songkhla (1.3% or 4/314 acts), Raman in Yala (1.3% or 4 acts), Su-ngai Padi in Narathiwat (1.3% or 4/314 acts), Chanae in Narathiwat (1.3% or 4/314 acts), Bang Klam in Songkhla (1.3% or 4/314 acts), Na Thawi in Songkhla (1.0% or 3/314 acts), Mai Kaen in Pattani (1.0% or 3/314 acts), Panare in Pattani (1.0% or 3/314 acts), and Chana in Songkhla province (1.0% or 3/ 314 acts).

What seems significant here is those results showcased that even in the southern provinces with the highest rates of business related terrorism, some Thai districts within them experienced very small rates of commercial terrorism. In other words, the patterns of terrorism dispersion were unequal across districts even in Thai provinces with very high rates of terrorism. In turn, when the Indian states with the top three rates of business related terrorism were scrutinized, similar patterns appeared where in Jharkhand, Manipur, and Bihar and Chhattisgarh (tie), some districts experienced less than one percent of all business related terrorism chronicled.[26]

[26] There were twenty two (22) ***districts*** in Thailand that accounted for less than one percent of all business related terrorism. Those districts included: (1) Hua Hin district in Prachuap Khiri Khan province (0.6% or 2/314 acts), (2) Khuan Niang district in Songkhla (0.6% or 2/314 acts), (3) Krong Pi Nang district in Yala province (0.6% or 2/314 acts); (4) Lam Luk Ka district in Pathum Thani

Frequencies

Statistics

District

N	Valid	314
	Missing	29

District

		Frequency	Percent	Valid Percent	Cumulative Percent
Valid	Mueang Narathiwat District	15	4.4	4.8	4.8
	Mueang Pattani District	58	16.9	18.5	23.2
	Yarang District	19	5.5	6.1	29.3
	Bannang Sata District	12	3.5	3.8	33.1
	Ra-ngae District	12	3.5	3.8	36.9
	Mueang Yala District	36	10.5	11.5	48.4
	Panare District	3	.9	1.0	49.4
	Khok Pho District	13	3.8	4.1	53.5
	Kapho District	1	.3	.3	53.8
	Sai Buri District	5	1.5	1.6	55.4
	Mai Kaen District	3	.9	1.0	56.4
	Mayo District	7	2.0	2.2	58.6
	Mae Lan District	2	.6	.6	59.2
	Rueso District	9	2.6	2.9	62.1
	Sungai Kolok District	15	4.4	4.8	66.9
	Sukhirin District	2	.6	.6	67.5
	Na Thawi District	3	.9	1.0	68.5
	Nong Chik District	7	2.0	2.2	70.7
	Thepa District	11	3.2	3.5	74.2
	Saba Yoi District	4	1.2	1.3	75.5
	Mueang Nonthaburi District	1	.3	.3	75.8
	Tak Bai District	6	1.7	1.9	77.7
	Raman District	4	1.2	1.3	79.0
	Yaha District	12	3.5	3.8	82.8
	Waeng District	1	.3	.3	83.1
	Sadao District	2	.6	.6	83.8
	Kabang District	5	1.5	1.6	85.4
	Yi-Ngo District	10	2.9	3.2	88.5
	Su-ngai Padi District	4	1.2	1.3	89.8
	Mueang Chiang Mai District	2	.6	.6	90.4

Fig. 7.10 Relative frequency of Thailand terrorist attacks by District, 2013–2018

District

		Frequency	Percent	Valid Percent	Cumulative Percent
	Sarapee District	1	.3	.3	90.8
	Mae Sot District	1	.3	.3	91.1
	Lam Luk Ka District	2	.6	.6	91.7
	Hat Yai District	1	.3	.3	92.0
	Betong District	1	.3	.3	92.4
	Ko Samul District	1	.3	.3	92.7
	Chanae District	4	1.2	1.3	93.9
	Krong Pi Nang District	2	.6	.6	94.6
	Hua Hin District	2	.6	.6	95.2
	Mueang Krabi District	1	.3	.3	95.5
	Mueang Chachoengsao	1	.3	.3	95.9
	Ban Pho District	1	.3	.3	96.2
	Chana District	3	.9	1.0	97.1
	Bacho District	1	.3	.3	97.5
	Khuan Niang District	2	.6	.6	98.1
	Bang Klam District	4	1.2	1.3	99.4
	Si Sakhon District	1	.3	.3	99.7
	Cho-airong District	1	.3	.3	100.0
	Total	314	91.5	100.0	
Missing	System	29	8.5		
Total		343	100.0		

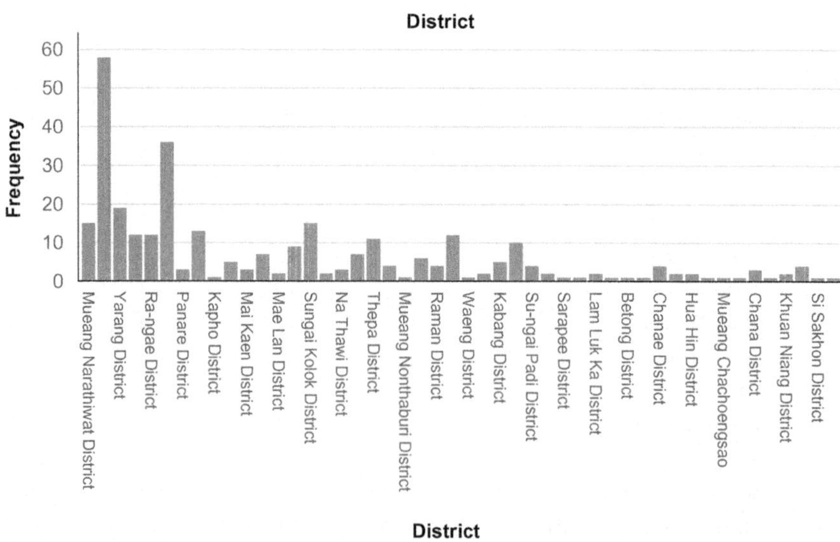

Fig. 7.10 (continued)

7.22 Terrorist Assaults by Tambon (Sub-district) Nakhon (City), Mueang (Town), and Ban (Village)

In the case of cities, towns, and villages in Thailand, there was a wide dispersion of terrorist assaults across those geographical locales. In a first tier of cities, towns, and villages, specific sites accounted for between a little over 11.0 to 5.0% of all business related terrorism in Thailand. The city of Pattani had the highest rate of business related terrorism at 11.0% with 26/236 acts, with the city of Yala closely behind it at 9.3% of the total (22/235 acts).[27] The town of Sungai Kolok ranked third with 5.1% (12/235 acts) of the total (see Fig. 7.11).

The second grouping of cities, town, and villages was comprised of those geographical locale with some 4.0% and to about 1.0% of the total amount of commercial based terrorism Thailand experienced between 2013 and 2018. Those venues included: the city of Bangkok with 3.8% (9/236 acts), Rusa Milae (tambon, Pattani) with 3.0% (7/236 acts), Paka Harang (tambon, Pattani) with 2.5% (6/236 acts), Bannang Sata (town, Yala) with 2.1% (5/236 acts), Tanyong Mat (town, Narathiwat) with 1.7% (4/236 acts), Yarang (town, Pattani) with 1.7% (4/236 acts), Ban Lamphu (town, Narathiwat) with 1.3% (3/236 acts), Ban Lidon (village, Yala) with 1.3% (3/236 acts), Chiang Mai (city, Chiang Mai) with 1.3% (3/236 acts), Danok (town, Songkhla) with 1.3% (3/236 acts), Phrai Wan (village, Narathiwat) with 1.3%, Pitumudi (tambon, Pattani) with 1.3% (3/236 acts), Sabarang (tambon, Pattani) with 1.3% (3/326 acts), Sawo (tambon, Narathiwat) with 1.3% (3/236 acts), Tanyongamas (tambon, Narathiwat) with 1.3% (3/236 acts), Ta Kae (tambon, Pattani) with 1.3% (3/236 acts), and Ban Lamphu (town, Narathiwat) with 1.3% (3/236 acts).[28]

---

province (0.6% 2/314 acts), (5) Mueang Chiang Mai district in Chiang Mai province (0.6% or 2/314 acts), (6) Mae Lan district in Pattani (0.6% or 2/314 acts), (7) Sadao district in Songkhla province (0.6% or 2/314 acts), (8) Sukhirin district in Narathiwat (0.6% or 2/314 acts), (9) Bacho district in Narathiwat (0.3% or 1/314 acts), (10) Ban Pho district in Chachoengsao province (0.3% or 1/314 acts), (11) Betong district in Yala province (0.3% or 1/314 acts), (12) Cho-airong district in Narathiwat (0.3% or 1/314 acts), (13) Hat Yai district in Songkhla (0.3% or 1/314 acts), (14) Ko Samui district on Samui Island (0.3% or 1/314 acts), (15) Kapho district in Pattani (0.3% or 1/314 acts), (16) Mueang Chachoengsao district in Chachoengsao province (0.3% or 1/314 acts), (17) Mueang Krabi district in Krabi province (0.3% or 1/314 acts), (18) Mae Sot district in Tak province (0.3% or 1/314 acts), (19) Mueang Nonthaburi district in Nonthaburi (0.3% of 1/314 acts), (20) Sarapee district in Chiang Mai province (0.3% or 1/314 acts), (21) Si Sakhon district in Narathiwat (0.3% or 1/314 acts), (22) Waeng district in Narathiwat (0.3% or 1/314 acts). These findings suggest that even in deep southern provinces with high rates of business related terrorism, some districts were relatively unaffected by terrorism against commercial interests.

[27] This relative frequencies test for "City, Towns, Villages" had an N set of 236 valid cases with 107 missing cases.

[28] There were ninety-one (91) ***tambons, cities, villages, or towns*** that accounted for less than one percent of all business related terrorism in Thailand. Those tambons, cities, towns, or villages included: (1) Ban Bure (village, Narathiwat) with 0.8% (1/236 acts); (2) Bana (tambon, Pattani) with 0.8% (2/236 acts), (3) Ban Bongo (tambon, Narathiwat) with 0.8% (2/236), (4) Bang Riang (tambon, Songkhla) with 0.8% (2/236 acts), (5) Bo Thong (Pattani) with 0.8% (2/236 acts), (6) Chana (tambon, Songkhla) with 0.8% (2/236 acts), (7) Hua Hin (town, Prachuap Khiri Khan) with 0.8% (2/236 acts), (8) Kaluwo Nuea (city, Narathiwat) with 0.8% (2/236 acts), (9) Kayu Boko

Frequencies

Statistics

CityTownsVill

N	Valid	236
	Missing	107

CityTownVill

		Frequency	Percent	Valid Percent	Cumulative Percent
Valid	Khok Khian	1	.3	.4	.4
	Pattani	26	7.6	11.0	11.4
	Pitumudi	3	.9	1.3	12.7
	Tanyongamas	3	.9	1.3	14.0
	Talubo	1	.3	.4	14.4
	Ta Kae	3	.9	1.3	15.7
	Barahom	1	.3	.4	16.1
	Yala	22	6.4	9.3	25.4
	Ban Tha Muang	1	.3	.4	25.8
	Ban Lua	1	.3	.4	26.3
	Ban Klong	1	.3	.4	26.7
	Ban Mor Saeng	1	.3	.4	27.1
	Ban Kayo	1	.3	.4	27.5
	Ban Plug Taen	1	.3	.4	28.0
	Ban Pa Mai	1	.3	.4	28.4
	Ban Palas	1	.3	.4	28.8
	Ban Cho Batu	1	.3	.4	29.2
	Bangkok	9	2.6	3.8	33.1
	Suwari	1	.3	.4	33.5
	Sungai Kolok	12	3.5	5.1	38.6
	Saba Yoi	2	.6	.8	39.4
	Ban Lamphu	3	.9	1.3	40.7
	Thai Sai	1	.3	.4	41.1
	Kero	1	.3	.4	41.5
	Sakom	2	.6	.8	42.4
	Danok	3	.9	1.3	43.6
	To Tee Tay	1	.3	.4	44.1
	Tapoyo	1	.3	.4	44.5
	Ban Bongo	2	.6	.8	45.3
	Tanyong Mat	4	1.2	1.7	47.0
	Ban Khlong Tae	1	.3	.4	47.5
	Tanyong Limo	1	.3	.4	47.9

Fig. 7.11 Relative frequency of Thailand terrorist attacks by Tambon (sub-district), Nakhon (city), Mueang (town) and Ban (village), 2013–2018

CityTownVill

	Frequency	Percent	Valid Percent	Cumulative Percent
Lo Jood	1	.3	.4	48.3
Chiang Mai	3	.9	1.3	49.6
Lat Sawai	2	.6	.8	50.4
Hat Yai	1	.3	.4	50.8
Sabarang	3	.9	1.3	52.1
Paka Harang	6	1.7	2.5	54.7
Rusa Milae	7	2.0	3.0	57.6
Bana	2	.6	.8	58.5
Sai Khao	1	.3	.4	58.9
Na Paradu	2	.6	.8	59.7
Betong	1	.3	.4	60.2
Sawo	3	.9	1.3	61.4
Samakkhi	1	.3	.4	61.9
Ban Tala Khosator	1	.3	.4	62.3
Ban Bluka	1	.3	.4	62.7
Ban Buere	2	.6	.8	63.6
Tha Muang	1	.3	.4	64.0
Muno	1	.3	.4	64.4
Bang Nak	1	.3	.4	64.8
Bang Po	1	.3	.4	65.3
Tha Rua	1	.3	.4	65.7
Talo Kapo	2	.6	.8	66.5
Bo Put	1	.3	.4	66.9
Baro	1	.3	.4	67.4
Sateng Nok	2	.6	.8	68.2
Khok Pho	1	.3	.4	68.6
Mayo	1	.3	.4	69.1
Ko Saba	1	.3	.4	69.5
Bo Thong	2	.6	.8	70.3
Koto Tuera	1	.3	.4	70.8
Panare	1	.3	.4	71.2
Ruangthip	2	.6	.8	72.0
Yarang	4	1.2	1.7	73.7
Kaluwo Nuea	2	.6	.8	74.6
Ban Mae Kang	1	.3	.4	75.0
Krawa	2	.6	.8	75.8
Tha Sap	1	.3	.4	76.3
Bannang Sata	5	1.5	2.1	78.4

Fig. 7.11 (continued)

CityTownVill

	Frequency	Percent	Valid Percent	Cumulative Percent
Ban Cho Bantang	1	.3	.4	78.8
Krong Pinang	1	.3	.4	79.2
Hua Hin	2	.6	.8	80.1
Ao Nang	1	.3	.4	80.5
Yaha	2	.6	.8	81.4
Na Muang	1	.3	.4	81.8
Tao Rabon	1	.3	.4	82.2
Bang Kro	1	.3	.4	82.6
Chana	2	.6	.8	83.5
Ban Phra Put	1	.3	.4	83.9
Tuyong	1	.3	.4	84.3
Ban Lidon	3	.9	1.3	85.6
Yingo	1	.3	.4	86.0
Pawang Nok	1	.3	.4	86.4
Bindiyor	1	.3	.4	86.9
Na Thawi	2	.6	.8	87.7
Baju	1	.3	.4	88.1
Taluban	1	.3	.4	88.6
Prom	1	.3	.4	89.0
Phrai Wan	3	.9	1.3	90.3
Moo 2 Village	1	.3	.4	90.7
Kabang	1	.3	.4	91.1
Talign Chan	1	.3	.4	91.5
Marue Botok	1	.3	.4	91.9
Kayu Boko	2	.6	.8	92.8
Ton Sai	1	.3	.4	93.2
Ban Nod	1	.3	.4	93.6
Chaloem	1	.3	.4	94.1
Puyut	1	.3	.4	94.5
Ban Khae	1	.3	.4	94.9
Ban Ae Lae	1	.3	.4	95.3
Tawan Ok	1	.3	.4	95.8
Ban Kuyae	1	.3	.4	96.2
Tanoh Puteh	1	.3	.4	96.6
Ban Thung Ya Mu	1	.3	.4	97.0
Bannang Dama	1	.3	.4	97.5
Ban Na	1	.3	.4	97.9
Bang Riang	2	.6	.8	98.7

Fig. 7.11 (continued)

CityTownVill

		Frequency	Percent	Valid Percent	Cumulative Percent
	Buenae Nakao	1	.3	.4	99.2
	Bango Dudung	1	.3	.4	99.6
	Ban Bo Thong	1	.3	.4	100.0
	Total	236	68.8	100.0	
Missing	System	107	31.2		
Total		343	100.0		

CityTownVill

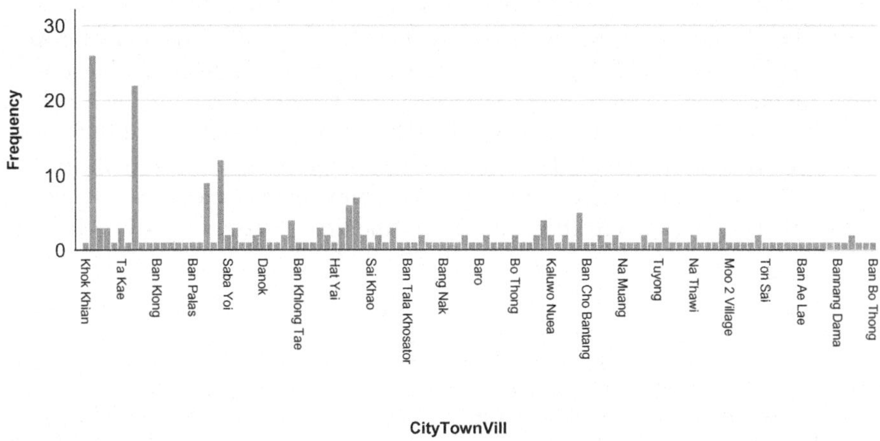

Fig. 7.11 (continued)

(tambon, Yala) with 0.8% (2/236 acts), (10) Krawa (tambon, Pattani) with 0.8% (2/236 acts), (11) Lat Sawai (town, Pathum Thani) with 0.8% (2/236 acts), (12) Na Pradu (tambon, Pattani) with 0.8% (2/236 acts), (13) Na Thawi (village, Songkhla) with 0.8% (2/236 acts), (14) Ruangthip (town, Narathiwat) with 0.8% (2/236 acts), (15) Sabai Yoi (town, Songkhla) with 0.8% (2/236 acts), (16) Sakom (town, Songkhla) with 0.8% (2/236 acts), (17) Sateng Nok (tambon, Yala) with 0.8% (2/236 acts), (18) Talo Kapo (tambon, Pattani) with 0.8% (2/236 acts), (19) Yaha (town, Yala) with 0.8% (2/236 acts); (20) Ban Bo Thong (Narathiwat) with 0.4% (1/236 acts); (21) Ao Nang (town, Krabi) with 0.4% (1/236 acts), (22) Bangu Dudung (village, Narathiwat) with 0.4% (1/236 acts), (23) Baju (village, Yala) with 0.4% (1/236 acts), (24) Ban Ae Lae (village, Yala) with 0.4% (1/236 acts), (25) Ban Bluka (village, Narathiwat), (26) Ban Cho Bantang (village, Yala) with 0.4% (1/236 acts), (27) Ban Cho Batu (village, Pattani) with 0.4% (1/236 acts), (28) Ban Kayo (village, Pattani) with 0.4% (1/236 acts), (29) Ban Khae (village, Yala, Tachi tambon) with 0.4% (1/236 acts), (30) Ban Khlong Tae (village, Yala) with 0.4% (1/236 acts), (31) Ban Klong (village, Pattani) with 0.4% (1/236 acts), (32) Ban Kuyae (village, Yala, tambon Sa-Eh) with 0.4% (1/236 acts), (33) Ban Lua (village, Pattani) with 0.4% (1/236 acts), (34) Ban Mae Kang (village, Pattani) with 0.4% (1/236 acts), (35) Ban More Saeng (village, Pattani) with 0.4% (1/236 acts), (36) Ban Na (tambon, Songkhla) with 0.4% (1/236 acts), (37) Ban Nod (tambon, Songkhla) with 0.4% (1/236 acts), (38) Ban Pa Mai (village, Pattani) with 0.4% (1/236 acts), (39) Ban Palas (village, Pattani) with 0.4% (1/236 acts), (40) Ban Phra Put (village, Songkhla) with 0.4% (1/236 acts), (41) Ban Plug Taen

7.23 Business Firms Attacked

There were 109 business firms that experienced terrorist assaults in Thailand between 2013 and 2016. The first cluster of business firms were attacked some five percent of the time to nearly eight percent of the time. At 7.8%, (13/167 acts) the American based firm 7–11 was the business target of choice with the highest rate of terrorist attacks. The Norwegian telecommunications firm Total Access Communication Public Co Ltd. (DTAC) ranked second with 5.4% of all attacks (9/167 acts), while True Move placed a close third with 4.8% (8/167 acts) (see Fig. 7.12).

A second tier of Thai firms were targeted from about 2.5% of the time to 3.5% of the time. Those included five Thailand government owned institutions: Electricity Generating Authority (EGAT) with 3.6% of the total (6/167 acts), the Bank for Agriculture and Agricultural Cooperatives (BAAC) with 3.0% (5/167 acts), the Government Savings Bank with 3.0% (5/167 acts), the Provincial Electricity Authority (PEA) with 2.4% (4/167 acts), and the PTT Public Company with 2.4% (4/167 acts).

In turn, there were firms in Thailand that were targeted about 1.0% of the time to almost 2.0% of the time. For example, the Diana Supermarket, the Islamic Bank, and the Krung Thai Bank, were attacked 1.8% of the time (3/167 acts), while Big Ben

---

(village, Pattani) with 0.4% (1/236 acts), (42) Ban Tala Khostar (village, Narathiwat) with 0.4% (1/236 acts), (43) Ban Tha Muang (city, Pattani) with 0.4% (1/236 acts), (44) Ban Thung Ya Mu (town, Yala) with 0.4% (1/236 acts), (45) Banang Dama (tambon, Yala) with 0.4% (1/236 acts), (46) Bang Kro (tambon, Pattani) with 0.4% (1/236), (47) Bang Nak (village, Narathiwat) with 0.4% (1/236 acts), (48) Bang Po (tambon, Narathiwat) with 0.4% (1/236 acts), (49) Barahom (tambon, Pattani) with 0.4% (1/236 acts), (50) Baro (tambon, Yala) with 0.4% (1/236 acts), (51) Betong (town, Yala) with 0.4% (1/236 acts), (52) Bindiyor (village, Pattani) with 0.4% (1/236 acts), (53) Bo Put (town, Surat Thani) with 0.4% (1/236 acts), (54) Buenae Nako (Narathiwat) with 0.4% (1/236 acts), (55) Chaloem (Narathiwat) with 0.4% (1/236 acts), (56) Hat Yai (city, Songkhla) with 0.4% (1/236 acts), (57) Kabang (tambon, Yala) with 0.4% (1/236 acts), (58) Kero (tambon, Yala) with 0.4% (1/236 acts), (59) Kho Saba (tambon, Songkhla) with 0.4% (1/236 acts), (60) Khok Khian (tambon, Narathiwat) with 0.4% (1/236 acts), (61) Khok Pho (tambon, Pattani) with 0.4% (1/236 acts), (62) Koto Tuera (tambon, Yala) with 0.4% (1/236 acts), (63) Krong Pinang (tambon, Yala) with 0.4% (1/236 acts), (64) Lo Jood (tambon, Narathiwat) with 0.4% (1/236 acts), (65) Marue Botok (tambon, Narathiwat) with 0.4% (1/236 acts), (66) Mayo (tambon, Pattani) with 0.4% (1/236 acts), (67) Moo 2 (village, Narathiwat) with 0.4% (1/236 acts), (68) Muno (tambon, Narathiwat) with 0.4% (1/236 acts), (69) Na Muang (tambon, Chachoengsao) with 0.4% (1/236 acts), (70) Panare (tambon, Pattani) with 0.4% (1/236 acts), (71) Pawang Nok (village, Yala) with 0.4% (1/236 acts), (72) Prom (village, Yala) with 0.4% (1/236 acts), (73) Puyut (tambon, Pattani) with 0.4% (1/236 acts), (74) Sai Khao (tambon, Pattani) with 0.4% (1/236 acts), (75) Samakkhi (tambon, Narathiwat) with 0.4% (1/236 acts), (76) Suwari (tambon, Narathiwat) with 0.4% (1/236 acts), (77) Talign Chan (tambon, Yala) with 0.4% (1/236 acts), (78) Talubo (tambon, Pattani) with 0.4% (1/236 acts), (79) Tanoh Puteh (tambon, Yala) with 0.4% (1/236 acts), (80) Ton Sai (tambon, Narathiwat) with 0.4% (1/236 acts), (81)Tao Rabon (tambon, Pattani) with 0.4% (1/236 acts), (82) Tapoyo (tambon, Narathiwat) with 0.4% (1/236 acts); (83) Tawan Ok (village, Yala) with 0.4% (1/236 acts), (84) Tayong Limo (tambon, Narathiwat) with 0.4% (1/236 acts), (85) Tha Muang (village, Songkhla) with 0.4% (1/236 acts), (86) Tha Ruae (tambon, Pattani) with 0.4% (1/236 acts), (87) Tha Sap (tambon, Yala) with 0.4% (1/236 acts), (88) Thai Sai (tambon, Nonthaburi) with 0.4% (1/236 acts), (89) To Tee Tay (tambon, Pattani) with 0.4% (1/236 acts), (90) Tuyong (tambon, Pattani) with 0.4% (1/236 acts), (91) Yingo (village, Narathiwat) with 0.4% (1/236 acts).

Frequencies

Statistics

FirmName

N	Valid	167
	Missing	176

FirmName

		Frequency	Percent	Valid Percent	Cumulative Percent
Valid	Nong Nad Karaoke	1	.3	.6	.6
	Paisal Shop	1	.3	.6	1.2
	Diana Supermarket	3	.9	1.8	3.0
	Big Ben Restaurant	2	.6	1.2	4.2
	Yarang Hospital	1	.3	.6	4.8
	7-11	13	3.8	7.8	12.6
	Rungruan Kanke Grocery	1	.3	.6	13.2
	Had Thip Co.	1	.3	.6	13.8
	DTAC	9	2.6	5.4	19.2
	The Islamic Bank	3	.9	1.8	21.0
	Cola Hotel	1	.3	.6	21.6
	Grand Palace Hotel	1	.3	.6	22.2
	Thep Viman Hotel	1	.3	.6	22.8
	Provisional Fishery Business	1	.3	.6	23.4
	Advanced Information Service PCL	1	.3	.6	24.0
	Agricultural Cooperative Office	1	.3	.6	24.6
	Provincial Electricity Authority PEA	4	1.2	2.4	26.9
	Toyota Motor Co.	1	.3	.6	27.5
	Thai Rai (newspaper)	1	.3	.6	28.1
	Asia Hotel	1	.3	.6	28.7
	Krung Thai Bank	3	.9	1.8	30.5
	Teck Bee Hang Corp.	1	.3	.6	31.1
	P. Parawood Corp.	1	.3	.6	31.7
	Yala Thamthong Corp.	1	.3	.6	32.3
	Union Plastic Ltd.	1	.3	.6	32.9
	Yang Paktai Factory	1	.3	.6	33.5
	Phithan Panich Motorcycle	1	.3	.6	34.1

Fig. 7.12 Relative frequency of Thailand terrorist attacks by Firm Name, 2013–2018

FirmName

	Frequency	Percent	Valid Percent	Cumulative Percent
Minimart	1	.3	.6	34.7
Nara Petroleum Ltd.	2	.6	1.2	35.9
Post Today	1	.3	.6	36.5
Coastal Fisheries R&D Centre	1	.3	.6	37.1
402 Thaksinsamphan Radio	1	.3	.6	37.7
McDonalds	1	.3	.6	38.3
Lotus Express	1	.3	.6	38.9
Blue Sky TV Channel	1	.3	.6	39.5
Oliver Hotel	1	.3	.6	40.1
Bangkok Bank	1	.3	.6	40.7
Siam Rath (newspaper)	1	.3	.6	41.3
Thai Public Broadcasting Service	1	.3	.6	41.9
PTT Public Co.	4	1.2	2.4	44.3
Andaman Seafood Restaurant	1	.3	.6	44.9
Chiangmai Beverage Co.	1	.3	.6	45.5
Racha Furniture Shop	2	.6	1.2	46.7
TOT Public Co.	1	.3	.6	47.3
Sri Samai Warehouse	1	.3	.6	47.9
Radio Democracy Network	2	.6	1.2	49.1
Daily News (newspaper)	1	.3	.6	49.7
Chulabhorn Hospital	1	.3	.6	50.3
Siam Commercial Bank (SCB)	1	.3	.6	50.9
Honda Motorcycle	1	.3	.6	51.5
Toyota Corp.	1	.3	.6	52.1
Suzuki Corp.	1	.3	.6	52.7
Super CD	1	.3	.6	53.3
Centro Supermarket	1	.3	.6	53.9
Esso	1	.3	.6	54.5
Royal Dutch Shell	1	.3	.6	55.1
Khok Pho Hospital	1	.3	.6	55.7
Chairat Parawood Co.	1	.3	.6	56.3
Bank for Agriculture and Agricultural Cooperatives BAAC	5	1.5	3.0	59.3
Holiday Hill Hotel	1	.3	.6	59.9

Fig. 7.12 (continued)

FirmName

	Frequency	Percent	Valid Percent	Cumulative Percent
Mayo Hospital	1	.3	.6	60.5
Sairung Bar	1	.3	.6	61.1
Krua Songkhla Bar	1	.3	.6	61.7
Maruey Karaoke Bar	1	.3	.6	62.3
Fan Ja Karaoke Bar	1	.3	.6	62.9
Advanced Info Service Public Co.	1	.3	.6	63.5
TrueMove	8	2.3	4.8	68.3
Siam Paragon Mall	1	.3	.6	68.9
Isuzu Public Co.	1	.3	.6	69.5
Po Kijcharoen Kansura Liquor	1	.3	.6	70.1
Thanasain Motorcycle	1	.3	.6	70.7
Central Festive Mall	1	.3	.6	71.3
Nongluck Clinic	1	.3	.6	71.9
Ban Ton Mai Plant Shop	1	.3	.6	72.5
Khrua Jenny Restaurant	1	.3	.6	73.1
Phat Nuea Katha Restaurant	1	.3	.6	73.7
Top Asia Hotel	1	.3	.6	74.3
Butsaba Karaoke	1	.3	.6	74.9
Caltex (gas)	1	.3	.6	75.4
Somchai Auto Parts	1	.3	.6	76.0
Saithong Restaurant	2	.6	1.2	77.2
Halal Food Industrial Estate	1	.3	.6	77.8
Sim To Ong (rubber)	1	.3	.6	78.4
Telewia (cell phone)	1	.3	.6	79.0
Nong Gift (noodle)	1	.3	.6	79.6
Nik Ma Phochana Restaurant	1	.3	.6	80.2
Government Savings Bank	5	1.5	3.0	83.2
JP Furniture	1	.3	.6	83.8
Alaiyon Auto Parts	1	.3	.6	84.4
Phitan Co. Ltd.	1	.3	.6	85.0
Sam Dao Parawood Co.	1	.3	.6	85.6
Rain Tree Bar	1	.3	.6	86.2
Johnny Bar	1	.3	.6	86.8
Tesco Lotus (market)	1	.3	.6	87.4
Anuchart Engineering Ltd.	1	.3	.6	88.0

Fig. 7.12 (continued)

FirmName

		Frequency	Percent	Valid Percent	Cumulative Percent
Valid	Burger King	1	.3	.6	88.6
	Southern View Hotel	1	.3	.6	89.2
	Manu Rock Plant	1	.3	.6	89.8
	Peerapol Sila Rock Plant	1	.3	.6	90.4
	SPV Parawood Ltd.	1	.3	.6	91.0
	Chinnawon Construction Co.	1	.3	.6	91.6
	Chalong Rubber Milk Factory	1	.3	.6	92.2
	Big C (department store)	2	.6	1.2	93.4
	Wang To Car Center	1	.3	.6	94.0
	Imperial Hotel	1	.3	.6	94.6
	Electricity Generating Authority in Thailand EGAT	6	1.7	3.6	98.2
	Kasikombank	1	.3	.6	98.8
	Seesan Max Tyre Centre	1	.3	.6	99.4
	Fai Sai Furniture Store	1	.3	.6	100.0
	Total	167	48.7	100.0	
Missing	System	176	51.3		
Total		343	100.0		

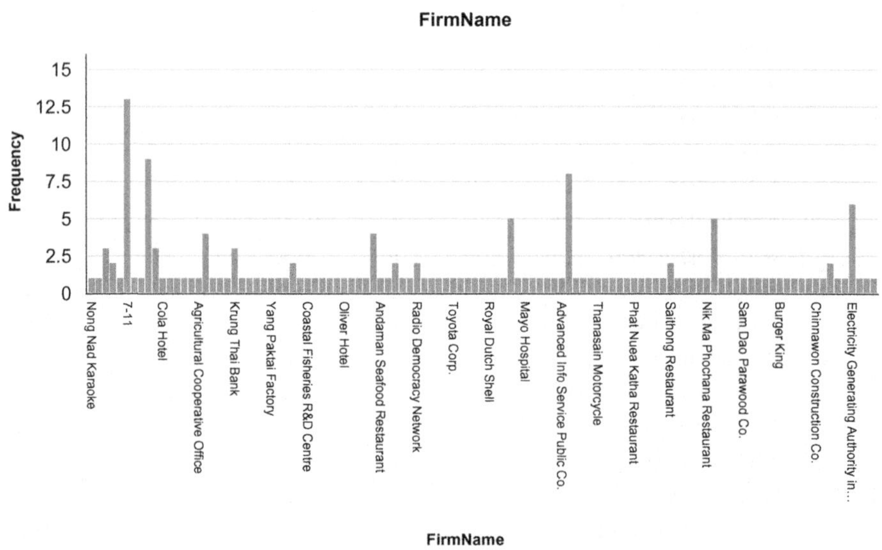

Fig. 7.12 (continued)

Restaurant, Big C Department Store, Nara Petroleum, Ltd., Racha Furniture Shop, Radio Democracy Network, and Saithong Restaurant, were each targeted 1.2% of the time (2/167 acts).

There were several targets that experienced one attack each that made up 0.6% of the total (1/167 acts). Those firms included bars and Karaoke bars, such as Butsaba

Karaoke, Fan Ja Karaoke Bar, Johnny Bar. Krua Songkhla Bar, Maruey Kaaraoke Bar, Nong Nad Karaoke, Rain Tree Bar, and Sairung Bar. It seems likely that such terrorist assault focus reflected an underlying theme in the literature, namely the "un-Islamic character" of those types of establishments.

In addition, hotels, restaurants, and food and grocery stores were also attacked at that same low rate of 0.6% (1/167 acts): the Asia Hotel, the Cola Hotel, the Grand Palace Hotel, the Holiday Hill Hotel, the Imperial Hotel, the Oliver Hotel, Southern View Hotel, Thep Viman Hotel, Top Asia Hotel, Andaman Seafood restaurant, Burger King, Khrua Jenny restaurant, McDonalds, Nik Ma Phochana restaurant, Nong Gift (noodle), Phat Nuea Katha restaurant, Provisional Fishery Business, Centro supermarket, Chiangmai Beverage Co., Halal Food Industrial Estate, Po Kijcharoen Kansura Liquor, Rungruan Kanke, and Tesco Lotus (market) grocery stores.

There were several oil firms, automotive companies, and medical/health facilities attacked one time (0.6% of the total) such as Alaiyon Autoparts (0.6%), Caltex (0.6%), Esso (0.6%), Honda Motorcycle (0.6%), Isuzu Public Co. (0.6%), Royal Dutch Shell (0.6%), Suzuki (0.6%), Toyota Motor Co. (0.6%), Pithan Panich Motorcycle (0.6%), Seesan Max Tyre Centre (0.6%), Somchai Auto Parts (0.6%), Thanasain Motorcycle (0.6%) and Wang To Car Center (0.6%). In the case of hospitals or medical facilities, there was one chronicled terrorist assault a piece against Yarang Hospital (0.6%), Chulabhorn Hospital (0.6%), Khok Pho Hospital (0.6%), Mayo Hospital (0.6%), and Nongluck Clinic (0.6%).

Other firms that experienced one terrorist assault a piece included, Advanced Information Service (PCL), Agricultural Cooperative Office, Anuchart Engineering Ltd., Bangkok Bank, Ban Ton Mai plant shop, Blue Sky Channel, Chalong Rubber Milk Factory, Central Festive Mall, Chairat Parawood Co., Chinnawon Construction Co., Coastal Fisheries R&D Centre, Daily News newspaper, Fai Sai Furniture Store, Had Thip Co., JP Furniture, Kasikornbank, Krungthal Bank, Lotus Express, Manu rock plant, Minmart, P. Parawood Corp., Paisal shop, Peerapol Sila rock plant, Phitan Co. Ltd., Post Today, Sam Dao Parwood Co., Siam Commercial Bank (SCB), Siam Paragon Mall, Siam Rath newspaper, Sim Tong On (rubber), SPV Parawood Ltd., Sri Samai Warehouse, Super CD, Teck Bee Hang Corp., Telewia (cell phone) Thai Public Broadcasting, Thai Rai (newspaper), TOT Public Co., Union Plastic Company, Yala Thamthong Corp., Yang Paktai Factory, and 402 Thaksinsamphan Radio.

7.24 Variable Analysis

7.24.1 Terrorist Group-Name X Business Target

This first crosstabulation test was conducted to determine if there was a statistically significant relationship found between "Terrorist Group-Name" and "Business Target." A Pearson Chi Square statistic of 8.877 with a "p-value" of 0.012 at two degrees of freedom (2 d.f.) makes it possible to reject the null hypothesis at the 0.05 level of confidence. There were 2 cells (33.3%) that had an expected count of less than 5. These findings were reported for fear of making a "Type II" error of failing to reject the null hypothesis of no relation between the variables. That is the case even though Norusis reports, "in general, you should not use the chi-square test if more than 20% of the cells have an expected value of less than 5." [6, 112, 147 n184; 43, 313–320].[29]

With respect to the strength of the relationship, a "Cramer's V" score of 0.426 with a "*p*-value" of 0.012 and, "Phi" score of 0.412 with a "*p*-value" of 0.012 suggests a moderate strength relationship exists between those variables, "Terrorist Group-Name" and Business Target." At the same time, a Goodman and Kruskal *tau* score of 0.181 with a significance score of 0.13 when "Group-Name" was the dependent variable, indicates a weak relationship between those variables (see Table 7.1).

The data distributions reveal that most Barisan Revolusi Nasional (BRN) had, at 10.01% (34/338 acts), the highest percentage of terrorist assaults linked to a terrorist group. That was followed by 5.0% of the total (17/338 acts) attributable to Runda Kumpulan Kecil (RKK). Other identifiable groups each comprised less than one percent of the total—Masorae Duerama Group with one act (0.3%), Hundum Musordee Group with one act (0.3%), and the Mayakoh Lateh Group with one act (0.3%).

When specific business target-types were considered, "private establishments" accounted for a full 56.5% (191/338 acts), followed by "banking and finance" targets with 17.5% (59/338 acts), and "telecommunications" targets with 11.8% (40/338 acts). In turn, newspaper/print targets comprised 1.2% of the total (4/338 acts) while "agriculture" targets accounted for a paltry 0.3% (1/338 acts). It was found that Barisan Nasional Revolusi focused on two primary business target types in terrorist assaults. For Barisan Nasional Revolusi, "private establishments" were targeted over one-third of the time at 35.3% (12/34 acts), while "energy/alloy" infrastructure was targeted nearly one-third of the time at 29.4% (10/34 acts).

In turn, Runda Kumpulan Kecil (RKK) placed emphasis on "private establishments" a full 76.5% of the time (13/17 acts), on "energy alloy" targets 11.8% of the time (2/17 acts) and on hospitals/medical facilities 5.9% of the time (1/17 acts). In addition the Masorae Duerama Group, Hundum Musordee Group, and the Mayokah Lateh Group each attacked "private establishments" 100.0% of the time (1/1 acts). To be sure, terrorist assaults aimed at "private establishments" were highlighted across identifiable terrorist groups and terrorist attacks carried out by anonymous actors (see Table 7.2).

[29] In this crosstabulation test, the variable, "Group Name" was recoded into "the same variable" to 2 → 2, 4 → 4, ELSE SYSMIS; while the variable "Business Target" was recoded into "the same variable" to 1 → 1, 4 → 4. ELSE SYSMIS. This test had a N set of 49 with 294 missing events.

Table 7.1 Relative frequency of group-name by Thailand Business Targets, 2013–2018 (summary statistics)

Case processing summary

	Valid		Cases missing		Total	
	N	Percent	N	Percent	N	Percent
GroupName * Bus.Target	49	14.3%	294	85.7%	343	100.0%

GroupName * Bus.Target Crosstabulation

			Bus.Target	
			Energy/Alloy	Private establishments
GroupName	Runda Kumpulan Kecil (RKK)	Count	2	13
		% within GroupName	12.5%	81.3%
		% within Bus.Target	16.7%	52.0%
		% of total	4.1%	26.5%
	Barisan Revolusi Nasional (BRN)	Count	10	12
		% within GroupName	30.3%	36.4%
		% within Bus.Target	83.3%	48.0%
		% of total	20.4%	24.5%
Total		Count	12	25
		% within GroupName	24.5%	51.0%
		% within Bus.Target	100.0%	100.0%
		% of total	24.5%	51.0%

			Bus.Target	
			Banking/Finance	Total
GroupName	Runda Kumpulan Kecil (RKK)	Count	1	16
		% within GroupName	6.3%	100.0%
		% within Bus.Target	8.3%	32.7%
		% of Total	2.0%	32.7%
	Barisan Revolusi Nasional (BRN)	Count	11	33
		% within GroupName	33.3%	100.0%
		% within Bus.Target	91.7%	67.3%
		% of Total	22.4%	67.3%
Total		Count	12	49
		% within GroupName	24.5%	100.0%
		% within Bus.Target	100.0%	100.0%

(continued)

Table 7.1 (continued)

			Bus.Target	
			Banking/Finance	Total
		% of total	24.5%	100.0%

Chi-square tests

	Value	df	Asymptotic significance (2-sided)
Pearson chi-square	8.877[a]	2	0.012
Likelihood ratio	9.591	2	0.008
Linear-by-linear association	0.186	1	0.667
N of valid cases	49		

Directional measures

			Value	Asymptotic standard error[b]
Nominal by Nominal	Lambda	Symmetric	0.025	0.123
		GroupName Dependent	0.063	0.303
		Bus.Target Dependent	0.000	0.000
	Goodman and Kruskal tau	GroupName Dependent	0.181	0.101
		Bus.Target Dependent	0.109	0.060

Directional measures

			Approximate T[c]	Approximate significance
Nominal by nominal	Lambda	Symmetric	0.200	0.841
		GroupName dependent	0.200	0.841
		Bus.Target dependent	[d]	[d]
	Goodman and Kruskal tau	GroupName dependent		0.013[e]
		Bus.Target dependent		0.005[e]

Symmetric measures

		Value	Approximate significance
Nominal by nominal	Phi	0.426	0.012

(continued)

Table 7.1 (continued)

Symmetric measures

		Value	Approximate significance
	Cramer's V	0.426	0.012
N of valid cases		49	

[a]2 cells (33.3%) have expected count less than 5. The minimum expected count is 3.92
[b]Not assuming the null hypothesis
[c]Using the asymptotic standard error assuming the null hypothesis
[d]Cannot be computed because the asymptotic standard error equals zero
[e]Based on chi-square approximation

7.25 Political Ideology X Business Targets

A bivariate analysis reveals there is a statistically significant and substantive relationship between the variables, "Group-Type" and "Business Target." That test produced a Pearson Chi Square statistic of 23.354 with a "*p*-value" of less than 0.001 at one degree of freedom (1 d.f.). A continuity correction measure of 21.934 with a *p*-value of less than 0.001 was produced for this 2 × 2 matrix. It was found there were 0.0% cells with an expected frequency of less than 5.[30] All of the foregoing makes it possible to reject the null hypothesis of no relation between the variables at the 0.05 level of confidence.

In terms of the strength of the relationship between those variables, a "Cramer's V" measure of 0.306 with a significance score of less than 0.001 and a "Phi" measure of 0.306 with a significance score of less than 0.0001, suggest a weak relationship. In turn, a Goodman and Kruskal tau score of 0.094 with a "*p*-value" of less than 0.001 when "Group-Type" is the dependent variable, also indicates a weak relationship between those variables (see Table 7.3).

Hypothesis One: Islamic Nationalist-Irredentist terrorist groups will have comparable rates of attacks against telecommunications targets, and private establishments.

This hypothesis derives from the "structuralist—non-structuralist" continuum framework presented in Chapter Two. On that target continuum, nationalist-irredentist groups were expected to put emphasis on "non-structuralist" targets representative or symbolic of individuals or groups of individuals. Therefore nationalist-irredentist groups should be positioned close to that continuum's "non-structuralist" pole. At the same time, "hybrid groups" such as Islamic extremist groups, have been found in previous work to fall towards the center of the target continuum in part because of a broad range of legitimate targets found in Dar al-Harb (House of War) [5; 6; 35, 29].

[30] N = 249 with 94 missing events. In this test, the variable "Group-Type" was recoded in the "same variable" with 3 → 3; 4 → 4; ELSE SYSMIS, and the variable "Business Target" was recoded 4 → 4; 7 → 7; ELSE SYSMIS. It is understood that "anonymous" is not a formal group type per se, but because there is one identifiable terrorist group-types and a very small number of identifiable terrorist groups in the contemporary Thai landscape, it is necessary to conduct the crosstabulation test with those categories.

Table 7.2 Relative frequency of group-name by Thailand Business Targets, 2013–2018

Case processing summary

	Valid		Cases missing		Total	
	N	Percent	N	Percent	N	Percent
GroupName * Bus.Target	338	98.5%	5	1.5%	343	100.0%

GroupName * Bus.Target Crosstabulation

			Bus.Target	
			Energy/Alloy	Hospitals/Medical
GroupName	Masorae Duerama Group	Count	0	0
		% within GroupName	0.0%	0.0%
		% within Bus.Target	0.0%	0.0%
		% of total	0.0%	0.0%
	Runda Kumpulan Kecil (RKK)	Count	2	1
		% within GroupName	11.8%	5.9%
		% within Bus.Target	5.4%	16.7%
		% of total	0.6%	0.3%
	Hundum Musordee Group	Count	0	0
		% within GroupName	0.0%	0.0%
		% within Bus.Target	0.0%	0.0%
		% of total	0.0%	0.0%
	Barisan Revolusi Nasional (BRN)	Count	10	0
		% within GroupName	29.4%	0.0%
		% within Bus.Target	27.0%	0.0%
		% of total	3.0%	0.0%
	Anonymous	Count	25	5
		% within GroupName	8.8%	1.8%
		% within Bus.Target	67.6%	83.3%
		% of total	7.4%	1.5%
	Mayakoh Lateh Group	Count	0	0
		% within GroupName	0.0%	0.0%

(continued)

Table 7.2 (continued)

GroupName * Bus.Target Crosstabulation

			Bus.Target	
			Energy/Alloy	Hospitals/Medical
		% within Bus.Target	0.0%	0.0%
		% of total	0.0%	0.0%
Total		Count	37	6
		% within GroupName	10.9%	1.8%
		% within Bus.Target	100.0%	100.0%
		% of total	10.9%	1.8%

			Bus.Target	
			Private establishments	Telecommunications
GroupName	Masorae Duerama Group	Count	1	0
		% within GroupName	100.0%	0.0%
		% within Bus.Target	0.5%	0.0%
		% of total	0.3%	0.0%
	Runda Kumpulan Kecil (RKK)	Count	13	0
		% within GroupName	76.5%	0.0%
		% within Bus.Target	6.8%	0.0%
		% of total	3.8%	0.0%
	Hundum Musordee Group	Count	1	0
		% within GroupName	100.0%	0.0%
		% within Bus.Target	0.5%	0.0%
		% of total	0.3%	0.0%
	Barisan Revolusi Nasional (BRN)	Count	12	1
		% within GroupName	35.3%	2.9%
		% within Bus.Target	6.3%	2.5%
		% of total	3.6%	0.3%

(continued)

Table 7.2 (continued)

			Bus.Target	
			Private establishments	Telecommunications
	Anonymous	Count	163	39
		% within GroupName	57.4%	13.7%
		% within Bus.Target	85.3%	97.5%
		% of total	48.2%	11.5%
	Mayakoh Lateh Group	Count	1	0
		% within GroupName	100.0%	0.0%
		% within Bus.Target	0.5%	0.0%
		% of total	0.3%	0.0%
Total		Count	191	40
		% within GroupName	56.5%	11.8%
		% within Bus.Target	100.0%	100.0%
		% of total	56.5%	11.8%

GroupName * Bus.Target Crosstabulation

			Bus.Target	
			Newspaper/Print	Banking/Finance
GroupName	Masorae Duerama Group	Count	0	0
		% within GroupName	0.0%	0.0%
		% within Bus.Target	0.0%	0.0%
		% of total	0.0%	0.0%
	Runda Kumpulan Kecil (RKK)	Count	0	1
		% within GroupName	0.0%	5.9%
		% within Bus.Target	0.0%	1.7%%
		% of total	0.0%	0.3%
	Hundum Musordee Group	Count	0	0
		% within GroupName	0.0%	0.0%

(continued)

Table 7.2 (continued)

GroupName * Bus.Target Crosstabulation

			Bus.Target	
			Newspaper/Print	Banking/Finance
		% within Bus.Target	0.0%	0.0%
		% of total	0.0%	0.0%
	Barisan Revolusi Nasional (BRN)	Count	0	11
		% within GroupName	0.0%	32.4%
		% within Bus.Target	0.0%	18.6%
		% of total	0.0%	3.3%
	Anonymous	Count	4	47
		% within GroupName	1.4%	16.5%
		% within Bus.Target	100.0%	79.7%
		% of total	1.2%	13.9%
	Mayakoh Lateh Group	Count	0	0
		% within GroupName	0.0%	0.0%
		% within Bus.Target	0.0%	0.0%
		% of total	0.0%	0.0%
Total		Count	4	59
		% within GroupName	1.2%	17.5%
		% within Bus.Target	100.0%	100.0%
		% of total	1.2%	17.5%

			Bus.Target	
			Agriculture	Total
GroupName	Masorae Duerama Group	Count	0	1
		% within GroupName	0.0%	100.0%
		% within Bus.Target	0.0%	0.3%
		% of total	0.0%	0.3%
	Runda Kumpulan Kecil (RKK)	Count	0	17
		% within GroupName	0.0%	100.0%

(continued)

Table 7.2 (continued)

			Bus.Target	
			Agriculture	Total
		% within Bus.Target	0.0%	5.0%
		% of total	0.0%	5.0%
	Hundum Musordee Group	Count	0	1
		% within GroupName	0.0%	100.0%
		% within Bus.Target	0.0%	0.3%
		% of total	0.0%	0.3%
	Barisan Revolusi Nasional (BRN)	Count	0	34
		% within GroupName	0.0%	100.0%
		% within Bus.Target	0.0%	10.1%
		% of total	0.0%	10.1%
	Anonymous	Count	1	284
		% within GroupName	0.4%	100.0%
		% within Bus.Target	100.0%	84.0%
		% of total	0.3%	84.0%
	Mayakoh Lateh Group	Count	0	1
		% within GroupName	0.0%	100.0%
		% within Bus.Target	0.0%	0.3%
		% of total	0.0%	0.3%
Total		Count	1	338
		% within GroupName	0.3%%	100.0%
		% within Bus.Target	100.0%	100.0%
		% of total	0.3%	100.0%

While information on the identities of many terrorist groups in contemporary Thailand is makeshift and incomplete, it is clear that nowadays, nationalist-irredentist terrorist organizations in Thailand have a significant Muslim hue to them based on what scholars call the "ethno-religious identity" of Malay-Muslims. It follows that it is possible to think about nationalist-irredentist terrorist groups with Islamic trappings in Thailand as Islamic nationalist irredentist terrorist organizations [35, 4; 65, 45–47, 54–55].

Hence, in the case of Thailand, it is expected that the traditional nationalist-irredentist terrorist group focus on targets representative of groups of people and individuals should be diluted somewhat because of Islam's influence on a what amounts to a nationalistic struggle. As a result, Thailand's Islamic nationalist-irredentist terrorist groups should be found in the middle part of that target continuum.

A breakdown of the data distributions reveals a full 50.9% (83/163 acts) of all Islamic national-irredentist group attacks were aimed at "private establishments"

Table 7.3 Relative frequency of group-type by Thailand Business Targets, 2013–2018 (summary statistics)

Case processing summary

	Valid		Cases missing		Total	
	N	Percent	N	Percent	N	Percent
GroupTy * Bus.Target	249	72.6%	94	27.4%	343	100.0%

GroupTy * Bus.Target crosstabulation

			Bus.Target		
			Private establishments	Banking/ Finance	Total
GroupName	Anonymous	Count	107	12	119
		% within GroupTy	89.9%	10.1%	100.0%
		% within Bus.Target	56.3%	20.3%	47.8%
		% of total	43.0%	4.8%	47.8%
	Islamic Nationalist-Irredentist	Count	83	47	130
		% within GroupTy	63.8%	36.2%	100.0%
		% within Bus.Target	43.7%	79.7%	52.2%
		% of total	33.3%	18.9%	52.2%
Total		Count	190	59	249
		% within GroupTy	76.3%	23.7%	100.0%
		% within Bus.Target	100.0%	100.0%	100.0%
		% of total	76.3%	23.7%	100.0%

Chi-square tests

	Value	df	Asymptotic significance (2-sided)	Exact significance (2-sided)	Exact significance (1-sided)
Pearson chi-square	23.354[a]	1	< 0.001		
Continuity correction[b]	21.934	1	< 0.001		
Likelihood ratio	24.747	1	< 0.001		
Fisher's exact test				< 0.001	< 0.001
Linear-by-linear association	23.260	1	< 0.001		
N of valid cases	249				

(continued)

Table 7.3 (continued)

Directional measures

			Value	Asymptotic standard error[c]
Nominal by Nominal	Lambda	Symmetric	0.135	0.072
		GroupTy Dependent	0.202	0.103
		Bus.Target Dependent	0.000	0.000
	Goodman and Kruskal tau	GroupTy Dependent	0.094	0.033
		Bus.Target Dependent	0.094	0.034

Directional measures

			Approximate T[d]	Approximate significance
Nominal by nominal	Lambda	Symmetric	1.752	0.080
		GroupTy dependent	1.752	0.080
		Bus.Target dependent	[e]	[e]
	Goodman and Kruskal tau	GroupTy dependent		< 0.001[f]
		Bus.Target dependent		< 0.001[f]

Symmetric measures

		Value	Approximate significance
Nominal by nominal	Phi	0.306	< 0.001
	Cramer's V	0.306	< 0.001
N of valid cases		249	

[a]0 cells (0.0%) have expected count less than 5. The minimum expected count is 28.20
[b]Computed only for a 2 × 2 table
[c]Not assuming the null hypothesis
[d]Using the asymptotic standard error assuming the null hypothesis
[e]Cannot be computed because the asymptotic standard error equals zero
[f]Based on chi-square approximation

(a "non-structuralist" target), while 28.8% (47/163 acts) of Islamic nationalist irredentist organization targets involved "banking/finance" institutions (a "structuralist target"). Both of those business target types accounted for 79.8% of all Islamic nationalist-irredentist terrorist attacks (see Table 7.4).

In turn, telecommunication targets (a "structuralist" target) comprised 2.5% of the total (4/163 acts) for Islamic nationalist irredentist groups, while "hospitals/ medical facilities" (a "non-structuralist" target) comprised 1.2% of the total (2/163 acts). There were no Islamic nationalist-irredentist terrorist assaults recorded for newspaper (print) or agricultural targets. Overall, the data results suggest that on the "structuralist-non-structuralist" target continuum, there was a broad range of different target-types associated with Thailand's Islamic nationalist-irredentist groups, and therefore, Hypothesis One is accepted as valid.

In one case, it was found that target type rates across Islamic nationalist-irredentist terrorist groups and anonymous terrorist assault perpetrators in Thailand were high. The anonymous terrorist attack rate against "private establishments" at 61.5% (107/ 174 acts) was comparable to the high rate 50.9% rate (83/163 acts) found for Islamic nationalist-irredentist groups. Likewise, in the case of "hospitals/medical facilities" targets, Islamic nationalist-irredentist acts (1.2%) and anonymous acts (2.3%) both had low rates.

However, anonymous terrorism in Thailand also showcased very different patterns in business target selection when compared to Islamic nationalist-irredentist terrorist group patterns. For example, the anonymous actor attack rate for "banking/finance" institutions at 6.9% (12/174 acts) was only about one-fourth of the 28.8% rate (47/ 163 acts) found for Islamic nationalist-irredentist groups. The anonymous attack percentage rate against energy/alloy targets at 5.7% (10/174 acts) was little more than one-third the 16.6% rate (27/163 acts) found for Islamic nationalist-irredentist terrorist organizations.

It was found that one-fifth of all anonymous terrorist attacks at 20.7% (36/174 acts) were directed at telecommunications targets. That rate was some eight times higher than the 2.5% rate for Islamic nationalist-irredentist attacks carried out against telecommunications communications. There was only one "agriculture" target chron icled in the data—an anonymous terrorist assault against an "agricultural cooperatives office building" in Mai Kaen district in Pattani province, on April 10, 2013 [28; 53].[31]

7.26 Business Target-Type X Number of Deaths

Hypothesis Two: Terrorist attacks against business targets that symbolize ethnic group or individuals ("non-structuralist" targets) will have a higher rate of terrorist attacks that caused between one and fifteen deaths than business terrorist attacks

[31] 2.5% X 8 = 20.0%

Table 7.4 Relative frequency of group-type by Thailand Business Targets, 2013–2018

Case processing summary

	Valid		Cases missing		Total	
	N	Percent	N	Percent	N	Percent
GroupTy * Bus.Target	337	98.3%	6	1.7%	343	100.0%

GroupTy * Bus.Target crosstabulation

			Bus.Target	
			Energy/Alloy	Hospitals/Medical
GroupTy	Anonymous	Count	10	4
		% within GroupTy	5.7%	2.3%
		% within Bus.Target	27.0%	66.7%
		% of total	3.0%	1.2%
	Islamic Nationalist-Irredentist	Count	27	2
		% within GroupTy	16.6%	1.2%
		% within Bus.Target	73.0%	33.3%
		% of total	8.0%	0.6%
Total		Count	37	6
		% within GroupTy	11.0%	1.8%
		% within Bus.Target	100.0%	100.0%
		% of total	11.0%	1.8%

			Bus.Target	
			Private establishments	Telecommunications
GroupTy	Anonymous	Count	107	36
		% within GroupTy	61.5%	20.7%
		% within Bus.Target	56.3%	90.0%
		% of total	31.8%	10.7%
	Islamic Nationalist-Irredentist	Count	83	4
		% within GroupTy	50.9%	2.5%
		% within Bus.Target	43.7%	10.0%
		% of total	24.6%	1.2%
Total		Count	190	40
		% within GroupTy	56.4%	11.9%
		% within Bus.Target	100.0%	100.0%

(continued)

Table 7.4 (continued)

			Bus.Target	
			Private establishments	Telecommunications
		% of total	56.4%	11.9%

			Bus.Target		
			Newspaper/ Print	Banking/ Finance	Agriculture
GroupTy	Anonymous	Count	4	12	1
		% within GroupTy	2.3%	6.9%	0.6%
		% within Bus.Target	100.0%	20.3%	100.0%
		% of total	1.2%	3.6%	0.3%
	Islamic Nationalist-Irredentist	Count	0	47	0
		% within GroupTy	0.0%	28.8%	0.0%
		% within Bus.Target	0.0%	79.7%	0.0%
		% of total	0.0%	13.9%	0.0%
Total		Count	4	59	1
		% within GroupTy	1.2%	17.5%	0.3%
		% within Bus.Target	100.0%	100.0%	100.0%
		% of total	1.2%	17.5%	0.3%

			Total
GroupTy	Anonymous	Count	174
		% within GroupTy	100.0%
		% within Bus.Target	51.6%
		% of total	51.6%
	Islamic Nationalist-Irredentist	Count	163
		% within GroupTy	100.0%
		% within Bus.Target	48.4%
		% of total	48.4%
Total		Count	337
		% within GroupTy	100.0%
		% within Bus.Target	100.0%
		% of total	100.0%

directed at "structuralist" targets (i.e., linked to "world systems" such as capitalism, globalization, modernization).

A Pearson Chi Square statistic of 11.758 with a "*p*-value" of less than 0.001 at one 1° of freedom (1.d.f.) makes it possible to reject the null hypothesis of no relation between the variables "Business Target-Type" and "Number of Deaths" at the 0.05 level of confidence. A Continuity Correction score of 10.406 with a significance score of 0.001 is also reported. Hence the null hypothesis of no relationship between the variables is rejected. There are 0 cells with an expected count of less than 5.

With respect to the strength of that relationship, both a "Cramer's V" value of 0.217 and a "Phi" value of − 0.271, and both with a significance score of less than 0.001, suggest a weak relationship between those variables. In addition, a Goodman and Kruskal *tau* measure of 0.047 with a significance score of less than 0.001 when "Business Target" is the dependent variable, also suggests a weak relationship (see Table 7.5) [18, 229–230 n30].[32]

A breakdown of the data distributions reveals that terrorist assaults against "private establishments" in Thailand had the highest rate of attacks that killed between one and fifteen people with one fifth of the total at 20.4% (39/191 acts). In terms of the other "non-structuralist" target-types considered, there were no terrorist assaults that killed between one and fifteen people recorded. Those other non-structuralist targets included agricultural targets, newspaper/print targets, and hospital medical targets (see Table 7.6).

In each case of the two "structuralist" target-types that experienced lethal attacks, "energy/alloy" targets had the highest rate of terrorist assaults that killed between one to fifteen people at 5.4% (2/37 acts), in comparison to the 1.7% rate found for "banking/finance" targets 1/59 acts). There were no lethal terrorist attacks chronicled for "structuralist" telecommunications targets (0.0%). The data distribution supported Hypothesis Two and it is accepted as valid.

7.27 Group-Type X Reaction to Political Events

Hypothesis Three: Most business-related terrorist assaults in Thailand will not be linked to political events in the region, such as diplomatic initiatives, the commemoration of religious or landmark events, or to counterterrorism activities (e.g., ground assaults).

A crosstabulation test was run with the variables, "Group-Type" and "Reaction to Political Events." With a Pearson Chi Square statistic of 30.266 with a "p-value" of less than 0.001 at two degrees of freedom (2 d.f.), it is possible to reject the null hypothesis of no relationship between those variables at the 0.05 level of confidence.

[32] In this crosstabulation test, the variable "Business Target" was recoded into the same variable, with 7 → 7; 4 → 4, ELSE SYMIS; the variable "Deaths" was recoded into the same variable as 0 = 0; 1 = 1 → 15, ELSE SYSMIS. This test had an N set of 338 with 5 missing events.

Table 7.5 Relative frequency of business type target by Deaths in Thailand Terrorist Attacks, (0 = 0; 1 = 1 through 15) (summary statistics)

Case processing summary

	Valid		Cases missing		Total	
	N	Percent	N	Percent	N	Percent
Bus.Target * Deaths	250	72.9%	93	27.1%	343	100.0%

Bus.Target * Deaths Crosstabulation

			Deaths		Total
			0	1	
Bus.Target	Private establishments	Count	152	39	191
		% within Bus.Target	79.6%	20.4%	100.0%
		% within deaths	72.4%	97.5%	76.4%
		% of total	60.8%	15.6%	76.4%
	Banking/Finance	Count	58	1	59
		% within Bus.Target	98.3%	1.7%	100.0%
		% within deaths	27.6%	2.5%	23.6%
		% of total	23.2%	0.4%	23.6%
Total		Count	210	40	250
		% within Bus.Target	84.0%	16.0%	100.0%
		% within deaths	100.0%	100.0%	100.0%
		% of total	84.0%	16.0%	100.0%

Chi-square tests

	Value	df	Asymptotic significance (2-sided)	Exact Sig. (2-sided)	Exact Sig. (1-sided)
Pearson chi-square	11.758[a]	1	< 0.001		
Continuity correction[b]	10.406	1	0.001		
Likelihood ratio	16.346	1	< 0.001		
Fisher's exact test				< 0.001	< 0.001
Linear-by-linear association	11.711	1	< 0.001		
N of valid cases	250				

Directional measures

			Value	Asymptotic standard error[c]
Nominal by nominal	Lambda	Symmetric	0.000	0.000
		Bus.Target dependent	0.000	0.000
		Deaths dependent	0.000	0.000

(continued)

Table 7.5 (continued)

Directional measures

			Value	Asymptotic standard error[c]
	Goodman and Kruskal tau	Bus.Target dependent	0.047	0.013
		Deaths dependent	0.047	0.013

Directional measures

			Approximate T	Approximate significance
Nominal by nominal	Lambda	Symmetric	[d]	[d]
		Bus.Target dependent	[d]	[d]
		Deaths dependent	[d]	[d]
	Goodman and Kruskal tau	Bus.Target dependent		< 0.001[e]
		Deaths dependent		< 0.001[e]

Symmetric measures

		Value	Approximate significance
Nominal by nominal	Phi	– 0.217	< 0.001
	Cramer's V	0.217	< 0.001
N of valid cases		250	

[a]0 cells (0.0%) have expected count less than 5. The minimum expected count is 9.44
[b]Computed only for a 2 × 2 table
[c]Not assuming the null hypothesis
[d]Cannot be computed because the asymptotic standard error equals zero
[e]Based on chi-square approximation

It was found that there were 0.0% cells with an expected count of less than 5 (see Table 7.7).

In terms of the strength of that relationship, both a "Cramer's V" score of 0.333 with a significance score of less than 0.001, and a "Phi" score of 0.333 with a significance score of less than 0.001 suggest a weak strength relationship exists between those variables. In addition, a Goodman and Kruskal *tau* measure of 0.111 with a significance score of less than 0.001 when "Group-Type" is the dependent variable also suggests a weak relationship between those variables.[33]

[33] In this crosstabulation test, the Variable "Group Type" was 3 → 3, 4 → 4, ELSE SYSMIS and the variable "reaction to Political Event" was recoded in the "same variable" to 0 → 0, 2 → 2, 5 → 5, ELSE SYSMIS. In this test N = 273 with 70 missing events.

Table 7.6 Relative frequency of business type target by Deaths in Thailand Terrorist Attacks, (0 = 0; 1 = 1 through 15)

Case processing summary

	Valid		Cases missing		Total	
	N	Percent	N	Percent	N	Percent
Bus.Target * Deaths	338	98.5%	5	1.5%	343	100.0%

Bus.Target * Deaths crosstabulation

			Deaths		
			0	1	Total
Bus.Target	Energy/Alloy	Count	35	2	37
		% within Bus.Target	94.6%	5.4%	100.0%
		% within deaths	11.8%	4.8%	10.9%
		% of total	10.4%	0.6%	10.9%
	Hospitals/Medical	Count	6	0	6
		% within Bus.Target	100.0%	0.0%	100.0%
		% within deaths	2.0%	0.0%	1.8%
		% of total	1.8%	0.0%	1.8%
	Private establishments	Count	152	39	191
		% within Bus.Target	79.6%	20.4%	100.0%
		% within deaths	51.4%	92.9%	56.5%
		% of total	45.0%	11.5%	56.5%
	Telecommunications	Count	40	0	40
		% within Bus.Target	100.0%	0.0%	100.0%
		% within deaths	13.5%	0.0%	11.8%
		% of total	11.8%	0.0%	11.8%
	Newspaper/Print	Count	4	0	4
		% within Bus.Target	100.0%	0.0%	100.0%
		% within deaths	1.4%	0.0%	1.2%
		% of total	1.2%	0.0%	1.2%
	Banking/Finance	Count	58	1	59
		% within Bus.Target	98.3%	1.7%	100.0%
		% within deaths	19.6%	2.4%	17.5%
		% of total	17.2%	0.3%	17.5%

Bus.Target * Deaths crosstabulation

			Deaths		Total
			0	1	
	Agriculture	Count	1	0	1
		% within Bus.Target	100.0%	0.0%	100.0%
		% within deaths	0.3%	0.0%	0.3%

(continued)

Table 7.6 (continued)

Bus.Target * Deaths crosstabulation

			Deaths		Total
			0	1	
		% of total	0.3%	0.0%	0.3%
Total		Count	296	42	338
		% within Bus.Target	87.6%	12.4%	100.0%
		% within deaths	100.0%	100.0%	100.0%
		% of total	87.6%	12.4%	100.0%

A breakdown of the data revealed the number of business-related terrorist assaults without connections to political events comprised a full 63.6% of all commercial based terrorism chronicled (211/332 acts). It follows that some 36.4% of all business-related terrorism in Thailand was linked to a set of political events, as defined in this study. A full 76.1% of all anonymous acts (134/176) acts were with readily discernable ties to political events, while 49.4% of Islamic nationalist-irredentist acts (77/156 acts) were without discernable ties to political events (see Table 7.8).

When the one identifiable terrorist group was analyzed, it was found Islamic nationalist-irredentist terrorist groups in Thailand had nearly one-fifth of all attacks against business targets linked to "landmark events" with 19.2% (30/156 acts) of the total. In turn, Islamic nationalist-irredentist terrorist group attacks in Thailand were linked to "religious holidays" 13.5% of the time (21/156 acts), while attacks linked to "ground assaults" by those types of organizations accounted for 10.9% of the total (17/156 acts) [16; 24; 32, 45–47, 55–56; 35, 37; 42; 46–57; 64].[34]

Further, business-related terrorist acts conducted by Islamic national-irredentist groups had ties to "government policies" 4.5% of the time (7/156 acts). Terrorist assaults with links to "secular holidays" only made up 1.3% (2/156 acts) of attacks taken by Islamic nationalist irredentist groups, while attacks by Islamic nationalist-irredentist groups with ties to "government assassinations" also made up 1.3% (2/156 acts).

The rate of all anonymous terrorist assaults in Thailand with discernable links to political events as defined was less than one-half the rate, at some 23.9%, than the corresponding rate of some 50.7% found for Islamic nationalist-irredentist groups.[35]

[34] In this test, "landmark events" ("5") included: anniversaries of both PULO and BRN's *establishment* (entries #71–#99), initial broadcast of Wuthipong "Ko Tee" Kotthammakhun's "pro-government," Radio 90.5 HMz (entry #130), the Narathiwat "arms heist" on January 4, 2002 (#108), the Bersatu charter's anniversary (entries # 134, #135), anniversary of King Bhumibal who became King on June 15, 1946 (entry #164), the overthrow of Prime Minister Yingluck Shinawatra (entry #184,); anniversary of the Tak Bai incident (entry # 268), the anniversary of Maroso Chantrawadee's death. In the case of "religious events," holidays included: Ramadan (e.g., entry #204), and Christmas (entries #106, #107). There were no recorded events tied to the Chinese New Year.

[35] For anonymous actors, the breakdown was "govt. policies" (7.4%) + "ground assaults" (4.0%) + "landmark events" (4.5%) + "religious holidays" (8.0%) = 23.9%. For Islamic nationalist-irredentist groups, the breakdown was "govt. policies" (4.5%) + "ground assaults" (10.9%) +

Table 7.7 Relative frequency of group-type by Political Event, 2013–2018 (summary statistics)

Case processing summary

	Valid		Cases missing		Total	
	N	Percent	N	Percent	N	Percent
GroupTy * ReacPol.Evnt	273	79.6%	70	20.4%	343	100.0%

GroupTy * ReacPol.Evnt crosstabulation

			ReacPol.Evnt	
			No relation	Ground assaults
GroupTy	Anonymous	Count	134	7
		% within GroupTy	89.9%	4.7%
		% within ReacPol.Evnt	63.5%	29.2%
		% of total	49.1%	2.6%
	Islamic Nationalist-Irredentist	Count	77	17
		% within GroupTy	62.1%	13.7%
		% within ReacPol.Evnt	36.5%	70.8%
		% of total	28.2%	6.2%
Total		Count	211	24
		% within GroupTy	77.3%	8.8%
		% within ReacPol.Evnt	100.0%	100.0%
		% of total	77.3%	8.8%

			ReacPol.Evnt	
			Landmark events	Total
GroupTy	Anonymous	Count	8	149
		% within GroupTy	5.4%	100.0%
		% within ReacPol.Evnt	21.1%	54.6%
		% of total	2.9%	54.6%
	Islamic Nationalist-Irredentist	Count	30	124
		% within GroupTy	24.2%	100.0%
		% within ReacPol.Evnt	78.9%	45.4%
		% of total	11.0%	45.4%
Total		Count	38	273
		% within GroupTy	13.9%	100.0%
		% within ReacPol.Evnt	100.0%	100.0%
		% of total	13.9%	100.0%

Chi-square tests

	Value	df	Asymptotic significance (2-sided)
Pearson chi-square	30.266[a]	2	< 0.001
Likelihood ratio	31.161	2	< 0.001
Linear-by-linear association	27.610	1	< 0.001

(continued)

Table 7.7 (continued)

Chi-square tests

	Value	df	Asymptotic significance (2-sided)
N of valid cases	273		

Directional measures

			Value	Asymptotic standard error[b]
Nominal by nominal	Lambda	Symmetric	0.172	0.035
		GroupTy dependent	0.258	0.055
		ReacPol. Evnt dependent	0.000	0.000
	Goodman and Kruskal tau	GroupT dependent	0.111	0.035
		ReacPol. Evnt dependent	0.080	0.026

Directional measures

			Approximate T[c]	Approximate significance
Nominal by nominal	Lambda	Symmetric	4.193	< 0.001
		GroupTy dependent	4.193	< 0.001
		ReacPol. Evnt dependent	[d]	[d]
	Goodman and Kruskal tau	GroupTy dependent		< 0.001[e]
		ReacPol. Evnt dependent		< 0.001[e]

Symmetric measures

		Value	Approximate significance
Nominal by nominal	Phi	0.333	< 0.001
	Cramer's V	0.333	< 0.001
N of valid cases		273	

[a]0 cells (0.0%) have expected count less than 5. The minimum expected count is 10.90
[b]Not assuming the null hypothesis
[c]Using the asymptotic standard error assuming the null hypothesis
[d]Cannot be computed because the asymptotic standard error equals zero
[e]Based on chi-square approximation

Table 7.8 Relative frequency of group-type by Political Event, 2013–2018

Case processing summary

	Valid		Cases missing		Total	
	N	Percent	N	Percent	N	Percent
GroupTy * ReacPol. Evnt	332	96.8%	11	3.2%	343	100.0%

GroupTy * ReacPol. Evnt crosstabulation

			ReacPol. Evnt		
			No relation	Govt.Policies	Ground assaults
GroupTy	Anonymous	Count	134	13	7
		% within GroupTy	76.1%	7.4%	4.0%
		% within ReacPol. Evnt	63.5%	65.0%	29.2%
		% of total	40.4%	3.9%	2.1%
	Islamic Nationalist-Irredentist	Count	77	7	17
		% within GroupTy	49.4%	4.5%	10.9%
		% within ReacPol. Evnt	36.5%	35.0%	70.8%
		% of total	23.2%	2.1%	5.1%
Total		Count	211	20	24
		% within GroupTy	63.6%	6.0%	7.2%
		% within ReacPol. Evnt	100.0%	100.0%	100.0%
		% of total	63.6%	6.0%	7.2%

			ReacPol.Evnt	
			Govt.Assassinations	Landmark events
GroupTy	Anonymous	Count	0	8
		% within GroupTy	0.0%	4.5%
		% within ReacPol. Evnt	0.0%	21.1%
		% of total	0.0%	2.4%
	Islamic Nationalist-Irredentist	Count	2	30
		% within GroupTy	1.3%	19.2%

(continued)

Table 7.8 (continued)

			ReacPol.Evnt	
			Govt.Assassinations	Landmark events
		% within ReacPol. Evnt	100.0%	78.9%
		% of total	0.6%	9.0%
Total		Count	2	38
		% within GroupTy	0.6%	11.4%
		% within ReacPol. Evnt	100.0%	100.0%
		% of total	0.6%	11.4%

			ReacPol.Evnt	
			Religious holidays	Secular holidays
GroupTy	Anonymous	Count	14	0
		% within GroupTy	8.0%	0.0%
		% within ReacPol. Evnt	40.0%	0.0%
		% of total	4.2%	0.0%
	Islamic Nationalist-Irredentist	Count	21	2
		% within GroupTy	13.5%	1.3%
		% within ReacPol. Evnt	60.0%	100.0%
		% of total	6.3%	0.6%
Total		Count	35	2
		% within GroupTy	10.5%	0.6%
		% within ReacPol. Evnt	100.0%	100.0%
		% of total	10.5%	0.6%

			Total
GroupTy	Anonymous	Count	176
		% within GroupTy	100.0%
		% within ReacPol. Evnt	53.0%
		% of total	53.0%
	Islamic Nationalist-Irredentist	Count	156

(continued)

Table 7.8 (continued)

			Total
		% within GroupTy	100.0%
		% within ReacPol. Evnt	47.0%
		% of total	47.0%
Total		Count	332
		% within GroupTy	100.0%
		% within ReacPol. Evnt	100.0%
		% of total	100.0%

The rate for anonymous terrorist attacks linked to "religious holidays," at 8.0% (14/176 acts) ranked first for anonymous stakeholders when terrorist assaults lined to political events were considered.

That 8.0% rate for "religious holidays" was followed very closely behind by anonymous terrorist attacks tied to "government policies," which accounted for 7.4% (13/176 acts) of the total. Anonymous terrorist acts with links to "ground assaults" followed with 4.0% of the total (7/176 acts), With the finding that some 63.6% of all business-related terrorist attacks were without discernable ties to political events, Hypothesis Three is accepted as valid.

7.28 Business Target X Province—Region

Hypothesis Four: There will be a higher rate of Islamic nationalist-irredentist terrorist attacks for "private establishments" and other "non-structuralist" business targets in Thailand's "deep south" compared to other Thai provinces outside the "deep south." [32, 88; 35, 29].[36]

This hypothesis stems from results for India that revealed a statistically significant relationship exists between the variable, "Business target-type" and the variable "Indian state." When Indian states were compared by region, the distributions indicated states in the "seven sister region" experienced a higher rate of "private establishments" attacks compared to other states in India. Those results were consistent with the idea that emphasis on targeting Indian "private establishments" (a "non-structuralist" target type), reflected links between "private establishments" and the ethnicity of business ownership or management.

"govt. assassinations" (1.3%) + "landmark events" (19.2%) + "religious holidays" (13.5%) + "secular holidays" (1.3%) = 50.7%

[36] As only 4 out of 16 districts of Songkhla (25.0%) constitute part of the "deep south," Songkhla was not included in the category "deep south." There were no chronicled business-related terrorist events that happened in Satun in this six-year time interval. Helbardt reports there are few if any "Southern separatist" terrorist organization constituent group supporters in Satun province. By contrast, Gunaratna and Acharya report that PULO constituent support exists in Satun.

A Pearson Chi Square statistic of 9.614 with a "*p*-value" of 0.008 at two degrees of freedom (2 d.f.) makes it possible to reject the null hypothesis of no relation between the variables "Business Target" and "Region" at the 0.05 level of confidence. There were 2 cells (33.3%) with an expected count of less than 5 but the results are reported for fear of making a "Type" II error of failing to reject the null hypothesis when it should be rejected.[37] The strength of this relationship was found to be weak with a "Phi" score of 0.310 with a significance score of 0.008 and a "Cramer's V" score of 0.310, each with a significance score of 0.008 (see Table 7.9).

The data distributions reveal that a full 83.3% (280/336 acts) of all business-related terrorist attacks chronicled took place in the "deep south." That rate was about five times higher than the 16.7% rate of business-related terrorist attacks (56/336 acts) found in non "deep south" provinces, inclusive of other southern provinces in Thailand. Those data distributions also reveal that rates of terrorist assaults for all business targets, except for "newspaper/print" targets, were higher in Thailand's "deep south" than in other parts of Thailand (see Table 7.10).

A full 100.0% (1/1 act) of "agriculture" targets happened in the "deep south." In turn, rates of attack in the "deep south" for five other business target types were closely clustered. For example, 86.4% of all terrorist attacks directed at "banking/finance" institutions (51/59 acts) happened in the "deep south." In turn, with a rate of 83.6% (158/189 acts), "private establishments" had the third highest rate of attack in the deep south. The 83.3% attack rate (5/6 acts) for "hospital/medical facilities" in Yala, Pattani, and Narathiwat ranked fourth, followed by "telecommunications" targets with 82.5% (33/40 acts) and "energy/alloy" targets with 81.1% (30/37 acts) that happened in those three provinces.

In the case of "Non-deep south" provinces in Thailand, "newspaper/print" targets had the highest rate of business-related terrorist attack by far at 75.0% (3/4 acts) outside of Thailand's "deep south."[38] In those "Non-deep south" areas, terrorist attacks against "energy/alloy" targets ranked a very distant second with 18.9% (7/37 acts), while "telecommunications" targets were the focus of attention 17.5% of the time (7/40 acts). In turn, 16.7% of all "hospitals/medical" facilities attacks (1/6 acts) happened outside the "deep south," followed by 15.9% of attacks against "private establishments" (30/189 acts) in those areas. Outside of the "deep south," "banking/finance" institutions experienced the lowest rate of business related terrorist attacks at 13.6% (8/59 acts).

The results revealed that in Thailand's "deep south," many "structuralist" business target types that symbolized "world systems" factors such as capitalism, globalism, and modernization, also experienced high rates of business-related terrorist assaults, in addition to "private establishments" and other "non-structuralist" targets.

---

[37] In this test, the variable, "Prov/State" was recoded into "a different variable," "Region" with value labels "Deep South" (1.00 = 1 → 1, 2 → 2, 3 → 3) and "non-Deep South" (2.00 = 4 → 4, 5 → 5, 6 → 6, 7 → 7, 8 → 8, 9 → 9, 10 → 10, 11 → 11, 12 → 12, 13 → 13, 14 → 14, ELSE SYSMIS). The variable "Business Target" was recoded into the "same variable," 1 → 1, 6 → 6, 7 → 7, ELSE SYSMIS).

[38] There were no chronicled business-related terrorist assaults in Satun province for the 2013–2018 time period under consideration.

Table 7.9 Relative frequency of business target by Region, 2013–2018 (summary statistics)

Case processing summary

	Valid		Cases missing		Total	
	N	Percent	N	Percent	N	Percent
Bus.Target * Region	100	29.2%	243	70.8%	343	100.0%

Bus.Target * Region crosstabulation

			Region		Total
			Deep South	Non-deep South	
Bus.Target	Energy/Alloy	Count	30	7	37
		% within Bus.Target	81.1%	18.9%	100.0%
		% within region	36.6%	38.9%	37.0%
		% of total	30.0%	7.0%	37.0%
	Newspaper/Print	Count	1	3	4
		% within Bus.Target	25.0%	75.0%	100.0%
		% within region	1.2%	16.7%	4.0%
		% of total	1.0%	3.0%	4.0%
	Banking/Finance	Count	51	8	59
		% within Bus.Target	86.4%	13.6%	100.0%
		% within region	62.2%	44.4%	59.0%
		% of total	51.0%	8.0%	59.0%
Total		Count	82	18	100
		% within Bus.Target	82.0%	18.0%	100.0%
		% within region	100.0%	100.0%	100.0%
		% of total	82.0%	18.0%	100.0%

Chi-square tests

	Value	df	Asymptotic significance (2-sided)
Pearson chi-square	9.614[a]	2	0.008
Likelihood ratio	7.055	2	0.029
N of valid cases	100		

Directional measures

			Value	Asymptotic standard error[b]
Nominal by Nominal	Lambda	Symmetric	0.034	0.033

(continued)

Table 7.9 (continued)

Directional measures

			Value	Asymptotic standard error[b]
		Bus. Target Dependent	0.000	0.000
		Region Dependent	0.111	0.105
	Goodman and Kruskal tau	Bus. Target Dependent	0.016	0.018
		Region Dependent	0.096	0.069

Directional measures

			Approximate T[c]	Approximate Significance
Nominal by Nominal	Lambda	Symmetric	1.005	0.315
		Bus.Target dependent	[d]	[d]
		Region dependent	1.005	0.315
	Goodman and Kruskal tau	Bus.Target dependent		0.204[e]
		Region dependent		0.009[e]

Symmetric measures

		Value	Approximate significance
Nominal by nominal	Phi	0.310	0.008
	Cramer's V	0.310	0.008
N of valid cases		100	

[a]2 cells (33.3%) have expected count less than 5. The minimum expected count is 0.72
[b]Not assuming the null hypothesis
[c]Using the asymptotic standard error assuming the null hypothesis
[d]Cannot be computed because the asymptotic standard error equals zero
[e]Based on chi-square approximation

Those business target types included, "energy/alloy," "telecommunications" and "banking/finance" institution targets. Therefore, Hypothesis Four, which posits that rates of business-related terrorism against "private establishments" and other "non-structuralist targets" in the "deep south" would be higher than in other provinces in Thailand outside the "deep south," is rejected.

Table 7.10 Relative frequency of business type target by Region, 2013–2018

Case processing summary

	Valid		Cases missing		Total	
	N	Percent	N	Percent	N	Percent
Bus.Target * Region	336	98.0%	7	2.0%	343	100.0%

Bus.Target * Region crosstabulation

			Region		Total
			Deep South	Non-deep South	
Bus. Target	Energy/Alloy	Count	30	7	37
		% within Bus.Target	81.1%	18.9%	100.0%
		% within region	10.7%	12.5%	11.0%
		% of total	8.9%	2.1%	11.0%
	Hospitals/Medical	Count	5	1	6
		% within Bus.Target	83.3%	16.7%	100.0%
		% within region	1.8%	1.8%	1.8%
		% of total	1.5%	0.3%	1.8%
	Private establishments	Count	159	30	189
		% within Bus.Target	84.1%	15.9%	100.0%
		% within region	56.8%	53.6%	56.3%
		% of total	47.3%	8.9%	56.3%
	Telecommunications	Count	33	7	40
		% within Bus.Target	82.5%	17.5%	100.0%
		% within region	11.8%	12.5%	11.9%
		% of total	9.8%	2.1%	11.9%
	Newspaper/Print	Count	1	3	4
		% within Bus.Target	25.0%	75.0%	100.0%
		% within region	0.4%	5.4%	1.2%
		% of total	0.3%	0.9%	1.2%
	Banking/Finance	Count	51	8	59
		% within Bus.Target	86.4%	13.6%	100.0%

(continued)

Table 7.10 (continued)

Bus.Target * Region crosstabulation

			Region		Total
			Deep South	Non-deep South	
		% within region	18.2%	14.3%	17.6%
		% of total	15.2%	2.4%	17.6%

Bus.Target * Region crosstabulation

			Region		Total
			Deep South	Non-deep South	
	Agriculture	Count	1	0	1
		% within Bus.Target	100.0%	0.0%	100.0%
		% within region	0.4%	0.0%	0.3%
		% of total	0.3%	0.0%	0.3%
Total		Count	280	56	336
		% within Bus.Target	83.3%	16.7%	100.0%
		% within region	100.0%	100.0%	100.0%
		% of total	83.3%	16.7%	100.0%

7.29 Conclusions

This chapter on Thailand starts with broad descriptions of the historical context of Thailand's centralized government and its corresponding approaches to exert control over the "deep south" provinces. It assesses the role of Bangkok's Buddhist assimilationist policies, that in turn interact with the "ethnoreligious" character of the Malay-Muslim population in the "deep south." That complex set of interactions has led to clarion calls by Malay-Muslims in the southern provinces for greater autonomy or independence from the regime in Bangkok.

What might constitute the final form of southern state autonomy or independence outright varies, as some separatist leaders envision the political goal of self-determination to be achieved as greater autonomy from Thailand. At the same time, other activists and at least some of their supporters aspire to establish an independent state. There is also underlying divergence about the nature of the government envisioned—be it an Islamic autonomous region or a full-blown secular independent state.

Still another layer to those political complexities is that among those who want an Islamic autonomous area or state, some want a "back to the future" establishment of an Islamic sultanate, rather than a more contemporary Islamic state or autonomous region. Indeed, Helbardt and other scholars point out that some contemporary activists seem have poorly articulated ideas about what is the final political objective to strive for, and for some scholars, that condition seems to stimulate a pursuit of violence for its own sake.

That idea of violence for its own sake, as Helbardt and others note, is consistent with Mary Kaldor's notion of "New Wars," where violence largely becomes an end as well as a means, in large part because of the interests of "political entrepreneurs" on both sides to continue the conflict. The Kaldor argument is that those "political entrepreneurs" or what Harris and Reilly call "ethnic entrepreneurs," utilize the conflict to maximize personal gain [34; 35, 27; 8, 1–34].

What was also significant here was the makeshift and incomplete condition of information about terrorist groups active in the contemporary political fray—a condition that reignited in 2004. As both Yusuf and Helbardt point out, a clear understanding about the precise nature of current terrorist campaigns waged by Malay-Muslim separatists is hard to acquire. It appears scholars know comparatively little about the exact organizational structure of some of those terrorist groups and in some cases, who particular terrorist chieftains are at particular moments of time [22, 24; 65, 52; 35, 2, 55, 43].

The reasons why there is a comparative lack of reliable information on terrorism in Thailand seems to be multifaceted. First, there is the absence of effective and sustained communications from terrorist group chieftains themselves about mission and specific ideological orientation. Second, there is in some cases, fundamental disagreement between experts about the sources and some of the characteristics of more established terrorist groups. Notwithstanding that, there is consensus among scholars that at the heart of the separatist struggle are what can be described as nationalist-irredentist terrorist groups with an Islamic hue. In this study, those groups are labelled as "Islamic nationalist-irredentist" terrorist organizations.

In this study, examples of authoritative academic disagreement about terrorist group sources and origins revolved around the terrorist groups Barisan Nasional Pembebasan (BNPP), and Gerakan Mujahideen Islam Pattani (GMIP). There were also different claims about terrorist organization activist size, especially as the size of identifiable terrorist groups seemed to fluctuate over several decades in part due to internecine conflict within groups and in part because of counterterrorism actions that included a series of "peace talks." Indeed, there are some differences of opinion about who exactly the most predominant stakeholders are in the contemporary political and military fray.

For example, some in the Thai government point to criminal syndicalists as the source of the problem, while some scholars seem to put misplaced emphasis on global Salafism/Jihadism that originates from countries such as Indonesia and the Philippines. A third and related problem is that Thai authorities have experienced intelligence difficulties, where inadequate intelligence compilation has compounded problems with acquiring solid data about terrorist groups [35, 43–44].

Still another important dimension of the separatist conflict that probably contributes to intelligence compilation problems and to overall counterterrorism effectiveness is the major role in the Thai political system of what Poocharoen calls "bureaucratic politics." [14, 307; 41, 26; 47, 194–195, 201, 191, 187]. That condition of "bureaucratic politics," which Allison describes at length, is characterized by a variety of upper crust decision makers in cliques who engage in political turf wars, stoke personal animosities, engage in professional jealousies, and battle over public policy direction [14, 307; 9, 68–70; 41, 26; 47, 194–195, 201, 191, 187].

That fierce political competition between stakeholders is entrenched in the Thai political system in profound and lasting ways. With fierce rivalries between actors critically important to the future of the "deep south." Those include, but are not limited to, Thailand's political parties, Thailand's Fourth Army, the National Security Council, and the Southern Border Province Administrative Centre (SBPAC). The results of that condition are spelled out clearly by McCargo and other scholars who note that "bureaucratic politics" has worked to provide "political space" for terrorist group formation and development [35, 229, n37; 40, 14–15, 11, 80, 87, 183–184, 8–9, 84, 36, 42]. The major role of nation-state structural factors and their effects on the separatist conflict and the prospect of its resolution was generally recognizable in the literature.

One other potential source of conflict that seems to have remained largely unrealized at this juncture is the potential friction points between Muslim-Malay Khana Khao "traditionalists" whose Islamic outlook about Islam is considered less stringent and as a result more fluid and open to interpretation, and Islamic "modernists" or the Khana Mai who are more stringent about Islamic interpretations. McCargo suggests that perhaps because the Khana Khao are more open to "free interpretation" of Islamic principles, the Khana Kao might be more receptive to nationalist-irredentist influences [22, 31; 40, 23, 20, 26, 28–29]. That could be a fissure or schism in Thailand's Islamic political landscape that outside Jihadist activists could exploit to their advantage.

In the case of the TABVI analysis, it was found Thailand ranked second behind India as the "host" country most afflicted by business related terrorism threat and corresponding vulnerability. Thailand's second place ranking on the TABVI threat/vulnerability continuum constructed was found to be almost at the midpoint of that spectrum, just past the outside parameter of the "middle level risk" domain for those developing host countries. In addition, a TABVI analysis was conducted for Thai industries; that made it possible for the reader be able to compare and contrast threat and vulnerabilities associated with different industries.

In fact, the TABVI analytic tool proved to be especially useful in the case of Thailand to capture variations of risk and vulnerability when business target-types were compared. That was the case because with only one identifiable terrorist group-type, in addition to anonymous terrorist assaults, the use of bivariate analysis was limited. It follows that other types of targets of interest to terrorists can also be fitted onto this TABVI measure. What is significant is the TABVI algorithm should prove useful for analysis of "terrorism systems" (e.g., at the nation-state, region, or city level) to capture variations in risk and vulnerability within countries, across industries, or across countries, especially when data about terrorism is as opaque as it was in the case of Thailand.

In terms of the quantitative analysis, the use of bivariate analysis (i.e., crosstabulation table analysis) was able to reveal statistically significant relationships between several pairs of Thai terrorist group and terrorist assault characteristics. That was the case even though there were some problems with the data with respect to terrorist stakeholder identification in some cases, and problems of differentiation associated with the extremely large number of anonymous terrorist assaults conducted between January 1, 2013 and December 31, 2018 [35, 5, 9, 18, 20].

For example, there were statistically significant relationships found for the following explanatory factor pairings: (1) Terrorist Group-Name X Business Target, (2) Political Ideology X Business Target, (3) Business Target-Type X Number of Deaths, (4) Terrorist Group-Type X Reaction to Political Events, and (5) Business Target X Province (recoded into Region). There were four hypotheses tested for validity, and out of four hypotheses tested, three were accepted as valid. Efforts were made conform the basic nature and structure of those hypotheses used for Thailand, to conform to, the basic hypotheses used in the case of India. The reason why was because in this study, bivariate analysis was only able to be used in the cases of India and Thailand. In the next chapter, some of the major qualitative and quantitative findings will be compared and summarized across the five developing world "host" countries under consideration.

References

1. Abuza Z (2016) Forging peace in Southeast Asia: insurgencies, peace processes, and reconciliation. Rowman & Littlefield
2. Allen R (1974) Imperialism and nationalism in the fertile crescent-sources and prospects of the Arab-Israeli conflict. Oxford University Press
3. Baldwin D (1971) The power of positive sanctions. World Pol 24(1):19–38
4. Baldwin D (1985) Economic statecraft. Princeton University Press
5. Chasdi RJ (1999) Serenade of suffering: a portrait of Middle East terrorism, 1968–1993. Lexington Books
6. Chasdi RJ (2002) Tapestry of terror: a portrait of Middle East terrorism, 1994–1999. Lexington Books
7. Hoffman B (1998) Inside terrorism. Columbia University Press
8. Kaldor M (2013) In defense of new wars. Int J Secur Develop 2(1):1–34
9. Lindblom CE (1980) The policy-making process, 2nd edn. Prentice Hall
10. Makarenko T (2004) The crime terror continuum: tracing the interplay between transnational organized crime and terrorism. Global Crime 6(1):129–145
11. Pearson FS (1974) Geographic proximity and foreign military intervention. J Conflict Resolut 18(3):432–460
12. Starr H, Most B (1976) The substance and study of borders in international relations research. Int Stud Quart 20(4):581–620
13. Abuza Z (2009) Conspiracy of silence: the insurgency in southern Thailand. United States Institute of Peace
14. Allison GT, Zelikow PD (1999) Essence of decision: explaining the Cuban Missile Crisis, 2nd edn. Addison Wesley Longman, Inc
15. Aslam MM (2022) Decoding the global security threat of COVID-19. In: Gunaratna RK, Aslam MM (eds) COVID-19 pandemic: the threat and response. Routledge
16. Benjakat A (2016, 26 October) Pattani blast suspects "known": 1 dead, 21 injured by bomb at noodle shop. The Bangkok Post. https://www.bangkokpost.com/thailand/general/1119197/pattani-blast-suspects-known

17. Chalk P (2008) Occasional paper—the Malay-Muslim insurgency in southern Thailand: understanding the conflict's evolving dynamic. National Defense Research Institute. Rand Corporation
18. Chasdi RJ (1995) The dynamics of Middle East terrorism, 1968–1993: a functional typology of different terrorist groups. Ph.D. dissertation, Purdue University
19. Chasdi RJ (2010) Counterterror offensives for the ghost war world: the rudiments of counterterrorism policy. Lexington Books
20. Chasdi RJ (2021) Prevention of major economic disruptions following acts of terrorism—the case of the Bali bombings of 2002 and 2005. In: Schmid AP (ed) Handbook of terrorism prevention and preparedness. ICCT Press Publications
21. Chongkittavorn K (2004) Thailand: international terrorism and the Muslim south. Southeast Asian Affairs 267–275. https://www.jstor.org/stable/27913265
22. Croissant A (2005) Unrest in South Thailand: contours, causes and consequences. Contemp Southeast Asia 27(1):21–43
23. Diamond L (1990) Nigeria: pluralism, statism and the struggle for democracy. In: Diamond L, Lintz JL, Lipset SM (eds) Politics in developing countries: comparing experiences with democracy. Lynne Rienner
24. Doksone T (2015, 2 February) Thai leader says blasts aimed at discrediting government. The Associated Press
25. Emmers R (2004) Non-traditional security in the Asia-Pacific: the dynamics of securitization. Eastern Universities Press
26. Esman MJ (1994) Ethnic politics. Cornell University Press
27. Funston J (2010) Malaysia and Thailand's southern conflict: reconciling security and ethnicity. Contemp Southeast Asia 32(2):234–257. https://openresearch-repository.anu.edu.au/bitstream/1885/50966/2/01_Funston_Malaysia_and_Thailand%27s_2010.pdf
28. Global Terrorism Database (GTD) Thailand. GTD ID: 201304100068. 10 Apr 2013
29. Global Terrorism Database (GTD) Thailand. GTD ID: 201405070017. 5 May 2014
30. Global Terrorism Database (GTD) Thailand. GTD ID: 201405070016. 7 May 2014
31. Guidere M (2017) Barisan Revolusi Nasional (BRN). In: Historical dictionary of Islamic fundamentalism, 2nd edn. Rowman & Littlefield. https://www.google.com/books/edition/Historical_Dictionary_of_Islamic_Fundame/NYYyDwAAQBAJ?hl=en&gbpv=1&dq=Guidere,+Mathieu+Barisan+Revolusi+Nasional&pg=PR7&printsec=frontcover
32. Gunaratna R, Acharya A (2013) The terrorist threat from Thailand: Jihad or quest for justice. Potomac Books
33. Gunaratna R, Acharya A, Chua S (2005) Conflict and terrorism in southern Thailand. Marshall Cavendish Academic
34. Harris P, Reilly B (eds) (1998) Democracy and deep rooted conflict: options for negotiators. IDEA. http://www.idea.int/publications/democracy/_and_deep_rooted_conflict/ebook_contents.htm
35. Helbardt S (2015) Deciphering south Thailand's violence: organization and insurgent practices of BRN-coordinate. ISEAS Publishing
36. Henry N (2013) Public administration and public affairs-twelfth edition. Pearson Education Inc
37. International Crisis Group (2022, 19 April) Sustaining the momentum in southern Thailand's peace dialogue. Briefing 172 Asia. https://www.crisisgroup.org/asia/south-east-asia/thailand/sustaining-momentum-southern-thailands-peace-dialogue
38. Lesser IO (1999) Countering the new terrorism: implications for strategy. In: Lesser IO, Hoffman B, Arquilla J, Ronfeldt D, Zanini M (eds) Countering the new terrorism. Rand
39. Mandaville P (2016) Islam and international relations in the Middle East from Umma to nation-state. In: Fawcett L (ed) International relations in the Middle East, 4th edn. Oxford University Press
40. McCargo D (2008) Tearing apart the land: Islam and legitimacy in southern Thailand. Cornell University Press

41. McDermott G (2014) The 2013 Kuala Lumpur talks: a step forward for southern Thailand. Peace Res 46(1):5–34. https://www.jstor.org/stable/24896051
42. Moore JM (2014, 9 January) Outside view: Thailand's southern insurgency turns up the heat. API.com. Nexis-Uni
43. Norusis MJ (1991) The SPSS guide to data analysis, 2nd edn. SPSS
44. Nye JS (1993) Understanding international conflicts: an introduction to theory and history. Harper Collins College Publishers
45. Ockey J (2011) Individual imaginings: the religio-nationalist pilgrimages of Haji Sulong Abdulkadir al-Fatani. J Southeast Asia Stud 42(1):89–119. https://www.jstor.org/stable/pdf/23020304
46. Parmentier G (2006) France. In: Alexander Y (ed) Counterterrorism strategies: successes and failures of six nations. Potomac Books
47. Poocharoen O-O (2010) The bureaucracy: problem or solution to Thailand's far south flames? Contemp Southeast Asia 32(2):184–207. https://www.jstor.org/stable/41756326
48. Rogan EL (2016) The emergence of the modern Middle East into the modern state system. In: Fawcett L (ed) International relations in the Middle East, 4th edn. Oxford University Press
49. Shelley LI (2013) Money laundering into real estate. In: Miklaucic M, Brewer J (eds) Convergence: illicit networks and national security in the age of globalization. Center for Complex Operations, Institute for National Strategic Studies, National Defense University
50. Shelley LI (2014) Identifying, counting and categorizing transnational criminal organizations. In: Sheptycki J (ed) Transnational organized crime, volume II: definitional and methodological issues, constructionist and critical perspectives. Sage Publications
51. Shelley LI, Picarelli J, Irby A, Hart DM, Craig-Hart PA, Williams P, Simon S, Abdullaev N, Stanislawski B, Covill L (2005) Methods and motives: exploring links between transnational organized crime and international terrorism. Trends Organ Crim 8(2). https://doi.org/10.1007/s12117-005-1024-x
52. Starr H, Most B (1985) Patterns of conflict: quantitative analysis and the comparative lessons of third world wars. In: Harkavy R, Neuman SG (eds) Approaches and case studies: volume 1 of the lessons of recent wars in the third world. Heath and Company
53. The Bangkok Post (2013, 11 April) Militants rampage in Pattani overnight. Nexis-Uni
54. The Bangkok Post (2014, 9 April) Cops narrow search for blast culprits. Nexis-Uni
55. The Bangkok Post (2016, 13 February) Four blasts rattle Narathiwat. Nexis-Uni
56. The Bangkok Post (2016, 14 February) Blasts mark three years since rebel defeat. Nexis-Uni
57. The Nation (Thailand) (2014, 31 March) Separate attacks on red radio station, army unit. Nexis-Uni
58. Waltz KN (1959) Man, the state and war: a theoretical analysis. Columbia University Press
59. Weimann G (2006) Virtual training camps: terrorists' use of the internet. In: Forest JJF (ed) Teaching terror: strategic and tactical learning in the terrorist world. Rowman & Littlefield Publishers Inc, pp 110–132
60. White JR (2002) Terrorism: an introduction, 3rd edn. Wadsworth Thomson
61. Wikipedia (n.d.) List of prime ministers of Thailand. https://en.m.wikipedia.org
62. World Economic Forum (2017) Business costs of terrorism. http://reports.weforum.org/global-competitiveness-index-2017-2018/competitiveness-rankings/#series=EOSQ033
63. World Economic Forum (2017) Appendix C. http://www3.weforum.org/docs/GCR2017-2018/04Backmatter/TheGlobalCompetitivenessReport2017%E2%80%932018AppendixC.pdf
64. Xinhua General New Service (2013, 9 October) Wave of violence hits S. Thailand. Nexis-Uni
65. Yusuf I (2009) Ethnoreligious and political dimensions of the southern Thailand conflict. In: Islam and politics: renewal and resistance in the Muslim world. Stimson Center. https://www.jstor.org/stable/pdf/resrep10936.9.pdf

Chapter 8
Conclusions

8.1 Qualitative Findings

8.1.1 The Interrelated Concepts of Vulnerability, Security, and Risk

This study puts focus on business vulnerabilities to terrorism with use of the TABVI analysis. In turn, the statistical analysis illuminates choices made about business target selection. It seems plausible that terrorist leader preferences for particular types of targets are both a cause and effect of those business target vulnerabilities. Therefore, it seems useful that findings about terrorism threat in specific developing world host countries should first be positioned within a framework that provides some description of what vulnerability, security, and risk are about, and the conceptual ties between them.

From the start, vulnerability contrasts with security in terms of passive and active qualities. Vulnerability is a reactive condition, reflective of threatening action, that itself is frequently perceived as proactive and proximate in chronological terms. In contrast, security, for those who experience it, is a positive empirical condition that presupposes and derives from proactive action that has removed explanatory factors outright or reduced their effects, which caused feelings of vulnerability in the first place.

Seen from a different angle, vulnerability is akin to the abject and reactive fear intrinsic to terrorism threat, while the confidence that derives from security is akin to effective and sustained counterterrorism capabilities or positive perceptions of those abilities. It is important to point out the manifestations of both those two conditions of vulnerability and security are not mutually exclusive; they can both be experienced, albeit in different degrees, between members of a group such as C-class executives, within communities, and even within an individual [29; 45, 59-64, 87].

R. J. Chasdi, *Corporate Security Surveillance*, Advanced Sciences and Technologies for Security Applications, https://doi.org/10.1007/978-3-031-39550-5_8

Another observation about the relationship between vulnerability and security stresses an attribute that both conditions have in common. What seems significant is that in addition to thinking about vulnerability and security as a "relational concept" with comparisons made to other stakeholders, both vulnerability and security can be experienced as more "stand-alone" conditions which do not require conscious and regular comparisons to other stakeholders or specific links to anticipated events [5; 6; 12, 84–85].

To be sure, individuals, groups of individuals, business executives, and nation-state populations can experience "stand-alone" feelings of vulnerability, sometimes vague but still deeply disturbing, from a variety of sources without specific and proximate threats posed by one or a combination of state, non-state, or individual actions. Those "stand-alone" dynamics of vulnerability are reflected in many of the legal systems of Western style democracies, which seek to alleviate feelings of vulnerability and similar sentiments.

Under domestic law, security in many Western style liberal democracies is more a function of legal protections afforded to groups and individuals, and law enforcement implementation of those protections, rather than on primary reliance on regular and immediate comparison to other groups and individuals about lurking or imminent threats, real or perceived. That is the case even though ethnic, religious, and racial groups, and people in regions frequently make comparisons to uphold the law. A comparison of laws in specific U.S. regions over abortion rights for example, is a case in point. In contrast, in authoritarian systems, groups are often favored by government or discriminated against, so that relative comparisons about threat and security across individuals, "in-groups," and "out-groups" become more constant, deeply entrenched, and acute.

That "stand-alone" perspective also appears to hold true, at least in some cases, for the concept of security in a regional, international context. For example, until Putin's invasion of Ukraine, many Scandinavian countries saw security in the broader sense primarily as a "stand-alone" condition that did not require making comparisons with many non-Scandinavian countries. From this security perspective, the qualities of social and economic conditions and balance between work and leisure time have been promoted in a non-military context.

To reiterate, what seems significant is that vulnerability and lack of security, and related feelings such as anxiety, can be experienced as more "stand-alone" conditions, sometimes vague and unsettling, in comparison to situations where relational comparisons are made about threat. What is also important is those psychological conditions are akin to the abject fear intrinsic to acts of terrorism. The conditions of vulnerability and "insecurity" in addition to the condition of "security" span across individuals, communities, C-class executives, and other leaders of international commerce.

Furthermore, while conditions of vulnerability and security can be conceived of from two different standpoints, the two different perspectives involved are not necessarily mutually exclusive in practice. From one standpoint, vulnerability and security can be more of an "absolute" or "abstract" psychological condition, absent of specific or consciously made comparisons to other stakeholders. As described in Chapter One, if a firm compares assets and revenue flow to the assets and revenue flows of its prime competitors, appraisal of vulnerability becomes a relational process much like Morton Deutsch's notion that "power is a relational concept." [12, 84–85].

This notion of vulnerability (i.e., insecurity) dovetails well with work that highlights how the intensity levels of vulnerability and security differ between individual government and business leaders. Jervis argues that government leaders experience either a higher or comparatively lower degree of "subjective security demand" sensitivities because of personal and professional experiences, such as a traumatic childhood or work in the intelligence or security fields [30, 174–176]. At a theoretical level, it follows that Jervis' notion of "subjective security demands" also applies to C-class executives as it does for government officials.

That notion of vulnerability, which as previously mentioned, is a passive condition, and more proactive efforts to achieve security, resonate throughout in an open -market system where firms strive to reduce vulnerability and increase security. At the same time, those business world conditions can influence the behavior of stakeholders in new industries that experience "first mover advantage." [11, 191–192, 185–186, 355, 21; 25, 348, 360, 130, 137, 81–82; 26, 338, 342–344; 39, 321–323, 60–62; 50, 42]. Scholars often describe the benefits of "first mover advantage" and traditionally, vulnerability and security issues in a monopoly or duopoly have focused on what firms can do, perhaps with the tacit support of one or two competing firms, to somehow "circle the wagons" and keep firms from easy entry into that industry [11, 191–192, 185–186, 355, 21; 25, 348, 360, 130, 137, 81–82; 50, 26, 338, 342–344; 39, 321–323, 60–62]. Nowadays, when business related terrorism is considered within the context of globalization, benefits linked to "first mover advantage" might be offset to some degree by the attention from terrorists that new firms receive for new technologies that are potentially valuable to terrorist organizations.

Moreover, the problem is those cutting-edge technologies likely make those firms have developed likely make those firms potential terrorist targets because new technologies associated with a new product are symbolic of Western technological and economic prowess, and by extension, Western norms, and values. For example, "CRISPER" is a new technology that revolves around gene splicing and editing; as such, it fits the bill with respect to having utility for terrorists, and symbolic importance of Western prowess. [4] It is probably fair to say that certain eco-terrorist groups such as the Individuals Tending Towards Savagery (ITS) in Mexico for example, might work to oppose that type of technological innovation and in the process, target those firms involved in crisper development. It follows the condition of vulnerability is increased for those researchers and technicians associated with such groundbreaking technologies.

The notion of security, as an elixir of sorts to the condition of vulnerability, defies attempts to craft one widely shared and generally recognizable definition of the term. For example, notions of security might be colored by what Wolfers calls the "protection of values," that in this case might boil down to the protection of enshrined Western business norms and values endorsed by government or enshrined in tradition. Those include efforts to keep government and the private sector at arm's length, with minimal government involvement in the private sector. As previously mentioned, security can also be appraised in an abstract "stand-alone" fashion or in relational terms [12, 84–85; 33; 63, 29–45].

What the foregoing notions of security and vulnerability suggest is government policies can have profound and lasting influence on the private sector in international business. For example, by contrast to expropriation or nationalization of foreign firms that is now considered crude, and at worst a national security risk for government leaders to undertake, there are efforts by some host country leaders to devalue their currency. Currencies are devalued in the hope of making products of their companies more competitive at home and abroad. At the same time, there are deleterious effects associated with currency devaluation. Not only does currency devaluation affect competition, but it devalues a firm's assets in a host country that in many cases, at lease to some degree, must be held in that host country's local currency. Equally important, as Wolfers might suggest, those types of economic policies violate Western business norms and values of minimal government influence or control over the private sector.

As such, Booth's idea of "survival plus," is presented in ways that seem to exemplify business conditions largely unfettered by government. Booth's idea of "survival plus" suggests "security" entails much more than simple survival. For Booth, a condition of security entails the capacity to thrive in effective and sustained ways—it means conditions are in place that facilitate "innovation" and presumably, other forms of corporate development [5, 39, 110].

Turning to the condition of "risk," risk is seen in this study as the glue that bonds vulnerability and security together. There is an inverse relationship between vulnerability and risk where an increase in security leads to a decrease in risk, and vice versa. Monahan defines risk in two ways- as "risk abatement" where risk is seen in actuarial terms as the probabilities of victimization, or risk as "risk reduction" where explanatory factors are removed [27, 149–153, 157, 200, 299; 31, 1–34; 43, 14–17, 6 n7, 4].

The notion of risk, whether it is defined in actuarial terms as "risk abatement" or in "risk reduction" terms, influences vulnerability and security conditions as those conditions are understood by the stakeholder [31, 1–34; 43, 14–17, 6 n7, 4]. Seen from a different angle, risk can be conceptualized as an intervening variable where the dependent variable is vulnerability or security, and "risk" is an intervening variable to a host of independent variables that affect vulnerability or security. Those independent variables include but are not limited to, terrorism, currency devaluation, expropriation/nationalization, political instability and social unrest, and war.

8.2 Joint Government and MNC Efforts to Manipulate Terrorist Group Splintering and Spinoff Group Formation

Another theme in this book involved a preliminary examination into what Lasswell calls the "terrorist group life cycle" for certain terrorist groups in several of the developing world host countries under consideration [7, 2, 229 n6, 29; 10, 127; 28, 238–255; 36, 35, 107, 110, 252–253; 37, 255–263; 38, 25]. While the Lasswell focus is on terrorist group "formation," "growth," "development," "maturity," and "decline," primary emphasis in this book is on terrorist group "splintering" and "spinoff" formation, within those phases of development.

For definitional purposes, terrorist group "splintering" is when members of an existing terrorist organization split directly from a parent organization. In turn, terrorist "spinoff group" formation is closely related to "splinter group" fragmentation, but the formation process is more indirect where factions of pre-existing groups or a fledgling splinter group might coalesce with each other or perhaps with new members, to form a "spinoff" terrorist organization [8, 456, 613, 731–732; 9, 48].

The reason why this topic is important is because both government officials and C-class business leaders, who have non-kinetic or "soft-line" counterterrorism options available to them, can work to manipulate the terrorist group splintering process to the advantage of government and business interests in host countries. If a fledgling terrorist group is engaged in copious and bloody attacks, perhaps to make a name for itself over the political landscape, government policy-makers could work to thwart the progress of that new group through efforts to foment additional splintering or cohesion of the parent terrorist group.

In contrast, if an already established terrorist group were to mount an especially dangerous campaign against government interests, those policymakers could encourage the splintering process to diminish the capacities of that established terrorist organization. In both cases, business leaders could coordinate with both "home" and "host" country governments to assist in this process to facilitate or inhibit splintering. That could be done through the provision or withholding of non-lethal technologies, funds for education, and medical facilities and supplies, for example. That approach also highlights the importance of joint public–private sector cooperation in "public–private partnerships" to achieve counterterrorism success [2; 3; 8, 41–43; 32, 95–120].

8.3 Dashboard of Possible Explanatory Factors Linked to Terrorist Group Fragmentation

The five developing world host country case studies suggests a six-point terrorism "cohesion-fragmentation" dashboard to help isolate and identify possible explanatory factors that contribute to terrorist group splintering or spin-off formation. In his work on public administration, Henry describes "...key performance indicators, which provide executives with 'a dashboard' that quickly informs them of progress towards larger goals." For our purposes, Henry's notion of "larger goals" equates terrorist group fragmentation or cohesion [24, 193].

This preliminary six-point dashboard reflects "contextual factor" conditions in particular countries [24, 193; 27, 125, 133]. It is understood this conceptualization, as it now stands, has basic limitations. For instance, it cannot take into account the interactive effects between explanatory factors for those splinter and spinoff processes.

Furthermore, this "cohesion-fragmentation" dashboard cannot account for predominant and subordinate terrorist group or terrorist proto-group dynamics. For example, it cannot account for the leader of terrorist group A's efforts to cohere or fragment terrorist groups C, D, and E to conform with the sub-national group interests of terrorist group A. Still, the hope is the basic rudiments of this dashboard might serve as a springboard for future research on terrorist group splintering and spinoff formation [41; 49, 149–173].[1] With the foregoing as caveats, the explanatory factors for this dashboard include: (1) number of terrorist groups; (2) number of terrorist groups with shared or similar ideology; (3) number of terrorist group "factions" or units; (4) monopoly or duopoly condition for terrorist group operation (5) government policies reflective of responsiveness or sensitivities towards terrorist group constituent demands and aspirations; (6) overall terrorist organization constituent support (see Fig. 8.1).[2]

---

[1] Mearsheimer's notion of "offensive realism" offers a useful template to think about terrorist fragmentation efforts against other terrorist groups. For instance, in Mearsheimer's discussion about "offensive realism" where states are power maximizers in pursuit of hegemony, Snyder reports state leaders sometimes have to prepare for deterrence against the prospect of exploitation from another state. They can do so by means of "balancing" to confront nation-state threats, or by "buck passing" to allies to cope with threats. For Mearsheimer, the central notion is that "buck passing" is more likely in a "***balanced***" multipolar system (without a hegemonic power) by contrast to an "***unbalanced*** system" ***with*** a hegemonic power, especially so where the geographical locale of the state making the threat is far away. If Mearsheimer's ideas about "balancing" and "buck passing" are overlaid onto terrorism systems as defined in this study, imagine a "***balanced***" terrorism system ***without*** a hegemonic terrorist group, where terrorist group B might have to deter another terrorist group (Terrorist Group A) from an act of exploitation. It might also be that in this "balanced system," terrorist group A is seeking hegemony. In response, terrorist group B's efforts at fragmentation of terrorist group A amounts to "balancing," especially if terrorist group B shares similar political ideology to terrorist group A. In a metaphysical sense, shared or similar (i.e., "close") political ideology is analogous to Mearsheimer's notion of "close geographical proximity." For example, it would be useful to test whether or not Terrorist Group C, another terrorist group but with a dissimilar political ideology to Terrorist Group A, "buck passes" its responsibility to confront a threat to it onto its (de facto) allies in ways consistent with Mearsheimer's model. Such analysis might also include examination of an "***unbalanced***" terrorist system ***with a hegemonic terrorist group power*** in place.

[2] It should be noted this is a first pass at conceptualization and that in future work some of these explanatory factors might be discarded and others added. For example, "government responsiveness" and "constituent support" might be confounding variables. Therefore, in future research, a bivariate correlations test with data for those two variables and a Spearman's rho (as the direction of the relationship is known—increased government responsiveness leads to a decrease in constituent

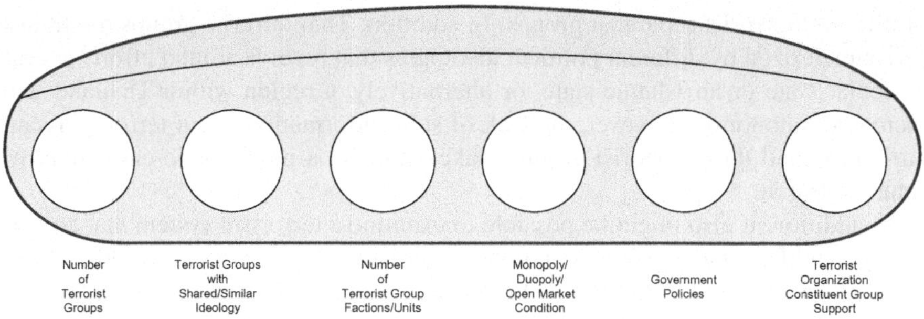

Fig. 8.1 Cohesion-fragmentation dashboard

In this work, it might be useful to focus on India, because of its very large number of active terrorist groups. The case of India illuminates dashboard variable one—the possible role that high numbers of terrorist groups in a country might play in splintering and spinoff group formation processes. India is marked by a saturated terrorism system where there is a (very) high number of terrorist groups. In addition, results for India resonate with dashboard variable two because many Indian terrorist groups have the same or similar political ideology such as Marxist-Leninism (i.e., Maoism). It follows that one hypothesis to explore for example, is the notion that if a country has a saturated terrorism system with high numbers of terrorist groups, then that saturated system structure will influence terrorist group fragmentation processes [40, 5, 11, 7; 61, 10–20].

Another related idea to test in future research is whether or not the presence of one or two predominant terrorist groups in a terrorist system has influence over terrorist group splintering or spinoff formation. In other words, the central idea is a terrorist system that resembles a market monopoly or a duopoly condition with one or two dominant terrorist groups (or terrorist group-types) that "sell" opportunities to join the ranks, will influence the splintering or spinoff process differently than an open market system [11, 181; 26, 162, 193n 34; 46].

It appears India might provide an example as good as any of what dashboard variable four captures—how terrorist group cohesion or fragmentation processes are affected by a terrorist group monopoly or duopoly system. This seems to be the case because of the ideological predominance of the Communist Party of India (CPI Maoist) and its splinter groups and because of the total number of terrorist assaults attributed to those terrorist groups (and that Marxist-Leninist/Maoist terrorist group-type) for the 2013–2018-time interval, where the Communist Party of India (CPI Maoist) alone had 15.5% of all attributed terrorist assaults (103/663 acts).

It would be useful to compare India to a country characterized by a large number of more equally balanced terrorist groups, both in ideological and numerical terms. Thailand is a country that might qualify as a country characterized by a large number

support) should be conducted. If the test produces high correlations measure of 1 or − 1, it might be necessary to reconceptualize or eliminate one data category [7].

of different terrorist separatist groups. In addition, Thai terrorist groups might also be characterized by different political ideologies that revolve around efforts to craft a secular state or an Islamic state, or alternatively, a region within Thailand with increased autonomy. However, the lack of solid information about terrorist assault attribution and those terrorist groups make Thailand a problematic case study for future research.

In addition, it also might be possible to examine a terrorism system that equates to or resembles a monopsony. In a monopsony-like condition, there would be many terrorist group "sellers" of slots to fill terrorist group ranks, but very few "buyers" (i.e., recruits). This analysis would make it possible to determine if splintering or spinoff group process patterns are similar or different across monopoly, duopoly, and open market conditions in specific countries as those apply to terrorist group cohesion and fragmentation conditions.

In this "cohesion-fragmentation" dashboard, explanatory variable three captures the idea that numbers of terrorist units or divisions which comprise a terrorist group, and high or low numbers of such units might influence terrorist group splintering or spin-off formation. Terrorism in India might also provide a useful case study to examine this notion. For example, in the case of the Communist Party of India (CPI Maoist), it was found that terrorist group was comprised of several "Naxal units" known as Dalam. In one CPI-Maoist administrative zone alone, Kujur reports some, "...30 military dalams functioning under the Dandokaranya Zonal Committee" in 2006 [34, 2, 5, 7; 52, 3–4; 56].[3]

Those Communist Party India (CPI Maoist) units included, Tippagardh Dalam, Devri Dalam, Kokadi Dalam, Here Dalam, Aheri Dalam, Etapalli Dalam, and Permili Dalam [34, 2, 5, 7; 52, 3–4; 56]. In some cases, those different CPI Maoist factions have engaged in competition, fierce competition between splinter or spinoff groups has also been commonplace to note. For example, in Nagaland, the National Socialist Council of Nagaland-Isak-Muivah (NSCN-IM), experienced armed conflict with its two splinter groups, namely NSCN-U (Unification) and NSCN-K (Khaplang) [51; 52, 6].

The dashboard's explanatory variable five captures the role of government policies as crucial external factors to the terrorist group, that affect the "life-cycle" trajectories of terrorist organizations. The role of government policies (e.g., responsiveness to potential terrorist group constituent supporters) and in the broader sense, government policies as they interact with terrorist groups over the political landscape, are explanatory factors for terrorist group trajectories widely cited in the terrorism literature, with government sponsored ceasefires, deradicalization and rehabilitation programs, and other incentives for terrorist to defect as examples [7, 8].

In addition to improved government responsiveness overall to diminish constituent support for terrorist groups, future research might examine if particular government

---

[3] While it might be intuitive to think the presence of a large number of units within a terrorist group might exacerbate the splintering process which itself is oftentimes rooted in differences of opinion, personal animosities, jealousies, and turf wars, it is equally plausible that a high number of terrorist units might serve as a disincentive to terrorist group splintering or spin-off group formation.

policies have potential to increase terrorist organization constituent group solidarity when terrorist group cohesion is the preferred outcome. Conversely, future research should isolate and identify government policies that foment splintering or terrorist group spinoff formation. Those counterterrorism policies might include efforts to play off terrorist group leader and constituent group supporter interests.

In future research, it will be necessary to scope out different government policy types. In the case of responsiveness, the issue revolves around the capacity or willingness of government to provide political opportunity structures to ensure platforms for non-violent political expression, and economic relief packages to specific regions and clusters of neighborhoods to meet the political demands and aspirations of different ethnic, racial, or religious communities traditionally neglected by national or state governments or both.

In the cases of India, Mexico, South Africa, and Thailand, the core narrative related to the use of illegal force, be it terrorism or criminal syndicalism or both, has revolved around the flawed or basically incomplete or makeshift nature of government policy to respond to citizen demands and aspirations. It seems likely that ineffective government policies have effects on what is captured in this dashboard's sixth explanatory factor, namely the level of constituent support for terrorist groups.

For example, the extant literature on Thailand underscores the suspicion, distrust, and other similar sentiments that many of the local population in the "deep south" experience vis a vis the Bangkok government, its overt military presence, and the quality and authentic interests of its political representatives in the "deep south." In turn, that increases the likelihood that a small percentage of the population in the Southern part of Thailand, inclusive of those states outside the "deep south," will gravitate towards terrorism.

In addition to the foregoing, there are other policies that need to be examined in future work about the relationships between government policies and terrorist group splintering or spin-off formation. Those include, but are not limited to, the effect of "peace talks" on terrorist group cohesion or fragmentation, "peace negotiations," police activities, military activities, and the lack of resolve on the part of government to tackle systemic corruption.

8.4 Terrorist Organizations, Criminal Syndicalists, and Terrorism: Conceptualizations

An important component of this research explores the question about whether or not it is suitable to call organized criminal syndicalists that use terrorism terrorist organizations; the answer is unequivocally no. At a theoretical level, work that clumps together traditional terrorist groups and organized criminal syndicalists as terrorist groups lacks precision and meticulousness—it ignores and discards some critically important differences between both of those types of organizations.

For example, White points out that those who gravitate towards the orbit of terrorism and those who gravitate towards the orbit of organized crime and common criminal activity are essential different in psychological composition. For White and other scholars, those who gravitate towards terrorism want to make an "imprint on history," to belong to something bigger than themselves, and to steer historical change with greater political goals in mind [9, 42, 197 n2; 62, 11–17].

In comparison, those who enter into the netherworld of organized crime and common criminal activities are characterized by the desire for profit. There are no coherent political ideologies that characterize organized crime and common criminals. One of the results of the qualitative analysis showcased how terrorist groups have a coherent political ideology and agenda that is directed towards government and to constituent groups.

Indeed, that stands in sharp contrast to certain organized criminal syndicalists whose "political" activities are largely framed within the context of the pursuit of economic profit. To be more specific, the "political" messages sent are usually ad hoc responses to perceived threat. Those threats can emanate from rival criminal organizations for example, and be transmitted to constituent groups that more often than not are coerced to support criminal groups.

Hence, the killings of informants for example, while they send a message of threat that mimics political terrorism in the message and abject fear it generates, is ad hoc—it lacks the type of coherent political agenda that characterizes terrorist organizations. All of the foregoing requires that we make separate pedagogical categories in scholarship: one for terrorist groups and another for organized criminal groups that use terrorism.

8.5 TABVI Scores: A Cross-Country Comparison

8.5.1 Aggregate TABVI Scores

The Terrorist Assault Business Vulnerability Index (TABVI) score results were divided into two sets of findings. The first set of results involved an aggregate TABVI score for each of the five developing world "host" countries used to compare overall terrorism threat and vulnerability to business targets across countries. The second set of TABVI results involved a cross country comparison of specific industry scores; that made it possible to compare terrorism threat and vulnerability associated with specific industries across those five countries, and to provide some preliminary findings for specific industries in Latin America and Asia.

The raw TABVI scores were standardized by dividing 156.6, the highest raw TABVI score obtained for India, by 1.566 to standardize to 100.00. In turn, the other raw TABVI scores host countries were also divided by 1.566.[4] In the case of aggregate

[4] In essence, 156.6 (India) $\times$ 0.638 = 99.91 provides the same result.

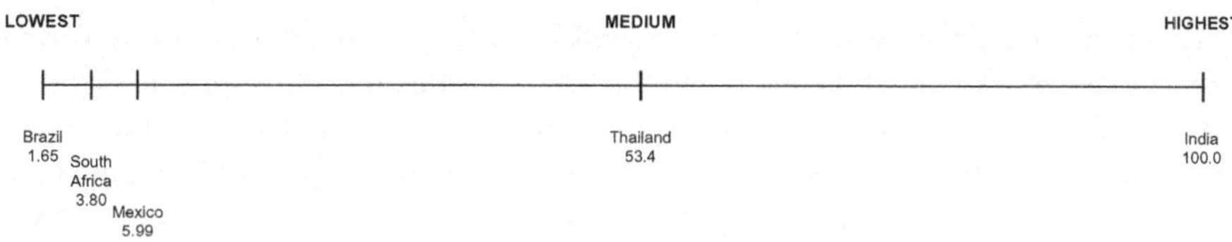

Fig. 8.2 Aggregate TABVI scores for five host countries (standardized scores) < 1 to 10 = low risk; 11 to 50 = medium risk; 51 to 100 = high risk

TABVI scores, it was found that India, with a standardized score of 100.0, ranked first among the five "host" countries examined. Thailand ranked a distant second, with a standardized score of 53.4 (83.7/1.566), and Mexico ranked third with a standardized score of 5.99 (9.375/1.566). At the other end of the spectrum, Brazil was found to have the lowest business target terrorism threat and vulnerability level of all host countries examined, with a standardized TABVI score of 1.64 (2.58/1.566). In turn, South Africa was positioned slightly higher than Brazil with a standardized TABVI score of 3.80 (5.95/1.566) (see Fig. 8.2).

In the broader sense, those aggregate TABVI scores and corresponding rankings conformed at least to some degree to the WEF rankings for countries when the degree of cost that terrorism imposed on business was appraised by business executives in each country by means of an WEF survey [64, 65]. While there were some variations in placement, the basic parameters of cost imposed by terrorism threat and rates of threat and vulnerability the TABVI appraised were very similar.

For example, the rankings of those five developing world "host" countries in the WEF survey from highest to lowest degree of cost imposed by terrorism threat were: 1. Thailand (WEF score of 4.1 with a #121/137 country ranking), India (WEF score of 4.2 with a #117/137 country ranking), South Africa (WEF score of 4.7 with a #92/137 country ranking) Mexico, (WEF score of 4.8 with an #87/137 country ranking). In turn, Brazil had the least amount of business costs inflicted by the threat of terrorism according to WEF survey respondents, with a WEF score of 6.2; that corresponded to a #8/137 country ranking for Brazil.

There were some country placement differences found between the TABVI results and the WEF rankings, when those standardized TABVI scores were placed on a continuum. As previously mentioned, Brazil (1.64) had the lowest terrorist threat vulnerability score, followed by South Africa (3.80), Mexico (5.99), Thailand (53.4) and India (100.0). In comparison, the rankings in the WEF survey data results were consistent with TABVI results for Brazil, Mexico, and South Africa. However, the placement of South Africa and Mexico were reversed, with Mexico appraised by WEF survey respondents with bearing higher business costs associated with terrorism. Interestingly enough, while the WEF ranking scores for Thailand ("4.1") and India ("4.2") were extremely close, the TABVI scores were not, with India at 100.0 and Thailand at 53.4. At first blush, it seems possible the results might have reflected, at least in part, the higher number of business related terrorist assaults recorded for India for the time period under consideration.

Likewise, in the case of the two countries that ranked highest for terrorism threat costs levied against business and the TABVI index used to appraise terrorism threat and vulnerability in host countries, the placement of Thailand and India were reversed. While the WEF ranking scores in the WEF survey results for Thailand (4.1) and India (4.2) were extremely close, the TABVI scores were not, with India at 100.0 and Thailand at 53.4. The results seem to reflect the higher number of business-related terrorist events recorded in India for the time period under consideration.

8.6 TABVI Scores by Target-Type

What follows is a breakdown of the TABVI scores by industry types within and across countries. In the case of specific industry type country findings, raw TABVI scores are presented, and in the case of cross-country comparisons, a set of standardized scores, with some one hundred percent as the highest possible TABVI value, are presented. In the case of India, it was found that "construction" "energy/alloy" and "private establishment" targets were the top three business targets most vulnerable to business related terrorism. The first two of those target-types are structuralist targets, where the target is symbolic of a "world systems" factor such as capitalism, globalization, or modernization.

In the case of Thailand, it was found that "private establishment" targets were most vulnerable to business related terrorism, followed by "banking and finance" targets and "telecommunications" targets. Unlike the case of India, construction targets were not of primary focus for terrorist groups in Thailand. While "private establishments" is non-structuralist target symbolic of people and groups targeted rather than a "world system," both "banking and finance" targets and "telecommunications" targets are structuralist targets. The expected observations by target-type were that results would be more similar because each country is found in the same region; hence, the observed findings for India and Thailand do not conform to expected results.

8.7 A First Pass Comparison of Three Host Countries by Region—Some Preliminary Findings

This comparison of India, Thailand, and South Africa is useful when the goal is to make comparisons between countries by region. Having said that, the analysis can only serve as preliminary findings for analysis about the influence that regional factors, such as socio-economic development and cultural factors, might have on terrorist group business target selection. The primary reason why is relatively straightforward—two countries in Asia and one in Africa do not begin to comprise a sufficiently large sample size of countries to make anything more than preliminary observations about the possible role of regional effects.

In addition, in the case of Thailand, many of the terrorist assaults chronicled had bits of data about terrorist assaults perpetrators, firm type, and links to political events that were makeshift and incomplete. Equally important, is that a full articulation of critical explanatory variables intrinsic to a study of regional explanatory factors is plainly beyond the scope of this book.

The TABVI scores for the industry types examined were standardized so that a cross country comparison of more specific degrees of business-related threat and vulnerability was possible. In each case study chapter, a three-point Likert ordinal scale was crafted with a range to correspond to those standardized scores. On this continuum, what amounts to "low level" terrorism threat and vulnerability was the range between 1 and 10. In turn TABVI scores in the range of between 11 and 50 constituted "medium" levels of threat and vulnerability, while TABVI scores of between 51 and 100 fell in the "high" range of terrorism threat and vulnerability [9, 89–91, 210 n69; 27, 157–159].

When India, South Africa, and Thailand were compared, the results suggest that with "private establishment" TABVI standardized scores of 60.96 for India, 100.0 for South Africa, and 99.57 for Thailand, "private establishments" in South Africa, Thailand, and India experienced a "high" level of terrorism threat and vulnerability in the time period examined. At the same time, the degree of business-related terrorism threat and vulnerability in Thailand and South Africa was higher than for India based on TABVI scores.[5]

In the case of "energy/alloy" targets, the standardized TABVI scores revealed that with India at 42.24, and Thailand at 19.35, such targets in India and Thailand both experienced a "medium" level of business- related threat and vulnerability.[6] In the case of South Africa, the appraised threat to "energy/alloy" targets was low with a standardized TABVI score of 4.36. At the same time, the degree of threat to "energy/alloy" targets in India was, at 42.24, a little more than twice as high as Thailand's score of 19.35.

In turn, terrorist threat and vulnerability to "newspaper (print)," "banking/finance," and "telecommunication" targets were assessed. When threat and vulnerability to "newspaper (print)" targets were compared across India and Thailand, it was found that such targets in India experienced "low" levels of threat and vulnerability with a score of 12.6.[7] For Thailand, the corresponding score for "newspaper (print)" targets

---

[5] There were many "construction firm" targets found in India, but none recorded for Thailand or South Africa.

[6] The highest raw TBVA score for India was 62.4 for "construction" targets. Therefore, 62.4 × ***1.60*** = 99.84 was calculated for standardization purposes. In turn, for Thailand, the highest raw TABVI score is 46.5 for "private establishments." Therefore, 45.6 × 2.145 = 99.957 for standardization purposes. It follows that for India, the standardized TABVI score for "energy/alloy" is 42.24 (26.4 × ***1.60*** = 42.24). For Thailand, the standardized TABVI score for "energy/alloy" is 19.35 (9.02 × ***2.145*** = 19.34).

[7] For India, the standard TABVI score for "newspaper (print)" targets is 12.6; it was obtained by multiplying the raw TABVI score of 7.86 × 1.60 = 12.6.

was 2.09.[8] There were no chronicled terrorist attacks against "newspaper (print)" targets in South Africa.

Accordingly, there was a "medium" level threat and vulnerability to "newspaper (print)" targets in India that was six times higher than the "low level" threat and vulnerability found for such firms in Thailand (2.09). The reverse was found for threat for "banking/finance targets." In India, the threat to "banking/finance" targets was gauged as "low" with a standardized TABVI score of 3.04.[9] In a similar vein, South Africa's standardized score for "banking/finance" was 4.35. In contrast, the threat appraisal for "banking/finance" targets in Thailand was higher, found in the "medium" range of the spectrum with 30.80.[10]

Turning to "telecommunication" targets, the standardized TABVI scores revealed that Indian telecommunication" targets had a standardized TABVI score of 25.6.[11] In turn, the standardized TABVI score for "telecommunication targets" in Thailand was 20.93.[12] The appraisal of terrorism threat level for "telecommunication" targets for those two countries was very close; both were found in the "medium" level range of that continuum. In comparison, South Africa had a much lower standardized TABVI score for "telecommunication targets" with 8.71. Likewise, "(private) transportation targets" experienced low threat with a standardized TABVI score of 4.35.[13]

In a similar vein, "hospitals/medical facilities" targets in India and Thailand were characterized by low standardized TABVI scores that were also very close in value. For India, a standardized TABVI score of 3.04 placed "hospitals/medical facilities" in the "low" range of terrorism threat appraisal, while for Thailand, a score of 3.13 positioned "hospital/medical facilities" targets in the same "low" level threat and vulnerability range.[14] Likewise, the extent of business related terrorism and vulnerability linked to "agriculture" targets in India and Thailand was also "low" for those

---

[8] For Thailand, the standard TABVI score for "newspaper (print)" targets is 2.09 where the raw TABVI score of 0.976 is multiplied by 2.145 = 2.093.

[9] For India, a standardized TABVI score for "banking/finance" is 3.04 where the raw TABVI score of 1.9 is multiplied by ***1.60*** = 3.04.

[10] For Thailand, a standardized TABVI score for "banking/finance" is 30.9, raw (TABVI) score of 14.4 × ***2.145*** = 30.9). For South Africa, a standardized TABVI score for "banking/finance" targets is 4.36 (TABVI raw score of 0.213 × ***20.45*** = 4.36). For South Africa, "private establishments" had the highest raw TABVI score of 4.89 (4.89 × 20.45 = 100.0).

[11] For India, a standardized TABVI score for "telecommunication" targets is 25.6 (TABVI raw score of 16.0 × 1.60 = 25.6).

[12] For Thailand, a standardized TABVI score for "telecommunication" targets is 20.93 (TABVI raw score of 9.76 × 2.145 = 20.93).

[13] For South Africa, a standardized TABVI score for "telecommunication" target is 8.71 (TABVI score of 0.426 × 20.45 = 8.71). In the case of "(private) transportation" a raw TABVI score of 0.213 was multiplied by 20.45 = 4.355.

[14] For India, the standardized TABVI score for "hospitals/medical facilities" is 3.04 (TABVI raw score of 1.9 × 1.60 = 3.04). For Thailand, the standardized TABVI score for "hospitals/medical facilities" is 3.13 (TABVI raw score of 1.46 × 2.145 = 3.13). There were no terrorist assaults against "hospital/medical facilities" chronicled for South Africa.

types of firms in both countries with a standardized TABVI score of 0.76 for India, and a score of 0.523 for Thailand.[15]

There were some TABVI results for business target types in India and Thailand that were consistent with the expected observation that at least some results for business related terrorism target-type should be similar in countries in the same region. For example, what was notable were similar findings across those two countries for "telecommunication" targets, and for agricultural targets. In the case of "telecommunication" targets, Mexico had a standardized TABVI score of 66.6 (3.33 × 20.0), while Brazil had a standardized TABVI score of 99.98 (1.61 × 62.1). In comparison, "telecommunications" target threat and vulnerability in South Africa was lower with a TABVI score of 8.71. To some extent, there were also similarities in results for "private establishments."

By contrast, there were results less than supportive of the notion that industry target choice is associated with region. In the case of "banking/finance" targets, that Indian industry with its standardized TABVI score of 3.04 was found to be much less vulnerable to threat than Thailand's "banking/finance" sector (30.88). In a similar vein, the appraised threat to the South African "banking/finance" sector was low at 4.36. There were no terrorist assaults against Mexico's "banking/finance" sector chronicled between 2013 and 2018. There were also no terrorist assaults against Brazil's "banking/finance" sector recorded between 2013 and 2018. In short, those findings comprise a springboard for future research (see Fig. 8.3). In the next section of this chapter, there is more in depth discussion about other industry results across the "host" countries examined.

8.8 The Cases of Mexico and Brazil; Examples of "Impure" Terrorism Systems

From the start, it is important to note certain caveats associated with a comparative interpretation of results from Mexico and Brazil to results from other "host" countries under consideration. That is the case because in Mexico and Brazil, it seems clear that drug kingpins account for much of the business-related terrorism chronicled. Those "hybrid" criminal organizations, as Shelley and Picarelli call them, are not terrorist group in the classical or traditional sense of the term [48, 52–67]. First, data remains incomplete and less than definitive about "hybrid" criminal groups that use terrorism. For example, there were many anonymous terrorist assaults most likely carried out by criminal syndicalist organizations that used terrorism.

Equally important, is that while it is possible to present results of TABVI scores across countries, interpretation of those TABVI scores across all five countries becomes problematic because India, Thailand, and South Africa are examples of

[15] For India, the standardized TABVI score for "agriculture" targets is extremely low at.76 (TABVI raw score of 0.476 × 1.60 = 0.7616). For Thailand, the standardized TABVI score for "agriculture" targets is also extremely low at 0.552 (TABVI raw score of 0.243 × 2.145 = 0.521).

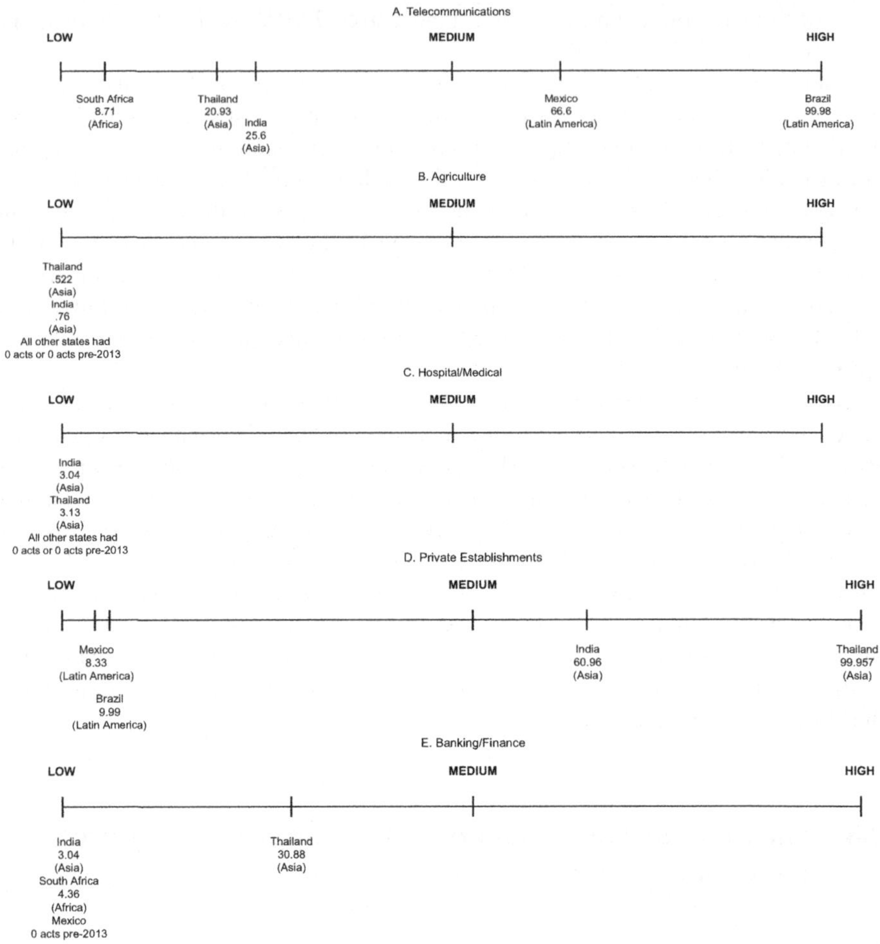

Fig. 8.3 Threat/Vulnerability spectrum by industry type, country, region < 1 to 10 = low risk; 11 to 50 = medium risk; 51 to 100 = high risk (standardized TABVI scores)

more traditional terrorism systems where traditional terrorist groups or proto-groups are involved with terrorism. For example, terrorism is South Africa for the 2013–2018 interval was often characterized by attacks on shops owned by proprietors from a particular ethnic group.

That stands in sharp contrast to the cases of Mexico and Brazil where organized criminal syndicalists who use terrorism predominate. As a result, efforts at (TABVI) data interpretation across traditional terrorism systems and criminally led terrorist systems should to take into account the differences in political systems, as well as the differences in organizational type involved, in political ideology and political goals, and overall objectives each type of organization pursues [45; 61, 10–20]. For example, ties between Mexico's government and drug kingpins comprise part of the shape or structure of Mexico's political system.

Hence, in the absence of more complete information for explanatory factor interpretation across terrorism systems that are dominated by traditional terrorist groups on the one hand, and criminal syndicalist organizations on the other, it is important for researchers to begin to think about political systems differences as those relate to the use of terrorism. Otherwise, analysis could amount to research efforts characterized by flawed assumptions and different starting points in the analysis, especially about the sources of government counterterrorism response for example, and assumptions about sources and origins of terrorist groups and terrorist assaults.

In this context, it might be useful to think about more "pure" terrorism systems, where the political landscape is dominated by traditional terrorist group assaults, by contrast to more "impure" terrorism systems, dominated by organized criminal syndicalist groups, or by a mixture of significant organized criminal organization terrorist activity in addition to the terrorism practiced by terrorist groups. For example, one issue found in "impure" terrorism systems is the set of possible interactive effects between organized crime and terrorist groups that might lead to "spinoff formation" of new organizations [35, 52–61].

Clearly, efforts to describe how "pure" and "impure" terrorism systems differ and to scope out even a few explanatory factor connections in each type of system are far beyond the scope of this book. At this stage, carefully framed interpretations of results across these "pure" and "impure" terrorism systems might be pursued with the aim to craft hypotheses to test. Such an approach might be useful to compare terrorism across India, Thailand, Mexico, and Brazil for example.

To recapitulate, for Mexico, it was found that "newspaper (print)" targets experienced the highest level of threat for the 2013–2018 time period with a raw TABVI score of 5.00 and a standardized TABVI score of 100.00.[16] In turn, Mexican "telecommunication" targets, that included bloggers, infrastructure and radio and television personalities, also experienced "high" threat and vulnerability levels with a standardized score of 66.6. In comparison, "private establishments" in Mexico experienced "low level" threat and by extrapolation, vulnerability from business related terrorism, reflected in a standardized TABVI score of 8.34.[17] The standardized TABVI score for NGO's was also 8.34 while the standardized TABVI score for "energy/alloy" "targets" ranked lowest in Mexico, with a standardized TABVI score of 4.16 [17, 18, 53].[18]

---

[16] For Mexico, the raw TABVI score of 5.00 for "newspaper/print" was multiplied by 20.00 for a standardized TABVI score of 100.00.

[17] In the case of "telecommunication targets" in Mexico, a raw TABVI score of $3.33 \times 20 = 66.6$. For "private establishments," a raw TABVI score of $0.416 \times 20 = 8.34$.

[18] Terrorist assaults against two NGO targets were included in the data in the case of Mexico because of their intrinsic importance to proto-terrorist group identification: "The settlers, Chol and Tzeltal Indians…." The standardized TABVI score of 8.34 for "NGO's" was the product of the raw TABVI score of 0.417×20.00. In turn, the "energy/alloy" target standardized TABVI score was the product of the raw TABVI score of $0.208 \times 20.00 = 4.16$.

In the case of Brazil, the rankings for the industries with the top levels of threat were the reverse of Mexico: "telecommunication" targets in Brazil had the highest level of business-related terrorism threat and vulnerability with a standardized TABVI score of 99.98, followed by a score of 50.0 for Brazilian "newspaper (print) targets." However, the threat appraised for Brazilian "private establishments," with a standardized TABVI score of 9.99 was lower for Brazil than for Mexico, while NGO's in the Brazilian context experienced low levels of threat that were similar to the Mexican case (8.32) with a standardized TABVI score of 9.99.[19] There were no "energy-alloy" targets recorded in the case of Brazil for that six-year period.

8.9 Quantitative Analysis

The limitations in the data with regards to overall numbers of terrorist events, coupled with high numbers of anonymous terrorist assaults, made it possible to conduct more complete bivariate analysis only for the "host" countries of India and Thailand. In the case of Mexico, some statistically significant relationships between variables also made it possible to test some of the hypotheses under consideration, but the scope of analysis for Mexico was much less than for India and Thailand.

One notable finding was that in the case of India, the majority of business-related terrorist assaults carried out ***were*** linked to political events as defined in this study. This was an unusual finding because in previous work on terrorism, and in the case of other host countries examined here, the majority of business-related terrorist assaults carried out ***were not*** related to political events. For example, a relative frequencies test for Mexico revealed that 87.8% (43/49 acts) were not related to political events. Similar results were found for Thailand in a crosstabulation test, where 211 out of 273 terrorist assaults (77.2%) were found to be unrelated to political events; where the relationship between "Group-Type" and "Reaction to Political Events" was found to be statistically significant.

Another set of findings for members of the business community that should be useful involved comparison of the percentage rate of business-related terrorist across countries that involved foreign business targets. In the case South Africa, the rate of business terrorist assaults against foreign business targets was very high at 71.4% (20/28 acts). This was most likely an artifact that reflected the condition of "foreign" merchants from states such as Somalia and Nigeria whose businesses or person were attacked because of South African xenophobia against other Africans commonplace to note in South Africa in this time interval.

In turn, Thailand ranked second with a 12.3% rate of business-related terrorist assaults (35/284 acts) against foreign business targets. That result is comparatively high, and suggests that if Thailand's essentially nationalist-irredentist struggle was

---

[19] For Brazil, a raw TABVI score of 1.61 for "telecommunication" targets was multiplied by 62.1 $= 99.98$. For "newspaper/print" targets, $0.806 \times 62.1 = 50.0$; for "private establishments," $0.161 \times 62.1 = 9.99$; for NGO's $0.161 \times 62.1 = 9.99$.

to expand its scope with increased foreign involvement with origins in Indonesia or the Philippines for example, those trends in foreign business target terrorist assaults, would be a good fit with Jihadist message-making about the importance of foreign targets as part of an eschatological struggle between Islam and the West.

The next three "host" states that ranked third, fourth, and fifth can be clustered in one grouping of developing world "host" countries. Mexico had a 7.4% rate of business-related attacks (6/81 acts) against foreign based business targets that ranked third, while the percentage rate for Brazil followed closely behind at 5.3% (1/19 acts). India was the host country with the lowest rate of business-related terrorist assaults against foreign business targets with 1.7% (11/646 acts).

A separate hand-count of terrorist assaults against hotels and motels was conducted for each "host" country under consideration. In the case of Thailand there nine (9) such terrorist events for the 2013–2018 time period. Those terrorist assaults were directed against the (1) the Oliver Hotel found in Danok Songkhla; (2) Cola Hotel located in Yala city, in Yala province; (3) the Grand Palace Hotel found in Yala city in Yala province; (4) Thep Viman Hotel, also found in Yala city in Yala province; (5) the Asia Hotel located in the town of Sungai Kolok in Narathiwat province; (6) the Holliday Hill Hotel in Betong district in Yala province [1; 19; 20, (entry #22, entry #24); 21, (entry # 42); 22 (entry #169); 42, 138; 44; 54; 55; 57]. In addition, the Top Asia Hotel located in Songai Kolok, Narathiwat (7); the Southern View Hotel in Pattani (8); the Imperial Hotel in Muang Narathiwat district, Narathiwat province (9) were also targeted by terrorists [23; 42, 58, 411; 58; 59].

In comparison, the Indian hotel/motel industry experienced four (4) terrorist assaults. Those terrorist assaults happened at: (1) the Kwality Hotel in the city of Dampur in Nagaland; (2) the Kalyan Hotel, found in the city of Thane in Maharashtra; the Ashiyana Hotel found in Deoghar District in Jharkhand; (4) the New Woodlands Hotel located in Chennai, in Tamil Nadu [13, (entry #224); 14 (entry 299); 15 (entry # 321); 16 (entry #415); 47; 60]. There were no terrorist assaults chronicled against hotels and/or motels in Mexico, Brazil, and South Africa.

8.10 India, Thailand, and South Africa

When India, Thailand, and South Africa were compared, it was found that construction targets, deemed to be structuralist targets in this study, had the highest rate of business-related terrorist attack in India. In terms of relative frequencies, Indian "private establishments," a non-structuralist target, ranked second, while Indian "energy-alloy" targets, a "structuralist target," ranked third.

For Thailand, "private establishments" ranked first, followed by "banking/finance" targets, and "telecommunication" targets. In South Africa, "private establishments" also ranked first, followed by "telecommunication" targets. In all three country cases "private establishments" played a predominant role in targeting selection. In two of the three countries examined here it ranked first in terms of target type. It seems likely this is due, at least in part, to the symbolism of "private establishments" as reflective of ethnic, regional, or religious identification and the role that plays with respect to terrorist group or "lone-operative" target choice.

In turn, "telecommunication" targets also ranked high across those three countries in terms of target selection. In two out of the three countries compared here, (i.e., South Africa and Thailand) "telecommunication" targets ranked second or third, behind "private establishments." This strong placement for "telecommunication" targets seems consistent with the central notion that target selection was somehow affected by "world systems" factors such as capitalism, globalization, and modernization, although the exact nature of those links remain unknown.

Nevertheless, it is incumbent to point out those links could also involve simple opportunity recognition, at least to some degree. Having said that, socio-economic development alters geographical locales where terrorists have traditionally operated to make terrorists more vulnerable to capture. As scholars of Indian terrorism and government officials point out, that might be the case with Indian terrorist group focus on construction target sites.[20] In the broader sense, it might also reflect perceptions that those involved in globalization, capitalism, and modernization continue to "win," while others lose out. It is probably fair to say that several possible interpretations about terrorist assault motivations especially in "pure" terrorism systems, are consistent with those findings.

8.11 Mexico and Brazil

The case of Mexico and the case of Brazil are two examples of more "impure" terrorism systems. In those two case studies, relative frequencies findings about target selection seem to have some similarities. Nevertheless, the TABVI analysis suggests that the overall order of rankings for two highly targeted industries in those two countries are reversed.

For Mexico, "newspaper/print" targets accounted for the largest portion of terrorist assaults with 43.8% (35/80 acts), followed by "telecommunication" targets with 25.0% (20/80 acts). In comparison, "telecommunication" targets in Brazil ranked highest with 55.6% of the total (10/18 acts), followed by "newspaper (print)" targets with 27.8% of the total (5/18 acts). Although no authoritative interpretations are available, it is probably fair to say that domestic "contextual factors" that influence the decision calculus of criminal syndicalists or terrorist groups, either within or outside the context organizational fragmentation, have effects on target selection.

[20] Somewhat ironically, that very same socioeconomic development will also alter geographical locales to the benefit of terrorists and criminal gangs -working to attract tourists that terrorists and criminal groups can attack or otherwise victimize.

8.12 Final Reflections

The underlying theme of this book is to provide a set of guideposts for C-class executives and other leaders of international enterprises for business conducted in developing world "host" countries. Those leaders, perhaps especially those in charge of firm security, need to have solid and detailed information about the prospective environmental risks that companies face, both before and after substantial investments like foreign direct investment (FDI) are made. The data provided here, which in many cases drills down to the city, towns, and villages that have experienced business-related terrorist assaults, seeks to provide the necessary data for environmental scanning operations as part of that decision-making process.

Effective environmental scanning for potential risk and vulnerabilities does not happen in a vacuum without taking into account political and economic events, and historical processes with profound and lasting influence. One of this book's goals is to help business executives increase their understanding about those events and processes, and the importance of political and social context to prepare for important investment decisions. Therefore, in-depth descriptions of terrorist groups, and in some cases the organized criminal syndicalists who use terrorism as "hybrid" organizations as Shelley and Picarelli put it, have been provided [48].

It is also important for business executives charged with security to understand the sources and origins of terrorist groups in specific host countries and the political systems within which they operate. This book aims to do just that, in the hope business executives will consider analysis of past terrorist group patterns of behavior and terrorism events in specific geographical locales in more effective and sustained ways. That is critical because the terrorist attack patterns of the past have some important predictive value in terms of anticipation of the types of terrorism and terrorism related threats that are likely to materialize and confront C-class executives and other business executives.

When C-class executives and other international enterprise leaders understand those threats more clearly and fully, it is possible to scope out specific defensive policies to augment multinational corporation and other international enterprise security. In my own discussions with business executive leaders and experts in corporate strategy and security, one matter that comes up for discussion repeatedly is a "mindset of insouciance" among many but certainly not all, business executives about the importance of counterterrorism preparations and the monetary allocations necessary for them. It seems reasonable to believe that in a world of "intensive globalization" there is and will be an increased need for anticipatory thinking about this crucial aspect of business security.

If these developing "host" country case studies, and political and historical processes described in this book are able to shift that mindset into one that more resembles an urgency mode of thinking, then this book has accomplished an important mission. For an in-depth discussion of those challenges and opportunities, readers are encouraged to review my previous work, *Corporate Security Crossroads:*

Responding to Terrorism, Cyberthreats, and Other Hazards in the Global Business Environment [9].

In closing, the continuously evolving international political system is matched by continuously evolving business strategies on the part of international business leadership. Those business leaders, in their quest to maximize profit, seek to reconfigure international business portfolios in the set of "host" countries where they have a presence, to take advantage of new economic opportunities. As discussed in Chapter One, changes in investment patterns and overall international involvement are standard operating procedures for international business executives; such events happen every few years or decades. It is my hope this book will provide corporate executives and leaders of other international enterprises with essential data, and new or modified perspectives about specific developing world "host" countries to assist in and contribute to that process of host country selection.

References

1. Agence France Presse—English (2014, 25 July) Three dead, dozens wounded in Thai car bomb
2. Baldwin D (1971) The power of positive sanctions. World Pol 24(1):19–38
3. Baldwin D (1985) Economic statecraft. Princeton University Press
4. Ben Zuk N, Sharan Y (2023) Gene editing: the CRISPER tool—flash scenario (unpublished manuscript)
5. Booth K (2007) Theory of world security. Cambridge University Press
6. Buzan B, Waever O (2003) Regions and powers: the structure of international security. Cambridge University Press
7. Chasdi RJ (2002) Tapestry of terror: a portrait of Middle East terrorism, 1994–1999. Lexington Books
8. Chasdi RJ (2010) Counterterror offensives for the ghost war world: the rudiments of counterterrorism policy. Lexington Books
9. Chasdi RJ (2018) Corporate security crossroads responding to terrorism, cyberthreats, and other hazards in the global business environment. ABC-CLIO Prager
10. Crozier B (1960) The rebels: a study of post war insurrections. Martinus Nijhoff
11. Cullen JB, Parboteeah KP (2014) Multinational management: a strategic approach, 6 edn. South-Western Cengage Learning
12. Deutsch M (1973) The resolution of conflict: constructive and destructive processes. New Haven Press
13. Global Terrorism Database (GTD) India. GTD ID: 201503250069. 25 Mar 2015
14. Global Terrorism Database (GTD) India. GTD ID: 201509070075. 7 Sept 2015
15. Global Terrorism Database (GTD) India. GTD ID: 201511200017. 20 Nov 2015
16. Global Terrorism Database (GTD) India. GTD ID: 201609120030. 10 Sept 2016
17. Global Terrorism Database (GTD) Mexico. GTD ID:201402490085. 27 Apr 2014
18. Global Terrorism Database (GTD) Mexico. GTD ID: 201405250056. 25 May 2014
19. Global Terrorism Database (GTD) Thailand. GTD ID: 201304070029. 4 Apr 2013
20. Global Terrorism Database (GTD) Thailand. GTD ID:201304070027. 7 Apr 2013
21. Global Terrorism Database (GTD) Thailand. GTD ID: 201305180011. 18 May 2013
22. Global Terrorism Database (GTD) Thailand. GTD: ID: 201407250017. 25 July 2014
23. Global Terrorism Database (GTD) Thailand. GTD: ID: 201608230010. 23 Aug 2016
24. Henry N (2013) Public administration and public affairs, 12th edn. Pearson Education Inc.
25. Hill CWL (2014) Global business today, 8th edn. McGraw Hill Irwin

26. Hill CWL, Hult GTM (2016) Global business today, 9th edn. McGraw Hill Education
27. Howard PD (2013) Official (ISC)2 guide to the CAP CBK, 2nd edn. CRC Press
28. Im EI, Cauley J, Sandler T (1987) Cycles and substitutions in terrorist activities: a spectral approach. Kyklos 40
29. Jervis R (1976) Perception and misperception in international politics. Princeton University Press
30. Jervis R (1978) Cooperation under the security dilemma. World Pol 30(2):174–176
31. Kaldor M (2013) In defense of new wars. Int J Secur Develop 2(1):1–34
32. Kayyem JN, Chang PE (2003) Beyond business continuity: the role of the private sector in preparedness planning. In: Kayyem J, Pagni RL (eds) First to arrive: state and local responses to terrorism. MIT Press
33. Kegley C (2007) World politics: trends and transformations, 11th edn. Thomson Wadsworth
34. Kujur RK (2006, 6 June) Left extremism in India: Naxal movement in Chhattisgarh & Orissa. In: Institute of peace and conflict studies, IPCS Special Report 25
35. Kupchan CA, Kupchan CA (1995) The promise of collective security. Int Secur 20(1):52–61
36. Lasswell HD (1935) World politics and personal insecurity. Whittlesey House, McGaw Hill
37. Lasswell HD (1978) Terrorism and the political process. Terrorism 1(4):255–263
38. Long DE (1990) The anatomy of terrorism. Free Press
39. Luthans F, Doh JP (2012) International management: culture, strategy, and behavior, 8th edn. McGraw Hill Irwin
40. Lynch III TF (2016) India's Naxalite insurgency: history, trajectory, and implications for U.S.—India security cooperation on domestic counterinsurgency, strategic perspectives 22. In: Institute for national strategic studies (INSS), National Defense University
41. Mearsheimer JJ (2001) The tragedy of great power politics. Norton, W.W
42. Mickolus E (2016) 2013–2015: a worldwide chronology. McFarland & Company, Inc.
43. Monahan J (2011, 10 October) The individual risk assessment of terrorism, psychology, public policy and law. Online first publication. https://doi.org/10.1037/a00257920
44. Moore J (2014, 9 January) Outside view: Thailand's southern insurgency turns up the heat. UPI.com
45. Nye Jr JS (1993) Understanding international conflicts: an introduction to theory and history. Harper Collins College Publishers
46. Porter ME (1990) The comparative advantage of nations. Free Press
47. Selvaraj A (2016, 13 September) Cauvery protests: four held for ransacking Chennai hotel. The Times of India
48. Shelley LI, Picarelli JT, Irby A, Hart DM, Craig-Hart PA, Williams P, Simon S, Abdullaev N, Stanislawski B, Covill L (2005) Methods and motives: exploring links between transnational organized crime and international terrorism. Trends Organ Crim 8(2):52–57. https://doi.org/10.1007/s12117-005-1024-x
49. Snyder GH (2002) Mearsheimer's world—offensive realism and the struggle for security: a review essay. Int Secur 27(1):149–173
50. Snyder GH (1984). The security dilemma in alliance politics. World Pol 36(4):462–495
51. South Asian Terrorism Portal (2001) National Socialist Council of Nagaland-Unification (NSCN-Unification). https://www.satp.org/terrorist-profile/india/national-socialist-council-of-nagaland-unification-nscn-u
52. Srivastava D (2009, May) Terrorism and armed violence in India: an analysis of events in 2008. In: IPCS Special Report 71. Institute of peace and conflict studies, pp 1–21. https://www.jstor.org/stable/pdf/resrep09368.pdf
53. Stevenson M (2014, 27 May) Environmentalist kidnapped, freed in Mexico. Associated Press News
54. Thai News Service (2013, 10 April) Thailand: Sunday's Yala bomb suspect nabbed
55. Thai News Service (2013, 21 May) Thailand: Six wounded in Narathiwat hotel bombing
56. The Asian Age (2019, 3 June) Maha cops detect explosives hidden under Gondia Bridge. https://www.asianage.com/metros/mumbai/030619/maha-cops-detect-explosives-hidden-under-gondia-bridge.html

57. The Bangkok Post (2013, 9 April) NSC presses on with South talks
58. The Bangkok Post (2015, 12 July) Ramadan bombers linked to 2014 blasts
59. The Bangkok Press (2016, 24 August) "Double tap" Pattani bombs kill one, wound 30
60. UNI (United News of India) (2015, 20 November) Crude bomb explodes inside eating joint in Deoghar; 1 hurt
61. Waltz KN (1973) The meaning of anarchy. In: Art RJ, Jervis R (eds) International politics: anarchy, force, imperialism. Little, Brown and Company
62. White J (2002) Terrorism: an introduction, 3rd edn. Wadsworth Thomson Learning
63. Wolfers A (1973) "National security" as an ambiguous symbol. In: Art RJ, Jervis R (eds) International politics: anarchy, force, imperialism. Little, Brown and Company
64. World Economic Forum (2017) Business costs of terrorism. http://reports.weforum.org/global-competitiveness-index-2017-2018/competitiveness-rankings/#series=EOSQ033
65. World Economic Forum (2017) Appendix C. http://www3.weforum.org/docs/GCR2017-2018/04Backmatter/TheGlobalCompetitivenessReport2017%E2%80%932018AppendixC.pdf

Appendix A

Methodological Appendix A—India

Case processing summary

	Valid		Cases missing		Total	
	N	Percent	N	Percent	N	Percent
Bus.Target * State	657	98.1%	13	1.9%	670	100.0%

Bus.Target * State crosstabulation

			State		
			Assam	Maharashtra	Nagaland
Bus.Target	Energy/Alloy	Count	22	1	2
		% within Bus.Target	20.0%	0.9%	1.8%
		% within State	30.1%	6.3%	16.7%
		% of total	3.3%	0.2%	0.3%
	Construction	Count	11	8	1
		% within Bus.Target	4.2%	3.1%	0.4%
		% within State	15.1%	50.0%	8.3%
		% of total	1.7%	1.2%	0.2%
	Hospitals/Medical	Count	1	0	1
		% within Bus.Target	12.5%	0.0%	12.5%
		% within State	1.4%	0.0%	8.3%
		% of total	0.2%	0.0%	0.2%

(continued)

R. J. Chasdi, *Corporate Security Surveillance*, Advanced Sciences and Technologies for Security Applications, https://doi.org/10.1007/978-3-031-39550-5

(continued)

Bus.Target * State crosstabulation

			State		
			Assam	Maharashtra	Nagaland
	Private establishments	Count	37	6	8
		% within Bus.Target	23.1%	3.8%	5.0%
		% within State	50.7%	37.5%	66.7%
		% of total	5.6%	0.9%	1.2%
	Telecommunications	Count	0	0	0
		% within Bus.Target	0.0%	0.0%	0.0%
		% within State	0.0%	0.0%	0.0%
		% of total	0.0%	0.0%	0.0%
	Newspapers/Print	Count	2	1	0
		% within Bus.Target	6.1%	3.0%	0.0%
		% within State	2.7%	6.3%	0.0%
		% of total	0.3%	0.2%	0.0%
	Banking/Finance	Count	0	0	0
		% within Bus.Target	0.0%	0.0%	0.0%
		% within State	0.0%	0.0%	0.0%
		% of total	0.0%	0.0%	0.0%
	Transportation	Count	0	0	0
		% within Bus.Target	0.0%	0.0%	0.0%
		% within State	0.0%	0.0%	0.0%
		% of total	0.0%	0.0%	0.0%
	Agriculture	Count	0	0	0
		% within Bus.Target	0.0%	0.0%	0.0%
		% within State	0.0%	0.0%	0.0%
		% of total	0.0%	0.0%	0.0%
Total		Count	73	16	12
		% within Bus.Target	11.1%	2.4%	1.8%
		% within State	100.0%	100.0%	100.0%
		% of total	11.1%	2.4%	1.8%

Bus.Target * State crosstabulation					
			State		
			Manipur	Bihar	Haryana
Bus.Target	Energy/Alloy	Count	11	8	0
		% within Bus.Target	10.0%	7.3%	0.0%
		% within State	12.6%	10.7%	0.0%
		% of total	1.7%	1.2%	0.0%
	Construction	Count	32	35	0
		% within Bus.Target	12.2%	13.4%	0.0%
		% within State	36.8%	46.7%	0.0%
		% of total	4.9%	5.3%	0.0%
	Hospitals/Medical	Count	3	0	0
		% within Bus.Target	37.5%	0.0%	0.0%
		% within State	3.4%	0.0%	0.0%
		% of total	0.5%	0.0%	0.0%
	Private establishments	Count	32	11	0
		% within Bus.Target	20.0%	6.9%	0.0%
		% within State	36.8%	14.7%	0.0%
		% of total	4.9%	1.7%	0.0%
	Telecommunications	Count	4	14	0
		% within Bus.Target	6.0%	20.9%	0.0%
		% within State	4.6%	18.7%	0.0%
		% of total	0.6%	2.1%	0.0%
	Newspapers/Print	Count	3	7	1
		% within Bus.Target	9.1%	21.2%	3.0%
		% within State	3.4%	9.3%	100.0%
		% of total	0.5%	1.1%	0.2%
	Banking/Finance	Count	2	0	0
		% within Bus.Target	25.0%	0.0%	0.0%
		% within State	2.3%	0.0%	0.0%
		% of total	0.3%	0.0%	0.0%
	Transportation	Count	0	0	0
		% within Bus.Target	0.0%	0.0%	0.0%
		% within State	0.0%	0.0%	0.0%
		% of total	0.0%	0.0%	0.0%
	Agriculture	Count	0	0	0
		% within Bus.Target	0.0%	0.0%	0.0%
		% within State	0.0%	0.0%	0.0%
		% of total	0.0%	0.0%	0.0%

(continued)

(continued)

Bus.Target * State crosstabulation					
			State		
			Manipur	Bihar	Haryana
Total		Count	87	75	1
		% within Bus.Target	13.2%	11.4%	0.2%
		% within State	100.0%	100.0%	100.0%
		% of total	13.2%	11.4%	0.2%

Bus.Target * State crosstabulation					
			State		
			Chhattisgarh	Meghalaya	Odisha (Orissa)
Bus.Target	Energy/Alloy	Count	17	17	1
		% within Bus.Target	15.5%	15.5%	0.9%
		% within State	23.9%	37.8%	1.7%
		% of total	2.6%	2.6%	0.2%
	Construction	Count	48	11	39
		% within Bus.Target	18.3%	4.2%	14.9%
		% within State	67.6%	24.4%	66.1%
		% of total	7.3%	1.7%	5.9%
	Hospitals/Medical	Count	0	0	0
		% within Bus.Target	0.0%	0.0%	0.0%
		% within State	0.0%	0.0%	0.0%
		% of total	0.0%	0.0%	0.0%
	Private establishments	Count	1	13	10
		% within Bus.Target	0.6%	8.1%	6.3%
		% within State	1.4%	28.9%	16.9%
		% of total	0.2%	2.0%	1.5%
	Telecommunications	Count	1	2	8
		% within Bus.Target	1.5%	3.0%	11.9%
		% within State	1.4%	4.4%	13.6%

(continued)

(continued)

Bus.Target * State crosstabulation

			State		
			Chhattisgarh	Meghalaya	Odisha (Orissa)
		% of total	0.2%	0.3%	1.2%
	Newspapers/Print	Count	1	1	0
		% within Bus.Target	3.0%	3.0%	0.0%
		% within State	1.4%	2.2%	0.0%
		% of total	0.2%	0.2%	0.0%
	Banking/Finance	Count	0	1	1
		% within Bus.Target	0.0%	12.5%	12.5%
		% within State	0.0%	2.2%	1.7%
		% of total	0.0%	0.2%	0.2%
	Transportation	Count	3	0	0
		% within Bus.Target	42.9%	0.0%	0.0%
		% within State	4.2%	0.0%	0.0%
		% of total	0.5%	0.0%	0.0%
	Agriculture	Count	0	0	0
		% within Bus.Target	0.0%	0.0%	0.0%
		% within State	0.0%	0.0%	0.0%
		% of total	0.0%	0.0%	0.0%
Total		Count	71	45	59
		% within Bus.Target	10.8%	6.8%	9.0%
		% within State	100.0%	100.0%	100.0%
		% of total	10.8%	6.8%	9.0%

Bus.Target * State crosstabulation

			State		
			Jharkhand	Tamil Nadu	West Bengal
Bus.Target	Energy/Alloy	Count	22	0	2

(continued)

(continued)

Bus.Target * State crosstabulation

			State		
			Jharkhand	Tamil Nadu	West Bengal
		% within Bus.Target	20.0%	0.0%	1.8%
		% within State	20.8%	0.0%	16.7%
		% of total	3.3%	0.0%	0.3%
	Construction	Count	57	0	2
		% within Bus.Target	21.8%	0.0%	0.8%
		% within State	53.8%	0.0%	16.7%
		% of total	8.7%	0.0%	0.3%
	Hospitals/Medical	Count	0	0	0
		% within Bus.Target	0.0%	0.0%	0.0%
		% within State	0.0%	0.0%	0.0%
		% of total	0.0%	0.0%	0.0%
	Private establishments	Count	11	5	5
		% within Bus.Target	6.9%	3.1%	3.1%
		% within State	10.4%	83.3%	41.7%
		% of total	1.7%	0.8%	0.8%
	Telecommunications	Count	11	1	0
		% within Bus.Target	16.4%	1.5%	0.0%
		% within State	10.4%	16.7%	0.0%
		% of total	1.7%	0.2%	0.0%
	Newspapers/Print	Count	2	0	1
		% within Bus.Target	6.1%	0.0%	3.0%
		% within State	1.9%	0.0%	8.3%
		% of total	0.3%	0.0%	0.2%
	Banking/Finance	Count	1	0	0
		% within Bus.Target	12.5%	0.0%	0.0%
		% within State	0.9%	0.0%	0.0%
		% of total	0.2%	0.0%	0.0%
	Transportation	Count	2	0	2
		% within Bus.Target	28.6%	0.0%	28.6%
		% within State	1.9%	0.0%	16.7%
		% of total	0.3%	0.0%	0.3%
	Agriculture	Count	0	0	0
		% within Bus.Target	0.0%	0.0%	0.0%
		% within State	0.0%	0.0%	0.0%
		% of total	0.0%	0.0%	0.0%

(continued)

(continued)

Bus.Target * State crosstabulation

			State		
			Jharkhand	Tamil Nadu	West Bengal
Total		Count	106	6	12
		% within Bus.Target	16.1%	0.9%	1.8%
		% within State	100.0%	100.0%	100.0%
		% of total	16.1%	0.9%	1.8%

Bus.Target * State crosstabulation

			State	
			Jammu and Kashmir	Madhya Pradesh
Bus.Target	Energy/Alloy	Count	1	0
		% within Bus.Target	0.9%	0.0%
		% within State	3.7%	0.0%
		% of total	0.2%	0.0%
	Construction	Count	0	1
		% within Bus.Target	0.0%	0.4%
		% within State	0.0%	25.0%
		% of total	0.0%	0.2%
	Hospitals/Medical	Count	2	0
		% within Bus.Target	25.0%	0.0%
		% within State	7.4%	0.0%
		% of total	0.3%	0.0%
	Private establishments	Count	2	0
		% within Bus.Target	1.3%	0.0%
		% within State	7.4%	0.0%
		% of total	0.3%	0.0%
	Telecommunications	Count	19	0
		% within Bus.Target	28.4%	0.0%
		% within State	70.4%	0.0%
		% of total	2.9%	0.0%
	Newspapers/Print	Count	1	3
		% within Bus.Target	3.0%	9.1%

(continued)

(continued)

Bus.Target * State crosstabulation

			State	
			Jammu and Kashmir	Madhya Pradesh
		% within State	3.7%	75.0%
		% of total	0.2%	0.5%
	Banking/Finance	Count	2	0
		% within Bus.Target	25.0%	0.0%
		% within State	7.4%	0.0%
		% of total	0.3%	0.0%
	Transportation	Count	0	0
		% within Bus.Target	0.0%	0.0%
		% within State	0.0%	0.0%
		% of total	0.0%	0.0%
	Agriculture	Count	0	0
		% within Bus.Target	0.0%	0.0%
		% within State	0.0%	0.0%
		% of total	0.0%	0.0%
Total		Count	27	4
		% within Bus.Target	4.1%	0.6%
		% within State	100.0%	100.0%
		% of total	4.1%	0.6%

Bus.Target * State crosstabulation

			State		
			Uttar Pradesh	Tripura	Andhra Pradesh
Bus.Target	Energy/Alloy	Count	0	0	6
		% within Bus.Target	0.0%	0.0%	5.5%
		% within State	0.0%	0.0%	33.3%
		% of total	0.0%	0.0%	0.9%
	Construction	Count	0	2	6
		% within Bus.Target	0.0%	0.8%	2.3%

(continued)

(continued)

Bus.Target * State crosstabulation

			State		
			Uttar Pradesh	Tripura	Andhra Pradesh
		% within State	0.0%	50.0%	33.3%
		% of total	0.0%	0.3%	0.9%
	Hospitals/Medical	Count	0	0	0
		% within Bus.Target	0.0%	0.0%	0.0%
		% within State	0.0%	0.0%	0.0%
		% of total	0.0%	0.0%	0.0%
	Private establishments	Count	6	0	0
		% within Bus.Target	3.8%	0.0%	0.0%
		% within State	46.2%	0.0%	0.0%
		% of total	0.9%	0.0%	0.0%
	Telecommunications	Count	1	1	4
		% within Bus.Target	1.5%	1.5%	6.0%
		% within State	7.7%	25.0%	22.2%
		% of total	0.2%	0.2%	0.6%
	Newspapers/Print	Count	6	0	0
		% within Bus.Target	18.2%	0.0%	0.0%
		% within State	46.2%	0.0%	0.0%
		% of total	0.9%	0.0%	0.0%

(continued)

(continued)

Bus.Target * State crosstabulation

			State		
			Uttar Pradesh	Tripura	Andhra Pradesh
	Banking/Finance	Count	0	1	0
		% within Bus.Target	0.0%	12.5%	0.0%
		% within State	0.0%	25.0%	0.0%
		% of total	0.0%	0.2%	0.0%
	Transportation	Count	0	0	0
		% within Bus.Target	0.0%	0.0%	0.0%
		% within State	0.0%	0.0%	0.0%
		% of total	0.0%	0.0%	0.0%
	Agriculture	Count	0	0	2
		% within Bus.Target	0.0%	0.0%	100.0%
		% within State	0.0%	0.0%	11.1%
		% of total	0.0%	0.0%	0.3%
Total		Count	13	4	18
		% within Bus.Target	2.0%	0.6%	2.7%
		% within State	100.0%	100.0%	100.0%
		% of total	2.0%	0.6%	2.7%

Bus.Target * State crosstabulation

			State			
			Mizoram	Kerala	Karnataka	Telangana
Bus.Target	Energy/Alloy	Count	0	0	0	0
		% within Bus.Target	0.0%	0.0%	0.0%	0.0%
		% within State	0.0%	0.0%	0.0%	0.0%
		% of total	0.0%	0.0%	0.0%	0.0%
	Construction	Count	1	1	0	3

(continued)

(continued)

Bus.Target * State crosstabulation

			State			
			Mizoram	Kerala	Karnataka	Telangana
		% within Bus.Target	0.4%	0.4%	0.0%	1.1%
		% within State	100.0%	11.1%	0.0%	75.0%
		% of total	0.2%	0.2%	0.0%	0.5%
	Hospitals/Medical	Count	0	0	0	0
		% within Bus.Target	0.0%	0.0%	0.0%	0.0%
		% within State	0.0%	0.0%	0.0%	0.0%
		% of total	0.0%	0.0%	0.0%	0.0%
	Private establishments	Count	0	7	3	0
		% within Bus.Target	0.0%	4.4%	1.9%	0.0%
		% within State	0.0%	77.8%	75.0%	0.0%
		% of total	0.0%	1.1%	0.5%	0.0%
	Telecommunications	Count	0	0	0	1
		% within Bus.Target	0.0%	0.0%	0.0%	1.5%
		% within State	0.0%	0.0%	0.0%	25.0%
		% of total	0.0%	0.0%	0.0%	0.2%
	Newspapers/Print	Count	0	1	1	0
		% within Bus.Target	0.0%	3.0%	3.0%	0.0%
		% within State	0.0%	11.1%	25.0%	0.0%
		% of total	0.0%	0.2%	0.2%	0.0%
	Banking/Finance	Count	0	0	0	0
		% within Bus.Target	0.0%	0.0%	0.0%	0.0%
		% within State	0.0%	0.0%	0.0%	0.0%
		% of total	0.0%	0.0%	0.0%	0.0%
	Transportation	Count	0	0	0	0
		% within Bus. Target	0.0%	0.0%	0.0%	0.0%

(continued)

(continued)

Bus.Target * State crosstabulation

			State			
			Mizoram	Kerala	Karnataka	Telangana
		% within State	0.0%	0.0%	0.0%	0.0%
		% of total	0.0%	0.0%	0.0%	0.0%
	Agriculture	Count	0	0	0	0
		% within Bus.Target	0.0%	0.0%	0.0%	0.0%
		% within State	0.0%	0.0%	0.0%	0.0%
		% of total	0.0%	0.0%	0.0%	0.0%
Total		Count	1	9	4	4
		% within Bus.Target	0.2%	1.4%	0.6%	0.6%
		% within State	100.0%	100.0%	100.0%	100.0%
		% of total	0.2%	1.4%	0.6%	0.6%

Bus.Target * State crosstabulation

			State		
			Punjab	Arunachal Pradesh	Delhi
Bus.Target	Energy/Alloy	Count	0	0	0
		% within Bus.Target	0.0%	0.0%	0.0%
		% within State	0.0%	0.0%	0.0%
		% of total	0.0%	0.0%	0.0%
	Construction	Count	0	2	0
		% within Bus.Target	0.0%	0.8%	0.0%
		% within State	0.0%	66.7%	0.0%
		% of total	0.0%	0.3%	0.0%
	Hospitals/Medical	Count	1	0	0
		% within Bus.Target	12.5%	0.0%	0.0%
		% within State	33.3%	0.0%	0.0%
		% of total	0.2%	0.0%	0.0%

(continued)

(continued)

Bus.Target * State crosstabulation

			State		
			Punjab	Arunachal Pradesh	Delhi
	Private establishments	Count	1	1	0
		% within Bus.Target	0.6%	0.6%	0.0%
		% within State	33.3%	33.3%	0.0%
		% of total	0.2%	0.2%	0.0%
	Telecommunications	Count	0	0	0
		% within Bus.Target	0.0%	0.0%	0.0%
		% within State	0.0%	0.0%	0.0%
		% of total	0.0%	0.0%	0.0%
	Newspapers/Print	Count	1	0	1
		% within Bus.Target	3.0%	0.0%	3.0%
		% within State	33.3%	0.0%	33.3%
		% of total	0.2%	0.0%	0.2%
	Banking/Finance	Count	0	0	0
		% within Bus.Target	0.0%	0.0%	0.0%
		% within State	0.0%	0.0%	0.0%
		% of total	0.0%	0.0%	0.0%
	Transportation	Count	0	0	0
		% within Bus.Target	0.0%	0.0%	0.0%
		% within State	0.0%	0.0%	0.0%
		% of total	0.0%	0.0%	0.0%
	Agriculture	Count	0	0	0
		% within Bus.Target	0.0%	0.0%	0.0%
		% within State	0.0%	0.0%	0.0%
		% of total	0.0%	0.0%	0.0%
Total		Count	3	3	1

(continued)

(continued)

Bus.Target * State crosstabulation

			State		
			Punjab	Arunachal Pradesh	Delhi
		% within Bus.Target	0.5%	0.5%	0.2%
		% within State	100.0%	100.0%	100.0%
		% of total	0.5%	0.5%	0.2%

Bus.Target * State crosstabulation

			State		
			Rajasthan	Gujarat	Total
Bus.Target	Energy/Alloy	Count	0	0	110
		% within Bus.Target	0.0%	0.0%	100.0%
		% within State	0.0%	0.0%	16.7%
		% of total	0.0%	0.0%	16.7%
	Construction	Count	1	1	262
		% within Bus.Target	0.4%	0.4%	100.0%
		% within State	100.0%	50.0%	39.9%
		% of total	0.2%	0.2%	39.9%
	Hospitals/Medical	Count	0	0	8
		% within Bus.Target	0.0%	0.0%	100.0%
		% within State	0.0%	0.0%	1.2%
		% of total	0.0%	0.0%	1.2%
	Private establishments	Count	0	1	160
		% within Bus.Target	0.0%	0.6%	100.0%
		% within State	0.0%	50.0%	24.4%
		% of total	0.0%	0.2%	24.4%
	Telecommunications	Count	0	0	67
		% within Bus.Target	0.0%	0.0%	100.0%
		% within State	0.0%	0.0%	10.2%
		% of total	0.0%	0.0%	10.2%
	Newspapers/Print	Count	0	0	33
		% within Bus.Target	0.0%	0.0%	100.0%
		% within State	0.0%	0.0%	5.0%
		% of total	0.0%	0.0%	5.0%
	Banking/Finance	Count	0	0	8

(continued)

(continued)

Bus.Target * State crosstabulation					
			State		
			Rajasthan	Gujarat	Total
		% within Bus.Target	0.0%	0.0%	100.0%
		% within State	0.0%	0.0%	1.2%
		% of total	0.0%	0.0%	1.2%
	Transportation	Count	0	0	7
		% within Bus.Target	0.0%	0.0%	100.0%
		% within State	0.0%	0.0%	1.1%
		% of total	0.0%	0.0%	1.1%
	Agriculture	Count	0	0	2
		% within Bus.Target	0.0%	0.0%	100.0%
		% within State	0.0%	0.0%	0.3%
		% of total	0.0%	0.0%	0.3%
Total		Count	1	2	657
		% within Bus.Target	0.2%	0.3%	100.0%
		% within State	100.0%	100.0%	100.0%
		% of total	0.2%	0.3%	100.0%

Appendix B

Methodological Appendix B—India

Statistics		
CityVillage		
N	Valid	575
	Missing	95

CityVillage		Frequency	Percent	Valid percent	Cumulative percent
Valid	Bongaiganon	2	0.3	0.3	0.3
	Ledo	1	0.1	0.2	0.5
	Menda	1	0.1	0.2	0.7
	Dimapur	9	1.3	1.6	2.3
	Imphal	42	6.3	7.3	9.6
	Badildeh	1	0.1	0.2	9.7
	Paschim Mamroni	1	0.1	0.2	9.9
	Narnaund	1	0.1	0.2	10.1
	Goh	1	0.1	0.2	10.3
	Dantewada	1	0.1	0.2	10.4
	Williamnaggar	5	0.7	0.9	11.3
	Betagon	1	0.1	0.2	11.5
	Aurangabad	1	0.1	0.2	11.7
	Noonmati	1	0.1	0.2	11.8
	Dangia	1	0.1	0.2	12.0
	Jamui	1	0.1	0.2	12.2

(continued)

R. J. Chasdi, *Corporate Security Surveillance*, Advanced Sciences and Technologies for Security Applications, https://doi.org/10.1007/978-3-031-39550-5

(continued)

CityVillage

	Frequency	Percent	Valid percent	Cumulative percent
Golgariba	1	0.1	0.2	12.3
Swangre	1	0.1	0.2	12.5
Kyang	1	0.1	0.2	12.7
Wageasi	2	0.3	0.3	13.0
Tiruvanna Malai	1	0.1	0.2	13.2
Bouserkuti	1	0.1	0.2	13.4
Mansai	1	0.1	0.2	13.6
Bengtol	1	0.1	0.2	13.7
Bhavanitola	1	0.1	0.2	13.9
Nender	1	0.1	0.2	14.1
Kudhni	1	0.1	0.2	14.3
Tilaparal-Bakenang	1	0.1	0.2	14.4
Kulgam	1	0.1	0.2	14.6
Tura	3	0.4	0.5	15.1

CityVillage

	Frequency	Percent	Valid percent	Cumulative percent
Bhopal	2	0.3	0.3	15.5
Pukhao	1	0.1	0.2	15.7
Badarpur	1	0.1	0.2	15.8
Chatra	3	0.4	0.5	16.3
Agartala	1	0.1	0.2	16.5
Laudha	1	0.1	0.2	16.7
Bitabari	1	0.1	0.2	16.9
Etawah	1	0.1	0.2	17.0
Chola	1	0.1	0.2	17.2
Kam biren	3	0.4	0.5	17.7
Mawlai	1	0.1	0.2	17.9
Shillong	3	0.4	0.5	18.4
Motphran	1	0.1	0.2	18.6
Miangpadar	2	0.3	0.3	19.0
Bishnupur	1	0.1	0.2	19.1
Tanda	1	0.1	0.2	19.3
Basaguda	1	0.1	0.2	19.5
Kumbhariput	2	0.3	0.3	19.8

(continued)

(continued)

CityVillage				
	Frequency	Percent	Valid percent	Cumulative percent
Tuisenphai	1	0.1	0.2	20.0
Chasingre	1	0.1	0.2	20.2
Thingou	1	0.1	0.2	20.3
Molandubi	1	0.1	0.2	20.5
Bage Bar	1	0.1	0.2	20.7
Simdega	1	0.1	0.2	20.9
Pajibali	1	0.1	0.2	21.0
Budhaniya	1	0.1	0.2	21.2
Nepa	1	0.1	0.2	21.4
Kalia Atala	1	0.1	0.2	21.6
Kharia	1	0.1	0.2	21.7
Nungba	1	0.1	0.2	21.9
Jiribam	1	0.1	0.2	22.1
Dhekiajuli	1	0.1	0.2	22.3
Chapagedda	3	0.4	0.5	22.8
Pedaarlagudem	1	0.1	0.2	23.0
Sasatgre	1	0.1	0.2	23.1
Chirudih	1	0.1	0.2	23.3
Sudikona	1	0.1	0.2	23.5
Mohanpur Misroliya	1	0.1	0.2	23.7

CityVillage				
	Frequency	Percent	Valid percent	Cumulative percent
Madurai	3	0.4	0.5	24.2
Sumandi	1	0.1	0.2	24.3
Mandu	1	0.1	0.2	24.5
Hazaribaugh	2	0.3	0.3	24.9
Somrei	1	0.1	0.2	25.0
Navinagar	1	0.1	0.2	25.2
Kulnung Khunou	1	0.1	0.2	25.4
Ahiapur	1	0.1	0.2	25.6
Nekhavaya	1	0.1	0.2	25.7
Majhowlia	1	0.1	0.2	25.9
Dumaria	2	0.3	0.3	26.3
Kirandul	3	0.4	0.5	26.8

(continued)

(continued)

CityVillage				
	Frequency	Percent	Valid percent	Cumulative percent
Rongrikimgre	1	0.1	0.2	27.0
Gasuapara	1	0.1	0.2	27.1
Barabadha	1	0.1	0.2	27.3
Pulwama	1	0.1	0.2	27.5
Ambabhona	1	0.1	0.2	27.7
Vijayawada	1	0.1	0.2	27.8
Bhadrachalam	1	0.1	0.2	28.0
Peeding	1	0.1	0.2	28.2
Dechlipetha	1	0.1	0.2	28.3
Balumath	1	0.1	0.2	28.5
Rangamati	1	0.1	0.2	28.7
Gaghra	2	0.3	0.3	29.0
Ghatshila	1	0.1	0.2	29.2
Kambesu	1	0.1	0.2	29.4
Kusumaguda	1	0.1	0.2	29.6
Sikarpai	1	0.1	0.2	29.7
Paralkot	1	0.1	0.2	29.9
Hesatu	1	0.1	0.2	30.1
Kalachand	1	0.1	0.2	30.3
Budhauli	1	0.1	0.2	30.4
Mirganj	1	0.1	0.2	30.6
Chintapalle	1	0.1	0.2	30.8
Srinagar	7	1.0	1.2	32.0
Urahiloga/Jagibeel	3	0.4	0.5	32.5
Uripok	1	0.1	0.2	32.7
Dalgaon	1	0.1	0.2	32.9

CityVillage				
	Frequency	Percent	Valid percent	Cumulative percent
Siladon	1	0.1	0.2	33.0
Senduwar	1	0.1	0.2	33.2
Ukhrul	2	0.3	0.3	33.6
Bhitia	3	0.4	0.5	34.1
Gora (Goda)	1	0.1	0.2	34.3
Rajivnagar	1	0.1	0.2	34.4

(continued)

(continued)

CityVillage

	Frequency	Percent	Valid percent	Cumulative percent
Madhwapur	1	0.1	0.2	34.6
Nungsai Tubung	1	0.1	0.2	34.8
Digboi	2	0.3	0.3	35.1
Pedapadu	1	0.1	0.2	35.3
Chulabhat	1	0.1	0.2	35.5
Mohanpur	1	0.1	0.2	35.7
Tinsukia	2	0.3	0.3	36.0
Rongara	1	0.1	0.2	36.2
Khelmati	1	0.1	0.2	36.3
Diphu	1	0.1	0.2	36.5
Chapi	2	0.3	0.3	36.9
Patgaon	1	0.1	0.2	37.0
Palakkad (Chandra Nagar)	2	0.3	0.3	37.4
Mariani (Jorhat)	1	0.1	0.2	37.6
Bangalore (Bengaluru)	2	0.3	0.3	37.9
Sivaganga	1	0.1	0.2	38.1
Umrangso	1	0.1	0.2	38.3
Tekulagudem	1	0.1	0.2	38.4
Ondrungula	1	0.1	0.2	38.6
Dhanora	1	0.1	0.2	38.8
Nawada	1	0.1	0.2	39.0
Manubothulagadda	1	0.1	0.2	39.1
Mananpur	1	0.1	0.2	39.3
Asansol-Jamuria	1	0.1	0.2	39.5
Sivasagar	1	0.1	0.2	39.7
Rankhorm Gaon	1	0.1	0.2	39.8
Nashik	1	0.1	0.2	40.0
Chawangkining	1	0.1	0.2	40.2
Neema	1	0.1	0.2	40.3
Chennai	2	0.3	0.3	40.7
Tikhali	1	0.1	0.2	40.9
Machadiha	1	0.1	0.2	41.0

CityVillage				
	Frequency	Percent	Valid percent	Cumulative percent
Wokha	1	0.1	0.2	41.2
Aulachowka	1	0.1	0.2	41.4
Chargaon	2	0.3	0.3	41.7
Tori	1	0.1	0.2	41.9
Baghmara	1	0.1	0.2	42.1
Churchu	1	0.1	0.2	42.3
Sapore	6	0.9	1.0	43.3
Banapar	1	0.1	0.2	43.5
Parswar	1	0.1	0.2	43.7
Shuwa	1	0.1	0.2	43.8
Dooru	2	0.3	0.3	44.2
Dangerpora	1	0.1	0.2	44.3
Panapur	1	0.1	0.2	44.5
Pattan	3	0.4	0:5	45.0
Bartola	1	0.1	0.2	45.2
Hajongpara	1	0.1	0.2	45.4
Handwara	1	0.1	0.2	45.6
Murki	1	0.1	0.2	45.7
Lumding	1	0.1	0.2	45.9
Bangsi Minol	1	0.1	0.2	46.1
Ganjeipadar	1	0.1	0.2	46.3
Bomai	1	0.1	0.2	46.4
Nangalbibra	1	0.1	0.2	46.6
Telenpali	1	0.1	0.2	46.8
Lathore	1	0.1	0.2	47.0
Damas	1	0.1	0.2	47.1
Moyyalagummi	1	0.1	0.2	47.3
Dudhiyatadi	1	0.1	0.2	47.5
Sorodo	1	0.1	0.2	47.7
Pitala	1	0.1	0.2	47.8
Dinanagar	2	0.3	0.3	48.2
Macca	1	0.1	0.2	48.3
Tisia	2	0.3	0.3	48.7
Orchha	1	0.1	0.2	48.9
Jamgai	1	0.1	0.2	49.0
Visakhapatnam	4	0.6	0.7	49.7

(continued)

(continued)

CityVillage				
	Frequency	Percent	Valid percent	Cumulative percent
Chitrakonda	2	0.3	0.3	50.1
Chandagre	1	0.1	0.2	50.3

CityVillage				
	Frequency	Percent	Valid percent	Cumulative percent
Chisikgre	1	0.1	0.2	50.4
Murki	1	0.1	0.2	50.6
Mahadev Ghat	1	0.1	0.2	50.8
Samanda	1	0.1	0.2	51.0
Geedam	1	0.1	0.2	51.1
Bhopalpatnam	1	0.1	0.2	51.3
Bhadrakali	1	0.1	0.2	51.5
Tarlaguda	1	0.1	0.2	51.7
Dudheda	1	0.1	0.2	51.8
Gumda	1	0.1	0.2	52.0
Bodhadih	1	0.1	0.2	52.2
Kuchai	1	0.1	0.2	52.3
Sukma	1	0.1	0.2	52.5
Hahaladdi	1	0.1	0.2	52.7
Murumgaon	1	0.1	0.2	52.9
Namrup	1	0.1	0.2	53.0
Chowka	1	0.1	0.2	53.2
Kathapada	1	0.1	0.2	53.4
Ramagiri	1	0.1	0.2	53.6
Chipakur	1	0.1	0.2	53.7
Ramgarh	2	0.3	0.3	54.1
Chirand	2	0.3	0.3	54.4
Sirigidi	1	0.1	0.2	54.6
Nuadihi	1	0.1	0.2	54.8
Loharam	1	0.1	0.2	55.0
Muskel	1	0.1	0.2	55.1
Magra	1	0.1	0.2	55.3
Pipghati	1	0.1	0.2	55.5
Yukharia	1	0.1	0.2	55.7
Jehanabad	1	0.1	0.2	55.8

(continued)

(continued)

CityVillage

	Frequency	Percent	Valid percent	Cumulative percent
Chhatarpur	1	0.1	0.2	56.0
Daliakhuji	1	0.1	0.2	56.2
Taupadar	1	0.1	0.2	56.3
Kasuguda	1	0.1	0.2	56.5
Borabandha	1	0.1	0.2	56.7
Zalembung	1	0.1	0.2	56.9
Sawombung	1	0.1	0.2	57.0
Muthbharo	1	0.1	0.2	57.2

CityVillage

	Frequency	Percent	Valid percent	Cumulative percent
Ganol Apal	1	0.1	0.2	57.4
Balu	1	0.1	0.2	57.6
Sevanan	1	0.1	0.2	57.7
Baraua	1	0.1	0.2	57.9
Darauli	1	0.1	0.2	58.1
Motihari	1	0.1	0.2	58.3
Pallemadi	1	0.1	0.2	58.4
Heirok	1	0.1	0.2	58.6
Guram Dato Tola	1	0.1	0.2	58.8
Turki	1	0.1	0.2	59.0
Bhabua (Kaimur)	1	0.1	0.2	59.1
Charhi	1	0.1	0.2	59.3
Gourapali	1	0.1	0.2	59.5
Rajnandgaon	1	0.1	0.2	59.7
Mangaluru	1	0.1	0.2	59.8
Tirtol	1	0.1	0.2	60.0
Aheri	1	0.1	0.2	60.2
Guijan	1	0.1	0.2	60.3
Ara	1	0.1	0.2	60.5
Bacheli	2	0.3	0.3	60.9
Maraigude	2	0.3	0.3	61.2
Bela	1	0.1	0.2	61.4
Kherem Murah	1	0.1	0.2	61.6
Dewaria	1	0.1	0.2	61.7

(continued)

(continued)

CityVillage

	Frequency	Percent	Valid percent	Cumulative percent
Mayyil	1	0.1	0.2	61.9
Natun Chariali	1	0.1	0.2	62.1
Gadiras	2	0.3	0.3	62.4
Chandanpur	1	0.1	0.2	62.6
Rayagada	1	0.1	0.2	62.8
Nuapari Khaliapur	1	0.1	0.2	63.0
Patna	1	0.1	0.2	63.1
Dogla Bathan	1	0.1	0.2	63.3
Thoubal	1	0.1	0.2	63.5
McCluskieganj	1	0.1	0.2	63.7
Upar Pakhi	1	0.1	0.2	63.8
Khangabok	1	0.1	0.2	64.0
Bagaha	1	0.1	0.2	64.2
Nat. Capital Terr. of Delhi	1	0.1	0.2	64.3

CityVillage

	Frequency	Percent	Valid percent	Cumulative percent
Nasirabad	1	0.1	0.2	64.5
Hisua	1	0.1	0.2	64.7
Suriya	1	0.1	0.2	64.9
Dengsupari	1	0.1	0.2	65.0
Chelakkad	1	0.1	0.2	65.2
Banchatara	1	0.1	0.2	65.4
Moreh	1	0.1	0.2	65.6
Hesakocha	1	0.1	0.2	65.7
Amratola	1	0.1	0.2	65.9
Darbhanga	1	0.1	0.2	66.1
Bhitarokota	2	0.3	0.3	66.4
Champijang	1	0.1	0.2	66.6
Fatehpura	1	0.1	0.2	66.8
Awangkhul	2	0.3	0.3	67.1
Sehjang	2	0.3	0.3	67.5
Margherita	1	0.1	0.2	67.7
Lamlai Khullen	1	0.1	0.2	67.8
Gadchiroli	1	0.1	0.2	68.0

(continued)

(continued)

CityVillage

	Frequency	Percent	Valid percent	Cumulative percent
Muzaffarpur	3	0.4	0.5	68.5
Khelari	1	0.1	0.2	68.7
Roam	1	0.1	0.2	68.9
Lidpura	1	0.1	0.2	69.0
Bharno	1	0.1	0.2	69.2
Latehar	1	0.1	0.2	69.4
Lukhambi	1	0.1	0.2	69.6
Latrutu	1	0.1	0.2	69.7
Annaram	1	0.1	0.2	69.9
Baddi	1	0.1	0.2	70.1
Hajipur	1	0.1	0.2	70.3
Bihubor	1	0.1	0.2	70.4
Belkhoria	1	0.1	0.2	70.6
Barachatti	1	0.1	0.2	70.8
Sandengleli	1	0.1	0.2	71.0
Kulhiamunda	1	0.1	0.2	71.1
Kathupani	1	0.1	0.2	71.3
Sangkini Dabgre	1	0.1	0.2	71.5
Dugdha	1	0.1	0.2	71.7
Naharkatia	1	0.1	0.2	71.8

CityVillage

	Frequency	Percent	Valid percent	Cumulative percent
Era Aning	1	0.1	0.2	72.0
Mankidi	1	0.1	0.2	72.2
Rompalli	1	0.1	0.2	72.3
Pedakurti	1	0.1	0.2	72.5
Borapadar	1	0.1	0.2	72.7
Panhala	1	0.1	0.2	72.9
Jaiprakash Nagar	1	0.1	0.2	73.0
Hathras	3	0.4	0.5	73.6
Ladpur	1	0.1	0.2	73.7
Tandwa	1	0.1	0.2	73.9
Muchnar	1	0.1	0.2	74.1
Sheikhbigh	1	0.1	0.2	74.3

(continued)

(continued)

CityVillage				
	Frequency	Percent	Valid percent	Cumulative percent
Datuta	1	0.1	0.2	74.4
Raghubari	1	0.1	0.2	74.6
Gurua	1	0.1	0.2	74.8
Dambuk	1	0.1	0.2	75.0
Birbanki	2	0.3	0.3	75.3
Busuputtu	1	0.1	0.2	75.5
Kangpokpi	1	0.1	0.2	75.7
Pombai	1	0.1	0.2	75.8
Majhi Gumandi	1	0.1	0.2	76.0
Kapasiya	1	0.1	0.2	76.2
Amjharia	1	0.1	0.2	76.3
Papermetia	1	0.1	0.2	76.5
Mankelli	1	0.1	0.2	76.7
Tarwadih	1	0.1	0.2	76.9
Cuttack	1	0.1	0.2	77.0
Tiskopi	1	0.1	0.2	77.2
Teokghat	1	0.1	0.2	77.4
Gagaguro	1	0.1	0.2	77.6
Sohra (Cherrapunji)	1	0.1	0.2	77.7
Anandpur	1	0.1	0.2	77.9
Mutanpal	1	0.1	0.2	78.1
Lumnongrim Dewlieh	1	0.1	0.2	78.3
Bagabandh	1	0.1	0.2	78.4
Dingdinga	1	0.1	0.2	78.6
Mawlai Nangmali	1	0.1	0.2	78.8
Lodhama	1	0.1	0.2	79.0

CityVillage				
	Frequency	Percent	Valid percent	Cumulative percent
Malewahi	1	0.1	0.2	79.1
Darliput	1	0.1	0.2	79.3
Kasaram	1	0.1	0.2	79.5
Barbaspur	1	0.1	0.2	79.7
Tarkhola	1	0.1	0.2	79.8
Dudhia	1	0.1	0.2	80.0

(continued)

(continued)

CityVillage

	Frequency	Percent	Valid percent	Cumulative percent
Kurseong	1	0.1	0.2	80.2
Ormanjhi	1	0.1	0.2	80.3
Mirik	1	0.1	0.2	80.5
Manpur	1	0.1	0.2	80.7
Jangai	1	0.1	0.2	80.9
Darjeeling	1	0.1	0.2	81.0
Kalimpong	1	0.1	0.2	81.2
Napet Palli	1	0.1	0.2	81.4
Nurmati	1	0.1	0.2	81.6
Kohkameta	2	0.3	0.3	81.9
Saun (Sawkala)	1	0.1	0.2	82.1
Mandai	1	0.1	0.2	82.3
Kunnoth	1	0.1	0.2	82.4
Ritu Kathalguri	1	0.1	0.2	82.6
Darakonda	1	0.1	0.2	82.8
Rajpora Chowk	1	0.1	0.2	83.0
Piparwar	1	0.1	0.2	83.1
Melakajoba	1	0.1	0.2	83.3
Shivpur	1	0.1	0.2	83.5
Mounasilli	1	0.1	0.2	83.7
Darna	1	0.1	0.2	83.8
Rekhabat	1	0.1	0.2	84.0
Tikak	1	0.1	0.2	84.2
Bilhaur	1	0.1	0.2	84.3
Ghatampur	1	0.1	0.2	84.5
Navani	1	0.1	0.2	84.7
Konapather	1	0.1	0.2	84.9
Kralcheck Keller	1	0.1	0.2	85.0
Mahuamilan	1	0.1	0.2	85.2
Savalvahi	1	0.1	0.2	85.4

(continued)

(continued)

CityVillage				
	Frequency	Percent	Valid percent	Cumulative percent
Andrahal	1	0.1	0.2	85.6
Sikandra	1	0.1	0.2	85.7

CityVillage				
	Frequency	Percent	Valid percent	Cumulative percent
Mirzadih	1	0.1	0.2	85.9
Konta	2	0.3	0.3	86.3
Kumkumpudi	1	0.1	0.2	86.4
Sahyara	1	0.1	0.2	86.6
Toylanka	1	0.1	0.2	86.8
Itkhori	1	0.1	0.2	87.0
Modakpal	1	0.1	0.2	87.1
Pandrasali	1	0.1	0.2	87.3
Thane	2	0.3	0.3	87.7
Dhina	1	0.1	0.2	87.8
Kudag	1	0.1	0.2	88.0
Kukud	1	0.1	0.2	88.2
Jamakana	1	0.1	0.2	88.3
Donaikala	2	0.3	0.3	88.7
Jagun	2	0.3	0.3	89.0
Muzaffarnagar	1	0.1	0.2	89.2
Mathili	1	0.1	0.2	89.4
Kangchup	1	0.1	0.2	89.6
Belagavi	1	0.1	0.2	89.7
Kalyan	1	0.1	0.2	89.9
Kanubari	1	0.1	0.2	90.1
Madded	1	0.1	0.2	90.3
Gatam	1	0.1	0.2	90.4
Edira	1	0.1	0.2	90.6
Borhat	1	0.1	0.2	90.8
Goju	1	0.1	0.2	91.0
Paji Bahali	1	0.1	0.2	91.1
Bhejji	1	0.1	0.2	91.3
Vardeltong	1	0.1	0.2	91.5
Amildhar	1	0.1	0.2	91.7

(continued)

(continued)

CityVillage

	Frequency	Percent	Valid percent	Cumulative percent
Kadambaguda	1	0.1	0.2	91.8
Ahmednagar	1	0.1	0.2	92.0
Balimaha	1	0.1	0.2	92.2
Thoubal Khunou	1	0.1	0.2	92.3
Dharampenta	1	0.1	0.2	92.5
Umpling	1	0.1	0.2	92.7
Pratappur	1	0.1	0.2	92.9
New Helipong	1	0.1	0.2	93.0

CityVillage

		Frequency	Percent	Valid percent	Cumulative percent
	Sarivella	1	0.1	0.2	93.2
	Sapekhati	3	0.4	0.5	93.7
	Simaluguri	1	0.1	0.2	93.9
	Samri	1	0.1	0.2	94.1
	Malappuram	1	0.1	0.2	94.3
	Pirtand	1	0.1	0.2	94.4
	Bhansi	2	0.3	0.3	94.8
	Rupai Siding	1	0.1	0.2	95.0
	Rodo	1	0.1	0.2	95.1
	Keeta	1	0.1	0.2	95.3
	Jatatari	1	0.1	0.2	95.5
	Dalki	1	0.1	0.2	95.7
	Metoda	1	0.1	0.2	95.8
	Meppadi	1	0.1	0.2	96.0
	Selenghat	1	0.1	0.2	96.2
	Bara	1	0.1	0.2	96.3
	Kashitand	1	0.1	0.2	96.5
	Jalandhar	1	0.1	0.2	96.7
	Kolkata	1	0.1	0.2	96.9
	Vangaichungpao	1	0.1	0.2	97.0
	Mumbai	1	0.1	0.2	97.2
	Brakpora	1	0.1	0.2	97.4
	Chouparan	1	0.1	0.2	97.6
	Pathalgada	1	0.1	0.2	97.7
	Aranpur	1	0.1	0.2	97.9

(continued)

(continued)

CityVillage

		Frequency	Percent	Valid percent	Cumulative percent
	Ekilsara	1	0.1	0.2	98.1
	Bautia	1	0.1	0.2	98.3
	Bamchuk Beel	1	0.1	0.2	98.4
	Mahuadanr	1	0.1	0.2	98.6
	Upampalli	1	0.1	0.2	98.8
	Bukru	1	0.1	0.2	99.0
	Demow	1	0.1	0.2	99.1
	Lewadih	1	0.1	0.2	99.3
	Kanglatongbi	1	0.1	0.2	99.5
	Etapalli	1	0.1	0.2	99.7
	Garu	1	0.1	0.2	99.8
	Kusumba	1	0.1	0.2	100.0
	Total	575	85.8	100.0	
Missing	System	95	14.2		
Total		670	100.0		

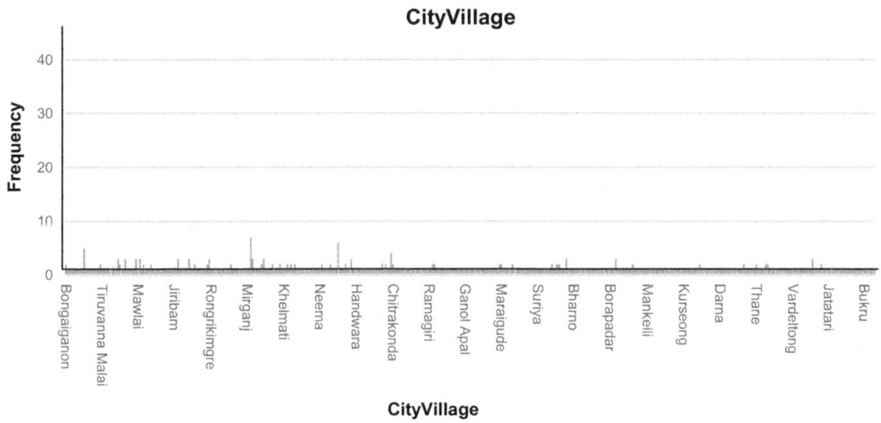

Index

R. J. Chasdi, *Corporate Security Surveillance*, Advanced Sciences and Technologies for Security Applications, https://doi.org/10.1007/978-3-031-39550-5

H

I

J

K

L

M